Companion to
Shakespeare

VOLUME III

Companion to Shakespeare

VOLUME III

WILLIAM BAKER AND KENNETH WOMACK

Facts On File
An Infobase Learning Company

Facts On File, Inc.
An imprint of Infobase Learning
132 West 31st Street
New York NY 10001

Library of Congress Cataloging-in-Publication Data
Baker, William, 1944–
    The facts on file companion to Shakespeare / William Baker and Kenneth Womack.
       p. cm.
    Includes bibliographical references and index.
    ISBN 978-0-8160-7820-2 (acid-free paper) 1. Shakespeare, William, 1564–1616—Encyclopedias.
I. Womack, Kenneth. II. Title.
    PR2892.B26 2011
    822.3'3—dc22   2010054012

Facts On File books are available at special discounts when purchased in bulk quantities for businesses, associations, institutions, or sales promotions. Please call our Special Sales Department in New York at (212) 967-8800 or (800) 322-8755.

You can find Facts On File on the World Wide Web at http://www.infobaselearning.com

Text design by Annie O'Donnell
Composition by Hermitage Publishing Services
Cover printed by Yurchak Printing, Landisville, Pa.
Book printed and bound by Yurchak Printing, Landisville, Pa.
Date printed: January 2012

Printed in the United States of America

10 9 8 7 6 5 4 3 2 1

This book is printed on acid-free paper.

Contents

Henry V

INTRODUCTION

Henry V concludes Shakespeare's second tetralogy (group of four plays), often called the Henriad, which begins with *Richard II,* followed by *Henry IV, Parts 1* and *2.* The play is a triumphant depiction of Henry V's victorious reign, culminating in his success at Agincourt and his marriage to Katharine, daughter of the king of France. Whereas *Richard II,* which depicts the downfall and death of the monarch, is tragic, *Henry V,* which ends in the promise of marriage, is comic.

Yet, it is also tragic in its own way, for the play shows the deaths of several of the characters whom audiences have come to know through the two parts of *Henry IV.* By play's end, Falstaff, Bardolph, Doll Tearsheet, and Mistress Quickly are dead, as are Nym and the Boy, whom Shakespeare introduced in this work. The epilogue also anticipates the death of Henry V and the disasters that will ensue under his son.

Chronologically, *Henry V* follows hard upon *Henry IV, Part 2* and shares with earlier works in the tetralogy some of its characters, images, and thematic concerns, such as the source of royal authority. It also presents a new ambiguity that will mark the other plays Shakespeare composed in this period, *Julius Caesar* and *Hamlet.*

In the late 20th and early 21st centuries, this work has attracted a significant amount of critical attention compared to Shakespeare's other history plays. In "Back by Popular Demand: The Two Versions of *Henry V,*" Annabel Patterson neatly summarizes the alternate visions that the play generates:

> More than almost any other play of Shakespeare's, and certainly more than any other "history," *Henry V* has generated accounts of itself that agree, broadly speaking, on the play's thematics—popular monarchy, national unity, militaristic expansion—but fall simply, even crudely, on either side of the line that divides belief from skepticism, idealism from cynicism, or, in contemporary parlance, legitimation from subversion. (72)

Henry V challenges its audiences either to decide for themselves on which side of the divide they will place the work or to attempt to bridge the two positions.

BACKGROUND

Shakespeare drew on earlier texts and contemporary events in crafting *Henry V.* John Dover Wilson and A. W. Pollard argued that the First Quarto, the first published version of the play, was based on an earlier work that Shakespeare had revised. Henry V had also been the subject of at least two earlier pieces for the stage. In the 1580s, the Queen's Men had performed *The Famous Victories of Henry the Fifth* (printed 1598). On November 28, 1595, Philip Henslowe, manager of the Lord Admiral's Men, recorded in his diary that his company had earned 3 6s for a new play, "Harey the v," which

Painting of Henry V by an unknown artist, late 16th or early 17th century

cannot be *The Famous Victories,* since it was by then hardly a new work. In 1592, Thomas Nashe wrote in *Pierce Penniless,* "What a glorious thing it is to have Henry the Fifth represented on the stage, leading the French king prisoner, and forcing both him and the Dauphin to swear fealty." In *The Famous Victories,* the Dauphin and Duke of Burgundy swear allegiance to Henry. Nashe's memory may have erred, since *Famous Victories* was not yet printed. Or, he may be referring to yet another work dealing with Henry's victorious reign.

Shakespeare drew heavily on *The Famous Victories* for both parts of *Henry IV* as well as *Henry V.* As in *The Famous Victories,* the three plays about Prince Henry (Hal) and then Henry V begin with the nonhistorical robbery at Gad's Hill (discussed initially in *Henry IV, Part 1,* Act I, Scene 2) and

end with the impending marriage of Henry V and Katharine of France (*Henry V,* Act V, Scene 2). Both omit any discussion of domestic affairs during Henry V's reign and concentrate on the war with France. Both also condense the king's French campaigns, showing only the siege of Harfleur (*Henry V,* Act III, Scenes 1–3) and the Battle of Agincourt. They then leap over five years to the Treaty of Troyes.

The structure of the two works is similar. In *Famous Victories,* Henry and the Archbishop of Canterbury discuss Henry's right to the French throne (*Henry V,* 1.2), and the French ambassador presents Henry with a carpet (not in Shakespeare's play) and "a Tunne of Tennis balles" (*Henry V* 1.2.255, 258) The following scene in both works turns to comic characters' setting off for France. In *Famous Victories,* John Constable weeps as he parts from his wife, just as Pistol grieves at parting from Mistress Quickly (2.3.3). Dericke and an unnamed Thief compose the remainder of the trinity of reluctant soldiers, corresponding to some extent to Bardolph and Nym (Nym's name means "thief"). *Famous Victories* omits the Southampton conspiracy (*Henry V,* 2.2), and Shakespeare devotes more attention to the siege of Harfleur (3.1–3). Katharine's English lesson (3.4) is Shakespeare's invention. *Famous Victories* and *Henry V* then turn to the Battle of Agincourt. At the end of scene 14 of *Famous Victories,* the stage directions read "The Battell," so that work may have included some actual fighting, whereas Shakespeare's play does not. Both works, however, present the French as overconfident and arrogant; in both, too, a French herald comes to Henry twice before the battle to ask for ransom, and Henry refuses to offer any. In *Famous Victories,* Derricke is captured by a French soldier, who demands ransom, but Derricke manages to trick the Frenchman and take him prisoner. This comic business resurfaces as Pistol's capture of Le Fer in *Henry V* (4.4). In *Famous Victories,* Dericke and John Cobbler discuss their impending return to England, where they intend to prey on the populace, just as Pistol says he will at the end of *Henry V* (5.1). Both works end with Henry's espousal to Katharine and the French king's naming Henry his heir to the throne of France.

Some of Shakespeare's lines are clearly lifted from *The Famous Victories*. For example, in the latter, Katherine asks Henry, "How should I love thee, which is my father's enemy?" In *Henry V,* Katharine asks, "Is it possible dat I sould love de ennemie of France?" (5.2.169–170). In *Famous Victories,* Henry asks Katherine, "Tush, Kate, but tell me in plain terms, canst thou love the king of England?" In Shakespeare's final scene, Henry asks her, "But, Kate, dost thou understand thus much English? Canst thou love me?" (5.2.193–194). When Henry learns that the Dauphin has sent him tennis balls, he replies, in Shakespeare's play, "We are glad the Dolphin is so pleasant with us" (1.2.258–259). In *Famous Victories,* the king says, "My lord prince *Dolphin* is very pleasaunt with me."

Shakespeare's other chief literary source is Raphael Holinshed's *Chronicles of England, Scotland, and Ireland* (second edition, 1587), which he used heavily for all his plays dealing with English history. Holinshed provides the details of the bill before Parliament that the clerics discuss in the opening scene of *Henry V.* Shakespeare essentially turns Holinshed's report into blank verse. The play also shares Holinshed's view of the Catholic clerics as conspirators, a common view of the Catholic clergy in Elizabethan England. Shakespeare similarly turns into poetry the Archbishop of Canterbury's long-winded justification of Henry's claim to the French throne (1.2.33–95), which in the *Chronicles* is "more cleere than the sunne," or, as Shakespeare's archbishop maintains, is "as clear as is the summer's sun" (1.2.86). Shakespeare seems to treat this assertion with greater irony than does his source. Shakespeare also turns into blank verse Holinshed's casualty list for the Battle of Agincourt.

Shakespeare would have found the details of the Southampton conspiracy (*Henry V,* 2.2) in Holinshed, though Holinshed makes clear that the motivation is not French bribery, as stated in the play, but rather a dynastic dispute that would eventually erupt as the Wars of the Roses. In both Holinshed and Shakespeare, Henry claims that he seeks no revenge for the plot against him, only for its threat against England. Bardolph's theft of a pax (3.6) derives from Holinshed's account of an unnamed soldier's stealing a pyx from a church. Holinshed and Shakespeare both discuss the ineffectual mining of Harfleur. Holinshed writes that after Harfleur surrendered, Henry ordered the city razed. In Shakespeare's play, the king orders his uncle, whom he appoints governor of the town, to "Use mercy to them all" (3.3.54). Whether Shakespeare knew it or not, his version is closer to the truth. Henry exiled some 2,000 French inhabitants but did not destroy the city.

Before the Battle of Agincourt, Henry ordered that his soldiers remain quiet. Fluellen tells Gower to "speak fewer" (4.1.65) on the eve of battle, and Gower agrees that he will speak more softly. Holinshed reports that before the fighting began, Henry delivered "a grave oration, moving them [his soldiers] to plaie the men, whereby to obtain a glorious victorie." This hint resulted in the great St. Crispin's Day speech that Shakespeare gives Henry (4.3). Holinshed also wrote that just before the battle, a soldier lamented, "I would to God there were with us now so manie good soldiers as are at this houre within England!" Westmoreland expresses this sentiment in the play: "O that we now had here / But one ten thousand of those men in England / That do no work today!" (4.3.16–18). According to Holinshed, Henry replied: "I would not wish a man more here than I have." Shakespeare's Henry expresses the same sentiment: "No, my fair cousin. / . . . I pray thee wish not one man more" (4.3.19–23). Before the battle, the French appear overconfident in the *Chronicles,* just as they do in both *The Famous Victories* and Shakespeare's play.

Holinshed provides two explanations for Henry's order to kill all his French prisoners. One is that when the French regrouped, Henry feared the prisoners would turn on their captors. The other motive was revenge for the French killing of the boys guarding the English baggage train. Both motives appear in Shakespeare's play (4.6, 4.7). Henry's encounter with Montjoy after the battle

(4.7) is yet another versification of Holinshed's account. Holinshed offered two reports of English casualties, one stating about 25, the other about 500. Shakespeare chose the lower figure to make the victory greater. Shakespeare condensed Holinshed's report of the first meeting of Henry and Katherine (the historical Catherine of Valois) at Melun in 1419 and their betrothal in 1420. The play shows only one meeting (5.2). The epilogue's phrase "small time" to describe Henry's reign also comes from Holinshed.

Another historical source for Shakespeare is Edward Hall's *The Union of the Two Noble and Illustre Famelies of Lancastre and Yorke* (1548). Whereas Holinshed makes the Dauphin's insulting gift of tennis balls a casus belli, in Hall and Shakespeare's play, Henry has already decided to go to war before he learns of the gift. Hall's reference to the reign of Henry IV as an "unquiet time" resurfaces in *Henry V* (1.1.4). In Hall, the Archbishop assures Henry that "they of the marches" (that is, border regions) will defend England against Scotland. In the play, he says: "They of those marches, gracious sovereign, / Shall be a wall sufficient to defend / Our inland from the pilfering borderers" (1.2.140–142). Hall refers to the "phantasticall braggynge" of the French, which Shakespeare repeatedly shows.

From the *Vita et Gesta Henrici Quinti* (translated to English in 1513), Shakespeare may have taken the kiss that Henry bestows on Katharine in 5.2, though the kiss recalls Petruchio's hasty wooing of another Kate, which concludes with his telling his bride-to-be, "And kiss me, Kate, we will be married a' Sunday" (*The Taming of the Shrew*, 2.1.324). (In *Famous Victories*, Henry and Katherine are to be married "The first Sunday of the next moneth.") The *Vita* also mentions the French boasting about their horses and armor, which Shakespeare depicts in Act III, Scene 7. The Archbishop's disquisition on the commonwealth of bees derives from John Lyly's *Euphues, the Anatomy of Wit* (1578). Henry's disguising himself to talk with his soldiers on the eve of battle may imitate Germanicus's action in his war against Arminius

as reported in Tacitus, though Germanicus only listens; he does not talk with his men as Henry does. An English translation of Tacitus appeared in 1598 (*The Annales of Cornelius Tacitus*). The *Vita* reports that Henry walked among his soldiers to encourage them but did so without concealment. Holinshed also writes of Henry's going among his soldiers, although in that instance, the king found two men outside the boundaries of the camp and ordered their execution. *The Wars of Cyrus* (1594) shows a king visiting his army on the eve of battle. Fluellen's comparing Henry V and Alexander the Great (4.7) recalls Plutarch's *Parallel Lives of the Greeks and Romans;* Plutarch pairs Alexander with Julius Caesar, the subject of Shakespeare's play immediately following *Henry V.* Shakespeare may thus imply similarities between Henry V and Caesar for good or ill; the Chorus before Act V compares Henry's entrance into London after Agincourt to Caesar's triumphant return to Rome, which serves as the opening scene of Shakespeare's Roman play.

Contemporary concerns also inform the play. *Henry V* is easy to date because it contains Shakespeare's only explicit reference to current events. The Chorus before Act 5 likens Henry's victorious entry into London to another anticipated triumphal return

> Were now the general of our gracious Empress,
> As in good time he may, from Ireland coming,
> Bringing rebellion broached on his sword.
> (5.0.30–32)

On March 12, 1599, Elizabeth commissioned Robert Devereux, earl of Essex, to command the English forces fighting the rebels in Ireland. Essex set off from London with great fanfare on March 27, and he returned alone and in disguise on September 28, having concluded an unauthorized truce with the rebel leader Hugh O'Neill, earl of Tyrone, who would not be defeated until 1603 by Charles Blount, Lord Mountjoy. *Henry V* may therefore be dated safely as having been composed before this last date and probably first staged between March and September 1599. Gower speaks of "a beard of the general's cut" (3.6.77), referring to Essex's distinctive square-cut beard. Henry's sparing Harfleur after it surrenders recalls Essex's generosity to Cádiz after he captured the city in 1596. The Irish wars were on the minds of Englishmen in 1599, so much so that in the First Folio, Shakespeare mistakenly has the queen of France greet Henry as "brother Ireland" (5.2.12), corrected in later folios to "brother England." The horrors of war and the worries over the plight of returning war veterans also surface in this work.

Another concern was Elizabeth's successor. The Virgin Queen had not produced an heir. The most likely claimant to the throne was James VI of Scotland, whose mother, Mary Stuart, Queen of Scots, traced her lineage back to Henry VII, the first Tudor king (whose family tree includes Katharine, wife of Henry V). Henry V bases his claim to France through a woman, the French wife of Edward II; the French reject that claim, stating that in France, inheritance can descend only through the male line. This question of inheriting the throne through female ancestors occupied the minds of Shakespeare's contemporaries.

Yet another subject much under discussion in the 1590s was the legitimacy of war and the duty of soldiers. In 1586, William Stanley had been appointed governor of the town of Deventer in the Netherlands as part of English support for the Dutch rebelling against the Spanish. The next year, Stanley surrendered the town to the Spanish because, he maintained, the Dutch were rebels and so the city rightly belonged to Spain. The Catholic cardinal William Allen defended Stanley's action. The author known as G.D., in *A Briefe Discoverie of Doctor Allen's Seditious Drifts* (1588), replied that as a subject, Stanley was obliged to obey the queen regardless of whether her cause was just or not. In Act VI, Scene 1 of *Henry V,* Michael Williams, and John Bates discuss the justice of the English invasion. Bates comments: "for we know enough, if we know we are the King's subjects. If his cause be wrong, our obedience to the King wipes the crime of it out of us" (130–133), the very position G.D.

had taken. John Norden's *The Mirror of Honor* (1597) is another work dealing with what makes a war just: "it is then lawful, when it is done by the authority of the Prince." Henry argues that "War is [God's] beadle, war is his vengeance; so that here men are punish'd for before-breach of the King's laws in now the King's quarrel" (4.1.169–171). This idea may derive from Matthew 26:52: "for all that take the sworde, shall perishe with the sworde," in the words of the Geneva Bible. John Eliot's *Discourses of Warre and Single Combat* (1591) quotes this passage in making the same point that Henry does in the play.

In the play, Henry's seeking the approval of the Archbishop of Canterbury for his French invasion is historical, but it also recalls the earl of Leicester's appeal in 1585 to the then archbishop for his sanction for England to aid the Dutch against Spain. The church's subvention for Henry's expedition also calls to mind Archbishop Whitgift's arranging for the convocation to support the English war effort financially in 1588 and again in 1593.

Date and Text of the Play

As noted, *Henry V* was first staged between March and late September 1599. On August 4, 1600, four plays were listed on a preliminary leaf of Register C in the Stationers' Register "to be staied," in other words, not to be printed:

> *as yow like yt:* / a booke
> *HENRY THE FFIFT:* / a booke
> *Euery Man in his humor.* / a booke
> *The commedie of muche A doo about nothinge.*
> / a booke

Ten days later, the Stationers' Register C, folio 63, recorded the transfer of ownership of "The historye of Henrye the vth wth the battell of Agencourt" to Thomas Pavier, who reprinted the play in 1602 (as the Second Quarto, or Q2) and again in 1619 (as the Third Quarto, Q3, which bears the false date of 1608). Both were set from the First Quarto (Q1), which appeared in 1600, printed by Thomas Creede, who also printed Q2 for Pavier. Creede owned the copyright of *The Famous Victories of Henry the Fifth,* which he had printed in 1598. Perhaps, under the cover of this title, he issued Q1.

The First Quarto may be a memorial reconstruction by the actors who played Pistol, Exeter, and Gower. Will Kempe left the Lord Chamberlain's Men in 1599. He may have played Pistol, as he specialized in clownish parts. Once he left the Lord Chamberlain's Men, he would have felt no loyalty to the company and might have offered his reconstructed text to a printer. Q1 is about half the length of the 1623 First Folio version (1,622 lines as opposed to 3,380). Q1 omits the choruses; Act I, Scene 1; Act III, Scene 1; much of Act III, Scene 3; almost all of Act IV, Scene 2 (the remaining one-and-a-half lines are transferred to 3.7), and the epilogue. Act IV, Scenes 4 and 5 are transposed. The roles of Jamy and Macmorris are cut, as are Henry's soliloquy about ceremony (4.1) and Burgundy's lament about the effects of war on France (5.2.34–62).

Q1 may be based on a provincial production, as it has 37 or 38 speaking parts, whereas the First Folio version contains 45. Q1 could be performed with 11 actors. In his 2005 New Cambridge Shakespeare edition of the *Henry V,* Andrew Gurr suggests that Q1 may not have been an acting version at all because in three places the text calls for a character to exit and immediately return, a practice eschewed on the Elizabethan stage. Gurr offers the possibility that Q1 was, therefore, intended to be read.

Although Q1 has many characteristics that suggest it was one of those "stolne, and surreptitious copies" that John Heminge and Henry Condell condemn in their preface "To the great Variety of Readers" in the First Folio, it may represent the version staged at the Globe after the earl of Essex returned to London in disgrace in late September 1599. In February 1599, John Haywood published his *History of Henry IV,* dedicated to Essex; the archbishop of Canterbury, John Whitgift, ordered the dedication removed. When a second edition appeared in June, it was ordered burned. Haywood was committed to the Tower of London in July 1600 and remained there until Elizabeth died in 1603. By February 1600, a heroic engraving of Essex by Thomas Cockson was circulating in England. In August, the Privy Council ordered it suppressed. Staged productions seem to have enjoyed more freedom than published works: The deposition scene in *Richard II* probably was acted during Elizabeth's reign, though it was not included in printed versions until after her death. Printing, however, was closely watched. On June 1, 1599, the bishops decreed that "noe English histories be printed excepte they bee allowed by some of her maiesties privie Counsell."

The praise of Essex in the Chorus before Act 5 had become anachronistic as well as dangerous by late 1599. The Lord Chamberlain's Men may have decided to eliminate all the choruses, not just the one. The First Quarto version is less subversive throughout. It sharply curtails or cuts speeches highlighting the horrors of war. It removes the contentions among the captains of various nationalities in Act III, Scene 2. Cambridge in Q1 does not even hint at having any motive in seeking to kill Henry other than French gold. Henry's right to the throne—and by extension the right of his Tudor descendants—thus goes unchallenged. Nym does not accuse Henry of running "bad humors on" Falstaff (2.1.121). Q1 also more accurately keeps the Dauphin away from the Battle of Agincourt. In Act III, Scene 6, Shakespeare has the king of France ordering him not to participate in the battle but then places him there anyway. Q1 substitutes Bourbon for the Dauphin as Henry's chief antagonist in the second half of the play. Even if the Lord Chamberlain's Men continued to perform the play as Shakespeare had written it, they may have thought it prudent to print a safer version. In *Shakespearean Suspect Texts* (1996), Laurie E. Maguire argues that Q1 is not a memorial reconstruction, since except for the last scene the play is coherent. The only problems with the text stem from stage directions. Q1 may, therefore, not be the piracy it seems after all but rather the version Shakespeare's company chose to have printed.

The First Folio version, meanwhile, seems to be based on Shakespeare's foul papers, with some use of Q3. The only scene division noted is Act I, Scene

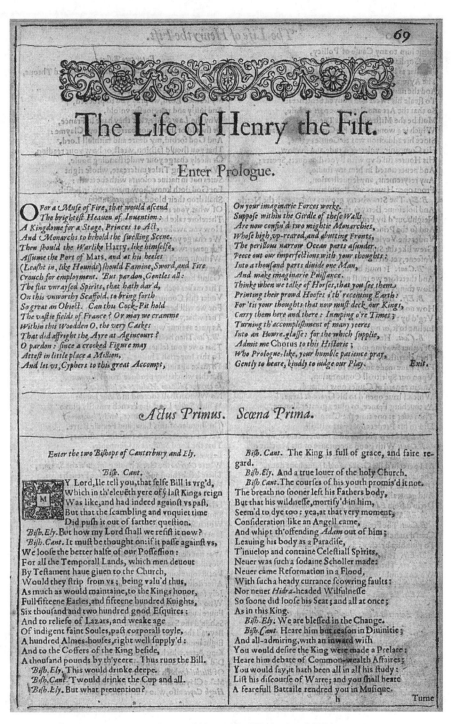

Title page of the First Folio edition of *Henry V*, published in 1623

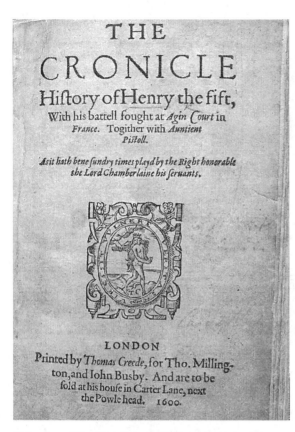

THE
CRONICLE
History of Henry the fift,
With his battell fought at *Agin Court* in
France. Togither with *Auntient*
Pistoll.

*As it hath bene sundry times playd by the Right honorable
the Lord Chamberlaine his seruants.*

LONDON
Printed by *Thomas Creede,* for Tho. Millington, and Iohn Busby. And are to be
sold at his house in Carter Lane, next
the Powle head. 1600.

Title page of the First Quarto (Q1) publication of *Henry V*, printed by Thomas Creede in 1600

1. Act II in the First Folio is the modern Act III; and Act III, the now-accepted Act IV. The First Folio begins Act IV at what is now Act IV, Scene 7; Act V corresponds to modern editorial practice. The First Folio lacks staging directions and regularized speech headings. For example, Mistress Quickly sometimes is labeled *"Woman."* In Act III, Scene 2, Fluellen, Macmorris, and Jamy are listed as *"Welch,"* *"Irish,"* and *"Scot,"* highlighting their generic quality, at least as Shakespeare initially conceived them.

SYNOPSIS
Brief Synopsis

Henry V begins on April 30, 1414, and ends (excluding the epilogue) on May 20, 1420, with the Treaty of Troyes. Henry V came to the throne in 1413 upon the death of his father, Henry IV. Henry V's accession serves as the culmination of Shakespeare's *Henry IV, Part 2.* Henry V soon renewed English claims to the French throne. As the action of *Henry V* begins, the Archbishop of Canterbury and the Bishop of Ely are discussing a bill pending in Parliament to seize lands deeded to the church by laypeople. This is the only domestic issue raised in the play.

To persuade the king to quash the bill, the Archbishop intends to offer Henry a large sum of money to finance a campaign in France, an invasion that the prelate encourages by supporting Henry's right to the French crown. In 1415, Henry assembles an English force at Southampton, where several noblemen are planning to kill him. This plot thwarted, Henry and his army sail for France. Included in the English forces are two of the king's former companions, the disreputable Bardolph and Pistol, along with a new partner in crime, Nym.

The king first besieges Harfleur, an important port that will serve as his base of operations. The city falls after a siege, but the English forces are so depleted by war and sickness and the season so advanced—medieval armies did not fight in the winter—that Henry resolves to withdraw to Calais without further fighting.

Trying to take advantage of the English army's weakness, the French block Henry's route, hoping for a decisive victory that will end Henry's military plans. The ensuing battle at Agincourt results in a decisive victory for the English. Although outnumbered four or five to one (10,000–15,000 English to 60,000 French), the English forces kill some 10,000 French, while suffering far fewer casualties themselves: 29, according to the play. Two non-fighting casualties are Bardolph and Nym, hanged for looting.

The play jumps from 1415 to 1420, suggesting (incorrectly) that the English victory at Agincourt led directly to the Treaty of Troyes, in which King Charles VI of France gives his daughter Katharine to Henry as wife and names Henry V and his descendants as heirs to the French throne. The Epilogue notes that after Henry V died in 1422 and his infant son, Henry VI, was crowned king, England lost France and sank into the civil war known as the Wars of the Roses (subjects of Shakespeare's first tetralogy dealing with English history).

Prologue

The Chorus, who appears before each act, begins by wishing for "a muse of fire" (l.1) that would inspire a play worthy of its subject. Such a play would have a kingdom for a stage, real rulers for actors, and actual armies engaging in battle. Lacking these, the Chorus asks the audience to imagine that the theater encompasses England and France and that each actor represents many soldiers. He calls upon the spectators to transport the players mentally from place to place and from year to year. The Chorus concludes with a plea for a kind reception to the play to follow.

Act I, Scene 1

The action begins in an antechamber of the king's London palace. The Archbishop of Canterbury and the Bishop of Ely are discussing a bill now before Parliament that would expropriate all the lands given to the church by the laity. The clerics interrupt this conversation to talk about Henry V's sudden transformation. As Prince of Wales he had been, or at least had seemed to be, a scofflaw and scapegrace who consorted with the demimonde. Yet, as soon as he ascended to the throne, he banished his former dissolute companions and began to govern soberly and justly.

The conversation then returns to the subject of church property. To persuade the king to quash the bill, the Archbishop of Canterbury proposes to offer Henry a large sum of money to help finance the pending invasion of France.

Act I, Scene 2

Henry and his council enter the presence chamber of the palace. The Archbishop and the Bishop of Ely soon follow. The king asks the Archbishop whether he (Henry) may justly claim the French throne, basing his right to it on his great-great grandmother, who was daughter of King Philip

IV of France. The French have rejected this claim, stating that the Salic law (named for a Frankish tribe that lived on the Sala River), which applies in France, bars inheritance through the female line. Henry wants to know whether the French position is justified.

In a lengthy reply that may not be totally disinterested, the Archbishop of Canterbury states that the Salic law does not apply to France. The Archbishop; the Bishop of Ely; the king's uncle, the duke of Exeter; and the Earl of Westmoreland urge the king to pursue his claim militarily. Henry worries that if England invades France, Scotland will seize the opportunity to invade England. Ely suggests that Henry subdue Scotland and then attack France, but the Archbishop and Exeter assure Henry that England can defend itself at home even as it fights the French. Henry resolves on war to gain the French crown.

The French ambassadors have been waiting to respond to Henry's demand for various dukedoms in their country. Now that Henry has decided he wants the entire country, he summons them to hear their answer. Their reply comes from the Dauphin, not the king. Knowing of Henry's reputation as a madcap prince, the Dauphin has sent him a barrel of tennis balls as more fitting his inclinations than the French territories he had demanded. Henry replies that the Dauphin's jest will ring hollow when the English army strikes the French crown out of the court. Henry dismisses the ambassadors and orders that preparations be made for the invasion.

Act II, Chorus

The Chorus declares that all the youth of England are eager to follow Henry on his quest to conquer France. Yet, the Chorus notes that three men close to the king—Richard, Earl of Cambridge; Henry, Lord Scroop of Masham, and Sir Thomas Grey—have been seduced by French bribes to kill Henry at Southampton before he can lead his flotilla across the English Channel. The Chorus promises to convey the audience to France and back again without causing seasickness, as the actors do not want to turn the viewers' stomachs.

Act II, Scene 1

The act opens at Eastcheap, a dubious part of London to which Henry used to resort before becoming king. One of his former criminal associates, Pistol, and a newcomer, Nym (whose name means "thief"), have quarreled over Mistress Quickly, owner of the Boar's-Head Tavern. She had been betrothed to Nym but then had married Pistol. When Nym and Pistol meet, they draw their swords and insult each other. Bardolph, another of the king's former friends, reconciles them.

A Boy enters to report that Sir John Falstaff is dying. Falstaff had been Henry's closest friend before the latter had become king and had banished Sir John and his associates. After Mistress Quickly and the Boy leave to attend Falstaff, Nym and Pistol quarrel again, this time over a gambling debt. Bardolph once more intervenes. Mistress Quickly reappears to summon the men to Falstaff's deathbed.

Act II, Scene 2

The scene shifts to Southampton. The king enters with his attendants, including the three men the Chorus has identified as traitors. Henry orders the release of a man who the previous day, while in his cups, had railed against the king. Scroop, Cambridge, and Grey protest this leniency, but Henry overrules them. They then ask for their letters appointing them commissioners and so allowing them to act in the king's absence. Henry gives them letters, but instead of naming them commissioners, these documents show that the king is aware of their plot to kill him.

The three confess and ask for mercy. Henry replies that their recent harsh counsel concerning the drunk man has stifled all clemency. He expresses disappointment at their betrayal. They reply that they are glad their plot failed. Henry says that for himself he seeks no vengeance, but since they have plotted against their country, he sentences them to death. After the three are led away, Henry orders the expedition to sail to France.

Act II, Scene 3

Back at Eastcheap in the Boar's-Head Tavern, Mistress Quickly asks to accompany her husband, Pistol, as far as Staines on the road to Southampton. Pistol is too emotionally wrought to allow her to do so. She, Bardolph, Nym, and the Boy discuss Falstaff's death. The men set off to join the English force about to invade France, which they hope to plunder.

Act II, Scene 4

At the palace in Paris, King Charles VI and his court discuss the impending English invasion. The Dauphin dismisses the threat. The Constable of France replies that the Dauphin underestimates Henry's abilities. The French king concurs with the Constable and reminds his nobles of Edward III's victory at Crécy (1346).

Exeter and other English lords arrive to demand the French crown for Henry. Exeter warns that if Charles refuses to surrender the throne, war will ensue. Exeter then conveys to the Dauphin Henry's message of contempt. The king promises to reply the next day. Exeter urges haste; Henry and his army are already in France.

Act III, Chorus

The Chorus urges the audience to envision the English fleet sailing from Southampton to France and then to picture in their minds the English siege of Harfleur. The English ambassadors have returned with an unsatisfactory answer: The French king offers Henry only some dukedoms and the hand of Katharine in marriage. So, the siege continues.

Act III, Scene 1

The battle for Harfleur is not going well for the English; they are retreating. Henry delivers a rousing speech to impel his soldiers back into battle.

Act III, Scene 2

Bardolph mocks Henry's speech while avoiding the fighting. Nym, Pistol, and the Boy also shun battle until Fluellen, a Welsh captain, drives the

William Devereux as the Constable of France in *Henry V* *(Photographed by Langfier)*

warfare. Macmorris laments the poor execution of the mining operation. Fluellen wants to debate with him about Roman military tactics. Macmorris replies that now is not a good time for such a conversation. Fluellen and Macmorris quarrel; Macmorris threatens to cut off Fluellen's head. Gower tries to pacify them. The scene ends as Harfleur sounds a trumpet to signal its willingness to negotiate.

Act III, Scene 3

Henry tells the citizens of Harfleur assembled on the walls that they must surrender or face the dreadful consequences of conquest. The town's governor enters to say that the aid he expected from the Dauphin will not arrive, so he yields the town. Henry appoints Exeter as governor of Harfleur and orders that the French be treated kindly. He announces his intent to withdraw to Calais for the winter.

Act III, Scene 4

In a comic interlude filled with sexual innuendo, but strategically placed in the middle of the play, Katharine receives an English lesson from Alice, an old gentlewoman who has been to England.

Act III, Scene 5

The king of France and his court lament Henry's progress through their country. They cannot understand how these "Norman bastards," as the Duke of Brittany calls them (l.10), can fight so well. The Constable is equally astonished that the dank English climate yields such warriors. King Charles orders his nobles to stop Henry's advance and capture the English king. The Constable regrets that Henry's army is so small. He is sure that Henry will offer to be ransomed as soon as the French army appears. The Dauphin wants to accompany the other nobles to the battlefield, but the king insists that he stay in Rouen.

Act III, Scene 6

The English march to Calais is interrupted by an encounter with a French force seeking to destroy a

men forward. The Boy remains behind to comment negatively on his three companions.

Gower, an English captain, enters to summon Fluellen to a conference to discuss the mining of Harfleur. Fluellen criticizes the Irish captain Macmorris for his lack of knowledge of military science. Macmorris enters with the Scottish captain Jamy. Fluellen praises the latter for his knowledge of ancient

bridge. The English forces thwart this effort. Pistol enters. According to Fluellen, Pistol has fought bravely during this skirmish. Pistol asks Fluellen to intercede for Bardolph, who has stolen a pax (a piece of metal stamped with the image of a crucifix) or pyx (a box holding communion wafers) from a church and therefore has been sentenced to death for looting. Fluellen refuses to intervene. Pistol curses Fluellen and leaves. Gower tells Fluellen that Pistol is a rogue.

Henry and his army appear. He asks Fluellen about the bridge. Fluellen replies that Exeter has gained the victory with no losses, except for a man about to be hanged for robbing a church. Henry replies that all who pilfer from the French will be executed because he wants to gain the goodwill of those he hopes will be his French subjects.

Montjoy, the French herald, arrives to demand reparations for the English depredations. Henry refuses. He tells the herald that the English wish to proceed peacefully to Calais, but if the French bar his way, he will fight.

Act III, Scene 7

The French army blocks Henry's path. On the eve of battle, the French nobles praise themselves, their armor, and their horses. The Constable and the Dauphin quarrel over the latter's fondness for his steed. After the Dauphin departs, the Duke of Orleans defends the prince, but the Constable continues to mock him. The two nobles agree, however, that the English are fools to invade France. Orleans predicts that by the next morning, each of them will have captured a hundred English prisoners.

Act IV, Chorus

The Chorus conjures up the image of the eve of battle. The rival camps are so close to each other that they can almost hear each other's whispers. He imagines the campfires, the horses neighing, the armorers mending coats of mail.

The French, he says, are so confident of victory that they already are dicing for English prisoners. In contrast, the English sit patiently and dejectedly beside their fires. Henry walks among the troops to cheer them. The Chorus concludes with an apology for the stage battle to come; it will not do justice to the reality of Agincourt.

Act IV, Scene 1

Henry encourages his brothers Humphrey, Duke of Gloucester, and John, Duke of Bedford. Henry borrows the cloak of Sir Thomas Erpingham to disguise himself. As soon as the others leave, Henry encounters Pistol. The king (former Prince of Wales, born in Monmouth) pretends to be a Welsh pikeman, a friend of Fluellen. Since Pistol has quarreled with Fluellen, Pistol insults the disguised king and departs.

The king overhears a conversation between Fluellen and Gower. Fluellen wants Gower to speak more softly because Pompey's soldiers whispered. When the captains leave, Henry comes upon three common soldiers: John Bates, Alexander Court, and Michael Williams. The king, still pretending to be a soldier like them, debates with the men about the king's ethical/religious responsibility for those who die in battle.

They quarrel even more heatedly when Henry says he has heard that the king has pledged not to be ransomed if the English lose. Williams does not believe the king's word. Henry says that if the king lies, he will never trust him again. Williams bristles at what he regards as a foolish statement: What can a commoner do if a king breaks a promise? The two exchange gloves, pledging to continue this quarrel after the battle.

The soldiers withdraw. Alone, Henry laments the hard lot of kingship. Sir Thomas Erpingham comes to summon him to a council of war. Erpingham leaves, and Henry resumes his interrupted soliloquy, now praying that God not punish him in battle for his father's usurpation of the throne and the murder of Richard II. Gloucester comes to summon the king again, and the two exit.

Act IV, Scene 2

In the French camp, the Constable orders the nobles to mount. He expects an easy victory.

Grandpré and the Dauphin echo his optimistic expectations.

Act IV, Scene 3

As the vastly outnumbered English prepare for battle, Westmoreland wishes for another 10,000 soldiers. Henry replies with the play's most famous speech. He declares that he does not want to share the day's honor with any more people. He tells the officers to announce that if anyone fears fighting, that man is free to leave and will receive money for his journey. Those who engage in today's battle, Henry says, will annually recount their deeds, and those men will be remembered forever. This speech so motivates Westmoreland that he wishes now that he and Henry alone were fighting the French.

Montjoy returns and again asks for ransom. Henry replies that the French should capture him first. He reminds the herald of the lion hunter who sold the beast's skin while the lion still lived; the hunter became the lion's dinner. Henry dismisses Montjoy, telling him to come no more. Montjoy departs. The Duke of York asks to lead the English vanguard, a request Henry grants.

Act IV, Scene 4

In the play's only battle scene, Pistol has captured a Frenchman, Monsieur Le Fer. Le Fer, who speaks no English, is even more cowardly than Pistol, who speaks no French. Shakespeare creates comedy out of their misunderstandings. The Boy serves as translator and arranges for Le Fer to pay 200 crowns in ransom. When the two men exit, the Boy states that Bardolph and Nym have been hanged. He goes off to guard the baggage train, which he notes would be easy prey for the French.

Act IV, Scene 5

The French nobles lament their defeat and resolve to attack again.

Act IV, Scene 6

Henry, Exeter, and their retinue enter with French prisoners. Exeter movingly reports the deaths of York and Suffolk. A trumpet announces that the French have regrouped for another attack. Henry orders that the French prisoners be killed; Shakespeare may have intended the order to be carried out onstage.

Act IV, Scene 7

Fluellen and Gower enter. Fluellen condemns the French attack on the baggage train and their massacre of the boys guarding it. According to Gower, the king has ordered the killing of the French prisoners in retaliation. Fluellen draws an elaborate comparison, in the manner of Plutarch, between Alexander the Great and Henry.

Henry enters, enraged at the killing of the boys. He orders his herald to tell the French, who remain on the battlefield, to fight or flee. If the French do not abandon the field, thus giving the English the victory, he will kill all his prisoners and spare no one the English capture.

As soon as the English herald departs on his mission, Montjoy arrives. Henry asks whether he has come again for ransom. Montjoy replies that he would like Henry to allow the French to bury their dead. Henry says he is not sure whether the victory is his, since French forces remain on the battlefield. Montjoy tells him that the English have triumphed.

Williams appears wearing King Henry's glove in his cap. Henry asks about the glove; Williams replies that he intends to beat the person who gave it to him. When Williams leaves, Henry instructs Fluellen to wear Williams's glove in his hat. Henry says that anyone who challenges that glove is a French ally. Fluellen exits. Henry sends Warwick and Gloucester after him to prevent mischief.

Act IV, Scene 8

Williams, seeing his glove in Fluellen's cap, assumes that Fluellen was the soldier with whom he had argued the previous night. Williams therefore strikes the Welshman. Fluellen accuses Williams of treason. Henry intervenes and confesses that he was Williams's antagonist. Henry instructs Exeter to fill the glove with crowns and give it to Williams, and Fluellen adds a shilling of his own to the sum. Williams refuses the money.

The English Herald delivers notes listing the French and English casualties. The French have lost 10,000 men, almost all of them nobles and knights. The English losses consist of the Duke of York, the Earl of Suffolk, a knight, an esquire, and 25 commoners. Henry orders that the English give God all credit for the victory. The English army resumes its march to Calais and thence back home.

Act V, Chorus

The Chorus describes Henry's triumphant return to London. In Shakespeare's only overt reference to current events, the Chorus imagines a similar scene were the earl of Essex to return victorious from the war in Ireland. The Chorus refers to the visit to England of Sigismund, Holy Roman Emperor, in 1416 to try to arrange a peace treaty between England and France. Peace was concluded only in 1420; the Chorus bridges the gap of five years between the Battle of Agincourt and the Treaty of Troyes (May 1420) and transports the audience back to France.

Act V, Scene 1

This scene seems to occur immediately after the victory at Agincourt. Pistol has insulted Fluellen's leek, a symbol of Wales. Fluellen makes Pistol eat a leek. Left alone, Pistol reports the death of his wife. He will return to England to steal and beg.

Act V, Scene 2

In a royal palace in France, Charles VI, Queen Isabel, and their daughter, Katharine, enter from one side with other French nobles, while Henry and his attendants enter from the other. The Duke Burgundy expresses a desire for peace, which Henry says is obtainable if the French accede to all his demands. While the others leave to conclude a peace treaty, Henry woos Katharine with clever wordplay. She agrees to marry him—she has no choice—and they seal their agreement with a kiss. The French king and queen and nobles return along with the English nobles and report that the French have accepted Henry's terms. Katharine will marry Henry, and

In this 1830 painting, Henry V gives a ring to Catherine of Valois at the conclusion of the Treaty of Troyes. This print was published by the London Printing and Publishing Company. *(Painting by William Hamilton; engraving by John Rogers)*

he and his children will become heirs to the French throne, thus disinheriting the Dauphin. Queen Isabel hopes that the union between Henry and Katharine, England and France, will endure in peace.

Epilogue

In a sonnet, the Chorus relates that Henry's successful reign was short-lived: he died in 1422. His infant son, Henry VI, was crowned king of England and France, but during his reign, the English would lose all that Henry had won abroad, and England would descend into the civil war known as the Wars of the Roses, the subject of Shakespeare's first tetralogy (*Henry VI, Parts 1, 2,* and *3* and *Richard III*).

CHARACTER LIST

King Henry V   King of England. A reformed scapegrace who becomes one of England's most successful leaders.

Chorus   He delivers the prologue and epilogue and introduces each act, briefly summarizing the action that ensues and identifies leaps in time and place.

Humphrey, Duke of Gloucester   Brother of Henry V.

John, Duke of Bedford   Brother of Henry V.

Duke of Clarence   Brother of Henry V.

Duke of Exeter   Henry V's uncle. He acts as the king's ambassador to France.

Duke of York   Henry V's cousin. He leads the vanguard of the English forces at Agincourt and dies in the battle.

Earl of Salisbury   Councillor to Henry V.

Earl of Westmoreland   Attendant of Henry V.

Earl of Warwick   Member of Henry's court.

Archbishop of Canterbury   Worried that Parliament will expropriate the church's temporal lands, the prelate seeks to persuade Henry to prevent this action and justifies Henry's claim to the French throne.

Bishop of Ely   The Archbishop's confederate. Ely suggests that Henry subdue Scotland before he invades France.

Earl of Cambridge   One of three conspirators who seek to kill Henry at Southampton.

Lord Scroop   A Southampton conspirator; close friend of Henry V.

Sir Thomas Grey   A Southampton conspirator.

Sir Thomas Erpingham   One of Henry's chief military officers.

Gower   An English captain.

Fluellen   A Welsh captain. This comic figure shows much concern for the military practices of the Romans.

Macmorris   An Irish captain.

Jamy   A Scottish captain.

John Bates   A common English soldier. He engages in a debate with the king on the eve of battle.

Alexander Court   A common English soldier.

Michael Williams   A common English soldier who debates with Henry V on the eve of battle and later quarrels with Fluellen.

Pistol   An old drinking companion of Henry V when the king was Prince of Wales. He serves as sutler (seller of provisions) to the English army. He is married to Mistress Nell Quickly.

Nym   A disreputable associate of Pistol and Bardolph. His name means "thief," and indeed he is hanged in France for looting.

Bardolph   One of Henry's former associates. He joins the English invasion of France in the expectation of plunder and is hanged for robbing a church.

Boy   Accompanies Pistol, Nym, and Bardolph to France. He offers pithy commentary about his three colleagues. The Boy is killed when the French attack the English baggage train at Agincourt.

English Herald   Bears the king's messages to the French army and provides the casualty lists after the Battle of Agincourt.

Charles VI   King of France.

Lewis   The Dauphin (or Dolphin), heir to the French throne and Henry's antagonist.

Duke of Burgundy   Member of the French court; urges peace between England and France.

Duke of Orleans   Member of the French court and a leader of the French army.

Duke of Bourbon   A leader of the French forces; captured by Henry V.

Duke of Brittany   French nobleman.

Duke of Berri   French aristocrat.

Duke of Beaumont   French aristocrat killed at Agincourt.

Constable of France   Officer in the French army. He warns against underestimating Henry and is killed at Agincourt.

Rambures   Master of the French crossbows. He is killed at Agincourt.

Grandpré   Another French nobleman killed at Agincourt.

Governor of Harfleur   French official who surrenders the town to Henry.

Montjoy   French herald who first comes to Henry confidently to demand ransom and later returns humbly to ask permission to bury the French dead.

Isabel   Queen of France who, like Burgundy, hopes for peace between the two countries.

Katharine   Daughter of the king and queen of France and later the wife of Henry V.

Alice   Katharine's Franglais-speaking attendant.

Mistress Nell Quickly   Owner of the Boar's-Head Tavern and married to Pistol. She dies of syphilis while Pistol is in France.

CHARACTER STUDIES
Henry V

Henry V is one of Shakespeare's most enigmatic characters. His treatment in this play raises two questions. The first concerns the extent to which he resembles Prince Hal in the two parts of *Henry IV.* In those plays, he associated with scapegraces and scofflaws. He spent his time drinking in the Boar's-Head Tavern in Eastcheap, a disreputable part of London, rather than participating in government at the royal palace in Westminster. Yet, at the end of *Henry IV, Part 2,* he banishes his old friends and promises to reform. The Archbishop of Canterbury and the Bishop of Ely allude to this transformation in the play's first scene. According the former, Henry V as king bears no resemblance to his former self:

> The breath no sooner left his father's body,
> But that his wildness, mortified in him,
> Seem'd to die, too; yea, at that very moment,
> Consideration like an angel came
> And whipt th' offending Adam out of him,
> Leaving his body as a paradise
> T' envelop and contain celestial spirits.
> Never was such a sudden scholar made;

King Henry V sentences the three traitors, Scroop, Cambridge, and Grey, to death in Act II, Scene 2 of *Henry V.* This is a print from the Boydell Shakespeare Gallery project, which was first conceived in 1786 and lasted until 1805. *(Painting by Henry Fuseli; engraving by Robert Thew)*

Never came reformation in a flood
With such a heady currance, scouring faults;
Nor never Hydra-headed willfulness
So soon did lose his seat (and all at once)
As in this king. (1.1.25–37)

The Archbishop maintains that Henry, as king, is a character totally different from the one Shakespeare presented earlier in the tetralogy. In one of Shakespeare's chief sources for this play, *The Famous Victories of Henry the Fifth,* the prince's metamorphosis is instantaneous and complete. Henry himself tells his former friend Falstaff, "Presume not that I am the thing I was, / For God doth know, so shall the world perceive, / That I have turn'd away my former self" (*Henry IV, Part 2,* 5.5.56–58).

Shakespeare's other sources also describe a sudden change. According to R. Fabyan's *Chronicle* (1559),

This man before the death of his father,
applied him unto all vyce and insolency,
and drewe unto him all riottours and wildly
disposed persons. But after he was admitted
to the rule of the lande, anon and sodainely
he became a newe man, and turned all that
rage and wildnessse into sobernesse and wise
sadnesse, and the vice into constant vertue.

According to Ely, Henry V's character is consistent with that of the Prince of Wales. As early as *Richard II,* when Percy reports that the prince intends to wear a prostitute's glove as a favor at the jousts at Oxford, Henry IV says that he sees in his son "some sparks of better hope, which elder years / May happily bring forth" (5.3.21–22). At the end of Act I, Scene 2, *Henry IV, Part 1,* Prince Hal delivers a soliloquy in which he anticipates his reformation. Whereas in *The Famous Victories* he indulges in robberies and assaults the Lord Chief Justice, in Shakespeare's *Henry IV* plays, the Prince of Wales never commits a crime and shows bravery and military skill at the Battle of Shrewsbury. When Hal's dying father says he fears "th' unguided days / And rotten times" that will ensue

under the new king (*Henry IV, Part 2,* 4.4.59–60), Warwick predicts a better future:

The Prince but studies his companions
Like a strange tongue, wherein, to gain the
  language,
'Tis needful that the most immodest word
Be look'd upon and learnt, which once
  attain'd,
Your Highness knows, comes to no further use
But to be known and hated. So, like gross terms,
The Prince will in the perfectness of time
Cast off his followers, and their memory
Shall as a pattern or a measure live,
By which his Grace must mete the lives of other,
Turning past evils to advantages. (4.4.68–78)

This question of continuity has engaged 20th-century critics. Evelyn May Albright sides with the Bishop of Ely and Warwick. She writes: "Shakespeare's trilogy on Henry V shows the development of a wise, humane, and, above all, courageous and patriotic king from a wayward, almost dissolute boy, impulsive and undignified, but warm-hearted and devoted to the welfare of his friends and to any inspiring cause (731). J. H. Walter and Norman Rabkin also see continuity. Alan Howard, who played Hal and Henry in the 1975 Royal Shakespeare Company productions of *Henry IV, Parts 1* and *2* and *Henry V,* also argued that Hal anticipates Henry V.

Robert Speaight, writing in *The Tablet* for September 8, 1951, sides with the Archbishop: "It is rarely possible to believe that these [Hal and Henry V] are one and the same person". Similarly, J. W. Lambert, reflecting in the *Sunday Times* on Richard Burton's 1951 Stratford-on-Avon portrayal of Hal and Henry, observed, "Perhaps the differences between the young Prince Hal and the soldier King are too great to allow the two to be welded into one developing character". E. M. W. Tillyard, too, found little similarity between the prince and the king: "Shakespeare [jettisoned] the character he had created and [substituted] one which, though lacking all consistency, satisfied the requirements both of the chroniclers and of popular tradition" (306).

In *Shakespeare after All* (2004), Marjorie Garber argues that the difference lies not in the character but in his circumstances. As king, Henry "will put aside private feelings and private friendships to become a public man" (396). In this view, she echoes James L. Calderwood in *Metadrama in Shakespeare's Henriad,* Richard II *to* Henry V (1979). Calderwood maintains that in *Henry V,* "Harry the man is now kept private, suppressed in favor of Harry the king, who is nearly always on public display" (141). Even earlier, Alvin Kernan had observed that in this final play of the Henriad, Henry almost never reveals his feelings. This critics imply that the question of continuity, therefore, is moot.

The other major debate over Henry concerns Shakespeare's attitude toward him. From his sources, Shakespeare inherited a favorable view of the king. Humphrey, the duke of Gloucester, commissioned Tito Livio to write a biography of his brother as a conduct manual for his nephew, Henry VI. In 1513 or 1514, an anonymous translator offered an English version of the original Latin text to Henry VIII, then fighting against France, just as Henry had done a century earlier. In *The Union of the Two Noble and Illustre Famelies of Lancastre and Yorke* (1548), Hall titled his chapter dealing with Henry V's reign as "The victorious acts of kyng Henry the V." Of that ruler, Hall writes: "Neither fire, rust, nor frettyng time shall amongst Englishmen either appall his honor or obliterate his glory, [who] in so few years and brief days achieved so great a conquest." Hall describes him as follows:

> a king whose life was immaculate and his living without spot . . . a shepherd whom his flock loved and lovingly obeyed . . . he was merciful to offenders, charitable to the needy; indifferent [impartial] to all men, faithful to his friends, and fierce to his enemies, toward God most devout, toward the world moderate, and to his realm a very father.

Holinshed's *Chronicles* (1587) refers to Henry as "a majestie . . . that both lived and died a paterne in princehood, a lode-starre in honour, and mirrour of magnificence." Samuel Daniel's *Civil Wars* (1595) calls Henry a "Mirror of virtue, miracle of worth" (145). In that poem, the king's ghost laments:

> O that our times had had some sacred wight
> Whose wordes as happie as our swords had bin
> To have prepar'd for us *Tropheis* aright
> Of undecaying frames t' have rested in. (143)

For some critics, Shakespeare's play continues this mood of panegyric. Tillyard regards Shakespeare's Henry V as an ideal ruler, the "paragon of kingly virtue" (305–306). Lily B. Campbell writes, in *Shakespeare's "Histories": Mirrors of Elizabethan Policy* (1947), "Henry V stands as the ideal hero in contrast with the troubled John, the deposed Richard, the rebel Henry IV; for the traditional conception of Henry V was of a hero-king, and about his dominant figure Shakespeare chose to fashion a hero-play" (255). Wilson, in his 1947 Cambridge University Press edition of the play, praises Henry. In his introduction to the 1954 Arden edition of the play, J. H. Walter claims that Henry is portrayed as an ideal Christian ruler. According to M. M. Reese, "If Shakespeare had any secret reservations about the character, they are not apparent on the stage, where Henry is virtuous, strong and gay, a born leader of men. . . . Henry is an appointed symbol of majesty, and the action of the play is directed with the most elaborate care to show him doing everything that the age expected of the perfect king" (320). Geoffrey Bullough maintains that in Shakespeare's play, "We see Henry V as the ideal man of action, reasonable, just, touched with some of his old impetuosity, but now entirely devoted to the service of his country, and aware of his grave responsibilities" (355). C. W. R. D. Moseley, in *Shakespeare's History Plays,* Richard II *to* Henry V (1988), echoes the Chorus's praise of Henry as "the mirror of all Christian kings" (2.0.6).

Others have taken a dimmer view of the king. William Hazlitt described him as "a very amiable monster" (133). For George Bernard Shaw, Henry is an imperial warmonger. E. K. Chambers described him as "the prototype of the blatant modern imperialist, with his insolent talk of 'little England.'". Mark Van Doren called Henry a "mere good fellow, a hearty undergraduate with enormous initials on his chest". Harold C. Goddard, in *The Meaning of Shakespeare* (1951), regards the king as hypocritical, a man who "made himself into something that comes too close for comfort to Machiavelli's ideal prince" (267).

A middle course finds partial truth in both positions. Anthony Quayle, who directed the two tetralogies at Stratford in 1951, maintained that Shakespeare did not seek to idealize Henry:

> Hal inherits some of his father's political astuteness and even ruthlessness, he lets us see a king who can lose his temper with a common soldier [4.1]. He lets us see a man. A man who, more than any other of the monarchs whom Shakespeare dramatized, possessed at least some of the qualities of the great king including that of the greatest quality: that of having and holding his people's love. (25–26)

Norman Rabkin's "Rabbit, Duck, and *Henry V*" nicely summarizes the diverging views about one of Shakespeare's most enigmatic characters. Rabkin takes his title from the Gestalt psychology experiment involving a picture that may be seen as the head of either a duck or a rabbit, but not both at the same time. According to Rabkin, Shakespeare has created "a subtle and complex study of a king who curiously combines strengths and weaknesses, virtues and vices" (295). Hence, like Julius Caesar, the title character of Shakespeare's next play, Henry can be seen as the best or worst of men, a power-hungry dictator or a benevolent ruler.

Chorus

The Chorus, too, prompts varying reactions. This device of the chorus was old fashioned by 1599,

and Shakespeare mocked its use in *Pyramus and Thisbe* in *A Midsummer Night's Dream* as well as in *The Murder of Gonzago* in *Hamlet*. Perhaps precisely because it was antiquated Shakespeare introduced it in a play dealing with events a century old. He would use a chorus again in *Pericles* (1609), in which the medieval poet Gower introduces each act. In that play's opening lines, Gower states: "To sing a song that old was sung, / From ashes ancient Gower is come" (1.0.1–2). An old device suits a play set in the distant past.

The Chorus in *Henry V* employs stately diction and neologisms that lend dignity to his speeches. Among his linguistic creations are "vasty" and "abutting" (Prologue, 12, 21), "sternage" (3.0.18), and "self-glorious" (5.0.20). He also inverts word order, as in "crowns imperial" (2.0.10) and "fleets majestical" (3.0.16). The Chorus praises Henry, and his admiration extends to his echoing the king's language. Thus, like the king, he employs many hortatory verbs, giving orders to the audience in the same way the king commands his subjects.

In *Henry V,* the Chorus serves two functions. One is to anticipate the action and thereby orient the audience. In this role, he repeatedly praises the king, who is "warlike Harry" (Prologue, 5), "the mirror of all Christian kings" (2.0.6), comforter of his troops the night before Agincourt (4.0), "free from vainness and self-glorious pride," a "conqu'ring Caesar" (5.0.20, 28). The other is to apologize for the deficiencies of the theater and to urge spectators to use their imaginations to "Piece out our imperfections with your thoughts" (Prologue, 23).

In his first role, though, the Chorus often seems inadequate. At the beginning of Act II, he says that "all the youth of England are on fire" (1) to follow Henry to France and advises the audience that "Unto Southampton do we shift our scene" (42). The act then moves to Eastcheap, London, where Nym, Pistol, and Bardolph appear none too eager to join the army. Indeed, the action that the Chorus describes occupies only one of the act's four scenes. In Act IV, Scene 1, contrary to the Chorus's assurance that Henry comforts his soldiers, the king quarrels with them. The Chorus also promises battle scenes; the play has only one, a comic scene. At the beginning of Act V, the Chorus transports the audience to London and thence back to France five years later; the scene that follows occurs a day or two after the Battle of Agincourt.

The Chorus thus disorients as much as he orients. The Chorus offers an orthodox interpretation of the action and the king, which the ensuing action then undercuts or at least questions. What Walter Benjamin observed about Bertolt Brecht's theatrical technique holds true for Shakespeare as well: "Epic theatre . . . derives a lively and productive consciousness from the fact that it is theatre. . . . elements of reality . . . are not brought closer to the spectator but distanced from him. When he recognizes them as real conditions it is not, as in naturalistic theatre, with complacency, but with astonishment" (4).

The Chorus's comments about the limitations of the stage are similarly ambiguous. Shakespeare's was a theater of convention rather than illusion. Plays were staged during the day; the outdoor theaters had no artificial illumination and so had to rely on London's (limited) sunlight. Yet, many scenes are set at night. When Bernardo and Francisco, at the beginning of *Hamlet,* announce that it is cold midnight, the audience accepts these assertions, even though the play may be unfolding on a balmy September afternoon. When Oberon, in *A Midsummer Night's Dream,* claims that he is invisible to Demetrius and Helena (2.1.186), the audience suspends its disbelief even as it looks straight at him. In noting the stage's physical deficiencies, the Chorus in fact highlights the power of the empty space. The audience follows the Chorus's instruction to "Piece out our imperfections with your thoughts" (Prologue, 23), to create what Shakespeare's contemporary Christopher Marlowe, in another context, described as "infinite riches in a little room" (6).

Fluellen

The Welsh captain has the most lines of any character in the play except for Henry himself. Fluellen first appears in Act III, Scene 2, driving the reluctant Pistol, Bardolph, and Nym into battle. Shortly afterward, he criticizes the Irish captain Macmorris for ignorance of "the true disciplines of the wars" (3.2.71–72), that is, military science, and praises the Scottish captain Jamy for his command of the subject. Fluellen wishes to debate the topic and gets into a heated argument with his Irish counterpart. Shakespeare introduced the Welshman, along with a Scotsman and an Irishman, to show that Henry had unified Britain under his banner, though the relationship among these proves less than harmonious. In reality, Welsh and Scottish troops fought alongside the French against the English and Irish at Agincourt.

Later in Act III, Pistol asks Fluellen to intercede for Bardolph, who has been sentenced to death for stealing from a church. Fluellen, consistent with his rigid belief in military discipline, refuses to help the condemned soldier. Fluellen's stance provokes another division within the army, which ends in Act V, Scene 1 with Fluellen's beating Pistol and forcing him to eat a leek, a Welsh symbol that Pistol had mocked, probably in anger over Fluellen's failure to try to save Bardolph.

On the eve of battle at Agincourt, Fluellen reprimands the English captain Gower for speaking too loudly, noting that Pompey's forces did not engage in "tiddle taddle nor pibble babble" (4.1.70–71); Fluellen's speech again reflects his obsession with military theory and history, especially the practices of the Romans. Fluellen's fascination with ancient warfare makes him a comic figure; he wishes to debate the subject even in the midst of battle. His accent and choice of words, too, would strike Elizabethan audiences as funny, as he generally pronounces "Jesu" as "Chesu," uses catchphrases such as "look you" and "I warrant you," and substitutes unvoiced stops for voiced ones: *f* for *v* and *p* for *b.* The result is the occasional malapropism, as when he refers to Alexander the Great as "Alexander the Pig" (4.7.13), intending Alexander the Big.

Shakespeare introduces this linguistic confusion for more than mere comic effect. This verbal misprision occurs at the beginning of Fluellen's comparing Henry V with Alexander, one of nine worthies, the most heroic figures from the classical, Hebrew, and medieval worlds. Yet, Dante placed Alexander in Hell among the wrathful, and though Shakespeare is unlikely to have read the great Tuscan poet, Fluellen's Plutarchan comparison of the two military leaders is ambiguous. The very epithet "pig" is hardly flattering. It can be dismissed as an effect of Fluellen's accent, or it may be read as an indictment. Henry has just ordered the killing of all the French prisoners, according to Gower, as retaliation for French raiders' killing the boys guarding the English baggage train and looting Henry's tent. Henry's response can indeed be seen as piggish.

Fluellen also observes that Alexander killed his best friend, Cleitus, in a drunken rage. Fluellen goes on to say that Henry's dismissal of Falstaff (whose death is reported in Act II, Scene 3) reflects the king's sound judgment. Again, one may agree with Fluellen that the king acted wisely in rejecting this lord of misrule. Conversely, one may regard Henry's behavior as cruel and heartless, as morally wrong as Alexander's action.

Fluellen may have been modeled on a real person. Charles Boyce in *Shakespeare A to Z* (1990) suggests that his name, a variation on the more common Welsh *Llewelyn,* may derive from Shakespeare's father's associate William Fluellen (198). Wilson proposed Sir Roger Williams (1540?–1595; not the founder of Rhode Island), a Welshman who spent much of his life fighting on the Continent. Wilson also offered, more plausibly, Sir John Smythe, for Williams in 1590 published *A Briefe Discourse of Warre,* in which, unlike Fluellen, he prized experience over theory. In 1595, Smythe published *Instructions, Observations, and Orders Military . . . ,* in which he praises "the orders, exercises and Discipline of our most valiaunt and worthie Auncestors" and notes that "great *Alexander* with small Armies of disciplined and exercised souldiers, did vanquish infinite and most great and huge Armies of his enemies." Smythe's emphasis on military theory in general and the practices of the ancients in particular may be a source for Fluellen's,

and the allusion to Alexander may have prompted Shakespeare to develop Fluellen's comparison.

Macmorris

Fluellen's Irish counterpart appears only in Act III, Scene 2 as sign of the unity, or lack thereof, of Britain under Henry V. Just as Fluellen's accent and name mark him as Welsh, Macmorris's reveal his origin. He turns the terminal *s* into "ish," as in "the work ish ill done" (3.2.88–89). He refuses to debate with Fluellen about military theory, noting correctly that they are in the midst of the battle for Harfleur, hardly the appropriate time for such a discussion. Fluellen, insistent, is about to say something about those of Macmorris's "nation" (3.2.121), which provokes Macmorris's retort, "Of my nation? What ish my nation? Ish a villain, and a bastard, and a knave, and a rascal. What ish my nation? Who talks of my nation?" (3.2.122–124).

As with so much else in this ambiguous play, Macmorris's retort may be understood in more than one way. If one wishes to interpret Shakespeare's introduction of four captains from four parts of Britain as a sign of unity, Macmorris is implying that, as an Irishman, his nation is the same as Fluellen's or the king's (whose birthplace was Monmouth, in Wales), that there is no separate Irish or Welsh or English nation but rather all are Britain. In *Richard II,* the king fought against the Irish; under Henry V, the Irish fight alongside the English king. Yet, even as audiences watched the first productions of *Henry V* in the spring and summer of 1599, English and Irish forces were fighting each other. The 1537 Act for the English Order, Habit, and Language sought to assimilate the Irish, and in 1541, the Irish parliament declared Henry VIII king of Ireland. Yet, Henry VIII and Elizabeth had banned intermarriage between Irish and English, and Shakespeare's contemporary the writer Edmund Spenser expressed surprise that the English in Ireland preferred Gaelic to their own language.

Macmorris may be seen as a caricature of an Irishman, with his quick temper and his accent. He threatens to decapitate Fluellen; the Irish rebels of the 1590s were rumored to cut off the heads of their enemies. Even if Macmorris is intended as a caricature, his eccentricities indicate that Irishness is indeed distinct from Englishness. Those laughing at the character would be implicated in recognizing the differences of the Irish. Macmorris's name may derive from, or might at least recall, James Fitzmorris Fitzgerald, who led an Irish rebellion against English rule under Elizabeth. Macmorris's question thus interrogates unity within the play and the larger issue of Irish nationality.

Jamy

This Scottish representative is also identifiable by his name and accent. He is another comic figure whose brogue would raise a laugh among his Elizabethan audiences. Like Macmorris, he appears only in Act III, Scene 2 and is less quarrelsome than his Irish and Welsh counterparts. By 1599, James VI of Scotland appeared to be Elizabeth's most likely successor; Jamy's name may derive from him. In his few lines, he promises to fight well against the French and takes no position in the argument between Fluellen and Macmorris, perhaps reflecting James VI's pacific approach to international affairs. In his later French campaigns, Henry V took James I of Scotland with him, so that earlier Scottish king could also be a source of Jamy's name.

John Bates, Alexander Court, and Michael Williams

Just as Shakespeare introduces representatives from all geographical parts of the British Isles to examine the idea of national unity or its absence under Henry V (and by implication Elizabeth), so, too, he includes in Henry's army all social classes, from the king and his brothers to common soldiers. In Act IV, Scene 1, the audience meets three such men. Shakespeare gives them full names to enhance their humanity. Alexander Court is aptly named: *court* means "short" in French, and he has a short part in the play—one line.

The other two men expose discontent within the ranks. Henry appears among them in disguise, pretending to be a common soldier like them. He seeks to sound out their feelings and to encourage them before the impending battle. John Bates says that he wishes he were back in London, even if that meant being submerged in the chilly Thames up to his neck. Henry doubts that Bates feels as he speaks, since the king's cause is just.

Michael Williams challenges that assertion. Bates replies that soldiers need not examine the legitimacy of war; their duty is to obey. Williams concurs but adds that if the king's cause is unjust, the king must bear the moral responsibility for all who die fighting for him.

Henry demurs. His long response begs the question but convinces Williams and Bates. Then Henry, trying to buck up the troops even more, says that the king will not be ransomed. Williams recognizes the ploy, though he does not know that he is speaking to the king. Henry has said what he has to to encourage his men, but after the battle, the king can do what he wants. Henry replies that if the king is ransomed, he will never trust his monarch again. Williams bridles at this comment. What can a commoner do about the actions of a ruler? The two quarrel, and they challenge each other to a fight after the battle, exchanging gloves.

After the English victory, Henry gives Fluellen Williams's glove and tells him that if anyone challenges it, that man is a traitor. Williams, spotting his glove in Fluellen's cap and mistaking the Welsh captain for his interlocutor, strikes him. Henry clears up the confusion and offers Williams a glove filled with gold coins for his pains; Fluellen adds a shilling of his own. Williams, indignant at Henry's treatment, rejects the money (though it is not clear in the text whether he rejects only Fluellen's or also Henry's) and stalks off.

The Chorus before Act IV says that when Henry walks among his troops the night before the battle, "That every wretch, pining and pale before, / Beholding him, plucks comfort from his looks" (4.0.41–42). In the course of his conversation with the disguised king, Bates says he intends to "fight lustily" for him (4.1.189), though whether this resolve results from their discussion is unclear. Henry's comment about the king's ransoming certainly does not comfort Williams.

In his discussion with the soldiers, Henry's refusal to accept responsibility for those who die in battle is of a piece with his blame shifting throughout the play. In Act I, he places the onus of war first upon the Archbishop of Canterbury and then the Dauphin, though Henry had already resolved on going to war. Prince John in *Henry IV, Part 2,* declares: "I will lay odds that ere this year expire, / We bear our civil swords and native fire / As far as France" (5.5.105–107). At the siege of Harfleur, Henry blames the inhabitants for any violence they suffer if they do not surrender. After the soldiers depart in Act IV, Scene 1, Henry, in a soliloquy again, complains that he is blamed for all ills, yet he is the source of the evils of this war.

Henry's encounter with the soldiers also highlights the chasm that yawns between king and commoner. Henry tries to show their common bonds; the soldiers emphasize that the king enjoys choices that they lack. In his soliloquy, Henry uses the Chorus's word "wretch" to refer to commoners ("wretched slaves," 4.1.268; "wretch," 4.1.278). He also uses the terms "lackey" and "slave" (4.1.272, 281) and speaks of the commoner's "gross brain" and "vacant mind" (4.1.282, 269), though Williams and Bates show intelligence in their conversation and dignity in their behavior. He also says that commoners sleep better than the king, even though he has just seen the anxious wakefulness of his men. The joke that Henry plays on Williams and Fluellen again shows the royal privilege: He finds a substitute to receive a blow on the ear. Even as Prince Hal, he could be cavalier toward his social inferiors. Falstaff can give as good as he gets, but in Act II, Scene 3 of *Henry IV, Part 1,* Prince Hal plays an unpleasant practical joke on the waiter Francis (whom he calls a "puny drawer," 2.3.30), who has just tried to befriend him. Henry V calls his army a "band of brothers" (4.3.60), but the play shows much strife within it.

Falstaff

The epilogue to *Henry IV, Part 2* promised that "our author will continue the story, with Sir John in it, and make you merry with fair Katherine of France, where (for anything I know) Falstaff shall die of a sweat" (27–30). Yet, Falstaff does not appear in *Henry V,* perhaps because Will Kempe, the actor who most likely played this character in the two parts of *Henry IV,* left the Lord Chamberlain's Men as Shakespeare was writing the play; Kempe departed in 1599, the year *Henry V* opened. Still, Falstaff appropriately looms large in this work. At the end of Act II, Scene 1, Mistress Quickly announces that the knight is suffering from a fever (the sweat promised in *Henry IV, Part 2*?), and in Act II, Scene 3, Bardolph, Nym, the Boy, and Mistress Quickly discuss his death. Nym observes that "The King hath run bad humors on the knight" (2.1.121–122), and Pistol concurs, saying that Henry's rejection of Falstaff at the end of *Henry IV, Part 2* has broken the knight's heart.

Fluellen defends Henry's action in dismissing his former friend as a troublemaker, but this action and its consequences suggest the king's callousness. The Henriad is framed by the deaths of two Johns: John of Gaunt in *Richard II* (2.1) and Sir John Falstaff in *Henry V*—a lean John and a fat one. Both deaths symbolize the passing of an older order. In the first instance, John of Gaunt symbolized the chivalric code and established order that Richard has violated as well as a belief in the divinity of kings that Bolingbroke is about to reject. Falstaff's death marks the loss of jovial conviviality and leisure as well as skepticism toward militarism that have no place in a world given over to war.

Pistol, Bardolph, and Nym

If Will Kempe had remained with Shakespeare's company for the opening of *Henry V* (and Falstaff had remained absent from play), the actor most likely would have played Pistol, a comic role, but a darker one than Falstaff's. The character must have been popular because Pistol is named on the title pages of the quarto editions of both *Henry IV, Part 2* and *Henry V* as an enticement to customers to buy these works. Pistol had been one of Prince Hal's drinking companions at the Boar's-Head Tavern, though in their only encounter in *Henry V* they fail to recognize each other. The king is disguised; Pistol is not. Pistol still expresses his

William Mollison as Pistol in a 1901 production of *Henry V*

comment indicates how Shakespeare imagined his part's being acted, with a booming voice and swaggering manner, suggesting the miles gloriosus, or bragging (and cowardly) soldier of Roman comedy. He has married Mistress Quickly, though she had been engaged to Nym. His motivation for the marriage seems more pecuniary than amatory. As he leaves for Southampton, he charges his wife, who had owned the Boar's-Head Tavern before marrying, "Look to my chattels and my moveables" (2.3.48); the tavern is now his. He does, however, reject her offer to accompany him at least part of the way to the port, "for my manly heart doth ern [grieve]" in parting from her (2.3.3).

As sutler (seller of provisions) to the army, Pistol will have ample opportunity to enrich himself, and he promises to share his ill-gotten gains with Nym, telling him "friendship shall combine, and brotherhood" (2.1.109). He, Nym, and Bardolph form a band of brothers, parodying and commenting on Henry's more elevated use of that term. The Boy observes that Pistol, Nym, and Bardolph "will steal any thing, and call it purchase" (3.2.42). Similarly, Henry maintains that his claim to France is legitimate.

The Chorus before Act 2 says that "all the youth of England are on fire" (2.1.1) to join Henry's French invasion. Pistol, Bardolph, and Nym prove exceptions to this statement. Pistol says, "Let us to France, like horse leeches, my boys, / To suck, to suck, the very blood to suck" (2.3.55–56). Pistol's motivation is ignoble, but the English army will, in fact, suck French blood. He thus serves as a commentary on Henry's enterprise.

In *Henry IV, Part 1*, Pistol holds the rank of ancient, or lieutenant, though he shows no taste for warfare. As the Boy says of him, "he hath a killing tongue and a quiet sword" (3.2.34). Fluellen must force him into battle at Harfleur. He remains faithful to Bardolph, though, and tries to save him from the gallows when he is caught stealing from a church. In the only battle scene in the play, he captures a French soldier, from whom he hopes to secure a ransom. His threat to kill his prisoner foreshadows Henry's order in Act 4, Scene 6. He

love for the king in his own idiom, which includes archaisms (such as "wight" for man), bombast, and syntactical inversions, assonance, and alliteration, even at the expense of sense (for example, "doting death" at 2.1.61) that may parody the speech patterns of older plays. The king, having rejected all his former Boar's-Head acquaintances, shows no such affection for Pistol.

Pistol's name suggests his loudness. As the Boy says of him, "I never knew so full a voice issue from so empty a heart; but the saying is true, 'The empty vessel makes the greatest sound'" (4.4.68–70). This had also proleptically parodied the king's order when he had threatened Nym with the cry, "*Couple a gorge!*" (2.1.71). The command to cut the French prisoners' throats (4.7) deprives Pistol of his prisoner Le Fer's ransom money, and his position as sutler also seems to prove less profitable than he had hoped. At the end of the campaign, he resolves to return to England to prey upon that country, as he had hoped to do in France.

Though Pistol's greed and cowardice render him unsympathetic in many ways, he highlights the problem of the discharged veteran in Elizabeth's age and any other. In June 1601, Shakespeare's town of Stratford-upon-Avon petitioned the government to be relieved of the expense of caring for Lewis Gilbert, a butcher who had been injured in the recent Irish campaign. After his return, he had broken into a shop, run up debts, and stabbed a neighbor to death in a quarrel, signs of post-traumatic stress disorder. Pistol's only wounds in France come from a beating he receives from Fluellen for mocking the Welshman's leek, but he is the lone survivor of his band of brothers who go to the war.

The other two adults have been hanged for stealing. (The Boy observes that Pistol owes his survival to his cowardice. Had he been as bold in stealing as Bardolph or Nym, he, too, would have been executed.) Nym, whose name reveals his trade, had not been among the prince's friends in the *Henry IV* plays. To the end of his speeches, he often tacks on the phrase "that's the humor of it." In 1598, the Lord Chamberlain's Men staged Ben Jonson's *Every Man in His Humour;* Shakespeare acted in this work. The following year, the same year as *Henry V*'s premier, Jonson's *Every Man Out of His Humour* was staged. These plays popularized the "humor" character, one motivated by a particular medical condition such as choler; Hamlet, with his melancholy, may be the most famous such figure, though he is so much more. Nym's catchphrase may be an attempt to capitalize on the popularity of Jonson's character type. George Chapman's *The Blind Beggar of Alexandria* (1596) includes a character who repeatedly uses this phrase and thus is another source for Nym's mannerism. Nym shares

Pistol's cowardice as well as his greed. He vanishes from the play after Act III, Scene 2; in Act IV, Scene 4, the Boy reports his death.

Of the three men in this group, Bardolph is the most sympathetic. In Act II, Scene 1, he reconciles Nym and Pistol. His peacemaking contrasts with the king's militarism. He also parodies Henry's heroic posturing. Before Harfleur, Henry urges his troops to continue fighting despite reverses: "Once more unto the breach, dear friends, once more" (3.1.1), which Bardolph then mocks: "On, on, on, on! To the breach, to the breach!" (3.2.1–2).

Although Bardolph was among Prince Hal's associates at the Boar's-Head Tavern, Henry does not save Bardolph from execution after the latter steals from a church. The king's decision may be viewed as just or cold-hearted. Shakespeare's source says that an unnamed soldier stole a pix, or pyx, a box that holds the sacramental wafer. Shakespeare changes the object to a pax (3.6.45), a piece of metal with a crucifix stamped on it. Even when the wind was not southerly, Shakespeare knew a pyx from a pax. His alteration of his source suggests that he was playing on the meaning of the Latin word for "peace." For stealing a "pax of little price" (3.6.45), Bardolph is hanged. For stealing the peace of France, Henry and his descendants become heirs to the throne of that country, and Henry is regarded as a hero. As the Emperor Jones says in Eugene O'Neill's eponymous play, "For de little stealin' dey gits you in jail soon or late. For de big stealin' dey makes you Emperor and puts you in de Hall o' Fame when you croaks."

The Boy

This nameless character is among the most endearing and tragic in the play. Just as Pistol, Nym, and Bardolph provide an antiheroic response to Henry, so the Boy serves as their Chorus, commenting on their characters and behavior. His comments show keen insight into his companions, whom he talks of abandoning, though he never does. In Act IV, Scene 4, he serves as Pistol's translator with the captured Le Fer. His death in the French attack on the English baggage train highlights the cost of Henry's war.

Archbishop of Canterbury

Shakespeare presents the Archbishop as a schemer who hopes to persuade Henry to go to war and so distract the king and Parliament from a pending bill that would strip the church of donated property. He has arranged for the church to offer Henry a large subvention to finance the war. Hence, when Henry asks him in Act I, Scene 2 whether he (Henry) may justly claim the throne of France, the Archbishop responds affirmatively. This justifying speech is so convoluted that at its end Henry must inquire again, "May I with right and conscience make this claim?" (1.2.96), though the Archbishop has said that the argument is "as clear as is the summer's sun" (1.2.86).

In the 1944 Laurence Olivier production, the Archbishop is presented as a figure of fun, a Polonius avant la lettre. Kenneth Branagh's 1989 version treats him as sinister. Just as the Archbishop seeks to use Henry to safeguard church property, Henry uses the Archbishop to justify a war he has already resolved on waging.

Earl of Cambridge, Lord Scroop, and Sir Thomas Grey

These three men appear only in Act II, Scene 3, in which their conspiracy is exposed. They object to Henry's leniency toward a drunken man who railed against him. After Henry overrides their objections, they ask for their letters appointing them commissioners in the king's absence. Henry knows of their intent to kill him before he and his army sail to France, but he pretends to give them the letters they request. Instead, the letters show them that their plot has been exposed. When they ask for mercy, Henry tells them that their attitude toward the drunken man has killed that quality in him, thus again shifting responsibility from himself. He says that he seeks no revenge for himself, but because they have endangered the kingdom, they must die. This seems a distinction without a difference. Henry's toying with the plotters, pretending to give them their commissions and instead presenting them with their death warrants, is coldly, cruelly calculating.

Henry's foreknowledge of the plot suggests Elizabeth's secret service and her "Rainbow" portrait of about 1600 showing her wearing a dress adorned with eyes and ears. Roy Strong interprets the portrait's iconography as representing "the Queen's use of her servants as seeing and hearing for her, yielding intelligence and preserving her safety" (Pomeroy 71). Though *Henry V* probably predates this painting, the play seems to embody the idea of an all-seeing, all-hearing government with its spies everywhere that the image conveys.

Henry accuses Scroop, Cambridge, and Grey of plotting against him because they were bribed by French gold. Only Cambridge indicates that he was not seduced by money yet does not explain his motive. From Holinshed it is clear that the three men acted to put Edmund Mortimer on the throne. Descended from Edward III's third son, Clarence (whereas Henry is descended from his fourth, John of Gaunt), and named Richard's successor, Mortimer had a stronger claim to the English crown than Henry. Though this dynastic issue is mooted here, it is raised repeatedly in the *Henry VI* plays, where it underlies the Yorkist claim to the throne, and it also surfaces in *Henry IV, Part 1* (1.3, 2.3.84–85, and 4.3.90–96). Shakespeare's audiences would thus have understood that this Southampton conspiracy, though it fails, questions Henry's legitimacy as king.

Henry singles out Scroop as the most culpable of the plotters because Henry loved him most. Henry likens Scroop's betrayal as "Another fall of man" (2.2.142). If Scroop is as noble, grave, learned, religious, abstemious, "Free from gross passion, . . . / Constant in spirit" (2.2.132, 133) as Henry says Scroop has seemed, and as Holinshed portrays him, perhaps his decision to turn against Henry is justified. He may be seen as a study for Brutus in Shakespeare's next play, a good man motivated by political idealism who falls to realpolitik.

The Dauphin (Dolphin)

The Dauphin serves as a foil to Henry. He is a diminished version of Henry Percy (Hotspur), Prince Hal's antagonist in *Henry IV, Part 1*. Like

Hotspur, he is impulsive, imprudent, eager for battle so that he may prove himself militarily, and fonder of his horse than of any woman. Whereas Hotspur is valiant, though, the Dauphin shares with his fellow Frenchmen in this play an arrogance and absurdity that render the outcome of Agincourt a foregone conclusion (as it, of course, was in 1599).

The Dauphin's folly precedes him. In Act I, Scene 2, he responds to Henry's demand for the French crown by sending the English ruler a barrel of tennis balls as more appropriate for the inclinations of the young king (Henry was 27 at the time) than governing would be. The Dauphin is taunting Henry with the king's reputed prodigal ways when he was Prince of Wales. Henry replies that the Dauphin's jest will prove costly, as indeed it does.

When the Dauphin first appears in Act II, Scene 4, he again dismisses Henry as a serious threat, calling him "a vain, giddy, shallow, humorous youth" (28). That description better fits the Dauphin: Harfleur falls to the English because the Dauphin, who was supposed to relieve the siege, is unprepared to act. He asks to participate in the military operation against the English; the king, his father, refuses to allow him to do so. Historically, the dauphin was not present at Agincourt, but Shakespeare places him there so that he may continue serving as an antagonist to Henry. On the night before the battle, the Dauphin exhibits his characteristic folly and self-assurance. He announces that he has composed a sonnet to his horse, and his bragging angers the Constable. Even his cousin Orleans, who defends him, asks him to cease praising his steed. The Dauphin thus provokes division within the French ranks. At the end of the battle, he laments the French defeat (4.5) and then vanishes from the play. His disappearance may result from the death of the real dauphin Lewis a few months after Agincourt. The real-life dauphin in 1420, when Act V occurs, was Charles, later to become King Charles VII.

Mistress Quickly and Katharine

At first blush, a great gulf seems to divide the hostess of the Boar's-Head Tavern, Mistress Nell Quickly, and the French princess who becomes queen of England and, through her second marriage to Owen Tudor, the founder of the Tudor dynasty. Yet, their similarities outnumber their differences in the play. Nym and Pistol fight over the hostess; Henry claims that Katharine is his chief demand in going to war with France. Through his marriage with Mistress Quickly, Pistol becomes owner of her tavern. Through marriage with Katharine, Henry becomes heir to the French throne. Both women also serve as comic figures through

Sarah Brooke as Katharine in a 1905 Imperial Theatre production of *Henry V (Photographed by Langfier)*

their misuse of language, which can result in bawdy double meanings.

Mistress Quickly may actually have more autonomy than Katharine. She chose her husband; Katharine cannot. Henry woos the French princess in Act V, Scene 2, but when she says she will act as it pleases her father, Henry replies that their marriage "will please him well, Kate; it shall please him, Kate" (5.2.248–249). That *shall* is a third-person imperative. The king must accede to the demands of the victorious Henry, and so must Kate. Mistress Quickly cannot accompany Pistol on his way to Southampton because he forbids it. Mistress Quickly dies from syphilis, "a malady of France" (5.1.82), just as Katharine may be viewed as a prisoner carried off by her conqueror.

Charles VI, King of France, and Isabel, Queen of France

In *Henry V,* Shakespeare panders to English anti-French sentiment. Most of the French nobility appear overconfident and foolish. However, the French king and queen prove exceptions to this generalization. When the Dauphin dismisses the English threat, the king responds, "Think we King Henry strong" (2.4.48), a more accurate assessment than his son's. When Exeter, as leader of the English embassy to France, demands the French throne for Henry, the Dauphin replies peevishly, "if my father render fair return, / It is against my will" (2.4.127–128). Although Charles VI refuses to abdicate, he speaks diplomatically and prudently to the English ambassadors and offers Katharine and some French dukedoms in an effort to prevent war.

Failing in that effort, he orders his nobles to defeat Henry. They cannot do so, but the king's speech is dignified and appropriate. He is courteous to Henry when they meet in the play's last scene, and he yields to Henry's demands with good grace. Both he and his queen express a hope for peace. The king speaks of reconciliation between England and France. Isabel talks first of domestic happiness between Henry and Katharine and then

of international union, putting the personal ahead of the political.

DIFFICULTIES OF THE PLAY

Because *Henry V* deals with historical events, students may think that to understand the play they need to acquaint themselves with the reign of this monarch. Reading a modern history of Henry V's reign can indeed prove helpful, but even more useful for understanding Shakespeare's play is studying Shakespeare's sources, which are discussed in the "Background" section.

Such an examination will reveal what Shakespeare knew about Henry V's reign and what he chose to emphasize and to ignore. For example, Holinshed's *Chronicles* discusses Henry's domestic concerns as well as his foreign wars. Yet, war is the only subject of the play, except for some consideration of a bill that anticipates Henry VIII's dissolution of the monasteries. Henry V engaged in several campaigns in France, but for dramatic effectiveness, Shakespeare condenses these into one and implies that the victory at Agincourt in 1415 led directly to the 1420 Treaty of Troyes that named Henry V heir to the French throne. Shakespeare's sources informed him that the dauphin was not present at Agincourt, but to augment the dauphin's role as Henry V's foil, Shakespeare placed him there anyway.

While such background knowledge is useful, it is not essential for an understanding of the play. When the work premiered in 1599, some in the audience would have had a solid grasp of early 15th-century English history. Others, like the groundlings, are unlikely to have had much knowledge of the subject beyond what they might have gleaned from other plays dealing with the topic. Hence, Shakespeare provides everything that the audience needs to know to follow the action and understand the characters. Shakespeare is writing a history play, not history; he is offering art, not facts. Many of the characters bear names of historical figures, but they live on the stage as the playwright's creations. The play is based on real events, but these have been adapted to suit the demands of art.

More challenging, and more important, than correlating events in the play to the historical record is discerning Shakespeare's attitude toward those events. Shakespeare lived in a world of censorship. When the unhappily named John Stubbs questioned, in *The discoverie of a gaping gulf . . .* (1579), Queen Elizabeth's proposed marriage to the duke of Anjou, he had his right hand cut off. William Page, who had helped distribute the work, suffered the same fate. Haywood's dedication of a play to the earl of Essex led to the writer's prolonged imprisonment. Every play required the approval of the Lord Chamberlain before it could be performed; every publication was supposed to be licensed by the Stationers' Company before it could be printed. Subversive plays were still staged, and subversive literature was still published, but such actions were dangerous. Shakespeare witnessed firsthand the fate of indiscreet fellow dramatists. Marlowe was killed at the age of 29. Thomas Kyd was tortured and died shortly afterward. Jonson and Haywood were imprisoned.

Because open expression of opinions was dangerous, Shakespeare masked his. Are the Catholic clerics in Act 1 conspiring against England's best interests in offering to help fund the war with France? Or, are they patriotic? Does Henry invade France to support his just claim to the French crown? Or, is he following his crafty father's advice to "busy giddy minds / With foreign quarrels" (*Henry IV, Part 2*, 4.5.213–214)? Is Henry the legitimate king of England, a question that related to the Tudor claim to the throne? The Southampton conspirators seem motivated by French gold, but in one line, Cambridge mentions that he had another reason, one that he never makes explicit. Astute audience members would recall, however, that Mortimer, Cambridge's brother-in-law, had a better claim to the throne than did Henry. After the victory at Agincourt, Henry orders that all credit for the victory be given to God. Is history then providential, the working out of God's plan, especially for England? The epilogue ascribes the disasters under Henry VI to human mismanagement, not divine retribution for the deposition of

Richard II. Shakespeare constantly teases his audiences into thought.

As *Henry V* is the last in a series of four plays, students may be unfamiliar with some characters who have appeared in earlier works. For example, the death of Falstaff is reported in Act II, Scene 3, but the character never appears in this work. In *Henry IV, Parts 1* and *2,* he was a major figure, and his relationship with Prince Hal was the most important in both men's lives in those works. Without recognition of Falstaff's wit, arrogance, and subversive behavior, students are unlikely to be moved by his death and may wonder why Shakespeare included this episode. Its poignancy depends on knowledge of the character gained from seeing the previous two plays in the tetralogy. Similarly, the king's failure to save Bardolph from execution in Act III, Scene 6 is less problematic if one does not know that he and Prince Hal had been drinking mates and had ostensibly been partners in crime in *Henry IV, Part 1.* Even the king himself gains in complexity if students can compare him to his former self.

Shakespeare's language tends to puzzle students, at least initially. His early modern English now seems archaic, and his poetry is dense with meaning. Even his first audiences would have had trouble unpacking at least some of his lines and understanding his neologisms. Adding to the confusion, Pistol employs terms that were old-fashioned, even in 1599; Jamy, Fluellen, and Macmorris speak in dialect; Katharine and her waiting woman have a scene almost entirely in French (3.4); and Mistress Quickly misuses words. Thus, she reports that Falstaff suffers from "a burning quotidian tertian" (2.1.119). Parsing the individual words poses a challenge; taken together, the phrase makes no sense, as literally it would mean that Falstaff has a daily fever that recurs every third day. Happily, modern editions offer glosses.

Despite the serious matters addressed in *Henry V,* the play is filled with humorous characters and incidents. Elizabethan humor, however, does not always translate into 21st-century laughs. Fluellen's beating of Pistol in Act V, Scene 1 or Pistol's threats to kill Le Fer in Act IV, Scene 4 can appear to modern audiences as cruel rather than funny. The French braggadocio before the Battle of Agincourt may strike 21st-century audiences as national stereotyping unworthy of Shakespeare's capacious soul, though the English of his day probably found these boasts amusing, especially in light of the thrashing that awaits those braggarts. Moreover, lines on a page may seem inert until they are spoken and performed by a skilled actor. Watching live or recorded productions of the play will enhance enjoyment and understanding.

KEY PASSAGES
Prologue, 1–34

CHORUS. O for a Muse of fire, that would ascend
The brightest heaven of invention!
A kingdom for a stage, princes to act,
And monarchs to behold the swelling scene!
Then should the warlike Harry, like himself,
Assume the port of Mars, and at his heels
(Leash'd in, like hounds) should famine, sword, and fire
Crouch for employment. But pardon, gentles all,
The flat unraised spirits that hath dar'd
On this unworthy scaffold to bring forth
So great an object. Can this cockpit hold
The vasty fields of France? Or may we cram
Within this wooden O the very casques
That did affright the air at Agincourt?
O, pardon! Since a crooked figure may
Attest in little place a million,
And let us, ciphers to this great accompt,
On your imaginary forces work.
Suppose within the girdle of these walls
Are now confin'd two mighty monarchies,
Whose high, upreared, and abutting fronts
The perilous narrow ocean parts asunder.
Piece out our imperfections with your thoughts,
Into a thousand parts divide one man,
And make imaginary puissance;
Think, when we talk of horses, that you see them

Printing their proud hooves i' th' receiving earth;
For 'tis your thoughts that now must deck our kings,
Carry them here and there, jumping o'er times,
Turning th' accomplishments of many years
Into an hour-glass: for the which supply,
Admit me Chorus to this history,
Who, Prologue-like, your humble patience pray,
Gently to hear, kindly to judge, our play.

In his first appearance, the Chorus apologizes for the inadequacies of the Elizabethan theater, a multisided timber polygon that he calls "this wooden O." Depending on when in 1599 *Henry V* was first staged, it would have opened at the Curtain, which Shakespeare's company was using after the Theater closed and before the Globe was completed, or at the new Globe. Shakespeare had already staged the Battle of Shrewsbury *(Henry IV, Part 1)* and various other conflicts *(Henry VI, Parts 1, 2,* and *3* and *Richard III)* without apology, so the Chorus's plea here seems disingenuous.

Although the answers to the Chorus's rhetorical questions seem to be in the negative, they actually emphasize the power of the Elizabethan theater of convention, which relied on the audience's imagination rather than on spectacle and special effects. This empty space could be England or France, court or battlefield, as the playwright wished. The Chorus charges the audience to use its imagination, to which the play's language will appeal. His speech even offers an example of the power of words. When he speaks of horses, the accents in the line "Printing their proud hoofs i' th' receiving earth" imitate hoofbeats. The audience actually hears the steeds cantering.

Throughout the play, the Chorus presents the official version of events. He serves as Henry's press secretary. His language reflects that role. Like Henry, he gives orders. In calling everyone in the audience "gentles," that is, gentlemen, even though many were apprentices and common laborers, the Chorus anticipates Henry's claim that for each English soldier who fights at Agincourt, "This day shall gentle his condition" (4.3.63). Yet, this opening speech also calls that official account into question. How should one understand the image of Henry as the god of war accompanied by "famine, sword, and fire"? Does one focus on the king's godlike power or on the destruction he wreaks?

Act III, Scene 1, 1–34

KING HENRY. Once more unto the breach,
  dear friends, once more,
Or close the wall up with our English dead.
In peace there's nothing so becomes a man
As modest stillness and humility;
But when the blast of war blows in our ears,
Then imitate the action of the tiger;
Stiffen the sinews, conjure up the blood,
Disguise fair nature with hard-favor'd rage;
Then lend the eye a terrible aspect;
Let it pry through the portage of the head
Like the brass cannon; let the brow o'erwhelm it
As fearfully as doth a galled rock
O'erhang and jutty his confounded base,
Swill'd with the wild and wasteful ocean.
Now set the teeth and stretch the nostril wide,
Hold hard the breath, and bend up every spirit
To his full height. On, on, you noblest English,
Whose blood is fet from fathers of war-proof!
Fathers that, like so many Alexanders,
Have in these parts from morn till even
  fought,
And sheath'd their swords for lack of argument.
Dishonor not your mothers, now attest
That those whom you call'd fathers did beget
  you.
Be copy now to men of grosser blood,
And teach them how to war. And you, good
  yeomen,
Whose limbs were made in England, show us
  here
The mettle of your pasture; let us swear
That you are worth your breeding, which I
  doubt not;
For there is none of you so mean and base

That hath not noble luster in your eyes.
I see you stand like greyhounds in the slips,
Straining upon the start. The game's afoot!
Follow your spirit; and upon this charge
Cry, "God for Harry, England, and Saint
  George!"

The siege of Harfleur is not going well. The English have been repulsed, and Henry here seeks to rally his troops. He appeals to the various social orders individually, beginning with the noblest and proceeding downward to yeomen and those below them in status. Although he seeks a unified effort to take the city, this speech highlights division. Perhaps this rhetorical approach explains its failure to rally everyone; the next scene shows Bardolph, Nym, and Pistol hanging back until Fluellen forces them into the fray. Harfleur will surrender in Act III, Scene 3 not because the English overcome its defenses but because the Dauphin will not be able to lift the siege.

The speech shows the dehumanizing effects of war. Henry likens soldiers to tigers and greyhounds. The images of set teeth and flaring nostrils suggest animals rather than humans, as do the references to "pasture" and "breeding." Henry also compares his fighters to cannons and rocks, which have no emotions or thoughts.

His mention of Alexander foreshadows Fluellen's comparing the king to the Macedonian conqueror, an analogy not necessarily flattering: Fluellen calls the ancient general "Alexander the Pig" (4.7.13). His Welsh accent creates a comic solecism for "Big," but "pig" reinforces the animal imagery of Henry's speech. Fluellen notes that in a drunken fit, Alexander killed his best friend. In Act II, Scenes 1 and 3, the audience has heard how Falstaff, Henry's companion in *Henry IV, Parts 1* and *2*, died of a broken heart after Henry had rejected him. Alexander died at age 33 after achieving great military success, and his empire immediately disintegrated. Henry V died at the age of 35 after conquering most of France. His son lost all that Henry had won and also the English throne. Henry refers to earlier English campaigns in France under Edward III that produced

King Henry delivers a speech to his soldiers in Act III, Scene I of *Henry V*. This drawing was designed for the Chiswick edition of Shakespeare, published in 1900. *(Illustration by John Byam Lister Shaw)*

great victories but no lasting gains. The same will prove true of Henry's conquest. The king's likening his soldiers' ancestors to Alexander's underscores the futility of the current invasion. Henry's warlike speech deconstructs itself, showing the folly of the effort it seeks to encourage.

Act IV, Scene 3, 15–67

WESTMORELAND. O that we now had here
But one ten thousand of those men in England
That do no work today!

KING HENRY. What's he that wishes so?
My cousin Westmoreland? No, my fair cousin.
If we are mark'd to die, we are now
To do our country loss; and if to live,
The fewer men, the greater share of honor.
God's will, I pray thee wish not one man more.
By Jove, I am not covetous for gold,
Nor care I who doth feed upon my cost;
It yearns me not if men my garments wear;
Such outward things dwell not in my desires.
But if it be a sin to covet honor,
I am the most offending soul alive.
No, faith, my coz, wish not a man from
  England.
God's peace, I would not lose so great an honor
As one man more methinks would share
  from me,
For the best hope I have. O, do not wish one
  more!
Rather proclaim it, Westmoreland, through my
  host,
That he which hath no stomach to this fight,
Let him depart, his passport shall be made,
And crowns for convoy put into his purse.
We would not die in that man's company
That fears his fellowship to die with us.
This day is call'd the feast of Crispian:
He that outlives this day, and comes safe home,
Will stand a' tiptoe when this day is named,
And rouse him at the name of Crispian.
He that shall see this day, and live old age,
Will yearly on the vigil feast his neighbors,
And say, "To-morrow is Saint Crispian."
Then will he strip his sleeve and show his scars,
And say, "These wounds I had on Crispin's day."
Old men forget, yet all shall be forgot,
But he'll remember with advantages
What feats he did that day. Then shall our
  names,
Familiar in his mouth as household words,
Harry the King, Bedford and Exeter,
Warwick and Talbot, Salisbury and Gloucester,
Be in their flowing cups freshly remember'd.
This story shall the good man teach his son;
And Crispin Crispian shall ne'er go by,

From this day to the ending of the world,
But we shall be remembered—
We few, we happy few, we band of brothers,
For he to-day that sheds his blood with me
Shall be my brother; be he ne'er so vile,
This day shall gentle his condition;
And gentlemen in England, now abed,
Shall think themselves accurs'd they were not
  here;
And hold their manhoods cheap whilst any
  speaks
That fought with us upon Saint Crispin's day.

Whereas Henry's speech before Harfleur is rhetorically flawed and fails to rally the army to capture the city, Henry's address before Agincourt marshals the English language and sends it into battle. The earlier speech emphasized hierarchy among the ranks; this speech rejects all social distinctions. Henry proclaims that every man in the army, from Pistol to Henry's brothers, are equal, a "band of brothers" (4.3.60). He even abandons the royal "we." In the one place he does employ the word, it may not be a personal pronoun but rather an inclusive use that embraces the entire army. In his soliloquy in Act IV, Scene 1, Henry had shown that he recognized the vast gulf that separates king and commoner. This same division is evident in the casualty report after the battle: No one below the rank of esquire is important enough to be named. But, for the moment, Henry unifies his forces; the result is a great victory.

Henry overcomes his men's fears by focusing not on the battle itself but on the years to come. By imagining that his soldiers will feast their friends and tell stories about this day, he assumes, and makes them assume, that they will survive. He dismisses their fears of injury by describing how eagerly they will show their wounds and use them to illustrate their accounts. He reminds them that they will be able to drop names that will forever be linked to their own, and he promises them a safeguard against oblivion. In his "Elegy Written in a Country Churchyard" (1751), Thomas Gray recognizes the desire of every person, no matter his station, to be remembered after death:

For who to dumb Forgetfulness a prey,
This pleasing anxious being e'er resigned,
Left the warm precincts of the cheerful day,
Nor cast one longing look behind?

Henry promises his soldiers that they will not prove prey for that dumb forgetfulness.

Henry's desire for honor recalls a different Henry's view—that of Henry Percy (Hotspur), who thought

it were an easy leap
To pluck bright honor from the pale-fac'd moon,
Or dive into the bottom of the deep,
Where fadom-line could never touch the
  ground,
And pluck up drowned honor by the locks,
So he that doth redeem her thence might wear
Without corrival all her dignities. (*Henry IV,*
  Part 1, 1.3.201–207)

Hotspur represents a view of chivalry outmoded in the world of Henry IV, and he dies at the Battle of Shrewsbury. Henry V is a sounder politician than Hotspur, yet in this instant before Agincourt, he reminds his army of the older, heroic values that inspire them to victory.

Shakespeare undercuts Henry's speech before Harfleur through Bardolph's mockery immediately afterward and by showing that Bardolph, Nym, and Pistol remain unmoved by the king's words. Here, Shakespeare reveals the effectiveness of this address as Westmoreland declares, "Perish the man whose mind is backward now!" (4.3.72). York comes forward to ask to lead the vanguard, and the next scene shows that even the cowardly Pistol has captured a Frenchman.

Epilogue, 1–14

CHORUS. Thus far, with rough and all-
  unable pen,
Our bending author hath pursu'd the story,

In little room confining mighty men,
Mingling by starts the full course of their
  glory.
Small time; but in that small most greatly lived
This star of England. Fortune made his sword;
By which the world's best garden he achieved,
And of it left his son imperial lord.
Henry the Sixt, in infant bands crown'd King
Of France and England, did this king succeed;
Whose state so many had the managing,
That they lost France, and made his England
  bleed;
Which oft our stage hath shown, and for their
  sake,
In your fair minds let this acceptance take.

Shakespeare's play ends triumphantly. Henry has defeated his enemies, foreign and domestic, been proclaimed heir to the French throne and secured his hold on the English, and become engaged to the princess he loves. He anticipates enduring peace between France and England, and he imagines that his son will successfully lead the crusade that Henry IV had promised at the end of *Richard II*.

Then, in the 14 lines of the play's concluding sonnet, Shakespeare undermines the previous five acts, indeed, the entire Henriad. In this epilogue, Shakespeare reminds his audience of the futility of the war with France, since in the next reign all that Henry won will be lost. Bolingbroke's usurpation of Richard II's crown and the civil wars he fought to keep it also prove to have been in vain, since the House of Lancaster will lose the throne to the House of York. The third line of the Epilogue assumes an additional tragic tone in echoing Marlowe's "infinite riches in a little room." Marlowe, too, "greatly lived," becoming England's greatest playwright in the late 1580s and early 1590s, but dying at age 29. The reference to "confining mighty men" in a small space may also suggest the graves to which all paths of glory lead.

For Shakespeare, history is circular, like the wheel of fortune. An individual may remain at the apex for "small time" only. Triumph ends in tragedy; the victor today is the vanquished tomorrow. Henry V leads to Henry VI. It is unlikely that when Shakespeare began writing about English history in the early 1590s he envisioned a series of eight works that would examine the sweep of the 15th century that led to the Tudor ascendancy. By 1599, however, he could look back on that period and perceive clearly the tragedy that had unfolded.

Like Puck's plea at the end of *A Midsummer Night's Dream*, Rosalind's at the end of *As You Like It*, and Prospero's at the end of *The Tempest*, the Epilogue here, delivered by the Chorus, asks the audience for its approval and applause. Although the Epilogue's opening line belittles the playwright's achievement, the sonnet quickly shifts tone to summarize the work's achievement. The Prologue asks, "Can this cockpit hold / The vasty fields of France? Or can we cram / Within this wooden O the very casques / That did affright the air at Agincourt?" (11–14). The Epilogue confirms what the audience has seen: The theater has succeeded in "confining mighty men" in a little space. The Epilogue also serves as an advertisement for Shakespeare's plays about the reign of Henry VI.

DIFFICULT PASSAGES
Act I, Scene 2, 33–95

ARCHBISHOP OF CANTERBURY. Then
  hear me, gracious sovereign, and you peers,
That owe yourselves, your lives, and services
To this imperial throne. There is no bar
To make against your Highness' claim to France
But this, which they produce from Pharamond:
"In terram Salicam mulieres ne succedant,"
"No woman shall succeed in Salique land";
Which Salique land the French unjustly gloze
To be the realm of France, and Pharamond
The founder of this law and female bar.
Yet their own authors faithfully affirm
That the land Salique is in Germany,
Between the floods of Sala and of Elbe,
Where Charles the Great, having subdu'd the
  Saxons,

There left behind and settled certain French;
Who holding in disdain the German women
For some dishonest manners in their life,
Establish'd then this law: to wit, no female
Should be inheritrix in Salique land;
Which Salique, as I said, 'twixt Elbe and Sala,
Is at this day in Germany call'd Meisen.
Then doth it well appear the Salique law
Was not devised for the realm of France;
Nor did the French possess the Salique land
Until four hundred one and twenty years
After the defunction of King Pharamond,
Idly suppos'd the founder of this law,
Who died within the year of our redemption
Four hundred twenty-six; and Charles the
  Great
Subdu'd the Saxons, and did seat the French
Beyond the river Sala, in the year
Eight hundred five. Besides, their writers say,
King Pepin, which deposed Childeric,
Did, as heir general, being descended
Of Blithild, which was daughter to King
  Clothair,
Make claim and title to the crown of France.
Hugh Capet also, who usurp'd the crown
Of Charles the Duke of Lorraine, sole heir male
Of the true line and stock of Charles the
  Great,
To fine his title with some marks of truth,
Though in pure truth it was corrupt and
  naught,
Convey'd himself as th' heir to th' Lady
  Lingare,
Daughter to Charlemain, who was the son
To Lewis the Emperor, and Lewis the son
Of Charles the Great. Also King Lewis the
  Tenth,
Who was sole heir to the usurper Capet,
Could not keep quiet in his conscience,
Wearing the crown of France, till satisfied
That fair Queen Isabel, his grandmother,
Was lineal of the Lady Ermengare,
Daughter to Charles, the foresaid Duke of
  Lorraine;

By the which marriage the line of Charles the
  Great
Was re-united to the crown of France.
So that, as clear as is the summer's sun,
King Pepin's title and Hugh Capet's claim,
King Lewis his satisfaction, all appear
To hold in right and title of the female,
And rather choose to hide them in a net
Than amply to imbar their crooked titles
Usurp'd from you and your progenitors.

Henry asks the Archbishop whether he (Henry) may justly claim the French throne. This speech is the Archbishop's response. Even though Shakespeare took his text, historical errors and all, directly from Holinshed, it is not clear whether he intended his audience to understand it. Even when one reads the lines slowly, the details seem overwhelming, repetitive, and incoherent. Heard, it would be almost impossible to digest. When the Archbishop finishes, Henry must ask again whether he may rightly claim the French crown. Despite the Archbishop's assertion, his response to Henry's initial query is hardly "as clear as is the summer's sun."

Close study exposes a contradiction between the Archbishop's affirmative response to Henry's question and the details he uses to support the king's right to reign in France. The Archbishop denies that the Salic law applies to France and names three rulers who claimed the French throne through female descent. Two were themselves usurpers, and the other was the son of a usurper (as is Henry V, whose father seized the throne from Richard II). This evidence suggests that in claiming the French throne because of his descent from the French wife of Edward II, Henry is also a usurper.

Furthermore, if female descent can confer royal rights, Henry's claim to the English throne is invalid. Edmund Mortimer was descended from the daughter of the third son of Edward III, while Henry traces his ancestry through the male line to Edward III's fourth son. Mortimer, thus, has a better claim to rule England than Henry does. As with so much else in *Henry V,* this speech can be interpreted in more than one way. It can support Henry's claim to the French throne, or it can show that he has no right even to the English crown.

CRITICAL INTRODUCTION
TO THE PLAY
Themes

One of the play's central concerns is language. Shakespeare composed some of the loftiest measures ever written and thus understood the power of the word to shape and misshape reality. Calderwood, in *Metadrama in Shakespeare's Henriad, Richard II to Henry V,* astutely comments that the Chorus focuses on the visual rather than the auditory aspects of drama because, since the deposition of Richard II, language has become debased. Word and object are severed in the opening play of the Henriad, so truth resides only in the visual.

Henry V enacts the power of language. Holinshed's *Chronicles* makes much of the tactics the English employed at Agincourt to defeat the French. Shakespeare does not mention this matter. This source also describes Henry's bravery in battle; on this subject, too, the play is silent. The climactic moment at Agincourt is Henry's speech in Act IV, Scene 3. Once Henry delivers those lines, the outcome of the battle is not in doubt. Earlier, Henry had captured Harfleur with a speech, which succeeds where English arms have failed.

Henry's speech is effective even though it is a lie. As the casualty report in Act IV, Scene 8 demonstrates, those who fight with him are not his brothers, are not remembered "from this day to the ending of the world," as he had promised (4.3.58); the commoners who die are not even named. Richard II's beautiful language deceived himself; Henry's powerful language deceives others. In grammar school, Shakespeare would have read the Roman orator Quintillian, who maintained that rhetoric "is an art that relies on moving the emotions by saying that which is false." Yet, it also, for small time, rallies the English army to a miraculous victory.

That the theme of language is key to the play is evident from the structure of the work. At the heart of *Richard II,* Shakespeare placed a garden scene (3.4) that bears no relationship to the play's action but emphasizes the central concern of the work: Under Richard's bad governing, England, that other Eden, has become a garden gone to seed—things rank and gross in nature possess it merely. In that same place in *Henry V* (3.4), Shakespeare inserts a language lesson. Katharine, princess of France, attempts to learn English. Her mispronunciations and sexual innuendos provide welcome comic relief after the horrors of war that Henry has just described in Act III, Scene 3 and the execution of Bardolph soon to follow (3.6). But, coming immediately after the fall of Harfleur, it foreshadows Henry's further victories. Katharine must surrender her French language; if the forces of France had triumphed, she would have had no need to learn English.

This issue of language concerned Shakespeare and his contemporaries. Though Wales had officially been annexed to England in 1537, it retained its own national identity. In *Henry IV, Part 1,* Mortimer has married the daughter of Owen Glendower, who is fighting to retain Welsh independence. The two cannot communicate because she speaks no English, and he no Welsh. In his *View of the Present State of Ireland,* Edmund Spenser expressed amazement that the English there were learning Gaelic and maintained that it would be more appropriate for the Irish to learn the language of the conquering English. In *Henry V,* Act III, Scene 2, the Welsh, Irish, and Scottish captains retain their own linguistic traits. It is perhaps fitting that Shakespeare's works should be among the most potent forces in the Englishing of the world.

Henry V also explores the nature of power. The king wishes to stake his claim to the French throne of "right and conscience" (1.2.96). The Archbishop of Canterbury has tried, in a speech analyzed earlier (see "Difficult Passages"), to assure him of the legitimacy of his pretensions. When Henry still questions his claim, the Archbishop abandons the issue of Salic law and tells Henry, "unwind your bloody flag, . . . / Go my dread lord, to your

Princess Katharine of France in Act V, Scene 2 of *Henry V*. This print is from Charles Heath's 1848 edition of *The Heroines of Shakspeare: Comprising the Principal Female Characters in the Plays of the Great Poet. (Painting by J. W. Wright)*

great-grandsire's tomb, / From whom you claim" (1.2.101–104). Henry's right to the French throne ultimately rests, not on nice points of the laws of inheritance, but on force, not on Edward II's marriage to the daughter of Philip IV, but on Edward III's victories at Crécy and Poitiers. Henry's right to the English throne also derives from conquest; his father deposed Richard II. On the eve of battle, Henry recalls this usurpation and prays that God will not visit the sin of his father upon him at Agincourt; this plea reminds the audience of the source of Henry's kingship. The Southampton conspiracy, too, underscores the tenuous Lancastrian claim to the English throne. In the play's final scene, Charles VI designates Henry as his heir, supplant-

ing the Dauphin, who as Charles's son should by his birthright inherit the French throne. He would, in fact, be crowned Charles VII through the agency of Joan of Arc's military successes. Shakespeare's plays repeatedly show that kings may be made and unmade. One may, as York does in *Richard II,* see in these transitions divine intent (5.2.34), or one may, as with Edmund in *King Lear,* reflect, "Fine word, 'legitimate'!" (1.2.18).

As Shakespeare was writing *Henry V,* England was at war in Ireland and on the Continent. The play builds to the Battle of Agincourt, and critics at least from the time of Samuel Johnson have found the fifth act anticlimactic (see "Extracts from Classical Criticism" below). War is the play's central concern, but how is one to view that endeavor? Laurence Olivier dedicated his 1944 film version of the play to "the Commandos and Airborne Troops of Great Britain"; the film was part of the British Ministry of Information's war effort. Of this film, which glorifies the English invasion and victory at Agincourt, Olivier declared, "I had a mission . . . my country was at war; I felt Shakespeare within me. I felt the cinema within him. I knew what I wanted to do, what he would have done" (*On Acting* 80). In Olivier's film, only two deaths occur: that of the Boy, killed by the French, and the Constable of France, whom Henry kills in single combat. Even Bardolph escapes; Olivier cut his execution and, indeed, about half the text. Olivier omitted Henry's order to kill the French prisoners, further sanitizing the war effort. In the Olivier movie, Henry's banner bears a red cross, making him into St. George, the embodiment of England's patron saint embarked on a crusade.

Kenneth Branagh's 1989 film version offers a grimmer take on war. He, too, cut about half the text, but he reveals, as Shakespeare and Olivier did not, the reality of battle, which is bloody and violent. He shows the execution of Bardolph, which is discussed in the text, though no stage direction indicates that it was staged at the Curtain or the Globe. Whereas Olivier had cut the Southampton conspiracy to suggest that England was united behind Henry, Branagh keeps that scene. Olivier had also cut Henry's menacing speech before Harfleur in Act III, Scene 3, in which the king promises rape and infanticide, "murther, spoil, and villainy" (3.3.32) if the city does not surrender. Branagh retains the speech.

The play allows multiple interpretations, which are conditioned by the milieu in which it is produced. Speaking of his 2003 Royal Shakespeare production, Nicholas Hytner stated, "As the [Iraq] war finished [sic] and as skepticism returned and we were looking at it with cooler heads, that which is propagandistic about the play and that within the play is hagiographic about the king felt very familiar" (www.nationaltheatre.org). Thomas Carlyle, meanwhile, found "a noble patriotism" in the play (59). Charles Kean, who played Henry V at Sadler's Wells in 1859, agreed: "However much the general feeling of the present day may be opposed to the evils of war, there are few amongst us who can be reminded of the military renown achieved by our ancestors on the fields of Crécy, Poictiers, and Agincourt, without a glow of patriotic enthusiasm" (5). Whether *Henry V* inspires such a glow or some other feeling will depend on each viewer and reader.

Structure

At first glance, *Henry V* resembles the episodic chronicle plays that Shakespeare was writing in the early 1590s rather than the more carefully constructed *Richard II* and *Henry IV, Part 1*. It is a play crowded with incidents, some of which—such as the scenes in Eastcheap (2.1, 2.3) or Katharine's English lesson (3.4)—seem irrelevant to the main action, Henry's conquest of France. Closer examination, however, reveals Shakespeare's skill in constructing this work.

One obvious organizing principle is the Chorus, who introduces the entire play, reappears at the beginning of each act, and concludes the production with an epilogue. The Chorus thus marks each major division in the play and prepares the audience for the ensuing action. The Prologue sets out the play's central concern, the struggle between "two mighty monarchies" (21). At his next appearance, the Chorus describes England's preparations for war and the Southampton conspiracy. Before Act III, the Chorus transports the audience from Southampton to Harfleur, and prior to the Battle of Agincourt in Act IV, he informs us of the conditions in the English camp. He bridges the five-year gap between Acts IV and V and in the Epilogue circles back to Shakespeare's first tetralogy, dealing with the Wars of the Roses.

At the same time that the Chorus informs the audience of events to follow, he also emphasizes the play's artifice, constantly drawing spectators away from the action. His accounts, which may be regarded as the official version, are called into question by the scenes that follow, thereby challenging the Chorus's heroic vision. Before Act II, the Chorus focuses on the action at Southampton, where, he says, "three corrupted men" (22) have been bribed by French gold to kill the English king before he can sail for France. The act opens, however, not at Southampton, but at Eastcheap, where the Chorus's claim that "honor's thought / Reigns solely in the breast of every man" (3–4) is undercut by the discussion among Pistol, Bardolph, and Nym. They are going to France because they expect that "profits will accrue" (2.1.112). Their intention is "To suck, to suck, the very blood to suck!" (2.3.56). When the action finally moves to Southampton, the plot that the Chorus mentioned is exposed, but the conspirators are not necessarily motivated by bribery. Cambridge says that he had another reason, which he does not explain but which at least some audience members would know was his desire to put his brother-in-law, Mortimer, on the throne. (Mortimer had a better claim to the crown than Henry.)

Before Act IV, the Chorus says that Henry walks among his soldiers on the eve of battle to encourage them, and that everyone "plucks comfort from his looks" (42). In the scene that follows, however, the soldier Williams challenges Henry to a duel once the battle ends. The Chorus also promises at least one battle scene, which the play undercuts in comic fashion. What the audience sees and hears differs, challenging official accounts not just of the Chorus but of other speakers as well. For instance, the English casualty report in Act IV, Scene 8 notes 29 English dead. Shakespeare's source offered varying figures that ranged as high as 500. Gower says in Act IV, Scene 7 that Henry ordered the killing of the French prisoners in retaliation for the French killing of the boys guarding the baggage train. Yet, at the end of Act IV, Scene 6, Henry had declared, "The French have reinforc'd their scatter'd men. / Then every soldier kill his prisoners" (36–37). Who provides the real reason for this slaughter?

The play's seemingly heroic account is further undermined by Shakespeare's juxtaposition of scenes. In Act II, Scene 2, Henry rebukes Scroop, one of the three Southampton conspirators, for betraying his friendship:

Thou that didst bear the key of all my counsels,
That knew'st the very bottom of my soul,
That (almost) mightst have coin'd me into gold,
Wouldst thou have practic'd on me, for thy
  use? (96–99)

Yet, one would feel more sympathy for Henry had this episode not been sandwiched between accounts of Falstaff's illness (2.1) and death (2.3). Falstaff had been Prince Hal's closest companion, more of a father to him than Henry IV was. At the end of *Henry IV, Part 2,* however, Henry V cruelly rejected him. To Falstaff's "God save thee, my sweet boy," Henry replied, "I know thee not, old man" (5.5.43, 47). Now as Falstaff lies dying, Mistress Quickly observes that "The King has kill'd his heart" (*Henry V,* 2.1.88). Nym comments, "The King hath run bad humors on the knight, that's the even of it" (2.1.121–122). Pistol concurs: "His heart is fracted and corroborate" (2.1.124).

The opening scene of Act II also comments on the one preceding it, in which the king resolves to go to war. Here, Bardolph makes peace between Nym and Pistol. At the end of Act II, Scene 2, Henry gives orders to sail to France, declaring, "The signs of war advance! / No king of England, if not king of France!" (192–193). In the next scene, Pistol's language echoes Henry's but exposes the dark reality beneath those brave words: "Let us to France, like horse-leeches, my boys, / To suck, to suck, the very blood to suck!" (2.3.55–56).

In Act III, Scene 1 Henry urges his soldiers to renew the attack on Harfleur that has not been going well. "Once more unto the breach, dear friends, once more" (1) he begins, and goes on for another 33 lines. His heroic speech is parodied in the next scene, which opens with Bardolph's mocking, "On, on, on, on on! To the breach, to the breach!" (3.2.1–2). Whatever the reason is for Henry's killing his French prisoners, his order is anticipated by Pistol, who in Act IV, Scene 4 declares he will cut

Charles LeClerck as Bardolph in the Booth's Theatre 1875 production of *Henry V (Photographed by Napoleon Sarony)*

the throat of Le Fer, whom he has captured in the fighting. Earlier in the play, Pistol had threatened to cut Nym's throat: "Couple a gorge!" (2.1.71). By linking Henry and Pistol, the play's structure yet again questions the king's heroic stature.

Style and Imagery

Like almost all of Shakespeare's other plays, *Henry V* combines poetry and prose. In general, the characters lower in status speak prose, whereas the upper classes speak in blank verse. However, Shakespeare gives Pistol, a rogue, the archaic poetic diction of old plays, and noble figures speak in prose in comic scenes, which the play intermingles with more serious ones. To convey the sense that so much of the play is set in France, the work includes an unusually large amount of foreign speech, including a scene (3.4) almost entirely in French.

The work is more rhetorical than poetic and therefore lacks a controlling image such as that of the garden in *Richard II* or of poison and disease in *Hamlet*. Still, various image patterns pervade the work and serve to highlight themes and reveal character. In a play dealing with war, it is not surprising that the word *blood* occurs 33 times in the work. It takes on two senses here. One invokes bloodshed, as when Henry warns, "For never two such kingdoms [as England and France] did contend / Without much fall of blood" (1.2.24–25), or when the king later warns Harfleur of the soldier's "bloody hand" (3.3.34) and the French king describes Henry's flags as "painted in the blood of Harfleur" (3.5.49). Such references highlight the horrors of war, which is no "merry march" to triumph (1.2.195).

Blood, however, also refers to genealogy, as when Ely tells Henry V that "The blood and courage that renowned them [Henry's ancestors] / Runs in your veins" (1.2.118–119). Henry reminds his men that their "blood is fet [derived] from fathers of warproof" (3.1.18), and Fluellen assures Henry that "All the water in Wye cannot wash your Majesty's Welsh plood out of your pody" (4.7.106–107).

These two senses combine when Henry declares before the Battle of Agincourt, "For he to-day that sheds his blood with me / Shall be my brother" (4.3.61–62). The bloodshed in battle will confer on the fighters the blood of royalty. The play may also imply through its double sense of the word that royal blood provokes the spilling of that fluid, as Henry makes war to claim a throne he maintains is his through descent from Philip IV's daughter.

Another set of images deals with animals. The Prologue states that at Henry's heels, famine, sword, and fire are "Leash'd in, like hounds" (7). Henry urges his men to "imitate the action of the tiger" and imagines them as standing "like greyhounds in the slips" (3.1.6, 31). The Constable of France likens the English to "mastiffs" (3.7.148), picking up Orleans's description of them as "curs" (3.7.143); Orleans refers to the French fighters as resembling a "Russian bear" (3.7.144). These French nobles are implicitly comparing the upcoming battle at Agincourt to the popular Elizabethan sport of bearbaiting, which regularly occurred near the Globe Theatre. This supposed sport generally did not end happily for the bear, so the French unwittingly foretell their own defeat.

Fluellen addresses Nym, Pistol, and Bardolph as "you dogs" (3.2.20) when they hang back from battle at Harfleur. He also maintains that the Irish captain Macmorris knows no more about Roman military practice than "a puppy-dog" and regards him as "an ass" (3.2.73, 70). When the French herald Montjoy asks Henry for ransom before the Battle of Agincourt, Henry reminds him, "The man that once did sell the lion's skin / While the beast liv'd, was kill'd with hunting him" (4.3.93–94), as will happen to 10,000 Frenchmen trying to capture the English king. Queen Isabel later laments that Henry's eyes "have borne in them . . . The fatal balls of basilisks" (5.2.15–17), the final word denoting both a type of ordnance and a mythical beast. This proliferation of references to animals implies that war turns men into beasts.

The Sun often serves as a royal device in literature, and so it does here. Henry tells Katharine that his heart resembles the Sun, "for it shines bright and never changes" (5.2.163–164). The king warns the French ambassadors, "I will rise there [in

France] with so full a glory / that I will dazzle all the eyes of France / Yea, strike the Dolphin blind to look on us" (1.2.198–200). The Chorus also links Henry to solar imagery, stating, "A universal largesse, like the sun, / His liberal eye doth give to everyone" (4.0.43–44). When Henry, disguised as a common soldier, tells Williams that if the king breaks his promise not to be ransomed, he will never trust the monarch again, Williams retorts, "You may as well go about to turn the sun to ice with fanning in his face with a peacock feather" (4.1.199–201). By associating Henry with the Sun, the play implies that he is the true king even though he is the son of a usurper.

Yet another set of images involves water, which here is almost always destructive, a metaphor for armies descending on a country. Henry wonders whether he should take an army into France because whenever English forces go abroad, the Scots "Come pouring like the tide into a breach" (1.2.149). The French king declares that "England his approaches makes as fierce / as waters to the sucking of a gulf" (2.4.9–10). He therefore instructs his nobles to "Rush on his host, as doth the melted snow / Upon the valleys" (3.4.50–51). This use of a word that so often is life-giving indicates how war distorts nature as well as humans.

Two image patterns in the play recur from earlier works in the tetralogy. The word *time* appears in the first line of *Richard II*, when Richard addresses his uncle as "Old John of Gaunt, time-honored Lancaster" (1.1.1). The word occurs again in the second line of *Henry IV, Part 1*, when that monarch seeks "a time for frighted peace to pant" (1.1.2). In the play's next scene, in which Prince Hal, the future Henry V, first appears in the tetralogy, Falstaff asks him, "what time of day is it, lad?" (1.2.1), and at the end of that scene Henry, in a soliloquy, promises that he will redeem "time when men think least I will" (1.2.217).

In *Henry IV, Parts 1* and *2*, Hal lives in a pastoral world outside time. He dismisses Falstaff's question as "superfluous" (1.2.11). For the court and the rebels in *Henry IV, Part 1*, time moves too quickly, but in Hal's Eastcheap retreat, leisure prevails. Shakespeare's treatment of time in *Henry V* shows that with his coronation, Hal has fallen into history. Exeter notes the change when he tells the French that Henry now "weighs time / Even to the utmost grain" (2.4.137–138). In the play's opening scene, Canterbury observes that Henry did not have time to listen to the Archbishop's justification of the English claim on the French throne. Henry speaks of "brief mortality" (1.2.28), and the Epilogue tells of Henry's "small time" (l. 7): Henry died at the age of 35, two years after the signing of the Treaty of Troyes (5.2). The play's "Turning th' accomplishments of many years / Into an hourglass" (Prologue, 30–31) reflects the brevity of the king's life and the pressure of events that he feels as ruler.

Another image that runs through the Henriad is that of the garden. John of Gaunt refers to England as "this other Eden, demi-paradise" (*Richard II*, 2.1.42) that Richard has neglected. Henry V redeems fallen England, as the play's imagery reveals. In the opening scene, Canterbury observes that when Henry V's father died,

> Consideration like an angel came
> And whipt th' offending Adam out of him,
> Leaving his body as a paradise
> T' envelop and contain celestial spirits.
>   (1.1.28–31)

Ely, too, uses garden imagery to describe Henry, comparing him to strawberry plants that flourish "beneath the nettle" and to "summer grass" that grows at night when no one sees (1.1.60, 65). The Constable of France recognizes that when Henry, as Prince of Wales, surrounded himself with disreputable associates, his actions imitated sound horticultural practices: "As gardeners do with ordure hide those roots / that shall first spring and be most delicate" (2.4.39–40).

Henry's redemption extends to his realms of England and France. Burgundy calls France "This best garden of the world" that has reverted to wildness because of Henry's wars but that will assume "her former qualities" with the return of peace (5.2.36, 66). The Epilogue says that Henry achieved "the world's best garden," (7), echoing Burgundy's description of France. The term extends to England, since Henry V solidified the Lancastrian claim to the English as well as to the French throne. As Henry had promised in *Henry IV, Part 1,* he redeems himself and his country, though England will again suffer in the next reign.

EXTRACTS OF CLASSIC CRITICISM
Samuel Johnson (1709–1784) [Excerpted from *The Plays of William Shakespeare* (1765). Both Johnson's admiration for Shakespeare's portrayal of Henry V and his objection to the wooing scene (5.2) have been shared by later critics. Johnson hints at questions about the relationship between the Prince Hal of the two parts of *Henry IV* and the King Henry in this work, as well the Chorus's function. These issues, too, would concern subsequent students of the piece.]

This play has many scenes of high dignity, and many of easy merriment. The character of the King is well supported, except in his courtship, where he has neither the vivacity of *Hal*, nor the grandeur of *Henry*. The humour of *Pistol* is very happily continued; his character has perhaps been the model of all the bullies that have yet appeared on the *English* stage.

The lines given to the chorus have many admirers; but the truth is, that in them a little may be praised, and much must be forgiven; nor can it be easily discovered why the intelligence given by the chorus is more necessary in this play than in many others where it is omitted. The great defect in this play is the emptiness and narrowness of the last act, which a very little diligence might have easily avoided.

August Wilhelm von Schlegel (1767–1845) [Excerpted from *A Course of Lectures on Dramatic Art and Literature . . . Translated from the Origi-*

King Henry on horseback, surrounded by knights and with his army gathering behind him, addresses Montjoy in Act IV, Scene 7 of *Henry V.* This print was published by Amies in 1888. *(Illustration by Felix Octavius Darley)*

nal German by John Black (1815). Schlegel's translation of Shakespeare (1797–1810) is a masterpiece of German literature and did much to popularize Shakespeare on the Continent. His observation here, that *Henry V* is epic rather than dramatic, would be repeated by other critics. The same is true of Schlegel's comments about the comic nature of the play as well as its Machiavellian undertones, though Schlegel is of the party that admires the king.]

King Henry the Fifth is manifestly Shakespeare's favorite hero in English history: he paints him as endowed with every chivalrous and kingly virtue; open, sincere, affable, yet, as a sort of reminiscence of his youth, still disposed to innocent raillery, in the intervals between his perilous but glorious achievements. However, to represent on the stage his whole history subsequent to his accession to the throne, was attended with great difficulty. The conquests in France were the only distinguished event of his reign; and war is a epic rather than a dramatic object. For wherever men act in masses against each other, the appearance of chance can never wholly be avoided; whereas it is the business of the drama to exhibit to us those determinations which, with a certain necessity, issue from the reciprocal relations of different individuals, their characters and passions. . . .

Before the battle of Agincourt he paints in the most lively colours the light-minded impatience of the French leaders for the moment of battle, which to them seemed infallibly the moment of victory; on the other hand, he paints the uneasiness of the English King and his army in their desperate situation, coupled with their firm determination, if they must fall, at least to fall with honour. . . . He has surrounded the general events of the war with a fullness of individual, characteristic, and even sometimes comic features. A heavy Scotchman, a hot Irishman, a well-meaning, honourable, but pedantic Welchman, all speaking in their peculiar dialects, are intended to show us that the warlike genius of Henry did not merely carry the English with him, but also the other natives of the two islands, who were either not yet fully united or in no degree subject to him. Several good-for-nothing associates of Falstaff among the dregs of the army either afford an opportunity for proving Henry's strictness of discipline, or are sent home in disgrace. But all this variety still seemed to the poet insufficient to animate a play of which the subject was a conquest, and nothing but a conquest. He has, therefore, tacked a prologue (in the technical language of that day *a chorus*) to the beginning of each act.

These prologues, which unite epic pomp and solemnity with lyrical sublimity, and among which the description of the two camps before the battle of Agincourt forms a most admirable night piece, are intended to keep the spectators constantly in mind, that the peculiar grandeur of the action described cannot be developed on a narrow stage, and that they must, therefore, supply, from their own imaginations, the deficiencies of the representation. As the matter was not properly dramatic, Shakespeare chose to wander in the form also beyond the bounds of the species, and to sing, as a poetical herald, what he could not represent to the eye, rather than to cripple the progress of the action by putting long descriptions in the mouths of the dramatic personages. . . .

However much Shakespeare celebrates the French conquest of Henry, still he has not omitted to hint, after his way, the secret springs of this undertaking. Henry was in want of foreign war to secure himself on the throne; the clergy also wished to keep him employed abroad, and made an offer of rich contributions to prevent the passing of a law which would have deprived them of half of their revenues. His learned bishops consequently are as ready to prove to him his indisputable right to the crown of France, as he is to allow his conscience to be tranquilized by them. . . . After his renowned battles, Henry wished to secure his conquests by marriage with a French princess; all that has reference to this is intended for irony in the play. The fruit of this union, from which the two nations promised to themselves such happiness in the future, was the weak and feeble Henry VI, under whom every thing was so miserably lost. It must not, therefore, be imagined that it was without the knowledge and will of the poet that a heroic drama turns out a comedy in his hands, and ends in the manner of Comedy with a marriage of convenience.

William Hazlitt (1778–1830) [Excerpted from *Characters of Shakespear's Plays* (1817). Hazlitt, as will be obvious from the extract below, had no time for kings in general and for Henry V in particular. He brings his political views to bear on his criticism, a tendency much in evidence in 20th- and 21st-century commentary. His negative assessment of Shakespeare's Henry V, though not universal, would be echoed by many others. Hazlitt notes Henry's tendency to shift onto others the blame for his own actions. Hazlitt also regards as sinister and self-interested the advice of the Archbishop of Canterbury, another interpretation shared by later criticism. His disappointment with the comic scenes will find echoes in subsequent discussions of the play. Despite his attitude toward the main character, Hazlitt admires Shakespeare's skill with language, something no critic of whatever political or philosophical leanings can impugn.]

Henry V is a very favorite monarch with the English nation, and he appears to have been also a favorite with Shakespear, who labours hard to apologize for the actions of the king, by showing us the character of the man, as "the king of good fellows." He scarcely deserves this honour. He was fond of war and low company:—we know little else of him. He was careless, dissolute, and ambitious— idle, or doing mischief. In private, he seemed to have no idea of the common decencies of life, which he subjected to a kind of regal license; in public affairs, he seemed to have no idea of any rule of right or wrong, but brute force, glossed over with a little religious hypocrisy and archiepiscopal advice. . . . Falstaff was a puny prompter of violence and outrage, compared with the pious and politic Archbishop of Canterbury, who gave the king *carte blanche,* in a genealogical tree of his family, to rob and murder in circles of latitude and longitude abroad—to save the possessions of the Church at home. This appears in the speeches in Shakespear, where the hidden motives that actuate princes and their advisers in war and policy are better laid open than in speeches from the throne or woolsack. Henry, because he did not know how to govern his own kingdom, determined to make war upon his neighbours. Because his own title to the crown was doubtful, he laid claim to that of France. . . . Henry declares his resolution "when France is his, to bend it to his awe, or break it all to pieces" [1.2.224–225]—a resolution worthy of a conqueror, to destroy all that he cannot enslave; and what adds to the joke, he lays all the blame of the consequences of his ambition on those who will not submit tamely to his tyranny. Such is the history of kingly power, from the beginning of the end of the world. . . . Henry V, it is true, was a hero, a king of England, and the conqueror of the king of France. Yet we feel little love or admiration for him. . . . How then do we like him? We like him in the play. There he is a very amiable monster, a very splendid pageant. As we like to gaze at a panther or a young lion in their cages in the Tower [among its functions over the centuries, the Tower of London served as a zoo], and catch a pleasing horror from their glistening eyes, their velvet paws, and dreadless roar, so we take a very romantic, heroic, patriotic, and poetical delight in the boasts and fears of our younger Harry, as they appear on the stage and are confined to lines of ten syllables; where no blood follows the stroke that wounds our ears, where no harvest bends beneath horses' hoofs, no city flames, no little child is butchered, no dead men's bodies are found piled on heaps and festering the next morning—in the orchestra!

So much for the politics of this play; now for the poetry. Perhaps one of the most striking images in all Shakespear is that given of war in the first lines of the Prologue. . . .

Rubens, if he had painted it, would not have improved upon this simile.

The conversation between the Archbishop of Canterbury and the Bishop of Ely relating to the sudden change in the manners of Henry V [1.1.22–69] is among the well-known *Beauties* of Shakespear. It is indeed admirable both for strength and grace.

Nothing can be better managed than the caution which the king gives the meddling Archbishop, not to advise him rashly to engage in the war with France, his scrupulous dread of the consequences of that advice, and his eager desire to hear and follow it. . . .

A more beautiful rhetorical delineation of the effects of subordination in a commonwealth can hardly be conceived than the following: . . . [quotes 1.2.183–213].

HENRY V is but one of Shakespear's second-rate plays. Yet by quoting passages, like this, from his second-rate plays alone, we might make a volume "rich with his praise." . . .

Of this sort are the king's remonstrance to Scroop, Grey, and Cambridge, on the detection of their treason [2.2.79–144], his address to the soldiers at the siege of Harfleur [3.1], the description of the night before the battle [Chorus to Act 4], and the reflections on ceremony put into the mouth of the king [quotes 4.1.233–284]. . . .

But we must have done with splendid quotations. The behaviour of the king, in the difficult and doubtful circumstances in which he is placed, is as patient and modest as it is spirited and lofty in his prosperous fortune. The character of the French nobles is also very admirably depicted; and the Dauphin's praise of his horse [3.7.11ff.] shows the vanity of that class of persons in a very striking point of view. . . . The comic parts of *Henry V* are very inferior to those of *Henry IV*. Falstaff is dead, and without him, Pistol, Nym, and Bardolph are satellites without a sun. Fluellen the Welshman is the most entertaining character in the piece. He is good-natured, brave, choleric, and pedantic. His parallel between Alexander and Harry of Monmouth [4.7.11–50], and his desire to have "some disputations" with Captain Macmorris on the disciplines of the Roman wars, in the heat of the battle [3.294ff.], are never to be forgotten. His treatment of Pistol is as good as Pistol's treatment of his French prisoner. There are two other remarkable prose passages in this play: the conversation of Henry in disguise with the three sentinels on the duties of a soldier [4.1.92–229], and his courtship of Katherine in broken French [5.2.98–280]. We like them both exceedingly, though the first savours perhaps too much of the king, and the second too little of the lover.

Georg G. Gervinus (1805–1871) [Excerpted from *Shakespeare Commentaries* (1863). In typical 19th-century fashion, Gervinus focuses on characters. He draws some fascinating parallels between Henry V and Henry Percy (Hotspur), a major figure in *Henry IV, Part 1*.]

The whole interest of our play lies in the development of the ethical character of the hero. After the poet has delineated his careless youthful life in the First Part of Henry IV. and in the Second Part has shown the sting of reflection and consideration piercing his soul as the period of self-dependence approaches, he now displays Henry as arrived at the post of his vocation, and exhibits the king acting up to his resolutions for the future. At the very beginning of the play we are at once informed of the utter change which has passed over him. The sinful nature is driven out of him by reflection, the current of reformation has suddenly scoured away the old faults; as the wholesome strawberry ripens best "neighboured by fruit of baser quality" [*Henry V,* 1.1.62], so his active practice, his intercourse with lower life and simple nature, has matured in him all those gifts which etiquette and court ceremony would never have produced in him, and which those now around him perceive in him with admiration. . . .

Berthe Girardin as Princess Katharine in an 1875 production of *Henry V* (*Photographed by Napoleon Sarony*)

In his fight at Agincourt he has before him even to surpass the warlike Edwards [Edward III and his son, Edward the Black Prince], when, with a little, weak, famished band, he has to withstand the brilliant force of the French. . . . And in this position he aspires truly after the wholly undiminished glory of a position so desperate; he prefers not to lose so much "honour as one man more would share from him" [4.3.32], who should come to his assistance from England.

In these expressions somewhat of that strained nature may seem to lie which we pointed out in Percy as opposed to Henry. . . . This would be a contradiction in his character, if anything were a contradiction in it; but we showed throughout that it belongs to his nature and essence to be every-

thing when occasion calls him and necessity claims him. . . . Once had *Prince* Henry said that he was "not yet of Percy's mind" [*Henry IV, Part 1*, 2.4.101–102], but the *King* is so now. . . .

Among the more serious popular characters . . . the Welshman Fluellen, the king's countryman, is the central point. . . . Compared with the former companions of the prince, he is like discipline opposed to license, like pedantry opposed to dissoluteness, conscientiousness to impiety, learning to rudeness, temperance to intoxication, and veiled bravery to concealed cowardice. . . . In common with his royal countryman, he is not what he seems. Behind little caprices and awkward peculiarities is hidden an honest, brave nature. . . . He speaks good and bad of his superiors, ever according to truth, deeply convinced of the importance of his praise and blame, but he would do his duty under each. . . . The self-contentedness of an integrity, unshaken indeed, but also never exposed to any temptation, is excellently designed in all the features of this character.

The pedantic-like discipline and love of order, the valour by line and level of the brave Fluellen, though it may appear in an old-fashioned light compared to the well-based and free virtue of the king, stands out on the other hand by its unassuming nature in advantageous contrast to the worthlessness of his boasting companions, Pistol, Nym, and Bardolph. . . . At the commencement of the important period they appear a little elevated, but circumstances again ruin them. Their seducer Falstaff is no longer with them; a better spirit accompanies them in the boy, . . . who honourably falls in battle with the boys. He characterises his three companions, whom he thought of leaving, so distinctly, that we require no other analysis. They are soon again "sworn brothers in filching" [3.2.44], and Bardolph and Nym bring themselves to the gallows. . . . Pistol is not so bold a thief as they, and he is, therefore, dismissed with the more lenient lesson from Fluellen, who makes him eat his Welsh leek, and "cudgels his honour" from his limbs [5.1.84–85].

Algernon Charles Swinburne (1837–1909)
[Excerpted from *A Study of Shakespeare* (1880). Best known as a pre-Raphaelite poet, Swinburne was also an important 19th-century critic of Renaissance drama who promoted the study of various of Shakespeare's contemporaries. In the following passage, he offers his negative assessment of the character of Henry V, although Swinburne notes that critics of his day divide on this issue. They continue to do so today.]

Henry V is the first as certainly he is the noblest of those equally daring and calculating statesmen-warriors whose two most terrible, most perfect, and most famous types are Louis XI. and Caesar Borgia. Gain, "commodity," the principle of self-interest which never but in a word and in jest could become the principle of Faulconbridge [the hero of Shakespeare's *King John*], . . .—is as evidently the mainspring of Henry's enterprise and life as of the contrast between King Philip and King John. The supple and shameless egotism of the churchmen on whose political sophistries he relies for external support is needed rather to varnish his project than to reassure his conscience. . . . No completer incarnation could be shown us of the militant Englishman—*Anglais pur sang* [pure-blooded Englishman]; but it is not only, as some have seemed to think, with the highest, the purest, the noblest quality of English character that his just and far-seeing creator has endowed him. The godlike equity of Shakespeare's judgment, his implacable and impeccable righteousness of instinct and of insight, was too deeply ingrained in the very core of his genius to be perverted by any provincial or pseudo-patriotic preposses-

sions; his patriotism was too national to be provincial.

William Butler Yeats (1865–1939)
[Excerpted from "At Stratford-on-Avon" (1903). Winner of the 1923 Nobel Prize in literature for his poetry and plays, Yeats also wrote many critical essays. Here, he joins the dispraisers of Henry.]

To pose character against character was an element of Shakespeare's art, . . . and so, having made the vessel of porcelain, Richard II, he had to make the vessel of clay, Henry V. He makes him the reverse of all that Richard was. He has the gross vices, the coarse nerves, of one who is to rule among violent people, and is so little "too friendly" to his friends that he bundles them out of doors when their time is over. He is as remorseless and undistinguished as some natural force, and the finest thing in his play is the way his old companions fall out of it broken-hearted or on their way to the gallows; and instead of that lyricism which rose out of Richard's mind like the jet of a fountain to fall again where it risen, instead of that fantasy too enfolded in its own sincerity to make any thought the hour had need of, Shakespeare has given him a resounding rhetoric that moves men as a leading article does to-day. His purposes are so intelligible to everybody that everybody talks of him as if he succeeded, although he fails in the end, as all men great and little fail in Shakespeare. His conquests abroad are made nothing by a woman turned warrior [Joan of Arc]. That boy he and Katharine were to "compound," "half French, half English," "that" was to "go to Constantinople and take the Turk by the beard," turns out a saint and loses all his father had built up at home and his own life [*Henry V*, 5.2.207, 208–209].

Shakespeare watched Henry V not indeed as he watched the greater souls in the visionary procession, but cheerfully, as one watches some handsome spirited horse, and he spoke his tale, as he spoke all tales, with tragic irony.

MODERN CRITICISM AND CRITICAL CONTROVERSIES

Modern criticism of Shakespeare's history plays begins with Tillyard's *The Elizabethan World Picture* (1943) and *Shakespeare's History Plays* (1944). Written in the midst of the chaos of World War II, these works evidence Tillyard's rage for order, which he transferred to the Elizabethans. Tillyard argued that the Elizabethans (whom he regarded as intellectually monolithic) turned to the past to find lessons for the present, and the chief lesson they found was that obedience to rulers was the only way to ensure stability in the realm. He posited an Elizabethan worldview that saw the world as directed by divine providence and rulers as God's minister on Earth. Rebellion was not just treason but also heresy. For Tillyard, Shakespeare's two tetralogies that trace English history from Richard II to Henry VIII show the dangers of usurpation. Robert Ornstein's *A Kingdom for a Stage* (1972) was to challenge Tillyard's view of the Tudor myth, denying that it existed. Also, Ornstein argued that Shakespeare's plays present secular history determined by individual action, not the working out of a divine plan.

Perhaps because Henry V succeeds, Tillyard found Shakespeare's play about him less effective than those dealing with his father and son, whose reigns were plagued by civil wars resulting from the overthrow of the rightful king. According to Tillyard, *Henry V* "shows a great falling off in quality" from the two parts of *Henry IV* (*Shakespeare's History Plays* 306). He regarded the verse as flat, the comic scenes irrelevant to the main action, the wooing of Katharine in Act V, Scene 2 as coarse and "curiously exaggerated; one can almost say hectic: as if Shakespeare took a perverse delight in writing up something he had begun to hate" (313). Tillyard concludes perversely that Henry, who is as at least as ambiguous as Julius Caesar, Brutus,

and Hamlet—all of whom Shakespeare created in 1599–1600—was too unambiguous to appeal to the playwright.

Campbell's *Shakespeare's "Histories": Mirrors of Elizabethan Policy* (1947) shares Tillyard's view that Shakespeare's plays serve as comments on Elizabethan concerns. She notes that Humphrey, duke of Gloucester, brother of Henry V and protector of England during King Henry VI's minority, had commissioned Tito Livio to write a Latin biography of Henry V as a conduct manual for the young ruler. An anonymous translation into English in 1513 or 1514 offered the text to Henry VIII, who was then fighting the French. The translator included moral commentary throughout and compared Henry V with the current ruler. For Campbell, Shakespeare's Henry V is the ideal hero-king, and she draws parallels between events in the play and in Elizabeth's England. Still, she regards Henry V's reign as an interlude in the civil strife that was divine retribution for Bolingbroke's usurpation and the working out of a providential plan to put the Tudors on the English throne.

Calderwood's *Metadrama in Shakespeare's Henriad*, Richard II *to* Henry V (1979) focuses on the ways in which the play comments on itself as well as on its subject. Calderwood argues that *Henry V* emphasizes unity in king, play, and country. Hence, the private Henry is suppressed. "In keeping with the theme of unity," Calderwood writes, "the private man is subdued by the public office" (141). The Chorus encourages a monolithic interpretation of the play, and it serves to unify the work by linking the acts. The Chorus in the theater invites audience members to help create the play by using their imaginations, just as Henry at Agincourt asks his soldiers to work together to achieve victory. "The unity of English spirit on the battlefield is mirrored by the unity of English minds in the theater" (178), Calderwood writes. The Epilogue notes that Henry's victories did not endure. For Calderwood, this statement comments on plays as well, which are evanescent. Each lasts for "small time," as the Epilogue says, "but in that small most greatly live" (5).

More recent critical approaches have reapproached the play's historical context. John Dollimore and Alan Sinfield's "History and Ideology: The Instance of *Henry V*" (1985) exemplifies the way cultural materialism, an offshoot of Marxist criticism, looks at a text. Like Tillyard, they find a kind of Tudor myth, in which obedience to authority is central to the dominant ideology of Shakespeare's England. They agree with Calderwood that unity is central to the play. But, where Calderwood finds that quality, for Dollimore and Sinfield, the play is less clear. They note that aristocrats seek to kill the king (2.2) and commoners question the war's legitimacy (4.1). This challenge to unity within the play extends to the political world beyond. Henry tries to unify his country, but that effort is repeatedly tested. Similarly, Elizabeth sought a unified realm, but she continued to face opposition to her authority, whether from Irish rebels or aristocrats like the earl of Essex who thought themselves more competent than she to rule the country. In a later piece, "History and Ideology, Masculinity and Miscegenation: The Instance of *Henry V*" (1992), Dollimore and Sinfield argue that challenges to authority in the play are contained, but these are present, nonetheless.

Whereas for cultural materialists literature may question the governing elite, for new historicists it always confirms the power structure. Stephen Greenblatt's "Invisible Bullets" (1981) agrees with the old historicists like Tillyard and Campbell that a play like *Henry V* is not a self-contained artifact but rather shares concerns with the social and intellectual debates occurring in the larger society. Greenblatt acknowledges that "the play deftly registers every nuance of royal hypocrisy, ruthlessness, and bad faith," but it still celebrates Henry, and by extension, Elizabeth (56). Greenblatt rejects Tillyard's claim that Machiavelli's political ideas had not yet permeated Elizabethan thought. On the contrary, Greenblatt maintains that "the Henry plays confirm the Machiavellian hypothesis that princely power originates in force and fraud" (65). But, the plays also foster in their audiences an acceptance of that power.

Katharine of France is presented to Henry V of England at the Treaty of Troyes. Print published by the London Printing and Publishing Company in the 19th century *(Painting by Thomas Stothard; engraving by John Rogers)*

Another late 20th-century critical approach reflects the rise of feminism. Jean E. Howard and Phyllis Rackin's 1997 *Engendering a Nation* provides, as its subtitle states, *A Feminist Account of Shakespeare's English Histories*. Feminist critics find that New Historicism ignores issues relating to gender; they seek to understand how Shakespeare defines not just women but also men and how his works have helped to define the way cultures imagine "gender and sexual difference, the institution of marriage, and the gulf between 'public' and 'private' life" (20–21). Howard and Rackin argue that in *Henry V* women are seen as possessions. For example, in his speech before Harfleur, Henry addresses the men of the city only, and he speaks of "*your* fresh fair virgins," "*your* pure maidens," "*your* shrill-shriking daughters" (3.3.14, 20, 35; italics added). The play values women not for their intelligence or abilities but only for their sexuality and the possessions they confer on their husbands. Mistress Quickly provides Pistol with a tavern; Katharine confers a country on Henry. Henry demonstrates his masculinity by winning Katharine's hand and by conquering France, which is portrayed as a woman to be overcome by a masculine English army. Pistol and Nym draw swords to contest for Mistress Quickly.

Coppélia Kahn's earlier "'The Shadow of the Male': Masculine Identity in the History Plays" (1981) notes the absence of women in Shakespeare's historical dramas. Men are defined by their relationships with other men. Even though Henry's supposed right to France derives from the mother of Edward III, the Archbishop directs Henry to go "to your great-grandsire's tomb, / From whom you claim; invoke his warlike spirit, / And your great uncle's, Edward the Black Prince" (1.2.103–105). She argues that the great love scene in *Henry V* is not the king's wooing of Katharine (5.2) but rather the described deaths of the Duke of York and the Earl of Sussex, who expire in each other's arms (4.6).

THE PLAY TODAY

Henry V is politically charged. Its popularity in the early 21st century in Britain and the United States perhaps reflects contemporary politics and the social concerns of nations at war overseas. In fact, the play has always seemed especially relevant in times of war. Gerald Gould's 1919 "A New Reading of *Henry V*" used the play to condemn the horrors of World War I. In 1938, a production was chased from the London stage because it was seen as promoting war in a country still hoping vainly for peace. In his 1944 movie version, Olivier used the work to inspire patriotism during the world war. Branagh's post-Vietnam, post–Falklands War 1989 film used the play to question the costs of militarism. The 2003 stage production at London's Royal National Theatre was decidedly antiwar, with disgruntled, cowardly soldiers and a cynical, amoral king.

Not surprisingly, critics today continue to examine the play for what it tells us about nations and leaders at war. They argue over whether Henry V himself should be viewed as a hero whom Shakespeare celebrates or as a warmongering tyrant, the murderer of innocent prisoners. In 2010, a Washington, D.C., theater company held a mock trial, whose judges included the Supreme Court justices Ruth Bader Ginsburg and Samuel Alito, to decide whether Shakespeare's Henry V was guilty of war crimes in killing the French prisoners (the court rejected Henry's justification for the killing).

Of course, great literature offers no answers, only questions. It does not tell us what to think; it tells us what to think about. *Henry V* offers multiple viewpoints about authority, warfare, gender roles, language, public versus private domains, nationalism, and religion. Just as the play continues to exercise the intellect, its language appeals to the emotions. No matter how one feels about patriotism or the current wars, Henry's speech before Agincourt rouses the senses, and the play's Epilogue makes the listener feel the sadness of faded glory.

FIVE TOPICS FOR DISCUSSION AND WRITING

1. **Shakespeare's depiction of Henry V:** In this play, does Henry V emerge as a hero-king, as he is portrayed in Shakespeare's sources? Or, is he a Machiavellian prince? Or, does he appear as a combination of ideal Christian ruler and cold calculator?

2. **Treatment of war:** Is *Henry V* an entirely antiwar play, or does it support at least some military undertakings as justifiable? Is the invasion in France, in particular, justifiable?

3. **Comic subplots:** Many critics have observed that the comic scenes of the play do not advance the action. What, if anything, would be lost if these were removed from the play? What is the importance of the scene in which Falstaff's death is described?

4. **Absence of battle scenes:** This work about one of England's greatest military victories includes only one battle scene, played comically, though Shakespeare had not shied away from these in the *Henry VI* plays or *Henry IV, Part 1*. Filmed versions, on the other hand, do include them. Would the play have been more (or less) effective if Shakespeare had supplied battle scenes?

5. **Religion:** Henry repeatedly mentions God. Does he emerge as truly religious, or as a hypocrite who uses church and religion to achieve his worldly goals?

Bibliography

Albright, Evelyn May. "The Folio Version of *Henry V* in Relation to Shakespeare's Times." *PMLA* 43 (1928): 722–756.

Benjamin, Walter. *Understanding Brecht*. New York: Verso, 2003.

Berman, Ronald, ed. *Twentieth Century Interpretations of* Henry V: *A Collection of Critical Essays*. Englewood Cliffs, N.J.: Prentice-Hall, 1968.

Bloom, Harold. *Shakespeare: The Invention of the Human*. New York: Riverhead Books, 1998.

Boyce, Charles. *Shakespeare A to Z: The Essential Reference to His Plays, His Poems, His Life and Times, and More*. New York: Facts On File, 1995.

Bradshaw, Graham. *Misrepresentations: Shakespeare and the Materialists*. Ithaca, N.Y.: Cornell University Press, 1993.

Bullough, Geoffrey. *Narrative and Dramatic Sources of Shakespeare*, vol. 4. New York: Columbia University Press, 1962.

Calderwood, James L. *Metadrama in Shakespeare's Henriad:* Richard II *to* Henry V. Berkeley and Los Angeles: University of California Press, 1979.

Campbell, Lily B. *Shakespeare's "Histories": Mirrors of Elizabethan Policy*. San Marino, Calif.: Huntington Library, 1947.

Cartyle, Thomas. *On Heroes and Hero Worship*. London: Chapman and Hall Limited, 1840.

Chernaik, Warren. *The Cambridge Introduction to Shakespeare's History Plays*. Cambridge: Cambridge University Press, 2007.

Daniel, Samuel. *The Poetical Works of Mr. Samuel Daniel. v. 2.* London: Printed for R. Gosling, 1718.

Dollimore, John, and Alan Sinfield. "History and Ideology: The Instance of *Henry V.*" In *Alternative Shakespeares,* edited by John Drakakis, 210–231. New York: Routledge, 1985.

Garber, Marjorie. *Shakespeare after All*. New York: Pantheon Books, 2004.

Goddard, Harold C. *The Meaning of Shakespeare*. Chicago: University of Chicago Press, 1951.

Gould, Gerald. "A New Reading of *Henry V.*" *English Review* 29 (1919): 42–55.

Greenblatt, Stephen. "Invisible Bullets." In *Shakespearean Negotiations*. Berkeley and Los Angeles: University of California Press, 1988, 21–65.

Gurr, Andrew, ed. *Henry V.* Cambridge: Cambridge University Press, 2005.

Hall, Joan Lord. Henry V: *A Guide to the Play.* Westport, Conn.: Greenwood Press, 1997.

Hazlitt, William. *Characters of Shakespear's Plays*. New York: Wiley and Putnam, 1845.

Holderness, Graham. *Shakespeare: The Histories*. New York: St. Martin's, 2000.

———. *Shakespeare's History*. New York: St. Martin's, 1985.

Holderness, Graham, Nick Potter, and John Turner. *Shakespeare: The Play of History*. Iowa City: University of Iowa Press, 1988.

Howard, Jean E., and Phyllis Rackin. *Engendering a Nation: A Feminist Account of Shakespeare's English Histories*. New York: Routledge, 1997.

Kahn, Coppélia. *Man's Estate: Masculine Identity in Shakespeare*. Berkeley: University of California Press, 1981.

Kean, Charles. Preface to *King Henry V,* by William Shakespeare. London: John K. Chapman and Co., 1859.

Kernan, Alvin. "The Henriad: Shakespeare's Major History Plays." *Yale Review* 59 (1969): 3–32.

Knowles, Ronald. *Shakespeare's Arguments with History*. New York: Palgrave, 2002.

Marlowe, Christopher. *The Jew of Malta*. New York: Charles E. Merrill, Co., 1892.

Moseley, C. W. R. D. *Shakespeare's History Plays,* Richard II *to* Henry V. London: Penguin, 1988.

Neill, Michael. "Broken English and Broken Irish: Nation, Language, and the Optic of Power in Shakespeare's Histories." In *Putting History to the Question: Power, Politics, and Society in English Renaissance Drama*. New York: Columbia University Press, 2000, 339–372.

Ornstein, Robert. *A Kingdom for a Stage: The Achievement of Shakespeare's History Plays*. Cambridge, Mass.: Harvard University Press, 1972.

Patterson, Annabel. "Back by Popular Demand: The Two Versions of *Henry V.*" In *Shakespeare and the Popular Voice*. Oxford: Basil Blackwell, 1989, 71–92.

Pearlman, E. *William Shakespeare: The History Plays.* New York: Twayne, 1992.

Pomeroy, Elizabeth W. *Reading the Portraits of Queen Elizabeth I.* Hamden, Conn.: Archon Books, 1989.

Quayle, Anthony, ed. *Shakespeare's Histories at Stratford, 1951.* New York: Theatre Arts Books, 1952.

Quinn, Michael. *Shakespeare:* Henry V, *a Casebook.* London: Macmillan, 1969.

Rabkin, Norman. "Rabbits, Ducks, and *Henry V.*" *Shakespeare Quarterly* 28 (1977): 279–296.

Reese, Max Meredith. *The Cease of Majesty: A Study of Shakespeare's History Plays.* New York: St. Martin's Press, 1961.

Ribner, Irving. *The English History Play in the Age of Shakespeare.* Rev. ed. London: Methuen, 1965.

Richmond, H. M. *Shakespeare's Political Plays.* New York: Random House, 1967.

Saccio, Peter. *Shakespeare's English Kings: History, Chronicle, and Drama.* 2d ed. Oxford: Oxford University Press, 2000.

Tillyard, E. M. W. *Shakespeare's History Plays.* London: Methuen, 1944.

Traversi, Derek. *Shakespeare: From* Richard II *to* Henry V. Stanford, Calif.: Stanford University Press, 1957.

Watt, R. J. C., ed. *Shakespeare's History Plays.* New York: Longman, 2002.

Wilders, John. *The Lost Garden: A View of Shakespeare's English and Roman History Plays.* Totowa, N.J.: Rowman & Littlefield, 1978.

FILM AND VIDEO PRODUCTIONS

Branagh, Kenneth, dir. *Henry V.* With Derek Jacobi, Kenneth Branagh, and Alec McCowen. BBC, 1989.

Dews, Peter, dir. *The Life of Henry V.* With Michael Bates, John Neville, Bernard Hepton, and John Wood. BBC, 1957.

Gauger, Neal J., dir. *Henry V.* Ad'Hoc Productions, 2003.

Giles, David, dir. *Henry V.* With David Gwillim, Alec McCowen, Tim Wylton, and Jocelyne Boisseau. BBC, 1979.

Olivier, Laurence, dir. *Henry V.* With Leslie Banks, Laurence Olivier, Renee Asherton, and Felix Aylmer. Two Cities Films, 1944.

Watts, Peter, dir. *Henry V.* With John Clements, John Garside, and Kay Hammond. BBC, 1953.

—Joseph Rosenblum

Henry VI, Part 1

INTRODUCTION

Henry VI, Part 1 is one of Shakespeare's earliest plays. It serves as the opening of what we now know as the playwright's first tetralogy, which also includes *Henry VI, Parts 2* and *3* and *Richard III*. Some scholars perceive flaws in the play's text, and it has attracted much criticism and speculation over authorship because it does not seem to show a fully formed genius at work in the way that we have come to expect from Shakespeare. Some critics believe that *Henry VI, Part 1* was written after the other two *Henry VI* plays, probably in collaboration with another playwright. Others disagree and insist that the *Henry VI* plays were written consecutively.

None of the *Henry VI* plays is particularly well known or well regarded among Shakespeare's work, but all three have received more attention in recent years, in part because of a few high-profile productions. *Henry VI, Part 1* can be exciting precisely because it shows a young dramatist finding his feet, perhaps working with other writers of his day, developing his skills. It is episodic in structure, but its scope is huge, covering the concluding years of the Hundred Years' War and the opening skirmishes in the Wars of the Roses and showing action in both England and France. *Henry VI, Part 1* is a fast-paced play; no sooner has one event happened than the audience is whisked along to another event, another battle, another scene of plotting and scheming. The young Henry VI does not appear until the middle of the play and has a very small part for being the eponymous character; neverthe-less, *Henry VI, Part 1* is full of characters, sometimes confusingly so, who battle for and against the king on both sides of the English Channel.

The characters of the play are sometimes criticized for being thematic and lacking depth; however, they represent a wide range of qualities: Beaufort, the plotting cardinal; Talbot, the chivalric hero; Plantagenet, the young gentleman wanting to regain his family's honor and title; Joan, the warrior woman. *Henry VI, Part 1* also includes what are arguably some of Shakespeare's strongest and most feisty female roles; indeed, one of the main plot lines presents a woman who fights in battle and wins but is burned at the stake for witchcraft. This woman, who confounds the men, provides one of the most exciting stories. At first, Shakespeare presents Joan sympathetically, but through differing French and English responses to her, he creates an ambiguous character until the final scenes. However, even when Shakespeare abandons his ambiguous portrayal of her, Joan's speeches are beautifully poetic and deliciously deceitful. This example of Shakespeare's contingent approach to the themes and characters is an engaging aspect of play: Shakespeare does not tell the audience what to think but rather, by presenting many varying facets, encourages the audience to draw its own conclusions.

BACKGROUND

The action of the play is set during the Hundred Years' War in the early 15th century and takes place in both England and France, following conflicts in

The Dauphin promises to share his crown with Joan la Pucelle in Act 1, Scene 6 of *Henry VI, Part 1*. *(Painting by Friedrich Pecht; engraving by Tobias Bauer)*

both countries: at home, disagreements are growing between nobles, while in France, a woman leads the French army against English forces. This plot line closely parallels concerns and events in Shakespeare's time. The English defeat of the Spanish Armada in 1588 provides a significant backdrop to *Henry VI, Part 1:* From an atmosphere of rejoicing, England had descended into a gloom by the early 1590s; England remained at war with France, and there were problems brewing regarding Ireland. Protestant fights with the Catholic League in France were current with English forces supporting French Protestant attempts to take power after the assassination of King Henry III of France in 1589, and a certain degree of Francophobia infused the atmosphere in England at this time. During 1591–92, when *Henry VI, Part 1* was written, Henry of Navarre was expected to triumph over Catholicism, and his attempts were supported

by Robert Devereux, the earl of Essex, who was at the Siege of Rouen in 1591. Significantly, these missions to France were marred by a lack of support from home, particularly from Queen Elizabeth, who, at times, failed to send sufficient money and supplies to aid the soldiers. This letdown from home is an important plot line in Shakespeare's play and, in real life, fed the fear of Elizabeth's capitulating to French Catholicism. This was not an unfounded fear as the queen had considered marrying a Frenchman, the duke of Alençon, later of Anjou. If Elizabeth had married this nobleman, she would have become something of a Catholic queen. In *Henry VI, Part 1,* Alençon and Anjou are separate characters, but they are both named by Joan as her lovers in her pleas before she is burned at the stake. This would suggest a clear and negative reference to Elizabeth.

In 1591, Elizabeth I had already been queen for 33 years, but anxiety related to female dominance and rule remained an issue. Elizabeth's sense of androgyny was apparent in her frequent references to herself as a "prince" and the "husband" of the nation, such language seeming to masculinize the woman and creating anxieties about male identity. Elizabeth's androgyny was never more apparent than at Tilbury, where, in 1588, Elizabeth, for a pre-Armada speech, appeared before her men dressed in male clothing and armor and claiming that "I have the body of a weak and feeble woman, but I have the heart and stomach of a king, and a king of England too." Whether Elizabeth's appearance at Tilbury and her speech actually took place is something that scholars have questioned; however, it has gained mythical status. The very real opposition of gender qualities presented in Elizabeth's speech infuses the presentation and questioning of gender throughout *Henry VI, Part 1,* particularly embodied in the characters of Joan la Pucelle and Talbot. That Joan is presented in a negative way throughout the play— she is a Catholic leading an army against England and ultimately presented as a lying witch—suggests that an attack is being made upon Elizabeth I.

Ireland was also a significant sociopolitical concern of the day: Munster and Ulster had been colonized with the intention of civilizing the native Irish or converting them to Protestantism. The Irish, however, did not take kindly to this mission; indeed, by the mid-1590s, the situation had deteriorated into the Nine Years' War. Although *Henry VI, Part 1* was written prior to this war, Ireland features considerably in the play. After the death of Walter Devereux, Lord Lieutenant of Ireland, in 1576, there had been a problem regarding leadership in that country. Nobles and their supporters squabbled over positions, creating a background to *Henry VI, Part 1,* where the conflict begins between Plantagenet and Somerset but moves on to the fall of English forces in France and the start of a civil war, which will become known as the Wars of the Roses and dominate the other two *Henry VI* plays.

Date and Text of the Play

Although there has been disagreement between scholars about when *Henry VI, Part 1* was written, it is usually accepted as being the "Harey the vj" listed as "ne," or new, in Philip Henslowe's diary. The diary entry marks the play's performance by Lord Strange's Men at the Rose theater on March 3, 1592. Assuming the play was indeed Shakespeare's *Henry VI, Part 1,* it would then be the play by Shakespeare that we can most accurately date. However, if that date of performance was also close to the date of composition, it would mean that Shakespeare wrote the play after those that we now know as *Henry VI, Parts 2* and *3,* as these are referred to in Robert Greene's 1592 pamphlet *A Groatsworth of Wit* (at the time, they were known as *The First Part of the Contention Betwixt the Two Famous Houses of York and Lancaster* and *The true Tragedie of Richard Duke of Yorke, and the death of good King Henrie the Sixt,* respectively). That the first part of the *Henry VI* trilogy was written after the later two should not be problematic; in fact, scholars have generally agreed that *Henry VI, Parts 2* and *3* are better written than *Henry VI, Part 1.* Nonetheless, many scholars believe it is more likely that the *Henry VI* plays were written consecutively. Thus, suggesting that the first part was written

after the second and third parts creates a range of issues. A way in which scholars have negotiated this problem is to suggest that Shakespeare did not write the whole of the play: Two theories put forward are that Shakespeare either wrote the play in collaboration with other writers or that he did not write the play at all but rather revised another writer's play. Collaboration was common in the period, and it is most likely that this was the way *Henry VI, Part 1* was composed. Indeed, some of Shakespeare's later plays, such as *Pericles* and *King Henry VIII,* were also written in collaboration with other writers. Who Shakespeare might have collaborated with on *Henry VI, Part 1* remains in dispute, but names put forward include Thomas Nashe, George Peele, Robert Greene, and Christopher Marlowe. For clarity, and because we can firmly name Shakespeare as a writer of the play, herewith the writer will simply be referred to as Shakespeare.

Henry VI, Part 1 was first printed in the First Folio of 1623: It did not appear, as other plays did, including *Henry VI, Parts 2* and *3,* in an earlier quarto version. This may be because, although the play is set during the early 15th century, it embodies, discusses, and responds to many social and political concerns of the late 16th century; therefore, printers may have been wary of taking on the play.

SYNOPSIS
Brief Synopsis

The Duke of Gloucester and the Bishop of Winchester disrupt the funeral of King Henry V with an argument. Messengers arrive with news of disastrous military defeats in France, where the army under the Earl of Salisbury is pinned down outside Orleans (Orléans).

After an assault occurs at the siege of Orleans, Charles VII, Alençon, and Reignier decide that they will abandon the town. Joan La Pucelle, who claims she was sent a vision from heaven, enters and convinces Charles to accept her offer of assistance.

Salisbury and Talbot, an English leading knight, appear on the turrets of Orléans to plan an attack on the city. A cannonball strikes and mortally

Title page of the First Folio edition of *Henry VI, Part I*, published in 1623

injures Salisbury. Charles and Joan arrive with an army to raise the siege. Though the English are initially driven back into their trenches, Talbot, Bedford, and the Duke of Burgundy, an ally of the English, eventually drive the French leaders over the walls.

Bedford, Burgundy, and Talbot mourn the dead Salisbury. An invitation arrives for Talbot from a French noblewoman, the Countess of Auvergne, who unsuccessfully attempts to capture Talbot when he goes to meet her.

During his argument with the Duke of Somerset, Richard Plantagenet plucks a white rose from a garden tree and calls on those who support him to do likewise. Somerset takes a red rose as his own emblem. When most support Plantagenet, Somerset insults Plantagenet's father before departing.

Plantagenet visits a dying relative, Mortimer, who is a prisoner in the Tower of London. Mortimer describes the deposition of King Richard II by Henry IV, head of the Lancastrian branch of the royal family. An attempt to install Mortimer, of the York branch, as king resulted in Mortimer's imprisonment for life. Mortimer's brother-in-law, who had been Richard Plantagenet's father, was executed for attempting to crown Mortimer. Mortimer names Plantagenet his successor before dying.

King Henry VI pleads for peace between Gloucester and Winchester before agreeing to restore Plantagenet as Duke of York. Gloucester announces that all the preparations have been made for Henry to be crowned King of France in Paris.

A skirmish outside the gates of Rouen culminates in a French defeat and Bedford's death. Joan convinces the Duke of Burgundy to desert the English.

Winchester crowns the king in Paris. Fastolfe arrives with a message from Burgundy, in which he declares his changed allegiance. Talbot departs to march against Burgundy. The king attempts to resolve the dispute between York and Somerset by dividing the command of the English forces.

Sir William Lucy arrives from Bordeaux, where a French force marches to attack Talbot, with an urgent plea for reinforcements from York. He is resisted by York, who accuses Somerset for not pro-

viding cavalry support. Lucy approaches Somerset with the same plea, and Somerset refuses, criticizing York for a bad plan.

Talbot, mortally wounded, mourns the death of his son, John, killed in the battle, and then dies also. Lucy appears, under a flag of truce, to retrieve the bodies of the two Talbots.

Gloucester tells King Henry that a peace treaty has been arranged and that a marriage, intended to secure the peace, has been proposed between the king and the daughter of a French nobleman. The king agrees.

Joan uses witchcraft to summon a group of fiends, but these spirits refuse to aid her against the reunited English army. York defeats Burgundy and takes Joan prisoner. Suffolk enters with Margaret of Anjou as his prisoner. He offers to marry her to King Henry and make her Queen of England if she will be his lover. After Suffolk agrees to her own conditions, Margaret accepts. Condemned to be burned, Joan dies at the stake.

Suffolk's description of Margaret's virtues has caused the King to desire her. Gloucester objects, citing the earlier marriage agreement. However, the king orders Suffolk to return to France to arrange a marriage to Margaret. The play closes with a soliloquy by Suffolk, in which he proposes to rule the kingdom himself, through Margaret.

Act I, Scene 1

The play opens in England with the funeral of Henry V: Various nobles praise the dead monarch, but they descend into squabbling. The friction between the Duke of Gloucester and Bishop of Winchester is particularly evident. The arguing is interrupted by a messenger telling of the loss of eight French towns, the spoils of Henry V's victory in France, through want of men and money as a result of disputes among nobles. As the assembled lords bemoan this loss, a second messenger enters to inform of the Dauphin's being crowned king of France. A third messenger then enters telling of the capture of the English warrior hero John Talbot. Each lord declares his intent to help regain France before Winchester is left alone to state his intention to seize English power by the stealing the infant Henry VI from Eltham, where he is staying.

Act I, Scene 2

In France, near Orleans, the French lords reflect on their victories and, in the glow of their success, decide to raise the English siege of Orleans. But, they are beaten back by the English, causing the French to describe the English as mad. The Bastard of Orleans introduces "a holy maid" (1.2.51), Joan la Pucelle, who has a heavenly prophecy that she will raise the siege. The heir to the French throne, the Dauphin, subjects Joan to two tests. In the first, Reignier, King of Anjou, poses as the Dauphin to test her skills of prophecy. Joan triumphs by immediately recognizing and naming the impostor. In private conversation with the Dauphin, Joan details her background as a shepherd's daughter who has seen visions of the Virgin Mary instructing her to free France from English rule. The Dauphin subjects Joan to a second test, one of single combat, in which he is overpowered by the woman. This immediately inspires sexual desire in him, but Joan states that she must remain chaste. Impressed, the French resolve to follow her lead and leave to raise the siege.

Act I, Scene 3

England, the Tower of London. The Duke of Gloucester arrives to inspect the Tower but is refused entry by the Bishop of Winchester's men. Gloucester instructs his own men to "Break up the gates" (1.3.13). Winchester enters, and the two lords bicker over each other's ambition to the crown. Fighting ensues between the two sets of men, broken up by the Mayor of London. A proclamation is made forbidding the wielding of weapons on pain of death, and the two factions part and exit.

Act I, Scene 4

France, Orleans. The Master Gunner of the town instructs his boy to keep watch for the English while he leaves the post, stating that the boy must call for him if he spots the enemy; however, after the Gunner has left, the boy states his intention not to do this. Talbot and the Earl of Salisbury enter unseen. Talbot has recently been ransomed for French prisoners and tells Salisbury of his imprisonment and how the French fear him. The men are spotted, and Salisbury and his companion, Gargrave, are shot. Gargrave is dead, and Salisbury is badly wounded. A messenger enters to tell Talbot that the French have regrouped and are coming to raise the siege. Talbot, vowing vengeance for Salisbury, carries the dying man off to his tent.

Act I, Scene 5

France, Orleans. Talbot meets Joan in battle. He describes the wonder of the warrior woman, something he thinks explicable only in terms of witchcraft. The two fight. However, Joan states that the time has not come for her to vanquish Talbot and leaves him in a state of bewilderment.

Act I, Scene 6

France, Orleans. The French triumph, rescuing Orleans from the English. The Dauphin attributes the success to Joan, stating that he will share his crown with her and that she will become France's saint.

Act II, Scene 1

France, Orleans. The English plan to retake Orleans while the French feel secure in their victory. Talbot, Bedford, and Burgundy question the ambiguous nature of Joan. The French are taken at night unawares and squabble over whose fault it is. The Dauphin and Joan enter together; the nature of their relationship is ambiguous and commented on by the other Frenchmen, but Joan encourages the Frenchmen to cease in-fighting, regroup, and plan a counterattack. An English soldier reflects on the power of Talbot's name, boasting that he has won many spoils simply by shouting "Talbot."

Act II, Scene 2

France. The English enter with Salisbury's dead body and pay homage. A messenger from the

Talbot's soldiers free him from the Countess of Auvergne in Act II, Scene 3 of *Henry VI, Part 1*, in this print published by Virtue & Company in the 19th century. *(Painting by William Quiller Orchardson; engraving by Charles William Sharpe)*

Countess of Auvergne enters, requesting a meeting between the Countess and Talbot.

Act II, Scene 3

France. Talbot visits the Countess of Auvergne, who is plotting to capture him. She mocks Talbot but is mocked in turn by the warrior, who shows that while he is a "shadow" his "substance" is his whole army (2.3.36–38). At his soldiers' surprise entrance, Talbot is freed.

Act II, Scene 4

England, the garden of the Temple Hall. Richard Plantagenet, the Duke of Somerset, the Earl of Warwick, the Duke of Suffolk, and other gentlemen have come into the garden to continue a quarrel chiefly between Richard Plantagenet and Somerset. To indicate whose side they favor, each lord plucks a red rose for Somerset or a white rose for Plantagenet. The quarrel is not resolved but set to go on and looks to become violent.

Act II, Scene 5

England, the Tower of London. Plantagenet visits the dying Edmund Mortimer in jail and is acquainted with his history and claim to the throne. Mortimer provides the back story to the play, detailing episodes from the *Henry IV* plays and *Henry V.* Mortimer dies, and Richard states his intention to regain his title.

Act III, Scene 1

England, Whitehall. The quarrel between Gloucester and Winchester continues, with Gloucester accusing Winchester of plotting against his and the king's lives. Each accuses the other of wanting power over the king. King Henry VI attempts to make peace between the two, while other lords take sides and Plantagenet plots for his own advancement. The Mayor of London enters telling of Gloucester and Winchester's men fighting in the streets with stones. Both sides are forced to an uneasy peace by King Henry and Warwick. Richard is restored as the Duke of York, and the king sets off to be crowned in France. Exeter remains alone to state his unease and sense of foreboding in relation to the dissension among the lords, referring to an old prophecy that Henry born at Monmouth should win all and Henry born at Windsor should lose all.

Act III, Scene 2

France, Rouen. The French enter Rouen, disguised as peasants bringing corn and take the city from the English. The French, refusing to fight, speak from the walls to the English, who are now outside, and leave. The English, leaving the dying Bedford sitting outside the city to inspire the soldiers, plan their attack. Alarums and excursions ensue followed by the French fleeing. Rouen has been retaken for England, and Bedford now dies. Talbot honors the dead lord after stating his intent to go to Paris to meet King Henry.

Act III, Scene 3

France. Joan reassures the French lords and plots to bring the Duke of Burgundy to the French side. As the English march to Paris, Joan intercepts Burgundy and "bewitches" him by describing the wrongs done to France and the French people by the English (3.3.58). Burgundy is won over and defects from the English to the French.

Act III, Scene 4

France, Paris. Talbot meets with King Henry and the English lords. As reward for his endeavors, Henry makes Talbot the Earl of Shrewsbury. Alone, Vernon and Basset continue the conflict between York and Somerset, almost coming to blows. The domestic conflict escalates.

Act IV, Scene 1

France, Paris. Henry is crowned in France but, as the Mayor of London is pledging allegiance, the ceremony is interrupted by Sir John Falstaff, who brings a letter from the Duke of Burgundy. Falstaff is berated by Talbot, who, supported by the other lords, strips Falstaff's garter from him for his cowardice in the Battle of Patay, where Talbot was captured. Falstaff is exiled. The letter from Burgundy tells of the duke's betrayal, and Talbot is sent by Henry to talk with the Frenchman. To show his favor, Henry makes York regent of France, and both York and Somerset are commanded to join their forces to send support to Talbot. Vernon and Basset enter, approaching the king to ask for a trial by combat against each other. This request draws the conflict between York and Somerset to the attention of the king, who chides the lords. In an attempt to highlight the folly in conflict, Henry picks the red rose to demonstrate that it is arbitrary and does not indicate he loves York any less than Somerset. However, York, when the others have left, reveals that he perceives this as a slight and begins to obliquely suggest he may aim for the crown. Alone, Exeter again acts as a chorus, telling the audience of his foreboding.

Act IV, Scene 2

France, Bordeaux. Talbot is denied entry to Bordeaux by the Captain, who states his allegiance to the Dauphin and tells Talbot that he is surrounded by French soldiers.

Act IV, Scene 3

A messenger informs York of the armies marching to fight Talbot. York bemoans Somerset's failure to supply troops. Sir William Lucy enters to urge York's support, but it is in vain. Lucy informs York that Talbot's son, young John Talbot, who has not seen his father for seven years, is on his way to fight the French alongside his father although both are now certain to die.

Act IV, Scene 4

Somerset blames York and Talbot's haste for their predicament and his failure to provide aid in time for the battle at Bordeaux. Lucy asks that private disagreements should not prevent provision of aid. Somerset again blames York, while Lucy points out that York blames Somerset. Lucy underlines that it is English squabbles that have betrayed Talbot, not French power.

Act IV, Scene 5

France, Bordeaux. Young John Talbot meets with his father and demands to be allowed to fight. The men argue about who should flee, both attempting to save the other in the name of honor. Talbot eventually concedes and allows John to fight with him.

Act IV, Scene 6

France, the battle at Bordeaux. Talbot details how he has saved Young John from death and encourages his son to flee, but John refuses and the battle continues.

Act IV, Scene 7

France, Bordeaux. Talbot, alone, bemoans and details the death of Young John on the battlefield. John's body is brought to Talbot, and in a moving scene, the father grieves and then dies holding his son in his arms. The French lords and Joan enter stating that the battle would have been harder for them had the English support arrived. In a mocking tone, Joan details her encounter with John. On seeing the bodies, the Dauphin prevents their degradation, granting the former "scourge of France" respect in death (4.7.15). Lucy enters stating that the French have won and requesting details of prisoners and freedom to account for the English dead. His grief for Talbot is undercut by Joan's mockery. Lucy leaves with Talbot's body, while the Dauphin exits in triumph.

Act V, Scene 1

England. Gloucester informs King Henry that the pope, the emperor, and the Earl of Armagnac all request a peace between England and France. Henry concurs, stating his belief that followers of the same religion should not be at war with one another. Gloucester also says that Armagnac has offered his daughter in marriage to Henry, but Henry is unsure, stating that he is too young for marriage. Winchester, now made Cardinal, enters with the ambassadors: Exeter comments on Winchester's promotion, remembering a prophecy made by Henry V that if Winchester became a cardinal, he would make himself equal to the king. King Henry announces that peace will be made with France, and Gloucester supports this, stating that Henry intends to take Armagnac's daughter as his queen. Henry sends a jewel to the daughter of the earl as a pledge of his affection. All except Winchester and the papal legate leave, and Winchester reveals that he has paid for his new position, giving the money in payment to the legate. Finally, Winchester confirms Exeter's fears, stating that he intends to make Gloucester stoop to him, thereby taking power over Henry, or else cause mutiny in England.

Act V, Scene 2

France. Charles, Burgundy, Alanson, the Bastard, Reignier, and Joan discuss the French victory and news that the Parisians are rebelling against the English and turning to France. A scout enters to report that the English army, which had been divided, is now united and intends to fight the French again. The men leave, and Joan, alone onstage, prays to her helpers, who, she reveals, are ruled by the devil. Joan's fiends appear, but despite her requests, they refuse to help her and leave, shaking their heads. Joan, forsaken, also leaves to the battle.

There are excursions: York enters fighting Burgundy, and the French enter and flee. Joan, alone, is captured by York, who accuses her of being an enchantress and takes her away to the stake.

After an alarum, Suffolk enters with Margaret as his prisoner, but he is besotted with her. After flirt-

Margaret in *Henry VI, Part 1*. This is a print from Charles Heath's 1848 edition of *The Heroines of Shakspeare: Comprising the Principal Female Characters in the Plays of the Great Poet. (Painting by J. W. Wright; engraving by W. Holl)*

ing and much debate with himself, Suffolk decides to engage Margaret to Henry as a means by which to bring peace to England and France and also to conduct an adulterous relationship with Margaret himself. Suffolk parleys with Reignier, Margaret's father, who gives consent for Margaret to marry Henry on the condition that, even though Margaret has no dowry, the counties of Maine and Anjou are returned to him. Suffolk consents and leaves to take this news to King Henry.

Act V, Scene 3

France. York and Warwick bring out Joan. Joan's father, a Shepherd, enters and claims that he has searched for her, but Joan asserts that she is of nobler birth and rejects him. In turn, the Shepherd leaves Joan to the flames. York commands that Joan be taken away, but she pleads for her life claiming her noble birth and divine inspirations as grounds for leniency. When this fails, Joan claims her virginity and, finally, that she is pregnant. In desperation, Joan names the father first as Alanson and then as Reignier. When none of her pleas succeeds, Joan resigns herself to her death and is taken away cursing the men.

Cardinal Winchester enters and informs York of the peace being made between England and France. York is displeased and tells Warwick that he foresees the complete loss of France. The Dauphin and lords enter to ask the terms of the peace. Winchester states that Charles must become a liegeman to Henry. The French reject this idea, stating that the Dauphin already holds half the French territories, the people of which regard him as king, but, at York's exclamation that refusing the offer will bring more war on France, the Dauphin agrees to the terms. However, Alanson says to the Dauphin that he could break the terms whenever he pleases.

Act V, Scene 4

England. Suffolk is talking with Henry, who is astonished by his description of Margaret. Henry agrees to marry Margaret. Gloucester is angry that the contract with Armagnac will be dishonorably broken, but Suffolk puts this down with claims that Armagnac is a mere earl while Reignier is King of Naples and Jerusalem. Exeter raises the issue of wealth and Margaret's lack of a dowry, but this is again rejected by Suffolk, who claims that thinking of money over love is an insult to Henry. Henry, inspired by lust, agrees to the marriage under Reignier's terms. As they leave, Gloucester voices his misgivings at the proposal. Suffolk, left alone, concludes the play by musing that now Margaret will be queen and rule Henry, and he will rule Henry and England through his relationship with Margaret.

CHARACTER LIST

King Henry VI   King of England (historical figure lived 1421–71). A devoutly religious king, he was only nine months old when he ascended the throne on the death of his father, Henry V.

Duke of Gloucester   Younger brother of Henry V (historical figure lived 1391–1447), uncle of Henry VI, and protector of the realm during Henry VI's childhood. Also known as Humphrey.

Duke of Bedford   Younger brother of Henry V and uncle of Henry VI. Bedford is a military leader who represents past, now-lost glories.

Duke of Exeter   Also known as Thomas Beaufort. Uncle of Henry (historical figure died in 1427), great-uncle and guardian of Henry VI. Exeter acts as a chorus prophesying the bad things that will happen as a result of other characters' actions or inaction.

Bishop of Winchester   Also known as Henry Beaufort. Great-uncle to Henry VI (historical figure died 1447). He becomes a cardinal during the play. Winchester is in conflict with Gloucester about power over the young Henry and plots to become more powerful in England.

Duke of Somerset   Also known as John Beaufort, although Shakespeare conflates the historical first and second dukes, John (1403–44) and Edmund (1406–55), into a single character. While arguing with Richard Plantagenet in the Temple Garden, he asks his followers to pick a red rose with him, later becoming a leader of the Lancastrian faction.

Richard Plantagenet   The historical figure lived from 1411 to 1460. Richard is the son of the Duke of Cambridge, who is executed in *Henry V* as a traitor. Richard initially seeks to regain his title and his family's honor and is made Duke of York during the play. However, after a meeting with his uncle, Edmund Mortimer, he increasingly has eyes for the crown. Plantagenet becomes a major protagonist of *Henry VI, Parts 2* and *3*.

Earl of Warwick   Councilor to the king (historical figure lived 1382–1439) and friend of

Richard Plantagenet. Although he acts in a conciliatory manner in *Henry VI, Part 1*, Warwick picks a white rose with Plantagenet. In the later *Henry VI* plays, the subsequent earls will become loyal allies to the House of York.

Earl of Salisbury Also known as Thomas de Montacute (historical figure lived 1388–1428). He fights alongside Talbot and is shot at Orleans. The use of a gun in his death makes Salisbury a symbol of the death of chivalry.

Duke of Suffolk Also known as William de la Pole (historical figure lived 1396–1450). Suffolk engages Henry to Margaret of Anjou with the intention of ruling England himself though an adulterous relationship with Margaret.

Sir John Talbot Created Earl of Shrewsbury during the play, Talbot is arguably the play's protagonist (historical figure died in 1453). He is a heroic warrior who is feared as the "scourge of France."

John Talbot Sir John Talbot's son (historical figure died in 1453). He joins his father at the Battle of Bordeaux.

Edmund Mortimer Fifth Earl of March (historical figure lived 1391–1425), he is a gentleman who is imprisoned in the Tower of London. This character may be Shakespeare's conflation of different Edmund Mortimers, suggesting that this character is supposed to be read as the Mortimer who rose against Henry IV and claimed kingship. Mortimer acquaints Richard Plantagenet with his history and Plantagenet's own claim to the throne.

Sir John Falstaff The First Folio refers to this character as Falstaff, although he is not the same character of that name who features in the *Henry IV* plays and *Henry V*. Falstaff is a cowardly knight. While with the king in Paris, Talbot strips this knight of his garter for cowardly actions at the Battle of Patay, where Talbot was captured, and the character is exiled.

Sir William Lucy A knight who pleads with both the Dukes of York and Somerset to send aid to Talbot at the Battle of Bordeaux. Historically there was no such character during this time in these battles; however, there was a William Lucy who was sheriff of Warwickshire during the reign of Henry VI, and Shakespeare's familiarity with his descendants may have inspired the character.

Sir Thomas Gargrave An English soldier who is shot outside Orleans and dies offstage.

Woodville Lieutenant of the Tower of London (historical figure of Richard Woodville died in 1441).

Vernon A fictional gentleman who suggests the picking of roses in the Temple Garden scene and sides with Richard Plantagenet. Vernon helps to bring the growing domestic quarrels to the attention of the king by asking to settle his dispute with Basset in a trial by combat.

Basset A fictional gentleman who takes the red rose with Somerset in the Temple Garden scene. He continues to feud with Vernon later in the play, asking for a trial by combat to settle the argument.

Dauphin Charles The historical Dauphin lived from 1403 to 1461. French prince at war with the English in France.

Reignier Duke of Anjou and Maine, King of Naples and Jerusalem (historical figure lived 1409–80). Reignier is a friend of Charles and the father of Margaret of Anjou.

Duke of Burgundy A French duke (historical figure lived 1396–1467) and coregent of France with the Duke of Bedford, who begins the play on the English side but is won over to the French by Joan.

Duke of Alanson One of the French commanders (historical figure lived 1409–76).

Bastard of Orleans One of the French commanders (historical figure lived ca. 1403–68). The Bastard introduces Joan to the Dauphin.

Margaret Daughter of Reignier, (historical figure lived 1430–82). She is captured by Suffolk on a French battlefield and engaged to Henry. She becomes Henry's queen in *Henry VI, Part 2* and is a major protagonist through the remaining three plays of the first tetralogy.

Countess of Auvergne   A fictional character who attempts but fails to capture Talbot.

Joan la Pucelle   The historical figure, better known as Joan of Arc, lived from 1412 to 1431). She is introduced to the Dauphin claiming she has seen visions of the Virgin Mary and is ordained to lead France against the English. The Dauphin and lords follow her. She is later captured by York and burned as a witch.

Shepherd   He claims to be the father of Joan la Pucelle, but she rejects him.

Mayor of London   Breaks up a fight in Act I, Scene 3.

Master Gunner   His order is disobeyed by a boy in Act I, Scene 4.

CHARACTER STUDIES
Joan la Pucelle

Joan la Pucelle (based on the historical figure better known as Joan of Arc) is one of the more intriguing and ambiguous of Shakespeare's female characters. Ambiguity, in fact, is central to her, so much so that it is embodied even in her name, which may be *Pucelle* or *Puzel,* whose various meanings are polar opposites (both virgin and whore). The contradictions in her name give the scorning English much to joke about: "Pucelle or puzzel, Dolphin or dogfish" (1.4.106). Talbot, here, mocks both Joan and the Dauphin through belittling their names. However, it is not only the English who question the virginity of the "holy maid" (1.2.51); Charles the Dauphin states that "Joan de Pucelle shall be France's saint" (1.6.29). The equating of a whore with a saint symbolizes Joan's ambiguity and suggests that even her name, when spoken by another character, dubiously creates the presentation of her character.

Joan's own presentation of herself has two significant moments: the first when she is presented to the Dauphin in Act I and the second in Act V when she is finally captured by the English. In Act I, Joan refers to her poor background as a shepherd's daughter, inspired by visions of the Virgin Mary:

Lo, whilest I waited on my tender lambs,
And to sun's parching heat display'd my cheeks,
God's Mother deigned to appear to me,
And, in a vision full of majesty
Will'd me to leave my base vocation
And free my country from calamity. (1.2.76–81)

Joan explicitly details her inspiration as divine. Her state was lowly, much like that of Mary when the angel Gabriel appeared to her, and she has been given a mission by God. That Joan has already shown her gifts by correctly identifying Reignier posing as the Dauphin and that she soon will show her martial prowess confirm this special presentation. However, this speech also presents the oratorical gifts that Joan possesses, which will be of great importance to her survival with the French: She

Joan la Pucelle declares her mission to the Dauphin in a 19th-century depiction of Act I, Scene 2 of *Henry VI, Part 1. (Painting by John Opie; engraving by John Rogers)*

wins over the Dauphin with this speech ("Thou hast astonished me with thy high terms" [1.2.93]), and she continues to quell French doubts with her language ("Dismay not, princes, at this accident, / Nor grieve that Roan is so recovered: . . . We'll pull his [Talbot's] plumes and take away his train; / If Dolphin and the rest will be but rul'd" [3.3.1–8]). Her power with words even wins the Duke of Burgundy over from the English to the French side ("I am vanquished. These haughty words of hers / Have batt'red me like roaring cannon-shot" [3.3.78–79]). And, it is words that are left to Joan when she is captured: Her only recourse after she is abandoned by her fiends is to curse (5.4.86–91).

Although Joan creates and re-creates herself (she initially says she is a shepherd's daughter but in Act V denies her father, claiming rather, noble birth), central to her presentation are the accounts of and responses to her by other characters. Joan confounds most men on their first encounter with her. After fighting her, Talbot is bewildered:

My thoughts are whirled like a potter's wheel,
I know not where I am nor what I do.
A witch by fear, not force, like Hannibal,
Drives back our troops and conquers as she lists.
 (1.5.19–22)

This short passage gives two important aspects of Joan's character. In the first two lines, Talbot suggests Joan has such power that she can confuse a man's sense of time, space, and identity. However, in the last two lines, Talbot defines the English response to Joan: Her martiality is explicable only through witchcraft, and she is a dishonorable fighter because she wins through inspiring fear rather than by force. This presentation is supported by other English fighters who find the idea of a warrior woman paradoxical: "BEDFORD. A maid? and be so martial?/ BURGUNDY. Pray God she prove not masculine ere long" (2.1.22–23).

Joan is presented as a paradox: She is a "holy maid," but one who is assigned the masculine task of raising the siege of Orleans and "[driving] the English forth the bounds of France" (1.2.53–54).

Joan's presentation is built on this kind of opposition. To the French, she is "Bright star of Venus" (1.2.144), "Divinest creature, Astraea's daughter" (1.6.4). The Dauphin's praise defines Joan in terms of femininity, despite that it is inspired by her martial acts. However, within this, there is a sense of opposition, as the presentation is at once both about virginity and sexuality. Joan's defeat of the Dauphin immediately inspires lust in him; indeed, his description of Joan as a star of Venus suggests this alignment of her character with love.

Shakespeare's final presentation of Joan resolves all ambiguity, as she is captured while praying to the devil, and her pleas at the stake are made up of lies and curses:

  Joan of Aire hath been
  A virgin from her tender infancy . . .
  Will nothing turn your unrelenting hearts?
  Then, Joan, discover thine infirmity,
  That warranteth by law to be thy privilege.
  I am with child, ye bloody homicides!
   (5.4.49–62)

Such a change in character may be explained through Joan's desperation at the stake, but her previous command of language no longer has the power that it possessed earlier, and Shakespeare leaves her a confused, hypocritical, lying woman, demonized through her prayers to the devil. Joan is perhaps one of the most engaging and sympathetic characters in *Henry VI, Part 1;* by demonizing her, Shakespeare creates an acceptable ending where the more Protestant-like Englishmen defeat the Catholic woman, and equilibrium is apparently restored.

Sir John Talbot

Talbot is a great English warrior who is representative of the honor and chivalry that belonged to the era of Henry V and is now dying. Talbot's first presentation is by other characters as it is announced that he has been captured in France:

Enclosed were they with their enemies.
A base Wallon, to win the Dolphin's grace,

Thrust Talbot with a spear into the back,
Whom all France with their chief assembled
   strength
Durst not presume to look once in the face.
   (1.1.136–140)

This early presentation by an unnamed messenger tells the audience a lot: The French are presented as cowards who literally stab people in the back, and Talbot is presented as so powerful that all of France together could not look him in the face. This is supported throughout the play, as Talbot is referred to variously as the "scourge of France" (2.3.15) and the "terror of the French" (1.4.42). Indeed, France is so afraid of Talbot that one English soldier declares that he could conquer simply by shouting out Talbot's name (2.1.78–81). Talbot has his own elevated ideas of his power; indeed, when telling Salisbury of his imprisonment, he states that "with a baser man of arms by far / Once in contempt they would have barter'd me; / Which I, disdaining, scorn'd, and craved death" (1.4.30–32). This highlights Talbot's concern with chivalry: He holds traitors and cowards in contempt but will fight for the honor of good men, as evidenced in his pursuit of revenge for Salisbury:

Now I have paid my vow unto his soul;
For every drop of blood was drawn from him
There hath at least five Frenchmen died.
   to-night (2.2.7–9)

Talbot is seen here to keep his word: He is noble and brutal in his search for revenge, something that takes on greater significance when seen against the French murder of Salisbury by gunshot. The gunner's boy, Salisbury's murderer, is in contrast unseen and unheroic.

His encounter with the Countess of Auvergne in Act II, Scene 3 is central to the presentation of Talbot: Not appearing in any chronicle source, this scene is entirely of Shakespeare's invention. That the scene does not in any way contribute to the furthering of the plot means that Shakespeare is using it for presentational purposes. The Countess of Auvergne

sets up the idea of Talbot, talking of "this dreadful knight" and his "achievements" (2.3.7–8) in order that this image might be challenged, as it is by the Countess's response to his entrance:

Is this the scourge of France?
Is this the Talbot, so much fear'd abroad
That with his name the mothers still their babes?
I see report is fabulous and false. (2.3.15–18)

Indeed, the Countess goes further than this; her response to his physical appearance seems to undermine all that the audience has so far been told about Talbot's greatness: He is not scary but "a child, a silly dwarf," a "weak and writhled shrimp" (2.3.22–23). That Talbot responds to these insults with politeness and respect, however, immediately contradicts the impression that the Countess is creating. Talbot is indeed chivalric, and his nobility is further demonstrated when he states, "I am but shadow of myself" (2.3.50), and in a coup de théâtre, Talbot's strength, his "substance" (2.3.63), is revealed in his soldiers. Thus, Talbot is presented as a warrior but not a lone fighter; he is rather shown to be a leader with a loyal following of soldiers.

The presentation of Talbot is also part of a wider discussion of fathers and sons that threads through the first tetralogy. Young John Talbot's arrival at battle instigates a long discussion about honor and whether one should flee or fight. Talbot's protective instincts are keenly felt, but the idea of inheritance, which is so strong in the tetralogy, is seen fully in the presentation of Young Talbot, who is fully his warrior father's son: "Is my name Talbot? and am I your son? / And shall I fly?" (4.5.12–13). The classical image of Daedalus and Icarus is used to illustrate the pair, and the tenderness with which Talbot receives his dead son seems to dismiss the previous presentations of his character; he is now simply a father: "Soldiers, adieu! I have what I would have, / Now my old arms are young John Talbot's grave" (4.7.31–32). In death, however, Talbot is once again a hero; Lucy honors the dead soldier by listing his titles:

Talbot grieves over his son's body in Act IV, Scene 7 in this illustration from the 1757 Lewis Theobald edition of Shakespeare's plays. *(Illustration by Hubert Gravelot; engraving by Gerard Van der Gucht)*

Valiant Lord Talbot, Earl of Shrewsbury,
Created, for his rare success in arms,
Great Earl of Washford, Waterford and
  Valence,
Lord Talbot of Goodrig and Urchinfield,
Lord Strange of Blackmore, Lord Verdon of
  Alton,
Lord Cromwell of Wingfield, Lord Furnival of
  Sheffield. (4.7.61–66)

And, the list goes on. This epitaph, although it details an account of a successful warrior, is stuffy and staid and is fittingly undercut by the vibrancy of Joan, who quite perceptively states, "Here's a silly stately style indeed" (4.7.73). Joan's interjection completes the death of heroic masculinity that began with the funeral of Henry V and is now finished by the death of the hero Talbot, who is not honorably beaten but a victim of political squabbles at home.

Richard Plantagenet

Although in some ways Richard Plantagenet in *Henry VI, Part 1* is an embryo of the character who will come to fullness in *Henry VI, Parts 2* and *3*, here begins the arc of development. Richard Plantagenet's character is greatly concerned with two issues: truth and injustice. As Winchester says of himself, that he is "Jack out of office" (1.1.175), so Plantagenet is also at the beginning of the play: He is simply a gentleman without title, "attainted" (2.4.92) by his father the earl of Cambridge's treachery during the reign of Henry V. This fact is clearly stated in the Temple Garden scene (2.4), with Somerset using it as an insult to Plantagenet:

> by his treason stand'st thou not attainted,
> Corrupted, and exempt from ancient gentry?
> His trespass yet lives guilty in thy blood,
> And till thou be restored thou art a yeoman.
> (2.4.92–95)

This is an important moment: The argument not only begins the feud that will develop into the Wars of the Roses; it also helps create the sense of injustice that fuels Plantagenet. His response to Somerset's comment here is to claim that "My father was attached, not attainted, / Condemn'd to die for treason, but no traitor" (2.4.96–97). The difference between *attainted* and *attached* is significant, as Plantagenet argues that by being attached, his father's crimes are not inherited by his offspring and, therefore, should not be borne by him. This difference in perception of fact reveals another key aspect of the character that will influence events over the three plays.

The issue of truth also comes firmly to the fore in the Temple Garden scene: Plantagenet begins the scene by asking, "Dare no man answer in a case of truth?" (2.4.2). The scene begins in the middle of an argument, although the topic of discussion is never revealed; rather, the emphasis is placed on both parties arguing for truth on their side. The effect of this is that truth ceases to have a definitive sense but becomes factionalized. Plantagenet's first and frequent use of the words *true* and *truth* suggests that he views the truth as peculiarly his. Plantagenet's question "Then say at once if I maintain'd the truth; / Or else was wrangling Somerset in th'error?" (2.4.5–6) would seem at first to be a fair inquiry; however, Plantagenet is asking the same thing, his wit doubly condemning Somerset. Plantagenet's invocation of the truth in this scene increases the sense of injustice that surrounds him and is fed by Mortimer's revelations in the scene that immediately follows.

Plantagenet's history is emphasized by Mortimer's chronicle of events, which occurred before *Henry VI, Part 1* begins. As injustice is important to the character, so the idea of inheritance is, too: Plantagenet has inherited the injustice done to his father not only through his execution but also through his support of Mortimer, which creates Plantagenet's royal claim: "I was the next by birth and parentage, . . . Thou art my heir" (2.5.73, 96). That all this is shown to the audience before Henry VI has even appeared on stage creates sympathy for Plantagenet and perhaps even an atmosphere of hostility to the king when he does appear. Certainly, Richard is presented as politically savvy: He is schooled by Mortimer to "With silence . . . be thou politic" (2.5.101), something that Plantagenet takes on board as shown at the Parliament in a brief aside to the audience:

Plantagenet, I see, must hold his tongue,
Lest it be said, "Speak, sirrah, when you should:
Must your bold verdict enter talk with lords?"
Else would I have a fling at Winchester.
 (3.1.61–64)

Richard Plantagenet learns of his claim to the throne from the dying Mortimer in Act II, Scene 5 of *Henry VI, Part 1*. This is a print from the Boydell Shakespeare Gallery project, which was first conceived in 1786 and lasted until 1805. *(Painting by James Northcote; engraving by Robert Thew)*

Although short, this is a revealing passage: Plantagenet exposes his assumptions about the attitudes of the other men; his bitterness at his position; which side he would take in the debate; and his sense of political pragmatism, which will be seen much more fully in his soliloquies in *Henry VI, Part 2*. Plantagenet also presents confidence in his own intelligence and scorn for the other men around him.

Plantagenet is the only character who changes name during *Henry VI, Part 1:* In Act 3, Scene 1, Henry restores Plantagenet's title, and he becomes

Duke of York, his prefix even changing in the stage directions. Again, truth is an important issue in this, as Henry states, "If Richard will be true, not that alone / But all the whole inheritance I give / That doth belong unto the house of York" (3.1.162–164). Of course, in relation to Plantagenet, the audience already knows truth to be a subjective matter, and in offering "the whole inheritance," Henry foreshadows Plantagenet's claims to the crown, which will dominate the next two plays in the tetralogy.

Duke of Gloucester and Bishop of Winchester

The feud between the Duke of Gloucester and the Bishop of Winchester represents one of the main plots of *Henry VI, Part 1*, alongside the war in France and the development of the argument between York and Somerset. Although Winchester is Gloucester's uncle, their relationship in *Henry VI, Part 1* is characterized by tension and disagreement that constantly threatens and occasionally spills over into violence. The conflict between the two is made immediately apparent during the funeral of Henry V in Act I, as ceremony and ritualized grieving descend into squabbling between the two about power over the young king:

> GLOUCESTER. None do you like but an
>   effeminate prince,
> Whom like a schoolboy you may overawe.
>
> WINCHESTER. Gloucester, whate'er we like,
>   thou art Protector,
> And lookest to command the Prince and
>   realm. (1.1.35–38)

Gloucester is, indeed, protector, a regent who, because of the king's youth, exercises authority on his behalf. Winchester is, by comparison, only a bishop and later a cardinal. However, Winchester's position suggests a level of threat because he explicitly represents the Catholic Church and papism. Although England was still a Catholic country during the 15th century, the English are presented largely in Protestant terms. Winchester's

overt Catholicism, then, and his authority coming from Rome would be perceived as a threat by an Elizabethan audience. Indeed, the sinister nature of Winchester is exposed at the end of the first act as he plots to steal the young king from Eltham, and the unstable balance of power is clearly suggested in Act I, Scene 3, when Winchester prevents Gloucester from accessing the Tower of London.

Gloucester and Winchester mutually present each other in their quarrels: At the Tower, Winchester calls Gloucester "ambitious [Humphrey]" (1.3.29), "usurping proditor," or traitor (1.3.31), while Gloucester describes his uncle as "Peel'd priest" (1.3.30) and "manifest conspirator" (1.3.33), and all this in an, albeit angry, exchange of greeting. It is interesting that each describes the other in similar terms, recognizing the pursuit of ultimate power in the other and the threat that this poses to each. Winchester is also the only character in the play to refer to Gloucester by his Christian name, Humphrey, a patronizing gesture used, apparently, to remind Gloucester of his place.

That Gloucester and Winchester's men fall to fighting with weapons and, later, stones in the streets of London is significant not only to these characters but to the atmosphere of the play in general. The fights demonstrate the devotion that each man inspires in his followers, again emphasizing that each reflects the other. That the Mayor of London has to plead for peace ("Pity the city of London, pity us!" [3.1.77]) demonstrates that peace in London and, by extension, England hangs on a thread, dependent on these peers.

DIFFICULTIES OF THE PLAY

> Margaret shall now be Queen, and rule the
>   King:
> But I will rule both her, the King, and realm
>   (5.5.107–108).

These words uttered by the Earl of Suffolk in the last two lines of *Henry VI, Part 1* close the play with a cliff-hanger. For what happens next, one must look to *Henry VI, Part 2* and follow the fortunes of the characters there. This is one of the difficulties of *Henry VI, Part 1*; by its very nature, as the opening play of a trilogy or tetralogy, it does not appear to conclude so much as to begin. The play, therefore, can be hard to engage with; and the plot, hard to follow. *Henry VI, Part 1* is an episodic play, constructed of many scenes depicting a lot of different action. That the action takes place in a number of venues, not least across two countries, compounds these difficulties. For example, the play features battles at Orleans, Rouen, and Bordeaux and depicts a coronation at Paris, factional fighting at the Tower of London, and squabbling in the Temple Garden, among other scenes that take place in unspecified locations in both England and France. This jumping about from one location to another can become somewhat confusing.

This confusion can be amplified by the 22 male characters in the play with different place-names as their noble names. Furthermore, many characters have more than one name: For example, Richard Plantagenet becomes Duke of York during the play, and his prefix changes from Plantagenet to York in the text; Beaufort, a bishop, becomes Cardinal Winchester during the play; Gloucester is also Humphrey; and Talbot is

> "Great Earl of Washford, Waterford, and
>   Valence,
> Lord Talbot of Goodrig and Urchinfield,
> Lord Strange of Blackmere, Lord Verdon of
>   Alton,
> Lord Cromwell of Wingfield, Lord Furnival of
>   Sheffield,
> The thrice-victorious Lord of Falconbridge."
> (4.7.63–67)

In addition, Talbot is made Earl of Shrewsbury during the play. It is, therefore, not surprising that readers and audience members can become confused. Further complicating matters is the play's plot: It is about nobles fighting for and scheming to take power in one way or another, so it is necessary not only to remember names but also which names are fighting on whose side and for what. (Characters such as Burgundy who change sides during the course of the play only increase the potential for confusion.) Often in productions, the Temple Garden scene, where characters involved in the York-Somerset feud pick red and white roses, can clarify allegiances. In many productions, in fact, the characters continue to wear this emblem of allegiance throughout the play, visually aiding the audience in following the growing dispute between the factions.

Henry VI, Part 1 is part of a trilogy. The next two plays are aptly known today as *Henry VI, Parts 2* and *3*; however, these other plays were originally published in quarto form as *The First Part of the Contention of the Two Famous Houses of York and Lancaster with the Death of the Good Duke Humphrey (Henry VI, Part 2)* and *The True Tragedy of Richard, Duke of York, and the Good King Henry the Sixth (Henry VI, Part 3)*. These titles, albeit in a rather lengthy manner, describe the plot of the narrative. In contrast, *Henry VI, Part 1*, which was first printed in the First Folio of 1623 with this title, does not give a brief summary of its plot, and Henry VI does not really feature in the play at all. Indeed, his character has a much broader part to play in the second and third parts of the plays that cover his reign. This is because Henry VI was a child when he became king (historically he was only nine months old, although he is often played by a young adult actor in productions today), and the play focuses instead on the characters around him who are actually governing the country. Where the quarto titles of *Parts Two* and *Three* describe the action of those plays, *Henry VI, Part 1* gives no indications and can itself be misleading for readers searching for an eponymous hero more like Henry V.

KEY PASSAGES
Act II, Scene 4, 1–134
PLANTAGENET. Great lords and gentlemen,
  what means this silence?
Dare no man answer in a case of truth?

SUFFOLK. Within the Temple Hall we were
  too loud,
The garden here is more convenient.

PLANTAGENET. Then say at once if I
  maintain'd the truth;
Or else was wringling Somerset in th'error?

SUFFOLK. Faith, I have been a truant in the
  law,
And never yet could frame my will to it,
And therefore frame the law unto my will.

SOMERSET. Judge you, my Lord of Warwick,
  then between us.

WARWICK. Between two hawks, which flies
  the higher pitch,
Between two dogs, which hath the deeper
  mouth,
Between two blades, which bears the better
  temper,
Between two horses, which doth bear him best,
Between two girls, which hath the merriest
  eye—
I have perhaps some shallow spirit of judgment;
But in these nice sharp quillets in the law,
Good faith, I am no wiser than a daw.

PLANTAGENET Tut, tut, here is a mannerly
  forbearance.
The truth appears so naked on my side
That any purblind eye may find it out.

SOMERSET. And on my side it is so well
  apparell'd,
So clear, so shining, and so evident,
That it will glimmer through a blindman's eye.

PLANTAGENET Since you are tongue-tied
  and so loath to speak,
In dumb significant proclaim your thoughts:
Let him that is a true-born gentleman
And stands upon the honor of his birth,
If he suppose that I have pleaded truth,
From off this brier pluck a white rose with me.

SOMERSET. Let him that is no coward nor
  no flatterer,

But dare maintain the party of the truth,
Pluck a red rose from off this thorn with me.

WARWICK. I love no colors; and without all
  color
Of base insinuating flattery,
I pluck this white rose with Plantagenet.

SUFFOLK. I pluck this red rose with young
  Somerset,
And say withal, I think he held the right.

VERNON. Stay, lords and gentlemen, and
  pluck no more,
Till you conclude that he upon whose side
The fewest roses are cropp'd from the tree
Shall yield the other in the right opinion.

SOMERSET. Good Master Vernon, it is well
  objected;
If I have fewest, I subscribe in silence.

PLANTAGENET. And I.

VERNON. Then for the truth and plainnesss
  of the case,
I pluck this pale and maiden blossom here,
Giving my verdict on the white rose side.

SOMERSET. Prick not your finger as you
  pluck it off,
Lest, bleeding, you do paint the white rose red,
And fall in my side so against your will . . .

PLANTAGENET. Now, Somerset, where is
  your argument?

SOMERSET. Here in my scabbard, meditating
  that
Shall dye your white rose in a bloody red.

PLANTAGENET Mean time, your cheeks do
  counterfeit our roses;
For pale they look with fear, as witnessing
The truth on our side.

SOMERSET. No Plantagenet;
'Tis not for fear, but anger, that thy cheeks
Blush for pure shame to counterfeit our roses,
And yet thy tongue will not confess thy error.

PLANTAGENET Hath not thy rose a canker,
  Somerset?

SOMERSET. Hath not thy rose a thorn,
  Plantagenet?

PLANTAGENET Aye, sharp and piercing, to
  maintain his truth,
Whiles thy consuming canker eats his
  falsehood. . . .
Come, let us four to dinner. I dare say
This quarrel will drink blood another day.

Act II, Scene 4 is more famously known as the Temple Garden scene. The action takes place in the garden of the Inns of Court, the characters moving outside because "Within the Temple Hall we were too loud." The characters have been arguing, as is apparent from Plantagenet's command "Then

English lords pick between a red and white rose during the argument between Richard Plantagenet and Somerset in Act II, Scene 4 of *Henry VI, Part 1,* in this print published by Virtue & Company in the 19th century. *(Painting by John Pettie; engraving by Frederick Augustus Heath)*

say at once if I maintain'd the truth; / Or else was wrangling Somerset in th' error?" However, what the characters were arguing over is never explained to the audience, and no evidence is put forward to show who was in the right. Indeed, it is more important simply for the audience to know that an argument has been taking place, and the audience's ignorance of the topic is essential: By not explaining what the topic is, the audience is not being drawn in and asked to take sides but rather merely to observe the argument. This will later help emphasize the rather petty nature of the beginning of the Wars of the Roses; because the audience has no investment in the argument, it is able to stand in judgment.

Judgment is an important issue in this scene. The language used emphasizes the ideas of truth, law, and justice: In the space of four lines, Plantagenet speaks the word *truth* twice, following it up and confirming his stance 15 lines later by stating that "The truth appears so naked on my side." This focus is underlined by references to "the law," "some shallow spirit of judgment," "nice sharp quillets of the law," and "true-born gentlemen." This language is not out of place in the setting: The Inns of Court housed the legal societies of London; indeed, one of the minor characters in the scene is simply called a Lawyer. However, this language establishes the importance of the issue being discussed. It is significant also that it is Plantagenet who forcefully and explicitly uses the term *truth* about his stance. Although Somerset believes himself equal but opposite to Plantagenet, he does not use the word at this point. This contrast creates a clear division between Plantagenet and Somerset and defines the importance of this scene, which sets in motion events that will continue not only through the rest of *Henry VI, Part 1* but into *Henry VI, Parts 2* and *3* and will conclude with *Richard III*. That Plantagenet is here emphasized with truth on his side creates a long-lasting presentation; however, it may be that, by being so explicit, he is attempting to convince the audience, both on and off stage, that he is in the right. Whether the audience believes him at this point may be significant later in the tetralogy as he begins to set his sights on the crown.

The Temple Garden scene is famous for the picking of the roses that will initiate the Wars of the Roses, and the language used in the scene becomes imbued with gardening metaphors and references as the "plucking" proceeds. However, it is a menacing sense of the garden that is created, as references to the flowers become inextricably linked with the body: Numerous references to bleeding seem to foreshadow the real bloodshed that will occur as a result of this quarrel. Somerset's comment to Vernon highlights not only this but also the arbitrary choices that are made and the haste with which characters will change sides in the battles to come:

> Prick not your finger as you pluck it off,
> Lest, bleeding, you do paint the white rose red,
> And fall on my side so against your will.

Here the rose becomes linked to the body by touch; however, the roses are also imagined as part of the body: Plantagenet says of Somerset "your cheeks do counterfeit our roses; / For pale they look with fear," and Somerset counters with "'Tis not for fear, but anger, that thy cheeks / Blush for pure shame to counterfeit our roses." The roses are part of the body, expressed though the color of the cheeks. It is notable that Plantagenet and Somerset express the color of the other's rose, again suggesting the arbitrary nature of the quarrel and that neither may be sure of what the argument is, just that it is against the other. The intense linguistic focus on the roses also fulfills the function of moving attention away from what the original quarrel was about: The issue between the two characters has now become about the flowers.

Act IV, Scene 5, 1–55

TALBOT. O young John Talbot, I did send
  for thee
To tutor thee in stratagems of war,
That Talbot's name might be in thee reviv'd,
When sapless age and weak unable limbs
Should bring thy father to his drooping chair.

But O malignant and ill-boding stars!
Now thou art come unto a feast of death,
A terrible and unavoided danger;
Therefore, dear boy, mount on my swiftest horse,
And I'll direct thee how thou shalt escape
By sudden flight. Come, dally not, be gone.

JOHN. Is my name Talbot? and I am your son?
And shall I fly? O, if you love my mother,
Dishonor not her honourable name
To make a bastard and a slave of me!
The world will say, he is not Talbot's blood,
The basely fled when noble Talbot stood.

TALBOT. Fly, to revenge my death, if I be slain.

JOHN. He that flies so will ne'er return again.

TALBOT. If we both stay, we both are sure to
  die.

JOHN. Then let me stay, and, father, do you fly.
Your loss is great, so your regard should be;
My worth unknown, no loss is known in me.
Upon my death the French can little boast;
In yours they will, in you all hopes are lost.
Flight cannot stain the honor you have won,
But mine it will, that no exploit have done.
You fled for vantage, every one will swear;
But if I bow, they'll say it was for fear.
There is no hope that ever I will stay,
If the first hour I shrink and run away.
Here on my knees I beg mortality,
Rather than life preserv'd with infamy.

TALBOT. Shall all thy mother's hopes lie in
  one tomb?

JOHN Ay, rather than I'll shame my mother's
  womb.

TALBOT. Upon my blessing I command
  thee go.

JOHN. To fight I will, but not to fly the foe.

TALBOT. Part of thy father may be sav'd in
thee.

JOHN. No part of him but will be shame in me.

TALBOT. Thou never hadst renown, nor canst
not lose it.

JOHN. Yes, your renowned name. Shall flight
abuse it?

TALBOT. Thy father's charge shall clear thee
from that stain.

JOHN. You cannot witness for me, being slain.
If death be so apparent, then both fly.

TALBOT. And leave my followers here to fight
and die?
My age was never tainted with such shame.

JOHN. And shall my youth be guilty of such
blame?
No more can I be severed from your side
Than can yourself yourself in twain divide.
Stay, go, do what you will, the like do I;
For live I will not if my father die.

TALBOT. Then here I take my leave of thee,
fair son,
Born to eclipse thy life this afternoon.
Come, side by side, together live and die,
And soul with soul from France to heaven fly.

This short scene takes place before the Battle of Bordeaux. Young John Talbot has come to be taught "stratagems of war" by his father, but Old Talbot, recognizing that he is surrounded and outnumbered, wants his son to flee to safety. John refuses, and an argument ensues. The scene is immediately established on contrasts: In Talbot's first speech his opening line emphasizes the youth of his son, while line 7 talks about "a feast of death." This contrast is embodied by the two characters: the old warrior and the young apprentice. The scene continues in this vein. Constructed of a couple of short speeches and single lines, Shakespeare employs stichomythia, a rhetorical effect in which dialogue is given in alternate lines to alternate characters in a fast exchange of thoughts. The device is characterized by antithesis and the taking up of the other character's words:

TALBOT. Upon my blessing I command
thee go.

JOHN. To fight I will, but not to fly the foe.

TALBOT. Part of thy father may be sav'd in
thee.

JOHN. No part of him but will be shame in me.

The quick exchange with the repetition of words creates the sense of an intense and closely matched argument. The scene is written in rhyming couplets, which adds rhythm to the dialogue and also further forges the links between each character's ideas. However, the use of antithesis, Talbot and John using the same terms but in completely opposite ways—for example, referring to John's mother as a "tomb" and a "womb"—underlines the contrast in each character's position, restating the unsuitable connection between youth and death with which Talbot opened the scene.

This is a powerful and moving passage, and as in earlier scenes, the relationship between fathers and sons is paramount. Although a warrior referred to as the "terror of the French," at this point Talbot is most concerned with the preservation of his son and tries to persuade John to flee: "dear boy, mount on my swiftest horse, / And I'll direct thee how thou shalt escape / By sudden flight." This again is a contrast. Talbot appears to have performed a 180-degree turn around and is now, rather than schooling his son in war, teaching him how to flee in fear. Young John's response, "Is my name Talbot? and am I your son? / And shall I fly?" presents him as more of a warrior and, indeed, demonstrates that he is Talbot's heir. In posing these questions to his father, questioning their own courage, John in fact confirms the same.

As is a feature of discourse throughout the play, inheritance features strongly in this argument. Talbot argues that in fleeing, John will preserve his honor because "Thou never hadst renown, nor canst not lose it"; however John counters this by stating that his reputation is already made by having his father's name: "Shall flight abuse it?" Honor and chivalry are presented as things that are inherited rather than earned and that, by fleeing, it would not only be John whose reputation would be damaged, but his father's, also. Fathers and sons are not simply presented in terms of inheritance, however, but as two of one: John's insistence that "No more can I be severed from your side / Than can yourself yourself in twain divide" and "For live I will not if my father die" demonstrates the interdependence that the son has with the father.

Talbot, representing classical chivalry, invokes classical ideas here. His references to "sudden flight" on "my swiftest horse" suggest stories of the winged horse Pegasus carrying soldiers from battle, and the constant references to his son flying and Talbot's life "eclipsing" John's paints John as Icarus, the mythical son who followed his father, Daedalus, on wings made from wax but flew too near the Sun and died. Talbot's use of this image (which he uses explicitly later in the scene) creates a doomed impression of the boy, even while his father tries to save him. Interestingly, flight is described negatively throughout the scene, until at the end, Talbot talks of the two "soul with soul from France to heaven fly" in a positive sense. Again, the argument is turned around, and this flight, because it is honorable, becomes positive.

Act V, Scene 3, 1–44

JOAN LA PUCELLE. The Regent conquers,
  and the Frenchmen fly.
Now help, ye charming spells and periapts,
And ye choice spirits that admonish me
And give me signs of future accidents. *[Thunder]*
You speedy helpers, that are substitutes
Under the lordly Monarch of the North,
Appear, and aid me in this enterprise.

[Enter FIENDS.]
This speedy and quick appearance argues proof
Of your accustom'd diligence to me.
Now, ye familiar spirits, that are cull'd
Out of the powerful regions under earth,
Help me this once, that France may get the field.
[They walk, and speak not.]
O, hold me not with silence over-long!
Where I was wont to feed you with my blood,
I'll lop a member off and give it you
In earnest of a further benefit,
So you do condescend to help me now.
[They hang their heads.]
No hope to have redress? My body shall
Pay recompense, if you will grant my suit.
[They shake their heads.]
Cannot my body nor blood-sacrifice
Entreat you to your wonted furtherance?
Then take my soul—my body, soul, and all,
Before that England give the French the foil.
[They depart.]
See, they forsake me! Now the time is come
That France must vail her lofty-plumed crest
And let her head fall into England's lap.
My ancient incantations are too weak,
And hell too strong for me to buckle with:
Now, France, thy glory droopeth to the dust.
                                    [Exit.]
[Excursions. BURGUNDY *and* YORK *(enter
  and) fight hand to hand. French fly.]*
*[*PUCELLE *is brought in captive.]*

YORK. Damsel of France, I think I have you
  fast:
Unchain your spirits now with charming spells,
And try if they can gain your liberty.
A goodly prize, fit for the devil's grace!
See how the ugly witch doth bend her brows,
As if, with Circe, she would change my shape!

JOAN LA PUCELLE. Chang'd to a worser
  shape thou canst not be.

YORK. O, Charles the Dolphin is a proper man,
No shape but his can please your dainty eye.

JOAN LA PUCELLE. A plaguing mischief
light on Charles and thee!
And may ye both be suddenly surpris'd
By bloody hands, in sleeping on your beds!

YORK. Fell banning hag, enchantress, hold
thy tongue!

JOAN LA PUCELLE. I prithee give me leave
to curse a while.

YORK. Curse, miscreant, when thou com'st to
the stake.
[*Exeunt.*]

Although it comes toward the end of the play, this passage is crucial to the presentation of Joan. Shakespeare has been ambiguous about the source of Joan's power throughout the play, but here, that presentation is resolved. Joan is left alone onstage and prays for help. Shakespeare presents Joan as a devil worshipper: She calls on the spirits under the "lordly Monarch of the North," and when her spirits enter, they are explicitly called "FIENDS." The monarch of the north is a name for Satan, who was thought to inhabit northern regions, and Joan's reference to him as "lordly" encourages a positive view of the devil. The use of the term *fiends* further supports this.

Joan's speech is constructed in a way that it builds up over the five verses, reaching a dramatic climax as the fiends do not help Joan and depart and an emotional climax in Joan's desperation: When the fiends do not speak, Joan offers blood; when they hang their heads, she offers her body; when they shake their heads, she offers her soul. Joan's desperation reaches a crescendo against the continued silence of the fiends when she offers her "body, soul, and all." The silence of the fiends accentuates the depravity of the words that Joan uses: Joan tells the audience that "I was wont to feed you with my blood," which suggests that she has been offering blood sacrifices throughout the events of the play. This colors the audience's response to the character's past, a negative impression that is compounded by her offer to "lop a member off" for

Joan la Pucelle rages as the fiends leave her in Act V, Scene 3 of *Henry VI, Part 1*. (*Illustration by John Thurston; engraving by Allen Robert Branston*)

diabolical help. This is again underlined as she says, "My body shall / Pay recompense." The breaks in the speech for the stage directions emphasize the build. The silence of the fiends, however, continues to paint this source of power ambiguously: It is Joan's language that demonizes her character. The fiends say nothing and refuse to offer help, which, in comparison to the presentation of Joan, suggests they are not as a bad as she is. Joan's final line ends this speech with a sense of grief; her statement that "France, thy glory droopeth to the dust" is full of sadness, but the reference to "dust" highlights that her glory has all been an illusion.

The negative presentation of Joan is furthered when her tone changes in interaction with York: Her desperation gives way to cursing. Through York's name-calling—"hag," "ugly witch," "enchantress"—Joan continues to be created and presented by other characters as she has been throughout the play, and it confirms the audience's new, unambiguous view of her character.

DIFFICULT PASSAGES
Act I, Scene 4, 70–94

[Here they shoot, and SALISBURY falls down (together with Gargrave).]

SALISBURY. O Lord, have mercy on us,
 wretched sinners!

GARGRAVE. O Lord, have mercy on me,
 woeful man!

TALBOT. What chance is this that suddenly
 hath cross'd us?
Speak, Salisbury; at least, if thou canst, speak.
How far'st thou, mirror of all martial men?
One of thy eyes and thy cheek's side struck off!
Accursed tower! accursed fatal hand
That hath contriv'd this woeful tragedy!
In thirteen battles Salisbury o'ercame;
Henry the Fift he first train'd to the wars;
Whilst any trump did sound, or drum struck up,
His sword did ne'er leave striking in the
 field. . . .
He beckons with his hand and smiles on me,
As who should say, "When I am dead and gone,
Remember to avenge me on the French."

The difficulty with the passage lies in that it is easy to underestimate its importance and consequently miss the significance of its inclusion in the play. Talbot, Salisbury, Gargrave, and Glansdale are hiding in the "suburbs" (1.4.9) outside Orleans, planning an attack on the town. The Master Gunner of Orleans leaves his boy with "A piece of ordnance" (1.4.15) to watch for the English. The English are spotted and fired on. Although it is unclear who has fired the fatal shots, the boy makes it clear that he will not obey his father's commands to call him if he sees the English: "I warrant you, take you no care, / I'll never trouble you, if I may spy them" (1.4.21–22). This demonstrates the duplic-

ity of the French. The use of guns in warfare was a relatively recent innovation in the medieval period, and because guns allow for killing without meeting face-to-face and without hand-to-hand combat, they are a dishonorable weapon. Talbot emphasizes this as he describes Salisbury's past: "In thirteen battles Salisbury o'ercame; / Henry the Fift he train'd to the wars; . . . His sword did ne'er leave striking in the field." That Salisbury trained Henry V makes him a great warrior, but that he fought honorably in 13 battles underlines the dishonor of this unseen French attack. This passage subtly presents the French in a negative manner, while suggesting the theme of chivalry, because the honorable sword cannot stand up to this innovation in battle.

Act II, Scene 5

MORTIMER. And now declare, sweet stem
 from York's great stock,
Why didst thou say, of late thou wert despis'd?

PLANTAGENET. First, lean thy aged back
 against mine arm,
And in that ease, I'll tell thee my disease.
This day, in argument upon a case,
Some words there grew 'twixt Somerset and me;
Among which terms he us'd his lavish tongue
And did upbraid me with my father's death;
Which obloquy set bars before my tongue,
Else with the like I had requited him.
Therefore, good uncle, for my father's sake,
In honor of a true Plantagenet,
And for alliance sake, declare the cause
My father, Earl of Cambridge, lost his head.

MORTIMER. That cause, fair nephew, that
 imprison'd me
And hath detained me all my flow'ring youth
Within a loathsome dungeon, there to pine,
Was cursed instrument of his disease.

PLANTAGENET Discover more at large what
 cause that was,
For I am ignorant and cannot guess.

MORTIMER. I will, if that my fading breath
  permit
And death approach not ere my tale be done.
Henry the Fourth, grandfather to this king,
Depos'd his nephew Richard, Edward's son,
The first begotten, and the lawful heir
Of Edward king, the third of that descent;
During whose reign the Percies of the north,
Finding his usurpation most unjust,
Endeavor'd my advancement to the throne.
The reason mov'd these warlike lords to this
Was, for that (young Richard thus remov'd,
Leaving no heir begotten of his body)
I was next by birth and parentage;
For by my mother I derived am
From Lionel Duke of Clarence third son
To King Edward the Third; whereas he
From John of Gaunt doth bring his pedigree,
Being but fourth of that heroic line.
But mark: as in this haughty great attempt
They labored to plant the rightful heir,
I lost my liberty, and they their lives.
Long after this, when Henry the Fift
(Succeeding his father Bullingbrook) did reign,
Thy father, Earl of Cambridge then, deriv'd
From famous Edmund Langley, Duke of
  York,
Marrying my sister that thy mother was,
Again, in pity of my hard distress,
Levied an army, weening to redeem
And have install'd me in the diadem.
But as the rest, so fell that noble earl,
And was beheaded. Thus the Mortimers,
In whom the title rested, were suppress'd.

PLANTAGENET. Of which, my lord, your
  honor is the last.

MORTIMER. True; and thou seest that I no
  issue have,
And that my fainting words do warrant death.
Thou art my heir; the rest I wish thee gather;
But yet be wary in thy studious care.

PLANTAGENET Thy grave admonishments
  prevail with me.
But yet methinks, my father's execution
Was nothing less than bloody tyranny.

MORTIMER. With silence, nephew, be thou
  politic.
Strong fixed is the house of Lancaster,
And like a mountain, not to be remov'd.
But now thy uncle is removing hence,
As princes do their courts, when they are
  cloy'd
With long continuance in a settled place.

PLANTAGENET. O uncle, would some part
  of my young years
Might but redeem the passage of your age!

MORTIMER. Thou dost then wrong me, as
  that slaughterer doth
Which giveth many wounds when one will kill.
Mourn not, except thou sorrow for my good,
Only give order for my funeral.
And so farewell, and fair be all thy hopes,
And prosperous be thy life in peace and war!

PLANTAGENET. And peace, no war, befall
  thy parting soul!
In prison hast thou spent a pilgrimage,
And like a hermit overpass'd thy days.
Well, I will lock his counsel in my breast,
And what I do imagine, let that rest.
Keepers, convey him hence, and I myself
Will see his burial better than his life.
[*Exeunt Keepers, bearing out the body of
  MORTIMER.*]
Here dies the dusky torch of Mortimer,
Chok'd with ambition of the meaner sort;
And for those wrongs, those bitter injuries,
Which Somerset hath offer'd to my house,
I doubt not but with honor to redress.
And therefore haste I to the parliament,
Either to be restored to my blood,
Or make my will th'advantage of my good.

Plantagenet visits his dying uncle, Mortimer, in his jail in the Tower of London. This passage is central to establishing and building the character of Plantagenet and acquainting the audience with his history. What the reader immediately notices is that Shakespeare continues to use the language of the garden in phrases such as "sweet stem," "words there grew," "all my flow'ring youth," and "labored to plant the rightful heir." Although the sentiments expressed here appear unrelated, they are linked by the idea of natural growth: The argument between Plantagenet and Somerset is presented as something that happened naturally— the words grew between them—and Mortimer expresses the idea of inheritance as a natural progression. It is significant at this point that Mortimer refers to Plantagenet as "sweet stem from York's great stock," as this supports a sympathetic presentation of Plantagenet, who will later become the Duke of York. Mortimer is clearly presented as being on Plantagenet's side in the quarrel, but he also creates an agreeable image of the character for the audience, which may be important when York battles for the crown in the later *Henry VI* plays.

Plantagenet's words "declare the cause / My father, Earl of Cambridge, lost his head" tell the audience that he knows a certain amount about his family history. However, he encourages Mortimer to talk more about his background by stating, "Discover more at large what cause that was, / For I am ignorant and cannot guess." It seems very unlikely that Plantagenet would have been ignorant of his family's past; indeed, he has already shown that he knows something, and such a clumsy direct statement asks us to consider what Shakespeare is doing here. In the lines that follow, the audience is acquainted with the background to *Henry VI, Part 1,* which will later be written by Shakespeare in *Richard II,* the two parts of *Henry IV,* and *Henry V.* Indeed, any reader familiar with those plays will recognize some of the plot descriptions. Mortimer tells Plantagenet (and the audience) that Richard II, the rightful heir of Edward III, was deposed by Bolingbroke (who became Henry IV), Henry VI's grand-

father. During the reign of Henry IV, the Percies (who are a noble family in the north of England), thinking Henry IV's "usurpation most unjust," attempted to put Mortimer on the throne. In asking why the Percies were moved to do this, Mortimer tells us that Richard II had no heir and that Mortimer was rightfully next in line, not Henry IV. This was so because Mortimer's mother was daughter to Lionel, duke of Clarence, who was the third son of Edward III (Henry IV was descended through John of Gaunt who was fourth in line). This can be most confusing, and indeed, the Plantagenet family tree is confusing, but it is these various claims and counterclaims, the question of whose claim to the throne of England is strongest, that create the growing quarrel in *Henry VI, Part 1* and will dominate the later plays. It is, therefore, essential for Shakespeare to acquaint, or reacquaint, the audience with this family tree. Act II, Scene 5 is, therefore, a set-piece scene, intended to fill in the story so far.

Again, natural language is very important here. As the argument between Somerset and Plantagenet has been talked about in "growing" terms, so the idea of rightful kingship is also described in this way: Mortimer describes the Percies' attempts to make him king as their laboring "to plant" him, presumably so that he may grow. By mutual presentation, the usurper is unnatural; struggling against the unlawful king is therefore legitimized.

Mortimer continues to bring the tale up to date, detailing how Plantagenet's father attempted to install him as king but was beheaded for his efforts. Mortimer's presentation of the Lancastrians (Henry IV's family) paints them as unnaturally bad: Those whom they oppose, die (Richard II), but those who oppose them also die (the Percies and Plantagenet's father). This creates a powerful, almost mythically unassailable image of the Lancastrians, which will sit uneasily with the image of the youthful King Henry who is, as yet, unseen.

Mortimer is presented in two fashions here: He is both shown to have royal ideas in the language that he uses, for example, describing his death "As princes do their courts [remove]." Mortimer is the prince in this line. However, he also reveals a very politically savvy mind, schooling Plantagenet in political diplomacy as a means to an end: "With silence, nephew, be thou politic. / Strong fixed is the house of Lancaster."

In establishing Mortimer's claim to the throne, Shakespeare not only sets up this background to the play but looks to the future. Toward the end of the scene, Mortimer states: "thou seest that I no issue have . . . Thou art my heir." Mortimer's naming Plantagenet as his heir makes the history that has just been told politically alive and pertinent. As Mortimer's heir, Plantagenet has a strong claim to the throne, perhaps stronger than that of Henry

VI, a theme that will be thoroughly explored in the rest of the trilogy. This scene then sets in motion and legitimates Plantagenet's quest. At the end of the scene, after Mortimer's death, Plantagenet states that he will be "restored to my blood." On one level, he simply means regaining his title that was lost when his father was beheaded (as Somerset details in 2.4); however, this now takes on another meaning, referring also to the kingship. This is the first time that the audience will think of Plantagenet in royal terms, and it will not forget it over the coming scenes. That this is the penultimate line of this scene leaves this idea in the mind.

In Act II, Scene 5 of *Henry VI, Part 1*, Richard Plantagenet learns of his claim to the throne from Mortimer before he dies. This print is from the Boydell Shakespeare Gallery project. *(Painting by William Hamilton; engraving by Isaac Taylor)*

CRITICAL INTRODUCTION TO THE PLAY
Sources and Structure

Thus far, with rough and all-unable pen,
Our bending author hath pursu'd the story,
In little room confining mighty men,
Mangling by starts the full course of their
 glory.
Small time; but in that small most greatly lived
This star of England. Fortune made his sword;
By which the world's best garden he achieved,
And of it left his son imperial lord.
Henry the Sixt, in infant bands crown'd king
Of France and England, did this king succeed;
Whose state so many had the managing
That they lost France, and made his England
 bleed. (*Henry V*, Epilogue, 1–12)

Henry V concludes with this epilogue from the Chorus. Although written some time after *Henry VI, Part 1*, the Epilogue refers directly to all three of the *Henry VI* plays, covering the major themes of each in the last two lines: too many nobles mismanaging the state and leading to the loss of France and civil war in England. It is the mismanagement leading to the loss of France that forms the plot of *Henry VI, Part 1*. The play is set in the 15th century during the closing years of the Hundred Years' War and as the Wars of the Roses are in their most embryonic stages. The action takes place in England and France, and although named for the king of England, the play focuses on the activities of a number of nobles, King Henry first appearing in the middle of the play and, even then, not to lead but to misguidedly fuel conflict. Shakespeare used two chronicle histories as his major sources, Holinshed's *The Chronicles of England, Ireland, and Scotland* (first published in 1578, although Shakespeare used the second edition, which was published in 1587) and Hall's *The Union of the Two Noble and Illustre Families of Lancaster and York* (published in 1548). Although some events in the play seem to be almost lifted directly from the chronicles, such as parts of the story of Joan la Pucelle, Shakespeare has manipulated history to fulfill his thematic and narrative aims. For example, the time line begins with the funeral of Henry V in 1422 and stretches to the death of Talbot in 1453. The play also includes the capture of Joan of Arc (1430) and Suffolk's courtship of Margaret (1444). Shakespeare condenses the time line somewhat so that Talbot meets Joan in battle, a meeting that never took place, and has Talbot die before both Joan's capture and Suffolk's meeting with Margaret. These events are moved around in the play to enhance the dramatic structure and the discussion of the loss of France and the collapse of Henry V's legacy. This is also the case where different battles have become single military encounters and different nobles have become a single character.

The play is, in comparison to some of Shakespeare's later plays, more basic in its themes and depth. The characters seem to lack complexity and simply represent a thematic, didactic position. A central concern of the play is the death of the heroic as embodied by Henry V, and it is informed by a number of themes: ceremony, chivalry, history, and gender. When considered as part of the trilogy of *Henry VI* plays, the implications of the collapse of chivalry are seen in the ensuing chaos of the second and third parts, coming to fulfillment in the evil of *Richard III* at the end of the tetralogy. However, as part of an octology, or series of eight plays, that begin with *Richard II*, *Henry VI, Part 1* can be seen as part of a broader providential history.

The problems that England experiences in *Henry VI, Part 1*—the loss of French territories, the death of England's great warriors, the growing factionalism at home—can be related back through the preceding four plays (although, in fact, Shakespeare wrote those plays later) to the usurpation of Richard II by Bolingbroke. This "Tudor myth" begins with the usurpation of Richard II and concludes by divine providence with the accession of Henry VII, punishing England along the way. However, this is problematic. How, for example, is the glory of Henry V accounted for in such a theory when it occurs in the middle of the series? Despite these problems, *Henry VI, Part 1* can indeed be viewed as having an exterior providential theme that links it to the other plays, and certainly the issue of rightful inheritance begins to emerge as being at the center of the Wars of the Roses.

In telling the history of the loss of France and the disintegration of English society, *Henry VI, Part 1* follows three different plot lines: the conflict between Gloucester and Winchester; the growing feud between York and Somerset; and the war in France. This narrative structure is built on a framework of oppositions that mirror and reflect the growing tensions, creating a sense of conflict. These oppositions include that between France and England, Joan and Talbot, femininity and masculinity, and, within the English side, between Talbot and the nobles and between old heroism and youthful political pragmatism. Indeed, because the play focuses so strongly on the issue of conflict, the characters (particularly the English characters) are largely defined by who they are for and against. The play is structured so that the action moves backward and forward between English and French and between England and France. This creates the episodic feel of the play but enhances the sense of sides being taken.

Ceremony

Henry VI, Part 1 is infused with ceremony: Each episode is marked with a ceremony, using ceremonial language. Throughout the play, ceremonies act both as a means to unify the characters and as a barometer by which to measure the growth of factionalism and social disintegration. The play opens with the funeral of Henry V:

> Hung be the heavens with black, yield day to
>   night!
> Comets, importing change of times and states,
> Brandish your crystal tresses in the sky,
> And with them scourge the bad revolting stars
> That have consented unto Henry's death:
> King Henry the Fift, too famous to live long!
> England ne'er lost a king of so much worth.
>   (1.1.1–7)

Bedford's exclamation sets the tone for the play: England is in mourning for the greatest king it ever had. Indeed, Henry V was so great a king that the stars revolted against him and the heavens themselves are now in mourning. Bedford's speech is supported in turn by the obsequies that follow from Gloucester, Exeter, and Winchester, the most powerful nobles in England, all mourning Henry in hyperbolic terms: "What should I say? his deeds exceed all speech: / He ne'er lift up his hand but conquered" (1.1.15–16), says the Duke of Gloucester, followed by Exeter's demand to know "We mourn in black, why mourn we not in blood?" (1.1.17). It is significant that this is Henry's funeral: The play that bears the name of Henry VI begins by emphasizing the loss of his hero father. Gloucester's speech seems to invoke and glorify the dead king, conjuring images of

> His brandish'd sword [which] did blind men
>   with his beams:
> His arms spread wider than a dragon's wings;
> His sparkling eyes, replete with wrathful fire,
> More dazzled and drove back his enemies
> Than mid-day sun fierce bent against their
>   faces. (1.1.10–14)

Exeter's speech, meanwhile, quite bluntly emphasizes the loss: "Henry is dead and never shall revive" (1.1.18). Rather than invoking the heroism of the dead king, Exeter underlines the most significant point: the absence of that king. This absence ironically makes the ceremony empty, the death of the king marking the beginning of the disintegration of the ties that bind these nobles, a fact that is realized at this early point as the funeral speeches give way to bickering between Gloucester and Winchester:

> WINCHESTER. The Church's prayers made
>   him so prosperous.
>
> GLOUCESTER. The Church? where is it?
> (1.1.32–33)

It is significant that as Bedford attempts to bring the focus back to what now appears a delicately unstable ceremony, the funeral is fatally interrupted by messengers, each telling of losses and defeats in France, crowned by the capture of the warrior Talbot. The death of Henry seems to have begun a process of collapse of his victories and the values that he represented. This death is embodied not just in the failures in France and the bickering of his nobles but also in the presence of Henry V's opposite, an "effeminate" (1.1.35) child on the throne. This opening ceremony is an inauspicious indicator of what is to come: "With Henry's death," as Joan la Pucelle will later state, "the English circle ends" (1.2.136).

The symbolic usage of ceremony is continued through the play, superficially seeming to unify the characters. As the nobles are unified over Henry's corpse in the opening scene, so ceremonies are explicitly used as attempts to unify the factions throughout, notably at Parliament in Act 3, Scene 1, which "Call'd for the truce of Winchester and Gloucester" [2.4.118]), and in the coronation of Henry VI in France to "[engender] love / Amongst his subjects and his loyal friends" (3.1.180–181). However, Parliament is in fact characterized by bickering, opening with Winchester's somewhat aggressive "Com'st thou with deep premeditated lines, / With written pamphlets studiously devis'd, / Humphrey of Gloucester?" (3.1.1–3) and continuing through the scene in the insults directed between Gloucester and Winchester, which give way physically to the skirmishes between each noble's men. Nevertheless, as Bedford attempted to reunify the men in the first scene, so King Henry here attempts the same by physically joining his uncles' hands and extracting a truce. However, as the funeral is characterized by absence, so this ceremony is shown also to be empty, as both Gloucester and Winchester publicly shake hands but privately express doubt and hypocrisy:

GLOUCESTER. I fear me, with a hollow
  heart . . .

WINCHESTER. So help me God, as I intend
  it not! (3.1.136, 141)

This dissembling, the contrast between shape and substance, represents the growing divisions and conflicts beneath the surface of unification. Henry VI is shown to be naive and powerless in contrast to the all-commanding, perfect king figure invoked at the opening of the play.

Thus, ceremony serves in *Henry VI, Part 1* to underline the growing disunity among nobles, an effect compounded by the constant interruptions and empty words. However, ceremony is not only used in attempts to unify the characters but also in the fundamental moments of dissension, where, rather than appearing empty, the ceremony, in fact, strengthens the pledges made. This is most evident in the Temple Garden scene, where the ritual of picking flowers is represented verbally in the rhetorical construction of the scene. The use of antithesis and stichomythia (the use by both parties of the same terms and words) and the invocation of the truth create a sound akin to an incantation, solidifying the vows made. It is ironic that this ceremony of dissension is allowed to proceed to its end, whereas those that glorify the dead are constantly interrupted and undermined, not just in the funeral of Henry V but also evident in Lucy's mourning speech for Talbot, whose lengthy titles are undercut by Joan's irreverent "Here's a silly stately style indeed" (4.7.72).

English lords pick between a red and white rose during the argument between Richard Plantagenet and Somerset in Act II, Scene 4 of *Henry VI, Part 1*. Print from the Boydell Shakespeare Gallery project *(Painting by Josiah Boydell; engraving by John Ogborne)*

Chivalry

It is significant that the unheroic Joan undermines the remembrance of Talbot. *Henry VI, Part 1* is a play that is deeply concerned with history, not just of Shakespeare's past but with representations of the history of the characters and stories concerned. The play, consequently, is steeped in remembrances of the dead and past glories, showing the present to be somewhat mediocre and sordid in comparison. Much of this is embodied in the theme of chivalry and the apparent death of the heroic, which is personified in the character of Talbot.

Attention is first drawn to the death of chivalry at Henry V's funeral; Gloucester and Exeter's speeches decry the loss of the hero-king, referring to his superhuman deeds and strength. This heroism is seen only in its absence and begins a disintegration of heroism that threads through the whole play. Indeed, Henry V is already dead at the beginning of the play, and by the end, Bedford, Salisbury, and Talbot, Henry's contemporaries at Agincourt, are also dead. Significantly, these men are representatives of that bygone heroic age, and, as such, in contrast to the growing conflict between

Gloucester and Winchester and Suffolk and York, are seen to be dying out. This is emphasized by Talbot's eulogies after the deaths of Salisbury and Bedford. His accounts of them are funereal remembrances of the dead:

> Within their chiefest temple I'll erect
> A tomb wherein his corpse shall be interred,
> Upon the which, that everyone may read,
> Shall be engraved the sack of Orleans,
> That treacherous manner of his mournful
>   death. (2.2.12–16)

The play is structured so as to suggest a gathering of momentum; beginning with the funeral of Henry, then Salisbury's death at Orleans, followed by Bedford at Rouen and by Talbot at Bordeaux. Each is remembered with a heroic eulogy, only broken and stopped by Joan after Talbot's demise. With each step, the community surrounding Talbot grows smaller: He is betrayed by Burgundy between Orleans and Bordeaux, abandoned by English lords before the Battle of Bordeaux, and finally left with his son during the battle, this moment representing the total death of the heroic. Talbot is no longer defined as a soldier but simply as a father.

Most other characters in the play are presented in light of Talbot's character: York and Somerset are shown to be unheroic because they lack the values that Talbot represents, and the French Joan is directly opposed to the English soldier in all ways: her gender, her nationality, her cunning. This is most clearly evident in Talbot's discussion of his imprisonment by the French and his dealings with the figure of Falstaff. Talbot describes to Salisbury how he was ransomed for French prisoners but states that "with a baser man of arms by far / Once in contempt they would have barter'd me: / Which I, disdaining, scorn'd, and craved death" (1.4.30–32). Talbot's account details the alignment of chivalry with class: He would have rather have died than be bartered with a "baser" man. This stance is supported a few lines later as Talbot refers to "the treacherous Falstaff . . . Whom with my

bare fists I would execute" because of his cowardice (1.4.35–36). In this way, Talbot is set in opposition to the coward, consequently presenting himself as chivalric. This is further supported at Henry VI's coronation, where Talbot physically removes the knight's garter from Falstaff on account of his cowardice (4.1).

Gender

The Countess of Auvergne scene underlines the chivalry of Talbot in English terms against the vanity of the French noblewoman. In this scene, chivalry and heroism are presented in gendered terms, and in the play, the presentation of gender is intertwined with the presentation of nationality: The English are masculine, heroic warriors, contrasted sharply with the effeminate French. Even though the English do become more selfish and arrogant in the younger generation, they remain masculine, nevertheless, and opposed to the French, who are more given to cowardice and led by a transgressive warrior woman. History plays are, almost by definition, about men, and there are no significant women on the English side in *Henry VI, Part 1*. Indeed, despite the presence of strong, powerful women in the play, there are no women with the authority to legitimately wield power. It is significant, therefore, that the three strong, articulate, and powerful women dominate the French party: Gender is used as a means by which to demonize the French.

Despite the presence of a woman on the English throne in the 16th century, the figure of the martial woman remained a negative and dangerous image. Encapsulated in Bedford's questions "A maid? And be so martial?" (2.1.22), the contradictions of femininity and martiality represent a fundamental transgression of gender boundaries: women playing the men. The French are led by a "woman clad in armour" (1.5.3), and there is a general reversal of gender roles in the French characters: The female figures exhibit more masculine traits, while the men, the Dauphin and his nobles, appear more effeminate, overshadowed particularly by Joan but also by the crafty Countess of Auvergne and Margaret of Anjou. This is in direct opposition to the masculine men of the English forces.

Joan has become one of the most memorable characters in the play a result of her ambiguous presentation that appears to be ultimately misogynistic. Joan is first presented as a "holy maid" (1.2.51) whose account of her life as a lowly "shepherd's daughter" (1.2.72) seems entirely sincere. However, Joan is problematic even at the earliest point of her presentation: She is a woman, yet she wants to lead, thereby merging femininity and a masculine role. Joan has also apparently received a divine calling to lead France; however, this calling is attributed to the Virgin Mary, a female Catholic symbol, as opposed to the masculine Protestant god of the English. In contrast to this problematic yet virginal divinity, Joan inspires lust as she defeats the Dauphin in single combat, a sexual transgression on Joan's part that emasculates the Dauphin:

> Impatiently I burn with thy desire;
> My heart and hands thou hast at once subdu'd.
> Excellent Pucelle, if thy name be so,
> Let me thy servant, and not sovereign be.
>   (1.2.108–111)

In defeating the Dauphin and placing him in the submissive position, Joan is seen to directly attack and threaten the masculine role.

The threat to masculinity continues as Joan dons armor at the Battle of Orleans. The reports of this generate the confused and bewildered responses from the English: "Pray God she prove not masculine ere long, / If underneath the standard of the French / She carry armor as she hath begun" (2.1.2–25). Burgundy's words here suggest that Joan's appropriation of male dress implies an ambiguity about gender: She may, in fact, be male underneath her clothes. However, significantly, Joan is not gender ambiguous, as the English accounts of a monster or a witch might suggest: Unlike female characters in Shakespeare's comedies who disguise themselves as men and take male names, Joan is not disguised but fights as herself. The wearing of male clothing is a necessary appropriation for this woman to be able to play a public, military role. However, by doing so, Joan blurs gender lines, further threatening and calling male identity into question.

The role of the Frenchwoman who challenges English male identity is also shared by the Countess of Auvergne. The Countess is a crafty woman, using her feminine wiles, as opposed to masculine strength, to lure Talbot into her trap and there defeat him. The other English men fighting with Talbot mock how the end of a battle effeminizes the man:

> Is it even so? Nay, then I see our wars
> Will turn unto a peaceful comic sport,
> When ladies crave to be encount'red with.
>   (2.2.44–46)

This is compounded by the Countess, who denigrates Talbot's physical appearance against the portrait she has of him. The expectation of the Countess seems to be that Talbot will respond to her vanity in kind and be enamored of the fame she showers on him:

> Long time thy shadow hath been thrall to me,
> For in my gallery thy picture hangs;

Talbot's soldiers free him from the Countess of Auvergne in Act II, Scene 3 of *Henry VI, Part 1*. Print from the Boydell Shakespeare Gallery project (*Painting by John Opie; engraving by Robert Thew*)

But now the substance shall endure the like,
And I will chain these legs and arms of thine.
    (2.3.36–39)

However, the woman is unable to appreciate the honor of Talbot, who describes his substance as being in his army. The Frenchwoman here, then, as with Joan, represents an antichivalry.

Margaret is the final woman to appear in the play, and although she appears only in a single scene, her character will become one of the protagonists of the next two plays and will appear in a major role in *Richard III*. Margaret already possesses some of the qualities associated with Frenchwomen: She is apparently virginal but inspires lust in men. Her appearance at the end of the play while Joan is making her final exit is significant as the two characters become symbiotic: Joan may be burned at the stake, but her demonic qualities are transferred to Margaret, who will become the "tiger's heart wrapp'd in a woman's hide!"of *Henry VI, Part 3* (1.4.137). Indeed, some modern directors have emphasized this by editing the text so that the scene of Joan's death occurs directly before Margaret's entrance, thus underlining the link between the characters. This is further significant as, although the events of *Henry VI, Part 1* are not referred to in the later plays, Joan is seen to influence the disintegration of England in the later wars. The Frenchwomen not only bring about the downfall of England in France but the collapse of England at home, as well.

EXTRACTS OF CLASSIC CRITICISM
Thomas Nashe (1567–ca.1601) [Excerpted from *Pierce Pennilesse his Supplication to the Divell* (1592). Elizabethan pamphleteer, poet and satirist, Nashe may have had a hand in the writing of *Henry VI, Part 1*. This extract contains a discussion of the value of history plays and a contemporary account of performances of *Henry VI, Part 1*.]

Is it not then better (since of foure extreames all the world cannot keepe them but they will choose one) that they should betake them to the least, which is Playes? Nay, what if I prooue Playes to be no extreame: but a rare exercise of vertue? First, for the subiect of them (for the most part) it is borrowed out of our English Chronicles, wherein our forefathers valiant acts (that haue line long buried in rustie brasse, and worme-eaten bookes) are reuiued, and they themselues raised from the Graue of obliuion, and brought to pleade their aged Honours in open presence: than which, what can be a sharper reproofe to these degenerate effeminate dayes of ours.

How would it haue ioyed braue *Talbot* (the terror of the French) to thinke that after he had lyne two hundred yeares in his Tombe, hee should triumphe againe on the Stage, and haue his bones newe embalmed with the teares of ten thousand spectators at least, (at seuerall times) who in the Tragedian that represents his person, imagine they behold him fresh bleeding.

Samuel Johnson (1709–1784) [Excerpted from his edition of Shakespeare's plays (1765). Dr. Johnson was one of the greatest English critics. According to one of Johnson's modern editors, Walter Raleigh, Johnson "was not an Elizabethan specialist, but his brief account of the principal causes of Shakespeare's obscurities has never been bettered" (xvi). The sections on the usage of rhyming verse for the Talbots' scenes is of particular interest, showing that explanations for oddities of *Henry VI, Part 1* have been found from the beginning of critical interest in the play.]

For what reason this scene [Act IV, Scene 5] is written in rhyme I cannot guess. If *Shakespeare* had not in other plays mingled his rhymes and blank verse in the same manner, I should have suspected that this dialogue had been a part of some other poem which was never finished, and that being loath to throw his labour away, he inserted it here.

The return of rhyme where young *Talbot* is again mentioned [Act IV, Scene 6], and in no other place, strengthens the suspicion, that these verses were originally part of some other work, and were copied here only to save the trouble of composing new.

Of this play there is no copy earlier than that of the folio in 1623, though the two succeeding parts are extant in two editions in quarto. That the second and third parts were published without the first may be admitted as no weak proof that the copies were surreptitiously obtained, and that the printers of that time gave the publick those plays not such as the author designed, but such as they could get them. That this play was written before the two others is indubitably collected from the series of events; that it was written and played before *Henry the Fifth* is apparent, because in the epilogue there is mention made of this play and not of the other parts.

> Henry the sixth in swaddling bands
> Of France and England, did this king
>   succeed;
> Whose state so many had the managing,
> That they lost France, and made his
>   England bleed;
> Which oft our stage has shewn

France is lost in this play. The two following contain as the old title imparts, the contention of the houses of *York* and *Lancaster*.

The two first parts of *Henry* VI. were printed in 1600. When *Henry* V. was written we know not, but it was printed likewise in 1600, and therefore before the publications of the first and second parts, the first part of *Henry* VI. had been *often shown on the stage,* and would certainly have appeared in its place had the author been the publisher.

August Schlegel (1767–1845) [Excerpted from *A Course of Lectures on Dramatic Art and Literature* (1815). Schlegel was a German poet, translator, and critic.]

The three parts of *Henry the Sixth,* as I have already remarked, were composed much earlier than the preceding pieces. Shakespeare's choice fell first on this period of English history, so full of misery and horrors of every kind, because the pathetic is naturally more suitable than the characteristic to a young poet's mind. We do not yet find here the whole maturity of his genius, yet certainly its whole strength. Careless as to the apparent unconnectedness of contemporary events, he bestows little attention on preparation and development: all the figures follow in rapid succession, and announce themselves emphatically for what we ought to take them; from scenes where the effect is sufficiently agitating to form the catastrophe of a less extensive plan, the poet perpetually hurries us on to catastrophes still more dreadful. The First Part contains only the first forming of the parties of the White and Red Rose, under which blooming ensigns such bloody deeds were afterwards perpetrated; the varying results of the war in France principally fill the stage. The wonderful saviour of her country, Joan of Arc, is portrayed by Shakespeare with an Englishman's prejudices: yet he at first leaves it doubtful whether she has not in reality a heavenly mission; she appears in the pure glory of virgin heroism; by her supernatural eloquence (and this circumstance is of the poet's invention) she wins over the Duke of Burgundy to the French cause; afterwards, corrupted by vanity and luxury, she has recourse to hellish fiends, and comes to a miserable end. To her is opposed Talbot, a rough iron warrior, who moves us the more powerfully, as, in the moment when he is threatened with inevitable death, all his care is tenderly directed to save his son, who performs his first deeds of arms under his eye. After Talbot has in vain sacrificed himself, and the Maid of Orleans has fallen into the hands of the English, the French provinces are completely lost by an impolitic marriage; and with this the piece ends. The conversation between the aged Mortimer in prison, and Richard Plantagenet, afterwards Duke of York, contains an exposition of the claims of the latter to the throne: considered by itself it is a beautiful tragic elegy.

Samuel Taylor Coleridge (1772–1834)
[Excerpted from *Shakspeare, with Introductory Remarks on Poetry, the Drama, and the Stage* (1818). Coleridge, best known for poems such as "The Rime of the Ancient Mariner," was also an inventive critic.]

Act I. sc. 2. Bedford's speech:—

> Hung be the heavens with black, yield
>   day to night!
> Comets, importing change of times and
>   states,
> Brandish your crystal tresses in the sky;
> And with them scourge the bad revolt-
>   ing stars
> That have consented unto Henry's
>   death!
> King Henry the fifth, too famous to live
>   long!
> England ne'er lost a king of so much
>   worth.

Read aloud any two or three passages in blank verse even from Shakespeare's earliest dramas, as Love's Labour's Lost, or Romeo and Juliet; and then read in the same way this speech, with especial attention to the metre; and if you do not feel the impossibility of the latter having been written by Shakespeare, all I dare suggest is, that you may have ears,—

for so has another animal,—but an ear you cannot have, *me judice*.

George Bernard Shaw (1856–1950)
[Excerpted from Shaw's introduction to his play *Saint Joan* (1924). Irish playwright and critic, Shaw wrote *Saint Joan* in part as a response to Shakespeare's harsh treatment of the character.]

There is the first part of the Shakespearean, or pseudo-Shakespearean trilogy of Henry VI, in which Joan is one of the leading characters. This portrait of Joan is not more authentic than the descriptions in the London papers of George Washington in 1780, of Napoleon in 1803, of the German Crown Prince in 1915, or of Lenin in 1917. It ends in mere scurrility. The impression left by it is that the playwright, having begun by an attempt to make Joan a beautiful and romantic figure, was told by his scandalized company that English patriotism would never stand a sympathetic representation of a French conqueror of English troops, and that unless he at once introduced all the old charges against Joan of being a sorceress and harlot, and assumed her to be guilty of all of them, his play could not be produced. As likely as not, this is what actually happened: indeed there is only one other apparent way of accounting for the sympathetic representation of Joan as a heroine culminating in her eloquent appeal to the Duke of Burgundy, followed by the blackguardly scurrility of the concluding scenes. That other way is to assume that the original play was wholly scurrilous, and that Shakespear touched up the earlier scenes. As the work belongs to a period at which he was only beginning his practice as a tinker of old works, before his own style was fully formed and hardened, it is impossible to verify this guess. His finger is not unmistakeably evident in the play, which is poor and base in its moral tone; but he

The Maid of Orleans, Joan la Pucelle, in Act I, Scene 2 of *Henry VI, Part I*.

may have tried to redeem it from downright infamy by shedding a momentary glamour on the figure of The Maid. . . .

Now there is not a breath of medieval atmosphere in Shakespear's histories. His John of Gaunt is like a study of the old age of Drake. Although he was a Catholic by family tradition, his figures are all intensely Protestant, individualist, sceptical, self-centered in everything but their love affairs, and completely personal and selfish even in them. His kings are not statesmen: his cardinals have no religion: a novice can read his plays from one end to the other without learning that the world is finally governed by forces expressing themselves in religions and laws which make epochs rather than by vulgarly ambitious individuals who make rows. The divinity which shapes our ends, rough hew them how we will, is mentioned fatalistically only to be forgotten immediately like a passing vague apprehension. To Shakespear as to Mark Twain, Cauchon would have been a tyrant and a bully instead of a Catholic, and the inquisitor Lemaître would have been a Sadist instead of a lawyer. Warwick would have had no more feudal quality than his successor the King Maker has in the play of Henry VI. We

should have seen them all completely satisfied that if they would only to their own selves be true they could not then be false to any man (a precept which represents the reaction against medievalism at its intensest) as if they were beings in the air, without public responsibilities of any kind. All Shakespear's characters are so: that is why they seem natural to our middle classes, who are comfortable and irresponsible at other people's expense, and are neither ashamed of that condition nor even conscious of it. Nature abhors this vacuum in Shakespear; and I have taken care to let the medieval atmosphere blow through my play freely.

MODERN CRITICISM AND CRITICAL CONTROVERSIES

Criticism of *Henry VI, Part 1* has evolved over time. Bibliographical debates regarding authorship segued into discussions of the disintegration of the nation, coming more recently to focus on discussions of the representation of women in the play, and finally of the play in performance. The authorship debate, which began in the earliest criticism and tried to explain some of the flaws of the text, has, to some extent, stunted the growth of criticism of the play, as doubt over whether the play belonged to the Shakespearean canon created doubt as to whether the play was worthy of serious criticism. Nevertheless, over the last century, the acceptance of the play back into the canon and the development of a body of productions have encouraged the growth of serious scholarly criticism of the play.

The authorship debate is one of the most contentious issues surrounding *Henry VI, Part 1*: Although before the 20th century, it was generally held that Shakespeare did not write the whole of the play, postwar criticism from critics such as E. M. W. Tillyard suggested otherwise. Tillyard is a famous critic of the histories, arguing in his 1944 book *Shakespeare's History Plays* that Shakespeare had planned a unified cycle of plays that recounted the Tudor myth. However, although his theories remain famous, Tillyard's providential cycle has largely been discredited in subsequent studies of the histories. That said, the argument for Shakespeare as sole author of *Henry VI, Part 1* was also claimed by Andrew Cairncross, the editor of the 1960 Arden edition of the play. However, there is little consensus: Geoffery Bullough casts doubt on the authorship of the play in his *Narrative and Dramatic Sources of Shakespeare* (1966), as does Kenneth Muir in his *Sources of Shakespeare's Plays* (1977). More recently, Gary Taylor, coeditor of the Oxford Shakespeare, has entered the debate in his thorough study of the play's authorship, "Shakespeare and Others," concluding that Shakespeare wrote Act II, Scene IV, and Act 4, Scenes 2 to 7. Taylor also concludes that Nashe wrote Act I, while claiming two other writers, Y and Z, wrote other parts: Act III and most of Act V being written by Y, while Z wrote Act II and Act 4, Scene 1. The identities of Y and Z remain a mystery.

Tillyard brings the play into an octology, which was purposely built by Shakespeare and linked together by providence. In *Patterns of Decay*, Edward Berry discusses the history plays in terms of "an underlying conception of historical process that provides each work with a thematic center and binds together the entire series" (ix); however, he is stingingly articulate in his criticism of Tillyard's conception of the plays as a providential Tudor myth. Berry asserts that Tillyard's idea of "God's vengeance for the deposition and murder" (11) of Richard II being played out through the eight plays is flawed, because as Berry argues "*1 Henry VI* contains no reference to such a curse". Indeed, Berry goes on to say: "The discussion between Plantagenet and Mortimer . . . is singularly free of providential overtones and focuses instead with characteristic Yorkist straightforwardness on political realities" (11). Berry's own work focuses on disorder at home, which spreads through all the relationships and settings in the play. He sees Talbot as a representative of a heroic ideal, with all other characters defined against him, this being particularly evident in the Countess of Auvergne scene. Talbot's death, in Berry's work, therefore, represents the "climactic moment of social disintegration" (2).

In "Frame of Disorder," J. P. Brockbank points out the difference between watching and reading *Henry VI, Part 1*, stating that the play is "more moving to watch than to read" (75). Brockbank discusses the play as a part of a trilogy about "a cataclysmic movement of events for which responsibility is communal and historical" (73). In *Henry VI, Part 1*, Brockbank argues, Shakespeare is looking at the "poignant contrast between the past nostalgically apprehended through its monuments and the past keenly re-enacted in the present" (75). Robert C. Jones takes up this thread, emphasizing the role of remembrance in the history plays and describing *Henry VI, Part 1* as illustrating "more positively than any other play until *Henry V* . . . how the leader of the past can survive as a vital presence in those who properly emulate [him]" (2).

The discussion of gender in the play began with David Bevington's influential study of "The Domineering Female in *1 Henry VI*" in 1966. Bevington's article appears to have grown out of the early debates surrounding authorship, as he writes that his purpose "is to bolster appreciation of structural integrity, by tropological analysis of a Renaissance commonplace: the relationship of men and women" (51). In a close study of the sexual domineering of Joan, Margaret, and the Countess of Auvergne, Bevington shows how "The theme of feminine supremacy echoes the larger theme of discord and division throughout *1 Henry VI* and the tetralogy." This would appear to be a negative account of female power in the play. Indeed, Carol Chillington Rutter, in 2006, wrote that the character of Joan has "borne the brunt of misogynist backlash" since 1963. Although in this statement, Rutter was writing about the character in productions, the same could be said for the character's experience in criticism.

The negative presentation of women in both the text and criticism is something that feminist critics have sought to address, attempting to rehabilitate the women in the play. Jean E. Howard and Phyl-

Joan la Pucelle in *Henry VI, Part 1*. Print from Charles Heath's 1848 edition of *The Heroines of Shakspeare: Comprising the Principal Female Characters in the Plays of the Great Poet. (Painting by J. W. Wright; engraving by B. Eyles)*

lis Rackin's seminal feminist critique of the history plays, *Engendering a Nation,* sees the plays as part of building the English nation, addressing "a public longing for narratives of strong male heroes" (9). Howard and Rackin portray Joan, Margaret, and the Countess of Auvergne as threats to masculinity as embodied by Talbot; Joan is particularly noted as a "threat to English historical renown" (54) and the Countess of Auvergne "threatens to subvert the English historical project by calling attention to the difference between Talbot's unimpressive physical presence . . . and the verbal record" (59). Although expressly a feminist account, Howard and Rackin have been criticized by Carol Banks, who states that *Engendering a Nation* "serves . . . to negate

rather than promote the women in these plays" (Lavanagh, 2007). Banks points out that although Joan may be transgressive, she "fights as a woman" and "[draws] attention to her female body" rather than disowning her femininity. Indeed, Banks argues that "Shakespeare's plays may be less a backlash against female power and supremacy than an attempt to re-examine old fashioned military heroism in a society in which attitudes to masculinity were evidently changing." Naomi Liebler and Scancella Shea support this by noting that "Joan draws strength from her female roles, of which she has several" (Pendleton, 2001). However, the main feminine role, Liebler and Shea point out, is that of the virgin going on to highlight the role of military leader, which is arguably a masculine role, and witch, which is a somewhat negative feminine role.

THE PLAY TODAY

After its first performances in the 1590s, *Henry VI, Part 1* seemed to fall off the radar of Shakespearean production. The acceptance of the play back into the canon in the 20th century and a number of large-scale cycle performances of the histories have contributed to a growing interest in the early history plays over the past century and into the 21st century. *Henry VI, Part 1* now enjoys a degree of scholarly interest, with critics continuing to focus on the powerful women it depicts. Most recently, Kristin Smith wrote about "Martial Maids and Murdering Mothers: Women, Witchcraft and Motherly Transgression in *Henry VI* and *Richard III*," discussing how Joan and Margaret are presented as degenerate, transgressive women through the language they use and viewing Richard III as the Scourge of God "birthed" by these illegitimate women.

Critical interest in performance of the *Henry VI* plays has also grown, encouraged by a number of high-profile productions. However, the play has not returned to the repertoire unscathed. Although what may be considered the first of modern stagings, Barry Jackson and Douglas Seale's 1953 production of the history cycle for the Birmingham Repertory Theatre, used an unabridged text of

Henry VI, Part 1, subsequent productions by Seale in 1957, Peter Hall and John Barton in 1963–64, and Michael Bogdanov and Michael Pennington for the English Shakespeare Company in 1986, all used abridged and adapted texts combining *Parts 1* and *2* of *Henry VI* into a single play. More recently, this has been the case in Barrie Rutter's production of *The Wars of the Roses* for Northern Broadsides in 2006 and also in a production by Edward Hall entitled *Rose Rage.*

Despite the continued absence of *Henry VI, Part 1* in individual, stand-alone productions, the history cycles have been important, epic stagings of Shakespeare's histories that are themselves significant in theater history. And *Henry VI, Part 1* has occasionally been performed in its entirety: Terry Hands in 1977 and Adrian Noble in 1988 staged cycles that included full productions of *Henry VI, Part 1.* At the turn of the 21st century, the Royal Shakespeare Company staged all eight plays of the first and second tetralogy, including *Henry VI, Part 1,* in full. The productions were staged in Stratford-upon-Avon and London, and the first tetralogy, directed by Michael Boyd, also traveled to Michigan for a residency at the University of Michigan in Ann Arbor. This production was critically acclaimed and was revived for Boyd's full staging of *The Histories* in 2006–08 (the original Boyd staging in 2000–01 was part of a project that saw three other directors and companies take the other plays of the second tetralogy). The interest in studying the play in performance has mirrored this growth in productions of the play, which has also been seen on television directed by Jane Howell in the BBC-TimeLife production in 1981. Stuart Hampton Reeves and Carol Chillington Rutter have published a thorough study of the three *Henry VI* plays in performance, and the actress Fiona Bell, who played both Joan La Pucelle and Margaret in the Boyd productions, has written about her experience of creating the roles in Robert Smallwood's series of Players of Shakespeare books.

Scholars also continue to study the historical context of the play. More recently, the two disci-

plines of textual study and performance criticism have combined: Ben Spiller, in an article entitled "Warlike Mates?" writes about modern performances of Joan and sees the continued use of armor costuming for her character, specifically in Boyd's productions, as a visual reference back to Elizabeth I at Tilbury.

FIVE TOPICS FOR DISCUSSION AND WRITING

1. **Chivalry:** What are some examples of chivalrous behavior in the play? Is chivalry only an English attribute, or can the French be described as chivalrous, too? Which characters represent chivalry?
2. **History:** *Henry VI, Part 1* can be described as a chronicle history play. How is history figured in the play? Other than being a historical story, is history important to the characters? In what ways? Which characters are associated with history? Why?
3. **Gender and transgression:** How are gender issues presented and discussed in the play? What are some examples of gender transgression? How does the theme of gender interact with the theme of nationality?
4. **Opposition:** What oppositions are depicted in the play? How do these oppositions relate to theme and structure? What are their effects?
5. **Witchcraft:** What examples are there of witchcraft appear in the play? Is any particular character associated with witchcraft? How are the characters associated with witchcraft? Is witchcraft a negative or a positive in the play? Does this change during the play? Is this a fair presentation?

Bibliography

Berry, Edward I. *Patterns of Decay: Shakespeare's Early Histories.* Charlottesville: University Press of Virginia, 1975.

Bevington, David. "The Domineering Female in *1 Henry VI.*" *Shakespeare Studies* 2 (1966): 51–58.

Brockbank, J. P. "The Frame of Disorder: *Henry VI.*" In *Early Shakespeare,* edited by John Russell Brown and Bernard Harris, 73–99. London: Edward Arnold Publishers, 1961.

Bullough, Geoffrey. *Narrative and Dramatic Sources of Shakespeare,* Vol. 3: *Earlier English History Plays.* London: Routledge, 1966.

Cavanagh, Permot. *On Shakespeare's Histories and Counter-Histories.* Manchester, U.K.: Manchester University Press, 2007.

Grene, Nicholas. *Shakespeare's Serial History Plays.* Cambridge: Cambridge University Press, 2002.

Hampton-Reeves, Stuart, and Carol Chillington Rutter. *The Henry VI Plays.* Manchester, U.K.: Manchester University Press, 2006.

Holderness, Graham. *Shakespeare: The Histories.* Basingstoke, U.K.: Macmillan, 2000.

Pendleton, Thomas, ed. *Henry VI: Critical Essays.* New York: Routledge, 2001.

Howard, Jean E., and Phyllis Rackin. *Engendering a Nation: A Feminist Account of Shakespeare's English Histories.* London: Routledge, 1997.

Jones, Robert C. *These Valiant Dead: Renewing the Past in Shakespeare's Histories.* Iowa City: University of Iowa Press, 1991.

Marcus, Leah. *Puzzling Shakespeare: Local Readings and Its Discourses.* Berkeley and Los Angeles: University of California Press, 1988.

Raleigh, Walter. Introduction to *Johnson on Shakespeare,* by Samuel Johnson. London: Henry Frouide, 1908.

Riggs, David. *Shakespeare's Heroical Histories:* Henry VI *and Its Literary Tradition.* Cambridge, Mass. Harvard University Press, 1971.

Simpson, Richard. "The Political Use of the Stage in Shakespeare's Time." *New Shakespeare Society Publications* 1, no. 2, part 2 (1875).

Smith, Kristin M. "Martial Maids and Murdering Mothers: Women, Witchcraft and Motherly Transgression in *Henry VI* and *Richard III.*" *Shakespeare* 3, no. 2 (August 2007): 143–160.

Spiller, Ben. "Warlike Mates? Queen Elizabeth and Joan La Pucelle in *1 Henry VI.*" In *Goddesses and Queens: The Iconography of Elizabeth I,* edited by Annaliese Connolly and Lisa Hopkins. Manchester, U.K.: Manchester University Press, 2007.

Taylor, Gary. "Shakespeare and Others: The Authorship of *Henry the Sixth, Part One.*" In *Medieval and Renaissance Drama in England,* Vol. 7, edited by Leeds Barroll, 145–205. London: Associated University Press, 1995.

Tillyard, E. M. W. *Shakespeare's History Plays.* London: Chatto & Windus, 1944.

FILM AND VIDEO PRODUCTIONS

Howell, Jane, dir. *Henry VI, Part One.* With Peter Benson, Brenda Blethyn, Trevor Peacock, Ron Cook, and Brian Protheroe. BBC, 1983.

—Kate Wilkinson

Henry VI, Part 2

INTRODUCTION

Although *Henry VI, Part 2* is not one of Shakespeare's most popular or well-regarded works, it and the rest of its tetralogy, or group of four plays (including the three *Henry VI* plays and *Richard III*) have begun to receive a renewed level of attention in recent years. This is partly due to a number of acclaimed postwar productions of the first tetralogy, from Peter Hall and John Barton's 1963 Royal Shakespeare Company (RSC) production of *The Wars of the Roses* to Michael Boyd's 2008 RSC production of *The Histories*. Productions such as these, along with tremendous critical debate about the play's positions on gender and class, have increased interest in the plays.

Written around 1590 or 1591, *Henry VI, Part 2* is one of the very first plays that Shakespeare ever wrote; in fact, some scholars believe that it was written before *Henry VI, Part 1,* which, according to this theory, was probably a collaboration with another playwright. Although *Henry VI, Part 2* has long been dismissed as an amateurish work, scholars interested in Shakespeare's development as a writer have now begun to look at the play as a representation of Shakespeare's early genius. The play is full of tremendously effective drama. Margaret and Suffolk's machinations to have Gloucester murdered and York's schemes to seize the crown are both exciting and powerful. There is genuine sadness in Gloucester's fall and genuine love in the parting of Margaret and Suffolk. There is also a host of action, as rebellions and battles place England into turmoil. At the same time, the play's presentation of the horrors of war and civil strife has helped to make the play relevant to generations of audiences and readers. The play's historical subject, the Wars of the Roses, also means that the play should be popular with those who are interested in that terrible and fascinating period in English history.

BACKGROUND

Perhaps it is not surprising that Shakespeare would choose to dramatize the Wars of the Roses, for their relation to contemporary events was fairly strong. *Henry VI, Part 2* was written during a time of great turmoil in England. Although England had recently emerged victorious against the Spanish Armada in 1588, years of war had been incredibly draining on England's resources. Elizabeth I would rule for another 10 years, but already anxiety had begun about what would happen after she died without an heir. These anxieties over war and the perils of succession were explored in Shakespeare's two principal sources for *Henry VI, Part 2*: Edward Hall's *The Union of the Two Noble and Illustre Families of Lancaster and York* (1548) and Raphael Holinshed's *Chronicles of England, Scotland, and Ireland* (1577, second edition 1587).

Both of these works deal with the turmoil that engulfed England following the deposing of Richard II (1367–1400) in 1399 by Henry IV (1366–1413). Henry IV's son Henry V (1386–1422) was one of England's most famous heroes, principally remembered for his victory over the French at the Battle of Agincourt (1415). Henry V's son Henry VI (1421–71) was not as well remembered as his

York and Buckingham arrest Eleanor and Hume for conjuring a prophetic spirit in Act 1, Scene 4 of *Henry VI, Part 2*. This is a print from the Boydell Shakespeare Gallery project, which was first conceived in 1786 and lasted until 1805. *(Painting by John Opie; engraving by Robert Thew)*

father. Crowned at the age of nine months, Henry VI spent most of his reign dominated by others, first by his uncles such as Humphrey of Lancaster, the duke of Gloucester (1390–1447), and then by his wife, Margaret of Anjou (1430–82), and William de la Pole, duke of Suffolk (1396–1450). Henry VI's weaknesses inspired the ambitions of Richard Plantagenet, the duke of York (1411–60), to try to seize the crown for himself, an action that ultimately leads to the Battle of Saint Albans (1455) and the outbreak of the Wars of the Roses. It is an exciting period of English history, full of contemporary relevance and packed with a number of highly dramatic events. Shakespeare does follow the chronicles quite closely, but, being a dramatist, he rearranges, telescopes, and excises a number of historical events in order to make for a more compelling drama. In any case, Shakespeare chose a very exciting story to focus on in one of his earliest plays.

Date and Text of the Play

The Stationers' Register records the publication of the First Quarto—known as a "bad quarto," because of its faulty text—on March 12, 1594, under the title of *The First Part of the Contention between the Houses of York and Lancaster.* Most scholars believe that the play was actually written sometime around 1590 or 1591. An entry in the diary of Philip Henslowe records a production of a play called *Harey Vj* on March 3, 1592, although it is not entirely clear that it is Shakespeare's. According to Henslowe's diary, this play was very successful. Another indication of an earlier date for the play is Robert Greene's *Greene's Groatsworth of Wit* (1592). In this work, Greene famously makes reference to a line from *Henry VI, Part 3*, which suggests that both *Henry VI, Part 2* and *Henry VI, Part 3* were written and performed before 1592. The second quarto of the play was published in 1600 and a third was published in 1619 before the play's inclusion in the First Folio (1623).

SYNOPSIS
Brief Synopsis

The play begins with the Duke of Suffolk presenting Henry VI to his new bride, Margaret. The Lord Protector, Duke of Gloucester, is angered that this marriage brings no dowry and also means the loss of Anjou and Maine. He tries to tell the other nobles of his concerns, but they feel that he is too ambitious to be trusted and begin to plot against him. Whatever Gloucester's ambitions, the most ambitious man in the court is the Duke of York, who believes himself to be the rightful heir to the throne and who is merely biding his time until he can find the right opportunity to strike. Gloucester's wife, Duchess Eleanor, is also ambitious, but her husband tries to eschew this. Disgruntled, she attempts to raise a Spirit that will forecast her political future, not realizing that she is being set up by Gloucester's enemies, who seek to destroy him through her.

A petitioner named Peter Thump has accused Thomas Horner of declaring that York should be king, so a trial by combat is set up to settle the issue. Eleanor meets with the conjurers and a Spirit is raised, but as soon as the prophecies are told, she and the others are arrested for treason. Meanwhile, Gloucester is with Henry VI and the rest of the

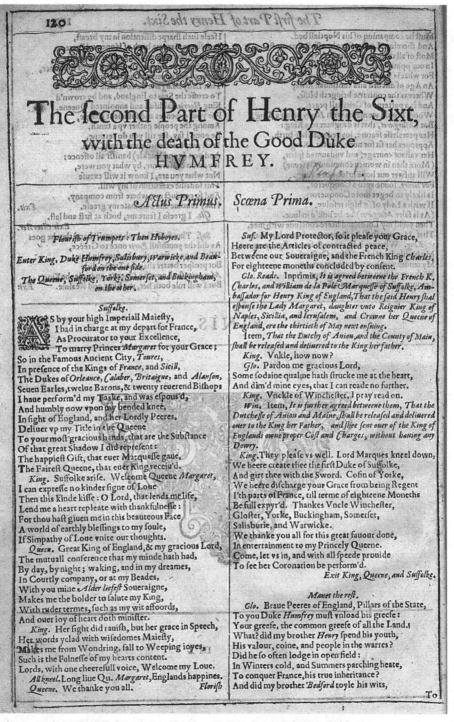

Title page of the First Folio edition of *Henry VI, Part 2*, published in 1623

court in Saint Albans. Gloucester exposes a con artist claiming to have been miraculously cured, but his victory is immediately tarnished when news arrives of Eleanor's arrest. At the same time, York has convinced the Earl of Salisbury and his son the Earl of Warwick that he is the rightful heir to the throne, and they agree to help him no matter what the cost. York tells them that he plans to let the other nobles destroy Gloucester, and then he will destroy them. At Eleanor's trial, she is ordered to do penance and then be banished to the Isle of Man. Gloucester is then stripped of his role as Lord Protector. Margaret and Suffolk are immensely pleased by this, for now they will have control over Henry VI. The trial by combat commences, and Horner is killed by Peter. Later, as Eleanor does her penitential walk on the way to exile, she warns Gloucester of his enemies and says that he is the one who has really been shamed. Gloucester ignores this and goes off to meet Henry VI.

Henry VI wonders why Gloucester has yet to arrive at court. Seizing the opportunity to slander him, Gloucester's enemies proceed to accuse him of every conceivable crime. Henry VI does not believe Gloucester to be guilty, but he is powerless to stop him from being arrested for treason. Gloucester's enemies—Margaret, Suffolk, Cardinal Beaufort, York, and Somerset—all fear that Henry VI may change his mind and release him, so they plan to murder the former Lord Protector. News arrives that an uprising has broken out in Ireland, so York is given an army to put it down. When the others have left, York excitedly exclaims that he now has the army to put his plan into motion. He has managed to get Jack Cade to start an uprising in Kent, an uprising York hopes to get the credit for putting down. Once this is done, York plans to take advantage of the turmoil and seize the crown for himself. Gloucester is dead, and although the conspirators try to act as though he died of natural causes, it quickly becomes clear to everyone that he was murdered. As a result of both his own anger and pressure from the Commons, Henry VI orders Suffolk sent into exile. Margaret is distraught at this, and she resolves to have her revenge. Gloucester's most hated enemy, the

Cardinal, is now dying, and in a delirious state he cries out in guilt over the crimes he has committed.

While on his way to exile in France, Suffolk is captured by pirates and beheaded. Rebellion has broken out all over England, for Cade has proclaimed himself to be the rightful heir to the throne. He and his followers defeat an army of the king's forces under the Staffords and begin to make their way to London. News of this arrives at court, inspiring Henry VI and Margaret to flee for safety and the Duke of Buckingham to meet the rebels with a larger army. Cade and his followers begin to rampage through London, burning London Bridge and executing Lord Saye and his son-in-law, whose heads are paraded through the city on poles. Buckingham and Old Clifford meet Cade and his followers and eventually manage to persuade the followers to forsake Cade, who immediately flees and goes into hiding. Henry VI is elated by news of Cade's fall, although his mood is dampened when news arrives that York has returned with his army determined to arrest the Duke of Somerset for treason. Alone and starving, Cade finds himself in the garden of Alexander Iden, an esquire of Kent. Iden kills Cade after a heated exchange and then decides to bring his head to Henry VI for a reward.

York arrives and is told that Cade has been defeated and Somerset is in the Tower of London. York agrees to disband his army and apologizes to Henry VI, but when he sees Somerset walking about freely with Margaret, he loses all control. He proclaims himself to be the rightful heir to the throne and demands that Henry VI step down from the throne. The battle lines are very quickly drawn, with Salisbury, Warwick, and York's sons supporting York, and everyone else supporting Henry VI. The Battle of Saint Albans then commences, which Henry VI and his army quickly lose. Somerset and Old Clifford are killed, and although his son Young Clifford swears revenge, he and Margaret manage to convince Henry VI to retreat to London in order to fight another day. The Yorks are jubilant about their triumph, but they, too, decide to try to get to London as quickly as possible in order to stop their enemies from regrouping.

Act I, Scene 1

The play opens at the royal palace in London. Henry VI and his court are assembled because William de la Pole has returned from France to present Margaret as the new queen of England. William had stood in as Henry VI's proxy at the marriage ceremony in France, leading some to believe that he and Margaret are lovers. Henry VI is not one of them, for he thanks William for his help. After everyone assembled has hailed Margaret as England's queen, William gives the Duke of Gloucester, as the Lord Protector, the articles of peace between England and France to read. Gloucester begins to read them but stops when he discovers that Henry VI has agreed to give Anjou and Maine to Margaret's father, the King of Naples, who has also not given Margaret any dowry. Unperturbed by this, Henry VI makes William the Duke of Suffolk. He also discharges the Duke of York as regent of France. After Henry, Margaret, and Suffolk exit, Gloucester turns to the nobles to complain about the marriage, the loss of English territory in France, and Suffolk's ambitions. Warwick and York agree with Gloucester, but Gloucester's enemy, Cardinal Beaufort, accuses Gloucester of having ambitions of his own. Angered, Gloucester exits, only to have the Cardinal begin to try to rally the remaining nobles against him. Many agree, but after the Cardinal makes his exit, Somerset and the Duke of Buckingham admit that they do not trust him, either. After Somerset and Buckingham have exited, the Earl of Salisbury, the Earl of Warwick, and York declare their intention to stand behind Gloucester. However, when Salisbury and Warwick exit and York is left alone, we learn of his true intentions. York has a claim to the throne through Edmund Mortimer, and he fully intends to take the crown for himself. Believing that Henry VI is too weak to be king, York declares that he is merely waiting for the right moment to strike.

Act I, Scene 2

At Gloucester's house, his wife, Duchess Eleanor, tries to persuade him that he should take the crown for himself. Gloucester refuses and tries to convince his wife to give up her ambitions. He then tells her of his dream, in which the staff he owns as Lord Protector was broken by his enemies. Eleanor dismisses this dream and continues to discuss Gloucester's chances of becoming king, only to have Gloucester angrily tell her once again to abandon such thoughts. Gloucester then exits to meet Henry VI in Saint Albans, leaving Eleanor behind with her thoughts. She ridicules her husband's mildness and declares that she has no intention to give up her ambitions. John Hume, a priest and her attendant, enters and tells Eleanor that he has found people who can conjure up a spirit that will answer her questions about her political future. Excited about what she may find out, Eleanor pays Hume and exits. It is then that we discover that Hume has betrayed Eleanor, for he has been paid by her enemies to get her to reveal her treasonous intentions. Musing that Eleanor's fall will also lead to Gloucester's, Hume simply laughs because he is getting paid by them all.

Act I, Scene 3

A group of petitioners enter with the intention of meeting Gloucester. Instead, they come across Suffolk and Margaret. Believing Suffolk to be Gloucester, one of the petitioners accidentally gives him his petition, which actually complains of Suffolk's actions in Melford. Another petitioner, Peter Thump, declares that his master, Thomas Horner, has said that York is the rightful heir to the crown. After they make their exit, Margaret tells Suffolk that she is distraught over the weakness of Henry VI and the power of Gloucester. She then goes on to list all her enemies at court, finally declaring that Eleanor is her greatest enemy, for many people mistake her for the queen. Suffolk placates Queen Margaret by informing her of his plan to bring about the ruin of Eleanor, Gloucester, and anyone else who stands in their way. Henry VI and his nobles enter, with the subject of whether York or Somerset should be regent of France still undecided.

Eleanor leaves after Queen Margaret boxes her ears in Act 1, Scene 3 of *Henry VI, Part 2*. This drawing was designed for the Chiswick edition of Shakespeare, published in 1900. *(Illustration by John Byam Lister Shaw)*

Soon, Gloucester finds himself a target, as Margaret, Suffolk, the Cardinal, and Buckingham turn on him in a quick succession of accusations. Gloucester leaves in a rage, leaving Eleanor to the mercy of Margaret, who proceeds to box her on the ear. Gloucester reenters as his wife makes her exit, proclaiming that York should be regent. This proclamation is challenged by Suffolk, who proceeds to bring forward Peter and his petition concerning York. Gloucester gives in and declares that Somerset should be regent, after which Henry VI declares that the case between Peter and Horner shall be decided in a trial by combat.

Act I, Scene 4

Hume, Margery Jourdayne, John Southwell, and Roger Bolingbroke enter and prepare for the conjuration. Eleanor then enters to have Bolingbroke and the others theatrically conjure up the Spirit that will answer her questions. The Spirit rises and answers a series of questions about the fates of Henry VI, Suffolk, and Somerset. The conjuration is interrupted by York and Buckingham, who have been watching from nearby and who arrest everyone present, including Hume. York then proceeds to read the Spirit's prophecies, which he dismisses as nonsense. Buckingham exits to tell Henry VI what has happened, while York decides to meet with Salisbury and Warwick to plan his course of action.

Act II, Scene 1

Henry VI and his nobles are engaged in falconry in Saint Albans, but when Gloucester's hawks fly higher than the rest, his enemies seize the opportunity to compare his hawks' flying to their master's ambitions. Henry VI tries to make peace between his warring nobles, only to have Gloucester and the Cardinal challenge each other to a duel out of his earshot. This is interrupted when the people of Saint Albans enter to declare that a miracle has taken place, for an apparently blind man named Sander Simpcox has regained his sight. Henry VI is overjoyed, but a suspicious Gloucester soon manages to show that it is all a fraud. His victory is soon tarnished, however, for Buckingham enters and declares that Eleanor has been arrested for treason. Gloucester tries to maintain his own innocence, but his enemies soon pounce on him and declare him to be a traitor, as well. Saddened, Henry VI declares his intention to return to London and look into the matter more thoroughly.

Act II, Scene 2

York proceeds to tell Salisbury and Warwick about his claim to the throne. York claims descent from Edmund Mortimer, who was prevented from taking the crown when the Lancaster Henry IV, Henry VI's grandfather, seized the crown from Richard II.

York declares that the Lancasters do not deserve to rule and that he, as the rightful heir, should be king. Salisbury and Warwick are convinced and declare their loyalty to York and his cause. York counsels them to remain quiet about their intentions until the time is right to strike. He believes that Gloucester will soon be destroyed by his enemies but that their victory will lead to their own destruction, too. Following this period of confusion, York will step forward to make his claim. Warwick promises that he will make York king, while York promises that he will make Warwick the second most powerful noble in England after York.

Act II, Scene 3

Henry VI makes his judgment in the trial of Eleanor and her coconspirators. The others will be executed, but Eleanor, as a noble, will do three days' penance and then be sent into exile. Gloucester is saddened by the losses of both his wife and his own prestige, but he feels completely powerless. Henry VI furthers this powerlessness by taking Gloucester out of his position as Lord Protector of England. Margaret and Suffolk are overjoyed, for now they will be the ones who are in charge of Henry VI and, by extension, the whole kingdom. Gloucester exits the stage as Peter and Thomas Horner enter, for this is the time designated for their trial by combat. Horner is drunk, and after some comic stage business, he is beaten by Peter. As he lies dying, Thomas Horner confesses his treason. Satisfied that justice has been properly meted out, Henry VI rewards Peter, and the court exits.

Act II, Scene 4

Gloucester stands on a street in London with his servant as he awaits Eleanor's penitential walk. Gloucester is ashamed, but he nevertheless refuses his servant's request that they rescue her. Eleanor enters barefoot and in a white penitent's sheet. She chastises her husband, declaring that her shame pales beside Gloucester's, for now the whole of London has seen how far he has fallen. She is angry, for she knows that Gloucester has done nothing to protect either her or himself from their enemies.

She declares that these enemies will bring about his destruction as well, and much sooner than he thinks. Believing himself safe so long as he remains loyal, Gloucester ignores his wife's warnings. A Herald enters demanding Gloucester's presence at court. Gloucester admits that this demand seems suspicious, but he agrees to go nevertheless. Before he exits, he asks Sir John Stanley to look after his wife. Stanley tries to cheer Eleanor, assuring her that she will still enjoy all of the comforts a duchess is accustomed to during her exile. Eleanor ignores these assurances about a comfortable exile and says that she will continue to wear the white penitent's sheet even after she is no longer required to do so.

Act III, Scene 1

Henry VI enters with his court and wonders aloud why Gloucester has not arrived yet. In a rapid succession of accusations, Margaret, Suffolk, the Cardinal, York, and Buckingham all declare Gloucester to be a traitor who has plans of seizing the throne for himself. Henry VI refuses to believe this, declaring that Gloucester is as innocent as a lamb or a dove. Unwilling to back down, Margaret insists that Gloucester is not as innocent as he appears to be. Somerset, who had been acting as regent of France, enters and declares that all of England's French possessions are now lost. Henry VI accepts this as the will of God, but York, who had hoped to rule France as well as England, expresses his anger in an aside. Gloucester finally enters, only to be immediately arrested by Suffolk for treason. Convinced of his innocence, Gloucester scorns his accusers; however, as accusation follows accusation, his ability to fight back is increasingly diminished. Henry VI still remains sure of Gloucester's innocence, but he is ultimately powerless to stop Margaret, Suffolk, the Cardinal, and the rest of Gloucester's enemies. Gloucester is thus committed to the Cardinal's care and is led away by guards. Distraught, Henry VI leaves the outcome of the trial to the others, for he believes that Gloucester has been wronged and he wants to play no part in destroying the duke. Yet, even though he is king, Henry VI seems unable to play a part in saving him. Henry VI exits with Buckingham, Salisbury, and Warwick, leaving Margaret, Suffolk, the Cardinal, Somerset, and York to debate about what to do next. Realizing that Henry VI may one day find the strength to save Gloucester, Margaret declares that they should have Gloucester murdered. The Cardinal argues that they should find a way to have him condemned and executed, but Suffolk counters this by arguing that Henry VI or the Commons could always manage to save him, whereas if he was murdered, the threat he poses would disappear forever. After discussing it further, the conspirators all agree that Gloucester must be murdered as soon as possible. A Post enters and brings news that a rebellion has broken out in Ireland and that English troops need to be sent there immediately in order to quell it. Perhaps because they believe him to be a dedicated coconspirator, the others all agree that York should be given an army to take to Ireland. The other conspirators exit, excitedly planning the murder of Gloucester while completely unaware of the degree to which York has tricked them all. The extent of this becomes clear as York congratulates himself on securing an army, which he will now use to further his ambitions for the crown. Earlier, he had declared his intention to wait for the right moment to strike; now he sees that that moment has come. While he is in Ireland quelling the rebellion, he has taken steps to ensure that England has a rebellion of its own. York has managed to get Jack Cade to begin an uprising and declare himself to be the rightful heir to the throne, hoping that the confusion this causes will make it all the easier for him to come back and seize the throne for himself.

Act III, Scene 2

Two Murderers enter and declare that now that they have killed Gloucester, they need to let Suffolk know that the deed is done. The second Murderer is racked with guilt, so he remains silent while the first Murderer relates to Suffolk that everything has gone according to plan. The Murderers make their exit as Henry VI and his nobles enter. Henry VI tells Suffolk to fetch Gloucester for his trial, to which Suffolk disingenuously complies. Henry

VI then declares his intention to have Gloucester tried fairly, to which Margaret insincerely agrees. This duplicity is soon taken even further, for now Suffolk enters and declares that Gloucester has been found dead in his bed, as though he had died of natural causes. Henry VI swoons at the news, only to revive and turn on those assembled around him for their falseness, for he believes that they may have had something to do with Gloucester's death. Suffolk takes the brunt of Henry VI's rage, inspiring Margaret to come to his defense. She accuses Henry VI of caring more for Gloucester than he does for her and protests that he could ever believe her responsible for such a thing. Her protest is interrupted by Salisbury and Warwick, who enter with a number of citizens and demand to know whether Gloucester was murdered. Henry VI allows them to enter Gloucester's bedchamber to investigate for themselves. Warwick then enters and shows Henry VI that regardless of whether Gloucester died in his bed, he certainly did not die of natural causes. Suffolk continues to proclaim his innocence, with Margaret backing him up on every point, so much so that she begins to seem more and more suspect. Warwick and Suffolk leave to settle their dispute, only to immediately reenter with a bruised Suffolk claiming that he has been beaten by the citizens. Now the Commons want nothing less than Suffolk's blood or banishment. Henry VI quickly acquiesces to their demands and orders the latter punishment. When Margaret protests, Henry VI turns on her with a fury that is quite uncharacteristic of him. Henry VI then exits with Salisbury and Warwick, leaving Margaret and Suffolk to make their tearful farewells. While this is going on, Vaux enters to announce that the Cardinal is dying. The news brings Suffolk even lower in spirits but has the opposite reaction on Margaret, for she ends the scene resolved not to let her enemies have the last laugh.

Act III, Scene 3

Henry VI, Salisbury, and Warwick enter the Cardinal's bedchamber to give him comfort in his last moments. Raving and acting as though he were mad, the Cardinal, believing Henry VI to be Death itself, says that he will give him all his riches if he can live still and feel no pain. The Cardinal then believes that he sees Gloucester, and his guilt over his part in the murder becomes overwhelming. After the Cardinal dies, Warwick declares that his monstrous death is a reflection on his monstrous life. Far more forgiving, Henry VI declares that everyone is a sinner and that he hopes that the Cardinal's soul will find peace.

Act IV, Scene 1

A disguised Suffolk is now one of a number of prisoners aboard a ship off the coast of Kent. They have been captured and are being divided among the crew. Walter Whitmore has been given Suffolk. The other prisoners are quick to offer money for their release, but Whitmore wants to have them all killed. The Lieutenant tries to stay Whitmore's blood lust, but Suffolk quickly begins to realize that he will not survive this voyage. Suffolk tells Whitmore that he is really the Duke of Suffolk in disguise, but Whitmore is not impressed. He becomes even less impressed when Suffolk tries to belittle him because of his lack of nobility. The Lieutenant orders for Suffolk to be beheaded for his numerous crimes: his relationship with Margaret, his role in the murder of Gloucester, his arrangement of Henry VI's marriage in order to suit his own ends, his responsibility for the loss of Anjou and Maine, and his role in the loss of France. The Lieutenant also expresses his support for York and reports that Kent has risen up in rebellion. Despite the entreaties of his fellow prisoners, Suffolk refuses to beg for his life from those he considers beneath him, and he goes to the chopping block, defiant to the end. Whitmore enters with Suffolk's head and body and the first Gentleman, who has been left behind because he paid his ransom, resolves to bring both back to Henry VI and Margaret.

Act IV, Scene 2

Two of Cade's rebels, Nick and George, enter with long staves. Both express hope that Cade will

change England and make conditions better for those who are not born noble. Cade enters with a large crowd of followers and begins to make the case for why he is the rightful heir to the throne; however, each and every point he brings up in his favor is mocked by Dick the Butcher and Smith the Weaver in a series of humorous asides that reveals Cade's origins are anything but royal. Cade then goes on to make a series of promises to his followers, many of which relate to cheap food and alcohol for all. After the Butcher famously declares their intention to kill all the lawyers, a clerk named Emmanuel enters only to find himself accused, tried, and executed in a matter of moments. One of Cade's followers, Michael, enters and informs Cade that Sir Humphrey Stafford and his brother William are coming with the king's forces to stop them. Undeterred by the news or by their pedigree, Cade knights himself in preparation for the coming battle. Stafford enters and orders Cade and his followers to lay down their arms if they want to return home alive. Contemptuous of both the Staffords and their demands, Cade once again makes the case for his rights to the throne. Despite the fact that his story is clearly false, Cade's followers continue to support him and mock the Staffords, inspiring Cade to begin to demand that he be made Lord Protector and that Lord Saye be executed. Angry, the Staffords proclaim their intention to do battle with Cade and his followers. Cade rallies his soldiers by telling them that they fight on behalf of the people and that none of the noblemen should be spared during the battle.

Act IV, Scene 3

A battle between King Henry's forces under the Staffords and Cade and his followers commences, during which both of the Staffords are slain. Cade rewards the Butcher for his bravery and then, after taking up Humphrey Stafford's sword, declares that the bodies of the Staffords shall be dragged behind his horse while he and his followers make their way to London. The Butcher suggests that they should free all of the prisoners in order to find more troops, an idea that Cade seconds.

Act IV, Scene 4

Margaret enters with Suffolk's head. At first she fears that her grief might destroy her, but then she decides to think of revenge in order to gain strength. Buckingham implores Henry VI to make a decision in regard to the rebels, for they have now sent him a supplication. Fearing further bloodshed, Henry VI considers sending a bishop to entreat the rebels to stop and even considers having a parley with Cade himself. Henry VI is concerned about Margaret's mourning, particularly since he feels that she mourns Suffolk's death far more than she would ever mourn his. A messenger arrives and brings news of both Cade's accusations against Henry VI and his actions inside London, where the defeat of the Staffords has given the rebels courage. Henry VI and his court decide to retreat to Killingworth until the rebels can be stopped. Lord Saye, who the rebels want dead, is asked to come along, but he refuses out of fear that his presence might endanger Henry VI. A second messenger arrives and announces that the rebels have almost taken London Bridge and that the city is beginning to slip into anarchy. Thus, Henry VI and Margaret make a hasty exit, leaving Buckingham to fight against the rebels and Lord Saye to fight to stay alive.

Act IV, Scene 5

At the Tower of London, Lord Scales asks if Cade has been killed. He is told by a citizen that Cade and his followers have take London Bridge and that the Lord Mayor needs Scales's help to defend the city. Scales agrees, although he worries that both the city and the tower might soon be overrun.

Act IV, Scene 6

Cade enters and strikes his staff on London Stone, pronouncing that he is now lord of the city. He then orders that anyone calling him anything other than Lord Mortimer be slain, an order that is quickly taken into effect when a Soldier calls Cade "Jack Cade" and is killed. The soldier was carrying a message that the Butcher now picks up and reads. The king's forces are gathering in Smithfield. Cade resolves to fight them but not before ordering that both London Bridge and the Tower of London be burned.

Act IV, Scene 7

Cade and his followers win another victory, and he orders that both the Savoy and the Inns of Court be destroyed. The Butcher expresses his hope that Cade will create the new laws in England, a hope that fills Nick and the Weaver with dread. Cade then orders that all of the records be burned and that he will be the mouth of Parliament from now on. A messenger enters with a captured Lord Saye, and Cade accuses him of a variety of crimes, such as attempting to enforce the rules of grammar and making life more difficult for those who cannot read or write. Saye scorns Cade and his charges and then goes on to defend himself and his actions, insisting that he cares far more for the people than Cade does. His defense is so compelling that even Cade, in an aside, admits to feeling pity for him. However, this pity does not keep Cade from ordering the death of both Saye and his son-in-law, Sir James Crowner, adding further that their heads should be placed on large wooden poles. Cade declares that all of the peers shall be treated in the same way if they do not pay him tribute. His followers enter with the heads placed on poles, motivating Cade to call for them to be placed next to each other as though they were kissing. He says that the rebels will ride through the streets and perform the same ceremony at every corner they reach.

Act IV, Scene 8

Cade and his followers continue to run riot throughout London, only to be stopped by Buckingham and Old Clifford. Cade asks his followers why they have stopped, only to be told by Buckingham that his followers can return home safely if they forsake Cade. Old Clifford then conjures the memory of Henry V, which leads the rebels to forsake Cade. Angered, Cade berates his followers and says that they will either be killed or at least punished by the nobles. Conjuring the memory of their past hardships, Cade manages to win his followers back to him. Undeterred, Old Clifford once again brings up Henry V, only now he does so to warn the rebels that their actions are making England vulnerable to attack from France. He also tells the rebels that they will be financially rewarded for their loyalty. Perhaps because of this, the rebels forsake Cade once again. Seeing that he has lost, Cade flees the scene. Buckingham orders that a reward be given for Cade's arrest and then tells the rebels that he will find a way to reconcile them to Henry VI.

Act IV, Scene 9

Henry VI and his court are assembled at Kenilworth Castle, where Henry VI laments having become king. Buckingham and Old Clifford arrive with the rebels. Cade has not been found yet, but the rebels have forsaken him, and they now beg Henry VI for clemency, which Henry VI quickly grants. A messenger arrives to say that York has come back from Ireland with a large force and the intention of removing Somerset from power. Henry VI orders Buckingham to meet York in the field and also orders that Somerset be taken to the Tower of London. Henry VI despairs at this news, for no sooner has one crisis ended than another begins. He wonders aloud about whether England will curse his reign.

Act IV, Scene 10

Starving and alone, Cade stumbles his way into Alexander Iden's garden. Iden enters, praising the joys of the country over that of the city and the court. Believing that Iden has come to claim the reward for his life, Cade comes forward and challenges him. Even though he is not aware who Cade is, Iden is angered by his challenge and so responds in turn. The two men fight, and Cade is killed. As Cade dies, Iden realizes who he is and resolves to cut off his head and bring it to Henry VI.

Act V, Scene 1

York enters with his army and boldly declares that he is the rightful king of England. However, when Buckingham enters, York decides to forgo pushing for his claim and contents himself merely with his

charges against Somerset. Buckingham informs York that Somerset has been sent to the Tower of London, so York disbands his army and insists that he is still loyal to Henry VI. Henry VI enters and is told that York only kept his army in order to stop Cade's rebellion and bring Somerset to justice. At this point, Iden enters with Cade's head, a sight that so pleases Henry VI that he makes Iden a knight and rewards him with money. Margaret then enters with Somerset by his side, a sight that so enrages York that he immediately declares that Henry VI is a usurper and that he, York, is the rightful king. Somerset orders that York be arrested, but York merely scoffs at this and declares that he and his sons will make his bail and fight to maintain their rights. York's sons Edward and Richard enter, as do Old Clifford and Young Clifford, who both support Henry VI. York continues to insist that he is the king over them all, and he is soon seconded by the newly arriving Salisbury and Warwick, who both support York. Henry VI is shocked by their lack of support for him, but Salisbury insists that York is the rightful king. Henry VI reminds Salisbury of his oath to him, but Salisbury argues the sin of breaking a solemn oath is less than the sin of keeping a sinful oath. Henry VI calls for Buckingham to prepare the king's forces, and so the two sides—York and Lancaster—prepare to do battle.

Act V, Scene 2

The Battle of Saint Albans has begun. Warwick enters and challenges Old Clifford to come and meet him in the field. York then enters and declares that he wants to kill Old Clifford himself, which he does once Warwick exits and Old Clifford enters. Young Clifford enters and declares that the king's forces have been defeated by the Yorks and are now in total retreat. Young Clifford resolves not to retreat and, after seeing his father dead on the battlefield, also resolves to have his revenge on all of the Yorks, even the York children. York's son Richard enters fighting Somerset, whom he quickly kills. Henry VI and Margaret now enter, and Margaret tells Henry VI that he must get a grip on himself. The day is lost, but if they retreat now, they will be able to fight on again someday. Despite his own desire to destroy the Yorks, even Young Clifford agrees that they must retreat for the time being back to London, where they may be able to rally more troops and stop the advance of the Yorks.

Act V, Scene 3

Having won the Battle of Saint Albans, York asks if Salisbury is alive and well. Richard tells his father that he saw and helped Salisbury three times during the battle and that Salisbury insisted on fighting on to the very end. Salisbury enters and thanks Richard for his brave assistance during the battle. He then reminds York that they need to pursue Henry VI and his forces in order to keep them from regrouping and fighting again. York believes that Henry VI is on his way to London to call a parliament, so he and the rest resolve to arrive there first. Warwick ends the play with the hope that the victory they enjoyed today is only the precursor to the victories to come.

CHARACTER LIST

King Henry VI King of England. Despite his good intentions, Henry VI has tremendous difficulty running his kingdom throughout the play. Seen by some as being too pious and by others as being too weak, Henry VI finds himself dominated by those around him. Margaret and Suffolk contrive to ruin Gloucester so that they can better control the king, and York plans to take advantage of Henry VI's weakness so that he can seize the crown for himself. Henry VI tries to do the right thing, but he is powerless when it comes to saving Gloucester, and he fails to deal with the threats of both Jack Cade and York.

Queen Margaret Queen of England. Margaret has come from France to marry Henry VI, but the marriage terms and her relationship with Suffolk anger many in the court. In an attempt to gain more power, Margaret connives first to bring Gloucester down and then to murder him. After Suffolk's murder, she vows to take revenge on her enemies, especially York.

Duke Humphrey of Gloucester The Lord Protector of England. Gloucester is Henry VI's uncle and most trusted adviser. His power in the court makes him several enemies, and after his wife Eleanor's arrest and exile, he is stripped of his status as Lord Protector. His enemies first conspire to have him arrested for treason, and then they decide to murder him when they fear that Henry VI may relent and set him free.

Duchess Eleanor Gloucester's wife. Eleanor is highly ambitious and tries to get Gloucester to seize the crown for himself. When Gloucester refuses, Eleanor attempts to conjure up a Spirit that will prophesy her political future, not realizing that she has been set up by Gloucester's enemies, who seek to ruin him by ruining her. After she is arrested, Eleanor is forced to do a penitential walk through the streets of London before going into exile on the Isle of Man.

Cardinal Beaufort, Bishop of Winchester The Cardinal is Gloucester's most hated enemy. First, he ruins Gloucester's attempts to warn the court of Suffolk's ambitions, and then, he joins Margaret, Suffolk, and the others in the murder of Gloucester. After the murder, the Cardinal is suddenly taken ill, and he dies in delirium over his crimes.

William de la Pole, Duke of Suffolk After arranging the marriage between Henry VI and Margaret, William becomes the Duke of Suffolk. Suffolk is Margaret's most ardent supporter in the court, so much so that there is some speculation that the two are lovers. Suffolk arranges for Eleanor to be arrested, and he takes part in the arrest and murder of Gloucester. After the murder is discovered, Suffolk is banished to France by Henry VI, but the ship carrying him there is taken and Suffolk is beheaded by pirates.

Duke of Somerset Somerset is York's most hated enemy. He becomes regent of France, and when France is lost, York brings an army to England in an attempt to have him arrested for treason. Margaret sets him free, causing York to announce his claim to the crown. Somerset is killed during the Battle of Saint Albans by York's son Richard.

Duke of Buckingham Buckingham is present at the arrest of Eleanor, and he also leads the army that defeats Jack Cade's rebellion. Buckingham also leads the army that comes out to confront York. He initially accepts York's story, but when York declares himself the rightful heir, Buckingham gives his support to Henry VI.

Lord Clifford A supporter of Henry VI. He manages to win over Jack Cade's followers by evoking the memory of Henry V. York kills him during the Battle of Saint Albans.

Young Clifford Lord Clifford's son and a supporter of Henry VI. After his father is killed at the Battle of Saint Albans, Young Clifford swears to revenge himself upon the entire House of York, including the children.

Richard Plantagenet, Duke of York York claims the throne through Edmund Mortimer, although he does not want to proclaim this until the time is right and Henry VI is weak enough. York manages to win Salisbury and Warwick over to his side. He also takes part in the conspiracy to kill Gloucester, whom York sees as an obstacle in his path. York is given an army to quell a rebellion in Ireland, although he uses it to further his own ambitions. He gets Jack Cade to start a rebellion in England to unsettle the country and provide York with the opportunity for seizing the crown. York returns with the intention to arrest Somerset, but when Somerset is released, York declares himself to be the rightful heir to the crown. This leads to the Battle of Saint Albans, during which York kills Old Clifford and wins a victory over King Henry's forces.

Edward, Earl of March York's son.

Richard York's son. At the Battle of Saint Albans, he kills Somerset and saves Salisbury's life three times.

Earl of Salisbury A supporter of York. After the murder of Gloucester, Salisbury and Warwick enter with the Commons declaring justice, which leads to Suffolk's banishment. Salisbury supports York when he declares himself to be the rightful heir to the crown, and he also takes part at the Battle of Saint Albans, fighting on bravely despite his advanced age.

Earl of Warwick Salisbury's son and a supporter of York. Warwick takes part in the exposure and exile of Suffolk. He also takes part in the Battle of Saint Albans. York sees Warwick as his strongest supporter, so much so that Warwick is eventually known as the "Kingmaker."

Thomas Horner An armorer. Horner is accused by Peter of declaring that York should be king. Thomas refutes this, but he confesses after he is defeated in a trial by combat.

Peter Thump Thomas Horner's apprentice. Peter makes the accusation against his master and later defeats him during a trial by combat.

John Hume A priest and Eleanor's attendant. Eleanor pays him to gather the conjurer who will call forth a Spirit for her. Hume betrays Eleanor to her enemies, but he is later betrayed when her enemies have him arrested and executed along with the rest.

John Southwell A priest. Southwell is hired by Eleanor to conjure up the Spirit that will tell her political future. He is later arrested and executed for treason.

Margery Jourdayne A witch. Margery is hired by Eleanor to conjure up the Spirit that will tell her political future. She is later arrested and executed for treason.

Roger Bolingbroke A conjurer. Roger is hired by Eleanor to conjure up the Spirit that will tell her political future. He is later arrested and executed for treason.

Spirit Either a genuine spirit or a theatrical trick used to trick Eleanor. The Spirit makes a number of prophecies about Henry VI, Suffolk, and Somerset, all of which turn out to be true.

Sander Simpcox A citizen of Saint Albans. Simpcox claims to have been cured of his blindness as a result of a miracle, but Gloucester quickly shows that this is a hoax. Gloucester orders that he be whipped through every market town for punishment.

Simpcox's Wife   A citizen of Saint Albans. Simpcox's wife supports her husband's story until Gloucester proves it to be false. Although she claims that they only did it out of necessity, Gloucester orders her to be whipped, too.

Mayor of Saint Albans   A supporter of Sander Simpcox's story until it is shown to be false.

Alderman of Saint Albans   A supporter of Sander Simpcox's story until it is shown to be false.

Beadle of Saint Albans   Gloucester orders the Beadle to whip Sander Simpcox in order to prove that he can walk. After one hit, Simpcox jumps up in pain, proving his story to be false.

Gloucester's Servants   During Eleanor's penance, one of Gloucester's servants asks if they should free her, but Gloucester refuses.

Sheriff of London   Accompanies Eleanor during her penitential walk.

Sir John Stanley   Governor of the Isle of Man. Gloucester asks him to look after Eleanor, and he responds by trying to raise her spirits.

Herald   Arrives to tell Gloucester of a meeting at court with Henry VI.

Two Murderers   After the murder of Gloucester, the second Murderer expresses tremendous feelings of guilt, so it is left to the first Murderer to give the details to Suffolk.

Commons   Angered by the news of Gloucester's murder, the Commons enter the court and demand that Suffolk be either executed or banished in the name of justice.

Lieutenant   The commander of the ship that captures the ship that was carrying Suffolk into exile. He accuses Suffolk of a variety of crimes before ordering that he be beheaded.

Master of the Ship   A member of the crew on the Lieutenant's ship.

Master's Mate   A member of the crew on the Lieutenant's ship.

Walter Whitmore   A member of the crew on the Lieutenant's ship. He gets into a heated exchange with Suffolk and later beheads him at the orders of the Lieutenant.

Two Gentlemen   Suffolk's fellow prisoners on the Lieutenant's ship. They both try to offer money for their release from the pirates. After being allowed to go free, the first Gentleman decides to bring Suffolk's head back to England.

Jack Cade   The leader of the rebellion that begins in Kent and soon spreads to London. Cade claims to be the rightful heir to the throne, and he and his followers initially have a great deal of success against the king's forces. They manage to take London, but Cade is soon betrayed, and his followers forsake him. Cade flees London, only to be killed by Alexander Iden when he enters Iden's garden in search of food.

Dick the Butcher   A follower of Jack Cade.

Smith the Weaver   A follower of Jack Cade.

Sawyer   A follower of Jack Cade.

John   A follower of Jack Cade.

Emmanuel   A London clerk who is accused, tried, and executed by Cade and his followers.

Sir Humphrey Stafford   Leads the king's forces against Cade and his followers, only to be killed in the ensuing battle.

William Stafford   Leads the king's forces against Cade and his followers, only to be killed in the ensuing battle.

Lord Saye   Lord Chamberlain and Treasurer of London. Saye is targeted by Jack Cade and his followers when they enter London. Henry VI asks Saye to flee with him, but Saye refuses for fear of endangering the king's life. When he is finally caught, he is accused of a number of crimes, although his impassioned defense moves even Cade to pity. Despite this, Cade orders that Saye be executed and his head paraded throughout London.

Lord Scales   Defender of the Tower of London.

Matthew Gough   A soldier in the king's forces. He is killed during a battle in London.

Alexander Iden   An esquire of Kent. Jack Cade enters his garden in search of food, but after a heated exchange, Iden kills Cade. He then takes Cade's head to Henry VI, who is so pleased that he makes Iden a knight.

Vaux   A messenger. He brings news of the Cardinal's imminent death.

Post   A messenger. He brings news that rebellion has broken out in Ireland.

Soldier   He calls Jack Cade by his own name and is killed for insubordination.

CHARACTER STUDIES
King Henry VI

It is quite telling that Henry VI is not the first character to speak in a play that is named after him, for, in many ways, Henry VI is a character dominated by those around him. It is also quite telling that the first action described in the play, Suffolk's marriage to Margaret as Henry VI's proxy, is one that has been taken on Henry VI's behalf rather than by Henry VI himself. Unlike his father, Henry V, Henry VI is not a man of action. Some have ascribed his passivity to saintly piousness, while others have ascribed it to frail powerlessness. Crowned when he was only nine months old, Henry VI has always been ruled instead of ruling himself. In fact, one of the key issues in the play is the question of who will rule Henry VI. Will it be Gloucester? Will it be Margaret and Suffolk? Will it be the Cardinal? Henry VI's inability to rule on his own behalf makes him a victim of the ambitions of others, culminating in York's attempt to steal the crown from him directly.

As Act I, Scene 1 draws to a close, Henry VI angers those in the court by giving up Anjou and Maine in exchange for Margaret's hand. He also fails to see that others might be affronted by Suffolk's sudden rise in power and York's sudden fall. At the end of the scene, Henry VI both literally and figuratively leaves the stage for those in the court to plot and maneuver. Henry VI's insistence on leaving the running of his kingdom to others ensures that there will be very violent rivalries among those wanting to fill the power vacuum. This attitude is perfectly summed up by Henry VI's response to the question of whether York or Somerset should be regent of France: "For my part, noble lords, I care not which; / Or Somerset, or York, all's one to me" (1.3.104–105). Henry VI may not care, but his nobles certainly do.

Although Henry VI sometimes seem nonchalant and uncommitted when it comes to his responsibilities as king, he does try to maintain the peace between his feuding nobles, be they Margaret and Eleanor (1.3) or Gloucester and the Cardinal (2.1). He is genuinely grieved when Eleanor is convicted of treason, but this does not keep him from excusing Gloucester as Lord Protector as a result: "Henry will to himself / Protector be; and God shall be my hope, / My stay, my guide and lantern to my feet" (2.3.23–25).

Despite these hopes that God will guide him in ruling England, the removal of Gloucester really just means that Margaret and Suffolk will now hold sway over Henry VI. Perhaps this explains why Henry VI, even though he is convinced that "Gloucester is as innocent / From meaning treason to our royal person / As is the sucking lamb or harmless dove" (3.1.69–71), does nothing to stop his uncle from being arrested for treason. Although he feels powerless to stop Gloucester's arrest, Henry VI does put his foot down after his uncle is murdered, for he angrily banishes Suffolk from England despite, or perhaps because of, Margaret's objections. Henry VI's anger here is quite uncharacteristic of him, so much so that everyone seems shocked when he upbraids Margaret for defending Suffolk so forcefully: "Ungentle Queen, to call him gentle Suffolk! / No more, I say; if thou dost plead for him / Thou wilt but add increase unto my wrath" (3.2.290–292). His anger abates somewhat when news arrives of the Cardinal's sudden illness, and after his death, Henry VI prays that the Cardinal will find some peace: "Forbear to judge, for we are sinners all. / Close up his eyes, and . . . let us all to meditation" (3.3.31–32).

Henry VI's pity for the Cardinal indicates a return back to his former self. Powerless to stop Cade's rebellion, Henry VI considers sending a "holy bishop to entreat" the rebels to stop (4.4.9). He even considers the possibility of a "parley with Jack Cade their general" (4.4.13), indicating his naïveté about just how perilous the situation has become. Some have suggested that this naïveté is actually saintliness, as indicated by Henry VI echoing Jesus Christ as he describes the rebels: "O, graceless men! They know not what they do" (4.4.38). Whether this is true, Henry VI does begin to feel that he is no longer fit to wear the crown. Lamenting that he wished he had been born a subject, Henry VI wonders whether "England" will "curse" his "wretched rein" (4.9.49). These doubts on Henry VI's part no doubt inspire York to make his claim for the crown. Henry VI is shocked by this claim (5.1), a claim that leads to the Battle of Saint Albans and ends in the defeat of the king's forces and the victory of the Yorks. After the defeat, Henry VI believes that it is impossible to escape providence or "outrun the heavens" (5.2.73), which leads Margaret to berate him for his refusal to fight the Yorks or flee to save his life. Others have argued that Henry VI has also refused to take on the responsibilities of his office, although whether such a judgment is justified is a matter of debate.

Queen Margaret

Although many characters within the play and commentators on it consider Margaret to be a villain, one could make a strong claim that she is forced into her actions. Even before she begins to play the game, the odds against her are very high. She is from France, and several characters therefore view her as an intruder. Her marriage actually means the loss of English territory rather than the acquisition of more, and her father did not provide her with any dowry. Finally, many in the court believe that her relationship with Suffolk is romantic. She perhaps does not help matters by making Suffolk her constant companion throughout the play, the man to whom she comes to unload her grievances and woes. Her marriage leaves much to be desired, for Henry VI relies too heavily on "Gloucester's surly governance" and he is too "bent on holiness" (1.3.50–57) to concern himself with his responsibilities as husband. Margaret is also jealous of Gloucester's wife, Eleanor, who makes her feel like an inferior even though she is queen. Seeing that Gloucester stands in the way

Queen Margaret in *Henry VI, Part 2*. This is a print from Charles Heath's 1848 edition of *The Heroines of Shakspeare: Comprising the Principal Female Characters in the Plays of the Great Poet. (Painting by J. W. Wright; engraving by B. Eyles)*

between her and real power, Margaret does all she can to undermine his authority: "If [Henry VI] be old enough, what needs your grace / To be Protector of his excellence?" (1.3.120–122).

After Eleanor has been arrested, Margaret does all that she can to convince Henry VI that Gloucester should lose his place as Lord Protector. She exults in her victory when Henry acquiesces: "Why, now is Henry King and Margaret Queen" (2.3.39). This is not enough though, so Margaret tries to have Gloucester arrested for treason. She and Suffolk and their allies go over a very long list of Gloucester's supposed crimes. Henry VI is convinced of Gloucester's innocence, but Margaret persists, wondering aloud "who cannot steal a shape, that means deceit" (3.1.79). Margaret succeeds, but she fears that Henry VI is "too full of foolish pity" (3.1.225) and that he might eventually free Gloucester, so she tells Suffolk and her allies that "this Gloucester should be quickly ride the world, / To rid us from the fear we have of him" (3.1.233–234). Gloucester's murder does not rid Margaret of trouble, for Henry VI turns on Suffolk and her with a vengeance, banishing the former and publicly chastising the latter.

Margaret is clearly distraught over Suffolk's banishment and her chastisement, so much so that she engages in a little chastisement herself, accusing Henry VI of being more concerned with Gloucester than he is with her: "Is all thy comfort shut in Gloucester's tomb? / Why then Queen Margaret's was ne'er thy joy" (3.2.78–79). Despite her pleas, or perhaps because of them, Margaret is unable to save Suffolk from banishment, and so the two share a tearful farewell. Suffolk seems to give himself completely over to despair, but Margaret actually gains strength from her resolve for revenge against her enemies. This resolve is strengthened further when news arrives of Suffolk's murder: "Oft have I heard that grief softens the mind / And makes it fearful and degenerate; / Think therefore on revenge and cease to weep" (4.4.1–3). She had certainly been strong even when Suffolk was alive, but now that he is dead, she becomes an even stronger character. Margaret's greatest enemy is York, so she defiantly disregards his order that Somerset be arrested: "For thousand Yorks he shall not hide his head, / But boldly stand in front him to his face" (5.1.85–86). This defiance shows itself during the Battle of Saint Albans, for Margaret is one of the only Lancastrians to keep her head after the Yorks are victorious. She chastises Henry VI for his lack of strength and promises that she will continue the fight against the Yorks. Some argue that Margaret is one of Shakespeare's greatest villains, while others insist that she is one of his strongest heroines. Whatever one's ultimate opinion of her, it is clear that Margaret is one of the most compelling characters of the first tetralogy.

Duke Humphrey of Gloucester

As Lord Protector, Gloucester begins Act 1, Scene 1 as the strongest noble in the realm; However, by the end of the play's first scene, he has already begun to face challenges on all fronts. The marriage between Henry VI and Margaret and the advancement of Suffolk both prove to be great blows to Gloucester's power, so much so that he tries to convince the other nobles that they are all in danger: "Brave peers of England, pillars of the state, / To you Duke Humphrey must unload his grief, / Your grief, the common grief of all the land" (1.1.75–77). His pleas fall on deaf ears, for many in the court are fearful and resentful of his influence over Henry VI. This influence inspires Gloucester's wife, Eleanor, to try to convince him to seize the crown for himself. Loyal to Henry VI, Gloucester angrily refuses to even consider such a thing: "may that hour, when I imagine ill / Against my King and nephew, virtuous Henry, / Be my last breathing in this mortal world!" (1.2.19–21).

Unfortunately, Gloucester's loyalty does not keep him safe, for he is constantly under attack by those who wish to remove him from his position as Lord Protector. Gloucester tries to hold his own against them, but it is becoming increasingly clear that he is fighting a losing battle. Gloucester does achieve a small victory when he uncovers a false miracle in Saint Albans, but this is almost immediately undone when news arrives of Eleanor's arrest for treason, news that brings the strongest noble in the realm to the very depths of despair: "Sorrow and grief have vanquished all my powers, / And, vanquished as I am, I yield to thee / Or to the meanest groom" (2.1.183–185). Despite his despair, Gloucester refuses to be disloyal to Henry VI, even if it means losing his wife to exile: "Eleanor, the law, thou seest, hath judged thee: / I cannot justify whom the law condemns" (2.3.15–16). Gloucester even refuses to disobey when Henry VI strips him of his position as Lord Protector, an act that leaves him vulnerable to his enemies.

Gloucester tries to do the right thing, but he is destroyed by those who do not share his moral convictions. One begins to wonder whether loyalty such as Gloucester's is actually detrimental. This question comes to the forefront as Gloucester prepares to view Eleanor's penitential walk through the streets of London (2.4). Gloucester worries about his wife's shame, but Eleanor angrily informs him that he is the one who is being shamed, for his enemies have managed to show all of London just how far Gloucester has fallen. She warns him to defend himself against these enemies, but Gloucester refuses to listen, for he believes himself to be safe so long as he remains loyal: "I must offend before I be attainted. / And had I twenty times so many foes, / And each of them had twenty times their power, / All these could not procure me any scathe / So long as I am loyal, true and crimeless" (2.4.59–63).

When Gloucester returns to the court, however, he realizes just how wrong he is, for he is immediately arrested by Suffolk for treason. Gloucester boldly defends himself against the accusations of treason, but such boldness is not enough to save him from the Tower of London. Gloucester is sent away under the control of the Cardinal, his most hated enemy in the entire realm. Although he knows that the end is near, Gloucester's thoughts still turn loyally toward the fate of Henry VI now that he can no longer protect him: "Thus is the shepherd beaten from [Henry VI's] side, / And wolves are gnarling who shall gnaw [Henry VI] first. / Ah, that my fear were false; ah, that it were! / For, good King Henry, thy decay I fear" (3.1.191–194). Gloucester's enemies fear that Henry VI may relent and try to set him free, so they conspire to have Gloucester murdered (3.2). Gloucester's loyalty to Henry VI and his refusal to bend the rules actually leave him vulnerable to those who plot his destruction, so much so that one begins to wonder whether he should have acted the way he did. However, if he had done otherwise, it is doubtful he would have been known, as he was during Shakespeare's time, as Good Duke Humphrey.

Duchess Eleanor

Although Gloucester is often characterized by his loyalty to Henry VI, Eleanor does her best to convince her husband to disobey his king and seize the crown for himself: "Put forth thy hand, reach at the

glorious gold. / What, is't too short? I'll lengthen it with mine" (1.2.11–12). Eleanor is more than willing to help Gloucester in this endeavor, but to her chagrin, Gloucester wants no part of it. Still determined to have her way, Eleanor tells her husband of her dream the night before, when she imagined herself at Westminster with "Henry and Dame Margaret kneeled to me, / And on my head did set the diadem" (1.2.39–40). Gloucester tries to quash these dreams, but Eleanor will not listen. After her husband has left, she recruits Hume to gather conjurers to bring forth a spirit to prophesy her political future. She is quite excited about what the spirit may reveal, but she does not realize that she has been betrayed, for Hume has been paid by her enemies who plan to have her charged with treason. Although Margaret certainly would like to see Eleanor fall, the main reason why she is targeted is because her husband's enemies want to use this as an excuse to bring down Gloucester.

Eleanor is arrested after the conjuration (1.4), which leads Henry VI to sentence her to do a penitential walk through the streets of London before going into exile on the Isle of Man, a sentence she despairingly accepts: "welcome is banishment, welcome were my death" (2.3.14). This despair soon turns to anger though when Eleanor runs into Gloucester during her walk of penitence. Gloucester is saddened by her shame, but she assures him that he is the one who is really being shamed, for now all of London can see how weak he has become: "Come you, my lord, to see my open shame? / Now thou dost penance too. Look how they gaze!" (2.4.19–20). Gloucester asks her to accept her punishment with stoical patience, the very thing she cannot do. She is angry that he has done nothing to save her, but she is angrier still that he is doing nothing to save himself: "be thou mild and stir not at my shame, / Nor stir at nothing, till the axe of death / Hang over thee, as sure it shortly will" (2.4.48–50). Gloucester still will not listen to her advice and warnings, and he leaves her with only his tears. His exit fills Eleanor with despair once again, and she now desires nothing more than "death, at whose name [she] oft have been afeared, / Because

[she] wished this world's eternity" (2.4.39–90). She also says that she will never remove the penitential sheet, even though she is now allowed to do so: "My shame will not be lifted with my sheet: / No, it will hang upon my richest robes / And show itself, attire me how I can" (2.4.107–109). Despite her fall, one stops short of simply characterizing her as a villain. Her advice to her husband may seem overly ambitious, but if Gloucester had listened to at least some of it, he might not have been destroyed and killed by his enemies. Perhaps, if her husband can be categorized as a loyalist, Eleanor can be categorized as a realist, for her warnings show that she understands the dangers of the court far more clearly than he does.

Duke of Suffolk

Suffolk is an interesting character, for he rises higher and falls lower than probably any other character in the play. William de la Pole is made the Duke of Suffolk by Henry VI in return for arranging the royal marriage, but his new position, his relationship with Margaret, and the terms of the marriage earn him many enemies. His relationship with Margaret, be it romantic or otherwise, is certainly quite strong. They both turn to each other as they try to gain a foothold of power in the often perilous court, as he reminds her: "As I was cause / Your highness came to England, so will I / In England work your grace's full content" (1.3.68–70). He has already laid the trap that will lead to Eleanor's arrest, and he assures Margaret that her other rivals will all soon be removed: "one by one we'll weed them all at last, / And you yourself shall steer the happy realm" (1.3.102–103). He continues his aid by casting aspersions on Gloucester's character, and after Eleanor has been arrested, Suffolk's is one of the strongest voices for Gloucester's removal from the post of Lord Protector.

Despite this removal, Suffolk and Margaret continue to see Gloucester as their biggest threat, so they desperately try to convince Henry VI that Gloucester should be arrested for treason. Suffolk uses every rhetorical device at his disposal to do this, claiming that Gloucester himself was behind Eleanor's actions and reminding Henry VI that although Gloucester seems loyal, "the fox barks not when he would steal the lamb" (3.1.55). Henry VI is not convinced by Suffolk's rhetorical flourishes, but he is powerless to stop him from arresting Gloucester, which he does before Gloucester has a chance to defend himself. Gloucester's arrest would seem to be a triumph, for now Margaret and Suffolk are the most powerful nobles in the realm. However, this is not enough for them, for they fear that Henry VI may eventually change his mind and set Gloucester free.

This fear inspires Margaret and Suffolk to conspire with others to murder Gloucester. The Cardinal argues that Gloucester could be tried and executed, but Suffolk argues that murder is the only way to ensure that Gloucester does not escape: "The King will labour still to save [Gloucester's] life, / The commons haply rise to save his life; / And yet we have but trivial argument, / More than mistrust, that shows him worthy death" (3.1.239–242). All of the conspirators want Gloucester dead, but Suffolk is undoubtedly the one who is most thirsty for his blood: "And do not stand on quillets how to slay [Gloucester]; / Be it by gins, by snares, by subtlety, / Sleeping or waking, 'tis no matter how, / So he be dead" (3.3.261–264). He is so thirsty that he even volunteers to do the job himself, despite the fact that the Cardinal wants to do it. Suffolk hires the murderers and rewards them after the deed is done, but his ruse quickly falls apart when Henry VI sees through his attempts to pretend that Gloucester died of natural causes. Perhaps because he suspects Suffolk to be the ringleader and perhaps also because he fears Suffolk's relationship with Margaret, Henry VI directs all of his rage at the subject he had raised so high at the beginning of the play. Suffolk tries to defend himself, and Margaret speaks most passionately in his defense, but Henry VI will not yield.

And so, when the Commons demand either Suffolk's death or his banishment, Henry VI orders that Suffolk leave England immediately. Suffolk realizes that he has been tricked by York, Salisbury, and Warwick, but aside from a few barbs and challenges directed toward the latter, Suffolk accepts

Suffolk and Queen Margaret make their tearful farewells after King Henry VI banishes Suffolk for the murder of Gloucester in Act III, Scene 2 of *Henry VI, Part 2.* Print from the Boydell Shakespeare Gallery project *(Painting by William Hamilton; engraving by Isaac Taylor)*

his way to France (4.1). However, although he is afraid, he has nothing but scorn for his captors, for he reminds them that their "prisoner is a prince, / The Duke of Suffolk, William de la Pole" (4.1). Suffolk's list of stations is interesting, for it goes from the highest down to the lowest. Suffolk had started the play as William de la Pole. He had risen to be one of the strongest nobles in the realm, but now he has fallen even lower, for he is disguised in rags, a prisoner about to be beheaded by pirates. Perhaps this awareness of how far he has fallen inspires the degree of Suffolk's contempt for the pirates gathered around him, for he goes into elaborate detail about just how low their station is in comparison with his. Of course, his description of all that he has enjoyed only helps to make the extent of his fall all the more palpable. It certainly does not awe the pirates, for they quickly behead him for the number of crimes they believe he has committed against England: his relationship with Margaret, his role in the murder of Gloucester, his arrangement of Henry VI's marriage in order to suit his own ends, his responsibility for the loss of Anjou and Maine, and his role in the loss of France. The man who had once risen to the very heights of power and prestige is thus executed onboard the deck of a pirate ship as though he were a common criminal.

Richard Plantagenet, Duke of York

York is one of the most complex characters in the play, for although several characters harbor ambitions for more power, York is the one who seeks the crown itself by virtue of his descent through Edmund Mortimer. At first, York does not feel that the time is right to make his move, and he spends much of the play maneuvering in the background and waiting for the opportunity to strike. He reveals his thoughts and ambitions in a number of speeches directed at the audience, speeches that outline his plans for becoming king of England. The first of these comes at the end of Act I, Scene 1, as York bemoans the loss of English territory and the rise of Suffolk. York plans to make Salisbury and Warwick his allies, and although he will

Henry VI's sentence and begins to fall into despair. He then shares an emotional farewell with Margaret, arguably one of the most heartfelt moments in the play, for Suffolk's words to her show just how much he loves her: "where thou art, there is the world itself, / With every several pleasure in the world; / And where thou art not, desolation" (3.2. 361–364). His final words to her recall Shakespeare's sonnets and the anguish of lovers parted forever.

Suffolk's despair and anguish might seem only heightened when he is captured by pirates on

make a show of friendship toward Gloucester, he will take advantage of his troubles with the other members of the court. Henry VI is weak, but York will wait until he is even weaker before taking full advantage of the situation: "And force perforce I'll make [Henry VI] yield the crown, / Whose bookish rule hath pulled fair England down" (1.1.258–259).

His plans are initially dashed when he loses his post as regent of France (1.1) and becomes tainted by the accusations of Peter Thump concerning his ambitions (1.3), but he quickly rebounds from these setbacks when he arrests Eleanor for treason (1.4) and manages to convince Salisbury and Warwick that he is the rightful heir to the throne and that the Lancasters hold the crown "by force and not by right" (2.2.30). Warwick wants to strike quickly, but York smartly tells him that the time is not yet right to strike. He can see that Gloucester will soon be destroyed by Margaret and Suffolk, so he wants them to hold back quietly until England is in a state of turmoil and ripe for the plucking. Even though he sees Margaret and Suffolk as his enemies, he joins them in their conspiracy to first arrest and then murder Gloucester (3.1). The others do not realize that they are playing into York's hands, so much so that they even give him an army when news arrives of a rebellion in Ireland. An army is just what York needed, for now he has the power to really make a claim for the crown, as he reveals in his address to the audience: "'Twas men I lacked, and you will give them me; / I take it kindly, yet be well assured / You put sharp weapons in a madman's hands" (3.1.345–347). To further his designs even more, York has arranged for Jack Cade to begin a rebellion in England, a rebellion York hopes to gain the credit for quelling: "Why then from Ireland come I with my strength / And reap the harvest which that rascal sowed. / For Humphrey being dead, as he shall be, / And Henry put apart, the next for me" (3.1.380–383).

York's plan succeeds, for after Gloucester is murdered, the conspirators are quickly thrown into turmoil and disrepute. This is furthered by Cade's rebellion, which forces Henry VI to flee and which almost brings down the entire city of London. These victories make York confident—perhaps too confident—as he makes his way back to England with his army. He claims that he merely wants to quell the rebellion and arrest his hated enemy Somerset for treason, although it is becoming clear to everyone that York has set his sights much higher. York freely admits as much to the audience: "from Ireland thus comes York to claim his right / And pluck the crown from feeble Henry's head" (5.1.1–2). However, York's hubris at this moment makes him act rashly and forget his usual cleverness and discretion. Seeing that Somerset has not been arrested as promised, York's rage gets the better of him, and he publicly berates Henry VI and proclaims himself to be the rightful heir to the crown: "False king, why hast thou broken faith with me, / Knowing how hardly I can brook abuse? / 'King' did I call thee? No, thou art not king" (5.1.91–93). York's rage surprises everyone in the court, so much so that Henry VI wonders if he has gone mad. All throughout the play, York has been waiting for the right moment to play his hand, and now he has played it too soon. However, since he cannot take it back, York decides to dive in headfirst. He scorns Somerset's attempts to arrest him and calls forward all of his supporters, a move that ultimately leads to the Battle of Saint Albans. York kills Old Clifford, and the Yorks win the battle, the first in the Wars of the Roses. Exuberant about their victory, York and his followers determine to race to London to capitalize on it. This rashness on York's part does lead to victory in this play, but one wonders whether it might lead to his eventual downfall. It is easy to plan to take the crown when one is safely far from everyone's thoughts. It is far less easy, and far less safe, to carry that plan to fruition, for now his enemies know York's intentions, and they will do everything they can to stop him.

Jack Cade

Although he had long been seen simply as a dangerous rabble-rouser, in recent years, Cade has come to be seen in a much less hostile light. Although he only appears in one act of the play,

Cade has begun to receive a tremendous amount of attention from critics, particularly in relation to the condition of the poor in early modern England and the tradition of popular protest. Is Cade simply an agent of destruction, or does he provide a moment of hope, however brief, for an oppressed populace? York certainly sees him as the former when he describes to the audience how he manages to persuade Cade to start the rebellion. However, one's view of Cade may change as the rebellion gets under way. Cade's first speech in the play regards his supposed descent from the Mortimers, a speech that is mocked by some of Cade's own followers. This mockery begins to die down, though, as Cade begins to promise that he will make "seven halfpenny loaves sold for a penny; the three-hooped pot shall have ten hoops, and [he] will make it a felony to drink small beer" (4.2.70–72). His followers cheer Cade's promises of cheaper food and alcohol, but they also cheer his promise that "all the realm shall be in common" and that "there shall be no money" and everyone will wear "one livery" (4.2.72–79).

Such promises make Cade seem like a revolutionary until one notices at the end of his speech that, although all shall be "brothers," all shall "worship [Cade] their lord" (4.2.80–81). It is this contradiction in Cade—this promise of liberation on the one hand and this desire to fill the place of the oppressor with himself on the other—that makes Cade such an interesting character. This contradiction is complicated further as he begins to deal with those he considers to be enemies of the people. Although the accused may sometimes be guilty, Cade's desire to be sole judge, jury, and executioner makes one wonder just how revolutionary this rebellion really is. Nevertheless, Cade does show bravery as he stands up to the Staffords and the king's forces (4.2), and he even manages to defeat the royal army (4.3). He rewards Dick the Butcher for his bravery in battle (4.3), but he also orders the execution of a soldier for calling him "Jack Cade" rather than "Lord Mortimer" (4.6). Is Cade fighting on behalf of the people, or is he fighting on behalf of himself?

Regardless of who he is fighting for, there is no doubt that Cade is a good fighter. Not only does he manage to defeat the royal army, but he also manages to take almost the whole city of London. However, his fighting spirit is tainted somewhat by his desire for destruction, for he orders that both London Bridge and the Tower of London be burned to the ground (4.6). He also orders that "all the records of the realm" be burned (4.7.16), an act seen by some as being destructive and by others as being revolutionary, for these records have ruined the lives of many of the poor in England. This revolutionary zeal is tempered somewhat by Cade's declaration that his "mouth shall be the parliament of England" (4.7.17). Once again, Cade becomes more difficult to pin down. What are his real motivations? He gives a number of reasons—some logical, others less so—for executing Lord Sayes, but his delight in ordering that Sayes and his son-in-law's heads should be placed on poles makes one wonder if Cade is too bloodthirsty to be a real liberator (4.7). At the same time, his desire to kill all of the nobles seems to be motivated less by a desire to help the people and more by a desire to clear a path to power for himself: "the proudest peer in the realm shall not wear a head on his shoulders, unless he pay me tribute; there shall not a maid be married, but she shall pay to me her maidenhead ere they have it" (4.7.126–129).

Is Cade a liberator, or has he, just like the nobles in Henry VI's court, become mad with power? There are certainly grounds for arguing, as several critics have done, that Cade's rebellion serves as a parody of both York's grab for power in particular and the power-thirstiness of the court in general. Whatever his rebellion may say about the nature of power in the court, Cade's own power has reached its peak, and after the peak, comes the fall. A new royal army under Buckingham and Old Clifford manages to win Cade's followers away from him (4.8). Cade manages to momentarily win them back when he reminds them of the burdens that await them, but ultimately, he loses ground and is forced to flee. And so, the man who had once succeeded in taking London is now forced to break into a garden in Kent in search of food (4.10). Mistakenly assuming that the owner of the garden, Alexander Iden, has come to kill him for the reward, Cade challenges Iden to a fight and is killed. Perhaps not surprisingly, Cade is defiant to the end: "Iden, farewell, and be proud of thy victory. Tell Kent from me she hath lost her best man, and exhort all the world to be cowards. For I, that never feared any, am vanquished by famine, not by valour" (4.10.77–81). It is this defiance that makes Cade, regardless of his faults, such a gripping character. York may simply see Cade as a pawn in his own game for the throne, but Cade shows the audience that, whatever else he may be, he is no pawn.

DIFFICULTIES OF THE PLAY

As the rather long list of characters and character studies may suggest, one of the chief difficulties of *Henry VI, Part 2* is the large number of characters that the audience must remember and keep track of. In fact, *Henry VI, Part 2* has more characters than any other Shakespeare play. The difficulties arising from having such a large cast are further complicated by the numerous factions and counterfactions that are constantly at on another's throats throughout the play, not to mention the often confusing alliances, betrayals, and political maneuvers that make up much of the play's action. Furthermore, this play is one of four plays dealing with the reigns of Henry VI, Edward IV, and Richard III, so some audience members and readers may feel that *Henry VI, Part 2* is unintelligible on its own without reference to the other three plays. Such a view has no doubt influenced modern producers and directors of the play, who generally perform it along with the rest of the first tetralogy rather than on its own.

There is a tremendous amount of debate over whether *Henry VI, Part 2* can be seen as a single play or as merely one part of a larger cycle. The play opens with Suffolk's description of his marriage—as Henry VI's proxy—to Margaret in France, an event that saw its genesis at the end of *Henry VI, Part 1*. At the same time, *Henry VI, Part 2* ends with the Yorks' resolution to capital-ize on their victory by racing to London, which occurs at the beginning of *Henry VI, Part 3*. This can make the play difficult to understand, particularly for modern audiences unfamiliar with the large host of historical information Shakespeare packs into the play, information here discussed in the "Background" section. These audiences are largely unfamiliar with the historical works of Hall and Holinshed or even with the Wars of the Roses, so the play can almost seem too complicated to really appreciate.

Nevertheless, there are a number of plot strands that do give the play a unity and enables it to stand on its own. In fact, these strands are explicitly laid out on the title page to the first quarto of the play (1594): *"The First part of the Contention betwixt*

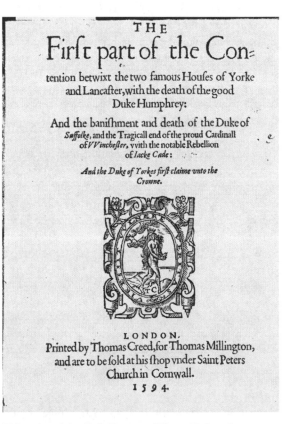

Title page of the First Quarto of *Henry VI, Part 2*, published in 1594

the two famous Houses of Yorke and Lancaster, with the death of the good Duke Humphrey: And the banishment and death of the Duke of Suffolke, and the Tragicall end of the proud Cardinal of Winchester, with the notable Rebellion of Jack Cade: and the Duke of Yorke's first claim unto the Crowne." This play contains the fall and murder of Gloucester; the rise, fall, and murder of Suffolk; the death of the Cardinal; Cade's rebellion; and York's maneuvers to gain the crown for himself, which leads to the first battle of the Wars of the Roses. These five plot strands, all of which help to culminate in the first contention between Lancaster and York, help give the play a unity that is often overlooked by those who feel that they play is seamless on its own or unintelligible without reference to the rest of the tetralogy. By keeping this in mind, one can truly begin to appreciate *Henry VI, Part 2* as a play that, whatever its strengths as part of a larger cycle, has more than enough to offer as a single demonstration of Shakespeare's genius.

Of course, the play's detractors do not only cite the play's plot or its place within the tetralogy. For many, *Henry VI, Part 2,* as an early play, does not possess the same beautiful language one associates with Shakespeare's later plays. However, *Henry VI, Part 2* does contain some very well written passages, and others are fascinating examples of Shakespeare's early experiments with the nature of both verse and prose.

KEY PASSAGES
Act 1, Scene 1, 75–122

GLOUCESTER. Brave peers of England,
  pillars of the state,
To you Duke Humphrey must unload his grief,
Your grief, the common grief of all the land.
What! did my brother Henry spend his youth,
His valour, coin and people, in the wars?
Did he so often lodge in open field,
In winter's cold and summer's parching heat,
To conquer France, his true inheritance?
And did my brother Bedford toil his wits,
To keep by policy what Henry got?
Have you yourselves, Somerset, Buckingham,

Brave York, Salisbury, and victorious Warwick,
Received deep scars in France and Normandy?
Or hath mine uncle Beaufort and myself,
With all the learned council of the realm,
Studied so long, sat in the council-house
Early and late, debating to and fro
How France and Frenchmen might be kept in
  awe,
And had his highness in his infancy
Crowned in Paris in despite of foes?
And shall these labours and these honours die?
Shall Henry's conquest, Bedford's vigilance,
Your deeds of war and all our counsel die?
O peers of England, shameful is this league!
Fatal this marriage, cancelling your fame,
Blotting your names from books of memory,
Razing the characters of your renown,
Defacing monuments of conquer'd France,
Undoing all, as all had never been!

CARDINAL. Nephew, what means this
  passionate discourse,
This peroration with such circumstance?
For France, 'tis ours; and we will keep it still.

GLOUCESTER. Ay, uncle, we will keep it, if
  we can;
But now it is impossible we should:
Suffolk, the new-made duke that rules the roast,
Hath given the duchy of Anjou and Maine
Unto the poor King Reignier, whose large style
Agrees not with the leanness of his purse.

SALISBURY. Now, by the death of Him that
  died for all,
These counties were the keys of Normandy.
But wherefore weeps Warwick, my valiant son?

WARWICK. For grief that they are past recovery:
For, were there hope to conquer them again,
My sword should shed hot blood, mine eyes
  no tears.
Anjou and Maine! myself did win them both;
Those provinces these arms of mine did
  conquer:

And are the cities, that I got with wounds,
Delivered up again with peaceful words?
Mort Dieu!

This extended scene at the very opening of the play showcases the degree of duplicity and treachery running through Henry VI's court. Immediately following the exit of Henry VI, Margaret, and Suffolk, Gloucester turns to the remaining nobles to complain about the new state of affairs. He is angry about both Suffolk's sudden advancement and the loss of English territory and France, and he tries to persuade the other nobles that they should be angry too: "shall these labours and these honours die? / Shall Henry's conquest, Bedford's viligance, / Your deeds of war and all our counsel die?" The other nobles share Gloucester's discontent, but at the same time, they are wary of his power and influence.

Later in the scene after Gloucester exits, the Cardinal declares that Gloucester is the real threat to the realm: "'tis known to you he is mine enemy, / Nay more, an enemy unto you all, / And no great friend, I fear me, to the King." The other nobles seem receptive to the Cardinal's warnings, but after he makes his exit, they express much the same doubts about him. For example, Somerset warns Buckingham that the Cardinal really only wants Gloucester's position for himself: "let us watch the haughty Cardinal; / His insolence is more intolerable / Than all the princes' in the land beside. / If Gloucester be displaced, he'll be Protector." After Somerset and Buckingham make their exit, Salisbury warns Warwick and York that none of them can be trusted. Warwick and York both agree with Salisbury, but when York is left alone onstage, he reveals that he himself is the greatest threat to the realm, for he seeks nothing less than the crown itself: "when I spy advantage, claim the crown, / For that's the golden mark I seek to hit." This dizzying array of reversals leaves one wondering if anyone in Henry VI's court can be trusted, for everyone has just betrayed everyone else. How will these betrayals play themselves out?

Act II, Scene 4, 48–63

ELEANOR. But be thou mild and blush not
  at my shame,
Nor stir at nothing till the axe of death
Hang over thee, as, sure, it shortly will;
For Suffolk, he that can do all in all
With her that hateth thee and hates us all,
And York and impious Beaufort, that false
  priest,
Have all limed bushes to betray thy wings,
And, fly thou how thou canst, they'll tangle
  thee:
But fear not thou, until thy foot be snared,
Nor never seek prevention of thy foes.

GLOUCESTER. Ah, Nell, forbear! thou
  aimest all awry;
I must offend before I be attainted;
And had I twenty times so many foes,
And each of them had twenty times their
  power,
All these could not procure me any scathe,
So long as I am loyal, true and crimeless.

Eleanor stops during her penitential walk through London to berate her husband, Duke of Gloucester, both for failing to protect her and for failing to protect himself. Gloucester thinks that he is witnessing Eleanor's shame, but she informs him that actually London is witnessing his, for now everyone can see just how far he has fallen. What rankles Eleanor most is Gloucester's unwillingness to realize that his enemies are holding "the axe of death" over his head. Not only does Gloucester not realize this, but he also insists on doing nothing about it. Even when Eleanor specifically names all of Gloucester's enemies, he still accuses her of aiming "all awry" with her accusations. Believing that he "must offend before [he] be attainted," Gloucester feels that he is safe "so long as [he is] loyal, true and crimeless." What Gloucester does not realize is that loyalty cannot save him from those who are disloyal, false, and criminal. Eleanor's advice seems harsh, but is she wrong? Given what happens to Gloucester in the end, one won-

Eleanor berates Gloucester during her penitential walk in Act II, Scene 4 of *Henry VI, Part 2*, in this 1740 engraving. *(Illustration and engraving by Hubert Gravelot)*

ders if perhaps he should have listened more to his wife's harsh advice.

Act III, Scene 1, 4–65

QUEEN MARGARET. Can you not see? or will ye not observe
The strangeness of his alter'd countenance?
With what a majesty he bears himself,
How insolent of late he is become,
How proud, how peremptory, and unlike himself?
We know the time since he was mild and affable,
And if we did but glance a far-off look,
Immediately he was upon his knee,
That all the court admired him for submission:
But meet him now, and, be it in the morn,
When every one will give the time of day,
He knits his brow and shows an angry eye,
And passeth by with stiff unbowed knee,
Disdaining duty that to us belongs.
Small curs are not regarded when they grin;
But great men tremble when the lion roars;
And Humphrey is no little man in England.
First note that he is near you in descent,
And should you fall, he as the next will mount.
Me seemeth then it is no policy,
Respecting what a rancorous mind he bears
And his advantage following your decease,
That he should come about your royal person
Or be admitted to your highness' council.
By flattery hath he won the commons' hearts,
And when he please to make commotion,
Tis to be fear'd they all will follow him.
Now 'tis the spring, and weeds are shallow-rooted;
Suffer them now, and they'll o'ergrow the garden
And choke the herbs for want of husbandry.
The reverent care I bear unto my lord
Made me collect these dangers in the duke.
If it be fond, call it a woman's fear;
Which fear if better reasons can supplant,
I will subscribe and say I wrong'd the duke.
My Lord of Suffolk, Buckingham, and York,
Reprove my allegation, if you can;
Or else conclude my words effectual.

SUFFOLK. Well hath your highness seen into this duke;
And, had I first been put to speak my mind,
I think I should have told your grace's tale.
The duchess, by his subornation,
Upon my life, began her devilish practises:
Or, if he were not privy to those faults,

Yet, by reputing of his high descent,
As next the king he was successive heir,
And such high vaunts of his nobility,
Did instigate the bedlam brain-sick duchess
By wicked means to frame our sovereign's fall.
Smooth runs the water where the brook is deep;
And in his simple show he harbours treason.
The fox barks not when he would steal the lamb.
No, no, my sovereign; Gloucester is a man
Unsounded yet and full of deep deceit.

CARDINAL. Did he not, contrary to form of
law,
Devise strange deaths for small offences done?

YORK. And did he not, in his protectorship,
Levy great sums of money through the realm
For soldiers' pay in France, and never sent it?
By means whereof the towns each day revolted.

BUCKINGHAM. Tut, these are petty faults
to faults unknown.
Which time will bring to light in smooth
Duke Humphrey.

Gloucester is late coming to Henry VI's court, so his enemies seize the opportunity to present him to Henry VI in the worst possible light. Margaret begins by saying that Gloucester's demeanor has changed lately and that he is now acting as though he should be ruling the realm. This accusation is furthered by Margaret's charge that Gloucester is trying to rally the Commons to his side in order to start a rebellion: "By flattery hath he won the commons' hearts; / And when he please to make commotion, / 'Tis to be feared they all will follow him." Suffolk complements Margaret's charges by reminding Henry VI that Gloucester is next in line to the throne and that he "did instigate the bedlam brainsick Duchess / By wicked means to frame our sovereign's fall." This charge is particularly baseless, for Suffolk knows that Gloucester has had nothing to do with his wife's treachery. Nevertheless, he and the others continue until Bucking-

ham suggests that these known faults pale beside Gloucester's unknown ones: "Tut, these are petty faults to faults unknown / Which time will bring to light in smooth Duke Humphrey."

Henry VI does not believe them, so, as the scene continues, they apply even more pressure. If Gloucester seems innocent, that is only because he is doing his best to hide his guilty heart: "Ah, what's more dangerous than this fond affiance? / Seems he a dove? His feathers are but borrowed, / For he's disposed as the hateful raven." Gloucester's enemies eventually succeed in having him arrested, although their victory is due as much to Henry VI's weakness as it is to their rhetorical prowess. Nevertheless, their accusations do reveal something quite interesting. Although they are ostensibly talking about Gloucester, every accusation they level against him can be just as easily leveled against themselves. They say that Henry VI should fear Gloucester's ambitions, but they are the ones who are ambitious, for they desire to take Gloucester's place once he is gone. With so much duplicity and deceit, can anyone ever really be trusted to speak the truth?

Act IV, Scene 2, 68–81

CADE. Be brave, for your captain is brave, and
vows reformation. There shall be in England
seven half-penny loaves sold for a penny; the
three-hooped pot shall have ten hoops, and
I will make it a felony to drink small beer.
All the realm shall be in common, and in
Cheapside shall my palfrey go to grass. And
when I am king, as king I will be—

ALL. God save your majesty!

CADE. I thank you, good people.—There
shall be no money, all shall eat and drink on
my score, and I will apparel them all in one
livery, that they may agree like brothers and
worship me their lord.

Jack Cade's opening remarks to his followers are interesting, for in many ways they reveal the incredibly contradictory nature of both his character and the rebellion that he has begun. After having gone through the supposed justification for why he should be the king of England, Cade goes on to make his promises to his followers. He first tells them that he "vows reformation," suggesting that he genuinely desires to change the conditions for the poor in England. He then goes on to say that there will be cheap food and alcohol for all of the people. Making food cheaper would certainly be a reform for the better, but the promise of cheap alcohol threatens to turn a fight for liberation into a drunken riot. Cade promises that "all the realm shall be in common" and that enclosure will be stopped, two measures that would seem to be good for the people. However, Cade's populist rhetoric is soon taken down a notch when he begins to speculate about his coming kingship. These contradictions continue when Cade says that all shall be appareled "in one livery," indicating an attempt to bring everyone together, but then says that all shall "agree like brothers and worship me their lord." Where does Cade really stand? Is he fighting on behalf of the people, or is he fighting on behalf of himself? Does Cade want to liberate the people from their oppressors, or does he simply want to take the oppressors' place? Cade is a contradictory character, and his motives are never clear, especially as indicated by the above speech.

Act V, Scene 1, 142–156

YORK. Look in a glass, and call thy image so:
I am thy king, and thou a false-heart traitor.
Call hither to the stake my two brave bears,
That with the very shaking of their chains
They may astonish these fell-lurking curs:
Bid Salisbury and Warwick come to me.
[Enter WARWICK and SALISBURY]

CLIFFORD. Are these thy bears? we'll bait
  thy bears to death.
And manacle the bear-ward in their chains,
If thou darest bring them to the baiting place.

RICHARD Oft have I seen a hot o'erweening
  cur
Run back and bite, because he was
  withheld;
Who, being suffer'd with the bear's fell
  paw,
Hath clapp'd his tail between his legs and
  cried:
And such a piece of service will you do,
If you oppose yourselves to match Lord
  Warwick

This passage is short, and York's son Richard's speech seems to be oddly awkward, so much so that the sense of his lines are not all that easy to understand. Nevertheless, the speech does point to one of the larger themes of the play: the bestial nature of humanity, particularly during times of war. York has called forward Salisbury and Warwick, whom he refers to as his "two brave bears." Warwick's heraldic device was a bear, so there is a straightforward explanation for calling them so. Nevertheless, the reference to the bear brings to mind other things as well. Mocking both York and Warwick, Old Clifford imagines himself in a baiting place where he defeats both the bearherd York and the bear Warwick. Richard warns Old Clifford not to mock, for Warwick is far more dangerous than he realizes. During Shakespeare's time bearbaiting was an incredibly popular activity, so it is no surprise that he should include references to it in his plays. However, his reference to it here brings to mind a compelling image: a bear that seems placid but is actually about to break its chains and wreak violent havoc. This is an interesting metaphor for what is happening in this scene, for the Yorks and the Lancasters are exchanging relatively harmless verbal attacks in the court before exchanging very harmful physical attacks on the battlefield. At the same time, war, like the unchained bear, is very difficult to restrain once it has been let loose. And so, this image of a bear that is about to break its chains seems very appropriate at the very moment that the Wars of the Roses are about to begin.

DIFFICULT PASSAGES
Act III, Scene 2, 73–121

QUEEN MARGARET. Be woe for me, more
  wretched than he is.
What, dost thou turn away and hide thy face?
I am no loathsome leper; look on me.
What! art thou, like the adder, waxen deaf?
Be poisonous too and kill thy forlorn queen.
Is all thy comfort shut in Gloucester's tomb?
Why, then, dame Margaret was ne'er thy joy.
Erect his statue and worship it,
And make my image but an alehouse sign.
Was I for this nigh wreck'd upon the sea
And twice by awkward wind from England's
  bank
Drove back again unto my native clime?
What boded this, but well forewarning wind
Did seem to say 'Seek not a scorpion's nest,
Nor set no footing on this unkind shore'?
What did I then, but cursed the gentle gusts
And he that loosed them forth their brazen
  caves:
And bid them blow towards England's blessed
  shore,
Or turn our stern upon a dreadful rock
Yet Æolus would not be a murderer,
But left that hateful office unto thee:
The pretty-vaulting sea refused to drown me,
Knowing that thou wouldst have me drown'd
  on shore,
With tears as salt as sea, through thy
  unkindness:
The splitting rocks cower'd in the sinking
  sands
And would not dash me with their ragged
  sides,
Because thy flinty heart, more hard than they,
Might in thy palace perish Margaret.
As far as I could ken thy chalky cliffs,
When from thy shore the tempest beat us back,
I stood upon the hatches in the storm,
And when the dusky sky began to rob
My earnest-gaping sight of thy land's view,
I took a costly jewel from my neck,
A heart it was, bound in with diamonds,
And threw it towards thy land: the sea
  received it,
And so I wish'd thy body might my heart:
And even with this I lost fair England's view
And bid mine eyes be packing with my heart
And call'd them blind and dusky spectacles,
For losing ken of Albion's wished coast.
How often have I tempted Suffolk's tongue,
The agent of thy foul inconstancy,
To sit and witch me, as Ascanius did
When he to madding Dido would unfold
His father's acts commenced in burning Troy!
Am I not witch'd like her? or thou not false
  like him?
Ay me, I can no more! die, Margaret!
For Henry weeps that thou dost live so long.

Not only is this the longest speech (49 lines) in *Henry VI, Part 2*, but it is also one of the most difficult to understand. Some have even questioned its place in the play, and many productions choose to cut it out altogether. Furthermore, the speech never receives a reply. Although it sometimes deals with other issues, the main purport of the speech is that Henry VI, by caring so much about Gloucester's death, shows that he no longer cares about Margaret: "Is all thy comfort shut in Gloucester's tomb? / Why the Queen Margaret was ne'er thy joy." Margaret actually takes this one step further as she begins to question her husband; not only does he love Gloucester more, but he actually wishes that his wife was dead. She goes on to describe the many trials and tribulations she had to endure on her sea voyage to England: "What did I then, but cursed the gentle gusts / And he that loosed them forth their brazen caves / And bid them blow towards England's blessed shore / Or turn our stern upon a dreadful rock." These ordeals did not abate, for many times did she almost perish along the way. She even threw "a costly jewel" into the ocean as an expression of how much she loved Henry VI. Suffolk had told Margaret many stories about Henry VI, stories that were so compelling that she fell in love with him before she even set foot on English soil. However, just as Dido was tricked into loving Aeneas, so too was Margaret tricked into loving Henry VI, for he does not love her at all. The speech is rich in rhetorical devices and classical allusions, but what purpose does it serve the action? Some have argued that it serves none, but that is not necessarily true. Perhaps Margaret is trying to avert Henry VI's rage at Suffolk. Perhaps she is trying to win his sympathy for herself. Even if she fails on either or both counts, that does not mean that the speech is redundant, for it would then showcase the degree to which Margaret's role in Gloucester's murder has caused a rift between her and Henry VI that might never be healed.

CRITICAL INTRODUCTION
TO THE PLAY

The historical period presented in *Henry VI, Part 2* is important to understand, but this is complicated by Shakespeare's tendency to rearrange, telescope, and excise key historical events. Of course, Shakespeare was a dramatist, not a historian, and he was willing to change his historical material in order to suit the demands of the stage. Nevertheless, Shakespeare does stay closer to the chronicles than one might expect, and some critics have actually praised him for his keen historical understanding. In terms of historical time, it is important to keep in mind that the play begins with the marriage of Henry VI and Margaret in 1445 and ends with the first battle of Saint Albans in 1455—not to be confused with the second battle of Saint Albans in 1461. Although this means that the play has a historical time frame of 10 years, Shakespeare does not indicate that the events he presents occur over 10 years. Events come fast and furious, and Shakespeare even includes events that occurred both before 1445 and after 1455.

All the same, an understanding of the historical period that Shakespeare presents is necessary to an understanding of the play. *Henry VI, Part 2* opens with England in possession of a large part of France. These possessions come into almost immediate peril when Henry VI agrees to give up both Anjou and Maine in exchange for Margaret's hand in marriage. They come into further peril when Henry VI removes York from his position as regent of France and replaces him with Somerset. Unlike *Henry VI, Part 1*, which contains a number of scenes set in France and deals with the war between English and French forces, *Henry VI, Part 2* does not mention France again until news arrives that all of the English territories have been lost (3.1), a reference to the loss of Normandy in 1448–49. Although there are a host of historical, political, and military reasons to explain the loss of French territory, many characters in the play blame the actions of Margaret, Suffolk, and Somerset. One of the reasons given by the Lieutenant who orders Suffolk's execution is that he is responsible for "Anjou and Maine [being] sold to France" and the loss of both Normandy and Picardy (4.1). Likewise, York demands Somerset's arrest because of his role in the loss of French territory (5.1).

Another important historical event that occurs during *Henry VI, Part 2* is the start of the Wars of the Roses. Both Henry VI's weakness and York's ambitions are presented as the primary causes behind this civil conflict, a conflict whose consequences Shakespeare would fully explore in *Henry VI, Part 3*. Shakespeare agrees with the historical chronicles in presenting Henry VI as a king too weak to keep control of his kingdom and the feuding nobles in his court. This weakness was exacerbated by the death of Gloucester in 1447, or Act III, Scene 2 of *Henry VI, Part 2*. Although there is still some speculation about whether the historical Gloucester was actually murdered, Shakespeare presents the conspiracy to kill Gloucester in great detail (3.1). The murderers even appear onstage to be rewarded by Suffolk in Act III, Scene 2. Historically, Suffolk became the power behind the throne for almost three years following Gloucester's death, but in *Henry VI, Part 2* the murder of Gloucester leads to Suffolk's immediate banishment (3.2) and later execution aboard the pirate ship (4.1). Shakespeare is correct in pairing the deaths of Gloucester and the Cardinal so closely together, for both nobles died within less than two months of each other.

In both the chronicles and in *Henry VI, Part 2,* the deaths of Gloucester, the Cardinal, and Suffolk lead to turmoil in England, for Jack Cade's rebellion broke out in 1450, the same year as Suffolk's death. The circumstances surrounding the historical Cade's rebellion are different from those of his dramatic counterpart in *Henry VI, Part 2,* which seem to be just as much inspired by the Peasant's Revolt of 1381, but both in the chronicle and on the stage, the results of the rebellion are the same: even more turmoil in England. Although in *Henry VI, Part 2,* York makes his play for the crown before the rebellion is even over, the historical York did not do so until 1452, nearly two years after the rebellion was over and Cade was killed. Nevertheless, the results of York's actions are the same both in the chronicle and *Henry VI, Part 2,* for in both, they lead to the Battle of Saint Albans in 1455 and the outbreak of the Wars of the Roses. In *Henry VI, Part 2,* Shakespeare takes a very complicated and unyielding part of English history and manages to turn it into a very compelling and exciting drama.

Themes

Given that *Henry VI, Part 2* deals with the outbreak of the Wars of the Roses, it is perhaps not surprising that many of the play's themes are political in nature: the dangers of factionalism; the nature of ambition; the nature, and perhaps limits, of loyalty; the dangers of having a weak leader; the nature of war; the causes behind, and outcomes of, popular uprisings; the destruction that ultimately comes from civil strife. However, the play also deals with a number of other themes: the nature of deceit, the dangers of xenophobia, the nature of jealousy, the conflict between stoicism and despair, the nature of love, the nature of misogyny and the role of women, the concerns of the poor, and the joys of the country over the care of the court.

As with other Shakespearean plays, these themes are explored in a number of interesting ways, be it setting, character, language, or otherwise. Given that the play is concerned with politics, the themes are, of course, dealt with on the public level. How-ever, the themes are also dealt with on the private level, as many characters find themselves questioning their positions and beliefs as a result of their experiences. For example, Gloucester and Eleanor debate the nature of loyalty, with the former believing in it wholeheartedly and the latter arguing that loyalty should not keep one from achieving one's ambitions. As they are both powerful members of the kingdom, this debate has public ramifications. However, as they are husband and wife, too, the debate also has private ones, for although Gloucester remains loyal to King Henry VI, he allows his wife, Eleanor, to be accused, arrested, and tried for treason. This intermingling of the private and public spheres is emphasized by Shakespeare's staging of the debates between Gloucester and Eleanor, for the first time they see each other, they are in the privacy of their own home (1.2), while the last time they see each other, they are in the very public streets of London (2.4). Likewise, although the conflicts among Henry VI's nobles initially seem to be largely confined to his court, the rebellion of Cade and his followers indicates that these conflicts are no longer private, but public.

Sometimes Shakespeare chooses to illustrate a theme by comparing and contrasting two characters' very different responses to it. For example, the theme of kingship could be explored by looking at the actions of Henry VI, the king of England, and of York, the man who wants to be the king of England. Henry VI was crowned when he was only nine months old, but he has never wanted the position of king: "Was never a subject so longed to be a king / As I do long and wish to be a subject" (4.9.5–6). Henry VI's reluctance to rule means that the other characters in the play spend most of their time fighting one another for control of both the king and the country. Henry VI tries to keep the peace, but he is ultimately powerless to save even his beloved uncle Gloucester, standing aside while the others seal his fate: "My lords, what to your wisdoms seemeth best / Do, or undo, as if ourself were here" (3.1.195–196). Although there is certainly an element of poignant sadness to Henry VI, one also can see the dangers of having a

Henry VI makes York the regent of France in this 18th-century depiction of Act 1, Scene 1 of *Henry VI, Part 2. (Illustration by Dietrich; engraving by Franke)*

king so weak. Unlike Henry VI, York wants to be king, and unlike Henry VI, York would never allow those around him to have so much control. There is something exhilarating about York's energy, cleverness, and strength, characteristics that are almost entirely lacking in Henry VI. However, these characteristics ultimately lead York to take part in Gloucester's murder, engineer a rebellion in England, and start the Wars of the Roses. Weakness in a king can be disastrous, but it can also be disastrous to act as York does.

Shakespeare also explores themes through language, be it in the form of poetry or prose. Shakespeare is often regarded as the greatest writer in the English language, a writer who used that language to express some of the most moving and inspiring speeches ever committed to paper. However, although Shakespeare was well aware of language's

capacity to move and inspire, he was also aware of the many ways in which language could mislead and deceive. Some of the greatest speeches in the play are concerned with this very topic. For example, York's addresses to the audience, particularly at the end of Act I, Scene 1 and Act III, Scene 1 are incredibly compelling and exciting pieces of dramatic writing: The audience is being compelled and excited by a character who is outlining his plan to bring down Henry VI and seize the crown for himself. At the same time, Margaret, Suffolk, and Gloucester's other enemies use every rhetorical tool at their disposal to convince Henry VI that Gloucester is a dangerous traitor. In speeches that seem more and more convincing, they warn Henry VI not to be deceived by Gloucester's show of loyalty: "What's more dangerous than this fond affiance? / Seems he a dove? His feather are but borrowed, / For he's disposed as the hateful raven. / Is he a lamb? His skin is surely lent him, / For he's inclined as is the ravenous wolves" (3.1.74–78). What makes speeches like this so interesting is that beautifully wrought poetry is being used to point away from the truth. If anything, Gloucester's enemies are the ravens and the wolves, not Gloucester himself. Language can be used to bring the truth into the light, but it can also be used to shift the light in the wrong direction. Ingeniously, Shakespeare chose to explore the deceitful nature of language and poetry through the use of language and poetry.

Structure
Many critics have complained that *Henry VI, Part 2* is a poorly constructed play, something that they attribute to the play being one of Shakespeare's earliest. However, the play is far less poorly constructed than it seems. For example, if one of the major themes of *Henry VI, Part 2* is the nature of both loyalty and treachery, then the first act of the play explores this theme in a variety of interesting ways. The play opens with the marriage between Henry VI and Margaret and the advancement of Suffolk, both of which inspire the entire court to publicly rejoice. Yet, the moment Henry VI,

Margaret, and Suffolk leave the stage, Gloucester tries to warn the other courtiers about the dangers of both the marriage and the ambitions of Suffolk. Although Gloucester is often seen as being a very loyal figure, it is interesting that he should wait until after Henry VI has exited to make these accusations. No one besides the Cardinal publicly challenges Gloucester, but the moment Gloucester leaves the stage, they all begin to complain about his influence over the king. They seem to be aligning themselves with the Cardinal, but the moment the Cardinal leaves the stage, Buckingham and Somerset both say that they do not trust the Cardinal any more than they trust Gloucester. After they leave the stage, Salisbury, Warwick, and York all agree that they do not trust Suffolk, the Cardinal, Buckingham, or Somerset. Finally, after Salisbury and Warwick leave the stage, York declares that he does not trust any of them, for he wants to seize power for himself alone.

The theme of loyalty and treachery continues in Act I, Scene 2, as Eleanor tries to convince Gloucester to betray Henry VI and become king. Gloucester refuses, but Eleanor continues to try to find a way to put her husband and herself on the throne. However, her servant, Hume, betrays her plan to Gloucester's enemies, who seek to destroy Gloucester via Eleanor. This theme is pursued further in Act I, Scene 3, as Peter betrays his master, Thomas, of treachery, and York, who the audience knows is a traitor, acts completely shocked when it is even suggested that he might have ambitions for the crown. York is also involved in the arrest of Eleanor, who has been betrayed by Hume, who has been betrayed by Suffolk, for he is interested along with the rest. All of this betrayal prepares the audiences for the betrayals that will begin to come with increasing speed as the play progresses.

Aside from Act II, Scene 2, which deals with York's recruitment of Salisbury and Warwick in his bid for the crown, the rest of the second act is devoted to the fall of Gloucester. This is explored through the Gloucester's triumph at Saint Albans, which is immediately followed by news that Eleanor has been arrested (2.1), the sentencing of Elea-

nor and Gloucester's loss of his position as Lord Protector (2.3), and Eleanor's penitential walk through London and her warnings to Gloucester to be careful and beware of the ambitions of others (2.4). This then builds up to the very dramatic third act, which deals with Gloucester's arrest and the conspiracy to murder him (3.1), York's plans to take the crown as a result of the turmoil that will be caused by Gloucester's murder (3.1), and Gloucester's murder and its aftermath (3.2). Perhaps it is not surprising that York's act of recruitment and his declaration of his plans are interspersed throughout these two acts, two acts that are primarily concerned with Gloucester's fall and murder. York is the one who will benefit the most from this murder, which he needs to happen in order to make his plans come to fruition.

Another part of that plan is the rebellion of Cade and his followers, which York hopes will cause so much confusion in England that he will be able to easily seize control. This rebellion takes up the whole of the fourth act: It is first reported by the Lieutenant (4.1), and it ends with Cade's death at the hands of Iden (4.10). It is worth noting that almost every scene in the fourth act features the rebellion. Even the two that do not feature it (4.4 and 4.9) deal with the consequences of it: They are two very short scenes featuring Henry VI's feeble reactions to the rebellion that threatens to topple him from power. The brevity of these scenes may seem a failing, but in fact they indicate the degree to which Henry VI's inability to act puts him ever more on the sidelines while everyone else determines who will rule. The degree of Henry VI's failings as king and the question of who should rule in his place are, thus, already prepared for by the time York reenters the play at the beginning of the fifth act, the act that features his declaration of his claim to the throne and the drawing of battle lines (5.1), the Battle of Saint Albans itself (5.2), and the result of the Yorks' victory (5.3). And so, although the structure of *Henry VI, Part 2* may seem too wide-ranging and episodic, it is actually far better structured and designed than many of its critics give it credit for.

Style and Imagery

As with all of Shakespeare's plays, imagery is used to elucidate themes and explore their potential. Three of these themes are loyalty and disloyalty, the bestial behavior of human beings, and the nature of ambition.

The Cardinal begins to elaborate on this first theme when he warns the others in the court not to be taken in by Gloucester's show of loyalty to Henry VI: "Look to it, lords; let not his smoothing words / Bewitch your hearts; be wise and circumspect" (1.1.156–157). Of course, the Cardinal is trying to bewitch them with his own smoothing words, and they should be wise and circumspect when it comes to him, as well. York also plans to hide his true intentions behind a facade of loyalty, reminding himself that he must not let anyone else know what he is really up to: "Then, York, be still awhile, till time do serve. / Watch thou and wake, when others be asleep, / To pry into the secrets of the state" (1.1.248–250). The use of the word *secrets* is telling, for York plans to be secretive about his true intentions. Suffolk is also secretive about his intentions, and he tells Margaret that they should make a show of being friends with the Cardinal and the others in order to use them: "Although we fancy not the Cardinal, / Yet must we join with him and with the lords / Till we have brought Duke Humphrey in disgrace" (1.3.97–99). York gives similar advice to Salisbury and Warwick when he tells them that they must do as he does "in these dangerous days" and use "silent secrecy" to hide their real plans (2.268–69).

This strong emphasis on pretence and show becomes even more explicit as Margaret, Suffolk, and the others try to convince Henry VI that Gloucester's expressions of loyalty cloak his true desires, for "Gloucester is a man / Unsounded yet and full of deceit" and anyone can "steal a shape, that means deceit" (3.1.56–57, 79). What is interesting is that their own emphasis on the nature of Gloucester's deceit is in itself an act of deceit, for they really only want Gloucester out of the way so that they can seize his power for themselves. Those who, like Gloucester, try to avoid such deceptive language are destroyed by those who use deception to their advantage. None of the characters is willing to show his or her true self or true intentions to the others, and the language of the play reflects this atmosphere of treachery and suspicion.

Such an atmosphere often results in the most inhumane forms of behavior, so perhaps it is not surprising there are many instances where language is used to compare human behavior to the behavior of beasts. For example, when Henry VI and his court are hawking in Saint Albans, Gloucester's high-flying hawk is compared to its master's potential ambitions: "My Lord Protector's hawks do tower so well, / They know their master loves to be aloft, / And bears his thoughts above his falcon's pitch" (2.1.10–12). Gloucester is later described as a shepherd (2.2), implying that Henry VI is his lamb, a comparison that is used again and again throughout the play, particularly in the third act. If Henry VI is described as a lamb, Gloucester is later described as "a great lion," as a "fox" that "would steal the lamb," as a "hateful raven," and as a ravenous wolf (3.1.55, 76, 78). When Gloucester is arrested, he warns Henry VI that he is not the wolf and that the others are waiting to take the first to bite: "Thus is the shepherd beaten from thy side, / And wolves are gnarling who shall gnaw thee first" (3.1.191–192). This animalistic imagery continues throughout the play, from Cade threatening Iden that he will make him "eat iron like an ostrich" (4.10.30) to York calling Salisbury and Warwick his "two brave bears" who will help him slaughter his enemies (5.7.10). All of this seems to imply something savage, much like the savagery that characterizes the arrest and murder of Gloucester, the violence of Cade's rebellion, and the bloodshed during the Battle of Saint Albans. These images, thus, make one reexamine the often bestial behavior of human beings, particularly during times of war.

Ambition often involves the rise of some with the fall of others, and the language of the play often uses plant imagery as a means of exploring the nature of ambition. When outlining his plans to the audience, York declares his desire for "fertile England's soil" (1.1.238), and he and others rely on similar imagery throughout the play. For example, Suffolk describe his and Margaret's rivals as plants that must be weeded out in order for them to seize power: "So one by one we'll weed them all at last, / And you yourself shall steer this happy realm" (1.3.102–103). In a similar vein, Warwick describes York and his descendants as plants that are about to bloom (2.2). When Eleanor has been sentenced and Gloucester has lost his position, Suffolk describes it all as though it were a tree falling: "Thus droops this lofty pine and hangs his sprays; / Thus Eleanor's pride dies in her youngest days" (2.3.45–46). Eleanor uses this imagery herself when she warns Gloucester of the ax that will soon cut him down (2.4). Warning Henry VI of the danger that Gloucester poses, Margaret argues that Gloucester must be weeded out before he has time to grow: "Now 'tis the spring, and weeds are shallow-rooted; / Suffer them now and they'll o'ergrow the garden / And choke the herbs for want of husbandry" (3.1.31–33). When news arrives that France has been lost, York decries the losts of territory he believes to be his: "Thus are my blossoms blasted in the bud, / And caterpillars eat my leaves away" (3.1.89–90). These comparisons between ambition and nature are taken one step further when Iden enters his garden and compares its tranquillity with the treachery of the court. However, even this pastoral image is complicated by the struggle for power. Iden beheads Cade and buries his body under a dunghill. He then says that he will leave Cade's "trunk for crows to feed upon" (4.10.90). The use of the word *trunk* is interesting, for although it can mean "torso," it can also refer to the trunk of a tree and, perhaps thus, all of the ambitious trees that sprang up in *Henry VI, Part 2*, only to be cut down. Perhaps it is no accident that this play is concerned with a conflict named after a plant: the Wars of the Roses.

EXTRACTS OF CLASSIC CRITICISM
Nicholas Rowe (1674–1718) [Excerpted from his edition of Shakespeare's plays (1709). Rowe is generally regarded as the first modern editor of Shakespeare's plays.]

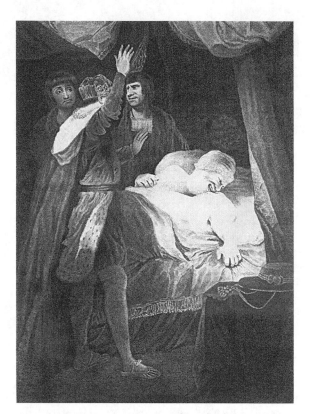

King Henry VI, Salisbury, and Warwick visit the guilt-ridden Cardinal on his deathbed in Act III, Scene 3 of *Henry VI, Part 2*. Print from the Boydell Shakespeare Gallery project *(Painting by Joshua Reynolds; engraving by C. Watson)*

There is a short scene [3.3] in *The Second Part of Henry VI* which I cannot but think admirable in its kind. Cardinal *Beaufort*, who had murder'd the Duke of *Gloucester*, is shown in the last Agonies on his Death-Bed with the good king praying over him. There is so much Terror in one, so much Tenderness and moving Piety in the other as must touch anyone who is capable either of Fear or Pity.

August Wilhelm Schlegel (1767–1845) [Excerpted from his *Lectures on Dramatic Art and Literature* (1815). Schlegel's translations of Shakespeare into German helped encourage interest in Shakespeare's work in that country during the 19th century.]

[On and whether the first tetralogy is really a single unified work or four separate plays] I say advisedly *one* of his works, for that poet evidently intended them to form one great whole. It is, as it were, an historical heroic poem in the dramatic form, of which the separate plays constitute the rhapsodies.

William Hazlitt (1778–1830)   [Excerpted from *Characters of Shakespear's Plays* (1817). Hazlitt is arguably one of the most important Shakespearean critics of the 19th century, particularly in regard to his interest in character and his attempts to politicize the interpretations of Shakespeare's plays.]

During the time of the civil wars of York and Lancaster, England was a perfect bear garden. . . . The three parts of *Henry VI* convey a picture of very little else.

Hermann Ulrici (1806–1884)   [Excerpted from *Shakespeare's Dramatic Art* (1876). Ulrici was an important German critic of Shakespeare.]

[Regarding Margaret's] energy and enormity, this shameful display of evil [is] an embodiment of the prevailing vices and crimes, a character in which was concentrated the whole demoralisation of the age . . . to unfold the meaning and significance of his drama. . . .

[Cade's rebellion] form[s] a parody on the substance of historical action, and exhibit— much in the same manner as the Falstaff episode in "Henry IV."—evil as irrational, stupid, ridiculous, which, in reality, it always is, in spite of its deep serious significance. . . .

[On the difference between Henry VI and Margaret,] the character of the king,

which had become effeminate and unmanly, required, as an organic contrast, a woman who had become masculine and depraved in character.

William   James   Courthope (1842–1917) [Excerpted from *A History of English Poetry,* volume 4 (1903).]

The whole tetralogy . . . forms a study of Machiavellism on a large scale, a dramatic comment on the theory "Might is Right."

. . . Indicative above all of Shakespeare's wonderful growth in imaginative power are the admirable scenes representing Cade's insurrection. Here, for the first time, the dramatist manifests his unequalled insight into the character of the crowd. With something of the resolute force of Tamburlaine, Cade combines the absurd self-sufficiency and ignorance of Dogberry and Bottom, and, like those masterful personages, he is able to impose his will on his still more ignorant followers, some of whom are quite capable of measuring his pretensions.

MODERN CRITICISM AND CRITICAL CONTROVERSIES

Henry VI, Part 2 has an interesting critical history, particularly since it did not really begin to acquire much attention until after World War II, and even then, critics generally tended to discuss the play primarily in relation to the first tetralogy as a whole rather than as a single, self-contained play. A tremendous amount of critical debate was instigated by the publication of E. M. W. Tillyard's *Shakespeare's History Plays* (1944). Tillyard argued that Shakespeare's plays, following the lead of Hall and Holinshed's chronicles, presented a providential view of English history. This view, which has come to be known as "the Tudor myth," suggests that the deposing of Richard II in 1399 led to a disastrous period in English history, a period that did not end until Henry Tudor became Henry VII, king of England, following the death of Richard III in 1485. This interpretation has been hotly contested by a number of critics, particularly those of the New Historicist school, who feel that Shakespeare's history plays challenge this providential view of history as much as they may uphold it.

This debate inaugurated a renewed interest in the first tetralogy, including *Henry VI, Part 2*. For example, in *Patterns of Decay* (1975), Edward Berry argues that *Henry VI, Part 2* deals with the collapse of justice and law, culminating in the outbreak of the Wars of the Roses. A host of reasons have been given for this collapse. In *The Weak King Dilemma in the Shakespearean History Plays* (1973), Michael Manheim attributes it to Henry VI's inability to govern his own realm, while in "The Frame of Disorder—*Henry VI*" (1961), J. Philip Brockbank attributes it to the influence of Machiavelli's theories about politics. At the same time, the question of *Henry VI, Part 2*'s structure or lack thereof is discussed in works such as Emrys Jones's *The Origins of Shakespeare* (1972), G. R. Hibbard's *The Making of Shakespeare's Dramatic Poetry* (1981), and John W. Blanpied's "Breaking Ground: The *Henry VI* Plays" (1983).

In recent years, the status of Margaret and the nature of Cade's rebellion have begun to spur a considerable amount of critical interest, as the former begins to be seen less as a villain and the latter is regarded less as simply a violent disordered melee. In regard to Margaret, much feminist criticism has finally begun to rescue her from the moniker of villain that had been so strongly applied to her for so many years. Jean E. Howard and Phyllis Rackin's "*Henry VI, Part II*" (1997) deals with the incredibly misogynistic attitudes displayed toward Margaret, while Rackin's *Stages of History: Shakespeare's English Chronicles* (1990) delves even further into the question of gender in relation to the history plays. In regard to Cade's rebellion, Thomas Cartelli's "Jack Cade in the Garden: Class Consciousness and Class Conflict in *2 Henry VI*" (1994) explores the tensions between the propertied rich and the landless poor in early modern England, particularly in regard to Act 4, Scene 10 of the play. Were there any dangers in exploring such tensions on the public stage? In "Murdering Peasants: Status, Genre, and the Representation of Rebellion" (1983), Stephen Greenblatt is concerned with the degree to which Shakespeare was able or unable to present popular rebellion on the public stage, while in "The Peasant's Toe: Popular Culture and Popular Pressure" (1989), Annabel Patterson examines the long tradition of popular protest inherited by Shakespeare.

The question of where Shakespeare's sympathies lay in regard to the rebellion has also come under scrutiny. Richard Helgerson's "Staging Exclusion" (1992) argues that Shakespeare was firmly against both Cade and his rebellion, while Chris Fitter's "Emergent Shakespeare and the Politics of Protest: *2 Henry VI* in Historical Contexts" (2005) argues that Shakespeare's politics were actually far more left-leaning than many might assume. Whatever one's ultimate opinion of any of these positions, one should at least be thankful that *Henry VI, Part 2* has finally begun to get the critical attention and recognition it deserves.

THE PLAY TODAY

While the first tetralogy has recently begun to receive more critical attention and recognition, most audiences are still not very familiar with the plays. This, too, has begun to change, however, for the first tetralogy has been theatrically performed several times in recent years. For instance, Edward Hall staged the first tetralogy at the Watermill Theatre as *Rose Rage* (2001), and Michael Boyd staged it at the Royal Shakespeare Company (RSC) as *The Histories* (2000, 2001, and 2008). There are still a disappointingly small number of movie versions of the first tetralogy, all of which are filmed for television. Many of these are based on famous stage productions of the plays, such as Peter Hall and John Barton's famous 1963 production of *The Wars of the Roses* at the RSC. Although it is somewhat dated, the best of these is probably Jane Howell's 1983 production for BBC television. She cut almost nothing from the text, so her version is perhaps the best example of just how well *Henry VI, Part 2* works as a piece of dramatic literature in its own right. It is to be hoped that more film versions of both *Henry VI, Part 2* in particular and the first tetralogy in general will continue to appear so that more audiences can become familiar with these little-known but nevertheless wonderfully captivating Shakespeare plays.

FIVE TOPICS FOR DISCUSSION AND WRITING

1. **Loyalty versus disloyalty:** In the dangerous world of Henry VI's court, where everyone seems to have an agenda, is it possible to be loyal? Gloucester tries to remain loyal, but his lack of guile places him at the mercy of those who do not share his moral scruples. York is disloyal to Henry VI, but *Henry VI, Part 2* ends with the Yorks' victory at Saint Albans. How are the themes of loyalty and disloyalty explored in *Henry VI, Part 2*?

2. **The weak king:** Henry VI tries to be a good king, but his weaknesses make him prey to the machinations of others. Many critics have noted the influence of Machiavelli's writings on the first tetralogy. How can these ideas be applied to *Henry VI, Part 2*? Is it possible to be both a good man and a good king?

3. **The nature of ambition:** *Henry VI, Part 2* is filled with a host of ambitious characters who all try to seize power in one form or another throughout the course of the play. However, almost all of these characters meet disastrous ends and bring about the ruin of those around them. How is the nature of ambition explored in *Henry VI, Part 2*? To what ends?

4. **Masculinity and femininity:** Many recent critics have begun to explore the nature of gender in the first tetralogy, particularly in relation to the character of Margaret. Is she simply a villain who plots to seize power, or is she one of Shakespeare's strongest and most compelling female characters? At the same time, although Margaret is criticized for being too masculine, Henry VI is criticized for being too feminine. How does Shakespeare handle the subject of gender in *Henry VI, Part 2*?

5. **Rebellion or revolution:** Many recent critics have begun to look at Jack Cade's rebellion in an entirely new light. What had previously been seen as a violent and destructive rampage is now being considered in light of its populist and revolutionary potential. Is Jack Cade a destructive villain, or is he a potential liberator of the people? Does Shakespeare take a positive or negative view of rebellion in *Henry VI, Part 2*?

Bibliography

Bate, Jonathan. *The Genius of Shakespeare*. London: Picador, 1997.

———. *Soul of the Age: A Biography of the Mind of William Shakespeare*. New York: Random House, 2009.

Bate, Jonathan, and Russell Jackson, eds. *The Oxford Illustrated History of Shakespeare on Stage*. Oxford: Oxford University Press, 1996, 2001.

Berry, Edward. "The Histories." In *The Cambridge Companion to Shakespeare Studies,* edited by Stanley Wells, 249–256. Cambridge: Cambridge University Press, 1986, 1987.

———. *Patterns of Decay: Shakespeare's Early Histories.* Charlottesville: University Press of Virginia, 1975.

Bevington, David. *Shakespeare's Ideas.* Oxford, U.K.: Wiley-Blackwell, 2008.

Blanpied, John W. "Breaking Ground: The *Henry VI* Plays." *Time and the Artist in Shakespeare's English Histories.* Newark: University of Delaware Press, 1983.

Briggs, Julia. *This Stage-Play World: Texts and Contexts, 1580–1625.* Oxford: Oxford University Press, 1997.

Brockbank, J. Philip. "The Frame of Disorder—*Henry VI.*" In *Early Shakespeare,* edited by John Russell Brown and Bernard Harris, 73–99. London: Edwin Arnold, 1961.

Carroll, William. "Theories of Kingship in Shakespeare's England." In *A Companion to Shakespeare's Works,* Vol. 2: *The Histories,* edited by

Richard Dutton and Jean E. Howard, 125–145. Malden, Mass.: Blackwell, 2003.

Cartelli, Thomas. "Jack Cade in the Garden: Class Consciousness and Class Conflict in *2 Henry VI*." In *Enclosure Acts: Sexuality, Property, and Culture in Early Modern England,* edited by Richard Burt and John Michael Archer, 48–64. Ithaca, N.Y.: Cornell University Press, 1994.

Chernaik, Warren. *The Cambridge Introduction to Shakespeare's History Plays.* Cambridge: Cambridge University Press, 2007.

Courtney, Richard. *Shakespeare's World of War: The Early Histories.* Toronto, Canada: Simon & Pierre, 1994.

Fitter, Chris. "Emergent Shakespeare and the Politics of Protest: *2 Henry VI* in Historical Contexts." *English Literary History* 72 (2005): 129–158.

Garber, Marjorie. *Shakespeare after All.* New York: Pantheon Books, 2004.

Goy-Blanquet, Dominique. *Shakespeare's Early History Plays: From Chronicle to Stage.* Oxford: Oxford University Press, 2003.

Greenblatt, Stephen. "Murdering Peasants: Status, Genre, and the Representation of Rebellion." *Representations,* no. 1 (1983): 1–29.

———. *Will in the World.* New York: W. W. Norton & Co., 2004.

Grene, Nicholas. *Shakespeare's Serial History Plays.* Cambridge: Cambridge University Press, 2007.

Hattaway, Michael, ed. *The Cambridge Companion to Shakespeare's History Plays.* Cambridge: Cambridge University Press, 2002.

Helgerson, Richard. "Staging Exclusion." *Forms of Nationhood: The Elizabethan Writing of England.* Chicago: University of Chicago Press, 1992.

Hibbard, G. R. *The Making of Shakespeare's Dramatic Poetry.* Toronto, Canada: University of Toronto Press, 1981.

Howard, Jean. E., and Rackin, Phyllis. "*Henry VI, Part II.*" *Engendering a Nation: A Feminist Account of Shakespeare's Histories.* London: Routledge, 1997.

Hussey, S. S. *The Literary Language of Shakespeare.* London: Longman, 1982.

Jones, Emrys. *The Origins of Shakespeare.* Oxford: Oxford University Press, 1972.

Kastan, David Scott. "Shakespeare and English History." In *The Cambridge Companion to Shakespeare,* edited by Margreta de Grazia and Stanley Wells, 167–182. Cambridge: Cambridge University Press, 2001, 2006.

Kermode, Frank. *The Age of Shakespeare.* New York: Modern Library, 2004.

———. *Shakespeare's Language.* New York: Penguin, 2000.

Knowles, Ronald. "The Farce of History: Miracle, Combat, and Rebellion in *2 Henry VI*." *The Yearbook of English Studies* 21 (1991): 168–186.

———. *Shakespeare's Arguments with History.* Basingstoke, U.K.: Palgrave Macmillan, 2002.

Leggatt, Alexander. *Shakespeare's Political Drama: The History Plays and the Roman Plays.* London: Routledge, 1989.

Manheim, Michael. *The Weak King Dilemma in Shakespearean History Plays.* Syracuse, N.Y.: Syracuse University Press, 1973.

McDonald, Russ. *Shakespeare and the Arts of Language.* Oxford: Oxford University Press, 2001.

Moseley, C. W. R. D. *Shakespeare's History Plays.* New York: Penguin, 1991.

Norwich, John Julius. *Shakespeare's Kings.* New York: Scribner, 1999.

Nuttall, A. D. *Shakespeare the Thinker.* New Haven, Conn.: Yale University Press, 2007.

Ornstein, Robert. *A Kingdom for a Stage: The Achievement of Shakespeare's History Plays.* Cambridge, Mass.: Harvard University Press, 1972.

Patterson, Annabel. "The Peasant's Toe: Popular Culture and Popular Pressure." *Shakespeare and the Popular Voice.* Cambridge, Mass.: Blackwell, 1989.

Rackin, Phyllis. *Stages of History: Shakespeare's English Chronicles.* Ithaca, N.Y.: Cornell University Press, 1990.

Ribner, Irving. *The English History in the Age of Shakespeare.* 1957. Reprint, New York: Barnes & Noble, 1965.

Riggs, David. *Shakespeare's Heroical Histories.* Cambridge, Mass.: Harvard University Press, 1971.

Saccio, Peter. *Shakespeare's English Kings: History, Chronicle, and Drama.* 1977. Reprint, Oxford: Oxford University Press, 2000.

Seward, Desmond. *The Wars of the Roses.* New York: Penguin, 1995.

Shakespeare, William. *Henry VI, Parts One, Two, and Three.* Edited by David Bevington. New York: Bantam, 1988.

———. *King Henry VI, Part 2.* Edited by Ronald Knowles. London: Thomson Learning/Arden Shakespeare, 1999, 2001.

———. *Henry VI, Part Two.* Edited by Roger Warren. Oxford: Oxford University Press, 2003.

———. *The Second Part of Henry VI.* Edited by Michael Hattaway. Cambridge: Cambridge University Press, 1991.

Smallwood, R. L. "Shakespeare's Use of History." In *The Cambridge Companion to Shakespeare Studies,* edited by Stanley Wells, 143–162. Cambridge: Cambridge University Press, 1986, 1987.

———. "Twentieth Century Performance: The Stratford and London Companies." In *The Cambridge Companion to Shakespeare on Stage,* edited by Stanley Wells and Sarah Stanton, 98–117. Cambridge: Cambridge University Press, 2002.

Spiekerman, Tim. *Shakespeare's Political Realism: The English History Plays.* Albany: State University of New York Press, 2001.

Taylor, Michael. *Shakespeare Criticism in the Twentieth Century.* Oxford: Oxford University Press, 2001.

Taylor, Neil. "Two Types of Television Shakespeare." In *Shakespeare and the Moving Image,* edited by Anthony Davies and Stanley Wells, 86–98. Cambridge: Cambridge University Press, 1994, 1995.

Tillyard, E. M. W. *Shakespeare's History Plays.* 1944. Reprint, Edinburgh, Scotland: Peregrine, 1962.

Watt, R. J. C., ed. *Shakespeare's History Plays.* London: Longman, 2003.

Weir, Alison. *The Wars of the Roses.* New York: Ballantine Books, 1995.

Willems, Michèle. "The English History Play on Screen." In *Shakespeare and the Moving Image,* edited by Anthony Davies and Stanley Wells, 121–145. Cambridge: Cambridge University Press, 1994, 1995.

FILM AND VIDEO PRODUCTIONS

Bogdanov, Michael, dir. *Henry VI: House of Lancaster.* Vision Replays, 1990.

Hall, Peter, and John Barton, dirs. *The Wars of the Roses.* Royal Shakespeare Company, 1965.

Hayes, Michael, dir. *An Age of Kings.* BBC, 1960.

Howell, Jane, dir. *Henry VI, Part Two.* BBC, 1983.

—John Cameron

Henry VI, Part 3

INTRODUCTION

Henry VI, Part 3 is the third play in Shakespeare's early tetralogy, or group of four plays, which also includes the first two *Henry VI* plays and ends with *Richard III*. None of the *Henry VI* plays is particularly well known or well regarded among Shakespeare's work, but all have received more attention in recent years, in part because of a few high-profile productions. As one of Shakespeare's earliest plays, *Henry VI, Part 3* is uneven but at times lively and moving.

The Wars of the Roses reach a climax in *Henry VI, Part 3*. Captains and would-be kings pursue one another back and forth across the stage and England with murderous intent. The older generation—Richard Plantagenet, Duke of York, Lord Clifford, and Warwick the Kingmaker, all key players in the previous plays—meets violent ends, clearing the way to the throne for the York sons Edward and Richard. The saintly but ineffectual Henry VI is defeated, imprisoned in the Tower of London, and stabbed by the evil Richard, Duke of Gloucester. From an audience's perspective, the number of double-crossings and broken allegiances has a real disadvantage; it can be very difficult to keep track of who is allied to whom at any one point in the play. But, as we consider this element of the drama, we come to realize that the changing alliances and almost interchangeable personalities echo and reinforce the brutality and treachery of civil war. Many of the characters in this play are not realistic in a modern sense of the word nor endowed with any real psychological depth. They exist primarily as figures of ambition, revenge, hatred, and murder. Only two figures are exceptions to this: King Henry and Richard of Gloucester, later Richard III.

In *Henry VI, Part 3*, the character of Richard, Duke of Gloucester, has two key scenes in which Shakespeare brilliantly dramatizes his transformation into the villain who will become the title character of *Richard III*. By the end of the play, Richard is poised for his next step, acknowledging his baby nephew with a Judas kiss and hypocritically vowing loyalty to his brother King Edward IV. Viewed from this perspective, the play becomes fascinating for its representation of Richard as arguably a more psychologically coherent or nuanced character than he is in the play that bears his name. In *Richard III*, Richard appears fully formed as an arch-manipulator, a deceiver, and a murderer. After his initial speech in which he mentions his deformed appearance as symbolic of his villainy, Richard moves on with supreme self-confidence until the play's conclusion. In *Henry VI, Part 3*, on the other hand, we see Richard becoming this villain and the background of revenge killings and betrayals that are a formative influence on him.

Richard's moral deformity, unlike his (fictional) physical deformity, is common to almost everyone in the play. *Henry VI, Part 3* repeatedly dramatizes a brutal cycle of murder and revenge; one need only take as an example Lord Clifford, whose father has been killed by the Duke of York. In revenge, he murders York's son, the noncombatant earl of Rutland (who in this play is only 11 years old), and

976

Warwick captures Edward in Act IV, Scene 3 of *Henry VI, Part 3*, as depicted in this print published in the 19th century. *(Painting by Max Adamo; engraving by Tobias Bauer)*

Clifford is in turn not only killed but his body hacked and tormented by York's surviving sons, Edward, George, and Richard. The play takes intergenerational conflict to an extreme, dramatizing the death not only of the older generation but also of the younger. Both the Yorkist and the Lancastrian sides lose children: the earl of Rutland and the young son of Henry VI, Prince Edward. Sole survivors are the young Richmond, who appears only long enough for Henry VI to offer a prophetic blessing to the future Henry VII, and the baby son of Edward IV and Elizabeth Woodville, doomed to become one of the Princes in the Tower.

Alexander Leggatt describes the *Henry VI* tetralogy as "stretching from the death of a hero to the birth of a monster". He is referring to the fact that the *Henry VI* plays begin with the death of Henry V and end with Richard of Gloucester's determination to seize the crown at any cost. In *Henry V*, Shakespeare arguably presents us with a king who combines personal strength, ruthlessness, and the ability to command loyalty, not to mention a victory that appears to indicate conclusively that God is on his side. Henry VI's inadequacies are made even more apparent by the fact that he is the son of this paragon. In the three plays that bear his name, Henry VI is portrayed as a child, a hen-pecked husband, and, in this play, a good man whose personal holiness is no match for the ruthlessness and ambition that surround him on all sides. In *Henry VI, Part 3*, Henry's personal sanctity is never questioned, but neither does it appear to excuse his complete inability to govern his nobles and indeed his propensity to be swayed by the last speaker. Henry is a pawn in the hands of his nobles and his wife, and his bitter lamentations over the state of his country do nothing to improve the situation. *Henry VI, Part 3* documents the rise to power of the three surviving Yorkist brothers—lecherous Edward, perjured Clarence, and deformed Richard. It dramatizes their murder of the king's son Edward, whose right to inherit the throne is as nearly incontestable as any such right can be within these plays, and although the play ends with a nod toward the destruction within their midst that Richard represents and with a timely reminder to the audience that salvation in the form of Henry Tudor awaits, the play nonetheless concludes with the triumph of might over right.

The play is hardly Shakespeare's masterpiece, but it contains some memorable scenes and speeches. The choric episode of the father who has killed his son, and the son who has killed his father, in particular, are emblematic of the universal tragedy that is civil war, while the dramatization of Richard's transformation into Machiavellian monster is a fantastic blending of history-driven narrative and psychological realism.

BACKGROUND

In format, the play is what is known as a chronicle, or history, play. These works had developed out of the older morality genre and drew on the history of England as it could be learned from chroniclers such as Raphael Holinshed's *Chronicles of England, Scotland and Ireland* (1577, 1585) and Edward Hall's *Union of the Two Noble and Illustre Famelies of Lancastre and Yorke* (1548). Another important source for Shakespeare, one with an overtly didactic purpose, was *A Mirror for Magistrates* (1599). Written by numerous different figures and building on a tradition of looking at history for the moral lessons it could impart, *A Mirror for Magistrates* was a collection of dramatic poems that enabled historical figures to tell their own stories and to warn their readers to avoid the various pitfalls of pride, tyranny, or oathbreaking into which they had fallen. The ghost of Richard, Duke of York, calls upon his listeners to "warne princes not to wade in warre, For any cause, except the realmes defence" (193) and in particular, not to attempt to gain titles prematurely—precisely the error into which York is lured by Richard in this play.

The play was first performed in the early 1590s, the final full decade of Elizabeth's life and one of increasing concern about succession to the throne. Elizabeth was in her 60s, childless, and refusing to name her successor. Civil war in France, in which England had become involved, sending troops under Robert Devereux, the earl of Essex, to support the Protestant Henry of Navarre in his struggle for the throne, not only afforded direct experience of the horrors of war for many but also resulted in an upsurge of militarily experienced, unemployed, and, hence, dangerous men returning to England from the wars. Although set more than 100 years earlier, the *Henry VI* plays, with their emphasis on succession and competition for the crown and, most important of all, a deeply cynical view of the extent to which issues such as legitimacy and genealogical lines could be manipulated in order to gain that crown, were both relevant and topical in the final decade of the 16th century.

Date and Text of the Play

As with most of Shakespeare's plays, there is some critical uncertainty over exactly when *Henry VI, Part 3* was written, and the importance of this debate lies in whether the *Henry VI* plays can be perceived as a genuine unit. *Henry VI, Part 1* appears to have been first performed on March 3, 1592, as mentioned in Philip Henslowe's diary. It was extremely popular, performed 14 times between March and that June, when the theaters were closed due to the plague. The first direct reference to *Henry VI, Part 3* also occurs in 1592, when the dying Robert Greene, in his attack on playwrights in general, paraphrased a line from the play: "A *Tygers hart wrapt in a Players hyde.*" The line is "O tiger's heart wrapped in a woman's hide," said by York to Margaret (1.4.137). This reference appears to predate the first performance of *Henry VI, Part 1.* In fact, many scholars believe that *Henry VI, Part 1* was written last among the *Henry VI* plays.

The publication history of *Henry VI, Part 3* is extremely complicated. A form of the play appeared in print in 1595 under the title *The true Tragedie of Richard Duke of Yorke, and the death of good King Henrie the Sixt, with the whole contention betweene the two Houses Lancaster and Yorke, as it was sundrie times acted by the Right Honourable the Earle of Pembrooke his servants.* This play, sometimes referred to as "O" for *octavo,* the size of the book (octavo means that a single sheet of paper, a folio, has been folded three times to make eight pages, cut and stitched together to form the book, so it would have been quite small), and a subsequent play with the same title was published in 1600. This latter one was published in quarto size (the sheet folded to make four pages, larger than the octavo) and is now referred to as Q2. The play appeared again, coupled together with an early version of *Henry VI, Part 2,* in a 1619 publication by William Jaggard, and attributed to Shakespeare. Finally, in 1623, a longer play appeared in what is now called the First Folio edition of Shakespeare's plays under the title of *The Third part of King Henry the Sixt.* This is the version reproduced in almost all editions of

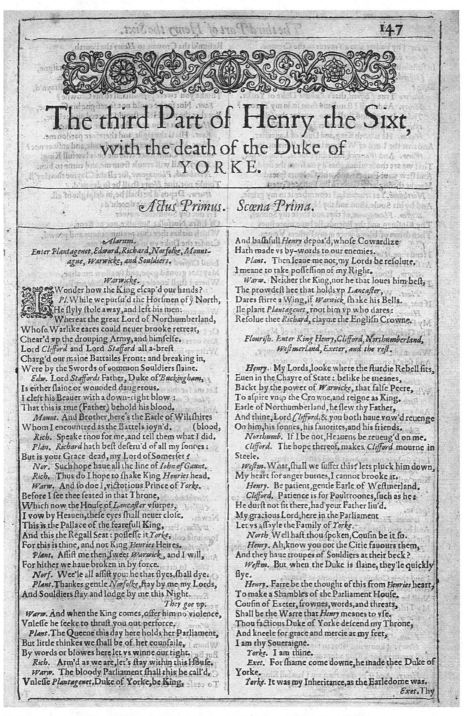

The third Part of Henry the Sixt,

with the death of the Duke of YORKE.

Actus Primus. Scœna Prima.

Alarum.
Enter Plantagenet, Edward, Richard, Norfolke, Mount-
ague, Warwicke, and Souldiers.

Warwicke.

Wonder how the King escap'd our hands?
Pl. While we pursu'd the Horsmen of ŷ North,
He slyly stole away, and left his men:
Whereat the great Lord of Northumberland,
Whose Warlike eares could neuer brooke retreat,
Chear'd vp the drouping Army, and himselfe,
Lord *Clifford* and Lord *Stafford* all a-brest
Charg'd our maine Battailes Front: and breaking in,
Were by the Swords of common Souldiers slaine.
Edw. Lord *Staffords* Father, Duke of *Buckingham*,
Is either slaine or wounded dangerous,
I cleft his Beauer with a down-right blow :
That this is true (Father) behold his blood.
Mount. And Brother, here's the Earle of Wiltshires
Whom I encountred as the Battels ioyn'd.   (blood,
Rich. Speake thou for me, and tell them what I did.
Plan. Richard hath best deseru'd of all my sonnes :
But is your Grace dead, my Lord of Somerset ?
Nor. Such hope haue all the line of *Iohn of Gaunt.*
Rich. Thus do I hope to shake King *Henries* head.
Warw. And so doe I, victorious Prince of *Yorke.*
Before I see thee seated in that Throne,
Which now the House of *Lancaster* vsurpes,
I vow by Heauen, these eyes shall neuer close.
This is the Pallace of the fearefull King,
And this the Regall Seat : possesse it *Yorke,*
For this is thine, and not King *Henries* Heires.
Plant. Assist me then, sweet *Warwick*, and I will,
For hither we haue broken in by force.
Norf. Wee'le all assist you : he that flyes, shall dye.
Plant. Thankes gentle *Norfolke*, stay by me my Lords,
And Souldiers stay and lodge by me this Night.
      They goe vp.
Warw. And when the King comes, offer him no violence,
Vnlesse he seeke to thrust you out perforce,
Plant. The Queene this day here holds her Parliament,
But little thinkes we shall be of her counsaile,
By words or blowes here let vs winne our right,
Rich. Arm'd as we are, let's stay within this House.
Warw. The bloody Parliament shall this be call'd,
Vnlesse *Plantagenet*, Duke of Yorke, be King,

And bashfull *Henry* depos'd, whose Cowardize
Hath made vs by-words to our enemies.
Plant. Then leaue me not, my Lords be resolute,
I meane to take possession of my Right.
Warw. Neither the King, nor he that loues him best,
The prowdest hee that holds vp *Lancaster*,
Dares stirre a Wing, if *Warwick* shake his Bells.
Ile plant *Plantagenet*, root him vp who dares:
Resolue thee *Richard*, clayme the English Crowne.

Flourish. Enter King Henry, Clifford, Northumberland,
Westmerland, Exeter, and the rest.

Henry. My Lords, looke where the sturdie Rebell sits,
Euen in the Chayre of State : belike he meanes,
Backt by the power of *Warwicke*, that false Peere,
To aspire vnto the Crowne, and reigne as King.
Earle of Northumberland, he slew thy Father,
And thine, Lord *Clifford*, & you both haue vow'd reuenge
On him, his sonnes, his fauorites, and his friends.
Northumb. If I be not, Heauens be reueng'd on me.
Clifford. The hope thereof, makes *Clifford* mourne in
Steele.
Westm. What, shall we suffer this? lets pluck him down,
My heart for anger burnes, I cannot brooke it.
Henry. Be patient, gentle Earle of Westmerland.
Clifford. Patience is for Poultroones, such as he :
He durst not sit there, had your Father liu'd.
My gracious Lord, here in the Parliament
Let vs assayle the Family of *Yorke.*
North. Well hast thou spoken, Cousin be it so.
Henry. Ah, know you not the Citie fauours them,
And they haue troupes of Souldiers at their beck ?
Westm. But, when the Duke is slaine, they'le quickly
flye.
Henry. Farre be the thought of this from *Henries* heart,
To make a Shambles of the Parliament House.
Cousin of Exeter, frownes, words, and threats,
Shall be the Warre that *Henry* meanes to vse.
Thou factious Duke of Yorke descend my Throne,
And kneele for grace and mercie at my feet,
I am thy Soueraigne.
Yorke. I am thine.
Exet. For shame come downe, he made thee Duke of
Yorke.
Yorke. It was my Inheritance, as the Earledome was.
      Exet. Thy

Shakespeare's plays. (The text of the *True Tragedy* [1595] is available at numerous online sites and was published as a facsimile edition in 1958.) To summarize, the two main versions of the play are *The True Tragedie of Richard Duke of York* (1595, 1600, 1619) and *The Third part of King Henry the Sixt* (1623; First Folio edition).

What is the relationship between the plays? The *True Tragedie of Richard Duke of York,* although shorter and differing widely in the development of its characters, is, nonetheless, closely affiliated with the play we now call *Henry VI, Part 3.* It is possible that the *True Tragedy* is the result of a "pirated" or reconstructed edition, made by individuals or actors who listened to or acted in the play and then transcribed what they had heard. This would enable them to create a playscript that could be sold. Thus, the *True Tragedy* becomes a "faulty version," so to speak, of Shakespeare's original work, a "bad quarto," described by Leo Kirschbaum in the following terms: "The simplest way to describe a bad quarto is to state that it cannot possibly represent a written transcript of the author's text" (20).

The idea that the *True Tragedy* represented a "bad quarto" had been originally mooted by Samuel Johnson, who had speculated that *Henry VI, Parts 2* and *3* were "copies taken by some auditor . . . during the representation" (225). Subsequent critics, most notably the great editor W. S. Greg, adopted this concept with the proviso that the "auditors" were, in fact, actors, thus accounting for any unevenness in the "reconstruction" of the "bad" text. Although Greg himself became dubious about the idea of "reported" texts later in his career, the concept of memorial construction increasingly became something of an article of faith in mainstream textual criticism of the 20th century. Peter Alexander, in *Shakespeare's* Henry VI *and* Richard III, endorsed the concept with relation to *Henry VI* and the *True Tragedy* in what became a key piece of scholarship for the *Henry VI* plays. Andrew Cairncross in his 1964 Arden edition of *King Henry VI, Part 3* asserts that "It is now generally agreed that Q *[The True Tragedy]* is a reported or bad version of the text later printed in

F, and not an early play or version of a play afterwards revised by Shakespeare" (XV). Michael Hattaway's New Cambridge edition (1993) also accepts the idea of memorial reconstruction.

The idea that such acts of piracy took place on a regular basis, however, has proved difficult to substantiate and has been challenged by scholars such as Steven Urkowitz. While Urkowitz used internal evidence to argue in 1988 that the memorial construction theory did not hold water, in 1990, Paul Werstine asserted that "there is no documentary evidence that any actor(s) ever memorially reconstructed a play." Werstine argues convincingly that the belief in the concept of memorial reconstruction owes as much to the 20th-century desire to ascribe agency to a "lone author or agent" as it does to any form of hard evidence. In making this statement, he is consciously moving the debate away from a historical-textual debate and locating it within fields of literary theory that debate the concept of an author. If we accept the famous statement of Roland Barthes that a text is not the product of a single author but rather a "tissue of quotations," then the argument itself becomes problematic, and any effort to valorize one play over another—as in to argue that the *True Tragedy* is inferior to the Folio version of *Henry VI, Part 3*—because it is essentially a faulty or unauthorized version of a play is inherently unsound. Graham Holderness in his 2003 book *Textual Shakespeare* develops this argument to the point where he is able to say, "Reviewing recent debates in textual theory and practice, I conclude that 'Shakespeare' is not a writer but a collection of documents, none of which can with any certainty be linked to whatever it was the author wanted to say. . . . According to modern literary studies the author is secondary to the text, and all texts are in any case copies, always already changed: there are no 'originals'" (x).

Another theory holds that the *True Tragedy* is a shortened version of *Henry VI, Part 3,* which was later revised into the form that appears in the First Folio. This suggestion was made in the 20th century by critics such as Robert E. Burkhart, who speculated that the *True Tragedy* was an abridge-

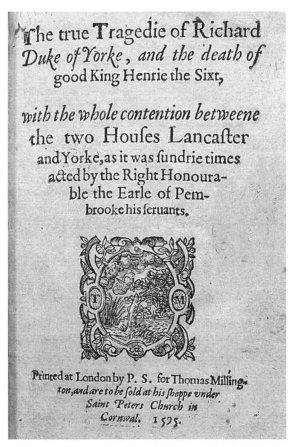

The true Tragedie of Richard Duke of Yorke, and the death of good King Henrie the Sixt,

with the whole contention betweene the two Houses Lancaster and Yorke, as it was sundrie times acted by the Right Honourable the Earle of Pembrooke his seruants.

Printed at London by P. S. for Thomas Millington, and are to be sold at his shoppe vnder Saint Peters Church in Cornwal. 1595.

Title page of the quarto *The True Tragedy*, a version of *Henry VI, Part 3*, published in 1595

ment of the longer play in order to render it playable on a provincial tour, adapted in terms of length and the number of actors the play required. Randall Martin, the editor of the 2001 Oxford Shakespeare edition of *Henry VI, Part 3*, debates this view extensively and after analyzing the type of variances between the two texts and assessing the casting requirement for both plays, considers that this is unlikely to have been the case.

Edward Malone's *Dissertation on the three parts of Henry the Sixth* (1790) suggested that *The True Tragedy* may have been at least partially an early version of *Henry VI, Part 3*. Stanley Wells and Gary Taylor adopted this viewpoint very visibly in the

1986 *William Shakespeare: The Complete Works*, in which they used the title *The True Tragedy of Richard Duke of York and the Good King Henry the Sixth* instead of the more familiar *Henry VI, Part 3*, arguing that this is the version of the play likeliest to have been seen by Shakespeare's audiences.

The textual history of *Henry VI* is contentious and inextricably linked to the history of textual criticism as a whole. Studies of the relationship between *The True Tragedy* and *Henry VI, Part 3* have contributed immeasurably to current understanding of Elizabethan staging practices, printing processes, and performance methods. Perhaps it would be too much to expect a single, final answer to the original question, as well.

SYNOPSIS
Brief Synopsis

Henry VI, Part 3 concludes the story of the traumatic reign of its eponymous monarch, and brings the wars between the houses of Lancaster and York to a temporary halt. The play opens with King Henry attempting to buy peace by naming the rebellious Richard, Duke of York, as his heir in exchange for York's promise to allow Henry to rule in peace for the rest of his life. This infuriates Henry's domineering wife, Margaret, and their son, Edward, who both vow to continue the struggle against York. Persuaded by his son Richard of Gloucester (later to be Richard III), York breaks his vow not to seek the crown during Henry's lifetime and takes up arms again, but his forces are defeated, and he himself is captured during the first of the battle scenes of this play, the Battle of Sandal. York is tormented by Margaret and her followers with the news that his youngest son, Edmund of Rutland, has been murdered, and later he himself is killed, with his head set above the gates of the city of York.

The battle and its bloody aftermath of humiliation and violent revenge killings set the tone for the rest of the play, with the tide of war flowing back and forth until eventually Henry's son Edward is defeated and killed and Henry himself is captured and murdered by Richard of Gloucester. Queen

Margaret, Henry's wife, is finally banished to France, and the Duke of York's son Edward, now Edward IV and married to Elizabeth Woodville, ascends the throne in the company of his brothers, his wife, and his infant son. Richard of Gloucester, however, continues to scheme, and although the play ends with the scene of a united family group, the audience is left in no doubt that the peace will not last.

Although the play is largely an ensemble piece, with most characters of secondary importance to the family unit to which they belong, it is notable for shaping and developing the character of Richard of Gloucester. At the play's beginning, Richard is a warrior, only marginally more brutal and cunning than many of his siblings and cousins. By the end of the play, he has become far more than that; he has become a rampantly egotistical and unscrupulous protagonist, glorying in his ambition and his ability to manipulate others and ready to dominate the stage in *Richard III*.

Act I, Scene 1

At the palace of Westminster, York, his sons Edward and Richard, along with the Earl of Warwick and other peers, regret the fact that King Henry has escaped and compare notes on the battle (of Saint Albans) that has just been fought, tallying up the names of the dead: Lord Clifford, Lord Stafford, and the Duke of Northumberland. Richard gains his father's warmest praise for the head of the Duke of Somerset, whom he has killed. Encouraged by Warwick, York enters Parliament and ascends the throne, when he is confronted by King Henry and his supporters, including Young Lord Clifford, whose father has been killed in the preceding battle. Following an angry debate in which both sides assert their claim to the crown, the central issue of Richard II's abdication in favor of Bolingbroke (later King Henry IV) is raised. Henry VI's claim to the throne stems from Bolingbroke's rebellion against Richard II; Bolingbroke took the crown from Richard by force, and therefore, Bolingbroke's grandson Henry VI is not the true king, or so it is asserted. The rights and wrongs of Henry's

ancestry are placed in the context of Henry VI's own shortcomings as king; his failures in the battlefields of England and in France are produced as evidence of his unworthiness to rule. The matter is settled, for the present, by Warwick, whose soldiers appear to enforce York's claim, and Henry offers a compromise: Henry will be allowed to reign as king during his lifetime and will make York his heir in place of his own son, Edward, Prince of Wales.

Disgusted by his weakness, Clifford, the Earl of Westmoreland, and the Earl of Northumberland leave to tell Queen Margaret about the latest turn of events. Having taken an oath of loyalty to Henry, York departs, followed by his supporters, and Henry is left to face his angry wife and son. Queen Margaret rejects Henry's plea that he was "enforced" and returns to her army with the intention of continuing the fight (1.1.229).

Act I, Scene 2

Richard persuades his father, the Duke of York, that he is not obliged to keep the oath he took to Henry, to be a loyal subject during the king's lifetime and to wait until Henry is dead before claiming the crown. York accedes to Richard's arguments and is further convinced by learning that Queen Margaret is leading an army against them. They leave for the battlefield.

Act I, Scene 3

York's son Edmund, the Earl of Rutland, a child too young to fight, is trying to escape with his tutor. He is captured by Clifford and, despite his pleas, is murdered in revenge: "Thy father slew my father; therefore die" (46). With Rutland's blood on his sword, Clifford leaves to seek the Duke of York.

Act I, Scene 4

Richard, Duke of York, has lost the battle and is captured by Margaret and her supporters, including her son, Prince Edward, and Lord Clifford. In mockery of his attempt to become king, York is given a paper crown to wear and, finally, a handkerchief soaked in his son Rutland's blood. He defies them and is stabbed by Margaret and Clif-

Clifford murders the young Earl of Rutland before the boy's tutor in Act 1, Scene 3 of *Henry VI, Part 3*. This is a print from the Boydell Shakespeare Gallery project, which was first conceived in 1786 and lasted until 1805. *(Painting by James Northcote; engraving by Charles Gauthier Playter and Thomas Ryder)*

ford. Margaret orders that his head be cut off and set above the gates of York: "So York may overlook the town of York" (180). Clifford has thus gained revenge for his father's death by killing both the Duke's son and the Duke himself.

Act II, Scene 1

Edward and Richard wonder what has happened to their father; both men applaud his bravery in the field. Three Suns appear in the sky, and Edward, whose family emblem is the Sun, interprets the omen to mean that the three adult sons of York should join together and gain victory. He affirms that hereafter his shield will carry this symbol. A messenger arrives to tell the brothers that their father and their brother Rutland are dead, and they vow revenge. Warwick and his forces arrive and tell Edward and Richard that his own army has also been defeated by Margaret and Henry at Saint Albans. The Lancastrians have now gone to Parliament to rescind the commitment made by Henry to York and reinstate Henry's son as heir to the throne. Spurred on by Richard, Edward (now Duke of York) and Warwick vow to continue fighting even though that they may be outnumbered and head toward London to confront Queen Margaret.

Act II, Scene 2

Outside York city, King Henry laments the sight of his cousin's head above the gates. When Margaret and Clifford scold him for his softness, he continues to resist their arguments, considering that an unmerited inheritance is worse than no inheritance at all. He knights his son with the reminder to draw his sword for the cause of right only, but Prince Edward receives it with the assurance that he will use it to assert his claim to the throne. York's sons Edward, George, and Richard confront Margaret, Henry, and Clifford, but the parley leads to no resolution. Edward places the blame for his family's insurrection firmly upon Margaret, arguing that her family's poverty, the loss of France which her marriage meant to the king, and her own rapaciousness are the cause of the war between the two families. Both sides leave, intent on battle.

Act II, Scene 3

The Battle of Towton: Warwick pauses for breath and begins to lose courage. Edward and George enter and confirm that the battle is not going their way, when Richard spurs them back into the fight with the news that Warwick's brother has been killed. They vow renewed commitment to one another and the Yorkist cause and head off to inspire their army with promises of rich rewards.

Act II, Scene 4

Richard and Clifford meet in single combat. Each taunts the other with the family members that they have killed, but they are interrupted by Warwick's arrival.

Act II, Scene 5

King Henry enters alone and mourns over the shifting tides of battle. Queen Margaret and Clifford have told him to leave the field because they have better fortune without him, and employing a traditional rhetorical *topos,* or theme, Henry yearns for the simple life of a shepherd, far away from the bloody politics that surround him. In Henry's imagination, the life of a shepherd is securely marked out by the seasons and by the needs of his flock and is far superior to the luxurious but troubled life of a prince. Henry's meditation on the vanity of high place is interrupted by the entry of two pairs of figures, a Son who has killed his Father and a Father who has killed his Son. In a lyrical set-piece that relies on formal patterning and mirroring lines, each couple laments the violent times that have led to the destruction of their families, while Henry prays for his country and laments the part he has played in the wars. The scene is interrupted by Margaret and her troops, who tell Henry that the battle is lost and sweep him away.

Act II, Scene 6

Clifford collapses from his wounds. In his final speech, he blames Henry's weakness and inability to rule for the civil war that has sprung up in England. Edward, George, Richard, Warwick, and their supporters enter and discuss their progress; troops are pursuing Queen Margaret and King Henry, and although they do not know what has happened to Clifford, he is likely to be dead. Hearing a groan from the dying man, Edward commands that any soldier, whatever his loyalty, should be treated gently but rescinds that command as soon as he realizes who it is. In a scene that echoes the taunting of their father, the York brothers and Warwick insult Clifford's body, and his head is cut off, to take the place of the Duke of York's over the city. Edward confers titles on his brothers—Duke of Clarence to George and

Duke of Gloucester to Richard—and Warwick announces that he will travel to France to arrange Edward's marriage to Lady Bona, sister of the French king Lewis XI.

Act III, Scene 1

Henry explains that while his wife and son are in France seeking help from the French king, he has left his refuge in Scotland in disguise to visit England once again. Arrested by two keepers, he sadly realizes that men's loyalty changes with whoever happens to be in possession of the crown, rather than adhering to any notion of absolute right or any previous oaths of obedience.

Act III, Scene 2

King Edward IV, as he is now known, is approached by the widow Elizabeth Woodville, Lady Grey, whose husband died in support of the Yorkist cause and whose lands have been forfeited. While George and Richard provide an amused commentary on the encounter, Edward attempts to seduce her, offering her back her lands in exchange for sexual favors, but she refuses the bargain, and Edward proposes marriage instead. Their dialogue is interrupted by news of Henry's capture and imprisonment in the Tower of London, and Richard is left alone on the stage. In the longest monologue in any of Shakespeare's works (71 lines), Richard's character radically develops, becoming a far more complex figure than the other contenders for the throne. Richard meditates on his ambition, recognizing the difficulties that lie before him and considering how they might be addressed. He describes his physical deformity as an obstacle that excludes him permanently and irrevocably from any form of loving relationship and consequently decides that his aim, henceforth, will be totally bent toward achieving the crown. He describes his talents: his willingness to stop at nothing in the achievement of his aims and his intelligence. He can, he says, outdo even the "Machiavel" (3.2.193) in his ability to dissemble and deceive everyone around him in the pursuit of his goal, the crown.

Act III, Scene 3

In France, King Lewis reassures Margaret of his willingness to help her, but their council is interrupted by the arrival of Warwick, seeking Lewis's friendship and the hand of his sister in marriage for Edward. Both Lady Bona and Lewis are swayed to Warwick's side and Bona agrees to become Edward's wife. Warwick becomes enraged upon receiving news of Edward's marriage to Lady Grey. Edward's refusal to follow the path Warwick has laid out for him reminds Warwick of the various insults he has received in the past at Yorkist hands, the death of his father in support of the Yorkist cause, and the poor thanks that he has received. In revenge, he pledges himself to the service of Queen Margaret and vows to reinstate Henry on the throne. An alliance is formed between Warwick, Margaret, and Lewis, and Warwick offers the hand in marriage of his eldest daughter, Anne, to Margaret's son, Prince Edward, in token of his future loyalty. In a final soliloquy, however, Warwick acknowledges that he is supporting Henry not in any recognition of royal title but purely in revenge for Edward's disloyalty.

Act IV, Scene 1

Edward confronts his brothers and lords with his marriage to Elizabeth Woodville and challenges them to state any reasons they may have for disliking the alliance. Richard, George, and the other peers point out that Edward has made an enemy of both Warwick and the French king and, furthermore, that Edward is now favoring his wife's relatives at the expense of his brothers. A messenger enters bringing declarations of war from France, Margaret, and Warwick, and George precipitately abandons his brother's court. Edward rallies his remaining peers around him (including Richard who falsely proclaims his loyalty but who, like Warwick, informs the audience that it is proximity to the crown and not brotherly loyalty that keeps him on Edward's side) and prepares for battle.

Act IV, Scene 2

Warwick meets George and the Duke of Somerset. He has some misgivings about George's loyalty but includes him in plans to surprise Edward and take him prisoner.

Act IV, Scene 3

Edward's decision to remain in a tent on the field of battle rather than rest safely within the town proves disastrous, as he is attacked and captured. Warwick triumphs over him and sets off to restore Henry to the throne.

Act IV, Scene 4

Queen Elizabeth and her brother, Anthony Woodville, Lord Rivers, discuss the news of Edward IV's capture, and Elizabeth, now pregnant with Edward's child, retreats to sanctuary.

Act IV, Scene 5

Richard, Lord Hastings, and William Stanley rescue Edward and take ship for Flanders.

Act IV, Scene 6

King Henry thanks the Lieutenant of the Tower for his care of him and thanks Warwick for restoring him to the throne. However, he feels unfit for the burdens of government and asks Warwick to take on the role of Lord Protector

Richard and Stanley rescue Edward in Act IV, Scene 5 of *Henry VI, Part 3*. Print from the Boydell Shakespeare Gallery project *(Painting by William Miller; engraving Jean-Baptiste Michel and William Leney)*

of the realm. After some polite debate, Warwick and, George, Duke of Clarence, agree to share the responsibility while Henry devotes himself to a private life of prayer, having first urged that Margaret and Prince Edward be brought to England. Catching sight of Henry Tudor, the Earl of Richmond, Henry VI blesses him and prophesies that the boy will prove the savior of his country (he will become Henry VII of England). News of Edward's escape disturbs them, and Richmond is sent to Brittany for safety from the civil wars, thus isolating and, indeed, quarantining him from the moral and civil disorder that pervades England.

Act IV, Scene 7

Having returned to England, Edward convinces the citizens of York to open their gates to him by falsely promising that he has returned solely to regain his title of Duke of York, ironically echoing a similar claim made by Bolingbroke on his return to England before overthrowing Richard II. He rapidly abandons this position and once again proclaims himself king of England, setting off to confront Warwick and Clarence.

Act IV, Scene 8

Henry, Warwick, and Clarence hold a council of war, and Clarence and Warwick leave to defend the king. Henry reassures himself and the Duke of Exeter that his gentle and altruistic reign will secure him the loyalty of his peers and of the Commons, an argument that is proved totally fallacious by Edward's triumphant entry. Henry is recaptured and returned to the Tower of London.

Act V, Scene 1

Edward and Richard take Warwick by surprise and encamp outside his walls. Warwick defies them and becomes more confident as peer after peer enters the town in his support. When Clarence arrives, however, he defects back to his brother's side (in an early version of the play dated 1595 this happens as a result of Richard's persuasions), and the two armies march off to battle.

Act V, Scene 2

Warwick dies, lamenting over his past glories and the death of his brother, the Marquess of Montague, and urging his supporters to seek safety with Queen Margaret.

Act V, Scene 3

Edward rallies his victorious troops and departs to confront Queen Margaret at Tewkesbury.

Act V, Scene 4

Margaret urges her soldiers and councillors to remain committed to their cause in an elaborate series of metaphors, likening herself and her son to the helmsmen of the ship of state, with the York brothers, Edward, George, and Richard, as rocks, waves, and quicksand that threaten their vessel. Edward and Margaret, in almost identical speeches, urge their soldiers to this final confrontation.

Act V, Scene 5

Edward IV has captured Margaret and two of Margaret's supporters, the Earl of Oxford and Somerset, who are promptly dispatched to execution. Edward, Prince of Wales, is also captured and, after a taunting exchange between him and the York brothers, is stabbed in front of his mother by Edward, Richard, and George. Margaret's pleas to die as well are refused by Edward, and Richard rushes away to the Tower to deal with Henry.

Act V, Scene 6

Henry and Richard confront each other in the tower. Henry learns of his son's death and prophesies the evil that Richard brings with him, both for himself and for England as a whole. Richard interrupts Henry's catalog of his moral and physical deformities and stabs him before meditating on the same issue and embracing the villainy that his misshapen body and unnatural birth appear to predict. Finally dissociating himself from any of the family loyalties that he displayed earlier in the play and in previous plays, Richard affirms that his loyalty henceforth will be solely to himself and that he will set to work to destroy his brothers.

Act V, Scene 7

Edward IV sits in splendor on his throne, surrounded by his brothers, his wife, and his newborn son. Queen Margaret is banished to France, and Edward celebrates his newfound security, unaware that his brother Richard is plotting his ruin. Richard kisses his nephew but likens himself to Judas in doing so. The stage is thus set for the final episode of the tetralogy: *Richard III.*

CHARACTER LIST

King Henry VI Son of the warrior-king Henry V, he inherited his father's throne as a baby. By the beginning of this play, he has lost most of his father's French conquests and is married to the ruthless and domineering Margaret. Henry is personally gentle and, indeed, saintly, but is easily swayed, indecisive, and haunted by the fear that his right to the throne has been tainted by the manner in which his grandfather acquired the crown: the deposition and subsequent murder of Richard II.

Queen Margaret Niece of the French king Lewis XI. Her marriage with King Henry, undertaken by proxy at the end of *Henry VI, Part 1,* was deeply unpopular as she brought no dowry with her, and, in fact, Henry agreed to cede the provinces of Maine and Anjou to the French as part of the marriage agreement. In the plays, she is portrayed as dynamic, aggressive, vindictive, and cruel but passionately attached to the rights of her son and devastated by his death.

Lewis XI King of France, courted by both the Lancastrian and the Yorkist factions. He is alienated from the Yorkist faction by Edward's rejection of his sister, Lady Bona.

Edward, Prince of Wales Only son of Henry VI and Queen Margaret, although doubt is cast on his paternity by some (In *Henry VI, Parts 1* and *2* Margaret is portrayed as having a very close relationship with the Duke of Suffolk). In this play, he is portrayed as more like his mother than his father; he is determined to fight for the crown. He is defeated and stabbed by the Yorkists at Tewkesbury.

Henry, Earl of Richmond A nonspeaking but crucial role. Henry Tudor, later King Henry VII, is recognized in this play by Henry VI as the figure who will restore peace to England. Henry is blessed by Henry VI in Act IV, Scene 6 before being sent to safety in France, whence he will return in *Richard III* to defeat Richard and finally unite the families of York and Lancaster.

Duke of Somerset The second Duke of Somerset's head is carried onto the stage by Richard in Act I, Scene 1. The play does not distinguish between the third and fourth dukes (although Edward does refer to the three Somersets who have withstood him). For the purposes of this play, Somerset is a Lancastrian supporter who is briefly in favor with the Yorkists (4.1.) but reverts to Lancastrian loyalty and is executed after the Battle of Tewkesbury.

Duke of Exeter Lancastrian supporter who is part of the negotiations whereby Henry VI will name York his heir in place of his son.

Earl of Oxford Lancastrian supporter who will later join Henry Tudor's invasion against Richard III.

Earl of Northumberland Lancastrian supporter who assists in the capture of York in Act I, Scene 4 but is moved by York's grief for the death of his son the Earl of Rutland.

Earl of Westmoreland Lancastrian supporter. Along with the Earl of Northumberland, he is disgusted by Henry's weakness but remains loyal to Queen Margaret and Prince Edward.

Lord Clifford Lancastrian supporter and key to the revenge motif in the play. Shakespeare depicts Clifford as killing the Earl of Rutland in revenge for his father's death at the hands of the Duke of York and later taunting York with the fact before killing the Duke. Richard fatally wounds Clifford in revenge, and in his dying speech, Clifford blames the civil war on Henry for weak rule.

Richard Plantagenet, Duke of York Father of Edward, George, Richard, and Rutland, head of the house of York, and claimant to the

English throne. Although he has promised to live as a loyal subject to Henry VI provided that he inherits the throne after Henry's death, he is persuaded to break this promise by Richard and is attacked by Margaret's army. He is defeated, captured, and killed by Margaret and Clifford.

Edward (later Edward IV) The eldest son of Richard Plantagenet and, thus, later on Duke of York and, eventually, king of England (Edward IV). He is courageous but easily manipulated by his brother Richard, and his sexual self-indulgence leads him to marry Elizabeth Woodville instead of the politically advantageous marriage with the Lady Bona that Warwick has been negotiating. Edward's marriage alienates both Warwick and the king of France and causes discontent within his family. Although this play ends with Edward enthroned as king, the audience is not permitted to forget that his security is both illusory and transitory; Richard is already waiting for the opportunity to seize the crown for himself.

George (later Duke of Clarence) Son of Richard Plantagenet, brother of Edward. He is alienated by Edward's marriage and throws in his lot with Warwick but rejoins his brothers at a crucial point, enabling Edward to defeat Warwick.

Richard (later Duke of Gloucester) Son of Richard Plantagenet, brother of Edward. He begins the play as a loyal son and brother but by the end of the play, has declared his own ambition and is plotting for the crown against his brothers. He is manipulative and bloodthirsty, killing both Prince Edward and Henry VI.

Edmund, Earl of Rutland Son of Richard Plantagenet. A young boy and noncombatant, he is killed by Clifford in revenge for his father's death.

Earl of Warwick Richard Neville, known as "the Kingmaker," is one of York's most important supporters. Throughout the play, his support or opposition determines who holds the crown of England. Although he is loyal to the Yorkists

for most of the play, Edward's decision to marry Elizabeth Woodville rather than Lady Bona infuriates Warwick, and he defects to Henry's side in revenge for the insult. He is finally defeated and killed at the Battle of Barnet.

Duke of Norfolk John Mowbray, a Yorkist supporter.

Marquess of Montague Brother of Warwick who changed sides, along with his brother, and died at the same battle.

Earl of Pembroke and Lord Stafford Nonspeaking roles. Both are Yorkist supporters who appear at Edward's court in Act IV, Scene 1.

Lord Hastings and William Stanley Yorkist supporters who, along with Richard, rescue Edward from captivity in Act IV, Scene 5. Both will be important figures in *Richard III*.

Sir John Mortimer and Sir Hugh Mortimer Uncles of the Duke of York who die fighting for York at the Battle of Wakefield (1.4).

Anthony Woodville, Lord Rivers Brother of Elizabeth Woodville.

Elizabeth Woodville, Lady Grey (later Queen Elizabeth) Historically a Lancastrian partisan, Shakespeare here depicts her as a Yorkist who appeals to Edward for the restoration of her late husband's lands. Her beauty and refusal to submit to Edward's sexual demands lead Edward into marrying her.

Sir John Montgomery A Yorkist supporter who encourages Edward to assert his claim to the throne against Henry and Warwick in Act IV, Scene 7.

Sir John Somerville Lancastrian supporter.

Tutor to Rutland He is unable to protect his charge, but his life is spared by Clifford because he is a cleric.

Mayor of York Thomas of Beverley, who is rather easily persuaded by Edward to open the gates to the city, thus enabling Edward to begin his campaign to regain the crown.

Mayor of Coventry John Brett, loyal to Warwick.

Lieutenant of the Tower Henry VI's jailer, whom he thanks for his careful treatment of him.

Lady Grey in *Henry VI, Part 3*. This is a print from Charles Heath's 1848 edition of *The Heroines of Shakspeare: Comprising the Principal Female Characters in the Plays of the Great Poet. (Painting by J. W. Wright; engraving by B. Eyles)*

A Son who has killed his Father and a Father who has killed his Son Figures from the Yorkist and Lancastrian sides who in their namelessness represent all victims of civil war.

CHARACTER STUDIES
Henry VI

Historically, Henry Plantagenet was born in 1421, the grandson of Henry Bolingbroke (Henry IV) and son of Henry V, the hero of Agincourt. Henry V died when his son was a baby, and although Henry inherited two crowns—that of England and of France—he proved incapable of retaining them. He was subject to fits of mental instability (although Shakespeare does not portray this), and for much of his adult life, he was controlled by his wife, Queen Margaret, and her faction. *Henry VI, Parts 1,* and *2* describe Henry's growth to adulthood and the infighting between his regents, the loss of France, and his marriage to Margaret of Anjou. The marriage, a costly one for England, which had to cede lands to France rather than receive any dowry for Margaret, was detrimental in other ways. The enmity between Margaret and Richard Plantagenet, the duke of York, and his faction led to civil war and eventually to Henry's murder. *Henry VI, Part 3* documents the final years of Henry's life.

Shakespeare's portrayal of Henry in this play and the earlier ones is that of an ineffectual and weak king whose personal virtue does not make up for his inability to rule and to maintain order. From the beginning of the play, Henry is depicted as being fatally flawed as a monarch on three counts: first, his fear that his claim to the throne is in fact less strong than it should be and that York's claim to the throne is more legitimate; second, his personal gentleness, which leads him to attempt to avoid conflict whenever possible; and third, his willingness to be dominated by other, stronger characters and to hand over the responsibility of decision making to others. Thus far, it might appear that Henry is without any redeeming characteristics, but Shakespeare has created a more nuanced character than this. Henry, alone in the play, is motivated neither by personal nor familial ambition, and he is genuinely, if ineffectually, concerned for what is right rather than what is personally profitable. Act II, Scene 2 demonstrates this when Henry is rebuked by Clifford for his regret over his cousin the Duke of York's death. In response to Clifford's argument that even irrational animals are able to seek the best for their young, and that Henry's failure to protect his son the Prince of Wales's inheritance is the sign of an unnatural parent, Henry presents the counter-argument that an unlawful inheritance is worse than none at all:

But Clifford tell me, didst thou never hear
That things ill got had ever bad success?
(2.2.45–46).

He knights his son with the injunction to "draw thy sword in right" (2.2.62), in other words to fulfill the duties of a knight to use force only in a good cause. His son, Edward, however, in keeping with the other characters of the play, responds with the determination to use his sword in order to further his own interests, irrespective of right or wrong:

My gracious father, by your kingly leave,
I'll draw it as apparent to the crown,
And in that quarrel use it to the death.
(2.2.63–65)

Henry's downfall comes in part, indeed, from his desire to do what is right as opposed to what is expedient, and to his expectation that other people will do likewise. Thus, in the scene where he returns to England from Scotland and is captured by two keepers, he asks them to recollect the oaths of loyalty they have taken to him in the past only to be confronted with their blunt real politik. Their oaths of loyalty held good only when he was king; now that another man sits in Westminster, their loyalty is to him instead: "we were subjects but while you were king" (3.1.80). Equally, when Edward's army is storming the Bishop of London's palace, Henry remains convinced that the majority of his peers will remain loyal to him because of his gentle rule right up to the point where he is taken prisoner and returned to the Tower of London for the final time.

Henry's unworldliness emphasizes the extent to which the struggle for the crown of England is based on superior force rather than issues of divine appointment or legitimate right to rule within this play. Although in Act I, Scene 1 there is some show of reasoned debate over whose claim to the throne is more legitimate, this quickly gives way to the question of who has more soldiers and who has won the most recent battle.

One of Henry's most important scenes is Act II, Scene 5, which is set apart from the action of the play but acts in many ways as a distillation of the play's main concerns, in particular the dangers and consequences of civil conflict. In this scene, Henry uses the image of a shepherd to express his yearning for a quiet life, ordered by the changing rhythm of the seasons. The image of the ruler as a shepherd is one commonplace in literature, from the Bible to the classics, and Henry's repeated use of the shepherd image, both in this scene and elsewhere in the play, indicates the kind of ruler he desires to be: one who guides and protects his subjects. Henry is the only figure in the play who recognizes the duties and responsibilities of monarchy, and the fact that he is such a failure as a monarch emphasizes the moral bankruptcy of the world that Shakespeare is portraying. In a play that dramatizes harsh political realities, Henry's virtues are the very issues that make him a failure as a king, and notwithstanding his desire for peace, Henry's inability to hold the crown and rule firmly are, at least in part, the cause of all the deaths he laments. The only good man within this play is thus almost comically ineffectual, frightened of his wife, and despised by almost everyone around him. His son does not listen to him, and his wife and her supporters tell him that they will do better on the battlefield without him. The only element of moral authority left to Henry is when, in a prophetic moment, he recognizes the young Henry Tudor as being "England's hope" (4.6), the boy who will grow up to defeat Richard and bring the Wars of the Roses to an end. Henry VI is powerless to restore peace, but he is at least able to prophesy it.

In creating Henry, Shakespeare drew on sources such as *A Mirror for Magistrates,* in which Henry portrays his marriage and his belief that as monarch, he was entitled to do as he pleased as the two faults that led to his downfall. The character that Shakespeare has created is one that, in his failures but also in his virtues, is a far more three-dimensional figure, one whose failures as a monarch are ruthlessly highlighted, but whose moral qualities also serve to emphasize the near-total lack of adherence to principles of right and wrong anywhere else in the play.

Margaret

The historical Margaret, or Marguerite of Anjou, was born in 1430. She was the daughter of René, duke of Anjou and nominally king of Sicily and Jerusalem, and the cousin of King Lewis IX. She was married to King Henry VI of England by proxy (the duke of Suffolk represented her husband) in 1445, when she was 15, and was crowned later that year at Titchfield. The marriage was deeply unpopular in England as she brought no dowry with her but rather Henry had given the lands of Anjou and Maine back to the French as part of the marriage agreement. In life, as in the play, she appears to have been an intelligent and strong-minded woman, who, particularly during her husband's periods of mental weakness, more or less took over the governance of the kingdom. By the commencement of *Henry VI, Part 3,* she is a battle-hardened warrior whose only concern is to secure her son's inheritance as the next king of England. She is contemptuous of what she sees as her husband's weakness and inability to withstand pressure from York and furious when he signs away her son's inheritance. While Henry pleads ineffectually that he was coerced by York and Warwick, Margaret leaves to seek the military force that will safeguard her son's right to the crown.

Although up to this point Margaret might be considered to be more sinned against than sinning, and, indeed, her refusal to allow her husband to compromise her son's future is understandable, she loses audience sympathy in the final scene between herself and her nemesis, the Duke of York. Here, York has been captured and is at Margaret's mercy. With increasing brutality, she and Clifford join in humiliating their prisoner. In a scene reminiscent of the tormenting of Christ before the crucifixion, York is made to stand on a molehill and have a paper crown placed on his head, and finally, Margaret taunts him with evidence of his young son's murder; a handkerchief stained with Rutland's blood is offered him to wipe his face. Shakespeare used the chronicles of Hall and Holinshed as his inspiration for this scene, but in neither of the chronicles is Margaret present, and the bloody handkerchief seems also to be Shakespeare's own, a motif popular in the revenge drama of the time. Margaret's participation in the scene confirms the audience's perception of her as being "unwomanly." Her previous concern for her son's inheritance is understandable and even creditable; a sign of her natural feelings as a mother, but her brutality toward York allows her moral authority to evaporate even as she asserts her physical supremacy over him. Hence, from being an oath-breaker who has been fairly defeated, York becomes a victim, and his speech in response to her mockery of him emphasizes the extent to which she, rather than her husband, is responsible for the Wars of the Roses.

Margaret is a woman and foreign. Both of these elements render her a sinister and powerful figure in the play. In her mockery of York, her language takes on a parody of a maternal, domestic tone:

> Where are your mess of sons to back you now,
> The wanton Edward and the lusty George?
> And where's that valiant crookback prodigy,
> Dicky your boy, that with his grumbling voice
> Was wont to cheer his dad in mutinies?
> Or with the rest, where is your darling,
>   Rutland? (1.4.73–78)

Her violation of conventional expectations of womanly behavior renders her cruelty more horrific, and York's response reminds her, and the audience, that she is unnatural:

> She-wolf of France, but worse than wolves of
>   France,
> Whose tongue more poisons than the adder's
>   tooth,
> How ill-beseeming is it in thy sex
> To triumph like an Amazonian trull
> Upon their woes, whom fortune captivates.
>   (1.4.111–115)

York emphasizes Margaret's failings as a woman; the Amazons were a by-word for bloodthirsty, emasculating women, and the rest of his speech describes her as utterly unnatural, indeed inhuman:

> Women are soft, mild, pitiful, and flexible;
> Thou stern, indurate, flinty, rough, remorseless.
>   (1.4.141–142)

Margaret's cruelty renders her monstrous; no true woman, York argues, could possibly behave as she has done. The unnaturalness of Margaret's behavior is further emphasized by Northumberland's sympathetic response to York:

> Had he been slaughter-man to all my kin
> I should not for my life but weep with him,
> To see how inly sorrow gripes his soul.
>   (1.4.169–171)

Northumberland sheds tears where Margaret, a woman, does not. In every possible way in this scene, Shakespeare constructs Margaret's character as one that has been warped by taking part in this war. Although Margaret was not present at Rutland's murder, York conflates her and Clifford as being equally guilty of child murder and argues that the crime they have committed will remain a stain on them no matter who wins their encounter. Only in the final lines of his speech does he refer to the actual cause of their enmity: the crown. By focusing his speech on Margaret's defects, York renders the enormity of the crime she has committed disproportionate to their quarrel and thus constructs himself as a victim of her cruelty rather than an opponent who has been fairly defeated.

York builds up an image of Margaret to the audience as unnatural, unwomanly, and foreign, the emblem of a disastrous marriage and the loss of the lands that had been gained through the heroic exploits of Henry V. Margaret therefore symbolizes the extent to which England has declined from its conquering past, when it was able to bring other lands under its control. Now Margaret, the foreigner, has invaded England and is bringing about its destruction. In this manner, Shakespeare enables displacement of the blame away from Henry

VI himself and onto Margaret as the unwomanly intruder whose cruelty and untrustworthiness make her the author of all England's ills.

As the play develops, Margaret remains the center of the Lancastrian cause. She is active and articulate; Shakespeare depicts her rallying her armies, engaging in desperate diplomacy with King Lewis of France on her son's behalf, and finally holding her forces together in the face of disaster. The speech in which she rallies her forces before the Battle of Tewkesbury, the final battle of the play, is an elaborate conceit on the ship of state. In this speech, Shakespeare depicts Margaret as a master of formal rhetoric, constructing herself and her son as substitutes for the king as the pilot of the ship, and depicting her enemies as the rocks, waves, and quicksand on which the ship might well founder. In this and her following speech to her troops, Margaret is presented with dignity and authority, a very different figure to York's sadistic tormentor. Her final appearance in the play is a tragic one in which, with poetic justice, her own son is murdered in front of her, by the sons of the man whom she mocked and ordered killed. As she begs Edward and Clarence to kill her as well, Richard rushes away to the Tower to kill her husband. Margaret is finally banished to France by Edward but will (unhistorically) return as a witness to events in *Richard III*.

Richard

With the exception of Henry, the aristocratic characters of *Henry VI, Part 3* share similar qualities: All are self-seeking, courageous warriors who are driven by family pride, personal honor, and ambition. At first glance, the Duke of York's son Richard appears to be not dissimilar from any of the others. Like his brothers, he competes for his father's approval at the beginning of the play by displaying his war trophies. Like his brothers, he urges his father not to wait for Henry to die but to fight for the crown immediately, and like his brothers and Warwick, he vows vengeance for his father's death. If we consider Richard's character from a psychoanalytic perspective, it is tempting

and prowess in battle, and appears to value himself only to the extent that he is his father's son. In other words, Richard's perception of himself is shaped by his relationship to other people, particularly his father. On hearing the news of his father's death, Edward reacts with tears but Richard with the determination to revenge:

> Richard, I bear thy name; I'll venge thy death,
> Or die renowned by attempting it. (2.1.87–88).

While Richard is certainly not alone in his determination to take revenge for his father's death, it is significant that he does so using a phrase that emphasizes the deep connection between himself and his father. Given this emphasis on his family connections, furthermore, the taunts of characters like Margaret become more deadly:

> But thou art neither like thy sire nor dam,
> But like a foul misshapen stigmatic,
> Marked by the Destinies to be avoided,
> As venom toads, or lizards' dreadful stings.
>   (2.2.135–138)

By describing Richard in these terms, Margaret is denying him the family connection that appears to have been all-important to him in the previous scenes, and in a very real way, she is helping create the monster that Richard will become when he says:

> I have no brother, I am like no brother;
> And this word "love," which greybeards call
>   divine,
> Be resident in men like one another,
> And not in me: I am myself alone. (5.4.80–83)

Thus, Richard becomes the product of his time, the creation of those around him. Although there is no evidence to suggest that Richard's physical deformity was anything other than Tudor propaganda, from an Elizabethan point of view, Shakespeare was working within the context of known historical material: Richard was deformed; he did become the tyrant king and murderer depicted

King Edward proposes marriage to Lady Grey while George and Richard look on in Act III, Scene 2 of *Henry VI, Part 3*. Print from the Boydell Shakespeare Gallery project *(Painting by William Hamilton; engraving by Thomas Holloway)*

to argue that it is his father's death that drives Richard toward his path of lonely ambition. The following words are Richard's he and his brother Edward await news of their father:

> I cannot joy until I be resolv'd
> Where our right valiant father is become . . .
> Methinks 'tis prize enough to be his son.
>   (2.1.9–10, 20)

At this stage in the play, Richard appears, like any of the other characters, to possess strong bonds of family loyalty. He celebrates his father's courage

by Sir Thomas More, among others. Therefore, Shakespeare's dramatic treatment of Richard, as with all the other historical figures whom he was dramatizing, needed to conform to the familiar outcome. Within that context, the process by which Shakespeare depicts Richard's alienation and renders it psychologically convincing is remarkable.

Not only is Richard a psychologically developed figure; he is also crucial to the development of others. While it is true to say that his ambition and desire for revenge is typical of others in the play—Clifford is as bloodthirsty as Richard, Edward is as determined to achieve the crown—it is notable that Shakespeare has woven Richard into the story as the motivating force behind key decisions in a way that does not appear in the sources that he used. It is worth noting, thus, that Richard's arguments persuade his father to break his oath to remain Henry's subject during his lifetime; Richard urges Edward, George, and Warwick to fight on at Towton; and Richard at least encourages George in his dissatisfaction with Edward's marriage and subsequent favoring of his wife's family over his own. Although Shakespeare does not portray Richard here as the smooth-tongued manipulator to the same extent as in *Richard III,* he is, nonetheless, the figure who encourages others to take decisions that will lead to further warfare and revenge.

Moral and physical deformity were seen in Shakespeare's day as being related. Francis Bacon in his essay "On Deformity" stated:

> DEFORMED persons are commonly even with nature; for as nature hath done ill by them, so do they by nature; being for the most part (as the Scripture saith) void of natural affection; and so they have their revenge of nature. Certainly there is a consent, between the body and the mind; and where nature erreth in the one, she ventureth in the other . . . Therefore it is good to consider of deformity, not as a sign, which is more deceivable; but as a cause, which seldom faileth of the effect. Whosoever hath anything fixed in his person, that doth induce contempt, hath also a perpetual spur in himself, to rescue and deliver himself from scorn. Therefore all deformed persons, are extreme bold. First, as in their own defence, as being exposed to scorn; but in process of time, by a general habit. Also it stirreth in them industry, and especially of this kind, to watch and observe the weakness of others, that they may have somewhat to repay. (296)

This essay could have been written for Richard, for whom deformity is at once a reason for his evil and a consequence of his evil. In the play *Richard III,* Richard's natural evil is represented by his physical deformity. In *Henry VI, Part 3,* the situation appears rather more complex as the emphasis placed by characters such as Margaret, Henry, and their son, Prince Edward, on Richard's deformity seem to provide a motivation for Richard to become evil.

DIFFICULTIES OF THE PLAY

The most immediate problem of *Henry VI, Part 3* is its assumption of prior knowledge. From the first line of the play, "I wonder how the king escap'd our hands!" we are in the middle of a story, not at the beginning. The play is located at the end of a series, and anyone new to the plays or not having a grasp of the basics of the Yorkist and Lancastrian feuds is going to have difficulties. Without understanding the play's background, *Henry VI, Part 3* will appear to be a collection of battles between person or persons unknown, loosely held together by arguments. Briefly then, here is a guide to the main events and characters.

The *Henry VI* plays as a whole are concerned with the power vacuum created when the monarch is unable or unwilling to rule properly. Both the families of Lancaster and York have good claim to the crown, and Henry VI's ineffectiveness and unwise marriage has led his cousin the Duke of York to demand the throne. Henry is hampered by his own gentleness and desire to do right, while York is driven by ambition and by dislike of Margaret. The Earl of Warwick perceives himself as the puppet-master whose support is essential to the throne of England, and when Edward reveals his own feckless nature in marrying Elizabeth Woodville, Lady Grey, Warwick is driven to change sides.

The bond between parent and child, and particularly father and son, is important in these plays. Clifford's obsessive need to avenge his father's death, Margaret's passionate devotion to her son's interests, and even Richard's statement about his father, "Methinks 'tis prize enough to be his son" (2.1.20) all testify to the supreme importance of family relationships within the play—and their destruction. The central scene of the Father who has killed his Son and the Son who has killed his Father, epitomizes the connection between civil and familial conflict.

A further difficulty with *Henry VI, Part 3* is that the various battles and revenge killings can appear confusing and interchangeable; there are no real heroes or absolute villains in the play. Even Richard of Gloucester is really no more bloodthirsty than any other character within it, and the play is arguably lacking a straightforward conflict between good and evil that can be firmly resolved. Rather than a narrative that pushes the action forward from *a* to *d* through *b* and *c*, *Henry VI, Part 3* is a play about consequences. It takes the familiar figure of speech that describes the king as the "father of his country" literally. Henry's failure as monarch is dramatized in the form of familial and intergenerational breakdown, and the "happy family" image that concludes the play—Edward IV and his wife with their baby son, and George and Richard looking on—is all the more compelling because it is completely false.

Henry VI, Part 3 is deeply rooted in English history. Some find it overly historical, requiring too much contextual understanding from audiences and readers. This need not necessarily be the case, however. Ambition, revenge, betrayal, and civil war have not (unfortunately) become outdated, and any reading or performance of the play should reflect this.

KEY PASSAGES
Act I, Scene 1, 102–148

YORK. Will you we show our title to the crown?
If not, our swords shall plead it in the field.

KING HENRY. What title hast thou, traitor,
  to the crown?
Thy father was as thou art, Duke of York,
Thy grandfather Roger Mortimer, Earl of March.
I am the son of Henry the Fifth,
Who made the Dauphin and the French to stoop,
And seized upon their towns and provinces.

WARWICK. Talk not of France, sith thou hast
  lost it all.

KING HENRY. The Lord Protector lost it
  and not I.
When I was crowned I was but nine months old.

RICHARD. You are old enough now, and yet
  methinks you lose.
Father, tear the crown from the usurper's head.

EDWARD. Sweet father do so, set it on your head.

MONTAGUE. Good brother as thou lov'st
  and honour'st arms,
Let's fight it out and not stand cavilling thus.

RICHARD. Sound drums and trumpets, and
  the King will fly.

YORK. Sons, peace.

KING HENRY. Peace thou, and give King
  Henry leave to speak.

WARWICK. Plantagenet shall speak first. Hear
  him lords,
And be you silent and attentive too,
For he that interrupts him shall not live.

KING HENRY. Think'st thou that I will leave
  my kingly throne

Wherein my grandsire and my father sat?
No, first shall war unpeople this my realm.
Ay, and their colours often borne in France—
And now in England to our heart's great
  sorrow—
Shall be my winding-sheet. Why faint you lords?
My title's good, and better far than his.

WARWICK. Prove it Henry, and thou shalt be
  King.

KING HENRY. Henry the Fourth by
conquest got the crown.

YORK. 'Twas by rebellion against his king.

KING HENRY. *[aside]* I know not what to
say, my title's weak.—
Tell me, may not a king adopt an heir?

YORK. What then?

KING HENRY. And if he may, then am I
  lawful king,
For Richard in the view of many lords
Resigned the crown to Henry the Fourth,
Whose heir my father was, and I am his.

YORK. He rose against him, being his
  sovereign,
And made him to resign his crown perforce.

WARWICK. Suppose, my lords, he did it
  unconstrained,
Think you 'twere prejudicial to his crown?

EXETER. No, for he could not so resign his
  crown,
But that the next heir should succeed and reign.

KING HENRY. Art thou against us, Duke of
  Exeter?

EXETER. His is the right, and therefore
  pardon me.

In the preamble to this scene, the Duke of York has taken the royal throne in Parliament, the geographic center of the English state. Together, the king and Parliament form the supreme legislative English body, a concept known as "king (or queen) in parliament," and it is through this combination that laws are enacted. Thus, when York assumes the throne in Parliament, he is not simply appropriating a symbol of royalty, he is occupying the monarch's place of supreme power in England.

This scene summarizes the tangle of issues that push forward the play's narrative and demonstrates the extent to which figures from the past dominate the present. York's claim against Henry is twofold: first, that Henry's title to the crown—his right to rule—is not as good as York's, and second, that Henry is proving a poor monarch—he has lost France, which his father had won for England. The matter of inheritance refers us to the original act of usurpation in which Richard II was forced to "adopt" Bolingbroke (the present Henry's grandfather) as his heir, deposed, and subsequently murdered. Henry VI, therefore, owes his seat on the throne to an act of rebellion and usurpation. York's claim stems from his mother, Anne Mortimer, whose father, Roger Mortimer, had been Richard's natural heir and whose uncle Edmund has passed his claim to Richard in a scene in *Henry VI, Part 2*. Thus, although Henry had the right of immediate inheritance behind him, York's claim to the throne was less tainted by violent usurpation. Clearly, however, from this scene and elsewhere, the question of legitimate right to rule is overlaid by ability to rule and the military force to take the crown; as Montague says, "Let's fight it out." Henry's reference to the hero-king Henry V, his father, serves only to highlight Henry's own shortcomings. Henry's father won France, but Henry himself has lost it, and at this stage in the play, Warwick and Edward have more soldiers.

Another important issue that this episode in the play highlights is the question of whether it is possible for a king to nominate a successor outside the normal line of succession. In theory, the Acts of Succession passed in 1536 and 1543 enabled Henry VIII and his successors to dispose of the crown as they saw fit, but as it was passed from Henry to Edward to Mary to Elizabeth in proper lineal order, the theory never had to be put to the test. However, by the 1590s, when Elizabeth would clearly not produce a child herself nor openly nominate her successor, the question of whether the monarch had the right to nominate an heir who was not the direct lineal successor was once again an important issue. Thus, the debate here, over whether Richard II was in fact legitimately able to nominate who should succeed him—Henry Bolingbroke—over his nearest lineal successor—Roger Mortimer—had a very direct bearing on Elizabethan politics of the 1590s.

Act I, Scene 4, 66–168

QUEEN MARGARET. Brave warriors,
  Clifford and Northumberland,
Come, make him stand upon this molehill here,
That raught at mountains with outstretched
  arms,
Yet parted but the shadow with his hand.
What! was it you that would be England's king?
Was't you that revell'd in our parliament,
And made a preachment of your high descent?
Where are your mess of sons to back you now?
The wanton Edward, and the lusty George?
And where's that valiant crook-back prodigy,
Dicky your boy, that with his grumbling voice
Was wont to cheer his dad in mutinies?
Or, with the rest, where is your darling
  Rutland?
Look, York: I stain'd this napkin with the blood
That valiant Clifford, with his rapier's point,
Made issue from the bosom of the boy;
And if thine eyes can water for his death,
I give thee this to dry thy cheeks withal.
Alas poor York! but that I hate thee deadly,
I should lament thy miserable state.
I prithee, grieve, to make me merry, York.
What, hath thy fiery heart so parch'd thine
  entrails
That not a tear can fall for Rutland's death?
Why art thou patient, man? thou shouldst be
  mad;

And I, to make thee mad, do mock thee thus.
Stamp, rave, and fret, that I may sing and
  dance.
Thou wouldst be fee'd, I see, to make me sport:
York cannot speak, unless he wear a crown.
A crown for York; and lords bow low to him:
Hold you his hands whilst I do set it on.
[She puts a paper crown on his head.]
Ay, marry, sir, now looks he like a king.
Ay, this is he that took King Henry's chair,
And this is he was his adopted heir.
But how is it that great Plantagenet
Is crown'd so soon, and broke his solemn oath?
As I bethink me, you should not be king
Till our King Henry had shook hands with
  death.
And will you pale your head in Henry's glory,
And rob his temples of the diadem,
Now in his life, against your holy oath?
O, 'tis a fault too too unpardonable!
Off with the crown, and with the crown his
  head;
And, whilst we breathe, take time to do him
  dead. . . .

YORK. She-wolf of France, but worse than
  wolves of France,
Whose tongue more poisons than the adder's
  tooth!
How ill-beseeming is it in thy sex
To triumph, like an Amazonian trull,
Upon their woes whom fortune captivates!
But that thy face is, vizard-like, unchanging,
Made impudent with use of evil deeds,
I would assay, proud queen, to make thee
  blush.
To tell thee whence thou camest, of whom
  derived,
Were shame enough to shame thee, wert thou
  not shameless.
Thy father bears the type of King of Naples,
Of both the Sicils and Jerusalem,
Yet not so wealthy as an English yeoman.
Hath that poor monarch taught thee to insult?

It needs not, nor it boots thee not, proud
  queen,
Unless the adage must be verified,
That beggars mounted run their horse to
  death.
'Tis beauty that doth oft make women proud;
But, God he knows, thy share thereof is small:
'Tis virtue that doth make them most admired;
The contrary doth make thee wonder'd at:
'Tis government that makes them seem divine;
The want thereof makes thee abominable:
Thou art as opposite to every good
As the Antipodes are unto us,
Or as the south to the septentrion.
O tiger's heart wrapt in a woman's hide!
How couldst thou drain the life-blood of the
  child,
To bid the father wipe his eyes withal,
And yet be seen to bear a woman's face?
Women are soft, mild, pitiful and flexible;
Thou stern, obdurate, flinty, rough,
  remorseless.
Bids't thou me rage? why, now thou hast thy
  wish:
Wouldst have me weep? why, now thou hast
  thy will:
For raging wind blows up incessant showers,
And when the rage allays, the rain begins.
These tears are my sweet Rutland's obsequies:
And every drop cries vengeance for his death,
'Gainst thee, fell Clifford, and thee, false
Frenchwoman.

NORTHUMBERLAND. Beshrew me, but his
  passion moves me so
That hardly can I check my eyes from tears.

YORK. That face of his the hungry cannibals
Would not have touch'd, would not have
  stain'd with blood:
But you are more inhuman, more inexorable,
O, ten times more, than tigers of Hyrcania.
See, ruthless queen, a hapless father's tears:
This cloth thou dip'dst in blood of my sweet
  boy,

And I with tears do wash the blood away.
Keep thou the napkin, and go boast of this:
And if thou tell'st the heavy story right,
Upon my soul, the hearers will shed tears;
Yea even my foes will shed fast-falling tears,
And say 'Alas, it was a piteous deed!'
There, take the crown, and, with the crown,
  my curse;
And in thy need such comfort come to thee
As now I reap at thy too cruel hand!
Hard-hearted Clifford, take me from the world:
My soul to heaven, my blood upon your heads!

This passage is important in a number of ways.
Shakespeare has drawn inspiration for it from
Holinshed's account of York's death:

> Some write that the duke was taken alive, and
> in derision caused to stand upon a molehill,
> on whose head they put a garland in steed of
> a crowne, which they had fashioned and made
> of sedges or bulrushes; and having so crowned
> him with that garland, they kneeled downe
> afore him (as the Jewes did unto Christ) in
> scorne, saieng to him; Haile king without rule,
> haile king without heritage, haile duke and
> prince without people or possessions. And at
> length having thus scorned him with these and
> diverse other the like despitefull words, they
> stroke off his head, which . . . they presented to
> the queene. (269)

There are three important elements to this narrative and to the inspiration that Shakespeare took
from it. First, there is the comparison of the Duke
of York to Christ before the Jews, with all its implications of innocence and unjustified cruelty, which
casts the Duke in the role of the martyred victim
rather than a political opponent. Second, Shakespeare has reconstructed the scene with Queen
Margaret as its primary instigator, when, according
to the records, she was not even present. In making
Margaret, rather than Clifford or any other soldier,
the instigator of the violence and ridicule inflicted
upon York, Shakespeare not only enables one of his

principal characters to remain onstage but keeps the focus firmly on the element of personal hatred that is such a corrosive influence within the play. Finally, Shakespeare has added a further layer to the scene by having Margaret taunt York with the death of his son Rutland.

Margaret's taunting of York reproduces the previous scene in which York had assumed Henry's royal throne in the Parliament—but in a manner that transforms York's earlier assumption of power into a mockery. The royal throne is now a molehill, and York is transformed into the shadow of a king, a player king designed to amuse the real queen. In this manner, Margaret attempts to render York's earlier bid for power nothing more than a temporary aberration, the sort of inversion of authority associated with Yuletide festivities, when hierarchical structures of authority were traditionally turned upside down, and Margaret's use of the phrase "revelled in our parliament" emphasizes the implication that York and his allies are nothing but rogues, servants who have been permitted for a time to ape their betters but who must now be reminded of their true position. The paper crown that York is given is designed not only to humiliate him in the present but to belittle his previous claims, as well.

Again, the struggle for the crown of England is expressed in terms of family and family relationships. Each side competes to have a family tree that justifies a claim to the crown, and while military force and competence to rule are both vital issues, lineal right is also important. The death of Rutland is not merely the death of a son; it is an attack on the entire family line, on the possibility of continuity that children represent. The news of Rutland's death is Margaret's ultimate weapon in breaking her opponent's heart. In adding this element to the scene, Shakespeare creates a direct thematic connection between family destruction and civil conflict. Of course, it also prefigures the moment when Margaret will lose her own son, when he is stabbed in front of her at the end of the play. Shakespeare's careful patterning and shaping of the drama matches death with death, child with child.

Margaret's status and the balance of power between herself and her antagonist change dramatically in this passage. At the beginning of the scene, Margaret is wholly in control. She is able to force York to adopt any ridiculous or humiliating position that she chooses, with the molehill a deliberate insult to his aspirations (here, she implies, is a man who has attempted to make a mountain out of a molehill). In the view of her soldiers and, of course, the audience, Margaret enacts her authority upon York, imposing an identity upon him that is of her choosing rather than his (York perceives himself as the legitimate heir to the English throne, while Margaret perceives him as a deluded rebel against legitimate authority whose pretensions would be pitiable "but that I hate thee deadly"). Her use of Rutland's blood to torment his father, however, goes too far and gives York the opportunity to seize the rhetorical upper hand. York attacks her, not on the grounds of their political opposition, but on more personal issues. He begins by defining her as inhuman: "she-wolf of France," more poisonous than an adder, a "tiger's heart wrapped in a woman's hide," worse than a Hyrcanian tiger (a country conventionally associated with fierce tigers), a foreigner who can be compared to anything that is opposite to goodness and to England. Margaret's poor background and the economic cost her marriage represented to England (fully represented at the beginning of *Henry VI, Part 2*) is here returned to the audience's attention. York goes on to list the various ways in which Margaret fails as a woman; she lacks beauty, virtue, self-control (governance). To establish himself, rather than Margaret, as the arbiter of conduct, despite their relative positions, York appeals to the audience and to the other characters onstage as a father. He succeeds in reducing Margaret to a shrewish, vicious woman whose crimes will remain with her whatever becomes of the crown.

Act II, Scene 5, 55–124

SON. Ill blows the wind that profits nobody.
This man, whom hand to hand I slew in fight,
May be possessed with some store of crowns;

And I, that haply take them from him now,
May yet ere night yield both my life and them
To some man else, as this dead man doth me.
Who's this? O God! it is my father's face,
Whom in this conflict I unwares have kill'd.
O heavy times, begetting such events!
From London by the king was I press'd forth;
My father, being the Earl of Warwick's man,
Came on the part of York, press'd by his master;
And I, who at his hands received my life, him
Have by my hands of life bereaved him.
Pardon me, God, I knew not what I did!
And pardon, father, for I knew not thee!
My tears shall wipe away these bloody marks;
And no more words till they have flow'd their
  fill.

KING HENRY. O piteous spectacle! O bloody
  times!
Whiles lions war and battle for their dens,
Poor harmless lambs abide their enmity.
Weep, wretched man, I'll aid thee tear for tear;
And let our hearts and eyes, like civil war,
Be blind with tears, and break o'ercharged
  with grief.
[*Enter a Father that has killed his Son, bringing
  in the body,*]

FATHER. Thou that so stoutly hast
  resisted me,
Give me thy gold, if thou hast any gold:
For I have bought it with an hundred blows.
But let me see: is this our foeman's face?
Ah, no, no, no, it is mine only son!
Ah, boy, if any life be left in thee,
Throw up thine eye! see, see what showers
  arise,
Blown with the windy tempest of my heart,
Upon thy words, that kill mine eye and heart!
O, pity, God, this miserable age!
What stratagems, how fell, how butcherly,
Erroneous, mutinous and unnatural,
This deadly quarrel daily doth beget!
O boy, thy father gave thee life too soon,
And hath bereft thee of thy life too late!

KING HENRY. Woe above woe! grief more
  than common grief!
O that my death would stay these ruthful deeds!
O pity, pity, gentle heaven, pity!
The red rose and the white are on his face,
The fatal colours of our striving houses:
The one his purple blood right well resembles;
The other his pale cheeks, methinks, presenteth:
Wither one rose, and let the other flourish;
If you contend, a thousand lives must wither.

SON. How will my mother for a father's death

Take on with me and ne'er be satisfied!

FATHER. How will my wife for slaughter of
  my son
Shed seas of tears and ne'er be satisfied!

KING HENRY. How will the country for
  these woful chances

SON. Was ever son so rued a father's death?

FATHER. Was ever father so bemoan'd his son?

KING HENRY. Was ever king so grieved for
  subjects' woe?
Much is your sorrow; mine ten times so much.

SON. I'll bear thee hence, where I may weep
  my fill.
[*Exit with the body.*]

FATHER. These arms of mine shall be thy
  winding-sheet;
My heart, sweet boy, shall be thy sepulchre,
For from my heart thine image ne'er shall go;
My sighing breast shall be thy funeral bell;
And so obsequious will thy father be,
Even for the loss of thee, having no more,
As Priam was for all his valiant sons.
I'll bear thee hence; and let them fight that will,
For I have murdered where I should not kill.
[*Exit with the body.*]

KING HENRY. Sad-hearted men, much
  overgone with care,
Here sits a king more woful than you are.

This iconic episode is one of the play's finest. Inspiration for the passage probably came from Edward Hall's description in *Hall's Chronicle* of the Battle of Towton, one of the bloodiest in the entire conflict, with approximately 24,000 casualties:

This conflict was in maner unnaturall, for in it the sonne fought against the father, the brother against the brother, the nephew against the uncle, and the tenaunt against his lord, which slaughter did not onely sore debilitate and muche weken the puyssance of this realme, considering that these dedde men, when thei were livyng had force ynough to resist the greatest princes power of all Europe.

Shakespeare takes the most powerful of all these divisions, that of father and son, and uses it to dramatize the devastation of civil war. Politics that have nothing to do with the common people have divided the family; the Son who has killed

A Son who has killed his Father and a Father who has killed his Son come upon King Henry in Act II, Scene 5 of *Henry VI, Part 3*. This is a print from the Boydell Shakespeare Gallery project. *(Painting by Josiah Boydell; engraving by John Ogborne)*

his Father is fighting on the king's side simply because he was in London, while his Father, having remained at home in Warwick, has equally been conscripted into Warwick's army; there is no sense that either individual has the least concern over the rights and wrongs of the situation.

Most productions depict this scene as a highly formal, almost choric episode, with the Son and the Father on either side of Henry. In structure and impact, it has a close relationship to the morality play, an earlier dramatic form that relied on allegory and symbolism rather than psychological development. The anonymity of these two men enables their loss to transcend all of the individual deaths and revenges that the play has dramatized: Rutland, York, Prince Edward, even Clifford. As Everyman figures, they represent the universality of the civil war's destruction and are emblematic of all destroyed families.

Henry's lamentations in this scene sum up the best and the worst in him. He is both painfully aware of the devastation that has been wrought upon his country and powerless to do anything about it. In his detachment from the battle and from the hatred that permeates both sides and motivates, for example, his wife and Clifford, Henry appears almost a holy innocent whose appeal to heaven for an end to the fighting, regardless of which "rose" wins, indicates, at the least, a disinterested desire for the good of the country rather than any personal ambition. However, his prayers are interrupted by his wife and son urging him to flee with them because their forces have met with defeat. Henry's prayers and dreams of peace are thus interrupted by harsh political reality, and he trails unhappily in their wake.

Act IV, Scene 6, 65–76

KING HENRY. My Lord of Somerset, what
  youth is that,
Of whom you seem to have so tender care?

SOMERSET. My liege, it is young Henry, Earl
  of Richmond.

KING HENRY. Come hither, England's hope.

[Lays his hand on his head.]
If secret powers
Suggest but truth to my divining thoughts,
This pretty lad will prove our country's bliss.
His looks are full of peaceful majesty,
His head by nature framed to wear a crown,
His hand to wield a sceptre, and himself
Likely in time to bless a regal throne.
Make much of him, my lords, for this is he
Must help you more than you are hurt by me.

This scene endows Henry with prophetic powers when he catches sight of Henry Tudor, Earl of Richmond, who in *Richard III* will return to defeat the tyrant. Once again, Shakespeare was following Edward Hall's account of the encounter in which Henry says, "'Lo, surely this is he, to whom both wee and our adversaries levyng the possession of all thynges, shall hereafter give rome and place'" *(Hall's Chronicle)*. Following victory at the Battle of Bosworth, Henry Tudor would bring the Wars of the Roses to an end by marrying Elizabeth Plantagenet, the eldest daughter of Edward IV, and thus uniting the two houses of Lancaster and York. This scene creates a visual link between the virtuous Henry, soon to die at the hands of Richard, and the young boy who will avenge Henry's death. Henry Tudor's brief presence within this play (he is sent to safety in France immediately following this speech) links the Tudor dynasty, under whom Shakespeare was writing, to the Plantagenet line and implies that Henry Tudor is in some sense Henry VI's spiritual heir.

DIFFICULT PASSAGES
Act II, Scene 6, 2–30

CLIFFORD. Here burns my candle out; ay,
  here it dies,
Which, whiles it lasted, gave King Henry light.
O Lancaster, I fear thy overthrow
More than my body's parting with my soul!
My love and fear glued many friends to thee;
And now I fall, thy tough commixture melts.
Impairing Henry, strengthening misproud
  York,
The common people swarm like summer flies;
And whither fly the gnats but to the sun?
And who shines now but Henry's enemies?
O Phoebus, hadst thou never given consent
That Phaethon should check thy fiery steeds,
Thy burning car never had scorch'd the earth!
And, Henry, hadst thou sway'd as kings
  should do,
Or as thy father and his father did,
Giving no ground unto the house of York,
They never then had sprung like summer flies;
I and ten thousand in this luckless realm
Had left no mourning widows for our death;
And thou this day hadst kept thy chair in
  peace.
For what doth cherish weeds but gentle air?
And what makes robbers bold but too much
  lenity?
Bootless are plaints, and cureless are my
  wounds;
No way to fly, nor strength to hold out flight:
The foe is merciless, and will not pity;
For at their hands I have deserved no pity.
The air hath got into my deadly wounds,
And much effuse of blood doth make me faint.
Come, York and Richard, Warwick and the rest;
I stabb'd your fathers' bosoms, split my breast.

This passage is dense with classical and political imagery that can prove difficult to follow. It is Clifford's dying speech in which he, as one of Henry's most loyal supporters, reflects on the probable consequences of his death and finally blames Henry himself for the weak rule that has enabled the House of York to rebel against the king. The imagery that he uses to express these thoughts is complex and interesting. The lighted candle, which is a synonym for Clifford's own life, is gradually absorbed into the Sun, which is the emblem of the House of York. Although he does not mention the reference directly, when Clifford says that "My love and fear glued many friends to thee; And now I fall, thy tough commixture melts," the images are reminiscent of the figure of Icarus, the boy whose father made him wax wings and who, disregarding his father's warnings not to fly too close to the Sun, fell into the sea when the wings melted. Phoebus and Phaethon are more images of heat and overachieving; Phaethon was the son of Phoebus, the sun god, who persuaded his father to lend him his chariot. He lost control of the horses and traveled too close to the Earth, which began to burn. In order to protect the Earth from further damage, Jupiter was forced to strike Phaethon with a thunderbolt. Here, Clifford is likening Phoebus's overindulgence toward his son, which resulted in mass destruction, to Henry's inability to restrain his subject York. Shakespeare takes the images of the candle, heat, and Sun and weaves them together into a political homily: Clifford, as a loyal subject, has been a candle that has illuminated his monarch, while York, given too much freedom, has become an out-of-control Sun who draws the common people toward him as he simultaneously scorches the Earth. This is possibly the most direct moment of blame for Henry, made all the more powerful by the fact that it is Clifford's death speech.

Act V, Scene 4

MARGARET. Great lords, wise men ne'er sit
  and wail their loss
But cheerly seek how to redress their harms.
What though the mast be now blown
  overboard,
The cable broke, the holding-anchor lost,
And half our sailors swallowed in the flood?
Yet lives our pilot still. Is't meet that he
Should leave the helm and like a fearful lad
With tearful eyes add water to the sea
And give more strength to that which hath too
  much,
Whiles, in his moan the ship splits on the rock,
Which industry and courage might have saved?
Ah, what a shame, ah what a fault were this!
Say Warwick was our anchor, what of that?
And Montague our topmost, what of him?
Our slaughter'd friends the tackles, what of
  these?
Why, is not Oxford here another anchor?

And Somerset another goodly mast?
The friends of France our shrouds and
  tacklings?
And, though unskilful, why not Ned and I
For once allow'd the skilful pilot's charge?
We will not from the helm to sit and weep,
But keep our course, though the rough wind
  say no,
From shelves and rocks that threaten us with
  wreck.
As good to chide the waves as speak them fair.
And what is Edward but ruthless sea?
What Clarence but a quicksand of deceit?
And Richard but a ragged fatal rock?
All these the enemies to our poor bark.
Say you can swim; alas, 'tis but a while!
Tread on the sand; why, there you quickly sink:
Bestride the rock; the tide will wash you off,
Or else you famish; that's a threefold death.
This speak I, lords, to let you understand,
If case some one of you would fly from us,
That there's no hoped-for mercy with the
  brothers
More than with ruthless waves, with sands and
  rocks.
Why, courage then! what cannot be avoided
'Twere childish weakness to lament or fear.

An immediate source for this speech was Arthur Brooke's *The Tragical History of Romeus and Juliet* (1562), which was also Shakespeare's source for his play *Romeo and Juliet*. In Brooke's play, a very similar speech is offered by the Friar in order to convince Romeo not to give up or to simply bemoan his difficulties but rather to tackle them with courage and determination. Here, Shakespeare uses the concept of the government as a ship of state; Henry, the "pilot," is still alive, even though they are in stormy seas, and Margaret urges her men to accept her and her son as Henry's deputies. This figure of speech can be traced back to Plato, who used it in the following manner:

Imagine a fleet or a ship in which there is a captain who is taller and stronger than any of the crew, but he is rather deaf, and blind, and he doesn't know much about navigation either. The sailors are quarrelling with one another about the steering—every one believes that he has a right to steer, though he has never learned the art of navigation and cannot say who taught him or when he learned, and will further assert that it cannot be taught, and they are ready to murder any one who contradicts them. They throng about the captain, begging and praying him to commit the helm to them; and if at any time they do not prevail, but others are preferred to them, they kill the others or throw them overboard, and having first chained up the noble captain's senses with drink or some narcotic drug, they mutiny, take possession of the ship and make free with the stores . . . He who is their partisan and cleverly aids them in their plot for getting the ship out of the captain's hands into their own . . . they compliment with the name of sailor, pilot, able seaman . . . but the idea that the true pilot must pay attention to the year and seasons and sky and stars and winds . . . and that he must and will be the steerer, whatever other people think—the possibility of this union of authority with the steerer's art has never seriously entered into their thoughts or been made part of their calling. Now in vessels which are in a state of mutiny and by sailors who are mutineers, how will the true pilot be regarded? Will he not be called by them a prater, a star-gazer, a good-for-nothing? (321)

Plato's image promotes the value of absolute monarchy (always provided that the monarch, or pilot in question, is suitably wise). The common people bicker over who will steer the ship, each of them believing him- or herself capable but none of them possessing the combination of art and authority to make a good job of it. The image is a complex one, but Shakespeare has used it here to construct Margaret and her followers as the legitimate pilots of the ship with delegated authority from Henry, the true pilot. Plato's quarrelling sailors are clearly

the rebellious lords here, but Margaret develops the image to support her position further. Margaret represents herself, her son, and their supporters as the men and artifacts that keep the ship afloat and depicts Edward, George, and Richard as parts of the natural world that reflect their personalities: George, whose loyalty has wavered several times, is likened to quicksand, emotional Edward is the sea, and Richard's unrelenting personality is compared to a rock. Her allegory enables her to define the Yorkists, not as competitors for the crown, but as elements that are, by their nature, irreconcilable with good governance and, indeed, humanity.

CRITICAL INTRODUCTION TO THE PLAY

The play takes place against a family conflict that has been going on for approximately 60 years. Richard II, who had had no children, had been usurped and murdered by his cousin, Henry Bolingbroke, the duke of Lancaster. Bolingbroke's son, Henry V, had been one of England's most successful kings, at least in military terms: He had won substantial victories in France in the ongoing Hundred Years' War, and the Treaty of Troyes, signed in 1420, appointed Henry the heir of the French king Charles VI. Although Henry V's early death, in 1422, precluded his being crowned king of France, he left a double inheritance of France and England to his nine-month-old son, Henry VI, although, of course, a substantial faction in France rejected the treaty and disputed Henry's claim. England was ruled by a series of regents, or protectors, until Henry, who was crowned king of England in 1429 and king of France in 1431 (in response to the coronation at Rheims of the rival French king Charles VII by Joan of Arc), was declared of age in 1437. The factional quarrels that had characterized Henry's minority did not then end, however; Henry's own personal weakness and willingness to cede responsibility meant that the court continued to be dominated by favorites and political factionalism. Increasing political instability in England, Henry's deeply unpopular marriage to Margaret of Anjou, and resistance in France to English rule, led and inspired by Joan of Arc, created an explosive situation. The ensuing civil war between the king's Lancastrian party and the Yorkist party later came to be known as the Wars of the Roses and was depicted by Tudor historians as one of the worst periods of English history. Drawing on the chronicles of Hall and Holinshed, the *Henry VI* plays depict a spiral of increasing violence as England descends into chaos.

Shakespeare's two plays about Henry VI's earlier life, the first two parts, cover these events, while *Henry VI, Part 3* represents the worst of the civil war, when concepts such as moral authority and legitimate right to rule are depicted as increasingly hollow words that can be appropriated for political purposes by anyone with the military strength to do so. *Henry VI, Part 1,* opens with the funeral of Henry V, a reminder of past glory and conquest that will be lost over the course of this and the succeeding plays. In place of Henry V's unifying authority, his son's weakness unleashes destructive English rivalries that, coupled with the rise of Joan of Arc in France, lead to chaos. In the first part, Richard Plantagenet, Duke of York, is introduced as the leader of the faction opposing the king, the white and the red roses are chosen, and Henry VI breaks an agreement to marry the daughter of the Duke of Armagnac instead to marry Margaret. The play ends on an ominous note with the Duke of Suffolk resolving that while Margaret will rule Henry, he will rule her and, thus, the realm of England.

Henry VI, Part 2 begins with the consequences of Henry's marriage, the terms of which contract have been deeply disadvantageous to England. This is a constantly recurring theme in both this part and the following; Henry's marriage to Margaret has introduced a foreign element into England and one, moreover, that has impoverished the country and, in particular, stripped away much of the French lands conquered by Henry V. This play's focus is on England, rather than France, with rebellion and murder reaching into the king's court and Margaret becoming an increasingly contentious figure. In this play, the Duke of York is told that he, not Henry, is the true heir to England, his sons Edward

and Richard are introduced, and the play dramatizes the breakdown of political order in England and York's own formal claim to the English throne.

Thus, *Henry VI, Part 3* is very much a part of a series. It has been considered as the climax of the *Henry VI* plays or, indeed, as the "prequel" to *Richard III,* but to take either of these points of view without considering the play as an individual entity is to overlook the particular themes and unities this play has as an independent dramatic work.

Structure and Unity

The play as a whole is underpinned by three battles: Wakefield, Towton, and Barnet. Each of these concludes in a significant death or deaths and dramatizes the gradual decline of the Lancastrian fortunes. Thus, the first battle of the play, the Battle of Wakefield, is won by the Lancastrians, and the point is hammered home by the destruction of the older and the younger Yorkist generation, York himself and his young son Rutland (1.3, 1.4). However, Margaret may have won the battle at Wakefield, but she has lost the moral victory, and her brutality drives the surviving York sons into engaging in a further cycle of revenge. The Battles of Towton and Barnet are both won by the Yorkists, but Towton, in particular, depicts an England where there are no real victors. The scene of the Father who has killed his Son and the Son who has killed his Father (2.5) serves as a microcosm of the destruction that is being meted out upon the state as a whole. The desecration of Clifford's dead body in revenge for their father and brother's death by the surviving Yorks confronts the audience with the ultimate futility of revenge and the extent to which it degrades the perpetrators. Clifford, after all, is past feeling any pain, and the audience is treated to the unedifying spectacle of a human body being taunted and stabbed by the would-be king of England.

The Battle of Barnet mirrors the Battle of Wakefield, this time with Warwick and Edward, Prince of Wales, as the figures marked for death. Whereas York represented the senior military generation of the Yorkists and Rutland the innocent victim of the

This print, published by Virtue & Company in 1865, depicts the death of the Earl of Warwick at the Battle of Barnet in Act V, Scene 2 of *Henry VI, Part 3*. (Painting by John Adam Houston; engraving by T. Brown)

war, now Warwick does likewise for the Lancastrians, and Prince Edward, who in this scene is made to appear younger than he does elsewhere within the play, is also killed, bringing to an end the direct Lancastrian line and closing the cycle of revenge killings that began in this play with Rutland's death.

Revenge

Within the broad narrative of the struggle for the crown of England, the revenge subplot, with its series of increasingly brutal murders, drives the story forward and gives *Henry VI, Part 3* internal coherence. Although it adds interest to understand the reasons for the enmity between Clifford and York, all that is necessary to know for the purposes of this play is Clifford's simple statement to Rutland: "Thy

father slew my father, therefore die" (1.4.47). Clifford's confrontation with Richard and the matching speeches emphasize the extent to which both sides have been equally brutalized by the war:

> RICHARD. Now, Clifford, I have singled thee
>   alone.
> Suppose this arm is for the Duke of York,
> And this for Rutland, both bound to revenge,
> Wert thou environed with a brazen wall.
>
> CLIFFORD. Now, Richard, I am here with
>   thee alone.
> This is the hand that stabbed thy father York
> And this the hand that slew thy brother
>   Rutland,
> And here's the heart that triumphs in their
>   death (2.4.1–8).

The speech patterns for both parts match each other in content, sequence, and imagery. The use of similar words—*alone, York, Rutland*—and the assertion that each man embodies the spirit of revenge emphasize that Richard and Clifford are indistinguishable in their blood lust. This is a particularly important point to remember when we consider that Richard is known to the audience as the figure who will become the tyrant king Richard III, child murderer par excellence. Richard's development into a monster is not an anomaly; he is, instead, quite literally, a child of his time. The extent to which he and Clifford resemble each other in this scene emphasizes the fact that it is the ongoing cycle of violence that both shapes such men as Richard and enables them to rise to the top of such societies.

Monarchy

The crown in *Henry VI, Part 3* is at once a corrupting and a sanctified concept. On the one hand, the structure of society that exists in the *Henry VI* plays demands a king; the chain of power is designed to culminate in one person. Monarchy meant far more than simple political power, particularly in post-Reformation England where monarchy was also imbued with a religious awe previously inherent in the Catholic Church. The spiritual and secular swords had been united in the person of the monarch. In *Henry VI, Part 3*, the consequences of having a monarch who is unable to sustain this position are depicted. The tetralogy as a whole depicts the transformation of the crown from a symbol of divinely ordained kingship to an emblem of political force that can be captured by anyone with the military force to do so. The expositions of lineal right to the crown become increasingly perfunctory until we reach Richard's expression of ambition for the crown, which he desires despite the fact that he knows he has no right to it.

A close analogical and symbolic relationship existed between the family and the state, and the king himself naturally played a crucial part in this relationship. The loyalty and obedience due from a child to his father was in the same order as that due from a subject to a king, and the commandment to "honor thy father and thy mother" was used in religious sermons and homilies to enforce political obedience. Patricide, the murder of one's father, was punished by the state as a crime of treason, and likewise, the obligations of a king toward his subjects were compared with the duties of a father toward his children. As Desiderius Erasmus, the great scholar and humanist of the early 16th century, put it in his popular book *The Education of a Christian Prince:* "The good prince ought to have the same attitude toward his subjects, as a good *paterfamilias* [father of the family] has toward his household—for what else is a kingdom but a great family? What is the king if not father to a great multitude?" (63).

The king as the father of a family and the family as a microcosm of society were commonplace metaphors in Elizabethan and Jacobean culture. The abolition of the Catholic Church in England and the fact that the English monarch was now head of the church completed the circle. The sovereign was both the legitimate father of the commonwealth and its spiritual parent, also. When everything in the kingdom is running smoothly, this way of representing the political system—aligning benevolent rulership with domestic bliss—is one that is immensely flattering to the monarch and was, indeed, used by both Queen Elizabeth I and her successor, King James I, to emphasize the devoted care and love that they felt for their subjects.

It is, however, a metaphor that lends itself just as easily to harsh criticism of the monarchy. It is an image that posits a reciprocal relationship between the monarch and his or her subjects, with requirements on both sides. In the case of *Henry VI, Part 3*, the failure of Henry as a king is illustrated by the disintegration of the families around him, including his own. The crown is, for York and later for his sons Edward and Richard, a temptation that leads them to break their oaths and shed blood. In Henry's hands, the crown is also a moral vacuum; Henry may be a good man, but he has failed to exercise the moral authority that monarchy should carry with it, and in so doing, he has permitted the civil and familial disintegration that is depicted in this play. This brings the choric scene of Act II, Scene 5 into greater prominence as a condemnation of Henry as king; the killing of the Son by the Father and the Father by the Son symbolically portrays the consequence of the bad king-father who has failed to govern his family. Desire for the crown is sufficient to cause any form of oath breaking or betrayal; as Edward says, "I would break a thousand oaths to reign one year" (1.2.17).

The speech in which Richard persuades his father to break his oath to live as Henry's subject until Henry's death begins with the argument that as Henry is not the lawful king, he cannot administer any binding oaths, and therefore, the oath that York has made is not valid: "An oath is of no moment being not took / Before a true and lawful magistrate, . . . Your oath my lord is vain and frivolous" (1.2.22–23, 27). This casuistic, overly subtle piece of reasoning abruptly descends to the language of raw ambition: "And father do but think / How sweet a thing it is to wear a crown, / Within whose circuit is Elysium" (1.2.28–30). York succumbs to the temptation: "Richard enough, I will be king or die" (1.2.35). This exchange, which is

Shakespeare's own invention, clearly establishes the link between political ambition and the bloodshed that is to follow.

The transformation of York from peaceful subject into violent rebel in search of the crown prefigures Richard's own far more sinister transformation in search of the same object. In his long soliloquy of Act III, Scene 2, Richard expresses his ambition openly. Having just watched his brother Edward attempt to seduce and then decide to marry Lady Grey, Richard moves from his frustration that so many brothers and their offspring stand between himself and the crown to consideration of any alternatives available to him. Recognizing that his physical deformity will not allow him the kind of sexual conquests that his brother delights in, Richard likens himself to "a chaos or an unlicked bear whelp, / That carries no impression like the dam" (3.2.161–162). According to classical belief as expressed in Ovid's *Metamorphoses,* bear cubs were born shapeless and were literally "licked into shape" by their mothers. Richard, seeing himself as having lacked that fashioning influence that would have allowed him to find some acceptable substitute for royal position, proceeds to lick himself into shape—as a monster:

> Then, since the earth affords no joy to me. . .
> I'll make my heaven to dream upon the crown
> And whiles I live t'account this world but hell,
> Until my misshaped trunk that bears this head
> Be round impaled with a glorious crown.
> And yet I know not how to get the crown . . .
> (3.2.165–172)

The repetition of the word *crown* three times in these lines allows Shakespeare to depict the extent of Richard's obsession. As he ponders on how to achieve his aim, he likens himself to someone lost in a forest, until he resolves

> And from that torment I will free myself,
> Or hew my way out with a bloody axe
> (3.2.180–181).

The staccato monosyllables emphasize the violence of the creature that he is becoming, and in the rest of the speech, Shakespeare uses a series of attributes and qualities to fashion the image of would-be king and tyrant for the benefit of the audience: Richard can smile as he murders, be more subtle than Machiavelli himself—a byword for amorality and unscrupulousness—outdo the greatest manipulators of classical legend—Ulysses and Sinon who together, through deceit, brought about the fall of Troy. Each phrase or comparison adds another dimension to Richard's new persona as tyrant in waiting.

Morality and Vice

A key facet of morality plays was the Vice figure, an element of the genre that retained its popularity even as the morality play itself was becoming outdated. Bernard Spivack in his highly influential work *Shakespeare and the Allegory of Evil* (1958) explains that the origins of the Vice figure lay in the Evil Angel figure, which sought to bring about the fall of humankind. Thus, a Vice figure in drama was primarily engaged in corrupting the human protagonist. Richard's character may be seen to have much in common with a Vice figure in that (although perfectly willing to commit crimes himself) he is frequently seen encouraging other people to do so. His role in persuading his father to break his oath to Henry has been discussed above, but other incidents in which Richard is the instigator to the next wave of violence occur in the play: He urges Edward toward revenge and is the most bloodthirsty of all the brothers toward Clifford's dead body. While Richard's personal ambition is a quality that he shares with almost all other characters within the play, the extent to which he is portrayed as the instigator of other peoples' misdeeds is specific to Richard and prefigures his role in *Richard III.*

Symbolic Imagery

Within this play are three major sets of symbolic images related to animals, the Sun, and the elements of wind and water. We have already seen that York denigrates Margaret by comparing the gentler qualities of wolves and tigers favorably with her own. Rutland compares Clifford to a lion, a creature also noted for its ferocity but believed to spare any creature who humbled itself before him (a well-known proverb was "The lion spares the suppliant"). Thus, Rutland's speech

> So looks the pent-up lion o'er the wretch
> That trembles under his devouring paws;
> And so he walks, insulting o'er his prey,
> And so he comes to rend his limbs asunder.
> (1.3.12–15)

implicitly begs Clifford to emulate the lion and to pity Rutland's defenselessness. Later on, Clifford will use the same image to reproach Henry for his dismay at seeing York's head mounted upon the wall and to justify aggression toward his enemies:

> To whom do lions cast their gentle looks?
> Not to the beast that would usurp their den.
> Whose hand is that the forest bear doth lick?
> Not his that spoils her young before her face . . .
> The smallest work will turn, being trodden on,
> And doves will peck in safeguard of their
>   brood. (2.2.11–18)

Henry is here compared unfavorably to the wild animals that have enough natural feeling to protect their offspring, whereas Henry has proved himself willing to sign away his son's inheritance. By using examples taken from the natural world, Clifford manages to imply that Henry's actions are unnatural, repugnant to any right-feeling man.

One of the most significant symbols in this play is the Sun. The image of Phaethon, the boy who, as discussed above, took his father's chariot and drove it out of control until he had to be struck down by Jupiter, occurs at least twice in the play. The Jupiter-Phoebus-Phaethon relationship is an interesting one to consider in the context of commentary on monarchy within the play. The story of Phaethon is that of an overindulgent father who is unable to prevent his child from harming himself and others around him so that Jupiter is forced to intervene. Thus, when Clifford refers to York as "Now Phaeton has tumbled from his car" (1.4.33), he is addressing an implicit reproach to Henry that becomes explicit in the later use of this image (2.6). Henry has ruled leniently and indulgently, and York's rebellion is as much Henry's doing as it is York's.

Clifford's association of York with Phaethon has implications for the Sun symbol, which was one of the emblems of the House of York. Phaethon is the story of a boy who wrongly tries to possess the Sun for his own purposes; York's rebellion is, in Clifford's eyes, an equal attempt at wrongful possession. However, York manages to appropriate the figure of speech for his own purposes when he takes the image of Phaethon's charred remains and transforms them into a symbol of regeneration:

> My ashes, as the phoenix, may bring forth
> A bird that will revenge upon you all,
> And in that hope I throw my eyes to heaven.
> (1.4.35–37)

The phoenix rising out of York's ashes is of course Edward, and Richard continues his father's metaphor when he adjures his brother:

> Nay, if thou be that princely eagle's bird,
> Show thy descent by gazing 'gainst the sun.
> (2.1.91–92)

The eagle was believed to be able to gaze at the Sun without harm, and Richard's line encourages Edward to prove that he is his father's son by continuing his father's struggle for the crown. These lines follow the manifestation of three Suns in the sky (2.1), an omen mentioned in Shakespeare's source chronicles. Edward interprets the sign to mean that he and his two brothers will join together to defeat Lancaster, but his optimism and faith in his brothers is undermined by Richard:

EDWARD. . . . henceforth will I bear
Upon my target three fair-shining suns.

RICHARD. Nay, bear three daughters . . .
     (2.1.40–41)

Richard's mocking play on *sun* and *son* ominously prefigures the famous reference to the "sun of York" with which Richard will begin the next play.

It is interesting to note that while Shakespeare uses Sun imagery primarily in the Yorkist context, the imagery associated with the Lancastrians Henry and Margaret is related to winds, tides, and the sea. Not only in the elaborate image of

Edward IV sits on the throne next to his wife and newborn son, while a plotting Richard creeps in the shadows in Act 5, Scene 7 of *Henry VI, Part 3*. Print from the Boydell Shakespeare Gallery project *(Painting by James Northcote; engraving by Jean-Baptiste Michel)*

the ship of state used by Margaret (5.4) but also elsewhere in the play, Shakespeare uses the images of ships, winds, and tides in Henry's speeches and in speeches about Henry, in a manner that reflects and at times dictates the pace of the narrative.

Retreating from Towton, Henry describes the battle in terms of a stormy sea:

Now sways it this way, like a mighty sea
Forced by the tide to combat with the wind.
Now sways it that way, like the selfsame sea
Forced to retire by fury of the wind.
Some time the flood prevail, and then the wind;
Now one the better, then another best.
     (2.5.5–10)

Margaret will later describe Edward as the "ruthless sea," and Edward refers to Margaret as a "fretting gust," as we shall see, so that Henry's comparison of the battle to the conflict between wind and tide at once emphasizes the all-encompassing, elemental nature of the fight. If the conflict between Margaret and the Yorkists is a tempest, then Henry seems at this point to be literally in the eye of the storm. His figure of speech provides a symbolic context for the change of pace this scene represents and for its shift from the microcosmic focus on the personal details of the civil war to the macrocosmic focus on the country as a whole, represented by the anonymous Son and Father.

As the current king, however beleaguered, Henry is the pilot of the ship of state, for control of which both Margaret and Edward are battling. In Plato's original metaphor, he argues that the best king must also be a philosopher, for only the philosopher will have the requisite virtue and wisdom to act for the good of all, rather than selfishly. Act II, Scene 5 gives Henry the space that he needs to play the philosopher, to lament his own position and that of his country, but the contempt with which he is viewed by others is articulated by Edward in the following speech:

Some troops pursue the bloody-minded
     Queen,

That led calm Henry, though he were a king,
As doth a sail filled with a fretting gust
Command an argosy to stem the waves.
  (2.6.34–37)

Here, the metaphor of the king as the pilot of the ship of state has been transformed into the image of the king as an "argosy," a large merchant ship. It could be argued that this turn of phrase offers some indication of how Edward views the crown—not as a responsibility that must be cherished but as a potential source of rich pickings—but more to the purpose, Edward's speech articulates the extent to which Henry is Margaret's tool, blown in any direction that she pleases. It also continues the association of Margaret with the wind, with its implications of fickleness and changeability. The final reference to Margaret in the play, when Edward is asked what shall be done with her, plays again on wind imagery: "Away with her and waft her hence to France" (5.7.41). Edward's use of the term *waft* emphasizes his dismissive tone; a waft of air is nothing more than a light breeze, but, at the same time, the transformation from "fretting gust" to "waft" represents the extent to which Margaret's power has diminished.

As can be seen in these examples, the symbolic language in the play not only illustrates certain situations but also lends continuity to the drama as a whole. The battles on stage are echoed and reflected by the rhetorical struggles for command of the symbolic language, which is an abstract but equally important battlefield.

EXTRACTS OF CLASSIC CRITICISM
Robert Greene (1558–1592) and Ben Jonson (1572–1637) [The first known reference to *Henry VI, Part 3* was made by Robert Greene in his *Groatsworth of Wit* (1592), in which Greene warned his contemporary playwrights to beware "the upstart crow . . . beautified with our feathers, that with his Tygers hart wrapt in a Players hyde, supposes he is as well able to bombast out a blank verse as the best of you: and being an absolute *Johannes fac totum,* is in his owne conceit the only Shake-scene in the country." This line, relating as it does to York's attack on Margaret as having "A tiger's heart wrapped in a woman's hide" (1.4.137), indicates that the play had been sufficiently popular for the public to remember such a line. Ben Jonson in the prologue to his play *Every Man in His Humour* referred to plays in which actors: "with three rusty swords, / And help of some few foot-and-half-foot words, / Fight over York and Lancaster's long jars: (9–11). Contemptuous though Jonson's reference may be, it clearly indicates that the *Henry VI* plays as a group enjoyed popularity with Elizabethan audiences. In subsequent centuries, however, the plays were less celebrated. While the tragedies, in particular, generated massive critical interest, the early history plays were discounted to the extent that their worthiness to remain within the Shakespearean canon was debated. Criticism of the early works is in many ways more interesting for its participation in the grand project of fashioning Shakespeare's identity as national genius than for what is said about the plays themselves.]

Alexander Pope (1688–1744) [Excerpted from the *Preface to Shakespeare* (1728). Pope's edition of Shakespeare was not among his greatest successes, but he may be credited with being among the first to discuss the relationship between the plays as they appear in the folio editions (published after Shakespeare's death) and the versions that appeared during his lifetime (usually called quarto publications). Pope used the *Henry VI* plays as evidence that Shakespeare had redrafted if not entirely rewritten his work, contradicting Ben Jonson's famous assertion that "he never blotted [deleted or revised] a line." Pope's words are worth noting for the emphasis they place on piecing together an image of Shakespeare as scholar and reviser, as well as natural genius.]

But in reality (however it has prevailed) there never was a more groundless report, or to the contrary of which there are more undeniable evidences. As, the Comedy of the *Merry Wives of Windsor,* which he entirely new writ; the *History of Henry VI,* which was first published under the Title of the *The Contention of York and Lancaster;* and that of *Henry V,* extremely improved . . .

Samuel Johnson (1709–1784) [Johnson's nine-volume *The Plays of William Shakespeare* (1765) was accompanied by a preface that contributed substantially toward the "deification" of Shakespeare as the pinnacle of English dramatists. Aligning Shakespeare with the great classical authors of Greece and Rome, Johnson demands that Shakespeare and, by extension, the English nation and culture within which Shakespeare wrote are worthy of the same level of veneration and respect offered to the classical civilizations. For Johnson, Shakespeare's plays have a value that goes beyond the merely topical; he takes up and expands Ben Jonson's famous line "He was not of an age, but for all time." Nonetheless, Johnson does not adopt the extremes of Bardolatry that may be seen elsewhere. Simply because a play was not a work of untrammelled genius did not automatically disqualify it from being attributed to Shakespeare, and Johnson makes this plain in his notes to *Henry VI, Part 3.*]

The three parts of *King Henry VI* are suspected, by Mr. Theobald [one of the earliest and most important scholarly editors of Shakespeare], of being supposititious, and are declared, by Dr. Warburton [another editor], to be certainly not Shakespeare's. Mr. Theobald's suspicion arises from some obsolete words; but the phraseology is like the rest of our author's style, and single words, of which however I do not observe more than two, can conclude little.

Dr. Warburton gives no reason, but I suppose him to judge upon deeper principles and more comprehensive views, and to draw his opinion from the general effect and spirit of the composition, which he thinks inferior to the other historical plays.

From mere inferiority nothing can be inferred; in the productions of wit there will be inequality. Sometimes judgement will err, and sometimes the matter itself will defeat the artist. Of every author's works one will be the best, and one will be the worst. The colours are not equally pleasing, nor the attitudes equally graceful, in all the pictures of Titian or Reynolds.

Dissimilitude of style and heterogenousness of sentiment, may sufficiently show that a word does not really belong to the reputed author. But in these plays no such marks of spuriousness are found. The diction, the versification, and the figures, are Shakespeare's. These plays, considered, without regard to characters and incidents, merely as narratives in verse, are more happily conceived, and more accurately finished than those of *King John, Richard II,* or the tragick scenes of *King Henry IV* and *V.* If we take these plays from Shakespeare, to whom shall they be given? What author of that age had the same easiness of expression and fluency of numbers? Of these three plays I think the second the best. The truth is, that they have not sufficient variety of action, for the incidents are too often of the same kind; yet many of the characters are well discriminated. King Henry, and his Queen, King Edward, the Duke of Gloucester, and the Earl of Warwick, are very strongly and distinctly painted.

Elizabeth Griffiths (1727–1793) [Excerpted from *The Morality of Shakespeare's Drama Illustrated* (1775). Griffiths was an actress, translator, playwright, and author whose writing enabled her to support herself and her family at various times in her life. Griffiths's work is interesting as an early piece of literary criticism written by a woman and also for its construction of Shakespeare as a national playwright. Griffiths's work was inspired in part by the need to uphold this image against foreign critics such as Voltaire, who had described the Bard as "a savage with some imagination who has written some good lines but whose work only meets with favour in London. It's a poor indication of national taste when that taste isn't shared by anyone else" (Voltaire to Bernard Joseph Saurin, December 4, 1765). Voltaire's words were widely resented in England, and just as an insult to Shakespeare became an insult to the English nation, so a defense of Shakespeare was tantamount to an expression of national loyalty. Griffiths's work offers a fascinating example of the 18th-century constructions of Shakespeare as a moral and patriotic touchstone.

Griffiths begins her chapter on *Henry VI, Part 3* by acknowledging the authorship debate, and considering the question of whether the plays may be considered to be by Shakespeare.]

Mr. Theobald suspects the three parts of this Drama to be spurious, on account of some obsolete expressions in them, *alderlivest, unneath, mailed, me-seemeth, darraign, exigent* . . . If I was to offer an objection to the authenticity of these Pieces, it should be rather from their barrenness of sentiment, or reflection; though I think there is enough of the stile and manner of Shakespeare, in them all, to evince them to be his.

[Griffiths's ascription of authorship or lack thereof on the basis of a judgment of quality rather than the issues of contemporary attribution to Shakespeare, internal consistency, or lack of a viable alternative (all issues discussed by Samuel Johnson) illustrates the extent to which, by the 18th century, the figure of Shakespeare had become a national icon and the name *Shakespeare* was used to indicate work of the highest moral and literary quality rather than simply authorship.

Griffiths's aim in her popular work was to identify the moral lessons contained in each of Shakespeare's plays, a difficult task for a drama such as *Henry VI, Part 3,* which depicts a world of unremitting moral bankruptcy. However, by focusing on elements of a series of scenes, she succeeds in extracting a brief moral lesson. Her first example is Act II, Scene 3, in which Clifford reminds Henry of his duty of care toward his son by reference to animals caring for their young, even at the cost of their own lives (passing over the fact that Clifford has just killed the innocent Rutland).]

There is a natural instinct, even stronger than that of self-preservation, implanted in all the brute creation for the safety of their young— The simplest animals manifest an art, and the most pusillanimous shew a courage, in the defence of their progeny; but this, only till they become capable of taking care of themselves. Account for this Providence, upon the principle of uninspired *mechanism,* if ye can, ye *unphilosophic* Sophisters!

[In these lines, Griffiths enlists Shakespeare in a contemporary philosophical debate over the relationship between God, humankind, and the universe, using Shakespeare's example of the self-sacrificing love shown by parent animals for their infants as evidence of an active Divine Providence rather than a universe governed purely by natural laws. Act II, Scene 6, which is now more often used to exemplify the dangers of civil war, is used by Griffiths to point a slightly different moral; Henry's musings on the happiness of a shepherd's life in comparison to his own is mentioned, and his later assertion that he possesses a crown that few kings have—a crown called "content"—(3.1.65) is discussed by her in a manner that casts Shakespeare in the role of moral arbiter.]

In the last line we may see that Shakespeare takes one of his many occasions to humble ambition, and depreciate greatness. He is eternally acting the part of the slave placed behind the triumphal car; not, indeed, to shew his own envy, but to abate another's pride.

William Hazlitt (1778–1830) [Excerpted from *Lectures on the Literature of the Age of Elizabeth and Characters of Shakespear's Plays* (1817). Hazlitt, a contemporary of William Wordsworth and Samuel Taylor Coleridge, was an essayist and journalist whose collection of essays about Shakespeare's plays were among his most popular and successful works. The essays take the form of personal responses to the plays and characters, and rather than dealing with textual matters, which is where the interest of critics such as Samuel Johnson and Edmond Malone lay in terms of the *Henry VI* plays, Hazlitt lay his interest in character and theme. He addresses the *Henry VI* plays as a single entity, thereby anticipating a number of modern productions of the plays, and his interest focuses on Henry himself, along with Richard. In common with many other of his contemporaries, he does not think highly of the *Henry VI* plays.]

Richard stabs Henry a second time in Act V, Scene 6 of *Henry VI, Part 3*, in this print published by Amies in 1888. *(Illustration by Felix Octavius Darley)*

During the time of the civil wars of York and Lancaster, England was a perfect bear-garden, and Shakespear has given us a very lively picture of the scene. The three parts of *Henry VI* convey a picture of very little else; and are inferior to the other historical plays. They have brilliant passages, but the general groundwork is comparatively poor and meagre, the style flat and unraised.

We shall attempt one example more in the characters of Richard II and Henry VI. The characters and situations of both these persons were so nearly alike, that they would have been completely confounded by a common-place poet. Yet they are kept quite distinct in Shakespear. Both were kings, and both unfortunate. Both lost their crowns owing to their mismanagement and imbecility; the one from a thoughtless, wilful abuse of power, the other from an indifference to

it. The manner in which they bear their misfortunes corresponds exactly to the causes which led to them. The one is always lamenting the loss of his power which he has not the spirit to regain; the other seems only to regret that he had ever been king, and is glad to be rid of the power, with the trouble; the effeminacy of the one is that of a voluptuary, proud, revengeful, impatient of contradiction, and inconsolable in his misfortunes; the effeminacy of the other is that of an indolent, good-natured mind, naturally averse to the turmoils of ambition and the cares of greatness, and who wishes to pass his time in monkish indolence and contemplation. Richard bewails the loss of the kingly power only as it was the means of gratifying his pride and luxury; Henry regards it only as a means of doing right, and is less desirous of the advantages to be derived from possessing it than afraid of exercising it wrong. In knighting a young soldier, he gives him ghostly advice.

> Edward Plantagenet, arise a knight,
> And learn this lesson, draw thy sword in
> right.

Richard II in the first speeches of the play betrays his real character. In the first alarm of his pride, on hearing of Bolingbroke's rebellion, before his presumption has met with any check, he exclaims—

> Mock not my senseless conjuration, lords:
> This earth shall have a feeling, and these
> stones
> Prove armed soldiers, ere her native king
> Shall faulter under proud rebellious arms
> . . .
> Not all the water in the rough rude sea
> Can wash the balm from an anointed king;
> The breath of worldly man cannot depose
> The Deputy elected by the Lord.
> For every man that Bolingbroke hath
> prest,
> To lift sharp steel against our golden
> crown,
> Heaven for his Richard hath in heavenly
> pay
> A glorious angel; then if angels fight,
> Weak men must fall; for Heaven still
> guards the right.

Yet, notwithstanding this royal confession of faith, on the very first news of actual disaster, all his conceit of himself as the peculiar favourite of Providence vanishes into air.

> But now the blood of twenty thousand
> men
> Did triumph in my face, and they are
> fled.

All souls that will be safe fly from my
side;
For time hath set a blot upon my pride.

Immediately after, however, recollecting that "cheap defence" of the divinity of kings which is to be found in opinion, he is for arming his name against his enemies.

> Awake, thou coward Majesty, thou
> sleep'st;
> Is not the King's name forty thousand
> names?
> Arm, arm, my name: a puny subject
> strikes
> At thy great glory.

King Henry does not make any such vapouring resistance to the loss of his crown, but lets it slip from off his head as a weight which he is neither able nor willing to bear; stands quietly by to see the issue of the contest for his kingdom, as if it were a game at push-pin, and is pleased when the odds prove against him.

When Richard first hears of the death of his favourites, Bushy, Bagot, and the rest, he indignantly rejects all idea of any further efforts, and only indulges in the extravagant impatience of his grief and his despair, in that fine speech [from *Richard II*] which has been so often quoted:

> AUMERLE. Where is the duke my
> father, with his power?

> KING RICHARD. No matter where: of
> comfort no man speak:
> Let's talk of graves, of worms, and
> epitaphs,
> Make dust our paper, and with rainy eyes
> Write sorrow in the bosom of the earth!
> Let's chuse executors, and talk of wills:
> And yet not so—for what can we
> bequeath,

Save our deposed bodies to the ground?
Our lands, our lives, and all are
  Bolingbroke's,
And nothing can we call our own but
  death,
And that small model of the barren earth,
Which serves as paste and cover to our
  bones.
For heaven's sake let us sit upon the
  ground,
And tell sad stories of the death of Kings:
How some have been depos'd, some
  slain in war;
Some haunted by the ghosts they
  dispossess'd;
Some poisoned by their wives, some
  sleeping kill'd;
All murder'd:—for within the hollow
  crown,
That rounds the mortal temples of a king,
Keeps death his court: and there the
  antic sits,
Scoffing his state, and grinning at his
  pomp!
Avowing him a breath, a little scene
To monarchize, be fear'd, and kill with
  looks;
Infusing him with self and vain conceit—
As if this flesh, which walls about our life,
Were brass impregnable; and, humour'd
  thus,
Comes at the last, and, with a little pin,
Bores through his castle wall, and—fare-
  well king!
Cover your heads, and mock not flesh
  and blood
With solemn reverence; throw away
  respect,
Tradition, form, and ceremonious duty,
For you have but mistook me all this
  while:
I live on bread like you, feel want, taste
  grief,
Need friends, like you;—subjected thus,
How can you say to me—I am a king?

There is as little sincerity afterwards in his affected resignation to his fate, as there is fortitude in this exaggerated picture of his misfortunes before they have happened. When Northumberland comes back with the message from Bolingbroke, he exclaims, anticipating the result,

What must the king do now? Must he
  submit?
The king shall do it: must he be depos'd?
The king shall be contented: must he lose
The name of king? O' God's name let
  it go.
I'll give my jewels for a set of beads;
My gorgeous palace for a hermitage;
My gay apparel for an alms-man's gown;
My figur'd goblets for a dish of wood;
My sceptre for a palmer's walking staff;
My subjects for a pair of carved saints,
And my large kingdom for a little grave—
A little, little grave, an obscure grave.

How differently is all this expressed in King Henry's soliloquy during the battle with Edward's party:

This battle fares like to the morning's war,
When dying clouds contend with grow-
  ing light,
What time the shepherd blowing of his
  nails,
Can neither call it perfect day or night.
Here on this mole-hill will I sit me
  down;
To whom God will, there be the victory!
For Margaret my Queen and Clifford too
Have chid me from the battle, swearing
  both
They prosper best of all whence I am
  thence.
Would I were dead, if God's good will
  were so.
For what is in this world but grief and
  woe?

O God! methinks it were a happy life
To be no better than a homely swain,
To sit upon a hill as I do now,
To carve out dials quaintly, point by
point,
Thereby to see the minutes how they run:
How many make the hour full complete,
How many hours bring about the day,
How many days will finish up the year,
How many years a mortal man may live.
When this is known, then to divide the
times:
So many hours must I tend my flock,
So many hours must I take my rest,
So many hours must I contemplate,
So many hours must I sport myself;
So many days my ewes have been with
young,
So many weeks ere the poor fools will
yean,
So many months ere I shall shear the
fleece:
So many minutes, hours, weeks, months,
and years
Past over, to the end they were created,
Would bring white hairs unto a quiet
grave.
Ah! what a life were this! how sweet,
how lovely!
Gives not the hawthorn bush a sweeter
shade
To shepherds looking on their silly
sheep,
Than doth a rich embroidered canopy
To kings that fear their subjects'
treachery?
O yes it doth, a thousand fold it doth.
And to conclude, the shepherds' homely
curds,
His cold thin drink out of his leather
bottle,
His wonted sleep under a fresh tree's
shade,
All which secure and sweetly he enjoys,
Is far beyond a prince's delicates,

Hid viands sparkling in a golden cup,
His body couched in a curious bed,
When care, mistrust, and treasons wait
on him.

This is a true and beautiful description of a naturally quiet and contented disposition, and not, like the former, the splenetic effusion of disappointed ambition.

In the last scene of *Richard* II, his despair lends him courage: he beats the keeper, slays two of his assassins, and dies with imprecations in his mouth against Sir Pierce Exton, who "had staggered his royal person." Henry, when he is seized by the deer-stealers, only reads them a moral lecture on the duty of allegiance and the sanctity of an oath; and when stabbed by Gloucester in the tower, reproaches him with his crimes, but pardons him his own death.

MODERN CRITICISM AND CRITICAL CONTROVERSIES

Henry VI, Part 3, like many of Shakespeare's plays, has a complex and, indeed, a confusing critical history. Early criticism treated the three *Henry VI* plays as a single unit (which in many ways they are) and regarded the plays' dramatic or poetic shortcomings as reasons to consider them as having been written by someone other than Shakespeare. The growing stature of Shakespeare as national poet, however, made it increasingly problematic to acknowledge that he was capable of writing anything that was less than brilliant. In the 20th century, *Henry VI, Part 3* has been primarily addressed by critics in two areas: the chronology of composition and performance and the question of what, if any, political or theological motive could be assigned to the plays.

Regarding the chronology of the *Henry VI* tetralogy, the question of whether the plays were written in the order that they appear in the First Folio has been extensively debated and has of course major implications for any scholar wishing to argue that the plays form a coherent whole with thematic and stylistic development from play to play. The basic problems are as follows.

On March 3, 1592, Philip Henslowe, a businessman, theatrical entrepreneur, and diarist, noted that the play *"Harey vj"* had done well at the box office. It had taken 3 pounds and 16 shillings, compared with the previous day's 13 shillings for *Matchavell.* Henslowe marks the play as "ne," which generally, in his diary, means "new." The popularity of this *Henry VI* is further confirmed by Thomas Nashe, who wrote "How it would have joyed brave *Talbot* (the terror of the French) . . . that he should triumph again on the stage" (212). These references are quite clearly to the play now known as *Henry VI, Part 1.* Then, in September of the same year, Robert Greene's posthumous pamphlet, *A Groatsworth of Wit,* mentions the "Tygers hart wrapt in a Players hyde," clearly a reference to *Henry VI, Part 3.*

In order for the three plays to have been published in their chronological order, therefore, we would have to believe that *Henry VI, Part 1* was written in time to open in March 1592, and that the next two parts were performed with equal success in the same year, before June 23, 1592, when all theaters were closed due to the plague. A genius Shakespeare may have been, but it seems improbable that *Henry VI, Parts 2* and *3* could have been written, rehearsed, and performed over a period of no more than three months.

This time line, along with some internal evidence, has led 20th-century critics such as J. Dover Wilson and E. K. Chambers to assert that *Henry VI, Part 1* must have been written after *Henry VI, Parts 2* and *3,* a theory which itself raises questions, especially concerning Shakespeare's development as a playwright. Most critics believe that *Henry VI, Part 1* is a weaker play than the other two. One would therefore be asked to believe that Shakespeare had become less practiced as he went on. The argument also begs the question of why Shakespeare should have written what amounts to a "prequel" to the two plays, an unusual act for the time.

As with the textual debate, a range of answers has been put forward, including the theory that Shakespeare, on the strength of his success with the plays that became *Henry VI, Part 2* and *Henry VI, Part 3,* was asked to collaborate with another dramatist who was working on what amounted to a prequel. Nonetheless, Andrew Cairncross's influential Arden editions of the plays asserted that *Henry VI, Part 1* "has every mark of being written deliberately as an integral part of a tetralogy, (i) using the same chronicles and chronicle-material, (ii) according to the same method, (iii) at the exact points where each play supplements the others . . . in addition to preparing for the sequel in *Henry VI, Part 2.*"

As with the authorship debate, no final conclusion has been reached, nor is it likely to be without the emergence of radical new evidence. However, most content criticism since the 1970s tends to treat the plays as an organic whole and to assume that they were written consecutively.

Besides questions of textual criticism and debate over authorship and chronology, the plays were otherwise largely ignored by 19th- and early 20th-century critics, who considered their authorship to be questionable and referred to the plays as "drum and trumpet" affairs; "heaps of rubbish." Key critics such as A. C. Bradley passed over the early history plays entirely. Two scholars from either side of the Atlantic changed this attitude and focused significant critical attention on Elizabethan and Jacobean England's understanding and interpretation of its own past.

A significant strand of critical debate reads Shakespeare's history plays either as a narrative of English history that celebrates the Tudor dynasty on the throne at the time of writing or as an attempt to undermine other such celebratory narratives, or that they deconstruct any attempt to create such a narrative by focusing on the essentially destructive and amoral events that are represented within the history plays. E. M. W. Tillyard's 1944 publication, *Shakespeare's History Plays,* is fundamental in this area. His work and that of the American scholar Lily B. Campbell have shaped subsequent criticism of these works, whether the critic is agreeing or disagreeing with their ideas.

Both Tillyard and Campbell argued that Shakespeare—far from being the poet-dramatist who was not of one age but for all time and whose mind was far above contemporary political agendas (the popular 18th and 19th century construction of him)—was a dramatist who engaged closely and directly with significant contemporary concerns and elements of Elizabethan policy. Campbell, in her book *Shakespeare's Histories: Mirrors of Elizabethan Policy* (1947), argued that each of the history plays had "a special purpose in elucidating a political problem of Elizabeth's day and in bringing to bear upon this problem the accepted political philosophy of the Tudors" (125). Campbell thus discussed *Richard II,* for example, in terms of the dangers of deposing a king and *Henry IV* in terms of rebellion. Both Campbell and Tillyard viewed Shakespeare as working within a political as well as a moral universe, not one in which the history plays were simply patriotic celebrations, but one in which England's history had a divine as well as a political message.

While Campbell did not regard the *Henry VI* plays as worthy of attention, Tillyard did. Tillyard's concept of the "Elizabethan world picture" is worth describing here, because, while it has been variously critiqued, it has been enormously influential as much in generating disagreement and differing ideas as in the substantial number of scholarly adherents it has also attracted. Briefly, Tillyard argued that the Elizabethans perceived the universe as a divinely created entity in which all things had an assigned space within a fixed hierarchy: "As a chain, creation was a series of beings stretching from the lowest of inanimate creatures up to the angel nearest to the throne of God" (19). This divine order had, of course, been tarnished by the fall of man, but the relationships between each part of creation could still be perceived. Echoes of the universal order remained in society, and here Tillyard drew upon the 1547 Sermon of Obedience, portions of which, he points out, Shakespeare would have heard approximately nine times per year: "Almightie God hath created and appoync-

ted all thynges, in heaven, yearth, and waters, in a moste excellent and perfect ordre . . . Euery degree of people, in their vocacion, callyng, and office, hath appointed to them their duetie and ordre. Some are in high degree, some in lowe, some Kinges and Princes, some inferiors and subjectes . . . and euery one haue need of other, so that in all thynges is to bee lauded and praised the goodly ordre of God, without the whiche, no house, no citee, no common wealthe, can continue and endure. For where there is no right ordre, there reigneth all abuse, carnall libertie, enormitie, synne, and Babilonical confusion" (28).

Through a scholarly and detailed study of key moralists, historians, and political writers, Tillyard developed the thesis that Shakespeare's early history plays were deeply influenced by the morality dramatic tradition and that they had the figure of Respublica, England itself, as their protagonist. Tillyard read the early histories as having the clear authorial purpose of illustrating the dangers of civil war and disunity, drawing upon his historical sources: "The horror of civil war was common to the whole of western Europe at the time, but it took a special form in England. . . . there remained the terror that the Wars of the Roses might be fought again; and it was Catholic intrigue that the Elizabethans most feared as likely to start them. The monarchy was the safeguard against civil war and must at all costs be upheld" (72).

Essentially, Tillyard perceived the English history plays as making up an epic cycle that ran from the murder of Thomas of Woodstock (which initiates the events of *Richard II* and leads indirectly to Richard's own deposition and murder) through to the defeat of Richard III and the triumph of Henry VII. Shakespeare, according to Tillyard, was providing a view of English history in which Divine Providence punished the guilty and brought the House of Tudor to triumphant enthronement. Tillyard coined the phrase the *Tudor myth* to describe this process: "The union of the two houses of York and Lancaster . . . was the providential and happy ending of an organic piece of history. . . . Henry returns, wins the Battle of Bosworth, and providentially heals the old division by marrying the heiress of York. He is a successful politic king. Full fruition of the new order can only come from the issue of the union of the two houses" (67).

Tillyard's view of *Henry VI, Part 3*, therefore, is that the play represents the nadir of English history: "In the third part Shakespeare shows us chaos itself, the full prevalence of civil war, the perpetration of one horrible deed after another". He also views the play as being among the most uneven of Shakespeare's work: "There are indeed splendid things in it, but they are rather islands sticking out of a sea of mediocrity than hills arising from the valleys or undulations of an organic landscape. In the intermediate passages Shakespeare is either tired or bored: or perhaps both" (196).

Tillyard's ideas have been widely critiqued. His arguments for the thematic and structural coherence of the histories as an organic whole have been challenged, and the extent to which Divine Providence is perceptible as an operating force within the plays has been disputed by, for example, Henry Ansgar Kelly in *Divine Providence in the England of Shakespeare's Histories* and Robert Ornstein in *A Kingdom for a Stage*. A. L. French argues that rather than marching toward a triumphant restoration of order over chaos, the plays should be viewed as looking forward to the unjust world of the great tragedies rather than harking back toward the providentially oriented moralities. Likewise, Tillyard's assertion that Shakespeare's work wholeheartedly celebrates civil order and the Tudor regime has been attacked by critics who view the plays as morally ambiguous and who perceive the idea of a monolithic "world picture" as being insufficiently nuanced. Nonetheless, even those critics who dispute Tillyard's assertion of Shakespeare's political orthodoxy or who argue that his reading of the plays is oversimplified have been influenced by his work, and he was certainly an instrumental figure in bringing the early history plays to critical attention in the 20th century.

Later 20th-century criticism has seen in the history plays generally either a dramatist who uses political and historical material to consider the human condition or a political dramatist who is "exploratory" rather than possessing a fixed political agenda. New Criticism, spearheaded in Shakespeare studies by Gavin Wilson Knight and Caroline Spurgeon, drew attention away from the political or historical context of the plays and focused instead on patterns of language and imagery within the plays. Spurgeon, in her influential work *Shakespeare's Imagery and What It Tells Us* (1935), remarked on the "iterative imagery," metaphors or figures of speech that were repeated, in different forms, throughout, within *Henry VI, Part 3*. This reading enabled perception of a pattern and structure to the drama that were based on its language rather than the historical events it portrayed and that helped develop study of *Henry VI, Part 3* as an individual play rather than as part of a wider unit. A later, highly influential study of the *Henry VI* plays was written by J. P. Brockbank in his essay "The Frame of Disorder: *Henry VI*" (1961). Brockbank, like Spurgeon, argued strongly for internal unity and coherence within the play but disputed Tillyard's assertion that the play's events were generated by the Richard II-Bolingbroke dispute of the distant past. New Criticism, with its emphasis on the text as a single, comprehensible entity that exists and may be understood independently of historical context, has in its turn been variously critiqued but has remained, in the form of close reading, a key element of literary criticism.

The rise of New Historicism and its domination of Renaissance criticism in the late 1980s and 1990s harked back to a strongly politicized reading of the history plays in general, but one that now viewed the plays as being part of a ceaselessly renegotiated discourse of power, one in which the theater became simultaneously a place of subversion and containment, where monarchy itself was both celebrated and undermined. New Historicist critics, however, tend largely to focus on the later history plays. Feminist criticism of *Henry VI, Part 3*, meanwhile, has been notably lacking throughout the 20th century up until the 1980s. Thereafter, those critics who have considered *Henry VI, Part 3* have tended to focus on the only active female characters within the play, Margaret and Elizabeth Woodville (Lady Bona appears so briefly that she scarcely counts). Both Margaret and Elizabeth have been discussed mainly in terms of their supposed relationship to Joan la Pucelle of *Henry VI, Part 1*. Margaret, in particular, has been depicted as a continuation of the threat that Joan posed to the English in the earlier play, a threat that has become more dangerous as it has become domesticated, brought within the country of England (Leslie Fiedler, *The Stranger in Shakespeare*). Marilyn French similarly argued that "Margaret takes over the role Joan plays," asserting that the untrustworthiness of women is a theme of Shakespearean drama that intensified with age (41). The figure of Margaret as an independent character invites further study. As Cox and Rasmussen point out in their 2001 edition of *King Henry VI, Part 3*, "Margaret is the only character who appears in all four plays of the tetralogy: she is courted by Suffolk as his mistress (and incidentally as Henry's Queen) at the end of *Henry VI, Part 1*, becomes a major figure in English court politics in *Henry VI, Part 2*, emerges as *de facto* head of the Lancastrian faction when war breaks out in *Henry VI, Part 3* and survives unhistorically to curse the successful Yorkists at the height of their power in *Richard III*. . . . There is still, it appears, much to be said on behalf of Margaret" (141). A broader brush than specific character studies was deployed by Phyllis Rackin in her 1992 book *Stages of History*, which exposes the deeply patriarchal nature of Renaissance historiography and seeks to compensate by focusing on the importance of women in the history plays as objects of simultaneous veneration and mistrust: veneration for their capacity to bear children but mistrust for precisely the same reason—only a woman truly knows who is a child's father. Thus, Rackin argues, a historical narrative that ostensibly deals with the progression from father to son depends more than it would like to admit on the chastity of women as the only means of establishing that father-son relationship. In the ongoing debate over the role of history within the history plays, Rackin's work provided a vital emphasis on the gendered nature of

Edward, Prince of Wales, and Queen Margaret stand in front of Edward IV in Act V, Scene 5 of *Henry VI, Part 3*. Print from the Boydell Shakespeare Gallery project *(Painting by William Hamilton; engraving by Thomas Holloway)*

history and focused attention on the marginalized, mainly female figures of the history plays.

THE PLAY TODAY

Despite its popularity when first performed, *Henry VI, Part 3* fell off the theatrical map until the 20th century, and even today, it tends to be performed only in conjunction with other plays rather than as a standalone piece. With the civil war in England fresh in their minds, Restoration playwrights such as John Crowne produced conflated and adapted versions of the three *Henry VI* plays along with *Richard III*, under the title of *The Misery of Civil War* (1680–81).

Crowne was seeking royal patronage, and his play was unashamed in its condemnation of rebellion. Colley Cibber in 1700 was one of the most influential of Shakespearean adaptors when he appropriated Act 5, Scene 6 of *Henry VI, Part 3*—the scene of Henry's murder at Richard's hands—as the first scene in of an adaptation of *Richard III*. This conflation of *Henry VI, Part 3* with *Richard III* proved an extremely popular version, and similar conflations appeared, for example, Laurence Olivier's 1944 film production of *Richard III*.

Following World War II, the play became somewhat more popular, being performed either independently or, more often, as part of a cycle of plays. John Barton and Peter Hall, in 1963, produced two plays, *Henry VI* and *Edward IV,* together known as *The Wars of the Roses.* Barton and Hall, emphasized the political chicanery and bloodthirstiness of the plays, arguing that numerous parallels could be drawn with the present day: "In the middle of a blood-soaked century . . . a presentation of one of the bloodiest and most hypocritical periods in history would teach many lessons about the present" (Quoted in the Jisnel Classics edition of *Henry*). Subsequent productions have similarly engaged with contemporary political concerns, granting the plays a continuing life and freshness. Michael Bogdanov produced a new *Wars of the Roses* in 1987 with the English Shakespeare Company, again conflating elements of *Henry VI, Parts 2* and *3,* but this time producing a monumental cycle of seven plays running from *Richard II* to *Richard III.* Bogdanov's work also emphasized the contemporary relevance of the plays; costumes became increasingly modern as the cycle progressed, moving from Victorian to punk, although with the occasional classical reminder. Adrian Noble's production *The Plantagenets* was presented at the same time as Bogdanov's *Wars of the Roses.* Noble's production also conflated the *Henry VI* plays into two and performed them in conjunction with an adapted *Richard III.* The script was continuously adapted, even during rehearsal, and this tradition of adaptation and interpretation has continued for performances that have, at times,

been defined, not by their actors or by their directors, but by their political moment: A production in 1986 was dubbed a "post-Falkland's" production, while a performance by the Sydney Theatre Company (2009) called itself "post-Iraq." Reduced to two four-hour plays, Tom Wright and Benedict Andrews produced a fragmented, bloodsoaked text that drew mixed reviews but had as a specific focus the cynical use of overseas battles to distract attention from troubles at home.

While *Henry VI, Part 3* has never been made into a feature film as a single entity, parts of it appear in a number of films. A film made as early as 1906 of a pageant at Warwick Castle includes two scenes from the play, and a recording of John Barrymore—in what has been called "the first Shakespeare talking picture"—captures the great fin de siècle actor reciting a soliloquy from the play. Jane Howells directed *Henry VI, Part 3* for the camera as part of the BBC/Time-Life Shakespeare series, which captured all of the plays on film. The performance, like most of the other performances in this series, is set on a deliberately stylized stage with a minimum of props. The set is the same as that used for the preceding plays and has become increasingly battered as one play succeeds the next. Further emphasis is laid on the play's relationship to its predecessors and its conclusion, *Richard III,* by means of the introduction; the camera moving slowly over a pile of bodies, the number of which increases in each play.

Henry VI, Part 3 may never attract the kind of stature and reverence attached to, for example, *King Lear* or *Hamlet,* yet this enables different productions to retain freshness and relevance. Directors and producers feel empowered to adapt, conflate, even add lines to the play, where they would probably not dare to do so in the more "canonical plays." Indeed, Barton wrote 1,440 new lines for the performance of *Henry VI, Part 3* while stating that he "wouldn't dream of trying to write bits into *Lear.*" What all 20th- and 21st-century performances appear to have in common is the complete demystification of the monarchy that the plays, taken together, portray. Henry's ineptitude is in no way offset by any indication of divine authority, and most performances appear to portray the development of a moral vacuum in which no other authority than brute force exists. The oath breaking of York and Edward, Margaret's willingness to torment a man with the blood of his own son, Richard's development into monstrosity, all present an image of fallen humanity that Henry's impotent holiness is powerless to redeem. In a society that views its leaders with increasing cynicism and recognizes self-interest as one of the prime motivating factors behind a war, however concealed, the bleak moral world of *Henry VI* remains, tragically, as relevant and contemporary as it was in the 1590s.

FIVE TOPICS FOR DISCUSSION AND WRITING

1. **Revenge drama:** What are some of the motifs and characteristics of Elizabethan revenge drama? Do you think that *Henry VI, Part 3* should be considered a revenge drama rather than a history play?
2. **Women in the play:** This is a play with only three female parts. How have the three women—Lady Grey, Lady Bona, and Queen Margaret—been portrayed within this play? What, if any, conclusions might be drawn from Margaret's fate? Margaret herself is the only character to appear in all four plays of the tetralogy. Consider how this might affect our understanding of her as both queen and mother.
3. **Symbolic language within the play:** Many of the military battles in this play begin or end by a rapid dialogue between the opponents, when both sides seek to win their arguments by seizing control over the language and imagery used. Consider the implications of this technique for the structure of the play as a whole.
4. **Richard's deformity:** Much is made in this play of the fact that Richard is physically deformed. To what extent would it be fair to say that Richard's external deformity symbolizes the interior ambitions that render almost every character of the play monstrous in some way?

5. **Fathers and sons:** How significant do you think it is that Richard only states his desire for the crown after his father has been killed? Is he more in need of a therapist than a crown?

Bibliography

Alexander, Peter. *Shakespeare's* Henry VI *and* Richard III. Cambridge: Cambridge University Press, 1929.

Bacon, Francis. *The Works of Lord Bacon.* London: Henry G. Bohn, 1854

Barton, John, and Peter Hall. *The Wars of the Roses: Adapted for the Royal Shakespeare Company from William Shakespeare's* Henry VI, Parts 1, 2, 3 *and* Richard III. London: British Broadcasting Corporation, 1970.

Born, Lester K., trans. and intro. *The Education of a Christian Prince.* New York: Columbia University Press, 1964.

Bullough, Geoffrey. *Narrative and Dramatic Sources of Shakespeare,* Vol. 3: *The Earlier English History Plays.* London: Routledge, 1960.

Burkhart, Robert E. *Shakespeare's Bad Quartos: Deliberate Abridgements Designed for Performance by a Reduced Cast.* Paris: Mouton, 1975.

Cairncross, Andrew. *The First Part of King Henry the Sixth.* London: Methuen, 1962.

———. *King Henry VI, Part III.* London: Methuen, 1964.

Campbell, L. B. *Shakespeare's Histories: Mirrors of Elizabethan Policy.* Pasadena, Calif.: Huntingdon Library, 1947.

Chambers, E. K. *William Shakespeare: A Study of Facts and Problems.* Oxford, U.K.: Clarendon Press, 1930.

Cox, J., and E. Rasmussen. *King Henry VI, Part 3.* Arden Shakespeare. London: Methuen, 2001.

Erasmus, Desiderius and Lisa Jardine, ed. *The Education of a Christian Prince.* Edited by Lisa Jardine. Cambridge: Cambridge University Press, 2003.

Fiedler, Leslie. *The Stranger in Shakespeare.* London: Croom Helm, 1972.

French, A. L. "The Mills of God and Shakespeare's Early History Plays." *English Studies* 55 (1975): 313–324.

French, Marilyn. *Shakespeare's Division of Experience.* New York: Summit Books, 1981.

Haslewood, Joseph, ed. *Mirror for Magistrates.* London: Lackington, Allen, and Co. Finsbury Square, 1815.

Hattaway, Michael. *The Third Part of King Henry VI.* Cambridge: Cambridge University Press, 1997.

Holderness, Graham. *Textual Shakespeare: Writing and the Word.* Hertfordshire, U.K.: University of Hertfordshire Press, 2003.

Holinshed, Raphael. *Holinshed's Chronicles of England, Scotland, and Ireland, Volume 3.* London: Printed for J. Johnson, 1828.

Honigmann, E. A. J. *Shakespeare's Impact on His Contemporaries.* Totowa, N.J.: Barnes & Noble Books, 1982.

Johnson, Samuel. Notes to *The Plays of William Shakespeare in eight volumes, Volume 5.* London: Printed for J. and R. Tonson, 1765.

Jonson, Ben. *Every Man in His Humour.* Oxford: Oxford University Press, 1999.

Kelly, Henry Ansgar. *Divine Providence in the England of Shakespeare's Histories.* Cambridge, Mass.: Harvard University Press, 1970.

Kirschbaum, Leo. "An Hypothesis Concerning the Origins of the Bad Quartos." *Publications of the Modern Languages Association* 60 (September 1945): 697–715.

Leggatt, Alexander. *Shakespeare's Drama: The History Plays and the Roman Plays.* London and New York: Routledge, 1988.

Martin, Randall. "Reconsidering the Texts of the *True Tragedy of Richard duke of York* and *3 Henry VI.*" *Review of English Studies* 53 (2002): 8–30.

Martin, Randall, ed. *Henry VI, Part Three.* Oxford: Oxford University Press, 2001.

McDonald, Russ. "Review: *Shakespeare in His Time.*" *Shakespeare Quarterly* 34 (Winter 1983): 488–491.

Nashe, Thomas and Ronald B. McKerrow, ed. *The Works of Thomas Nashe, Volume 1.* London: Horace Hart, 1904.

Ornstein, Robert. *A Kingdom for a Stage: The Achievement of Shakespeare's History Plays.* Cambridge, Mass.: Harvard University Press, 1972.

Pendleton, Thomas. Henry VI: *Critical Essays.* London: Routledge 2001.

Plato and B. Iowett, trans. *The Dialogues of Plato, Volume 2.* London: Clarendon Press, 1871.

Rackin, Phyllis. *Stages of History: Shakespeare's English Chronicles.* Ithaca, N.Y.: Cornell University Press, 1991.

Rothwell, K., and A. Melzer. *Shakespeare on Screen: An International Filmography and Videography.* London: Mansell Publishing, 1991.

Rothwell, Kenneth S. *A History of Shakespeare on Screen.* Cambridge: Cambridge University Press, 1999.

Sherbo, Arthur, ed. *Johnson on Shakespeare.* New Haven, Conn.: Yale University Press, 1968.

Spurgeon, Caroline. *Shakespeare's Imagery and What It Tells Us.* Cambridge: Cambridge University Press, 1935.

Thomas, Sidney. "On the Dating of Shakespeare's Early Plays." *Shakespeare Quarterly* 39 (Summer 1988): 187–194.

Tillyard, E. M. W. *Shakespeare's History Plays.* London: Chatto & Windus, 1944.

Urkowitz, Steven. "'If I mistake in those foundations which I build upon': Peter Alexander's textual analysis of *Henry VI, Parts 2* and *3.*" *English Literary Renaissance* 18 (1988): 230–256.

Wells, Robin Headlam. "The Fortunes of Tillyard: Twentieth-Century Critical Debate on Shakespeare's History Plays." *English Studies* 66 (1985): 391–403.

Werstine, Paul. "Narratives about Printed Shakespeare Texts." *Shakespeare Quarterly* 41 (Spring 1990): 65–86.

Womersley, David. "The Politics of Shakespeare's *King John*" *Review of English Studies* 40 (1989): 497–515.

FILM AND VIDEO PRODUCTIONS

Howell, Jane, dir. *The Third Part of Henry the Sixth.* BBC Television Shakespeare, 1982.

—Helen Vella-Bonavita

Henry VIII

INTRODUCTION

Henry VIII, the full title of which is *The Famous History of the Life of King Henry the Eight, or All Is True*, is not one of Shakespeare's best-regarded plays today. Some critics believe it must have been a collaboration with the playwright John Fletcher. Nonetheless, the play successfully fulfills the audience's desire to observe the mercurial nature of politics and subterfuge amid pageantry, and at the same time, it depicts the maelstrom of the domestic life of this reputedly lion-hearted king. Some of the reviews of the play's performances have become legendary. Most notably, in a personal letter from Sir Henry Wotton to Sir Edmund Bacon on July 2, 1613, the same year in which the play was written, Wotton describes how the Globe Theatre was burned down during the performance when gunpowder discharged at the entrance of the king:

> The Kings Players had a new Play called *All is True,* representing some principal pieces of the Reign of Henry 8, which was set forth with many extraordinary circumstances of Pomp and Majesty, even to the matting of the stage; the Knights of the Order, with their Georges and Garter, the Guards with their embroidered Coats, and the like: sufficient in truth within a while to make greatness very familiar, if not ridiculous. Now, King Henry making a Masque at Cardinal Wolsey's House, and certain Canons being shot off at his entry, some of the Paper, or other stuff wherewith one of them was stopped, did light on the Thatch, where being thought at first but an idle smoke, and their eyes more attentive to the show, it kindled inwardly, and ran round like a train, consuming within less then an hour the whole House to the very grounds. This was the fatal period of that virtuous Fabrique; wherein yet nothing did perish, but a few forsaken Cloaks; only one man had his Breeches set on fire, that would perhaps have broiled him, if he had not by the benefit of a provident wit put it out with bottle ale (32).

The play henceforth became inextricably associated with the demise of The Globe Theatre in a most spectacular way. But, it also encapsulates the intrigue, the plots, and the regality that embodied the Tudor court. In the play, Henry VIII must find a way to rule over his kingdom without tearing it asunder and to usher in a new era with the birth of Princess Elizabeth, later Queen Elizabeth I. The rise and fall of the characters within the play and within the historical framework of the court engages the audience visually and ideologically. *Henry VIII* exemplifies the transition from the medieval to the Renaissance era, the displacement of the centrality of Catholicism to a new Protestantism, and the shift from the traditional nuclear family to the mixed family with which contemporary audiences have become most familiar.

BACKGROUND

Shakespeare's 17th-century audience gave their loyalty to King James I, who came to the throne in

King Henry VIII chooses Anne Bullen as his dance partner at Wolsey's banquet in Act I, Scene 4 of *Henry VIII*. This is a print from the Boydell Shakespeare Gallery project, which was first conceived in 1786 and lasted until 1805. *(Painting by Thomas Stothard; engraving by Isaac Taylor)*

1603. However, their hearts and minds, some historians argue, belonged to the Golden Age of Elizabeth. With this idea in mind, most experts believe that *The Famous History of the Life of King Henry the Eight, or All Is True* was written at the time of the king's daughter Princess Elizabeth's marriage to Prince Frederick, Elector Palatine, on February 14, 1613. Although James's empire was secured by the birth of Prince Charles, later Charles I of England, the marriage of Elizabeth evoked the Golden Age of Queen Elizabeth I's empire. James endeavored to continue this gilded era, particularly through the arts. The play concerns itself with ideas of succession, marriage, reformation, taxation, and rebellions but prophetically ends with the empire safely in the hands of Elizabeth, with clear support of Henry VIII, her father. In this manner, *Henry VIII* celebrates the survival of the monarchical system.

The authorship of *Henry VIII* has been argued ever since James Spedding raised the issue in 1850. Many critics suggest that the play was a collaboration between Shakespeare and Fletcher. Geoffrey Bullough asserts that Shakespeare wrote Act I, Scenes 1 and 2; Act II, Scenes 3 and 4; Act III, Scene 2, lines 1–203; and Act V, Scene 1. The critic Gordon McMullan suggests that the play can be seen as having three different "authors": Shakespeare by himself, Shakespeare and Fletcher, and the theater company that Shakespeare and Fletcher worked for:

> the play is Shakespeare's in the sense that it has, at least since the publication of the First Folio, been read, performed and witnessed in a Shakespearean context, with all the professional, cultural and political implications of that context, and in the sense that it engages with, and has a particular place among, the other plays in the Shakespearean canon. It is Shakespeare and Fletcher's, on the other hand, in the sense that a certain amount of evidence, mostly circumstantial, strongly suggests that, contrary to the impression given by its inclusion in the Shakespeare First Folio, the play was the product of two playwrights, William Shakespeare and John Fletcher, working together, and that to treat the plays as a collaboration in this restricted sense is to complicate its canonic status in a potentially productive manner. Again, it is the King's Company in the sense that it was written for, and belonged to, a particular acting company at a particular historical moment (198).

For convenience, this analysis of the play will refer to Shakespeare as the play's author for the remaining discussion.

Like other scholars, Brainerd Kellogg and William J. Rolfe identify several historical authorities for the play: Edward Hall's *Union of the Families of Lancaster and York* (1548) and Raphael Holinshed's *Chronicles of England, Scotland, and Ireland* (1577). Another source was George Cavendish's *Life and Death of Cardinal Wolsey* (probably written 1554–58), of which there were several manuscripts available well before its actual print date of 1641. Much of the final act appears to have been taken from John Foxe's *Acts and Monuments of the Church* (1563). Of each of the sources available to him, Shakespeare follows more closely certain main events from Holinshed.

Although Holinshed offers a rich source for the events of the play, Shakespeare, as usual, played with the history for the sake of his narrative. Alison Weir and John Bowle offer wonderful discussions on the historical facts surrounding Henry VIII. Some literary theorists have observed Shakespeare's manipulation of time in the play. For the purpose of the play's dramatic narrative, the playwright shifted some events which may not have been chronologically accurate. For instance, instead of performing the meeting of Kings Henry VIII and Francis I in the Field of the Cloth of Gold, Shakespeare uses two characters, Norfolk and Buckingham, to discuss the historic moment in Act I, Scene 1. The playwright uses this same strategy with Buckingham's trial. Also, notes McMullan, citing J. J. Scarisbrik, King Henry VIII was not in attendance for Princess Elizabeth's baptism, as Shakespeare represents in Act V. Realistically, the length of the play becomes an important consideration for the actual performance.

Despite moments of waning popularity, *Henry VIII* has enjoyed a colorful and lengthy performance history. Unlike many Shakespearean plays, observes Hugh Richmond, the play has been performed in an unbroken theatrical history since the time of the Bard himself. Perhaps the most notable production of the play was its first recorded performance. June 29, 1613, when the Globe burned. The reconstruction of the Globe was completed by June 30, 1614. After 1660, Sirs William Davenant and Thomas Killigrew's post-Restoration production of the play became a part of Charles II's effort to maintain ideological control over the performances, suggests McMullan. John Philip Kemble's production of the play at Drury Lane in November 1788 is notable for his sister Sarah Siddons's stunning portrayal of Queen Katherine. In 1848, William Charles Macready and Samuel Phelps staged the play before Queen Victoria and Prince Albert at Drury Lane featuring the compelling performance of American actress Charlotte Cushman. In 1910, Herbert Beerbohm Tree created a wonderfully historical spectacle

as he revived production features similar to Henry Irving's staging in 1892, observes McMullan. Later, in 1933, Terence Gray created "provocative productions" in the Festival Theatre at Cambridge where he "used cardboard figures" for some characters, according to Richmond (9). Tyrone Guthrie directed two productions of the play: a comic realist version in 1933 with Charles Laughton as Henry and another more energetic version in 1949 at Stratford, both of which were later revived in 1950 at the Old Vic and in 1953 for Elizabeth II's coronation. In 1969, Trevor Nunn directed Donald Sinden as Henry VIII and Peggy Ashford as Katherine in a Royal Shakespeare Company (RSC) production. In 1983, Howard Davies offered a postmodernist take on the play in another RSC production. In 1996, Greg Doran resurrected *Henry VIII* again in a somber RSC production reminiscent of Gray's earlier production, according to McMullan.

Perhaps the success of Henry VIII in performance owes to Shakespeare's ability to transcend other versions of the same story. For instance, Samuel Rowley's Henry VIII play, *When You See Me, You Know Me,* was performed in 1604 and reprinted in 1613. But, instead of modeling his play on Rowley's, Shakespeare wrote something completely different. He neither mocks, nor minimizes the importance of such seemingly ancillary characters as Gardiner and Cranmer. Shakespeare makes Wolsey a powerful political and religious force within the play, but also gives the character a recognizable humanity for his 17th-century audience. Amazingly, Shakespeare finds a way to create a compelling character in Queen Katherine but does not minimize the role that Lady Anne, later Queen Anne, plays in the future of the Tudor court.

Date and Text of the Play

The Famous History of the Life of King Henry the Eight was one of the last plays that Shakespeare wrote. It was performed in 1613 but not published until the First Folio of 1623, where it appears at the end of the section of history plays. The First Folio is the only text for this play; there were no earlier quarto publications.

205

The Famous History of the Life of
King HENRY the Eight.

THE PROLOGUE.

I Come no more to make you Laugh, Things now,
That beare a Weighty, and a Serious Brow,
Sad, high, and working, full of State and Woe:
Such Noble Scænes, as draw the Eye to flow
We now present. Those that can Pitty, heere
May (if they thinke it well) let fall a Teare,
The Subiect will deserue it. Such as giue
Their Money out of hope they may beleeue,
May heere finde Truth too. Those that come to see
Onely a show or two, and so a gree,
The Play may passe: If they be still, and willing,
Ile vndertake may see away their shilling
Richly in two short houres. Onely they
That come to heare a Merry, Bawdy Play,
A noyse of Targets: Or to see a Fellow
In a long Motley Coate, garded with Yellow,

Will be deceyu'd. For gentle Hearers, know
To ranke our chosen Truth with such a show
As Foole, and Fight is, beside forfeyting
Our owne Braines, and the Opinion that we bring
To make that onely true, we now intend,
Will leaue vs neuer an vnderstanding Friend.
Therefore, for Goodnesse sake, and as you are knowne
The First and Happiest Hearers of the Towne,
Be sad, as we would make ye. Thinke ye see
The very Persons of our Noble Story,
As they were Liuing: Thinke you see them Great,
And follow'd with the generall throng, and sweat
Of thousand Friends: Then, in a moment, see
How soone this Mightinesse, meets Misery:
And if you can be merry then, Ile say,
A Man may weepe vpon his Wedding day.

Actus Primus.   Scœna Prima.

Enter the Duke of Norfolke at one doore. At the other,
the Duke of Buckingham, and the Lord.
Aburgauenny.

Buckingham.

GOod morrow, and well met. How haue ye done
Since last we saw in France?
Norf. I thanke your Grace:
Healthfull, and euer since a fresh Admirer
Of what I saw there.
Buck. An vntimely Ague
Staid me a Prisoner in my Chamber, when
Those Sunnes of Glory, those two Lights of Men
Met in the vale of Andren.
Nor. 'Twixt Guynes and Arde,
I was then present, saw them salute on Horsebacke,
Beheld them when they lighted, how they clung
In their Embracement, as they grew together,
Which had they,
What foure Thron'd ones could haue weigh'd
Such a compounded one?
Buck. All the whole time
I was my Chambers Prisoner.

Nor. Then you lost
The view of earthly glory: Men might say
Till this time Pompe was single, but now married
To one aboue it selfe. Each following day
Became the next dayes master, till the last
Made former Wonders, it's. To day the French,
All Clinquant all in Gold, like Heathen Gods
Shone downe the English, and to morrow, they
Made Britaine, India: Euery man that stood,
Shew'd like a Mine. Their Dwarfish Pages were
As Cherubins, all gilt: the Madams too,
Not vs'd to toyle, did almost sweat to beare
The Pride vpon them, that their very labour
Was to them, as a Painting. Now this Maske
Was cry'de incompareable; and th'ensuing night
Made it a Foole, and Begger. The two Kings
Equall in lustre, were now best, now worst
As presence did present them: Him in eye,
Still him in praise, and being present both,
'Twas said they saw but one, and no Discerner
Durst wagge his Tongue in censure, when these Sunnes
(For so they phrase 'em) by their Heralds challeng'd
The Noble Spirits to Armes, they did performe

t 3   Beyond

Title page of the First Folio edition of *Henry VIII*, published in 1623

SYNOPSIS
Brief Synopsis

The play begins with the Dukes of Buckingham and Norfolk discussing the meeting of the kings of England and France in the Field of the Cloth of Gold. During this discussion, they reveal an antagonism against Cardinal Wolsey, particularly Buckingham. Norfolk warns Buckingham about the public display of his contempt for the cardinal. Later, Buckingham is arrested for high treason. Cardinal Wolsey tells King Henry VIII about the charges against Buckingham, and Queen Katherine tells the king about the burdensome taxation against his people. Later, the cardinal presents a masque at his home, where the king meets Anne Bullen. Buckingham is tried, several witnesses testify against him, and the duke is found guilty of treason. King Henry discloses the suffering of his conscience about his marriage to his brother's wife and the future of his daughter, Mary. At Blackfriars, Queen Katherine speaks in her own defense as she publicly pleads her virtue to King Henry before the bishops, the priests, the noblemen, and the judges Cardinals Wolsey and Campeius. Later, the cardinals privately seek to deter Katherine against opposing the king's desire for a divorce. In spite of the consequences, Katherine impugns the virtue of the cardinals and refuses to relinquish her crown. Cardinal Wolsey finds himself unsuccessfully defending several charges against him and refusing to surrender his seal of office to Norfolk and the Earl of Surrey. In the face of his impending doom, Wolsey reveals his destructive pride and ambition to Thomas Cromwell and asks him to serve the king well. King Henry's marriage to Katherine has been dissolved. Katherine, now the ailing Princess Dowager, has been removed to Kimbolton. Lady Anne becomes Queen Anne at her coronation. On this same day, many subjects receive new titles. After his arrest by the Earl of Northumberland at York, Cardinal Wolsey falls ill and eventually dies at the abbey at Leicester. On her deathbed, Katherine has a vision of her glorious reception in heaven. The new archbishop of Canterbury, Thomas Cranmer, must answer charges before the Privy Council, which later finds him guilty. However, King Henry rescues Cranmer from the malicious and unjust conviction and asks him to serve as godfather to his newborn daughter. At the baptism, Cranmer blesses the new princess, Elizabeth, and prophesizes her glorious reign. King Henry relishes this prophecy, and they all leave to celebrate.

Prologue

The Prologue explains the story of woe, not merriment. The tale is that of noble persons, consistent with the Aristotelian formula of tragedy. It should take place over the course of two hours. The Prologue also suggests that the audience may find truth, which is a major theme of the play. The play will not present fools. The audience should be saddened by the events of the play, in which noble personages will fall into misery.

Act I, Scene 1

The Duke of Buckingham, Lord Abergavenny, and the Duke of Norfolk discuss the kings of England and France, who have recently met to forge peace between their nations. Norfolk observes that Cardinal Wolsey handled the arrangements for said meeting. Buckingham despises the cardinal's ambition, and Norfolk distrusts the cardinal's meager origins. Abergavenny perceives a devilish demeanor to Wolsey. Buckingham fears that the shift in winds that occurred after the meeting of both England and France foreshadows a similar disturbance to the peace between the two nations. Norfolk warns Buckingham to discern carefully Wolsey's vengeful nature and the power that he wields. Later, when Wolsey enters, Buckingham does not hide his disdain of the cardinal, nor does the cardinal cloak his contempt for Buckingham. Wolsey seeks Buckingham's Surveyor and suggests that after having read the surveyor's deposition, Buckingham's scornful glances will wane. After Wolsey departs, Buckingham assures Norfolk that he will gather the evidence necessary to prove Wolsey's treason and corruption. He further assures Norfolk that he will say naught to King Henry before he has his proofs of Wolsey's cashiered honor. Later,

Buckingham is arrested for high treason along with Lord Montague, Buckingham's confessor, and his chancellor as witnesses in the underlying warrant. Buckingham and Abergavenny are taken to the Tower of London.

Act I, Scene 2

King Henry VIII of England enters and thanks Wolsey for defusing the Buckingham plot. Katherine of Aragon enters and tells the king about the complaints of the people, who are being assessed a 6 percent property tax. She explains his subjects' state of discontent and the potential for rebellion. Henry VIII denies knowledge of this taxation, and Wolsey takes the blame for the taxation of the people to pay for the king's war. Cardinal Wolsey defends the taxation, having sought the advice of learned judges, and suggests the ignorance of those who decry against the taxation. Henry VIII advises Wolsey to distribute letters of pardon to every shire for all who refused to pay the tax. Later, Henry VIII hears the evidence against the Duke of Buckingham on the charge of high treason. Katherine does not wholeheartedly accept the evidence, which Wolsey presents. Buckingham's Surveyor testifies to having witnessed the plot to usurp the throne of the king and revenge upon Cardinal Wolsey. Henry VIII demands Buckingham's trial so the law may either grant the duke mercy or find him a traitor.

Act I, Scene 3

Lord Chamberlain and Lord Sandys converse about the influence of French culture on Englishmen in terms of fashion and sexual mores explicitly and religion implicitly. Sir Thomas Lovell joins the discussion as well. Sandys expresses satisfaction that the French will soon leave English shores to return to their own country. They acknowledge the power of Cardinal Wolsey and the supposed slander against him by "a black mouth". They intend to join Cardinal Wolsey for dinner this evening.

Act I, Scene 4

Chamberlain, Sandys, and Lovell enter Wolsey's banquet, where Anne Bullen, other women, and

King Henry VIII holds the hand of Anne Bullen in Act I, Scene 4 of *Henry VIII,* as depicted in this print published in the 18th century.

guests are present. Sandys begins a discussion with Anne that moves from madness to sexual innuendo. Cardinal Wolsey enters, and later King Henry enters, along with others dressed as shepherds en masque. The masquers choose ladies to dance, and the king chooses Anne Bullen. Initially, Wolsey asks Chamberlain about the identity of the masquers, but eventually he identifies the king among them. Wolsey senses Henry's attraction to Anne and tries to distract the king by removing to the next chamber for the banquet.

Act II, Scene 1

Two Gentlemen enter discussing the trial of the Duke of Buckingham, which has occurred offstage. The duke has been found guilty of high treason based on the evidence presented by the king's attorney of examinations, proofs, confessions, and witnesses, including the duke's Surveyor; Sir Gilbert Park, his chancellor; John Court, his confessor; and Hopkins, a monk. The Gentlemen surmise that Cardinal Wolsey played a significant role in this guilty verdict, for, according to them, the common people hate Wolsey and love Buckingham. Buckingham enters from his arraignment and offers a great speech in which he accepts the guilty verdict but maintains that such a judgment lacks justice. He asserts that he forgives the unchristian-like behavior of his accusers and seeks the prayers of his friends. Buckingham also blesses King Henry VIII. The duke compares his predicament to the ill-fated end of his father, who died without a trial on the accusations of his servant at the hand of Henry VII. After the duke leaves, the two Gentlemen discourse upon the rumors of the king's separation from Katherine and the role that Cardinal Wolsey and Cardinal Campeius will play in this matter. The Gentlemen believe that this matter is an attempt at revenge against the Holy Roman Emperor Charles V, who is nephew to Katherine. They suggest that Cardinal Wolsey felt slighted by the emperor, who failed to bestow the honor of archbishopric of Toledo on Wolsey.

Act II, Scene 2

Chamberlain, the Duke of Suffolk, and Norfolk discuss King Henry's grief over having married his brother's wife. They suggest that the king is consumed by this matter, his conscience embattled with his circumstance. Norfolk blames Cardinal Wolsey for this problem. Both Norfolk and Chamberlain suggest that the king will eventually perceive the cardinal's true character. Suffolk maintains that until such time, they remain in bondage to the cardinal's will. Chamberlain leaves as the king enters. After Norfolk and Suffolk are asked to give the king privacy, Henry and Wolsey defer to Campeius's judgment in the matter of Queen Katherine. Wolsey establishes an alliance with the king's new secretary, Gardiner. The king commands Gardiner to deliver a message to the queen considering this matter of their marriage at Blackfriars.

Act II, Scene 3

Anne Bullen discusses with the Old Lady the honorable reputation that Queen Katherine pos-

sesses. Anne suggests that nothing could occur that would damage this reputation. The Old Lady concedes that the most hard-hearted person weeps for Queen Katherine's circumstance. In banter heavy with sexual connotations and double entendres, Anne maintains that she does not seek to become queen, while the Old Lady accuses Anne of hypocrisy with such denials. Later, Chamberlain enters and bestows upon Anne the title Marchioness of Pembroke, which includes the financial support of 1,000 pounds annually. Anne graciously accepts the honor and professes her obedience and blessings to the king. The Old Lady appears to be overwhelmed by the gift that the king has granted Anne, yet Anne presents a demeanor that is unruffled by the ostentatious gift.

Act II, Scene 4

The court proceeding at Blackfriars for King Henry's separation from Queen Katherine is called to begin by the Crier and the Scribe. The queen does not answer the call but kneels immediately before the king and begs him to give her justice as she has been "a true and humble wife" to him (l. 23) and the matter of her earlier marriage to Prince Arthur had been settled by his father, King Henry VII, and her father, King Ferdinand of Spain. Wolsey seeks to deter Katherine from her direct petition of Henry and to allow the learned men of integrity decide the matter. Cardinal Campeius encourages Queen Katherine to do the same. Katherine refuses to allow Cardinal Wolsey to be her judge as she considers him her enemy and the instigator in the strife between her and the king. Wolsey denies these accusations. She further accuses him of self-interest as opposed to spiritual interests. Katherine seeks to bring her appeal before the pope for his judicial determination. Thereafter, she leaves in spite of the calls for her return to court. King Henry attributes the queen's behavior to her noble birth and her love for him. Wolsey asks the king to confirm for the public that he has not instigated this matter as he is accused by Queen Katherine. Henry confirms this and proceeds to explain the impetus for his tortured conscience concerning his marriage and the consequent legitimacy of his daughter, Mary. He seeks to rectify his conscience. The king obtains his own confirmation through the Bishop of Lincoln. The king suggests that he seeks merely to prove his marriage lawful, and if so proven, he will remain with Queen Katherine. Campeius adjourns the court session. King Henry begins to doubt whether either of the cardinals take this court proceeding seriously. He is suspicious of Rome and diligently awaits the return of Thomas Cranmer.

Act III, Scene 1

The scene begins with Katherine and her women, who are working. She asks one of them to sing a song, which is of Orpheus with his lute. Cardinals Wolsey and Campeius seek a private word with the queen. Although she agrees to speak with them, she refuses to enter into a private chamber. Katherine speaks to them before her women, who serve as witnesses to this conspicuous interview. Wolsey and Campeius urge Katherine to allow King Henry to determine this matter of their marriage and forgo the trial by law, which she will fail. They endeavor to assure the queen that the king, who loves her, desires to protect her interests. They ask the queen to trust them. Katherine indicts the nature of the cardinals's service in which they seek a result that seems inconsistent with their religious profession. She questions their attempt to "comfort" her (l. 106). She warns them that they should be careful lest her fate become their own. Katherine concedes that she is without friends, hope, or pity in this land, not of her birth. The cardinals maintain that their profession, as "peacemakers, friends, and servants," requires them to provide a solution to her plight (l. 166). Katherine advises them to do as they will and offer her counsel, for she regrets the dire price that she must pay as queen.

Act III, Scene 2

Norfolk, Suffolk, the Earl of Surrey, and Chamberlain discuss Wolsey's imminent fall from the king's grace. Henry has discovered Wolsey's communications against the king's interest with the pope and,

in fact, possesses Wolsey's letters. The king has married Anne, and Suffolk hopes blessings will derive from the union. However, her coronation has not yet occurred. Wolsey detests Henry's union with Anne, now Marchioness of Pembroke, and seeks a more politically advantageous union with the king of France's sister, the duchess of Alençon. Wolsey and then the king enter. Henry questions Wolsey about all of the honors, wealth, and position that have been bestowed upon him not only by himself but also by the king's father, Henry VII. Wolsey confirms his gracious receipt of such honors and his complete loyalty to the king. The king exits ill-pleased with Wolsey. Wolsey worries over the king's disposition. Later, Norfolk, Surrey, Suffolk, and Chamberlain return to retrieve the great seal from Wolsey. Wolsey refuses to yield the seal in spite of their assurances that the request is made on the king's behalf. Surrey accuses Wolsey of being a traitor, laying fault at the cardinal's ambition. Thereafter, Surrey charges that Wolsey has committed extortion. Surrey, Suffolk, and Norfolk explain several of the complaints against Wolsey. Chamberlain beseeches them to leave such complaints to the law and seek not to correct him. Suffolk informs Wolsey that based upon said charges, he will "forfeit all [his] goods, lands, tenements, chattels, and whatsoever, and to be out of the king's protection" (l. 342–344). Wolsey realizes that no remedy exists that will cure this rift with the king. Later, Thomas Cromwell enters, and Wolsey asks him about the latest news. Cromwell tells him that the news includes the cardinal's strife with the king, Thomas More's replacement as Lord Chancellor, and the king's marriage to Anne Bullen. Wolsey advises Cromwell against the path that has led to his own fall, namely ambition, corruption, self-interest, and lies.

Act IV, Scene 1

The two Gentlemen attend Lady Anne's coronation. Other subjects, including Suffolk and Norfolk, also come forth to claim their new offices. The Gentlemen discuss the divorce trial that was held with Queen Katherine in abstentia. The court

Griffith describes the reception of Cardinal Wolsey to Queen Katherine in Act IV, Scene 2 of *Henry VIII*. Print from the Boydell Shakespeare Gallery project *(Painting by Richard Westall; engraving by Robert Thew)*

granted the divorce, and Katherine "was removed to Kimbolton," where she has fallen ill (34). The Second Gentleman describes Queen Anne as angelic. A Third Gentlemen enters and also praises the beauty, goodness, and similarly endearing qualities, which are expected of a new queen. The First Gentleman reveals that the cardinal's "York Place" has now become the king's "Whitehall." Stokesley, Bishop of London during Henry VIII's reign, and Gardiner have become reverend bishops. However, the Second Gentleman observes that Gardiner detests Cranmer, who has become the Archbishop of Canterbury. The Third Gentleman asserts that Cromwell has become the master of the jewel house and a member of the Privy Council. The Second and Third Gentlemen agree that Cromwell will rise higher than these offices.

Act IV, Scene 2

Katherine enters with Griffith and Patience, who help the ailing dowager. Katherine is "sick to death" (l. 2). Griffith tells Katherine of Wolsey's arrest and death. At his death, Wolsey was repentant, mournful, and full of regrets. Katherine discloses Wolsey's prideful and deceitful nature and his manipulation of the law for his own ends. She explains that he was no model cleric. With Kath-

erine's permission, Griffith expands upon Wolsey's virtues. Griffith explains Wolsey's scholarly nature, wisdom, and persuasive disposition. He notes that Wolsey "died fearing God" (l. 68) and was content with having been overthrown. Katherine has a vision of six personages in white robes, wearing garlands on their heads and golden vizards on their faces. Lord Caputius, the lord ambassador from Spain, comes to visit Katherine and dutifully agrees to send her blessings to King Henry VIII and seek the comforts of those servants who have loyally served the queen unto her death.

Act V, Scene 1

Gardiner and Lovell discuss Queen Anne's difficult labor. Gardiner hints at his suspicions of Cranmer and Cromwell, Queen Anne's chief supporters. He suggests that he has made enemies in the Privy Council by speaking against Cranmer, Archbishop of Canterbury. Later, Henry VIII discusses with Cranmer the complaints against him and how he must answer the charges before the Privy Council. The king tells him that he will be taken to the Tower of London. Henry believes Cranmer guiltless of the charges but doubts the archbishop's ability to prove himself so. Henry agrees, after Cranmer's supplication, to defend the archbishop. The Old Lady brings news: Queen Anne delivers Henry's heir, a daughter.

Act V, Scenes 2–3

Along with the king, Cranmer awaits his fate before the Privy Council. Once Cranmer enters the chambers of the Privy Council, the Lord Chancellor explains the charges, which include heresy, against Cranmer. Dismissing any notions of mercy, Gardiner interposes that such heresy leads to anarchy. Cromwell intercedes on Cranmer's behalf, and Gardiner accuses Cromwell of heretical affiliations, as well. Cranmer asks for mercy. The Lord Chancellor and Gardiner order Cranmer's removal to the Tower until King Henry's final determination. Finally, Cranmer displays the king's ring. Norfolk explains that the king will allow no harm to Cranmer. Suffolk and Chamberlain recognize the mistake of issuing charges against Cranmer. Cromwell responds in a self-satisfied manner. The king enters and berates each of the lords for their treatment of Cranmer, particularly Gardiner, who tries to assuage Henry with flattery. The Lord Chancellor defends the lords, who intended a fair trial without malice toward Cranmer. After demanding that the lords honor and accept Cranmer, King Henry asks Cranmer to be godfather to his newborn daughter. The king again demands that Gardiner embrace and love Cranmer. King Henry and Cranmer leave for the baptism, at which the Duchess of Norfolk and Lady Marquess Dorset will serve as godmothers.

Act V, Scene 4

The Porter and his Man prepare for the dining after the christening of the new princess. Their duties are portrayed as haphazard, comical, but quite political. Chamberlain enters and threatens the lackadaisical lot with imprisonment at Marshalsea should they fail to perform their prescribed duties.

Act V, Scene 5

Trumpets, along with the Garter, herald the christening of the new heir, Elizabeth. Her name is spoken for the first time in this scene. King Henry kisses her as a blessing and seeks divine protection for her. He also thanks the godparents. Cranmer, her godfather, offers an expansive prophecy of the glory that England will claim during the Virgin Queen Elizabeth's future reign. The king expresses his pleasure with this prophetic speech.

Epilogue

The Epilogue expresses an ambivalent reception of the play. These final words of the play suggest that the foregoing might find more pleasure by women, who will, of course, encourage the men to applaud.

CHARACTER LIST

Duke of Norfolk   He detests the influence of Cardinal Wolsey on Henry VIII and later serves on the Privy Council.

Duke of Buckingham   Enemy of Cardinal Wolsey but loyal to the king.

Lord Abergavenny   The Duke of Buckingham's son-in-law.

Cardinal Wolsey   Archbishop of York and Lord Chancellor.

Brandon   Conducts the arrest of Buckingham.

King Henry VIII   Son of Henry VII, husband to Katherine and later to Anne Bullen.

Sir Thomas Lovell   Reputed object in the Buckingham treason plot.

Katherine of Aragon   Queen of England. She later becomes Princess Dowager after Henry VIII divorces her.

Duke of Suffolk   One of Cardinal Wolsey's enemies.

Lord Chamberlain   Nobleman in charge of the king's household.

Anne Bullen   The historical Anne Boleyn, Katherine's lady-in-waiting and later Henry's second wife. Queen Anne gives birth to a daughter, the future Elizabeth I.

Sir Henry Guildford   Extends a welcome to the guests at Cardinal Wolsey's masque.

Sir Nicholas Vaux   Escorts Buckingham from his arraignment.

Cardinal Campeius   Papal legate.

Gardiner   King's secretary and, later, Bishop of Winchester.

Old Lady   Friend of Anne Bullen.

Bishop of Lincoln   One of the bishops in attendance at Blackfriars.

Griffith   Queen Katherine's gentleman usher (attendant).

Earl of Surrey   Buckingham's son-in-law.

Thomas Cromwell   Cardinal Wolsey's secretary and, later, secretary to the Privy Council.

Lord Chancellor   Highest-ranking government official. Historically, Sir Thomas More was Lord Chancellor at this time.

Third Gentleman   Witnesses the coronation of Lady Anne as the new queen.

Patience   Attendant to Queen Katherine.

Lord Caputius   Ambassador from the Holy Roman Emperor Charles V of Spain.

Sir Anthony Denny   Brings Cranmer to meet with the king.

Thomas Cranmer   Adviser to King Henry VIII and, later, Archbishop of Canterbury.

Doctor Butts   King's physician.

CHARACTER STUDIES
Henry VIII

Henry VIII has the most complex role in this play, beginning as merely a figure observing the pageantry of the monarchy, then becoming a tortured sovereign, and finally ending as a hopeful man resigned to placing his reign in the hands of the newly born Princess Elizabeth. McMullan and Richmond argue that in Act I, Scene 2, where Henry VIII makes his first entrance, the dependent king is quite passive, as the stage direction indicates: *"Enter King Henry, leaning on the Cardinal's shoulder."* When Queen Katherine enters, she is flanked by Norfolk and Suffolk. It is apparently the queen who, blaming Cardinal Wolsey, informs the king of the financial unrest among the commons. Henry VIII's conduct might appear not only passive and clinging but uninformed. Yet, Henry VIII ever embodies the clever politician. It is important for the audience and his court to believe that he was without blame in the assessment of taxes against his people. Later, by Act II, Scene 4, the king has moved from a visibly complacent sovereign to one who has become tortured by his conscience because of his marriage to his brother's wife. Katherine had been previously married to Henry's older brother, Arthur, before he died. Again, Henry looks to Cardinal Wolsey to aid him in removing God's judgment against him and the future of his realm without a male heir. This characterization of the marriage question portrays Henry as a king who decides this important matter, not for himself, but for the good of his kingdom. In Act V, Scene 2, the audience now sees a king who discerns the malicious element in his council, which seeks to fell yet another figure in the play, Cranmer. The king becomes Cranmer's most stalwart defender and offers his continued protection over the virtuous Cranmer, now Archbishop of Canterbury. Finally, in Act V, Scene 5, as evidence of the king's loyalty, Cranmer serves as godfather to Princess Elizabeth at her baptism. The king embraces Cranmer's "oracle of comfort" (5.5.67), in which Princess Elizabeth is prophesied to become a monarch where "in her days, every man shall eat in safety / Under his own vine what he plants, and sing / The merry songs of peace to all his neighbors" (5.4.33–35). The range of Henry VIII's character has sometimes, unfortunately, been abbreviated in performances, such as that of Herbert Beerbohm Tree's production in which Act 5 was deleted.

Cardinal Wolsey tries to distract King Henry VIII from Anne Bullen in Act 1, Scene 4 of *Henry VIII*, as depicted in this print published in the 19th century. *(Painting by Friedrich Pecht; engraving by Johann Leonhard Raab)*

Katherine

Queen Katherine's character enthralls the audience from her initial entrance at in Act I, Scene 2, flanked by the Dukes of Norfolk and Suffolk, to Act IV, Scene 2, where she is on her deathbed surrounded by loyal servants. She has four key scenes that exemplify her strength and intensity: her words on the issue of taxation, her plea to Henry VIII at Blackfriars, her quarrel with Wolsey and Campeius, and her deathbed scene. At her entrance, the queen fiercely defends the people and supports their complaints against the overburdening taxation. She does not hide her contempt for Cardinal

Helena Modjeska as Queen Katherine in an 1892 production of *Henry VIII (Photographed by Theodore C. Marceau)*

She deftly emphasizes her gender and her nationality—both of which place her on the outside of power in this matter. Campeius attempts to dismiss the moving speech by describing the queen as "obstinate, / Stubborn to justice, apt to accuse it, and / Disdainful to be tried by't" (2.4.119–121). As impassioned as the quite public Blackfriars scene is, the queen's character reaches its zenith in the more private scene with Cardinals Wolsey and Campeius in Act III, Scene 1. Although the cardinals try to placate the queen, she adeptly shuns their efforts. She exposes their lack of virtue and bonds to the church. She impeaches their conduct, their demeanor, and their intentions. After having swayed the audience at Blackfriars, Queen Katherine courageously exposes the truth as she sees it. She proclaims: "There's nothing I have done yet, o'my conscience, / Deserves a corner. Would all other women / Could speak this with as free a soul as I do" (3.1.30–32). The queen asks for counsel to defend her cause, yet after having been denied, she resigns herself to death. She tells her serving women: "Alas, poor wenches, where are now / your fortunes? / Shipwrecked upon a kingdom where no pity, / No friends, no hope, no kindred weep for me, / Almost no grave allowed me, like the lily / That once was mistress of the field and flourished, / I'll hang my head and perish" (3.1.148–153). The queen has no hope for her fortune nor for the fortune of other women as she, of royal blood, can be ejected from her marriage without the aid of true legal or spiritual counsel. In her final scene, in Act IV, Scene 2, Queen Katherine learns of Wolsey's death from Griffith and has a vision of her own death, which provides her solace. The vision evidences the virtuous life that she has led and the reward that she will have in the next life. Finally, she leaves Caputius with her final words, which demonstrate her loyalty and her love for her king and their daughter.

Wolsey

Cardinal Wolsey represents the malevolent antagonist from the moment the play begins. The cardinal enters at line 115 of the opening scene, but he

Wolsey and his machinations. The audience is able to attach her uncloaked insinuation against Wolsey to the revealing discussions that Norfolk and Suffolk have had about the cardinal's sinister character since the opening scene. Katherine displays her indomitable spirit here and again, in Act II, Scene 4 at Blackfriars, where the matter of her marriage is heard before Cardinals Wolsey and Campeius who serve as judges. In an emotionally charged scene, the royal lady kneels before her king and persuasively pleads her case, not before the cardinals and the retinue of bishops, but before her sovereign and husband, Henry VIII. She presents a figure of womanhood who is blameless before an entire audience of men who seek judgment against her.

is mentioned as early as line 45 by the Dukes of Buckingham and Norfolk. The audience becomes acquainted immediately with his repute for machinations and ambition. He becomes the key subject in this first scene. Norfolk warns Buckingham of the cardinal's malice and power: "You know his nature, / That he's revengeful, and I know his sword / Hath a sharp edge: it's long and't may be said / It reaches far, and where 'twill not extend / Thither he darts it" (1.1.108–112). Later in the same scene, as the stage directions specify, Wolsey *"fixeth his eye on Buckingham,"* which dooms the duke to his later fall. Wolsey, like King Henry, uses his "looks" to consign the fate of his enemy. Eugene Waith describes Wolsey as an "archintriguer" (120). Some of the cardinal's most compelling scenes involve how he answers his critics, most important, being the king at Act III, Scene 2. The cardinal secures his downfall when he denies his self-interested and ambitious nature before the king. He clings to a virtuous, pious, and selfless role of cardinal, not realizing the king's trust has begun to wane, although his perception has not. In an aside in Act II, Scene 4, the king reveals his disappointment in both Cardinals Wolsey and Campeius at Blackfriars: "I may perceive / These cardinals trifle with me. I abhor / This dilatory sloth and tricks of Rome" (2.4.232–234). After the king gives Cardinal Wolsey proof of his disloyalty, the Dukes of Surrey, Norfolk, and Suffolk verbally deliver to Wolsey the complaints against the cardinal, particularly those grounded in his aspirations to become pope (3.2). In the same scene, Wolsey gives a stirring speech in soliloquy about his prideful nature and his culpability, which contribute to his fall from greatness. The cardinal compares his fall to that of Lucifer, the devil (3.2.371). In his final moments, Cromwell informs him that Sir Thomas More will take the cardinal's place as Lord Chancellor, Cranmer is installed as Archbishop of Canterbury, and Lady Anne will soon be crowned the new queen of England. In the face of these rising new figures, the cardinal is at once surprised at Cranmer's position, hopeful for More, and rueful of Queen Anne. Verbally shunning Cromwell from his presence, Wolsey advises Cromwell to serve the king diligently but becomes regretful of his own fall: "Had I but served my God with half the zeal / I served my King, he would not in mine age / Have left me naked to mine enemies" (3.2.455–457). Throughout the play, Shakespeare creates a brilliant doubling effect for many of the characters. For instance, Cromwell offers a wonderful contrast to the figure of Wolsey. One of the final references to the cardinal is at Queen Katherine's bedside, when Griffith tells her of Wolsey's death and his virtues (4.2).

Buckingham

The Duke of Buckingham becomes intolerant of the malignity that reigns at this Tudor court through Cardinal Wolsey. He serves the king with loyalty and truth but becomes unable to contain his enmity against Wolsey. His complaints against the cardinal seem imbued with notions of class. He refers to the cardinal as "this butcher's cur" (1.1.120). Like the Duke of Norfolk, Buckingham apparently associates the cardinal's lack of noble lineage with his ignoble character. In spite of his own feelings about Wolsey, Norfolk advises Buckingham against his continued campaign against the powerful Wolsey, who has so close an ear and arm to the king. Yet, Buckingham expresses his displeasure with Wolsey visibly by demonstrating his disdain for the cardinal (1.1.115). Later in the scene, Buckingham is arrested based on the false testimony of his Surveyor. His fall becomes the first of several throughout the play. Buckingham is charged with high treason and tried by a jury, to which Wolsey later refers as evidence of Buckingham's lawful prosecution. Having previously identified the deceit within the court, Buckingham feels his doom before his trial: "Lo you, my lord, / The net has fall upon me: I shall perish / Under device and practice" (1.1.203–204). After hearing the false testimony of the Surveyor, the king deems Buckingham "a giant traitor" (1.2.199). Although evidence in the form of proofs, witnesses, and testimonies are presented in Buckingham's defense, the initial false confession that the Surveyor provides, along with the accusations and testimonies of Sir Gilbert Park, his chancellor; John Court, his confessor; and Hopkins, a monk, outweigh Buckingham's "sharp reasons to defeat the law" (2.1.14). The cardinal's role in the trial is publicly acknowledged. The First Gentleman observes: "whoever the King favours, / The Cardinal instantly will find employment— / And far enough from court, too" (2.1.47–49). At his arraignment (2.1), Buckingham acknowledges the judgment against him but bears the law no malice. He remains loyal to the king. He compares his fall to the fall of his father (2.1.119). Finally, he seeks the prayers of the listeners. Buckingham serves as a provocative contrast to Gardiner, who does not conceal his hatred of Cranmer.

Norfolk

The Duke of Norfolk's character demonstrates a political acuity and worldly experience that become evident in some key scenes: the description of the Field of the Cloth of Gold ceremony, the matter of the king's divorce, the removal of Wolsey from office, Cranmer's trial, and Elizabeth's baptism. Norfolk presents a more politically shrewd figure than either Buckingham or the Duke of Suffolk, the latter of whom does not appear until Act I, Scene 2. However, in the opening scene, the audience is immediately introduced to Norfolk, who describes the ceremony of the Field of the Cloth of Gold involving the kings of England and France, and his character makes a continuous appearance up to Act III, Scene 2; then later, Norfolk participates in Cranmer's trial (5.2) and makes his final, perfunctory appearance in Act V, Scene 4. In Act I, Scene 1, where Buckingham seems to rail at the malevolent behavior of Wolsey, Norfolk warns Buckingham against the choleric behavior that exposes his true feelings about Wolsey. Norfolk promotes reason and temperance. Buckingham ignores this advice and is immediately arrested. Later, in Act II, Scene 2, Norfolk discusses the matter of the king's divorce from Katherine with Suffolk and Chamberlain. Now, he purges his feelings about Cardinal Wolsey, which seem less politic. Norfolk blames Wolsey for counseling the king to divorce Queen Katherine. Norfolk exclaims: "He dives into the King's soul and there scatters / Dangers, doubts, wringing of the conscience, / Fears and despairs—and all these for this marriage. / And out of these, to restore the King, / He counsels a divorce, a loss of her / That like a jewel has hung twenty years / About his neck yet never lost her luster" (2.2.25–31). Norfolk reveals the true danger that Wolsey presents as the source of the success or failure of the nobles. In Act III, Scene 2, Norfolk informs Suffolk and Surrey that Wolsey's circumstances have changed since the cardinal failed to secure the king's divorce at Blackfriars: The king has evidence of Wolsey's disloyalty through the cardinal's "miscarried" letter to the pope in which the cardinal seeks a delay in the king's divorce judgment (3.2.30). A most compelling moment of Wolsey's fall occurs later in the same scene, when Norfolk takes the cardinal's seal of office from him at the king's behest. Norfolk, along with Suffolk, Surrey, and Chamberlain, detail the list of complaints against the cardinal. Specifically, Norfolk tells Wolsey that in his letter to Rome, the cardinal made it appear that the king was but his servant. Obstinately, the cardinal refuses to surrender the seal to Norfolk. In Act V, Scene 3, when the Privy Council finds Cranmer guilty, Norfolk, conspicuously does not say anything against Cranmer but acknowledges the king's protection. Still, the king chastises the Privy Council for its malice and extends his protection to Cranmer with his own ring. In Act V, Scene 5, the Duke and the Duchess of Norfolk attend the baptism of Princess Elizabeth, the duchess serving as godmother. Norfolk's character bears striking similarities to Suffolk's character. They seem to share the same alliances and many scenes throughout the play.

Anne Bullen

The character of Anne Bullen, though she has few lines, is fascinating because of the tremendous effect she has on the outcome of the play. She appears in three pivotal scenes. First, she meets

Anne Bullen in *Henry VIII*. This print is from Charles Heath's 1848 edition of *The Heroines of Shakspeare: Comprising the Principal Female Characters in the Plays of the Great Poet. (Painting by J. W. Wright; engraving by B. Eyles)*

King Henry VIII for the first time at Cardinal Wolsey's banquet (1.4). Next, Anne receives an honor from the king: She becomes the Marchioness of Pembroke, which includes "a thousand pound a year annual support" (2.3.63–64). Finally, she reappears at her coronation, yet the entire scene is described by the First, Second, and Third Gentlemen. Other scenes merely mention her but keep Anne uppermost in the minds of the audience and the other characters in the play. For instance, in Act III, Scene 2, Suffolk reads a letter that Cardinal Wolsey wrote to the pope: "'My King is tangled in affection to / A creature of the Queen's, Lady Anne Bullen'" (3.2.35–36). In the same scene, Wolsey disparages her Lutheran religion. Later,

after Anne's coronation, Lovell describes her by his conscience: "She's a good creature and, sweet lady, does / Deserve our better wishes" (5.1.24–26). Yet, Gardiner seeks her death and that of her agents, Cranmer and Cromwell. In that same scene, the Old Lady tells the king that Queen Anne has given birth to a girl. In Act V, Scene 5, Henry VIII encourages everyone to visit Queen Anne after the baptism of Elizabeth. Even though her appearance is brief within the play, Anne presents an intriguing character and a compelling contrast to Queen Katherine.

Cranmer

Thomas Cranmer's appearance, like Anne Bullen's, is brief but important. His character is not introduced until Act V, Scene 1, where he is facing a trial by his accusers. He has been warned by the king that these accusers are malicious and that Cranmer may find it difficult to defend himself. After having witnessed the fall of several great figures through the play, this final trial offers a different outcome. Instead, here, the audience witnesses King Henry rescuing Cranmer from an unjust conviction by the Privy Council. The king extends his protection to Cranmer, whom he describes as a good and honest man, and the now Archbishop of Canterbury becomes the godfather of Princess Elizabeth. In the final scene of the play, Cranmer makes a prophetic message of comfort not merely for the king but for the entire kingdom: Princess Elizabeth will become a solace for a nation that longs for what later will become the Golden Age.

DIFFICULTIES OF THE PLAY

One of the most striking aspects of *Henry VIII* is the way Shakespeare seems to meld several different genres into the play. Elements of history, tragedy, romance, and the court masque are all incorporated into the text, which becomes one of the key attributes in the long performance history of the play. This is part of the play's appeal but can be confusing to those studying it. Some critics believe the play suffers from a lack of organization.

Initially, the play seems to work well within the tragic genre. The successive falls of Buckingham, Wolsey, and Katherine hearken to Giovanni Boccacio's *De casibus* tradition of medieval tragedy, in which men and women fall from greatness, as exemplified by Geoffrey Chaucer's "Monk's Tale," John Lydgate's *The Fall of Princes,* or *A Mirror of Magistrates.* Citing Pooler, Frank Kermode suggests that the play is a "collection of tragedies." The audience watches as each man and woman is removed from a highly public station in life and eventually dies as a result of the fall. Critics attempt to distinguish the medieval tragedy, with its depiction of characters as noble warriors, from the Renaissance tragedy, with its seemingly ignoble cowards, observes McMullan. Yet, neither Buckingham nor Katherine appears to be vice-ridden weaklings. They are fearless in the face of the accusations and impending death. Wolsey serves his purpose as the villain in this play without taking from the designs of the tragic genre. His character brings in the elements of revenge, particularly in the fall of Buckingham, which is also found within the tragic genre.

Henry VIII also obviously fits within the genre of the history plays. It possesses an episodic structure, like *Henry VI,* and examines the origins of reformation, like *King John.* Finally, this drama most distinctively associates itself by reference to the events of *Richard III,* which ends with the crowning of King Henry VII. *Henry VIII* also includes figures from other Shakespearean history plays, such as Buckingham, Lovell, Norfolk, and Surrey, among other characters. In addition to these devices, the play seeks to present a reality or truth, as evidenced from its subtitle, *All Is True.*

Furthermore, taking poetic license with this moment in Tudor history, *Henry VIII* exhibits a number of romantic traits, as in such other late plays of Shakespeare as *The Tempest, Cymbeline, Pericles,* and *The Winter's Tale.* Like those, this drama focuses on a number of characters and features the supernatural, a redemptive father-daughter tableau, and a marked manipulation of time. Regarding the supernatural, Queen Katherine sees a vision of her heavenly reward. Archbishop Cran-

Cranmer prophesies England's future glory at the christening of Elizabeth, King Henry VIII's heir, in Act V, Scene 5 of *Henry VIII.* Print from the Boydell Shakespeare Gallery project *(Painting by William Peters; engraving by Joseph Collyer)*

mer also explains his prophetic vision of Princess Elizabeth leading Henry's kingdom to prosperity. Regarding the father-daughter relation, Henry VIII becomes a part of Elizabeth's baptism as she takes her rightful place in Tudor history. This affirmation of Elizabeth's place is repeated with each performance of the play. In this final scene, the playwright's manipulation of time and dramatic action is most pronounced, as he attempts to fit the framework of the play into its production demands.

Finally, the play also includes some conventions of the court masque, which was common in Renaissance comedy but will be unfamiliar to most of today's readers. The masque at Wolsey's house is where Anne Bullen meets Henry VIII and is also the first sign of doom for Queen Katherine. Within the masque's comic or romantic tradition, just as Buckingham, Wolsey, and Katherine fall, Anne, Cranmer and Cromwell's fortunes rise. The representation of Act V, Scene 4 becomes a comic scene, which is chiefly conducted between the Porter and his Man as they prepare for Princess Elizabeth's baptism. Yet, even in these comic moments, the play continues to grapple with ideological principles and political issues.

KEY PASSAGES
Act II, Scene 4, 170–203

KING HENRY. My conscience first received a
   tenderness,
Scruple and prick on certain speeches uttered
By th'Bishop of Bayonne, then French
   ambassador,
Who had been hither sent on the debating
A marriage 'twixt the Duke of Orleans and
Our daughter Mary. I'th' progress of this
   business,
Ere a determinate resolution, he—
I mean the Bishop—did require a respite,
Wherein he might the King his lord advertise
Whether our daughter were legitimate
Respecting this our marriage with the
   dowager,
Sometimes our brother's wife. This respite
   shook
The bosom of my conscience, entered me,
Yea, with a spitting power, and made to
   tremble
The region of my breast; which forced such
   way
That many mazed considering did throng
And pressed in with this caution. First,
   methought
I stood not in the smile of heaven, who had
Commanded nature that my lady's womb,
If it conceived a male child by me, should
Do no more offices of life to't than
The grave does to th' dead: for her male issue
Or died where they were made, or shortly after
This world had aired them. Hence I took a
   thought
This was a judgement on me, that my
   kingdom—
Well worthy the best heir o'th' world—should
   not
Be gladded in't by me. Then follows that
I weighed the danger which my realms
   stood in
By this my issue's fail, and that gave to me
Many a groaning throe. Thus hulling in
The wild sea of my conscience, I did steer

Toward this remedy where upon we are
Now present here together: that's to say,
I meant to rectify my conscience—

Henry VIII's entire speech, addressed to Cardinal
Wolsey, is important. Here, the play follows Holinshed's *Chronicles* quite closely. The business of marriage and divorce pervades this passage—specifically,
the king's daughter Mary's future marriage, her
legitimacy, and Henry's own divorce with Katherine.
If his marriage with Katherine becomes invalidated,
so does Mary's legitimacy. Princess Mary cannot
become contracted to marry the Duke of Orlean
as the French ambassador, the Bishop of Bayonne,
proposes. Henry later believes that Wolsey sought

**Edwin Booth as King Henry VIII in a 19th-century
production of *Henry VIII***

to avoid the matter by desiring "the sleeping of this business" (2.4.160). This passage also focuses on Henry's conscience, which serves as another significant theme in the play. Earlier, Henry VIII pleads: "O my Wolsey, / The quiet of my wounded conscience, / Thou art a cure fit for a king" (2.2.72–73). The king seeks to have Wolsey help him relieve himself from the "hulling in the wild sea of my conscience." The future of his realm rests on the ability to produce a viable heir for the Tudor court. Henry suggests that the matter of marrying his brother Arthur's wife, Katherine, has resulted in a biblical judgment that "shook the bosom of my conscience." A. D. Nuttall makes the comparisons between *Henry VIII* and the subject of marrying one's brother in *Hamlet,* where Claudius also marries his brother's wife. The marriage raises notions of incest, which were also considered by Sigmund Freud. In spite of the papal dispensation, now the good king seeks to "rectify [his] conscience." McMullan cites this speech as important in determining the audience's perception of the king. However, in performance, the speech is often consolidated. Hence, the speech may persuade the audience when the king is perceived as having been moved beyond his control in this business of marriage and his conscience.

Act III, Scene 1, 98–111

KATHERINE. Ye tell me what ye wish for
  both—my ruin.
Is this your Christian counsel? Out upon ye!
Heaven is above all yet: there sits a judge
That no king can corrupt.

CAMPEIUS. Your rage mistakes us.

KATHERINE. The more shame for ye. Holy
  men I though ye,
Upon my soul, two reverend cardinal virtues—
But cardinal sins and hollow hearts I fear ye.
Mend 'em for shame, my lords. Is this your
  comfort?
The cordial that ye bring a wretched lady,
A woman lost among ye, laughed at, scorned?

I will not wish ye half my miseries:
I have more charity. But say I warned ye.
Take heed, for heaven's sake take heed, lest at
  once
The burden of my sorrows fall upon ye.

Here, Queen Katherine confronts Cardinals Wolsey and Campeius as they "counsel" her on the business of her divorce proceeding. She scoffs at the advice that these "holy men," that is, these princes of the Roman Catholic Church, seek her to follow. The queen finds herself alone in a foreign country where she has no true advocate beyond God and the very distant pope. Their advice offers her no solace, no comfort, and no acceptable recourse. In this passage, Katherine unleashes her rage against these cardinals who abandon the law of the church for the more expedient and politic resolution that ultimately results in relinquishing her title as queen of England. The exchange in this passage becomes significant for later events in this play. The queen exclaims: "I will not wish ye half my miseries: I have more charity." She suggests that she has more charity, thereby impugning again the virtue of these two reverend cardinals. Katherine's speech serves as a foreshadowing of Wolsey's fall.

Act III, Scene 2, 203–227

CARDINAL WOLSEY. What should this
  mean?
What sudden anger's this? How have I reaped
  it?
He parted frowning from me, as if ruin
Leaped from his eyes. So looks the chafed lion
Upon the daring huntsman that has galled him,
Then makes him nothing. I must read this
  paper—
I fear, the story of his anger. 'Tis so:
This paper has undone me. 'Tis th'account
Of all the world of wealth I have drawn together
For mine own ends—indeed to gain the
  popedom
And fee my friends in Rome. O, negligence,
Fit for a fool to fall by! What cross devil

Made me put this main secret in the packet
I sent the King? Is there no way to cure this?
No new device to beat this from his brains?
I know 'twill stir him strongly. Yet I know
A way, if it take right, in spite of fortune
Will bring me off again. What's this? 'To th'
  Pope'?
The letter, as I live, with all the business
I writ to's Holiness. Nay then, farewell.
I have touched the highest point of all my
  greatness,
And from that full meridian of my glory
I haste now to my setting. I shall fall
Like a bright exhalation in the evening,
And no man see me more.

This speech is Wolsey's soliloquy after he has received the disapproving frown by the king and been accused of theft from royal accounts. This soliloquy follows closely Holinshed's *Chronicles* and is key in that it evokes a stark difference from Wolsey's responses to Henry VIII's previous accusations. In this moment, Wolsey considers whether he is ruined by the king's mere look of disapproval. As he looks at the papers that serve as proof "of all that world of wealth" that he has stolen for his own ambitious purposes—to become pope in Rome—Wolsey realizes his mistake in allowing these documents to be sent to the king. After he realizes the extent of the weight of this evidence, Wolsey tries to determine how he might remove himself from this predicament. He asks: "What cross devil / Made me put this main secret in the packet / I sent the King?" The cardinal considers the implications of having brought about his own ruin, having revealed the indisputable evidence of his crimes. Now, how should he pacify the king? Should Wolsey seek the pope's help in Rome? Then, with a sense of impending doom, the cardinal acknowledges that he has reached the heights of his "greatness" and now must resign himself to his impending "fall like a bright exhalation in the evening, / And no man see me more."

Act V, Scene 3, 130–147

KING HENRY. *[to Cranmer]* Good man, sit
  down. Now let me see the proudest—
He that dares most but wag his finger at thee.
By all that's holy, he had better, starve,
Than but once think his place become thee not.

SURREY. May it please your grace—

KING HENRY. No, sir, it does not please me.
I had thought I had had men of some
  understanding
And wisdom of my Council, but I find none.
Was it discretion, lords, to let this man,
This good man—few of you deserve that title—
At chamber door? And one as great as you are?
Why, what a shame was this! Did my commission
Bid ye so far forget yourselves? I gave ye
Power as he was a Councillor to try him,
Not as a groom. There's some of ye, I see,
More out of malice than integrity,
Would try him to the utmost, had ye mean,
Which ye shall never have while I live.

Here, as he did to Cardinal Wolsey before his fall, King Henry frowns in disapproval at his Privy Council, which includes Gardiner, Cromwell, Chamberlain, Suffolk, Surrey, and Norfolk. The king expresses his disappointment that this council, which he assumed possessed "some understanding and wisdom," seeks to punish Cranmer, "this good man." He detests the ill-treatment by the council. The king considers such treatment an abuse of the power that he has bestowed upon the council. He finds "malice than integrity." The king extends a protection over Cranmer against the council. This speech is similar to the king's speech to the Privy Council in Foxe's 1596 text.

DIFFICULT PASSAGES
Act I, Scene 1, 68–79

ABERGAVENNY. I cannot tell
What heaven hath given him—let some graver eye
Pierce into that—but I can see his pride
Peep through each part of him. Whence has
  he that?

If not from hell, the devil is a niggard
Or has given all before, and he begins
A new hell in himself.

BUCKINGHAM. Why the devil,
Upon this French going-out, took he upon him,
Without the privity o'th' King, t'appoint
Who should attend on him? He makes up the
    file
Of all the gentry, for the most part such
To whom as great a charge, as little honour
He meant to lay upon; and his own letter—
The honourable board of Council out—
Must fetch him in he papers.

This passage is an exchange between Abergavenny and Buckingham. Norfolk is also present. Here, Abergavenny struggles to see the godliness and virtue that should be synonymous with the position of Cardinal Wolsey, although he can easily see the prideful nature of the cardinal. Apparently, this pride becomes a quality that exudes his character. Abergavenny compares the cardinal to the devil, as do several characters throughout the play. Buckingham decries the cardinal's handling of state business, both foreign and domestic. He expresses his concern about Wolsey's proximity to the French. Buckingham believes that the cardinal is not even including King Henry in some of these decisions with the king of France. Buckingham also complains that the cardinal developed a list of the nobles and has issued a kind of tax upon them for any of the honors that they receive from the king. Buckingham criticizes that Wolsey also summons people on his own authority without consulting the Privy Council.

Act V, Scene 4, 31–39

MAN. What would you have me do?

PORTER. What should you do, but knock
    'em down by th' Dozens? Is this Moorfields
    to muster in? Or have we some strange
    Indian with the great tool come to court, the
    women so besiege us? Bless me, what a fry
    of fornication is at door! On my Christian

conscience, this One christening will beget a thousand: here will be Father, godfather, and all together.

This passage illustrates Scene 4 of Act V, which is jocular in tone. Holinshed does not include this scene in his *Chronicles*. Here, a Porter and his Man prepare themselves for the baptism of Princess Elizabeth. The Porter uses language that is sexualized, hinting at procreation and nuptials. In spite of its bawdy language, the scene emphasizes the religious importance of marriage, royal birth, an ecclesiastical blessing, and the celebration with the multitudes who witness the occasion. This moment could possibly allude to King James I's daughter Princess Elizabeth, who married the same year that this play was written. Still, the allusion to "strange Indian" evokes the foreign and England's expanding empire. Several years earlier, in 1605, Ben Jonson's *Masque of Blackness* was performed, in which the masquers, including Queen Anne, the wife of James I, were disguised as Africans. Later in 1616, Pocahontas of the Americas would be presented before the court of James I, as well. The allusion in this scene illustrates the contact between these other nations and this early modern court.

CRITICAL INTRODUCTION TO THE PLAY

At the broadest level, this play, like Shakespeare's other history plays, concerns itself with royal succession, civil wars, religion, and the expansion of its empire, as Kermode notes in his book *The Age of Shakespeare.*

Themes

The play is subtitled, *All Is True,* yet it is deeply concerned with treason, deception, corruption, tricks, and malice. As the play investigates truth, it utilizes the language of the law: warrant, examinations, proofs, confessions, witnesses. The play considers "truth" and, by extension, "deception" from different characters and perspectives. The Prologue suggests that here, in this play, the audience "may find truth" in the "chosen truth" that the performance offers (9, 18). Buckingham argues that "I am richer than my base accusers that never knew what truth meant" (2.1.104). The First and Second Gentlemen in the same scene discuss the matter of the king's separation from Katherine, which challenges Buckingham's notions of truth. Within the space of the play, what is rumor and slander one day "is found a truth" (2.1.155) the next day purportedly out of the machinations of Cardinal Wolsey. Such proofs, for these gentlemen, are found in the arrival of Cardinal Campeius. Yet, later in Act II, Scene 4, Wolsey defends himself against such accusations to Katherine by what he calls "my truth" (2.4.98). This phrase suggests that several versions of the truth exist differently for each character. In Act III, Scene 1, Queen Katherine boldly proclaims that "truth loves open dealing" (3.1.40). Yet, her demise suggests otherwise. In Act III, Scene 2, Wolsey doubts Surrey's loyalty and truth to the king. In Act IV, Scene 2, Katherine praises Griffith's "religious truth and modesty" (4.2.74). In Act V, Scene 1, Henry VIII reveals corruption in his realm and warns Cranmer that "truth and justice" are lacking (5.1.131). Later, Gardiner considers Cranmer's position as secretary as "plain truth," declaring "Your painted gloss discovers / To men that understand you, words and weakness" (5.3.7–72). Later, Cranmer prophesies Princess Elizabeth's great future, stating that the "truth will nurse her" (5.5.29). What does this all mean?

The deception encompasses trickery, malice, and corruption. For instance, the Duke of Norfolk tells Buckingham:

> I advise you—
> And take it from a heart that wishes towards you
> Honour and plenteous safety—that you read
> The cardinal's malice and his potency
> Together; to consider further that
> What his high hatred would effect wants not
> A minister in his power. (1.1.102–108)

Norfolk asks that Buckingham decipher truth from the deception that Wolsey presents cloaked in an as-yet-unarticulated malice. Later, the Second Gentleman also impugns Wolsey's character in the cardinal's treatment of Queen Katherine: "Either the cardinal, / Or some about him near, have, out of malice / To the good queen, possess'd him with a scruple / That will undo her" (2.1.156–159). Wolsey says "I mean your malice" (3.2.237) and later calls Suffolk, Surrey, and Norfolk "men of malice" (3.2.243) as they seek to take his seal, the evidence of his authority, away from him. The cardinal denies "any private malice" toward Buckingham's fall, citing the duke's "noble jury and foul cause" as witness (3.2.268–269). Wolsey maintains that Buckingham "by law / found his deserts" (3.2.266–267). Earlier, Buckingham swears: "the law bear I no malice for my death— / 'T has done upon the premises but justice" (2.1.62–63). In the trial of Cranmer, King Henry VIII warns Cranmer that he is "potently opposed, and with a malice / Of as great size" (5.1.134–135). The Tudor court possesses a great source of malefactors who through deception and malice work against truth. Later, Henry accuses Cranmer's judges: "I gave ye / Power as he was a Councillor to try him, / Not as a groom. There's some of ye, I see, / More out of malice than integrity, / Would try him to the utmost, had ye mean, / Which ye shall never have while I live" (5.3.142–147). The king exposes these malefactors for their work against truth and serves as a force to defend truth and administer justice.

The Role of the Law

Shakespeare's *Henry VIII* portrays the fall of four people: Buckingham, Wolsey, Cranmer, and Katherine. In the depiction of these tragic falls, the play presents several trials. The opening moments provide the rationale behind the fall of Wolsey. Yet, as Buckingham speaks against Wolsey, he provides the reasons for the cardinal to destroy him. Katherine's scene with Wolsey and Campeius foreshadows her fall. Thus, by the end, the audience wants to see Wolsey fall. Still, the play gives us a romantic ending in spite of the tragic circumstances that precede it. Elizabeth is baptized, and the drama portrays an order restored to the state. Several critics, including Kermode, Northrop Frye, and Waith, have examined the play's use of the *De casibus* tradition of portraying the fall of great men. Modern critics have, in particular, illuminated the function of the law within the tragic descent of all these characters. Specifically, the law is used to manipulate the tragic fall of several characters, yet in the end, it is a tool for restoration, as the last attempted fall is forestalled by Henry VIII, demonstrating a return of current and future order and prestige in the final years of the Tudor dynasty.

The first fall occurs when Buckingham is charged with high treason in the first scene. He has

Queen Katherine in *Henry VIII*. Print from Charles Heath's 1848 edition of *The Heroines of Shakspeare: Comprising the Principal Female Characters in the Plays of the Great Poet (Painting by J. W. Wright; engraving by W. H. Mote)*

a public trial at which evidence is presented, including witness statements and testimony. He defends himself well, yet the evidence becomes insurmountable, including the false testimony of his Surveyor. Buckingham is adjudged guilty and exits the play at Act II, Scene 1. Yet, when the motive is examined, it is clear that Cardinal Wolsey's hand guided Buckingham's fate. Wolsey used the law to fell this honorable man, who was well liked by the king.

Strikingly, the fall of women is not often told in the *De casibus* tradition. Queen Katherine is charged with having, in essence, failed her king whether the failure becomes a matter of maintaining the veracity of her proclaimed virtue at their marriage, giving birth to a viable son, or removing herself as queen. Her trial, the second fall, is conducted before the bishops, the king, and her judges, Cardinals Wolsey and Campeius. Instead of following the court procedure as Buckingham had, Katherine pleads her fate on bended knees before her king. She decries accusations that would taint her virtue or her loyalty to the king. She asks that God, or her king, decide her fate, and she abandons the proceedings. The queen seeks divine law or authority. Hence, the cardinals seek out the queen and try to negotiate a way out of the marriage that would please the king. Katherine berates them for their lack of piety, honor, and charity. Eventually, the divorce is granted, Queen Katherine becomes the Dowager Princess, and King Henry VIII marries Lady Anne. Katherine dies, but she blames Wolsey's manipulative hand, as do Norfolk and others. The audience, meanwhile, sees the motives of the king, who allegedly seeks the divorce for the quietude of his conscience.

In Act III, Scene 2, several charges are made against Cardinal Wolsey, yet the most compelling is the charge of extortion, siphoning the wealth of the king into his own coiffers. Wolsey's trial, the third fall, is set before the king, who allows the cardinal to show his own culpability with his verbal responses. Thereafter, the king gives the written proof of the cardinal's disloyalty and arguable treason. The motive for Wolsey's fall seems much more complicated than the other. The cardinal's letter to the pope is "miscarried" and taken to the king. The letter provides evidence that the cardinal asks the pope to "stay the judgment" of the king's divorce from Katherine, and he belittles Lady Anne. Noblemen, like Norfolk, Suffolk and Surrey, become concerned about the enormous power that Wolsey yields for the king. Their taxes, their honors, and their ultimate fate, as evidenced by Buckingham, bow to the cardinal's pleasure. Still, Wolsey confesses that his pride and his ambition are the cause of his fall.

The fourth fall is at least forestalled in Act V, Scene 1. Cranmer is charged with heresy. Here, the nature of the law impugned appears ecclesiastical. Gardiner proclaims that Cranmer is "a most arch heretic, a pestilence / that does infect the land" (5.1.45–46). His trial occurs before the Privy Council, where Suffolk, Surrey, Norfolk, Chamberlain, and Cromwell sit as his judges. The king has given them the authority to decide Cranmer's fate. Interestingly, the king warns Cranmer before his trial that his accusers are malicious and numerous. Cranmer despairs, but the king tells him to speak forthrightly on his own behalf. Against Cromwell's objections, the council determines a judgment against Cranmer, but the king safeguards Cranmer against their malicious devices. Henry VIII deems Cranmer a good and honest man and decries the council's judgment against such virtue. The motive behind this trial seems to be Gardiner's attempts to oust Cranmer for his alleged heresy, and later, Cromwell and Queen Anne.

Although the law serves as an instrument that aids the destruction of these men and women in four separate trials, this tool does not become the determining factor in their fate. The law becomes a place of tension against its own imperfections, ecclesiastical domains, and malice. In the end, the king becomes the key figure or instrument to safeguard his subjects from injustice.

Style and Imagery

The play focuses on imagery that highlights the truth by exposing the dark, the sinister, and the wicked. Some of this truth becomes illuminated by visual images; seeing, peeping, and perception become strongly connected to the themes of truth, treason, and deception. Also, the audience perceives the truth by the allusions to the Sun; strong parallels are made between "those suns of glory, those two lights of men" (1.1.6) and the king of England and the king of France by the Duke of Buckingham. Caroline Spurgeon observes that this same powerful image of authority may be found in *Henry V*. In an abrupt reversal, later in the scene, Buckingham says: "I am the shadow of poor Buckingham, / Whose figure even this instant cloud puts on / By darkening my clear sun" (1.1.225–227). In this complex passage, Buckingham's use of the word *Sun* becomes either an allusion to himself or the king, as McMullan similarly observes.

The play also illustrates an interesting contrast between virtue and vice. For instance, Cardinal Wolsey is likened to the devil as "venom-mouthed" (1.1.120) and as having a "witchcraft / Over the King in's tongue" (3.2.18–19). Yet, the figures of Queen Katherine and Princess Elizabeth embody biblical virtues. Katherine becomes likened to charity and honor. Elizabeth, through Cranmer's prophecy, becomes all that which is good, holy, and heavenly with the promise of "a thousand thousand blessings" (5.4.19).

Another image pervading the play is that of disease, where the state of the country and its people are sick. The image of sickness recurs throughout the play. Lord Abergavenny refers to the "sickened estates" (1.1.82) where Cardinal Wolsey now taxes the royals for any honor bestowed upon them. Late in the play, religious heresy is compared to "contagious sickness" (5.2.60). These discussions refer to the issue of reformation taking place. Yet, earlier, the image is more closely associated with the individual body. The king's sickness refers to the matter of his marriage to Queen Katherine and the issue of the legitimacy of not only his marriage but of his daughter, Mary, and the failure to conceive a male heir (2.4). The sickness of his conscience cannot be relieved until this matter of his marriage is rectified. Similarly, Katherine refers to her legal plight as her "sick cause" (3.1.118) where she has none other than Cardinals Wolsey and Campeius for aid. Later, sickness takes both Queen Katherine and Cardinal Wolsey.

EXTRACTS OF CLASSIC CRITICISM

Samuel Johnson (**1709–1784**) [Excerpted from *Preface to Plays of William Shakespeare* (1765). Johnson offers insight into the rationale for the playwright's narrative choices in the play.]

In his Henry VIII, that Prince is drawn with that greatness of mind, and all those good qualities which are attributed to him in any account of his reign. If his faults are not shewn in an equal degree, and the shades in this picture do not bear a just proportion to the lights, it is not that the Artist wanted either colours or skill in the disposition of 'em; but the truth, I believe, might be, that he forbore doing it out of regard to Queen *Elizabeth,* since it could have been no very great respect to the memory of his Mistress, to have expos'd some certain parts of her father's life upon the stage. He has dealt much more freely with the Minister of that great King, and certainly nothing was ever more justly written, than the character of Cardinal *Wolsey.* He has shewn him insolent in his prosperity; and yet, by a wonderful address, he makes his fall and ruin the subject of general compassion. The whole man, with his vices and virtues, is finely and exactly describ'd in the second scene of the fourth act. The distresses likewise of Queen *Catharine,* in this play, are very movingly touch'd; and tho' the art of the Poet has screen'd King *Henry VIII* from any gross imputations of injustice, yet one is inclin'd to wish, the Queen had met with a fortune more worthy of her birth and virtue.

William Hazlitt (**1778–1830**) [Excerpted from *Lectures on the Literature of the Age of Elizabeth* (1820) and *Characters of Shakespear's Plays* (1817). Hazlitt was a leading 19th-century critic and philos-

opher. He delves into the nature of representation, whether through plot or character. Here, his fascination with Shakespeare's depiction of Henry VIII becomes evident.]

This play contains little action or violence of passion, yet it has considerable interest of a more mild and thoughtful cast, and some of the most striking passages in the author's works. The character of Queen Katherine is the most perfect delineation of matronly dignity, sweetness, and resignation that can be conceived. Her appeals to the protection of the king, her remonstrances to the cardinals, her conversations with her women, show a noble and generous spirit accompanied with the utmost gentleness of nature. What can be more affecting than her answer to Campeius and Wolsey, whom come to visit her as pretended friends.

> "Nay, forsooth, my friends.
> They that must weigh out my afflictions,
> They that my trust must grow to, live
>   not here;
> They are, as all my comforts are, far hence,
> In mine own country, lords."

Dr. Johnson observes of this play, that "the meek sorrows and virtuous distress of Katherine have furnished some scenes, which may be justly numbered among the greatest efforts of tragedy. But the genius of Shakespear comes in and goes out with Katherine. Every other part may be easily conceived and easily written." This is easily said; but with all due deference to so great a reputed authority as that of Johnson, it is not true. For instance, the scene of Buckingham led to execution is one of the most affecting and natural in Shakespear, and one to which there is hardly an approach in any other author. Again, the character of Wolsey, the description of his pride and of his fall, are inimitable, and have, besides their gorgeousness of effect, a

Believe me, sir, she is the goodliest
woman
That ever lay by man: which when the
people
Had the full view of, *such a noise arose*
As th shrouds make at sea in a stiff
tempest,
As loud and to as many tunes—

The character of Henry VIII, is drawn
with great truth and spirit. It is like a very
disagreeable portrait, sketched by the hand
of a master. His gross appearance, his
blustering demeanour, his vulgarity, his
arrogance, his sensuality, his cruelty, his
hypocrisy, his want of common decency and
common humanity, are marked in strong
lines. His traditional peculiarities of expression complete the reality of the picture. The
authoritative expletive, "Ha!" with which
he intimates his indignation or surprise,
has an effect like the first startling sound
that breaks from the thunder-cloud. He is
of all the monarchs in our history the most
disgusting: for he unites in himself all the
vices of barbarism and refinement, without
their virtues. Other kings before him (such
as Richard III.) were tyrants and murderers
out of ambition or necessity: they gained or
established unjust power by violent means:
they destroyed their enemies, or those who
barred their access to the throne, or made
its tenure insecure. But Henry VIII's power
is most fatal to those whom he loves: he is
cruel and remorseless to pamper his luxurious appetites: bloody and voluptuous; an
amorous murderer: an uxorious debauchee.
His hardened insensibility to the feelings
of others is strengthened by the most prof-
ligate self-indulgence. The religious hypocrisy under which he masks his cruelty and
his lust, is admirably displayed in the speech
in which he describes the first misgivings of
his conscience and its increasing throes and
terrors, which have induced him to divorce

his queen. The only thing in his favor in
this play is his treatment of Cranmer: there
is also another circumstance in his favor,
which is his patronage of Hans Holbein.—
It has been said of Shakespear—"No maid
could live near such a man." It might with
as good reason be said—"No king could live
near such a man." His eye would have pen-
etrated through the pomp of circumstances
and the veil of opinion. As it is, he has represented such persons to the life—his plays are
in this respect the glass of history—he has
done them the same justice as if he had been
a privy councilor all his life, and in each successive reign. Kings ought never to be seen
upon the stage. In the abstract, they are very
disagreeable characters; it is only while living
that they are "the best of kings." It is their
power, their splendor, it is the apprehension
of the personal consequences of their favor
or their hatred that dazzles the imagination
and suspends the judgment of their favorites
or their vassals; but death cancels the bond
of allegiance and of interest; and seen *as*
they were, their power and their pretensions
look monstrous and ridiculous. The charge
brought against modern philosophy as inimical to loyalty is unjust, because it might as
well be brought against other things. No
reader of history can be a lover of kings. We
have often wondered that Henry VIII. as he
is drawn by Shakespear, and as we have seen
him represented in all the bloated deformity
of mind and person, is not hooted from the
English stage.

MODERN CRITICISM AND CRITICAL CONTROVERSIES

The play has not attracted as much attention in
the modern day as many of Shakespeare's others
plays, yet critics continue to find it fertile ground
for an examination of a variety of ideas, including
those related to history and culture. The critic
A. R. Humphreys in his book on Shakespeare's
history plays insists that *Henry VIII* depicts "a

With her women around her, Queen Katherine questions the motives of Cardinal Wolsey and Cardinal Campeius in Act III, Scene I of *Henry VIII*. This is a print from the Boydell Shakespeare Gallery project *(Painting by William Peters; engraving by Robert Thew)*

pathos, which only the genius of Shakespear could lend to the distresses of a proud, bad man, like Wolsey. There is a sort of child-like simplicity in the very helplessness of his situation, arising from the recollection of his past overbearing ambition. After the cutting sarcasms of his enemies on his disgrace, against which he bears up with a spirit conscious of his own superiority, he breaks out into that fine apostrophe—

"Farewell, a long farewell, to all my
greatness!
This is the state of man: to-day he puts
forth
The tender leaves of hope, to-morrow
blosssoms,
And bears his blushing honours thick
upon him;
The third day comes a frost, a killing
frost;
And-when he thinks, good easy man,
full surely
His greatness is a-ripening-nips his root,
And then he falls, as I do. I hae ventur'd,
Like little wanton boys that swim on
bladders,
These many summers in a sea of glory:
But far beyond my depth: my high-
blown pride
At length broke under me; and now has
left me,
Weary and old with service, to the mercy
Of a rude stream, that must for ever
hid me.
Vain pomp and glory of the world, I
hate ye:
I feel my heart new open'd. O how
wretched
Is that poor man, that hangs on princes'
favours!
There is betwit that smile we would
aspire to,
That sweet aspect of princes, and their
ruin,
More pangs and fears than wars or
women have:
And when he falls, he falls like Lucifer,
Never to hope again!"

There is in this passage, as well as in the well-known dialogue with Cromwell which follows, something which stretches beyond commonplace; nor is the account which Griffith gives of Wolsey's death less Shakespearian; and the candour with which Queen Katherine listens to the praise of "him whom I most hated living" adds the last graceful finishing to her character.

Among other images of great individual beauty might be mentioned the description of the effect of Ann Boleyn's presenting herself to the crowd at her coronation:

"While her grace sat down
To rest awhile, some half an hour or so,
In a rich chair of state, opposing freely
The beauty of her person to the people.

world of hearsay" and notes the play's dependence on opinion, report, insinuation, suspicions, and "grievous complaints, examinations, proofs, and trials" (280). Evidence of truth or deception is particularly important. As Norfolk warns Buckingham about having Wolsey as a foe, Buckingham responds: "by intelligence / And proofs as clear as founts in July when / We see each grain of gravel, I do know / To be corrupt and treasonous" (1.1.153–156). Buckingham says further: "I do pronounce him in that very shape / He shall appear in proof" (1.1.196–197). In spite of his innocence, false suspicions and testimonies were presented against Buckingham. The First Gentleman declares that "the King's attorney, on the contrary, / Urged on the examinations, proofs, / Of diverse witnesses, which the Duke desired / To have brought viva voce to his face" (2.1.15–18). False advisers seek to counsel Queen Katherine. False commissioners sit as judges over Cranmer. Yet, as a source of truth or revealed deception, letters abound in the play (1.1.77 and 2.2.1–8). Specifically, Wolsey's deception is revealed by his own "true" letter in Act 3, Scene 2.

Similarly, deception abounds during the trials of Buckingham and Queen Katherine. However, Wolsey's depravity and deception are exposed, too. Buckingham, Katherine, and Wolsey are all found guilty. Buckingham is put to death. Katherine and Wolsey languish before they expire. Cranmer is found guilty but saved by the king's merciful hands from an unjust conviction after Wolsey's death. Cranmer's true nature and actions are not only revealed but celebrated.

Other critics have examined the difficult question of the play's genre. In his 1972 book, Howard Felperin maintained that *Henry VIII,* like *Pericles,* was conceived in reaction to the romance plays that precede them. In *Henry VIII,* Shakespeare has moved from the fantastical world of *The Tempest* to the spectacular world surrounding the Tudor court.

Many critics, notably Jay Halio, in his introduction to the Oxford Shakespeare edition of the play have focused on the character of Henry, particularly on his presence and absence and on the transformation in his character. As in the other history plays, in *Henry VIII,* the key figure, the king, has a delayed entrance into the dramatic action. He is, however, mentioned at the outset of the play, when Buckingham, Abergavenny, and Norfolk discuss Henry and the king of France. The metaphoric mentioning of Henry and the Field of the Cloth of Gold in this opening scene of the play and the prophetic discussion of Elizabeth and her future reign place the play in an almost mythic Tudor history. Henry is also completely absent from Act IV, although he is often discussed. When he reappears later, his character has shifted. He becomes an aggressively stalwart defender of Cranmer and a proud father who anticipates the continuation of his realm through Princess Elizabeth, confirmed by Cranmer's prophecy. This disappearance and later transformed reappearance occurs in another history, *Richard II,* as Halio observes.

Halio and others have also examined the role of biblical allusions in the play. The use of these allusions creates evocative parallels that further illuminate the play's complex characters. The use of the Scriptures also reminds the audience of the ever-present threat of religion to create a schism in Henry's empire. Many references are from Psalms

The trial of Queen Katherine in *Henry VIII (Painting by Thomas Stothard; engraving by Louis Marie Normand)*

and the Gospels. Queen Katherine makes a reference to the lily of the fields (3.1) when she says: "Like the lily, / That once was mistress of the field and flourished, / I'll hang my head and perish" (150–152). Cranmer alludes to Luke 22:31 when Henry reveals the conspiracy against him: "I humbly thank your highness, / And am right glad to catch this good occasion / Most thoroughly to be winnowed, where my chaff / And corn shall fly asunder" (5.1.109–112). *Henry VIII*'s depiction of religious issues, in general, and, in particular, their role in the politics of the time have in general interested many critics.

THE PLAY TODAY

Henry VIII is performed less often than many of Shakespeare's plays, but it continues to have its appeal, perhaps because its pageantry and depiction of familiar historical characters. From John Philip Kemble's 1788 production at Drury Lane where Sarah Siddon played Queen Katherine, to Greg Doran's acclaimed Royal Shakespeare Company production in 1996, in which Jane Lapotaire played the rejected queen, the play's psychological aspects have been strongly emphasized. In 2010, the play received a notable production at the reconstructed Globe Theatre in London, with Dominic Rowan as the king.

In 1979, the British Broadcasting Company successfully brought the play to television under the title *The Famous History of the Life of King Henry the Eighth*. John Stride played Henry VIII, Claire Bloom played Katharine, and Timothy West captured audiences in the role of Cardinal Wolsey, under the direction of Timothy West.

Critics examining the play in recent years have often focused on the plays female characters and on its treatment of sexual politics, as in Susan Frye's "Queens and the Structure of History in Henry VIII." In addition, many critics continue to examine questions of the play's authorship, particularly the nature of the presumed collaboration between Fletcher and Shakespeare. In fact, the general topic of "Shakespeare as collaborator" has been very popular among scholars in recent years.

FIVE TOPICS FOR DISCUSSION AND WRITING

1. **Private versus public:** Norfolk explains to Buckingham: "Like it your grace, / The state takes notice of the private difference / Betweixt you and the Cardinal" (1.1.100–102). Why does Buckingham keep his grievances against Cardinal Wolsey private? Why would Wolsey have reasons to destroy Buckingham, even if his disdain for the cardinal had not become extremely public? If the state takes notice of Buckingham's grievances, does this fact mean that Henry VIII is also aware of the problem? If the king is aware, why does he not intervene on Buckingham's behalf as he does for Cranmer?

2. **Business:** The play emphasizes the theme of business. Henry VIII discloses to Wolsey: "You ever / Have wished the sleeping of this business, never desired / It to be stirred, but oft have hindered, oft, / The passages made toward it" (2.4.159–162). What interest would Wolsey have in maintaining "the sleeping of this business" of the king's divorce? Why has the business of marriage and divorce become the center of concern for Henry VIII and for the court?

3. **Law/crimes:** What are the crimes prosecuted in this play? How are they perceived by the individual characters and the audience? In this play about truth, is deception in general what is truly being punished here, considering the significant discussion of falsity, corruption, and malice in the play?

4. **Strange:** The "strange," or the unfamiliar and foreign, is a frequent topic of discussion in the play. What is the significance of this notion of the strange? What ideological and political concepts does this discussion invoke?

5. **Death/childbirth:** What is the significance of the issue of childbirth for Queen Katherine and Anne Bullen? What effect does the high rate of infant mortality have for Tudor succession?

Bibliography

Berry, Edward I. "Henry VIII and the Dynamics of Spectacle." In *Shakespeare Studies: An Annual Gathering of Research, Criticism, and Reviews,* vol.

12, edited by J. Leeds Barroll III, 229–246. New York: Burt Franklin & Co., 1979.

Boswell-Stone, W. G. *Shakespeare's Holinshed: The Chronicle and the Historical Plays Compared*. New York: Benjamin Blom, 1996.

Bowle, John. *Henry VIII: A Biography*. Boston: Little, Brown & Co., 1964.

Bruster, Douglas, and Robert Weimann. *Prologues to Shakespeare's Theatre: Performance and Liminality in Early Modern Drama*. London and New York: Routledge, 2004.

Bullough, Geoffrey. *Narrative and Dramatic Sources of Shakespeare*. London: Routledge & Kegan Paul, 1966.

Coleridge, Samuel Taylor. *Lectures and Notes on Shakespeare and Other Dramatists*. London: Oxford University Press, 1931.

———. *Shakespearean Criticism: In Two Volumes*. Edited by Thomas Middleton Raysor. London: J. M. Dent & Sons, 1960.

Duff, David. *Modern Genre Theory*. Harrow, U.K.: Longman, 2000.

Felperin, Howard. *Shakespearean Romance*. Princeton, N.J.: Princeton University Press, 1972.

Foakes, R. A. *Coleridge's Criticism of Shakespeare: A Selection*. London: Athlone Press, 1989.

Foxe, John. *Book of Martyrs*. Edited by G. A. Williamson. London: Secker & Warburg, 1965.

Frow, John. *Genre*. London and New York: Routledge, 2007.

Frye, Northrop. "The Tragedies of Nature and Fortune." In *Stratford Papers on Shakespeare*, edited by B. W. Jackson, 38–55. Toronto, Canada: W. J. Gage Ltd., 1961.

Frye, Susan. "Queens and the Structure of History in Henry VIII." In *A Companion to Shakespeare's Works: The Poems, Problem Comedies, Late Plays*, edited by Richard Dutton and Jean E. Howard, 427–444. Oxford, U.K.: Blackwell, 2003.

Halstead, William. *Shakespeare as Spoken: A Collation of 5,000 Acting Editions and Promptbooks of Shakespeare*. Ann Arbor, Mich.: University Microfilms International, 1978.

Hughley, Marty. "OSF's 'Henry VIII' Is Unemotional, but a Treat for Canon Completists."

Review of *Henry VIII*, dir. John Sipes. *Oregonian*, June 22, 2009. Available online. URL: http://www.oregonlive.com/performance/index.ssf/2009/06/theater_review_osfs_henry_viii.html. Accessed October 3, 2009.

Humphreys, A. R. *Shakespeare's Histories and "The Emotion of Multitude."* London: Oxford University Press, 1968.

Johnson, Samuel. *Johnson's Preface to Shakespeare: A Facsimile of the 1778 Edition with Introduction and Commentary by P. J. Smallwood*. Bristol, U.K.: Bristol Classical Press, 1985.

Jonson, Ben. *Masque of Blacknesse*. Cambridge, U.K.: Chadwyck-Healy, 1994.

Kermode, Frank. *The Age of Shakespeare*. New York: Modern Library, 2005.

———. "What Is Shakespeare's *Henry VIII* About?" In *Shakespeare: The Histories*, edited by Eugene M. Waith. Englewood Cliffs, N.J.: Prentice-Hall, 1965.

Knight, G. Wilson. *The Crown of Life: Essays in Interpretation of Shakespeare's Final Plays*. London: Methuen & Co., 1948.

McMullan, Gordon, ed. *King Henry VIII: All Is True* by William Shakespeare. London: Thomson Learning, 2000.

Micheli, Linda. Henry VIII: *An Annotated Bibliography*. New York and London: Garland Publishing, 1988.

Nicol, Allardyce, and Josephine Nicol. *Holinshed's Chronicle: As Used in Shakespeare's Plays*. London and New York: Everyman's Library, 1965.

Nuttall, A. D. *Shakespeare: The Thinker*. New Haven, Conn., and London: Yale University Press, 2007.

Ranald, Margaret Loftus. *Shakespeare and His Social Context: Essays in Osmotic Knowledge and Literary Interpretation*. New York: AMS Press, 1987.

Richmond, Hugh M. *King Henry VIII*. Manchester, U.K.: Manchester University Press, 1994.

"Saint-Saens at the Opera—Praises Metropolitan Opera Performance, *Henry VIII* to be sung next year." Review of *Traviata* by Guiseppe Verdi. *New York Times*, 2 December 1906. Available online. URL: http://query.nytimes.com/mem/archive-free/pdf?_r=1&res=9C02E3D7173EE733A2575

1C0A9649D946797D6CF. Accessed October 3, 2009.

Shakespeare, William. *Henry VIII.* Folger Shakespeare Library. Ed. Barbara A. Mowat and Paul Werstine. New York and London: Washington Square Press, 2007.

———. *King Henry VIII.* Ed. Jay L. Halio. Oxford: Oxford University Press, 1999.

Smith, D. Nicol. *Eighteenth Century Essays on Shakespeare.* Glasgow, Scotland: James MacLehose & Sons, 1903.

Spurgeon, Caroline. *Shakespeare's Imagery and What It Tells Us.* Cambridge: Cambridge University Press, 1935.

Waith, Eugene. *The Pattern of Tragicomedy in Beaumont and Fletcher.* New Haven, Conn.: Yale University Press, 1952.

Weir, Alison. *The Six Wives of Henry VIII.* New York: Grove Weidenfeld, 1991.

Wotton, Henry and Logan Pearshall Smith. *The Life and Letters of Sir Henry Wotton volume 2.* Oxford: Clarendon Press, 1907.

FILM AND VIDEO PRODUCTIONS

Bellafante, Gina. "Nasty but Not So Brutish and Short." Review of *The Tudors* creator, writer, executive producer Michael Hirst and actor Jonathan Rhys Meyers. *New York Times,* 28 March 2008. Available online. URL: http://www.nytimes.com. Accessed October 10, 2009.

Billington, Kevin, dir. *The Famous History of the Life of King Henry the Eight.* BBC-Time-Life Television, 2000.

Jarrott, Charles, dir. *Anne of the Thousand Days.* With Richard Burton, Genevieve Bujold, Irene Papas, and Anthony Quayle. Universal Pictures, 1969.

Korda, Alexandra, dir. *The Private Life of Henry VIII.* With Charles Laughton, Robert Donat, and Merle Oberon. United Artists Corporation, 1933.

Lubitsch, Ernst, dir. *Anna Boleyn* (1921). With Henny Porten, Emil Jannings, Ludwig Hartau, Hedwig Pauly-Winterstein, and Adolf Klein. Eureka Entertainment, 2010.

—Lisa Marie Barksdale-Shaw

Julius Caesar

INTRODUCTION

The ancient world fascinated Shakespeare and his fellow Elizabethans. The Renaissance, after all, is known for its revival of the intellectual spirit of antiquity. Ancient Rome, in particular, naturally appealed to Shakespeare's audience—so much so that Shakespeare would write three Roman plays over the course of his career: *Julius Caesar, Antony and Cleopatra,* and *Coriolanus. Julius Caesar* is the first of these.

The play appeals to audiences and readers today partly because it depicts one of the most significant moments in world history, the assassination of Caesar. However, this event occurs at the beginning of Act III, so Caesar is present for only half the play, and many, therefore, consider Marcus Brutus to be the play's main character. Caesar's presence, nonetheless, dominates the whole of the play. Before taking their own lives at the end of the play, two of the most notable conspirators against Caesar speak words for Caesar first, acknowledging Caesar's desire for revenge—even from the grave. As Harold Bloom argues, Shakespeare could not possibly have named this play after any character but the assassinated leader himself, simply because of the powerful associations Caesar's name immediately calls forth from viewers.

All of Shakespeare's plays have contributed familiar phrases to the English language, but *Julius Caesar* contains a particularly large number oft-quoted lines, such as "It's Greek to me" (1.2.286), "I am as constant as the northern star" (3.1.60), and "Friends, Romans, countrymen, lend me your ears" (3.2.78). But the play is more than the sum of its famous phrases. Readers might first assume that *Julius Caesar*'s themes are solely political, but this is wrong. The character of Caius Cassius reminds readers of the dangers of jealousy and envy; Mark Antony makes us think of what makes a person truly ambitious; and Brutus shows us how even a traitor can be noble. For these reasons and more, *Julius Caesar* remains vital today.

BACKGROUND

The Elizabethans believed that the people of ancient Greece and Rome provided them with the principles upon which they should base their own society. A. D. Nuttall, in *Shakespeare the Thinker,* suggests that the ancient world of Rome had special appeal to Shakespeare himself: "Shakespeare, who probably didn't know what a pyramid looked like and believed the Romans wore spectacles (*Coriolanus,* ii.i.206), is clearly interested in the cultural otherness of the Roman world. He read in Plutarch that the Romans were fascinated by 'maleness' and strength" (171–172). Though Shakespeare catered to the interests of his audience, he also wrote about subject matter he personally found interesting.

Julius Caesar appealed to Shakespeare's audience also because of its focus on the assassination of a ruler. In Shakespeare's time, more than 20 people attempted to assassinate Queen Elizabeth, none successfully. This play would clearly have been especially relevant (and troubling) to Elizabethans. Shakespearean scholars such as Marjorie Garber and Thomas

At Julius Caesar's funeral, Mark Antony shows the wounds on Caesar's body to the crowd, in Act 3, Scene 2 of *Julius Caesar*. *(Painting by Heinrich Spiess; engraving by Alfred Krausse)*

ably also used the following texts as sources for *Julius Caesar: The Histories of Sallust,* translated by Thomas Heywood; *The Roman History of Velleius Paterculus,* translated by Sir R. LeGrys; *The Historie of Twelve Caesars* by Suetonius, translated by Philemon Holland; Caesar's "complaint" in *A Mirror for Magistrates;* Ovid's *Metamorphoses* and Virgil's *Georgics I* (for descriptions about the omens and visions before Caesar's murder); and selections of Appian's *Auncient Historie and Exquisite Chronicle of the Romanes Warres, both Civile and Foren* (for Mark Antony's oration).

Shakespeare's use of Plutarch's *Lives* deserves the most analysis, however, as he borrowed so heavily from the work via North's translation. M. W. MacCallum, in *Shakespeare's Roman Plays and Their Background,* states that "in Plutarch he found practically all the stuff and substance for his play. . . . All the persons except Lucius come from him [Plutarch], and Shakespeare owes to him a number of their characteristics down to the minutest traits" (181). McCallum provides readers with an exhaustive list of what Shakespeare borrowed from North's translation. For example:

1. Cassius being described as *lean* and Antony as *sleek* (1.2).
2. Caesar suffering from epilepsy and Caesar's hubris (1.2).
3. The "disapproval with which the triumph over Pompey's sons was regarded" (1.1).
4. The Soothsayer's warning about the Ides of March (1.2).
5. Caesar being offered the crown during the Feast of Lupercal (1.2).
6. The way Flavius and Marullus suffered punishment for interfering with Caesar's decorations of triumph throughout the city (1.2).
7. Cassius talking privately with Brutus (1.2).
8. The anonymous letters the conspirators sent Brutus (2.1).
9. How the people respected Brutus.
10. Brutus's relationship with Portia (2.1).
11. Portia's demand that Brutus inform her of what has been bothering him (2.1).

McAlindon also point out that the play's focus on war and the threat of war was also particularly relevant to Shakespeare's audience, which had lived through conflicts with Spain, among other nations.

Shakespeare drew upon numerous sources when writing the play. The most important was Sir Thomas North's translation of Plutarch's *Lives of the Noble Grecians and Romans.* In his study *The Sources of Shakespeare's Plays,* Kenneth Muir asserts that Shakespeare must have read at least parts of North's translation of Plutarch's works by 1595, four years before he wrote *Julius Caesar,* paying most attention to Plutarch's depiction of the lives of Caesar, Marcus Brutus, and Mark Antony. According to Geoffrey Bullough in *Narrative and Dramatic Sources of Shakespeare,* Shakespeare prob-

12. The delight the conspirators felt when Brutus agreed to join their cause (2.1).
13. The conspirators agree not to kill Antony after Brutus tells them not to (2.1).
14. Caius Ligarius's "disregard of [Caesar's] illness" (2.1).
15. The omens predicting Caesar's death (2.2).
16. Calpurnia's dream (2.2).
17. Calpurnia arguing that Caesar stay home when Decius Brutus interferes (2.2).
18. Artemidorous's attempt to warn Caesar about the conspirators (2.3).
19. Portia's uneasiness and worry about Brutus's behavior (2.4).
20. The assassination scene (3.1).
21. Brutus's speech about Caesar (3.2).
22. Mark Antony's speech about Caesar (3.2).
23. The murder of Cinna, the poet (3.2).
24. The formation of the triumvirate (4.1).
25. The argument between Brutus and Cassius before the war (4.3).
26. The appearance of Caesar's ghost (4.3)
27. Portia's suicide (4.3).
28. The discussion Brutus and Cassius share about suicide (4.3).
29. How Cassius and Brutus commit suicide, using their own swords (5.3 and 5.5).
30. Lucilius's surrender (5.4).
31. Antony's final speech about Brutus (5.5) (168–186).

As MacCallum says, "There is thus hardly a link in the action that was not forged on Plutarch's anvil" (182).

In quite a few instances, Shakespeare even makes extensive use of the exact language North used in his translation. Consider this example MacCallum notes in his analysis of Lucilius's speech after Antony's soldiers capture him and bring him to their leader. In North's translation, Lucilius says the following:

> I dare assure thee, that no enemie hath taken, now shall take Marcus Brutus alive; and I beseech God keepe him from that fortune. Foe wheresoever he be found, alive or dead; he will be found like him selfe (182).

Shakespeare's Lucilius says (5.4.21–25):

> I dare assure thee that no enemy
> Shall ever take alive the noble Brutus:
> The gods defend him from so great a shame!
> When you do find him, or alive or dead,
> He will be found like Brutus, like himself.

Although he clearly borrowed some phrases, Shakespeare did make the story of Caesar's assassination his own. His narrative differs from Plutarch's in many respects, including Shakespeare's emphasis on Caesar's physical ailments (epilepsy and partial deafness). Shakespeare also chose to ignore the fact that Caesar actually died at the Theatre of Pompey; instead, Shakespeare has the conspirators murder him in the Capitol, which heightens the drama of the play.

Date and Text of the Play

Scholars assume Shakespeare composed *Julius Caesar* in 1599. Their rationale stems from a somewhat obscure detail concerning a German traveler and his diary, in which he remarks on seeing the play performed at the Globe Theatre on September 21, 1599. The text of the play was not published until 24 years later, in 1623, with the issuing of the First Folio. No earlier quarto texts have been discovered.

SYNOPSIS
Brief Synopsis

Having defeated Pompey, Julius Caesar returns to Rome to the people cheering him in the streets. Two tribunes confront a group of commoners, accusing them of being fickle in their loyalty as they had worshipped Pompey in the past. The tribunes leave and take down ornaments celebrating Caesar's victory.

During the celebration for Caesar, a Soothsayer tells Caesar to "Beware the ides of March" (1.2.17), but Caesar simply dismisses the man's ominous warning. In the meantime, Caius Cassius talks to Marcus Brutus about how Caesar acts as though he is mightier and better than all other Romans, even though Caesar is a mere human. Cassius tells Brutus that Caesar's ambitions will be

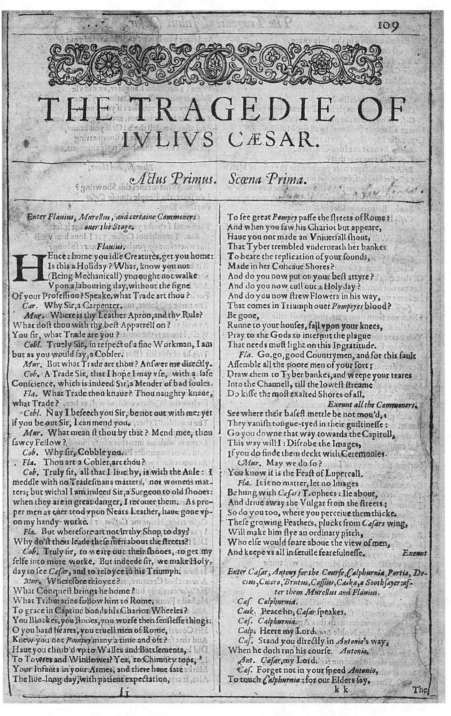

Title page of the First Folio edition of *Julius Caesar*, published in 1623

bad for Rome, a thought that Brutus ponders after the conversation's end. Caesar, spotting Cassius, grows suspicious of him.

Brutus contemplates joining a conspiracy to assassinate Caesar and soon finds himself visited by Cassius and the other conspirators, who discuss the plans to carry out the assassination the following day. Cassius suggests that they murder not only Caesar but also Mark Antony. Brutus argues that a double murder would make the conspirators like blood-hungry murderers instead of noblemen saving Rome from an ambitious leader. The conspirators leave, having won Brutus over. Portia, Brutus's wife, asks Brutus what troubles him; she has noticed that her husband does not seem himself. Brutus appreciates his wife's concern but hearing a knock at the door, sends her away, promising to tell her about his concerns at a later time.

On the ides (15th day) of March, Calpurnia tells her husband that she had a nightmare in which he was killed; she commands him not to go to the Capitol. Caesar agrees at first, but when Decius Brutus flatters Caesar and tells him that he would look foolish for staying home just because of a dream his wife had, Caesar decides to go to the Capitol. Meanwhile, Portia still has not had a chance to speak with Brutus about what bothers him, and she worries about him after he leaves for the Capitol.

Although several people attempt to warn Caesar of impending danger, Caesar simply casts them aside and goes to the Capitol. During a conversation there, some of the conspirators kneel at Caesar's feet. Casca stabs Caesar, and the others follow suit. Caesar feels especially betrayed by Brutus. Antony, devastated, praises Caesar's dead body but assures the conspirators that he wants to make friends with them. Antony asks Brutus if he can say a few words to the common people about his friend, the fallen Caesar, and even though Cassius disapproves of the plan, Brutus consents. The conspirators leave, and Antony, left alone, says that war will soon come to Rome. Meanwhile, Octavius, at his adoptive father Caesar's request, has been traveling to Rome. One of Octavius's servants sees Antony with Caesar's body, and Antony cautions the servant to tell his master not to enter Rome yet.

Brutus addresses the people of Rome, assuring them that the actions of the conspirators were noble because Caesar's ambition would have been hurtful to the welfare of Rome. The people agree with Brutus. Then Antony arrives, carrying Caesar's body. He speaks, and within minutes, the crowd decides that the conspirators behaved in the wrong and that Caesar was a noble, good leader who did not deserve to die. Brutus and Cassius leave Rome and prepare for battle with Octavius, who has joined forces with Antony and Lepidus, thereby forming the triumvirate.

Tension mounts between Brutus and Cassius; Cassius feels he has lost Brutus as an ally and tells him that he hopes he dies soon because he (Cassius) already feels devastated and betrayed by Brutus (who assures Cassius he is still his ally). The men reconcile, and Brutus informs Cassius that Portia has committed suicide. The triumvirate's power has grown, and Brutus convinces Cassius to have their forces march to meet them at Philippi. That night, Caesar's ghost appears to Brutus and says he will meet him again at Philippi.

At Philippi, the leaders (Octavius, Antony, Lepidus, Brutus, and Cassius) meet in battle. During the first engagement with the triumvirate, Cassius flees and asks his servant to kill him. After losing many of his men and acknowledging that Caesar—even in death—gains revenge, Brutus also eventually takes his own life. Antony states that Brutus was indeed a noble man: Whereas the other conspirators acted out of jealousy and revenge, Brutus acted only for the good of Rome.

Act I, Scene 1

Two tribunes, Flavius and Marullus, encounter a group of commoners who cheer Julius Caesar's victory over Pompey. The tribunes feel disgusted with the commoners, whom they consider fickle, and accuse them of being loyal to Pompey only until Caesar has defeated him. Flavius says that he will go through the streets removing any symbols of Caesar's victory.

Act I, Scene 2

Caesar enters, followed by a train of people. It is the celebration of the Feast of Lupercal (which celebrates fertility), and Caesar commands Calpurnia to stand in Mark Antony's way so that Antony will touch Caesar's wife and hopefully make her fertile. A Soothsayer calls from the crowd, warning Caesar to "beware the ides of March" (1.2.17), but Caesar disregards the man's warnings. Caius Cassius, during a private conversation with Marcus Brutus, tells his friend that Brutus is widely respected throughout Rome. The two men hear cheering, and Brutus confides that he hopes Caesar will not be king; Brutus emphasizes how much honor means to him and that he would die in the name of honor. Cassius also wishes that Caesar will not be king, but for reasons much different from Brutus's: Cassius argues that Caesar is a man, just like him, and that he would not kneel to the new king. Cassius relates to Brutus a tale in which Cassius and Caesar had a swimming race. Cassius had to save Caesar from drowning. Cassius also mentions Caesar's other physical ailments and feels outrage that Caesar, a man physically weaker than himself, will now be king.

During the Feast of Lupercal, a Soothsayer warns Caesar to "beware the ides of March" in this 19th-century depiction of Act I, Scene 2 of *Julius Caesar*. (Painting by Max Adamo; engraving by Jacob Deininger)

Caesar spies Cassius and tells Antony that he does not trust Cassius. Antony tells Caesar he should not be concerned about Cassius. Caesar asks Antony to come to his right side because he is deaf in his left ear. Cassius and Brutus ask Casca to inform them of what happened during Caesar's coronation: Casca reveals that Caesar refused the crown three times and that he experienced an epileptic fit. The men, except for Cassius, leave, and he vows to find a way to win Brutus to his cause of assassinating Caesar.

Act I, Scene 3

Casca meets another of the conspirators, Cicero, during the night. Casca tells Cicero of some of the extremely odd things he had seen that day and night, including an owl in the marketplace during the day, a lion at the Capitol, and a man with his hands on fire. Casca thinks these are omens of danger. Cicero leaves, and Cassius enters. Casca informs Cassius that the senate will crown Caesar king the next day; the men agree to stop this from happening, and Cassius reveals that he knows of other men who could help them. The men decide that they must convince Brutus to join their cause.

Act II, Scene 1

Brutus, at home, thinks about his conversation with Cassius earlier that day and worries that, indeed, Caesar will eventually be corrupted by his power, and in turn, Rome will suffer. Cassius arrives with the other conspirators, and they eventually convince Brutus to help them murder Caesar; they know that Brutus's participation will encourage the people of Rome to see the deed as noble. They know that without Brutus's cooperation, the assassination will look far worse than if Brutus were to participate.

Cassius tells Brutus that he thinks the group should murder Mark Antony, too, but Brutus disagrees, explaining that to kill Antony would be to shed too much blood. Brutus also says they must kill Caesar swiftly and efficiently so the conspirators do not appear to have relished in murdering him. A plan set, the men leave Brutus's home.

Portia, Brutus's wife, enters and asks her husband what has caused him to become so restless. Portia implores Brutus to reveal his troubles to her, reminding him that she is loyal and constant. Then she kneels at his feet. Brutus tells her not to kneel and says he feels unworthy of such an honorable wife as Portia. He promises to inform her about his troubles later.

Act II, Scene 2

Caesar prepares to leave for the Capitol when his wife, Calpurnia, stops him. She says that although she usually does not find herself influenced by superstitions, today she is, due to a terrible dream she had the night before. In the dream, Calpurnia saw monstrous things, including a statue of Caesar spouting blood. Caesar tells his wife not to worry, that she only had a bad dream, but Calpurnia warns her husband that he is too confident. Caesar concedes to his wife's wishes and says that Mark Antony can tell everyone that he is ill.

Decius Brutus, one of the conspirators, arrives at Caesar's home. When he learns that Caesar plans to stay home and have Mark Antony lie on his behalf, Decius capitalizes on Caesar's vanity and concern with appearances. Decius says that if anyone discovers the real reason that Caesar stayed away from the Capitol, he would be roundly mocked. Hearing this, Caesar agrees to go to the Capitol. The other conspirators arrive, as does Antony, and they all walk with Caesar to the Capitol.

Act II, Scene 3

Artemidorous writes a letter to Caesar, warning him about some of the conspirators and that they are intent on destroying Caesar. He plans to give the letter to Caesar, hoping to save his life.

Act II, Scene 4

Portia worries about her husband and sends their servant, Lucius, to see if Caesar has left for the Capitol. Portia encounters the Soothsayer and asks him whether Caesar has arrived at the Capitol; the Soothsayer tells her that Caesar has not yet made it to the Capitol. The Soothsayer intends to meet Caesar on his way and warn him, yet again, about the dangers of the day.

Act III, Scene 1

Caesar ignores the pleas of both Artemidorous and the Soothsayer. One of the conspirators diverts Antony so that the conspirators will be free to face Caesar without intervention. Metellus Cimber asks Caesar to allow his brother to return to Rome, but Caesar denies his request. Some of the other conspirators approach Caesar and kneel before him. The conspirators make their move and begin stabbing Caesar. Caesar utters the play's most famous line (3.1.77) *"Et tu, Brute?"* ("And you, Brutus?"), and dies. Antony, having missed the assassination, hears of it quickly. Antony's servant enters and tells Marcus Brutus that Antony would like to be friends with and serve the honorable Brutus. Cassius remains suspicious of Antony's intentions, but Brutus sends for Antony, sure that he will become their true ally.

Antony arrives, and Brutus assures him that the conspirators acted only in the best interest of Rome. Antony makes peace with the conspirators and asks if he can speak in front of the Roman people about the fallen leader. Though Cassius warns Brutus that Antony may sway the crowd against the conspirators, Brutus grants Antony his turn to speak. The conspirators leave for the Forum, and Antony, alone, acknowledges that Caesar will seek vengeance. Octavius, Caesar's adopted son, has been making his way to Rome and has now arrived. One of his servants sees Caesar's body, and Antony tells Octavius's servant to keep his master from entering the city until after the speeches in the Forum.

Act III, Scene 2

At the Forum, Brutus addresses the crowd first, assuring them that Caesar's ambition would have been greatly dangerous for Rome. The commoners agree with Brutus and view the conspirators as saviors, concerned only with the best interest of Rome. Antony arrives with Caesar's dead body in his arms. Brutus allows Antony to address the crowd. In a turn of masterly rhetoric, Antony completely sways the crowd and, by the end of his speech, has the commoners believing that it was the conspirators who acted ambitiously, not Caesar. He openly shows his grief at losing Caesar, touching many of the crowd; he also reads from Caesar's will, in which Caesar provided for the commoners, thus causing them to view Caesar as giving and kind and the conspirators as greedy and cruel. The crowd decides to gain revenge for Caesar, and they attack the conspirators. Octavius enters the city, and Cassius and Brutus flee.

Act III, Scene 3

Chaos rules the city, and a mad mob confronts a man, a poet, on his way to Caesar's funeral. His name is Cinna, the same as one of the conspirators (Trebonius Cinna). Consumed by revenge, the commoners ignore that the man they have encountered is not Cinna the conspirator, and they beat him relentlessly.

Act IV, Scene 1

Antony, Octavius, and Lepidus gather and decide who must be executed. When Lepidus leaves, Antony questions his abilities, saying that he does not think Lepidus is worthy of ruling Rome. Octavius assures Antony that Lepidus can be trusted and that he is a fine soldier. The men then focus on their plan to confront Brutus, Cassius, and the forces they have amassed.

Act IV, Scene 2

Cassius confronts Brutus, believing that Brutus has wronged him. Brutus invites Cassius into his tent to discuss the matter.

Act IV, Scene 3

Tempers flare, and a heated discussion ensues. Brutus and Cassius soon forgive each other, however, realizing they must remain allies. Brutus reveals that Portia has committed suicide by "swallowing fire," meaning she shoved hot coals down her throat. The men then discuss battle plans, upon which they disagree. Brutus thinks that they

Caesar's ghost visits Brutus in Act IV, Scene 3 of *Julius Caesar,* as depicted in this print published in 1832. *(Painting by Richard Westall; engraving by William Humphreys)*

should march to Philippi and meet the triumvirate and their army there. Cassius wants to wait, but eventually concedes to Brutus's suggestion. Brutus, in his tent, sees Caesar's ghost, who tells Brutus that he will meet him again at Philippi.

Act V, Scene 1

The opposing forces finally meet at Philippi. Antony attempts to direct the battle plan, but Octavius remains in charge of the attack. Antony begins calling Octavius "Caesar" and follows the fallen Caesar's adopted son's orders. The leaders meet and verbally spar, and Octavius vows vengeance. Before the war begins, Brutus and Cassius discuss their fates: Cassius worries about bad omens he has seen, and both men agree that they will not resort to being taken captive and paraded through Rome as traitors.

Act V, Scene 2

Brutus commands Messala to ride to Cassius and tell him to pursue their attack of Octavius; Brutus thinks that Octavius's troops only fight half-heartedly and that attacking them now might be beneficial to Brutus and Cassius.

Act V, Scene 3

The battle turns in favor of the triumvirate, whose troops begin infiltrating Cassius's camp. Frightened at the destruction occurring in his camp, Cassius flees to a different location on the field. Cassius's servant, Pindarus, meets him. Believing all is lost, Cassius asks Pindarus to kill him. Pindarus stabs him, and Cassius dies. In the meantime, Brutus's troops overpower Octavius's. When Brutus arrives and sees Cassius's body, Brutus acknowledges that Caesar has indeed met him at Philippi and is seeking vengeance. The war continues.

Act V, Scene 4

Lucilius walks onto the battlefield, pretending to be Brutus. Antony's soldiers capture him and bring him to their leader. Antony recognizes Lucilius as Brutus's servant but still praises his soldiers for bringing him a captive worth as much as Brutus. He commands his men to determine whether Brutus is still alive.

Act V, Scene 5

Brutus claims to have seen Caesar's ghost during battle. His soldiers implore Brutus to flee, and he tells them he will follow them shortly. As his men are leaving, Brutus asks Strato to stay behind with him; he then asks Strato to hold Brutus's sword out so that Brutus can commit suicide by thrusting himself onto the sword. Strato agrees, first asking his master for his hand. Brutus kills himself, but only after pleading with Caesar's spirit to rest. Antony and Octavius arrive. Antony says that Brutus was indeed a noble and honest man. Octavius

agrees to grant Brutus a proper burial. Octavius and Antony celebrate their victory.

CHARACTER LIST

Julius Caesar Rome's conquering general. Believing himself infallible, Caesar angers the conspirators to action, culminating in his death. Although he dies in Act 3, Scene 1 and has far fewer lines than the other major male characters, Caesar's presence looms throughout the entire play.

Marcus Brutus Noble Roman. He joins the conspirators against Caesar; his assistance in assassinating the Roman leader is particularly devastating to Caesar. Brutus feels that his actions remain pure of heart because he desires only a better Rome, rather than power for himself, like some of his fellow conspirators.

Mark Antony Caesar's confidante and a master rhetorician. Antony's ability to appeal to the Roman people and bend a crowd to his will thrusts him from a secondary position of power to a leader in Rome.

Caius Cassius Jealous man who leads the conspiracy against Caesar. Cassius convinces Brutus to join the conspirators and later leads an army with him in battle against Octavius.

Calpurnia Julius Caesar's wife. After an ominous dream, she implores Caesar not to go to the Senate. She attempts to warn Caesar of impending danger, but he ignores her.

Portia Marcus Brutus's loyal wife. She is the daughter of Cato (a man known for his integrity). Worried over Brutus's behavior, she entreats her husband to confide in her. Unsure of Brutus's fate after Caesar's assassination, she takes her own life.

Casca, Decius Brutus, Metellus Cimber, Trebonius Cinna, Labeo, and Caius Ligarius Conspirators against Caesar.

Cicero, Publius, and Popilius Lena Senators.

Cinna A poet. A crowd of plebeians attacks him mercilessly, simply because he shares the name of one of the men who conspired against Caesar.

Marullus A tribune. He berates some of the commoners for switching their allegiance so fickly from Pompey to Caesar. He is put to death for not demonstrating allegiance to Caesar.

Flavius A tribune. Like Marullus, he scolds a group of commoners for supporting Caesar. He commands that "no images be hung with Caesar's trophies" and is later executed for such behavior.

Soothsayer A truth teller, he warns Caesar to "beware the ides of March."

Octavius Caesar Julius Caesar's adopted son who takes the title of emperor. He joins forces with Antony and Lepidus after Caesar's death, forming the triumvirate. He is eager to gain power.

Lepidus Part of the triumvirate (with Antony and Octavius) that will rule Rome after the death of Caesar. Antony convinces Octavius that they should rid themselves of Lepidus once they gain power; Antony also mocks him and assigns him tedious, unimportant jobs.

Lucius Brutus's most kind and loyal servant. He is young and cares deeply about his master. He often plays music for Brutus to help his master find some peace.

Strato Brutus's servant who helps his master commit suicide.

Artemidorus A teacher of rhetoric who tries to warn Caesar about those conspiring against him.

Lucilius A member of Brutus and Cassius's army. He tells the opposing army that he is Brutus.

Titinius A member of Brutus and Cassius's army. He finds Cassius dead.

Messala A member of Brutus and Cassius's army.

Young Cato Portia's brother; the son of Cato.

Volumnius Brutus's friend who refuses to help him commit suicide.

Varro, Claudius, Clitus and Dardanius Brutus's servants.

Pindarus Cassius's servant.

Flavius A soldier.

Carpenter and Cobbler These two characters represent the fickle nature of the common people: Former worshippers of Pompey, they sud-

denly start cheering for Caesar after he defeats Pompey.

Plebeians Much like the Carpenter and Cobbler, Shakespeare uses the Plebeians to demonstrate how masterly rhetoricians (like Mark Antony) can bend the will of the masses to his own.

CHARACTER STUDIES
Marcus Brutus

Brutus, the "noblest Roman of them all" is usually considered the main character of *Julius Caesar*. Although he bloodies his hands with Caesar's murder, Brutus remains the only conspirator who acts for the good of Rome, rather than, as Antony says, out of envy of Caesar. When Brutus asks Cassius,

> Remember March, the ides of March
>   remember:
> Did not great Julius bleed for justice's sake?
> What villain touch'd his body, that did stab,
> And not for justice? (4.3.19–22)

Brutus speaks genuinely, and unknowingly, as the only conspirator that did stab "for justice." Readers learn about Brutus's reputation from other characters, who repeatedly attest to Brutus's conduct as an upstanding, honorable citizen. For instance, Cassius states that Caesar loves Brutus (1.2), and Casca says that Brutus

> sits high in all the people's hearts:
> And that which would appear offence in us,
> His countenance, like richest alchemy,
> Will change to virtue and to worthiness.
>   (1.3.159–162)

Brutus never attests to his own reputation, and he does not need to, especially when many others characters do so for him.

What readers and viewers do learn from Brutus is that he lacks "some part / of that quick sport that is Antony" (1.2). Brutus thinks things through carefully; he wrestles with becoming one of the conspirators against Caesar even though he freely

Basil Gill as Brutus in *Julius Caesar.* This photograph was published by Virtue & Company in the early 20th century. *(Photographed by J. & L. Caswall Smith)*

admits that he fears Caesar becoming king. After deciding to join the conspirators, Brutus dissuades them from simply attacking Caesar ruthlessly and, instead, shares a carefully crafted plan:

> Gentle friends,
> Let's kill him boldly, but not wrathfully;
> . . . And let our hearts, as subtle masters do,
> Stir up their servants to an act of rage,
> And after seem to chide 'em. This shall make
> Our purpose necessary and not envious:
> Which so appearing to the common eyes,
> We shall be call'd purgers, not murderers
>   (2.1.178–187).

Brutus wants to kill Caesar "boldly, but not wrathfully" to help illustrate to the Roman people that

the conspirators bloodied their hands only as much as necessary in executing Caesar. However, Brutus also wants to kill Caesar "boldly, but not wrathfully" because, of all the conspirators, Brutus is the only one who loves Caesar.

In his funeral oration for Caesar, Brutus admits his love for Caesar, exclaiming:

> If then that friend demand why Brutus rose
>   against Caesar, this is my answer:—Not that
> I loved Caesar less, but that I loved Rome
> more. Had you rather Caesar were living and
> die all slaves, than that Caesar were dead, to
> live all free men? (3.2.19–21)

This key passage also depicts another important element of Brutus's character: He is a true patriot. He acts on behalf of his fellow Romans, considering their welfare before thinking about his own. Antony reinforces this point at the close of the play, explaining that

> All the conspirators save only he
> Did that they did in envy of great Caesar;
> He only, in a general honest thought
> And common good to all, made one of them.
>   (5.5.75–78)

No character in the play possesses the same degree of nobility and honor as Brutus. As the model of the contemplative, composed Roman, Brutus—a kind, passionate man—teaches readers about the true definition of goodness and honor, unmatched in Shakespeare's canon.

Mark Antony

Readers and viewers remember Mark Antony for his masterly rhetoric, most obvious in his moving funeral oration for Caesar. Having lost a dear friend, Antony touches his audience, bends it to his will, and hence begins a war in Rome. He is not only a rhetorician but a manipulator. Characters like Brutus mistakenly consider the saddened Antony as an ally, but find they are sorely mistaken. Antony feels devastated by the loss of Caesar:

> O, pardon me, thou bleeding piece of earth,
> That I am meek and gentle with these
>   butchers!
> Thou art the ruins of the noblest man
> That ever lived in the tide of times.
>   (3.1.269–272)

This devastation, however, does not hinder him from developing a plan to avenge Caesar's death and gain power for himself. He first uses his expert rhetorical skills to pose as though he feels little—if any—animosity toward the conspirators. After Caesar's assassination, Antony tells the murderers: "Friends am I with you all and love you all, / Upon this hope, that you shall give me reasons / Why and wherein Caesar was dangerous" (3.1.232–234). Comments like these help convince Brutus that Antony poses no threat to him or his fellow conspirators; in turn, Brutus even encourages Antony to speak at Caesar's funeral, a fateful mistake that allows Antony to gain the crowd's support and sympathy.

Shakespeare made Antony a gifted rhetorician and manipulator, as well as a poor judge of character. When Caesar sees Cassius in Act 1, Scene 2, he tells Antony he thinks Cassius "has a lean and hungry look" (200) and considers such a disposition "dangerous" (201). Antony misjudges Cassius's character completely and tells Caesar: "Fear him not, Caesar; he's not dangerous; / He is a noble Roman and well given" (1.2). In contrast, Cassius remains suspicious of Antony, especially after Caesar's murder, and Cassius's concerns are proved valid. Though the Antony in *Antony in Cleopatra* seems far different from the Antony in *Julius Caesar*, at least one character trait remains constant: his poor judgment of character. His interpretation of Cassius is far from accurate, and in *Antony and Cleopatra*, he misjudges Cleopatra's devotion to him. A master rhetorician he is, but a person who understands the nature of others well, he is not.

Julius Caesar

Caesar may die at the hands of the conspirators at the beginning of Act III, looking like "a deer, stricken by many princes" (3.1.224), but critics agree that his presence looms throughout the rest of the play. Characters continually speak of him, and he even appears to Brutus as a ghost before the fateful battle at Philippi.

Shakespeare's Caesar symbolizes weakness, pride, and revenge. Shakespeare's source material for *Julius Caesar,* namely Plutarch's *Lives of the Noble Grecians and Romans,* does not emphasize Caesar's physical ailments, but Shakespeare does, drawing special attention to his epileptic fits and being partially deaf. Shakespeare highlights these physical ailments in Caesar as a way of symbolizing his mortality and fallibility. Though, as Cassius says, Caesar walks the world like a "Colossus" (1.2.136) and seems immune to the mortal fates of other men, Shakespeare reminds his audience of Caesar's mortality in an effort to depict him as a man subject to the same laws of nature as any other man.

Caesar, more than any other character in the play, epitomizes pride. Consider Caesar's comments to Antony that he would "rather tell thee

Four senators surround Julius Caesar (Amleto Novelli) in this photograph from the 1914 film version of *Julius Caesar.*

what is to be fear'd/Than what I fear; for always I am Caesar" (1.2.212–213). Caesar's hubris leads to his death: Had he not been flattered and swayed by Decius Brutus's comments, Caesar would have stayed home with Calpurnia, out of the path of danger. Instead, he dismisses her and makes his way to the Capitol. Further, Caesar repeatedly dismisses warnings and pleas from other characters such as the Soothsayer and Artemidorous, both of whom try to warn Caesar of his fate on several occasions. But, Caesar, as "constant as the northern star, of whose true-fix'd and resting quality there is no fellow in the firmament" (3.1.58–60), cares little about the prophecies of mortal men.

Caesar also represents revenge. Brutus, in his tent, finds himself confronted by Caesar's ghost, who promises to meet him at Philippi; while the apparition may be nothing more than a figment of Brutus's imagination, the appearance of Caesar symbolizes his unrest and desire for revenge, which he finally obtains when both Cassius and Brutus are killed with their own swords—but not without their first acknowledging Caesar and how, as Brutus says, Caesar, even in death, remains "mighty yet" (5.3.100).

Cassius

Cassius, more than any other character, represents envy. He makes the jealousy he feels for Caesar plain in Act I, Scene 2, when he tells Brutus that Caesar

> . . . Doth bestride the narrow world
> Like a Colossus, and we petty men
> Walk under his huge legs and peep about
> To find ourselves dishonorable graves.
> Men at some time are masters of their fates:
> The fault, dear Brutus, is not in our stars,
> But in ourselves, that we are underlings.
> Brutus and Caesar: what should be in that
>   "Caesar"?
> Why should that name be sounded more than
>   yours?
> Write them together, yours is as fair a name;
> Sound them, it doth become the mouth as well;
> Weigh them, it is as heavy; conjure with 'em,

Brutus will start a spirit as soon as Caesar (1.2.135–147).

Cassius's envy for Caesar shines here, as does his talent for manipulation. Hoping to convince Brutus to join the conspirators, Cassius draws comparisons between Caesar and Brutus instead of Caesar and himself. This way, Caesar's ambition becomes even clearer to Brutus. Cassius's talk with Brutus thrusts the noble Roman into a state of psychomachia, and after painful debate with himself, Brutus agrees to join the conspirators. The jealous, manipulative Cassius is victorious.

Brutus and the other conspirators do not suspect Cassius to be a hardened manipulator because they trust him. Caesar, however, does not. In an oft-quoted passage, Caesar tells Antony:

> Let me have men about me that are fat;
> Sleek-headed men and such as sleep o' nights:
> Yond Cassius has a lean and hungry look;
> He thinks too much: such men are dangerous.
>   (1.2.193–196)

Caesar suspects Cassius, although no one else does. Perhaps no other characters suspect Cassius because he is an excellent judge of character and would never reveal himself to someone he mistrusted. In stark contrast to Antony's skills at judging character, which are miserable, Cassius proves himself an excellent judge of character. While the conspirators discuss their plans for the assassination, Cassius says:

> Decius, well urged: I think it is not meet,
> Mark Antony, so well beloved of Caesar,
> Should outlive Caesar: we shall find of him
> A shrewd contriver; and, you know, his means,
> If he improve them, may well stretch so far
> As to annoy us all: which to prevent,
> Let Antony and Caesar fall together.
>   (2.1.162–168)

Brutus commands that the conspirators avoid killing Antony and then later affords Antony the opportunity to speak at Caesar's funeral, a decision Cassius rails against. Recognizing a fellow manipulator, Cassius realizes Antony can sway the crowd and says: "Have I a mind / That fears him much" (3.1.158–159). Cassius's fears do not go unfounded; Antony and the other members of the triumvirate—Octavius Caesar and Lepidus—conquer his and Brutus's army. Cassius orders his servant to kill him with his own sword. With him dies the envy that transformed him into one of Rome's great manipulators.

Calpurnia

Caesar's wife first appears when he thrusts her into the path of Mark Antony during the Feast of Lupercal, hoping that the touch of the young, robust Roman will break the curse of Calpurnia's infertility. She may appear to be objectified by Caesar in this episode, but she finds no difficulty in commanding her husband's actions, either, as evidenced by her line "What mean you, Caesar? Think you to walk forth? You shall not stir out of your house today" (2.2.8–9). When Caesar tells his wife that he was born in the same litter as a lion, but that he is "the elder and more terrible" (2.2.47), Calpurnia, without hesitation, tells her husband that his "wisdom is consumed in confidence", illustrating again that she is unafraid of making her opinion about her husband known to him.

Caesar, still entertaining the idea of going to the Capitol, finds himself confronted by his wife, who finally begs him to stay home, stating, "Let me, upon my knee, prevail in this" (2.2.54). In a stark contrast to the exchange between Portia and Brutus one scene prior, Caesar does not tell his wife to "kneel not" as Brutus did, a juxtaposition surely intended to emphasize Caesar's arrogance. The last time readers hear of Calpurnia, it is when Caesar exclaims, "How foolish do your fears seem now, Calpurnia!" (2.2.105). Caesar then goes to the Senate, where the conspirators assassinate him, justifying Calpurnia and her "foolish" fears.

Portia

Known for her constancy, Portia, Brutus's wife, symbolizes the ideal Roman woman and wife. Realizing her husband is not himself, Portia uses logic to appeal to her husband and convince him to share his troubles with her. She states that Brutus's withholding secrets from her makes her feel like "Brutus's harlot and not his wife" (2.1.299); in other words, a man may not tell a harlot much—or anything at all—but a wife deserves to know her husband's confidences. Stating that as his wife, Portia has the right to know what troubles her husband, she makes only one emotional plea with Brutus by kneeling before him, hoping this action will cause her husband to reveal his secrets. Brutus's command to "kneel not, gentle Portia" (2.1.290) demonstrates that Brutus considers his wife a partner and an equal.

Portia furthers her thread of logic by reminding Brutus that she is a "woman well-reputed" (2.1.307): She is Cato's daughter and Brutus's wife and, as such, is known for her morality and nobleness and worthy of being made privy to her husband's troubles. When Brutus still does not concede to inform her of his problems, she wounds herself in the thigh; this action aligns Portia with the stoic soldiers of Rome who wore battle scars like medals, further demonstrating her constancy and, inherently, her devotion.

Although Portia appears composed and governed by logic, her rational nature breaks after Brutus leaves for the Capitol, the very morning after she has implored her husband to confide in her. In her most famous passage, Portia begs:

> O constancy, be strong upon my side,
> Set a huge mountain 'tween my heart and
>   tongue!
> I have a man's mind, but a woman's might.
> How hard it is for women to keep counsel!
>   (2.4.6–9)

Her "man's mind," with its admiration for logic, leaves her as her anxiety begins to overcome her. With Portia's acknowledgment "Ay me, how weak a thing the heart of woman is!" (2.4.43–44), the usually poised Roman woman nears destruction. Portia deteriorates rapidly from a composed woman to a hysterical wife who eventually dies by "swallowing fire." Her method of death deserves analysis: Portia, who begged that a "mountain" be placed "'tween [her] heart and tongue" silences herself by shoving hot coals down her throat, a most painful and excruciating death. She preserves her image as a strong Roman woman by committing suicide, an action viewed as incredibly noble in the Roman world.

DIFFICULTIES OF THE PLAY

Every Shakespearean play presents challenges for its readers, but critics and educators alike typically consider *Julius Caesar* to be one of Shakespeare's least difficult plays. Harold Bloom, in *Shakespeare: The Invention of the Human,* reminisces about how *Julius Caesar* was the first Shakespearean play he read; educators often choose this play to introduce students to Shakespeare's canon because of its accessibility (along with its lack of sexual content).

The language in this play is more straightforward than that of Shakespeare's other Roman plays, *Antony and Cleopatra* and *Coriolanus.* However, like them, it presents the problem to modern readers of presupposing some knowledge of the ancient Roman world. Shakespeare and his audience would definitely have been familiar with the lives of the ancients, as chronicled by Plutarch, but most readers today lack a background in Roman history, so the play and its characters can be confusing and especially challenging. For instance, Portia's comment that she is the daughter of Cato has little effect, if any, on a reader with no knowledge of Cato. When one understands that Cato was known in Rome for his morality and steadfastness, Portia's comment becomes much more meaningful and significant. Nonetheless, a good edition of the play will usually explain such references.

A further difficulty for students is in identifying the tragic hero of the play. Although Julius Caesar is the title character, and a titanic historical figure, he dies halfway through the play, leaving Brutus as the focus of the tragedy for the rest of it. Some readers find the play to be less compelling, even anticlimactic, after Caesar's funeral, particularly after Antony's funeral oration. But, Brutus himself is an extremely compelling character, and his fate should not fail to interest the attentive student.

KEY PASSAGES
Act I, Scene 2, 132–177

BRUTUS. Another general shout!
I do believe that these applauses are
For some new honors that are heap'd on Caesar.

CASSIUS. Why, man, he doth bestride the narrow world
Like a Colossus, and we petty men
Walk under his huge legs and peep about
To find ourselves dishonorable graves.
Men at some time are masters of their fates:
The fault, dear Brutus, is not in our stars,
But in ourselves, that we are underlings.
Brutus and Caesar: what should be in that "Caesar"?
Why should that name be sounded more than yours?
Write them together, yours is as fair a name;
Sound them, it doth become the mouth as well;
Weigh them, it is as heavy; conjure with 'em,
Brutus will start a spirit as soon as Caesar.
Now, in the names of all the gods at once,
Upon what meat doth this our Caesar feed,
That he is grown so great? Age, thou art shamed!
Rome, thou hast lost the breed of noble bloods!
When went there by an age, since the great flood,
But it was famed with more than with one man?
When could they say till now, that talk'd of Rome,
That her wide walls encompass'd but one man?
Now is it Rome indeed and room enough,
When there is in it but one only man.
O, you and I have heard our fathers say,
There was a Brutus once that would have brook'd
The eternal devil to keep his state in Rome
As easily as a king.

BRUTUS. That you do love me, I am nothing jealous;

What you would work me to, I have some aim:
How I have thought of this and of these times,
I shall recount hereafter; for this present,
I would not, so with love I might entreat you,
Be any further moved. What you have said
I will consider; what you have to say
I will with patience hear, and find a time
Both meet to hear and answer such high things.
Till then, my noble friend, chew upon this:
Brutus had rather be a villager
Than to repute himself a son of Rome
Under these hard conditions as this time
Is like to lay upon us.

CASSIUS. I am glad that my weak words
Have struck but thus much show of fire from
  Brutus.

This passage, crucial to the plot of *Julius Caesar*, reveals Cassius's envy for Caesar and his manipulation of the noble Brutus. Shakespeare makes the jealousy Cassius feels for Caesar obvious in his first lines in this passage, in which Cassius asks why Caesar strides about the world like a giant, "a Colossus," while all other men must "walk under his huge legs." Perhaps the most famous lines of the passage are "The fault, dear Brutus, is not in our stars, / But in ourselves, that we are underlings." This quotation illustrates Cassius's life philosophy: He will be master of his own fate and will not sit idly by while Rome drops to its knees to worship Caesar, a man Cassius views as no better or mightier than any other Roman. Shakespeare depicts Cassius as wanting to dethrone Caesar because of his own needs and desires, which provides a striking contrast to Brutus, who later agrees to join the conspirators because of his concern for the fate of Rome, not for himself.

Knowing Brutus to be good and honorable, Cassius plays masterfully upon Brutus's patriotism by persuading him to think that Caesar will act only on his own accord and that with Caesar's rise to power Rome has "lost the breed of noble bloods." Cassius refers to Brutus's ancestors, known for their morality and nobility, and in doing so, Cassius expertly plays upon Brutus's strength—upholding honor—since,

as Brutus says, he would "rather be a villager / Than to repute himself a son of Rome / Under these hard conditions as this time / Is like to lay upon us."

Cassius's speech about Caesar incites concern in Brutus and encourages Brutus to hear more of what Cassius has to say about the dangers of Caesar ruling over Rome. Shakespeare also demonstrates Cassius's ability to manipulate others with his final lines to Brutus, in which he poses as humble—a man of "weak words"—who somehow is able to cause some emotion in the Stoic, noble Brutus.

Act II, Scene 1, 255–309

PORTIA. Dear my lord,
Make me acquainted with your cause of grief.

BRUTUS. I am not well in health, and that is all.

PORTIA. Brutus is wise, and, were he not in
  health,
He would embrace the means to come by it.

BRUTUS. Why, so I do. Good Portia, go to
  bed.

PORTIA. Is Brutus sick? and is it physical
To walk unbraced and suck up the humors
Of the dank morning? What, is Brutus sick,
And will he steal out of his wholesome bed,
To dare the vile contagion of the night
And tempt the rheumy and unpurged air
To add unto his sickness? No, my Brutus;
You have some sick offence within your mind,
Which, by the right and virtue of my place,
I ought to know of: and, upon my knees,
I charm you, by my once-commended beauty,
By all your vows of love and that great vow
Which did incorporate and make us one,
That you unfold to me, yourself, your half,
Why you are heavy, and what men to-night
Have had to resort to you: for here have been
Some six or seven, who did hide their faces
Even from darkness.

BRUTUS. Kneel not, gentle Portia.

PORTIA. I should not need, if you were
  gentle Brutus.
Within the bond of marriage, tell me, Brutus,
Is it excepted I should know no secrets
That appertain to you? Am I yourself
But, as it were, in sort or limitation,
To keep with you at meals, comfort your bed,
And talk to you sometimes? Dwell I but in the
  suburbs
Of your good pleasure? If it be no more,
Portia is Brutus' harlot, not his wife.

BRUTUS. You are my true and honorable wife,
As dear to me as are the ruddy drops
That visit my sad heart.

PORTIA. If this were true, then should I
  know this secret.
I grant I am a woman; but withal
A woman that Lord Brutus took to wife:
I grant I am a woman; but withal
A woman well-reputed, Cato's daughter.
Think you I am no stronger than my sex,
Being so father'd and so husbanded?
Tell me your counsels, I will not disclose 'em:
I have made strong proof of my constancy,
Giving myself a voluntary wound
Here, in the thigh: can I bear that with
  patience.
And not my husband's secrets?

BRUTUS. O ye gods,
Render me worthy of this noble wife!
[Knocking within]
Hark, hark! one knocks: Portia, go in awhile;
And by and by thy bosom shall partake
The secrets of my heart.
All my engagements I will construe to thee,
All the charactery of my sad brows:
Leave me with haste.
[Exit PORTIA.]

Shakespeare demonstrates here that Portia and Brutus have a true partnership in their marriage; more important, however, Shakespeare depicts Portia as the ideal Roman woman and wife. Portia, concerned for her husband, implores him to share his concerns with her. She reminds her husband that logically, she deserves to be made privy to his troubles since "the right and virtue of [her] place" entitles her to this knowledge. As a Roman woman, she must exude confidence and calm, rather than letting her emotions govern her. Kneeling is the most emotionally charged action she takes, preferring instead to rely on the Roman reverence for logic. When she kneels, Brutus says, "Kneel not, gentle Portia," implying that his wife is his partner, his equal, and that her logic has had an effect on him.

Portia remains unrelenting in her pursuit to discover what troubles her husband. She again

Portia in Act II, Scene 1 of *Julius Caesar.* This is a print from Charles Heath's 1848 edition of *The Heroines of Shakspeare: Comprising the Principal Female Characters in the Plays of the Great Poet. (Painting by J. W. Wright; engraving by W. H. Egleton)*

relies on logic to make her case and convince Brutus to reveal his pain to her. Some readers find Shakespeare's repeated line for Portia, "I grant I am a woman," troubling, as it seems to indicate that women are weak and emotional. Although this line could be read as misogynistic, one must also acknowledge the context of *Julius Caesar*, the Roman world, a context that automatically views women as the weaker sex. Portia's uttering "I grant I am a woman" does not insult fellow women but instead, acknowledges Roman beliefs about women. This acknowledgment paints Portia as something of a rhetorician herself, since by acknowledging the weakness on her own, Brutus cannot use this point against her.

Portia further strengthens her argument by stating she is Cato's daughter (a Roman known for his morality) and Brutus's wife (a point sure to touch the heart of Brutus). No point is more powerful, though, than Portia's willingness to wound herself to show her constancy to her husband. In ancient Rome, wounds represented strength and character. For instance, in *Coriolanus,* Volumnia brags about the number of wounds her son received while in battle. A wound, for a Roman, functioned as a medal. Inflicting a self-imposed wound allows Portia to compare herself to Roman soldiers, known for their bravery, dedication, and honor. This wound, in fact, serves as the tipping point for Brutus, who upon seeing it, agrees to divulge his concerns to his wife.

Portia receives her highest praise from Brutus, who calls her "true and honorable" and who also asks the gods to render him "worthy of this noble wife!" This scene is key to understanding *Julius Caesar* and the loving relationship between two of Rome's most noble citizens: Portia and Brutus.

Act II, Scene 2, 8–56

CALPURNIA. What mean you, Caesar? think you to walk forth?
You shall not stir out of your house to-day.

CAESAR. Caesar shall forth: the things that threaten'd me
Ne'er look'd but on my back; when they shall see
The face of Caesar, they are vanished.

CALPURNIA. Caesar, I never stood on ceremonies,
Yet now they fright me. There is one within,
Besides the things that we have heard and seen,
Recounts most horrid sights seen by the watch.
A lioness hath whelped in the streets;
And graves have yawn'd, and yielded up their dead;
Fierce fiery warriors fought upon the clouds,
In ranks and squadrons and right form of war,
Which drizzled blood upon the Capitol;
The noise of battle hurtled in the air,
Horses did neigh, and dying men did groan,
And ghosts did shriek and squeal about the streets.
O Caesar! these things are beyond all use,
And I do fear them.

CAESAR. What can be avoided
Whose end is purposed by the mighty gods?
Yet Caesar shall go forth; for these predictions
Are to the world in general as to Caesar.

CALPURNIA. When beggars die, there are no comets seen;
The heavens themselves blaze forth the death of princes.

CAESAR. Cowards die many times before their deaths;
The valiant never taste of death but once.
Of all the wonders that I yet have heard.
It seems to me most strange that men should fear;
Seeing that death, a necessary end,
Will come when it will come.
[Re-enter SERVANT.]
What say the augurers?

SERVANT. They would not have you to stir forth to-day.
Plucking the entrails of an offering forth,
They could not find a heart within the beast.

CAESAR. The gods do this in shame of
   cowardice:
Caesar should be a beast without a heart,
If he should stay at home to-day for fear.
No, Caesar shall not: danger knows full well
That Caesar is more dangerous than he:
We are two lions litter'd in one day,
And I the elder and more terrible:
And Caesar shall go forth.

CALPURNIA. Alas, my lord,
Your wisdom is consumed in confidence.
Do not go forth to-day: call it my fear
That keeps you in the house, and not your own.
We'll send Mark Antony to the senate-house:
And he shall say you are not well to-day:
Let me, upon my knee, prevail in this.

CAESAR. Mark Antony shall say I am not
   well,
And, for thy humor, I will stay at home.

Much like Portia with Brutus, Calpurnia exudes confidence in this exchange with her husband, depicting her, too, as a strong Roman woman. Unfortunately, Caesar does not observe his wife's request later in the scene. Shakespeare uses this conversation between Calpurnia and Caesar to foreshadow Caesar's doom and to emphasize Caesar's fateful degree of hubris. When Calpurnia reveals the omens of her dream, Caesar dismisses her, claiming "Caesar shall forth: the things that threaten'd me / Ne'er look'd but on my back; when they shall see / The face of Caesar, they are vanished." In other words, Caesar thinks that those who would threaten, instead, would "vanish" in fear upon seeing Caesar's face. Calpurnia tries furiously to rein her husband's prideful nature, arguing that when a man of Caesar's stature dies—or is fated to die—"the heavens themselves blaze forth."

Calpurnia, who never believed in omens or "stood on ceremonies" before, holds fast to the conviction that her dream reveals Caesar's fate, telling her husband, "Alas, my lord, / Your wisdom is consumed in confidence." And, though the passage analyzed here ends with Caesar conceding to his wife's plea, moments later Caesar, convinced by the flattery of Decius Brutus, leaves to meet the Senate and his death.

Act III, Scene 1, 52–83

BRUTUS. I kiss thy hand, but not in flattery,
   Caesar;
Desiring thee that Publius Cimber may
Have an immediate freedom of repeal.

CAESAR. What, Brutus!

CASSIUS. Pardon, Caesar; Caesar, pardon:
As low as to thy foot doth Cassius fall,
To beg enfranchisement for Publius Cimber.

CAESAR. I could be well moved, if I were as
   you:
If I could pray to move, prayers would
   move me:
But I am constant as the northern star,
Of whose true-fix'd and resting quality
There is no fellow in the firmament.
The skies are painted with unnumber'd sparks,
They are all fire and every one doth shine,
But there's but one in all doth hold his place:
So in the world; tis furnish'd well with men,
And men are flesh and blood, and
   apprehensive;
Yet in the number I do know but one
That unassailable holds on his rank,
Unshaked of motion: and that I am he,
Let me a little show it, even in this;
That I was constant Cimber should be
   banish'd,
And constant do remain to keep him so.

CINNA. O Caesar,—

CAESAR. Hence! wilt thou lift up Olympus?

DECIUS BRUTUS. Great Caesar,—

CAESAR. Doth not Brutus bootless kneel?

CASCA. Speak, hands for me!
[*CASCA first, then the other Conspirators and BRUTUS stab CAESAR.*]

CAESAR. Et tu, Brute! Then fall, Caesar.
[*Dies.*]

CINNA. Liberty! Freedom! Tyranny is dead!
Run hence, proclaim, cry it about the streets.

CASSIUS. Some to the common pulpits, and
cry out
"Liberty, freedom, and enfranchisement!"

BRUTUS. People and senators, be not
affrighted;
Fly not; stand stiff: ambition's debt is paid.

This passage reveals Caesar's hubris and the conspirators' relief and joy at Caesar's death. Caesar denies Metellus Cimber's request to save Publius, Metellus's brother, stating one of his most famous lines, one often quoted by modern politicians: "I am constant as the northern star, / Of whose true-fix'd and resting quality / There is no fellow in the firmament." This claim, that Caesar acts more resolutely and definitely than any other man, is perhaps his greatest, and his last, boast before his assassination.

The line "Et tu, Brute? [And you, Brutus?] Then fall Caesar," reminds readers of the dynamic of Brutus and Caesar's relationship: They loved and respected each other, so Brutus's betrayal in this scene feels especially treacherous to Caesar. However, Brutus (whether on his own accord or because of instigators such as Cassius) feels Caesar has betrayed him by acting ambitiously, rather than for the good of Rome. Brutus feels that the assassination of Caesar has allowed "ambition's debt to be paid" and that Rome will now flourish and not fail.

Act III, Scene 2, 11–54

THIRD CITIZEN. The noble Brutus is
ascended: silence!

BRUTUS. Be patient till the last. Romans, countrymen, and lovers! hear me for my cause, and be silent, that you may hear: believe me for mine honor, and have respect to mine honor, that you may believe: censure me in your wisdom, and awake your senses, that you may the better judge. If there be any in this assembly, any dear friend of Caesar's, to him I say, that Brutus' love to Caesar was no less than his. If then that friend demand why Brutus rose against Caesar, this is my answer:—Not that I loved Caesar less, but that I loved Rome more. Had you rather Caesar were living and die all slaves, than that Caesar were dead, to live all free men? As Caesar loved me, I weep for him; as he was fortunate, I rejoice at it; as he was valiant, I honor him: but, as he was ambitious, I slew him. There is tears for his love; joy for his fortune; honor for his valor; and death for his ambition. Who is here so base that would be a bondman? If any, speak; for him have I offended. Who is here so rude that would not be a Roman? If any, speak; for him have I offended. Who is here so vile that will not love his country? If any, speak; for him have I offended. I pause for a reply.

ALL. None, Brutus, none.

BRUTUS. Then none have I offended. I have done no more to Caesar than you shall do to Brutus. The question of his death is enrolled in the Capitol; his glory not extenuated, wherein he was worthy, nor his offences enforced, for which he suffered death.
[*Enter ANTONY and others, with CAESAR's body.*]

Here comes his body, mourned by Mark Antony: who, though he had no hand in his death, shall receive the benefit of his dying, a place in the commonwealth; as which of you shall not? With this I depart,—that, as I slew my best lover for the good of Rome, I have the same dagger for myself, when it shall please my country to need my death.

ALL. Live, Brutus! live, live!

FIRST CITIZEN. Bring him with triumph home unto his house.

SECOND CITIZEN. Give him a statue with his ancestors.

THIRD CITIZEN. Let him be Caesar.

FOURTH CITIZEN. Caesar's better parts
Shall be crown'd in Brutus.

The funeral orations given by Brutus and by Antony, which immediately follows, both require analysis. To begin, Shakespeare writes Brutus's oration in prose. Prose, the less-formal, less-elevated style (compared to Shakespeare's verse), implies that the subject of Brutus's speech—Caesar—is relatively unimportant, unworthy of verse. In contrast, Antony's oration is in verse, which implies greater respect for Caesar. Shakespeare's audience would have recognized the differences in form and language between the two orations and would have understood the implications of Shakespeare's choices.

Brutus begins his oration with "Romans, countrymen, and lovers" and in doing so, immediately appeals to the crowd's sense of nationalism, a key component that Brutus continues to refer to, claiming that the assassination of Caesar was committed for the good of Rome, for the good of his countrymen.

Another effective technique Brutus employs occurs during the following lines:

If there be any in this assembly, any dear friend of Caesar's, to him I say, that Brutus' love to Caesar was no less than his. If then that friend demand why Brutus rose against Caesar, this is my answer:—Not that I loved Caesar less, but that I loved Rome more.

Brutus, in acknowledging his love for Caesar, reminds the crowd that murdering Caesar was difficult for him, far from a ruthless, unfeeling act of anger. Brutus also reinforces his love for Rome, emphasizing that he did not act selfishly but for the good of all Romans.

Brutus's reference to his honor also warrants analysis, especially because Antony refers to Brutus's honor in his oration, as well. Brutus asks, "believe me / for mine honor, and have respect to mine honor," before he rationalizes the acts of the conspirators for the plebeians. Throughout the play, several characters mention that the public loves Brutus and views him as an honorable man, and Brutus partly relies on that perception of him in justifying the actions of the conspirators. Though the crowd accepts Brutus's explanation, and even wants to crown Brutus, they are quickly swayed by the master rhetorician, Antony.

Act III, Scene 2, 78–121

ANTONY. You gentle Romans,—

CITIZENS. Peace, ho! let us hear him.

ANTONY. Friends, Romans, countrymen,
  lend me your ears;
I come to bury Caesar, not to praise him.
The evil that men do lives after them;
The good is oft interred with their bones;
So let it be with Caesar. The noble Brutus
Hath told you Caesar was ambitious:
If it were so, it was a grievous fault,
And grievously hath Caesar answer'd it.
Here, under leave of Brutus and the rest—
For Brutus is an honorable man;
So are they all, all honorable men—
Come I to speak in Caesar's funeral.
He was my friend, faithful and just to me:
But Brutus says he was ambitious;
And Brutus is an honorable man.
He hath brought many captives home to Rome
Whose ransoms did the general coffers fill:
Did this in Caesar seem ambitious?

When that the poor have cried, Caesar hath
  wept:
Ambition should be made of sterner stuff:
Yet Brutus says he was ambitious;
And Brutus is an honorable man.
You all did see that on the Lupercal
I thrice presented him a kingly crown,
Which he did thrice refuse: was this ambition?
Yet Brutus says he was ambitious;
And, sure, he is an honorable man.
I speak not to disprove what Brutus spoke,
But here I am to speak what I do know.
You all did love him once, not without cause:
What cause withholds you then, to mourn for
  him?
O judgment! thou art fled to brutish beasts,
And men have lost their reason. Bear with me;
My heart is in the coffin there with Caesar,
And I must pause till it come back to me.

FIRST CITIZEN. Methinks there is much
  reason in his sayings.

SECOND CITIZEN. If thou consider rightly
  of the matter,
Caesar has had great wrong.

THIRD CITIZEN. Has he, masters?
I fear there will a worse come in his place.

FOURTH CITIZEN. Mark'd ye his words?
  He would not take the crown;
Therefore tis certain he was not ambitious.

FIRST CITIZEN. If it be found so, some will
  dear abide it.

SECOND CITIZEN. Poor soul! his eyes are
  red as fire with weeping.

THIRD CITIZEN. There's not a nobler man
  in Rome than Antony.

Antony has two advantages over Brutus, who spoke the first funeral oration, which immediately pre-cedes this one: Antony carries in Caesar's body and speaks in verse. Brutus himself commanded Antony to carry Caesar's body to the Forum; this decision was a grave mistake on Brutus's part. Imagine how much more moving Brutus's claim that he loved Caesar would have been, had Caesar been in his arms, or even somewhere near him? Instead, Antony's speech instantly has a more powerful effect on the crowd because Caesar, though dead, is also present. Unlike Brutus, who only referred to a Caesar no one could see, Antony can refer to Caesar and look at him, gesture toward him, cry over him, all actions that effect his listeners significantly.

The other advantage Antony has over Brutus was gifted to him by Shakespeare, who wrote Antony's oration in verse, a more serious form than

William Faversham as Mark Antony in a late 19th-century production of *Julius Caesar* *(Photographed by Napoleon Sarony)*

the prose he assigned to Brutus. As noted above, Shakespeare's audience would have perceived this difference, and the rhythmic verse of Antony's oration naturally would have sounded more pleasing to viewers, just as readers also appreciate the rhythm.

While Brutus began his oration with "Romans, countrymen, and lovers! hear me" (3.2.78), Antony addresses the crowd by asking "Friends, Romans, countrymen, lend me your ears." Brutus commands that the populace listen to him speak, whereas Antony asks for their attention, illustrating him as the more respectful of the two. Antony, Caesar's closest confidante, must also approach the crowd warily if he is to convince them of his views; asking for the crowd's attention instead of commanding it, then, demonstrates Antony's skill as a rhetorician. He must be sensitive to the views of the plebeians, who, at the start of his speech, already believe Brutus should be awarded a crown. Significantly, Antony addresses the crowd as his "friends"; Brutus speaks of those who were "friends" to Caesar but never identifies the crowd as his friends. Modern-day politicians employ Antony's tactic, hoping to appeal to and sway the people just as Antony did.

Antony also masterfully turns words and phrases used by Brutus to his own benefit, including *honorable* and *ambitious*. For instance, Antony states, Caesar "was my friend, faithful and just to me: / But Brutus says he was ambitious; / And Brutus is an honorable man." Consider, also, this example:

> For Brutus is an honorable man;
> So are they all, all honorable men—
> Come I to speak in Caesar's funeral.
> He was my friend, faithful and just to me:
> But Brutus says he was ambitious;
> And Brutus is an honorable man.

Brutus calls himself a man of honor and, knowing the plebeians' perception of him, does not even entertain the possibility of the crowd's questioning how honorable and noble he is. Conversely, Antony implicitly demands the crowd to reconsider their perception of Brutus; Antony uses *honorable* to refer to Brutus over and over again, and coupled with Antony's forthcoming revelation that Caesar provided for all Romans in his will, the crowd is swayed, incited to vengeance. Antony, a gifted rhetorician and manipulator, moves the crowd from wanting to crown Brutus to wanting him killed.

Act V, Scene 5, 68–75

ANTONY. This was the noblest Roman of
  them all:
All the conspirators save only he
Did that they did in envy of great Caesar;
He only, in a general honest thought
And common good to all, made one of them.
His life was gentle, and the elements
So mix'd in him that Nature might stand up
And say to all the world, "This was a man!"

This final passage of the play resonates with readers because of Antony's words about Brutus, whom he acknowledges as the "noblest Roman of them all." Although Shakespeare makes Antony the next-to-last character to speak, his words focus on Brutus, the central figure of the play, and in turn, Shakespeare and Antony both pay homage to Brutus, who was "honest," "good," and "a man."

DIFFICULT PASSAGES
Act IV, Scene 1, 1–21

ANTONY. These many, then, shall die; their
  names are prick'd.

OCTAVIUS. Your brother too must die;
  consent you, Lepidus?

LEPIDUS. I do consent—

OCTAVIUS. Prick him down, Antony.

LEPIDUS. Upon condition Publius shall not
  live,
Who is your sister's son, Mark Antony.

ANTONY. He shall not live; look, with a spot
  I damn him.
But, Lepidus, go you to Caesar's house;

Fetch the will hither, and we shall determine
How to cut off some charge in legacies.

LEPIDUS. What, shall I find you here?

OCTAVIUS. Or here, or at the Capitol.
[Exit LEPIDUS.]

ANTONY. This is a slight unmeritable man,
Meet to be sent on errands: is it fit,
The three-fold world divided, he should stand
One of the three to share it?

OCTAVIUS. So you thought him;
And took his voice who should be prick'd to die,
In our black sentence and proscription.

ANTONY. Octavius, I have seen more days
  than you:
And though we lay these honors on this man,
To ease ourselves of divers slanderous loads,
He shall but bear them as the ass bears gold,
To groan and sweat under the business,
Either led or driven, as we point the way;
And having brought our treasure where we will,
Then take we down his load, and turn him off,
Like to the empty ass, to shake his ears,
And graze in commons.

OCTAVIUS. You may do your will;
But he's a tried and valiant soldier.

ANTONY. So is my horse, Octavius; and for
  that
I do appoint him store of provender:
It is a creature that I teach to fight,
To wind, to stop, to run directly on,
His corporal motion govern'd by my spirit.
And, in some taste, is Lepidus but so;
He must be taught and train'd and bid go forth;
A barren-spirited fellow; one that feeds
On objects, arts and imitations,
Which, out of use and staled by other men,
Begin his fashion: do not talk of him,
But as a property. And now, Octavius,

Listen great things:—Brutus and Cassius
Are levying powers: we must straight make head:
Therefore let our alliance be combined,
Our best friends made, our means stretch'd
And let us presently go sit in council,
How covert matters may be best disclosed,
And open perils surest answered.

OCTAVIUS. Let us do so: for we are at the
  stake,
And bay'd about with many enemies;
And some that smile have in their hearts, I fear,
Millions of mischiefs.
[Exeunt.]

This passage presents difficulties for readers for several reasons. First, readers often feel confused by the sudden appearance of Lepidus as a speaking character; second, readers have trouble understanding the triumvirate's formation and dynamics; and third, and probably most confusing for readers, is Antony's attitude and behavior in the scene.

Although he appears in earlier scenes, Lepidus does not speak until this scene. Readers typically feel confused by his role, as Lepidus has, until now, appeared to be a very minor character. Lepidus, along with Octavius and Mark Antony, form the triumvirate, the group who hold power after Caesar's death. Lepidus was loyal to Caesar but agreed to his assassination. Lepidus also swore allegiance to the conspirators but instead abandoned them and joined forces with Antony and Octavius. Shakespeare, however, does not explain these events to his readers, so this passage remains hard to digest.

Mark Antony's attitude and behavior is even more confusing. Until now, unsuspecting readers may have viewed Mark Antony as one of Caesar's friends, devastated by his death; they may have even considered him manipulative based on his mastery of rhetoric and ability to sway a crowd to his will. But, here, Mark Antony's ruthlessness unveils itself, a characteristic some readers find confusing, especially in comparison to the Mark Antony of earlier in the play. In this scene, Antony agrees—without hesitation—to the death of his nephew (Publius).

He also reveals his disdain for Lepidus, comparing his fellow leader to a horse and urging Octavius to treat Lepidus as nothing more than "property." Antony's rage has been building since Caesar's assassination, and in this scene it erupts, demonstrating to readers that he is dangerous and intent on revenge and power.

CRITICAL INTRODUCTION TO THE PLAY
Honor and Nobility

Honor and nobility are perhaps the most significant themes in *Julius Caesar*. Shakespeare introduces these themes in the first scene of the play, during which Marullus and Flavius demonstrate their commitment to the fallen Pompey, attesting to his nobility and triumphs. When they find a group of commoners who once honored Pompey celebrating Caesar's arrival in Rome, they chastise them and then scout the town, removing any monuments to Caesar. The tribunes, honorable in their dedication to the fallen Pompey, provide the first examples of characters who live honorably and die nobly, as their refusal to support Caesar leads to their deaths. Shakespeare furthers his themes about honor and nobility in many of the play's characters, suggesting that, ultimately, acting honorably and nobly matters more than trying to preserve only honor.

Caesar acts to preserve honor. Consider how Caesar first agrees to Calpurnia's request that, after her dream full of harrowing portents, Caesar remain at home. He tells Calpurnia "for thy humor, I will stay at home" (2.2.56). But, after Decius Brutus arrives and tells Caesar that if he "hide himself," the senators will "whisper 'Lo, Caesar is afraid'" (2.2.100–101), Caesar feels concerned that his image, and his honor, could be tarnished. Had Caesar acted nobly, stuck to his convictions, and respected his wife's wishes, he might not have been killed; instead, Caesar merely tries to preserve his honor and, in the process, loses his life.

Portia provides a keen example of a character who becomes concerned with preserving honor instead of living honorably and nobly. Shakespeare introduces Portia as a truly honorable and noble woman: She describes herself as "A woman well-reputed, Cato's daughter" (2.1.295) and the "woman Lord Brutus took to wife" (2.1.293), highlighting her constancy, devotion, and excellence of character. She tells Brutus she is "stronger than her sex" (2.1.296), a comment that soon dooms her. Although she prides herself on being logical and rational, Portia breaks down after Brutus leaves for the Senate the following morning. Her composure crumbles, and instead of acting honorably and remaining silent out of personal strength, she acts to preserve her honor. Worried that she will divulge Brutus's confidences, she begs for a mountain to be placed "'tween her heart and tongue" (2.4.8). Fearing that she will compromise her status as "stronger than her sex," she swallows fire before she reveals any information Brutus shared with her. Romans viewed suicide as a noble act, but Portia takes her life to keep herself from talking and, in turn, preserves her image as Cato's daughter and Brutus's wife out of fear rather than acting truly honorably.

The most honorable and noble character in the play, undoubtedly, is Brutus. The conspirators plan to assassinate Caesar out of jealousy, but Brutus, beloved by all of Rome, acts with noble intentions. He only agrees to join the conspirators because he fears how Caesar's reign will affect Rome. He tells the people that he loved Caesar, but that he "loved Rome more" (3.2.23), an honorable justification for his participation in Caesar's assassination. Even Antony, who despises the conspirators, distinguishes Brutus and his motives from the rest, calling him "the noblest Roman of them all" (5.5.68). Caesar cares only about his image of honor; Portia fears her loss of honor and nobility; Brutus, however, acts with honor and nobility as his guides, and thus, Shakespeare presents a character worth admiring and emulating.

Ambition

Ambition is another theme crucial to *Julius Caesar*. Many characters act ambitiously, and the play suggests that based on one's intentions, ambition can be either a positive or a negative trait. The two

Brutus commits suicide by falling onto his sword, held by Strato, in Act V, Scene 5 of *Julius Caesar*. This print is from the Boydell Shakespeare Gallery project, which was first conceived in 1786 and lasted until 1805. *(Painting by Richard Westall; engraving by Samuel Noble)*

characters who exemplify ambition best are Caesar and Cassius, and each man's ambition leads eventually to his destruction.

Caesar, refusing the crown from Antony three times, demonstrates that he delights in pomp and circumstance. Further, Caesar's conviction that no man compares to him shows him to be arrogant and dangerous and serves as Cassius's rationalization for assassinating him. Caesar's ambition is the catalyst for the conspirators and, in turn, leads to his death.

Cassius, the ringleader of the conspiracy, grows ambitious out of jealousy. In Act I, Scene 2, Cassius tells Brutus a story about when he and Caesar had a swimming contest and Cassius had to rescue Caesar from drowning. Since this incident, Cassius

has grown wild with jealousy over the way Caesar, as mortal a man as any, thinks he is better than everyone else. Cassius's ambition grows and comes to a head when he develops the plan to assassinate Caesar. He feels he could rule Rome just as efficiently and expertly as Caesar, and in comparison to Brutus (who helped assassinate Caesar for the good of Rome), Cassius acts ambitiously for the good of himself.

Shakespeare suggests ambition can be a healthy attribute, as in Brutus's case, whose ambition to protect Rome and its people, was honorable. One's intentions make the difference. In men like Caesar and Cassius—who act in the best interest of themselves instead of others—ambition leads to death.

Superstition and the Supernatural

Julius Caesar is full of superstition and supernatural elements. Even logical and rational Romans, in tumultuous times, value omens and become superstitious.

The night before Caesar's assassination, Casca walks the streets of Rome and witnesses the following spectacles:

A common slave—you know him well by
  sight—
Held up his left hand, which did flame and burn
Like twenty torches join'd, and yet his hand,
Not sensible of fire, remain'd unscorch'd.
Besides—I ha' not since put up my sword—
Against the Capitol I met a lion,
Who glared upon me, and went surly by,
Without annoying me: and there were drawn
Upon a heap a hundred ghastly women,
Transformed with their fear; who swore they saw
Men all in fire walk up and down the streets.
And yesterday the bird of night did sit
Even at noon-day upon the market-place,
Hooting and shrieking. When these prodigies
Do so conjointly meet, let not men say
"These are their reasons; they are natural;"
For, I believe, they are portentous things
Unto the climate that they point upon.
(1.3.15–32)

Casca encounters a man who holds fire in his hand without being burned, a lion, men on fire, and an owl during the day, all disturbing images. Casca, uncertain of why these portents have appeared, guesses that they represent "civil strife in heaven" (1.3.11). Cassius, who calls Casca "dull" and tells him that "those sparks of life / That should be in a Roman you do want" (1.3.57–58), manipulates Casca into thinking that the portents actually foreshadow the chaos that Caesar, if crowned, would bring to Rome. Minutes later, Cassius's manipulative logic convinces Casca to join his cause to assassinate the "tyrant" Caesar. The following day, Casca, heartily convinced of Cassius's argument, stabs Caesar first.

Calpurnia's dream about supernatural events in Rome and Caesar's fate also includes supernatural elements:

> Caesar, I never stood on ceremonies,
> Yet now they fright me. There is one within,
> Besides the things that we have heard and seen,
> Recounts most horrid sights seen by the watch.
> A lioness hath whelped in the streets;
> And graves have yawn'd, and yielded up their
>   dead;
> Fierce fiery warriors fought upon the clouds,
> In ranks and squadrons and right form of war,
> Which drizzled blood upon the Capitol;
> The noise of battle hurtled in the air,
> Horses did neigh, and dying men did groan,
> And ghosts did shriek and squeal about the
>   streets.
> O Caesar! these things are beyond all use,
> And I do fear them. (2.2.13–26)

Visions of a lioness roaming the streets, corpses walking abroad, and blood running through the Capitol cause the usually rational Calpurnia, who has "never stood on ceremonies," to become superstitious and fear the portents of her dream. According to Caesar, Calpurnia also dreamed she saw his statue "Which, like a fountain with an hundred spouts, / Did run pure blood" (2.2.77–78). Convinced the events of her dream will be realized, Calpurnia asks her husband to remain home, but to no avail. With this passage, Shakespeare emphasizes that even the most rational people become superstitious if someone they love is threatened.

The other most significant example of superstition in the play occurs during Act 5, Scene 1, when Cassius believes the defeat of his and Brutus's army has been foretold based on the behavior of eagles, ravens, and other birds:

> Coming from Sardis, on our former ensign
> Two mighty eagles fell, and there they perch'd,
> Gorging and feeding from our soldiers' hands;
> Who to Philippi here consorted us:
> This morning are they fled away and gone;
> And in their steads do ravens, crows and kites,
> Fly o'er our heads and downward look on us,
> As we were sickly prey: their shadows seem
> A canopy most fatal, under which
> Our army lies, ready to give up the ghost.
>   (5.1.80–89)

The eagles descended, Cassius says, and ate from the soldiers' hands. Their disappearance signifies only one thing to Cassius: doom. Cassius divulges his belief in the superstition that "ravens, crows, and kites" symbolize impending death, proving that even someone fearless enough to assassinate a tyrant will himself fall prey to superstition in times of chaos.

The Fickle Public

Shakespeare gives the Roman public an important role in *Julius Caesar,* just as he does in *Richard III.* While the public in *Richard III* gauges Richard's appeal and serves as a guide for readers' feelings about the power-hungry monarch, the public of *Julius Caesar* serves a different purpose: to illustrate the fickleness of the masses and how easily they can be manipulated.

The first example of the public's fickleness occurs in the opening scene of the play when Marullus and Flavius confront a group of commoners cheering Caesar's return to Rome. The tribunes remind the commoners that they only recently showed devotion to Pompey but instead now champion the man who gained victory over Pompey. Marullus calls the commoners "blocks," "stones," and "worse than senseless things!" (1.1.40) The tribunes then remind the commoners that when Pompey ruled Rome,

> Many a time and oft
> Have you climb'd up to walls and battlements,
> To towers and windows, yea, to chimney-tops,
> Your infants in your arms, and there have sat
> The livelong day, with patient expectation,
> To see great Pompey pass the streets of Rome.
> (1.1.42–47)

The commoners feel untroubled by their sudden change in allegiance and stand idly by as the tribunes—still loyal to Pompey—remove signs of Caesar's victory, an action that leads ultimately to their deaths.

After Caesar's death, Brutus gives an oration; by the end of his speech, the public cries that Brutus, one of Caesar's assassins, should be crowned. Moments later, Antony employs sophisticated rhetoric and sways the public to agree with him. The public's opinion shifting so quickly, and monumentally, in a matter of minutes, emphasizes how shallow and petty the public can be.

No example better illustrates how senseless the public can be than the confrontation with Cinna the Poet after Antony's indictment of the conspirators:

> FIRST CITIZEN. Tear him to pieces; he's a conspirator.
>
> CINNA THE POET. I am Cinna the poet, I am Cinna the poet.
>
> FOURTH CITIZEN. Tear him for his bad verses, tear him for his bad verses.
>
> CINNA THE POET. I am not Cinna the conspirator.

Antony and the crowd mourn over Caesar's dead body in Act III, Scene 2, as depicted in an 1879 edition of *Julius Caesar*. (Painting by Julius Kleinmichel; engraving by Hugo Kaeseberg and Johann Feldweg)

> FOURTH CITIZEN. It is no matter, his name's Cinna; pluck but his name out of his heart, and turn him going. (3.3.33–37)

Although the crowd is clearly assaulting the wrong man, who merely shares the last name of a conspirator, the people do not care. In this passage, Shakespeare truly demonstrates how a group of fickle citizens is bound to act irrationally, a pattern demonstrated in their dismissal of Brutus and endorsement of Antony.

Letters

Letters are symbols of anxiety in *Julius Caesar*, especially the mock letter from the conspirators left for Brutus and Artemidorous's letter to Caesar. The letter Brutus receives from the conspirators states: "Brutus, thou sleep'st: awake, and see thyself. / Shall Rome, & c. Speak, strike, redress! / Brutus, thou sleep'st: awake!" (2.1). Symbolically, this letter represents both the conspirators' and Brutus's anxiety. The conspirators, eager to convince Brutus to join in their assassination of Caesar, feel anxious because without Brutus's participation, they will look like cold-blooded killers instead of men acting in the best interest of Rome. In Act 1, Cassius asks Brutus if he can see himself and how he appears to other men, since all men look to him as an example. When Brutus reads the lines "Brutus, thou sleep'st: awake!" he realizes that men in Rome look to him for action, and he, too, feels anxious about acting and, in turn, serving Rome well.

Artemidorous's letter symbolizes his anxiety over Caesar's fate. The letter reads:

> Caesar, beware of Brutus; take heed of Cassius; come not near Casca; have an eye to Cinna, trust not Trebonius: mark well Metellus Cimber: Decius Brutus loves thee not: thou hast wronged Caius Ligarius. There is but one mind in all these men, and it is bent against Caesar. If thou beest not immortal, look about you: security gives way to conspiracy. The mighty gods defend thee! Thy lover, ARTEMIDOROUS. (2.3.1–10)

Concerned for Caesar's safety, Artemidorous begs Caesar to read his letter before the other documents he has been given, hoping to alter the course of fate. But Caesar dismisses Artemidorous, saying "What touches us ourself shall be last served" (3.1.7). When Artemidorous responds by exclaiming, "Delay not, Caesar; read it instantly," Caesar asks if Artemidorous has gone mad (3.1.8). Caesar never reads the letter, and moments later, the conspirators assassinate him.

It is important to note regarding letters in *Julius Caesar* that the receiver's acknowledgment of the letter directly relates to that character's morality. Brutus, who receives an anonymous letter, reads it, takes the contents seriously, and acts upon the letter's request. Caesar, who receives a letter from an upstanding citizen of Rome, ignores both the letter and the man who composed it; minutes later he dies, though the contents of the letter could have saved him. Brutus, a moral and good man, heeds the words of an anonymous stranger for the good of Rome. Caesar, a prideful man, ignores the words of a friend to protect his image.

Women and the Home

Critics tend to agree that the women in the play—Portia and Calpurnia—represent private life in contrast to the public lives their husbands lead. Shakespeare shows intimate moments between Portia and Brutus and Calpurnia and Caesar that would not occur in public: Both wives question their husbands' choices. Portia appeals to Brutus to share his problems with her; the shocking comparison she draws between herself and a harlot works effectively on Brutus, but she is only able to say such a thing in the private world of their home. Even Portia's acknowledging that Brutus seems troubled would be an observation shared only in the private world like their home, not in the public domain. Brutus, a Roman Stoic, strives to present himself as collected and calm, never troubled.

Just like Portia, Calpurnia represents the private world—Caesar's private world, specifically. Only within the confines of Caesar's home can Calpurnia share her concerns with her husband and command him not to "walk forth," as she says (2.2.8). Persuaded by her arguments, Caesar agrees to stay home from the Senate. His compassion for his wife in this scene provides a striking juxtaposition to when Shakespeare first introduces Caesar and Calpurnia in Act I, Scene 1, during which Caesar commands his wife to stand in Antony's path so that during the Feast of Lupercal, Antony might touch her and make her fertile.

When Decius Brutus arrives, however, the dynamics of Caesar's home shift. The very private domain shared by Caesar, Calpurnia, and their servants becomes very public because of Decius Brutus's intrusion. Caesar suddenly disregards his wife's notions (with the help of some flattery on Decius Brutus's part) and transforms quickly into his public self, the Caesar who fears nothing.

In *The Shakespeare Book of Lists,* Michael LoMonico counted the occurrences of various words in the play. He noted the frequent occurrence of the word *men,* which appears more often than such words as *Rome* and *noble.* Clearly, *Julius Caesar* is a play about the world of men. Though women are present, their roles are minor, and some readers have even suggested that the play's forward movement is in no way affected by the women, making their roles seem insignificant.

Julius Caesar and the Roman Style

Shakespeare employs a very minimalistic style in *Julius Caesar*. Caroline Spurgeon describes the play as "straightforward, slow-moving, restrained, almost bare in style" (346). Maurice Charney notes the play's severely limited diction and neatly summarizes Shakespeare's stylistic choices: "The deliberate limiting of imaginative resources in *Julius Caesar* seems to indicate a stylistic experiment on Shakespeare's part. He appears to be attempting a special 'Roman' style for the play, one that can express the clarity of thought and forthrightness of action in the Roman subject matter" (16).

Charney also makes useful comparisons between *Julius Caesar* and Shakespeare's other Roman plays. He observes that they all share traits such as their source material (Plutarch's *Lives of the Noble Grecians and Romans*) and characters' fondness for committing suicide, an honorable decision in ancient Rome. *Julius Caesar*'s style differs from that of *Coriolanus* but differs most significantly from *Antony and Cleopatra*. Charney explains that "Actually, the Roman world in *Antony and Cleopatra* is very much like that in *Julius Caesar,* but it is 'overreached' by the world of empire and the splendors and perils of Egypt" (11). Similarly, the biggest stylistic difference between *Julius Caesar* and *Antony and Cleopatra* concerns Antony, who "abandons the Roman style and values of Octavius Caesar—they are public, political, and objective as is *Julius Caesar*—and enters into the Egyptian style and values of Cleopatra" (11). Charney adds that another significant difference between the styles of these two plays involves Shakespeare's imaginative powers. As mentioned earlier, Shakespeare seems to "limit" his imagination in *Julius Caesar,* but "in *Antony and Cleopatra* he appears to be trying to extend them 'past the size of dreaming'" (11). In sum, *Julius Caesar* lacks the ornate style of many of Shakespeare's other works. Instead, Shakespeare presents the story of Caesar's assassination in a clear, straightforward manner. This stylistic choice imitates the dynamics of the Roman world about which Shakespeare writes.

Imagery

Just as Shakespeare avoided ornate and complex style when he wrote *Julius Caesar,* he also decided not to include the lush, vibrant imagery found in most of his other plays. In terms of imagery and in comparison to Shakespeare's other Roman plays—*Antony and Cleopatra* and *Coriolanus*—*Julius Caesar* remains the simplest and barest. Spurgeon, in the landmark work *Shakespeare's Imagery and What It Tells Us,* writes that *Julius Caesar* "has relatively few images (less than half those in *Coriolanus,* and less than one-third those in *Antony and Cleopatra*)" (346). Charney, author of *Shakespeare's Roman Plays: The Function of Imagery in the Drama,* agrees with Spurgeon, classifying *Julius Caesar*'s imagery as "quite limited" (15). Spurgeon adds that "no leading or floating image" exists in the play (346), a claim Charney disagrees with, offering that the "chief image themes in *Julius Caesar* are the storm and its portents, blood, and fire" (42).

Charney recognizes the effective storm imagery in another of Shakespeare's tragedies: *King Lear.* The storm in *King Lear* represents Lear's tumultuous and deteriorating mental state. While Charney acknowledges that the storm in *Julius Caesar* does not compare to the storm in *King Lear,* he says that the imagery associated with the storms serve the similar purpose of representing chaos. The storm in this Roman play, however, represents more than mental chaos but the chaos of Rome and its citizens, especially the conspirators and Brutus. Charney also states that for Calpurnia, the storm represents Caesar's impending murder. Blood, too, functions as a significant image in *Julius Caesar* and reaches its height in Act 3, Scene 1, when the conspirators murder Caesar. The conspirators have committed a bloody deed and, like Caesar's corpse, find themselves drenched in the former emperor's blood.

Though Spurgeon argues there is no one dominant image in *Julius Caesar,* she recognizes a pattern in the imagery Shakespeare uses in the play: many of the images involve comparing characters to animals. Spurgeon provides the following examples:

1. Shakespeare compares Caesar to a wolf, lion, falcon, serpent's egg, adder, and a stricken deer.
2. The Romans are linked to sheep, hinds, and bees.
3. The conspirators are likened to apes and hounds.
4. Brutus calls himself a lamb.
5. Octavius calls Lepidus an ass and a horse.
6. Caesar calls Metellus and Casca curs. (346–347)

These animalistic images, Spurgeon states, "lack consistency of character" (347); for instance, Shakespeare variously compares Caesar to a wolf and a deer. Regardless, the prominent animal imagery in the play reinforces the beastly nature of the men, including Caesar, the selfish and prideful leader, and Cassius, the bloodthirsty ringleader of the conspiracy.

The Language of the Play

David Crystal and Ben Crystal, authors of *The Shakespeare Miscellany,* offer some valuable insight about the language of *Julius Caesar.* Nearly all of Shakespeare's plays include both verse and prose (with such exceptions as *Richard II* and *King John,* which Shakespeare wrote completely in verse). Crystal and Crystal observe that more than 90 percent of *Julius Caesar* is verse. This fact is unsurprising considering that Shakespeare follows a pattern evident in his entire canon: Members of higher social class (noblemen, gentlemen, monarchs, and so on) almost always speak in verse, while members of lower classes almost always speak in prose.

An exception to this rule occurs in *Julius Caesar,* however. Casca, one of the conspirators against Caesar, and of the same social class as Brutus and Cassius, speaks in prose. Shakespeare has Casca speak in prose during Act 1, Scene 2, when Brutus and Cassius stop Casca and ask him for details about when Antony attempted to present Caesar with the crown. Casca's attitude toward Caesar when he speaks in this scene is rude and demeaning: He focuses on Caesar's epileptic fit and then insinuates that Caesar only refused the crown three times because he enjoyed hearing the crowd cheer for him to finally receive it. Perhaps Shakespeare assigns Casca prose here because of the "low" subject matter Casca speaks about.

The most significant instance of prose in *Julius Caesar,* however, concerns the noble character Brutus. When Brutus addresses the Roman public in the Forum, after the murder of Caesar (3.2), he does so in prose; his speech during this scene provides a striking contrast to Antony the rhetorician's, whose speech is in verse. In sum, Shakespeare puts Brutus at a disadvantage by only assigning him prose at this key point in the play: Caesar's death, an event of great importance, deserves to be spoken about in the more complicated form of verse.

EXTRACTS OF CLASSIC CRITICISM

Samuel Johnson (1709–1784) [Excerpted from *Notes on Shakespeare's Plays* (1768). Johnson's writings remain some of the most influential of all Shakespearean criticism. Johnson's comments on *Julius Caesar* are minimal and focus on the scene where Brutus and Cassius make peace before the battle with Antony and Octavius. Johnson draws attention to the "Roman-ness" of the play, meaning that characters very often do not show emotion but remain stoic and reserved.]

Of this tragedy many particular passages deserve regard, and the contention and reconcilement of Brutus and Cassius is universally celebrated; but I have never been strongly agitated in perusing it, and think it somewhat cold and unaffecting, compared with some other of Shakespeare's plays; his adherence to the real story, and to Roman manners, seems to have impeded the natural vigour of his genius.

William Hazlitt (1778–1830) [Excerpted from *Characters of Shakespear's Plays* (1817). Hazlitt's groundbreaking analysis at the start of the 19th century influenced critics and readers of Shakespeare in his era and beyond.]

Shakespear's *Julius Caesar* is not equal as a whole, to either of his plays taken from the Roman history. It is inferior in interest to *Coriolanus,* and both in interest and power to *Antony and Cleopatra*. It however abounds with in admirable and affecting passages, and is remarkable for the profound knowledge of character, in which Shakespear could scarcely fail. If there is any exception to this remark, it is in the hero of the piece himself. We do not much admire the representation here given of Julius Caesar, nor do we think it answers the portrait of him given in his Commentaries. He makes several vapouring and rather pedantic speeches, and does nothing. Indeed, he has nothing to do. So far, the fault of the character is the fault of the plot.

The sprit with which the poet has entered at once into the manners of the common people, and the jealousies and heart-burnings of the different factions, is shewn in the first scene, where Flavius and Marullus, tribunes of the people, and some citizens of Rome, appear on the stage.

FLAVIUS. Thou art a cobbler, art thou?

COBBLER. Truly, Sir, *all* that I live by is the *awl;* I meddle with no tradesman's matters, nor woman's matters, but *with-al,* I am indeed, Sir, a surgeon to old shoes; when they are in great danger, I recover then.

FLAVIUS. But wherefore art not in thy shop to-day? Why dost thou lead these men about the streets?

COBBLER. Truly, Sir, to wear out their shoes, to get myself into more work. But indeed, Sir, we make holiday to see Caesar, and rejoice in his triumph.

To this specimen of quaint low humour immediately follows that unexpected and animated burst of indignant eloquence, put into the mouth of angry tribunes.

MARULLUS. Wherefore rejoice!—
What conquest brings he home?
What tributaries follow him to Rome,
To grace in captive-bonds his chariot
wheels?
Of you hard hearts, you cruel men of
Rome!
Knew you not Pompey? . . .

The well-known dialogue between Brutus and Cassius, in which the latter breaks the design of the conspiracy to the former, and partly gains him over to it, is a noble piece of high-minded declamation. Cassius's insisting of the pretended effeminacy of Caesar's character, and his description of their swimming across the Tiber together, "once upon a raw and gusty day," are among the finest strokes in it. But perhaps the whole is not equal to the short scene which follows, when Caesar enters with his train:

BRUTUS. The games are done, and
Caesar is returning.

CASSIUS. As they pass by, pluck Casca
by the sleeve,
And he will, after his sour fashion, tell you
What has proceeded worthy note today.

BRUTUS. I will do so, but look you,
Cassius—
The angry spot doth glow on Caesar's
brow,
And all the rest look like a chidden train.

Calpurnia's cheek is pale; and Cicero
Looks with such ferret and fiery eyes,
As we have seen him in the Capitol,
Being crost in conference by some
    senators.

CASSIUS. Casca will tell us what the
    matter is.

CAESAR. Antonius—

ANTONY. Caesar?

CAESAR. Let me have men about me
    that are fat,
Sleek-headed men, and such as sleep
    a-nights:
Yon Cassius has a lean and hungry look,
He thinks too much; such men are
    dangerous.

ANTONY. Fear him not, Caesar, he's
    not dangerous:
He is a noble Roman, and well given.

CAESAR. Would he were fatter; but I
    fear him not:
Yet if my name were liable to fear,
I do not know the man I should avoid
So soon as that spare Cassius. He reads
    much;
He is a great observer; and he looks
Quite through the deeds of men. He
    loves no plays,
As thou dost, Antony; he hears no music:
Seldom he smiles, and smiles in such a
    sort,
As if he mock'd himself, and scorn'd his
    spirit.
That could be mov'd to smile at any
    thing.
Such men as he be never at heart's ease,
Whilst they behold a greater than
    themselves;
And therefore are they dangerous.

I rather tell thee what is to be fear'd
Than what I fear; for always I am Caesar.
Come on my right hand, for this ear is
    deaf,
And tell me truly what thou think'st of
    him.

We know hardly any passage more expressive of the genius of Shakespear than this. It is as if he had been actually present, had known the different characters and what they thought of one another, and had taken down what he heard and saw, their looks, words, and gestures, just as they appeared.

The character of Mark Antony is farther speculated upon where the conspirators deliberate whether he shall fall with Caesar. Brutus is against it—

And for Mark Antony, think not of him;
For he can do no more than Caesar's arm,
When Caesar's head is cut off.

CASSIUS. Yet I do fear him:
For in th' ingrafted love he bears to Caesar—

BRUTUS. Alas, good Cassius, do not
    think of him:
If he love Caesar, all that he can do
Is to himself, take thought, and die for
    Caesar:
And that were much, he should; for he
    is giv'n
To sports, to wildness, and much
    company.

TREBONIUS. There is no fear in him;
    let him not die:
For he will live, and laugh at this hereafter.

They were in the wrong; and Cassius was right. The honest manliness of Brutus is however sufficient to find out the unfitness of Cicero to be included in their enterprize, from his affected egotism and literary vanity.

Antony kneels over Caesar's body and promises vengeance in Act III, Scene I of *Julius Caesar*. Print from the Boydell Shakespeare Gallery project *(Painting by Richard Westall; engraving by J. Parker)*

erate their own country fails from the generous temper and over-weening confidence of Brutus in the goodness of their cause and the assistance of others. Thus it has always been. Those who mean well themselves think well of others, and fall a prey to their security. That humanity and honesty which dispose men to resist injustice and tyranny render them unfit to cope with the cunning power of those who are opposed to them. The friends of liberty trust to the professions of others, because they are themselves sincere, and endeavour to reconcile the public good with the least possible hurt to its enemies, who have no regard to any thing but their own unprincipled ends, and stick at nothing to accomplish them. Cassius was better cut out for a conspirator. His heart prompted his head. His watchful jealousy made him fear the worst that might happen, and his irritability of temper added to his inveteracy of purpose, and sharpened his patriotism. The mixed nature of his motives made him fitter to contend with bad men. The voices are never so well employed as in combating with one another. Tyranny and servility are to be dealt with after their own fashion: otherwise, they will triumph over those who spare them, and finally pronounce their funeral panegyric, as Antony did of Brutus.

> O name him not: let us not break with
>   him;
> For he will never follow anything,
> That other men begin.

His skepticism as to prodigies and his moralising on the weather—"This disturbed shy is not to walk in" are in the same spirit of refined imbecility.

Shakespear has in this play and elsewhere shewn the same penetration into political character and the springs of public events as into those of every-day life. For instance, the whole design of the conspirators to lib-

> All of the conspirators, save only he,
> Did that they did in envy of great
>   Caesar:
> He only in a general honest thought
> And common good to all, made one of
>   them.

The quarrel between Brutus and Cassius is managed in masterly way. The dramatic fluctuation of passion, the calmness of Brutus, the heat of Cassius, are admirably described; and the exclamation of Cassius on hearing of the death of Portia, which he does not learn till after their reconciliation, "How 'scaped I killing when I crost you so?" gives double force to all that has gone before. The scene between Brutus and Portia, where she endeavours to extort the secret of the conspiracy from him, is conceived in the most heroical spirit, and the burst of tenderness in Brutus—

> You are my true and honourable wife;
> As dear to me as are the ruddy drops
> That visit my sad heart—

is justified by her whole behaviour. Portia's breathless impatience to learn the event of the conspiracy, in the dialogue with Lucius, is full of passion. The interest which Portia takes in Brutus and that which Calpurnia takes in the fate of Caesar are discriminated with the nicest precision. Mark Antony's speech over the dead body of Caesar has been justly admired for the mixture of pathos and artifice in it: that of Brutus certainly is not so good.

The entrance of the conspirators to the house of Brutus at midnight is rendered very impressive. In the midst of this scene, we meet with one of those careless and natural digressions which occur so frequently and beautifully in Shakespeare. After Cassius has introduced his friends one by one, Brutus says—

> They are all welcome,
> What watchful cares do interpose
>   themselves
> Betwixt your eyes and night?

> CASSIUS. Shall I entreat a word? *[They whisper.]*

> DECIUS. Here lies the east: doth not the day break here?

> CASCA. No.

CINNA. O pardon, Sir, it doth; and yon grey lines
That fret the clouds, are messengers of day.

CASCA. You shall confess, that you are both deceiv'd:
Here, as I point my sword, the sun arises,
Which is a great way growing on the south,
Weighing the youthful season of the year.
Some two months hence, up higher toward the north
He first presents his fire, and the high east
Stands as the Capitol, directly here.

We cannot help thinking this graceful familiarity better than all the fustian in the world.—The truth of history in *Julius Caesar* is very ably worked up with dramatic effect. The councils of generals, the doubtful turns of battles, are represented to the life. The death of Brutus is worthy of him—it has the dignity of the Roman senator with the firmness of the Stoic philosopher. But what is perhaps better than either, is the little incident of his boy, Lucius, falling asleep over his instrument, as his is playing to his master in his tent, the night before the battle. Nature has played him the same forgetful trick once before on the night of the conspiracy. The humanity of Brutus is the same on both occasions.

> It is no matter:
> Enjoy the honey-heavy dew of slumber.
> Thou hast no figures nor no fantasies,
> Which busy care draws in the brains of men.
> Therefore thou sleep'st so sound.

Samuel Taylor Coleridge (1772–1834) [Excerpted from *Lectures and Notes on Shakespeare and Other Dramatists* (1818). The famous poet

Coleridge came to be known as one of Shakespeare's defenders, praising the Bard's work while encouraging others to dismiss the conceited and self-righteous critics of the 18th-century who, in some cases (like that of Alexander Pope) thought they could revise Shakespeare's works for the better.]

The speeches of Flavius and Marullus are in blank verse. Wherever regular metre can be rendered truly imitative of character, passion, or personal rank, Shakespeare seldom, if ever, neglects it. . . . I say regular metre: for even the prose has in the highest and lowest dramatic personage, a Cobbler or a Hamlet, a rhythm so felicitous and severally appropriate, as to be a virtual metre. . . .

[Brutus's speech in Act 2, Scene 1, when Brutus debates about killing Caesar, and decides to do so because Caesar being crowned might "change his [Caesar's] nature"] is singular—at least, I do not at present see into Shakespeare's motive, his rationale, or in what point of view he meant Brutus' character to appear. For surely— (this I mean is what I say to myself, with my present quantum of insight, only modified by my experience in how many instances I have ripened into a perception of beauties, where I had before descried faults;) surely nothing can seem more discordant with our historical preconceptions of Brutus, or more lowering to the intellect of the Stoico-Platonic tyrannicide, than the tenets here attributed to him—to him, the stern Roman republican; namely, that he would have no objection to a king, or to Caesar, a monarch in Rome, would Caesar but be as good a monarch as he now seems disposed to be! How, too, could Brutus say that he found no personal cause, none in Caesar's past conduct as a man? Had he not passed the Rubicon? Had he not entered Rome as a conqueror? Had he not placed his Gauls in the Senate? Shakespeare, it may be said, has not brought these things forward. True— and this is just the ground of my perplexity. What character did Shakespeare mean his Brutus to be?

I know no part of Shakespeare that more impresses on me the belief of his genius being superhuman, than this scene between Brutus and Cassius. In the Gnostic heresy, it might have been credited with less absurdity than most of their dogmas, that the Supreme had employed him to create, previously to his function of representing, characters.

George Bernard Shaw (1856–1950)
[Excerpted from Shaw's essay "Better than Shakespear?" (1898) and a piece he wrote for the *Saturday Review* (1898). The great playwright Shaw, famous for his disdain for Shakespeare and the Renaissance, critiqued the Bard's canon in various forms, whether in scathing reviews of productions he had seen or essays on the plays. Shaw coined the term *Bardolatry,* used to refer to those who argued that Shakespeare was the greatest writer in the English language. His observations about *Julius Caesar* are particularly scathing.]

[From "Better than Shakespear?"] The truce with Shakespear is over. It was only possibly whilst Hamlet was on the stage. Hamlet is the tragedy of private life—nay, of individual bachelor-poet life. It belongs to a detached residence, a select library, an exclusive circle, to no occupation, to fathomless boredom, to impenitent mugwumpism, to the illusion that the futility of these things is the futility of existence, and its contemplation philosophy: in short, to the dream-fed gentlemanism of the age which Shakespear inaugurated in English literature: the age, that is, of the rising middle class bringing into power ideas taught it by its servants in the kitchen, and its fathers in the shop—ideas now happily passing away as the onslaught of modern democracy offers to the kitchen-taught and home-bred the alternative of achieving a real superiority or going ignominiously under in the class conflict.

It is when we turn to *Julius Caesar,* the most splendidly written political melodrama we possess, that we realize the apparently immortal author of *Hamlet* as a man, not for all time, but for an age only, and that, too, in all solidly wise and heroic aspects, the most despicable of all the ages in our history. It is impossible for even the most judicially minded critic to look without revulsion of indignant contempt at this travestying of a great man [Caesar] as a silly braggart, whilst the pitiful gang of mischief-makers who destroyed him are lauded statesmen and patriots. There is not a single sentence uttered by Shakespear's Julius Caesar that is, I will not say worthy of him, but even worthy of a Tammany boss. Brutus is nothing but a familiar type of English suburban preacher: politically he would hardly impress the Thames Conservancy Board. Cassius is a vehemently assertive nonentity. It is only when we come to Antony, unctuous voluptuary and self-seeking sentimental demagogue, that we find Shakespear in his depth; and in his depth, of course, he is superlative. Regarded as a crafty stage job, the play is a triumph: rhetoric, claptrap, effective gushes of emotion, all devices of the popular playwright, are employed with a profusion of power that almost breaks their backs. No doubt there are slips and slovenliness of the kind that careful revisers eliminate; but they count for so little in the mass of accomplishment that it is safe to say that the dramatist's art can be carried no further on that plane. If [Johann von] Goethe, who understood Caesar and the significance of his death— "the most senseless of deeds" he called it—

had treated the subject, his conception of it would have been as superior to Shakespear's as St. John's Gospel is to the Police News; but his treatment could not have been more magnificently successful. As far as sonority, imagery, wit, humor, energy of imagination, power over language, and a whimsically keen eye for idiosyncrasies can make a dramatist, Shakespear was the king of dramatists. Unfortunately, a man may have them all, and yet conceive high affairs of state exactly as Simon Tappertit did. In one of the scenes in *Julius Caesar* a conceited poet bursts into the tent of Brutus and Cassius, and exhorts them not to quarrel with one another. If Shakespear had been able to present his play to the ghost of the great Julius, he would probably have had much the same reception. He certainly would have deserved it.

[From the February 12, 1898, edition of the *Saturday Review.*] A fortnight ago I ventured to point out in these columns that Julius Caesar in Shakespear's play says nothing worthy, or even nearly worthy, of Julius Caesar. The number of humbugs who have pretended to be shocked by this absolutely incontrovertible remark has lowered my opinion of the human race. There are only two dignified courses open to those who disagree with me. One is to suffer in silence. The other, obviously, is to quote the passage which, in the opinion of the objectors, *is* worthy of Julius Caesar. The latter course, however, would involve reading the play; and they would almost as soon think of reading the Bible. Besides, it would be a waste of time; for since Shakespear is accepted as the standard of first-rate excellence, an adverse criticism of him need only be quoted to be accepted as damning evidence against itself. I do not mention this by way of complaint: if these gentlemen saw eye to eye with me they would all be G.B.S.'s; and a press written entirely in my style would be, like an exclusively Shakespearean municipal theatre, a little too much of a good thing. I merely wish to shew how the difficulty about guaranteeing the future good conduct of an endowed theatre can always be got over simply by mentioning our William's name. Assure the public that you will play Shakespear and that you will not play Ibsen, and your endowment fund will be second in respectability only to the restoration fund of a cathedral.

A. C. Bradley (1851–1935) [Excerpted from *Shakespearean Tragedy* (1904), Bradley's seminal work. Perhaps the greatest Shakespearean critic of his time, Bradley's theories about Shakespeare's method of composing his plays helped shape the course of 20th-century Shakespeare criticism.]

Shakespearean tragedy . . . is pre-eminently the story of one person, the "hero," or at most of two, the "hero" and the "heroine." . . . *Julius Caesar* is not an exception to this rule. Caesar, whose murder comes in the Third Act, is in a sense the dominating figure in the story, but Brutus is the "hero." . . .

Tragedy with Shakespeare is concerned always with persons of "high degree"; often with kings or princes; if not, with leaders in the state like Coriolanus, Brutus, and Antony. . . .

There is an outward conflict on persons and groups, there is also a conflict of forces in the hero's soul; and even in *Julius Caesar* and *Macbeth* the interest of the former can hardly be said to exceed the latter. . . .

Julius Caesar and *Coriolanus* [open] with a crowd in commotion: and when this excitement has had its effect on the audience, there follow quiet speeches, in which the cause of the excitement, and so a great part of the situation, are disclosed. . . . In the first scene of *Julius Caesar* and of *Coriolanus* those qualities of the crowd are vividly

shown which render hopeless the enterprise of the one hero and wreck the ambition of the other. . . .

When we are immersed in a tragedy, we feel towards dispositions, actions, and persons such emotions as attraction and repulsion, pity, wonder, fear, horror, perhaps hatred; but we do not *judge*. This is a point of view which emerges only when, in reading a play, we slip, by our own fault of the dramatist's, from the tragic position, or when, in thinking about the play afterwards, we fall back on our everyday legal and moral notions. But tragedy does not belong, any more than religion belongs, to the sphere of these notions; neither does the imaginative attitude in presence of it. While we are in its world we watch what is, seeing that so it happened and must have happened, feeling that it is piteous, dreadful, awful, mysterious, but neither passing sentence on the agents, nor asking whether the behaviours of the ultimate power towards them is just. And, therefore, the use of such language in attempts to render our imaginative experience in terms of understanding is, to say the least, full of danger. . . .

It is dangerous, I think, in reference to all really good tragedies, but I am dealing here only with Shakespeare's. In not a few Greek tragedies it is almost inevitable that we should think of justice and retribution, not only because the *dramatis personae* often speak of them, but also because there is something casuistical about the tragic problem itself. The poet treats the story in such a way that the question, Is the hero doing right or wrong? is almost forced upon us. But this is not so with Shakespeare. *Julius Caesar* is probably the only one of his tragedies in which the question suggests itself to us, and this is one of the reasons why that play has something of a classic air. Even here, if we ask the question, we have no doubt at all about the answer.

MODERN CRITICISM AND CRITICAL CONTROVERSIES

Modern critics, like those of the past, have focused on everything from the purpose of the play to its masterly rhetoric and, of course, its characters. Nuttall, in *Shakespeare the Thinker,* claims that the play "is about political ideology" (171). Nuttall explains that since the play takes place in a world far from Shakespeare's own, the piece becomes ripe for experimentation with politics: "The cultural separateness of the Roman world, its independence of Christianity, makes it a perfect laboratory for free-ranging political hypothesis. It may not be as far away in space as Thomas More's island of Utopia (the first such laboratory), but it is actually further off in time" (171). Yet, in *Shakespeare after All,* Garber notes that even though Shakespeare's focus in *Julius Caesar* is the ancient Roman world, the play abounds with themes that resonated with Shakespeare's audience, as well as audiences of today, including "the nature of kingship, the relationship of the public to the private self, the limits of reason, and the necessity of coming to terms with the irrational—the world beyond reason—as it presents itself in omens and portents, soothsayers and signs" (410).

Nuttall and Garber also focus on Shakespeare's use of rhetoric in *Julius Caesar.* Nuttall argues that while the play's focus remains on politics, it also concerns "rhetoric, the art of persuasion" (185). Both critics analyze Mark Antony and his oratory at the Forum after Caesar's death. Garber calls Antony a "master orator, a skillful manipulator of crowds" (421), and Nuttall asserts that "*Julius Caesar* contains the greatest oration in the English language, delivered by Mark Antony over the still-bleeding body of Caesar. Shakespeare is writing at the height of his powers" (186). Conversely, Garber argues that while Antony's speech is effective, the style is far from that of Shakespeare's typical elevated poetic style: Antony's speech, she says, "is designed to show Antony's facility in demagoguery. It is easy to memorize, easy to hear and follow, the perfect kind of language to reach and move the shallow masses" (421). Garber adds that the rhythm of Antony's speech makes it a popular choice for teachers when asking their students to memorize excerpts of Shakespeare.

Although some readers question the importance of the wives Calpurnia and Portia in the play, Harold Goddard, in *The Meaning of Shakespeare,* attests to their importance. He argues that Portia "is one of the first of a number of Shakespearean heroines who have brief roles of supreme importance," but emphasizes Calpurnia's importance as well with the following observation: "These women through their dreams and intuitions draw from deeper springs of wisdom than any to which their husbands have access. And Caesar because of his vanity and ambition, Brutus because of a strain of cold rationalism that runs through his nature, are in peculiar need of the insight of their wives" (313).

Goddard also reflects on Shakespeare's depiction of Caesar: "The unflattering character of the portrait Shakespeare draws of Julius Caesar is notorious. The name and spirit of Caesar ring as imperially through the play as they do through history. But the trembling epileptic the poet depicts seems like a parody of the figure that shook the ancient world" (309). Goddard's comments hearken back to the observations of those studying Shakespeare's source material and how Shakespeare emphasizes Caesar's physical ailments, insinuating that these, combined with his hubris, lead to his destruction.

Modern criticism focuses on Marcus Brutus more than any other character of the play. Garber writes: "The play is called *Julius Caesar,* but we might be justified in wondering why it is not called *Brutus*" (411). Bloom, in *Shakespeare: The Invention of the Human,* observes that "Brutus is such a puzzle that he is wonderfully interesting, to Shakespeare and to us" (112). Goddard explores the puzzle Bloom mentions and reflects on the two schools of thought concerning Brutus: Some believe he is "one of the most noble and lovable figures the poet ever created," while other readers "cannot conceal their scorn for him. He was a fool, they say, an egotist, an unconscionable prig. If this be true, it is a bit odd that almost everyone in the play seems to think highly of him" (310). Whether he is beloved or scorned, readers cannot deny Brutus's deep love for his wife, Portia, which makes Brutus very human and pitiable. Nuttall acknowledges that the expectations in Brutus's Rome would suggest that he keep his intimate feelings of loss to himself, as men must always appear strong and composed in public. Brutus's not sharing his feelings about Portia's death seems significant to Nuttall: "Brutus evidently loved Portia. His love for his wife and his grief at her death, "affections" Brutus is proud to be able to repress, actually redeem him as a human being. . . . The Shakespeare who can uncover so much frailty and continue to perceive goodness, the Shakespeare behind the plays, is a figure of immense, intelligent charity" (185).

Bloom, Nuttall, and Goddard pay specific attention to what the character of Brutus symbolizes, offering arguments ranging from patriotism and Stoicism to the average person. Bloom asserts that Brutus represents the ultimate patriot, but also says that this patriotism is itself a kind of flaw, since "he overidentifies himself with Rome, just as Caesar does" (109). If Brutus represents Roman patriotism, he could also easily symbolize Roman beliefs, such as that of Stoicism, a philosophy that, Nuttall believes, Shakespeare views as "a philosophy pathologically subject to degeneration and detachment" (184). Reflecting again on Brutus's refusal to share his grief at losing his wife, Nuttall states: "We begin to see that the Roman world as a whole is a place of malfunctioning emotion. In this society love is an ill-nourished, undeveloped thing . . . crushed by Stoic repression" (188).

Goddard argues that, more than anything else, Brutus represents the average person. Goddard calls Brutus "an exceptional man. Yet Brutus is an Everyman in the sense that every man is Brutus at some hour of his life. Whoever is aware of the disparity between what he would be and what the world seems bent on making him is a Brutus in the general sense" (312). Goddard adds that one reason why the character of Brutus appeals to so many readers is because of his willingness to

Brutus and the ghost of Caesar in an 1802 depiction of Act IV, Scene 3 of *Julius Caesar (Painting by Richard Westall; engraving by Edward Scriven)*

address injustice: "More specifically, Brutus is the man of sensitive nature who, outraged by cruelty and tyranny around him, sadly and reluctantly concludes that there is no way to oppose the world but with the world's weapons, that fire must drive out fire and force force" (312). The courageous Brutus, with the good of his fellow Romans at heart, resonates with readers and makes him a favorite subject of analysis for critics of all eras.

THE PLAY TODAY

Although *Julius Caesar* focuses on events that occurred more than two millennia ago, the play remains relevant and engaging today. As Bloom argues in *Shakespeare: The Invention of the Human,*

"Caesar is the grandest figure Shakespeare ever will represent, the person of most permanent historical importance" (106). Readers and viewers of this play will naturally gain insight into one of the most important events in world history, but complementing this history lesson is Shakespeare's analysis of themes relevant to all readers, including political upheaval, rebellion, jealousy, guilt, and ambition. Recent critics have examined all these traditional themes as well as more contemporary preoccupations, such as the play's depiction of masculinity and critique of social order

Recent notable theater performances have featured casts with some of the best Shakespearean actors of all time and even blockbuster movie stars. For instance, in 1977, *Julius Caesar* was performed at the Royal National Theatre, directed by John Schlesinger. In this production, one of the most celebrated Shakespearean actors of all time, Sir John Gielgud, played the title role in his last stage performance as one of Shakespeare's characters. In 2005, critics and viewers hotly anticipated the New York production of *Julius Caesar* in which Denzel Washington starred as Brutus. Although Washington's magic helped bring success to one of his earlier appearances in a Shakespearean play on film (*Much Ado About Nothing*), his talents and charm could not stave off poor reviews.

Marlon Brando playing the role of Mark Antony in Joseph Mankiewicz's 1953 production of *Julius Caesar* serves as the most famous contemporary image associated with Shakespeare's tragedy. Brando's robust and polished physique seemed to typify Caesar's Rome, where agile men like Brando's Antony, so unlike the "fat men" with which Caesar desired to surround himself, seek control, manipulate the common people, and always remain ready for war. Interestingly, Mankiewicz also directed *Cleopatra*, the celebrated version of the *Antony and Cleopatra* story (starring Elizabeth Taylor, Richard Burton, and Rex Harrison). In a 1970 film version of *Julius Caesar*, Charlton Heston played Mark Antony, Jason Robards played Brutus, and John Gielgud played Caesar.

FIVE TOPICS FOR DISCUSSION AND WRITING

1. **Ambition:** Antony accuses Brutus of being ambitious. While this accusation may ring true, discuss whether Antony is just as ambitious as Brutus. Do all the main characters suffer from being ambitious? Does Shakespeare suggest that ambition is a negative quality only?

2. **Genre:** Since the first publication of Shakespeare's collected plays in 1623, in the First Folio, *Julius Caesar* (known in the First Folio as *The Life and Death of Julius Caesar*) has been categorized as a tragedy. Why would this play have been classified under the genre of "tragedy" rather than "history," especially considering that the play focuses on one of world history's most important events?

3. **Shakespeare and his sources:** Shakespeare's primary source material for *Julius Caesar* was Plutarch's *The Lives of the Noble Grecians and Romans*, as translated by North. Shakespeare revises or adds to Plutarch's details about Caesar (and others). One such example is how Shakespeare emphasizes Caesar's physical disabilities and ailments, including the commander being partly deaf (see Act I, Scene 2) and how he suffers from epilepsy. Analyze the significance of Shakespeare's emphasizing these qualities in Caesar.

4. **Rhetoric:** The most valuable tool Antony possesses—his mastery of rhetoric—allows him to sway the crowd grieving over Caesar's corpse. Compare the speech Antony gives after Caesar's death to Brutus's, and discuss why Antony's speech remains the more moving and convincing of the two.

5. **Supernatural elements and superstition:** *Julius Caesar* resounds with references to the supernatural and superstitious characters, ranging from Calpurnia's dream about Caesar's death to the Soothsayer's ominous warning. Who believes in omens, and who disregards them? Examine who heeds superstition and

who discards it. What patterns do you recognize, especially about men and women in the play? What is significant about these patterns?

Bibliography

Asimov, Isaac. *Asimov's Guide to Shakespeare.* New York: Wings Books, 1970.

Bloom, Harold. *Shakespeare: The Invention of the Human.* New York: Riverhead Books, 1998.

———. *William Shakespeare: The Tragedies.* New York: Chelsea House, 1985.

Bloom, Harold, ed. *William Shakespeare's* Julius Caesar. New York: Chelsea House, 1988.

Bradley, A. C. *Shakespearean Tragedy.* 3rd ed. New York: St. Martin's Press, 1992.

Bullough, Geoffrey. *Narrative and Dramatic Sources of Shakespeare,* Vol. 5: *The Roman Plays.* London: Routledge, 1965.

Cantor, Paul A. *Shakespeare's Rome: Republic and Empire.* Ithaca, N.Y.: Cornell University Press, 1976.

Charney, Maurice. *Shakespeare's Roman Plays: The Function of Imagery in the Drama.* Cambridge, Mass.: Harvard University Press, 1961.

Clough, Arthur Hugh, ed. *Plutarch: The Lives of the Noble Grecians and Romans.* New York: Modern Library, 1932.

Coleridge, Samuel Taylor. *Lectures and Notes on Shakespeare and Other Dramatists.* Oxford: Oxford University Press, 1931.

Crystal, David, and Ben Crystal. *The Shakespeare Miscellany.* Woodstock, N.Y.: Overlook Books, 2005.

Garber, Marjorie. *Shakespeare after All.* New York: Pantheon Books, 2004.

Goddard, Harold C. *The Meaning of Shakespeare.* Chicago: University of Chicago Press, 1951.

Harbage, Alfred. *As They Liked It: A Study of Shakespeare's Moral Artistry.* New York: Harper, 1947.

Hazlitt, William. *The Characters of Shakespear's Plays.* London: Oxford University Press, 1947.

Johnson, Samuel. *Johnson on Shakespeare.* Oxford: Oxford University Press, 1908.

Kahn, Coppélia. *Roman Shakespeare: Warriors, Wounds, and Women.* London: Routledge, 1997.

Knight, George Wilson. *The Imperial Theme: Further Interpretations of Shakespeare's Tragedies, Including the Roman Plays.* London: Oxford University Press, 1931.

Kujawmíska-Courtney, Krystyna. *The Interpretation of the Time: The Dramaturgy of Shakespeare's Roman Plays.* Victoria, Canada: English Literary Studies, 1993.

Leggatt, Alexander. *Shakespeare's Political Drama: The History of the Roman Plays.* London: Routledge, 1988.

LoMonico, Michael. *The Shakespeare Book of Lists.* Franklin Lakes, N.J.: New Page Books, 2001.

MacCallum, M. W. *Shakespeare's Roman Plays and Their Background.* London: Macmillan & Co., 1925.

McAlindon, Thomas. *Shakespeare's Tragic Cosmos.* Cambridge: Cambridge University Press, 1991.

Muir, Kenneth. *The Sources of Shakespeare's Plays.* New Haven, Conn.: Yale University Press, 1978.

Nuttall, A. D. *Shakespeare the Thinker.* New Haven, Conn.: Yale University Press, 2007.

Schanzer, Ernest. *The Problem Plays of Shakespeare: A Study of* Julius Caesar, Measure for Measure, *and* Antony and Cleopatra. New York: Schocken, 1963.

Shaw, Bernard. *Shaw on Shakespeare: An Anthology of Bernard Shaw's Writings of the Plays and Production of Shakespeare.* Edited by Edwin Wilson. Freeport, N.Y.: E. P. Dutton & Co., 1961.

Spurgeon, Caroline. *Shakespeare's Imagery and What It Tells Us.* Cambridge: Cambridge University Press, 1935.

Thomas, Vivian. *Shakespeare's Roman Worlds.* London: Routledge, 1989.

Traversi, Derek. *Shakespeare: The Roman Plays.* Stanford, Calif.: Stanford University Press, 1963.

FILM AND VIDEO PRODUCTIONS

Bradley, David, dir. *Julius Caesar.* With Harold Tasker and Charlton Heston. Commonwealth United Entertainment, 1949.

Burge, Stuart, dir. *Julius Caesar*. With Charlton Heston, Jason Robards, and John Gielgud. Commonwealth United Entertainment, 1970.

Mankiewicz, Joseph L., dir. *Julius Caesar*. With James Mason, John Gielgud, and Marlon Brando. MGM, 1953.

Smedley, Ron, dir. *Heil Caesar*. With Anthony Bate, John Stride, and Frank Middlemass. BBC, 1974.

Wise, Herbert, dir. *Julius Caesar*. With Richard Pasco, Charles Gray, and Keith Michell. BBC, 1979.

—Karley K. Adney

King John

INTRODUCTION

King John is one of Shakespeare's lesser-known plays, but it continues to hold interest for the modern reader and playgoer. It is generally regarded as superior to Shakespeare's early *Henry VI* plays, and in particular, the character of the Bastard seems to mark an important advance in Shakespeare's art. The melodramatic plot—including a manipulative mother, corrupt kings, a papal conspiracy, and the blinding of a child with red-hot irons—makes for compelling theater. Unlike Shakespeare's nine other histories, which dramatize the deeds of kings, queens, and princes that lead to the founding of the Tudor dynasty and the reign of Queen Elizabeth, *King John* portrays events from more than 300 years before Elizabeth's birth. This distance in time gives Shakespeare the liberty to shape the play to his own ends. He omits two of the most famous subjects associated with King John: the adventures of Robin Hood and the signing of Magna Carta, the first document to grant legal rights to free men. Instead, Shakespeare explores questions of loyalty, legitimacy, succession, and fitness to rule.

The historical King John was the fifth son and the youngest of eight children of the powerful Henry II and Eleanor of Aquitaine. Even in the 12th century, it would have been hard to imagine that the fifth son of a king would inherit the crown; however, Henry II's first, second, and fourth sons died before the king did, so the crown passed to his third son, Richard I (the Lionheart). Richard died without a legitimate son, and his will named his brother John as the next king of England. This would have been the acceptable order of succession except that Henry II's fourth son, Geoffrey, had a son; Arthur, as Henry II's grandson by a son closer to the throne, should have become king. But, Arthur was only 12 years old when Richard died. By emphasizing that England had two possible kings, Shakespeare creates an ideal situation for political intrigue.

Shakespeare's audiences thrived on these soap opera–like tangles of royal succession. Queen Elizabeth herself had been accused of being illegitimate and became queen through her father Henry VIII's will only after the death of her younger half brother and older half sister. While questions of succession and legitimacy were appealing and relevant, on their own they did not make lively theater. Some kind of action was needed. As noted, Shakespeare for some reason preferred not to include reference to Magna Carta or Robin Hood, two of the most dramatic subjects associated with King John. Instead, he altered the historical record to squeeze about 15 years' worth of wars with France and disputes with the pope into a three-hour play.

To help hold together this series of conflicts, Shakespeare did something he had never done before (or again) in a history play: He included a fictional character. Known as the Bastard, because he is the illegitimate son of Richard I, this unhistorical character gives up his fortune and property to join the English army in its war against France. Once in the wars, he rescues the queen Eleanor from capture and takes revenge on the Duke of Austria, who

A dying King John lies on his couch in the garden of Swineshead Abbey in this depiction of Act V, Scene 7 of the 1865 Drury Lane Theatre's production of *King John*.

killed his father. Not just an energetic fighter, the Bastard shows an often dark sense of humor, perhaps best displayed when he walks around holding the Duke of Austria's head, putting it down only when the day becomes too hot to carry it anymore.

The play's interest for modern readers lies not only in the vivid, sometimes gruesome events but also in the questions it raises about responsibility, loyalty, and self-interest. In some ways, King John is caught in a position he never imagined for himself. His brother declared him king, and he has the support of his mother and the English lords. But his nephew Arthur has a valid legal claim to the throne, and John must decide how to deal with this threat. To make matters worse, the king of France, Philip, who has his eye on some English territories, supports Arthur's claim. And the pope wants John to submit to his authority in naming bishops in England. John must confront these challenges and make choices about the right thing to do, but he has difficulty separating his own interests from those of England.

While John is the play's title character, Shakespeare places nearly all the major characters into situations where they must choose between doing what is best for themselves and what is best for the greater good. Watching these characters confront such choices again and again and seeing the consequences of their actions make *King John* a powerful play to watch or read. Kings, servants, illegitimate children, and the rest of us all must make choices, and making the right one is not always easy.

BACKGROUND

Of Shakespeare's 10 history plays, *King John* stands alone, dramatizing actions nearly 200 years earlier than the others. As such, understanding its characters and events and their Elizabethan contexts requires knowledge of the historical king John and how Shakespeare's audiences regarded him.

History plays, whether by Shakespeare or other writers, were extremely popular with Elizabethan audiences in the 1580s and 1590s. These plays tended to focus on kings and conflicts that, according E. M. W. Tillyard, consistently revealed a providential force at work in English history, inexorably leading up to the Elizabethan age, superior to previous eras. Other critics, including Lily B. Campbell, have argued that history plays were didactic, using past events to reflect specific Elizabethan political and social concerns. More recently, scholars have seen history plays as heterogeneous. Rather than possessing a unified Elizabethan ideology, the plays are uneven, containing moments that challenge dominant ideology and moments that support it.

The Historical King John

John ascended the throne under unusual circumstances. His predecessor and brother, Richard I, the Lionheart (1157–99), was a popular and dynamic king who ruled an empire that stretched from Ireland through much of western France. When Richard died, however, he had no legitimate children to inherit the empire, so in his will, Richard declared that his younger brother John would succeed him. At this time in England, this type of succession was not unusual, so, with the support of the English nobility, many of the continental lords, and of his mother, Eleanor of Aquitaine, John quickly consolidated his power as king. He had a rival, however, in his nephew Arthur, son of John's brother Geoffrey. As the son of John's older sibling, Arthur also could claim the right of succession and, indeed, attempted to have himself declared king of England. Arthur found support primarily from King Philip II of France and other French nobility. These men, however, had

their own motives, especially a desire to gain control over continental provinces controlled by the English. The French went to war with England, claiming to be fighting for Arthur. A series of battles fought over five years (1199–1203), interrupted by the marriage of Louis, the dauphin of France, and John's niece Blanche, failed to resolve the disputes. John captured the teenage Arthur, and (probably) had him killed, but the French began slowly capturing most of the English possessions they desired. Several years afterward, John's conflict with the pope over the appointment of the archbishop of Canterbury erupted. It was resolved some years later, when John submitted to the church. John died in 1216 of dysentery, while fighting the French invasion. His nine-year-old son succeeded him and became Henry III.

Shakespeare's *King John*

Shakespeare's *King John* appeared at a time when England had recently defeated the Spanish Armada (1588) and was occupied with threats from the Catholic Church and questions of legitimacy and succession. Shakespeare's play addresses these issues by shifting the historical record of John's ascension to the throne in several ways. He compresses events into a brief period, lowers Arthur's age, amplifies the contention over John's legitimacy, blames the loss of English territories on John's poor negotiation with the French, makes the pope a more active agent in the conflicts with France, and has a vengeful monk poison John. In addition to creating dramatic tension, these changes allowed Shakespeare's audiences to see parallels with their own times.

For Elizabethans, King John was best known for his resistance to the pope. Protestant propagandists had portrayed him as an early martyr to Catholic tyranny, fighting for English autonomy in the face of an over-reaching pontiff. At least two plays, John Bale's *Kynge Johan* (ca. 1540) and the anonymous *The Troublesome Raigne of John King of England* (1591), portray the Catholic Church as corrupt and devious and John as its victim. John was also seen as patriotically resisting foreign interference, and his fall is an example of the dangers of discord and

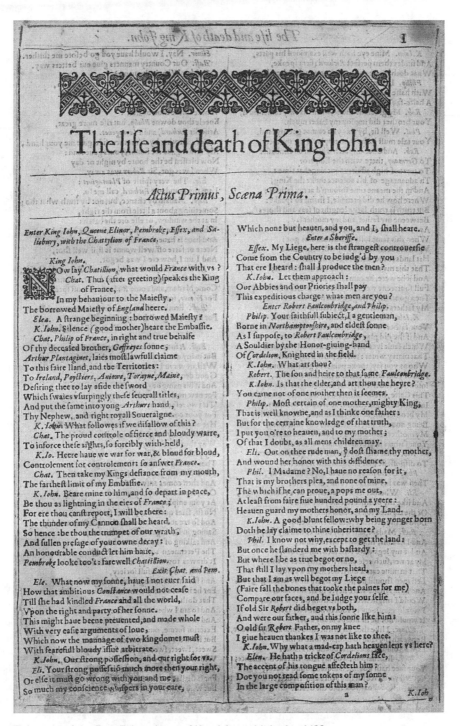

The life and death of King Iohn.

Actus Primus, Scæna Prima.

Enter King Iohn, Queene Elinor, Pembroke, Essex, and Salisbury, with the Chattylion of France.

King Iohn.

NOw say *Chatillion*, what would *France* with vs ?
　Chat. Thus (after greeting) speakes the King
　of France,
In my behauiour to the Maiesty,
The borrowed Maiesty of *England* heere.
　Elea. A strange beginning : borrowed Maiesty ?
　K. Iohn. Silence (good mother) heare the Embassie.
　Chat. Philip of France, in right and true behalfe
Of thy deceased brother, *Geffreyes* sonne,
Arthur Plantaginet, laies most lawfull claime
To this faire Iland, and the Territories :
To *Ireland, Poyctiers, Aniowe, Torayne, Maine,*
Desiring thee to lay aside the sword
Which swaies vsurpingly these seuerall titles,
And put the same into yong *Arthurs* hand,
Thy Nephew, and right royall Soueraigne.
　K. Iohn What followes if we disallow of this ?
　Chat. The proud controle of fierce and bloudy warre,
To inforce these rights, so forcibly with-held,
　K. Io. Heere haue we war for war, & bloud for bloud,
Controlement for controlement : so answer *France.*
　Chat. Then take my Kings defiance from my mouth,
The farthest limit of my Embassie.
　K. Iohn. Beare mine to him, and so depart in peace,
Be thou as lightning in the eies of *France* ;
For ere thou canst report, I will be there :
The thunder of my Cannon shall be heard.
So hence : be thou the trumpet of our wrath,
And sullen presage of your owne decay :
An honourable conduct let him haue,
Pembroke looke too't : farewell *Chatillion.*
　　　　　　　　　Exit. Chat. and Pem.
　Ele. What now my sonne, haue I not euer said
How that ambitious *Constance* would not cease
Till she had kindled *France* and all the world,
Vpon the right and party of her sonne.
This might haue beene preuented, and made whole
With very easie arguments of loue,
Which now the mannage of two kingdomes must
With fearefull bloudy issue arbitrate.
　K. Iohn. Our strong possession, and our right for vs.
　Eli. Your strong possessió much more then your right,
Or else it must go wrong with you and me,
So much my conscience whispers in your eare,

Which none but heauen, and you, and I, shall heare.
　　　　　　　　Enter a Sheriffe.
　Essex. My Liege, here is the strangest controuersie
Come from the Country to be iudg'd by you
That ere I heard : shall I produce the men ?
　K. Iohn. Let them approach :
Our Abbies and our Priories shall pay
This expeditious charge : what men are you ?
　　　　Enter Robert Faulconbridge, and Philip.
　Philip. Your faithfull subiect, I a gentleman,
Borne in *Northamptonshire*, and eldest sonne
As I suppose, to *Robert Faulconbridge*,
A Souldier by the Honor-giuing-hand
Of *Cordelion*, Knighted in the field.
　K. Iohn. What art thou ?
　Robert. The son and heire to that same *Faulconbridge.*
　K. Iohn. Is that the elder, and art thou the heyre ?
You came not of one mother then it seemes.
　Philp. Most certaine of one mother, mighty King,
That is well knowne, and as I thinke one father :
But for the certaine knowledge of that truth,
I put you o're to heauen, and to my mother ;
Of that I doubt, as all mens children may.
　Eli. Out on thee rude man, ŷ dost shame thy mother,
And wound her honor with this diffidence.
　Phil. I Madame ? No, I haue no reason for it,
That is my brothers plea, and none of mine,
The which if he can proue, a pops me out,
At least from faire fiue hundred pound a yeere :
Heauen guard my mothers honor, and my Land.
　K. Iohn. A good blunt fellow : why being yonger born
Doth he lay claime to thine inheritance ?
　Phil. I know not why, except to get the land :
But once he slanderd me with bastardy :
But where I be as true begot or no,
That still I lay vpon my mothers head,
But that I am as well begot my Liege
(Faire fall the bones that tooke the paines for me)
Compare our faces, and be Iudge your selfe
If old Sir *Robert* did beget vs both,
And were our father, and this sonne like him :
O old sir *Robert* Father, on my knee
I giue heauen thankes I was not like to thee.
　K. Iohn. Why what a mad-cap hath heauen lent vs here?
　Elen. He hath a tricke of *Cordelions* face,
The accent of his tongue affecteth him :
Doe you not read some tokens of my sonne
In the large composition of this man ?
　　　　　　　　　　　　　　　　　　K. Ioh

Title page of the First Folio edition of *King John,* published in 1623

infighting among the English. Shakespeare, however, tempers these elements, reducing the vilification of the Catholic Church and depicting John's personal flaws as the source of his troubles.

Legitimacy and succession were also of great interest in the 1590s because of the circumstances of Queen Elizabeth's rise to power in 1558 and her lengthy reign. The play suggests several similarities. Elizabeth had become queen via her father Henry VIII's will, although her cousin, Mary, Queen of Scots, daughter of Henry VIII's older sister, could make a legal claim to be queen of England. Furthermore, Elizabeth had been declared a bastard by her father and excommunicated by the pope. By the time the play was probably written, Elizabeth was in her 60s and, like Richard, had no children and would wait to name an heir until on her deathbed in 1603. In this context, Prince Henry's presence and the Bastard's speech at the play's end establish a reassuring sense of continuity. At the same time, it reminded playgoers that Elizabeth had not named an heir, and until she did, the matter of succession would be unresolved. As he often does, Shakespeare provides both causes for concern and moments of comfort but does not favor one over the other.

Shakespeare's Sources

One of Shakespeare's sources for *King John,* as with most of his history plays, was Raphael Holinshed's *The Chronicles of England, Scotland, and Ireland* (second edition, 1587). He also relied heavily on the 1591 play *The Troublesome Raigne of John* and the enormous work of Protestant propaganda, John Foxe's *Actes and Monuments* (1583). Extracts of these and other less important sources can be found in Geoffrey Bullough's *Narrative and Dramatic Sources of Shakespeare.*

Date and Text of the Play

The text we have of Shakespeare's play, *The Life and Death of King John,* first appears in the First Folio of 1623. Its date of composition and its sources are much more difficult to determine. Estimates for the play's composition range from 1590 to 1598,

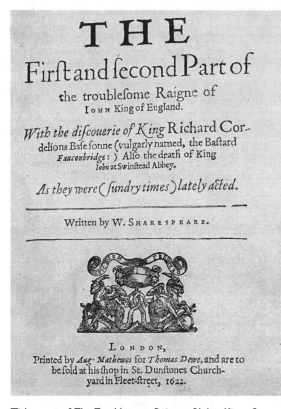

Title page of *The Troublesome Raigne of John, King of England,* a quarto published in 1591. Many scholars believe that Shakespeare adapted *King John* from this source.

all of which rely on supposition and guesswork using its similarities with other plays and possible references to a wide range of recent events. The majority of scholars favor the middle of the decade, 1595–96. One of the complicating factors is the existence of the anonymous play *The Troublesome Raigne of John, King of England,* printed in 1591. Though there are no exact correspondences in language, the events and the characters are so similar to Shakespeare's play that most experts agree that some relationship must exist between them. Until the 1950s, the majority of scholars believed that *King John* was a revision of *Troublesome Raigne.* A vocal minority, however, has argued the reverse, that someone used Shakespeare's play as a source for *Troublesome Raigne.* If true, this would require us to push back the date of *King John* to 1590, a difficult claim to accept because it is so early in Shakespeare's career. Most recently, scholarship such as Brian Vickers's study of Shakespeare and authorship has reinforced the first explanation. Vickers uses complex analysis of word use and style to propose that *Troublesome Raigne* was written by George Peele, a collaborator of Shakespeare's, and that Shakespeare revised the material into *King John*. Although not all scholars accept Vickers's arguments, the majority agree that Shakespeare adapted his play from *Troublesome Raigne*.

SYNOPSIS
Brief Synopsis

King Richard I died returning from a crusade, leaving no direct heir. In his will, he specified that his youngest brother, John, should become king. Legally, however, Arthur, the son of John's older brother Geoffrey could claim to be rightful king. With the support of his mother, Queen Eleanor, John has taken the throne, while Arthur and his mother, Constance, have remained in France to gather support for their case.

The play begins with King Philip II of France, supporting Arthur's legitimacy, sending an ambassador to John. The demands are that he abdicate or face war. John refuses to step down and prepares his army for an invasion of France. In the meantime, two brothers ask John to settle which of them is the true heir to their father's estate. The younger brother, Robert Faulconbridge claims that the older, Philip Faulconbridge, is illegitimate and that his father had said so on his deathbed. Philip claims that legitimate or not, as the eldest son of a married couple, he is the legal heir. John supports Philip's claim based on English law. He and Eleanor note Philip's resemblance to the dead king Richard. They offer him a knighthood and a commission in the English army if he renounces his claim to the land. He consents and is henceforth referred to as Sir Richard Plantagenet or the Bastard.

Once in France, the English army confronts the French and their ally, Austria, outside the town of Angiers. The townspeople refuse to acknowledge either king as their ruler, encouraging the two powers to fight. After an inconclusive battle, the Bastard suggests that the armies unite to attack the town. In response, the people of Angiers propose that the king of France's son, Louis, marry Blanche, John's niece, and the two sides negotiate a peace treaty. The marriage and treaty strengthen John's claim to the throne by eliminating France's support for Arthur. For Blanche's dowry, John provides a large sum of money and most of the English territories on the continent that he had been fighting to retain.

The peace between France and England is quickly broken when Pandulph, an emissary from Rome, arrives with a message from the pope that accuses John of disobeying the church. John has rejected the pope's candidate as archbishop of Canterbury. John refuses to recant and is excommunicated. Persuaded by Pandulph that they are once again enemies, the French ally with Austria to attack the English.

The English are successful, capture Arthur, and John orders his execution. Arthur's jailor, Hubert, is unable to kill the boy and frees him, but Arthur accidentally falls and dies. At the same time, the French have regrouped and invaded England. A number of English nobles, believing John is responsible for Arthur's death, agree to assist the French. The two armies fight with great losses. When a French noble reveals that the English traitors are to be executed, they return to the English side.

Pandulph appears again with a peace treaty that ends the conflict. John dies, having been poisoned by a monk. His son, Prince Henry, becomes king, and the English nobles swear to follow him.

Act I, Scene 1

The play begins in the throne room of King John of England, where he, his mother, Eleanor, and his nobles receive the French ambassador Chatillion. The message from Philip, the king of France, demands that John give up his claim to the English throne in favor of his nephew Arthur. The message's tone is insulting and angers Eleanor. John, however, calmly refuses to abdicate, and Chatillion threatens war. In response, John threatens to attack France first. After the ambassador departs, Robert

Queen Eleanor asks Philip Faulconbridge (the Bastard) to renounce his claim on his father's property in order to join the expedition against France in Act 1, Scene 1 of *King John*. This drawing was designed for the Chiswick edition of Shakespeare, published in 1900. *(John Byam Lister Shaw)*

and Philip Faulconbridge enter, requesting that the king resolve a dispute over which brother should inherit their father's property. Robert claims that, although he and Philip have the same mother, Philip is illegitimate; on his deathbed, their father revealed this to him and made him sole heir. Eleanor remarks to John that Philip looks remarkably like King Richard, so much so that they offer him the opportunity to join the expedition against France in return for renouncing his claim on the Faulconbridge property. Philip assents and as a bonus is knighted Sir Richard Plantagenet.

(Although characters in the play call him Sir Richard, his speech prefix is simply the Bastard.) Left alone for a moment, he delivers a soliloquy, meditating on how his change in status will improve his life but also expose him to flatterers and frauds. At the end of the act, Lady Faulconbridge enters and confirms to her son that King Richard is his biological father.

Act II, Scene 1

In front of the city of Angiers, an English possession in western France, King Philip and the Duke of Austria prepare a siege to uphold Arthur's claim to the English throne. Chatillion reports that his embassy has failed and that an ambitious English army is close behind him. King John, Eleanor, and the Bastard arrive and quickly begin to dispute with King Philip about Arthur's legitimacy. Eleanor and Arthur's mother, Constance, interrupt the two kings and initiate an argument of their own, with the young boy in the middle. The Bastard takes the opportunity to bait Austria, who claims to have slain King Richard and wears his legendary lion skin. Philip finally interrupts the argument and proceeds with the negotiations. Each king asks the people of Angiers to allow the true king of England to enter their city as lawful monarch. John points out that the French armies are prepared to attack the city and claims to be its king and savior. Philip draws attention to Arthur and argues that if the citizens accept him as king of England, they will have nothing to fear from the French. The citizens refuse to identify either as the true king and demand that either John or Arthur demonstrate their claim's validity. Philip and John take this as their cue to begin battle. After some offstage combat, the two kings meet again, both claiming to have won the advantage. The people of Angiers still refuse to choose, and the armies prepare to renew their conflict. Frustrated, the Bastard marvels at how ordinary citizens can manipulate monarchs and suggests the armies combine to attack the city, although he plans to use the opportunity to set France and Austria against each other. The townspeople realize their danger and resort to the language of courtly love to offer another solution. In florid language, they point out the beauty of Blanche of Spain, John's niece, and how Louis the Dauphin, heir to the French throne, would make a perfect match for her. The speech concludes with a peace treaty in which Blanche and Louis would marry to unite the English and French. Eleanor whispers to John that if the two marry and they give Blanche a rich dowry, Arthur's case will wither. John offers as dowry the lands of Anjou, Touraine, Maine, and Poitiers—nearly all England's territories in France. Louis and Blanche step forward and have an awkward brief courtship while the Bastard mutters cynically against it. The two kings agree to the marriage. John adds yet another English province and 30,000 marks of English money. Philip voices concern that Constance will feel that her son has been betrayed. To help content her, John gives Arthur the titles Earl of Richmond and Duke of Brittany and makes him Lord of Angiers. All parties exit in search of a church for the wedding but the Bastard, who delivers his second soliloquy, outraged at how easily the kings have broken their promises. He marvels at how self-interest alters the balance of the world, making it spin crookedly. By the end of his speech, however, the Bastard accepts that this is the way of the world and decides from now on to follow his own self-interest.

Act III, Scene 1

In the French camp, Constance cannot believe the news Salisbury brings her about the agreement. She claims that a king would never break his word to her. She despairs and attacks Salisbury when he tries to comfort her. Her son steps in, and she turns on him as well, wishing he were ugly so that she would not love him or care about him. Despondent, she sits on the ground as the French and English forces enter with John and Philip holding hands. When Constance sees them, she rises and accuses Philip of betraying her and Arthur. Her words' energy holds the other characters silent until Pandulph, the pope's legate, arrives with a message from Rome. The pope has accused John of disobeying him by refusing to allow Stephen Langton to become archbishop of Canterbury. John replies that as king, he answers only to God, not to the pope, and may appoint whomever he chooses. Because John has defied the pope, Pandulph excommunicates him, much to Constance's pleasure. Philip, however, is placed in a difficult position. He must choose between honoring the treaty with John, now a heretic, and risking excommunication or remaining faithful to the church, breaking his promise, and renewing war with John. The characters each take turns trying to persuade Philip one way or the other. Pandulph provides a complicated rationale for Philip to break the treaty with John, claiming that Philip has an obligation to honor his earlier promise to be a faithful Christian. Philip chooses his faith over his agreement and drops John's hand. The two sides trade insults and prepare to renew their conflict.

Act III, Scene 2

During the battle, the Bastard rescues Eleanor, decapitates Austria, and carries his head as a trophy. John captures Angiers and Arthur and appoints his servant Hubert to be the boy's jailer.

Act III, Scene 3

With the battle concluded, John prepares to return to England, leaving Eleanor in charge of the English territories in France. He sends the Bastard to England to gather money from the monasteries in order to prepare for continued conflict. Speaking to Hubert alone, John flatters him by praising his loyalty. Hubert accepts the compliments and reaffirms his faithfulness. John then confides that he regards Arthur as a threat. Hubert replies that he will see that Arthur will not interfere with John's plans. Unsatisfied with this answer, John indirectly suggests that Hubert kill Arthur. Hubert agrees to do so.

Act III, Scene 4

The English successes dishearten Philip. Constance is especially distraught at the capture of her son and, appearing with her hair down, grieves in such vivid language that Pandulph believes she has gone

King John appoints Hubert to be Arthur's jailor in Act III, Scene 2 of *King John*. This is a print from Malcolm C. Salaman's 1916 edition of *Shakespeare in Pictorial Art*. *(Painting by John Opie)*

mad. Inconsolable, Constance finally exits. Philip follows her, fearing that she will injure herself. Left alone with Louis, Pandulph tells him that while the circumstances do not look good, they may well give Louis a chance to claim the English throne. He predicts that John will kill Arthur to preserve his crown and that this death would allow Louis, via Blanche, to make his own legal claim to the English crown. Louis is unsure, and Pandulph adds that the young prince's demise will demoralize the English people and undermine John's authority. Not entirely convinced, Louis suggests that John will not execute Arthur but only keep him in prison. Pandulph replies that if Louis prepares to attack England, then John will certainly kill Arthur, hastening his peoples' revolt. Louis is intrigued, and they go to learn Philip's opinion on invading England.

Act IV, Scene 1

Hubert enters Arthur's prison cell with several executioners and tells them to heat some irons red-hot. Arthur notices that Hubert is upset, and when he asks why, Hubert shows him the warrant instructing him to burn out Arthur's eyes. The executioners return and give Hubert the irons, but Hubert dismisses them. Arthur pleads for his life, reminding Hubert of how friendly they have become. The boy's emotional speech touches Hubert's conscience, and he changes his mind. Hubert tells Arthur he will not hurt him but must tell the king that he has killed him. The two exit together.

Act IV, Scene 2

John sits upon his throne having been crowned king once again. His nobles are upset at his action, arguing that a second coronation was unnecessary and wasteful. The lords also request Arthur's release. The longer he is captive, the greater the public discontent grows. John, already having ordered Arthur's murder, readily agrees. Hubert arrives with the notice of Arthur's demise, at which the indignant nobles leave to find his body. Though he ordered it done, John is still shaken by Arthur's death and his nobles' anger. A messenger announces that the French army has landed and that both Eleanor and Constance have died, increasing John's uneasiness. The Bastard enters with Peter of Pomfret, a man who has prophesied that John will give up his crown before the next Ascension Day. John orders Pomfret incarcerated and, when his prediction proves false, instructs that he be hanged. He then sends the Bastard after the nobles to try to win them back. Hubert returns with word of the appearance of five Moons, an unfavorable portent, a French army having landed, and the peoples' distress at the rumors of Arthur's death. At the mention of the boy, John turns and accuses Hubert of forcing him to order the killing, claiming he had no desire to see Arthur dead. Hubert produces the death warrant with John's signature. Confronted with the evidence, John insists that it was Hubert's ugly appearance that forced him to sign the warrant. Hubert, seeking to redeem himself and restore John's confidence, reveals that Arthur is still alive. Pleased, John sends him to gather the nobles so they may be told the good news.

Act IV, Scene 3

Arthur, dressed as a sailor, appears on the walls of his prison. He tries to jump to freedom, falls on the rocks, and dies. The English lords enter discussing their plan to betray John and join the invading French. The Bastard enters and tries to persuade them to rejoin John. Together, they discover Arthur's body. The nobles assume Hubert killed Arthur under John's orders and vow revenge. The Bastard is skeptical and refuses to jump to conclusions. Hubert arrives and is nearly killed by the angry lords. He denies responsibility and begins to cry. Unsatisfied, the lords depart to meet with Louis. Hubert manages to persuade the Bastard that he did not kill Arthur. The Bastard instructs Hubert to care for Arthur's body and in a brief speech, reflects on England's dire situation.

Act V, Scene 1

In a ceremony reestablishing his loyalty to the pope, John hands his crown to Pandulph, who returns it. He asks Pandulph to keep his word and meet with the French to forestall the invasion. John reflects that Peter Pomfret had prophesied he would give up his crown but dismisses the portent because he gave up the crown willingly. The Bastard reports that the French have invaded and captured London, that the nobles have joined them, and that Arthur is indeed dead. John is distraught at the news, but the Bastard encourages him to fight the French. John is swayed and gives the Bastard, who has some doubts, command of the English armies.

Act V, Scene 2

The English lords swear their allegiance to Louis, who has their oaths written down. Salisbury dwells on their decision but believes that it is for the good of the country. Pandulph informs the dauphin that John has reconciled with the pope, and

therefore, the invasion of England is no longer necessary. Proud and confident of victory and the English crown, Louis refuses to obey Pandulph and declares that having provided no material support to his campaign, the church has no influence over him. The Bastard enters and learns that Pandulph's negotiation has failed. Equally proud, the Bastard declares in a flamboyant speech that the nearby English army will also ignore Pandulph and easily defeat the French.

Act V, Scene 3

Hubert reports to John, who is suffering from a fever, that the French army appears to have the advantage. John withdraws to an abbey at nearby Swinstead. A messenger reports that the dauphin has retreated and his reinforcements have been shipwrecked and lost.

Act V, Scene 4

Salisbury is surprised and worried that King John has gathered strong support and that the Bastard is such an effective leader. A fatally wounded French lord, Count Melun, discloses to the nobles that the dauphin, once he is victorious, plans to behead them. The English are skeptical, but Melun notes that as he is dying, he has no reason to lie. What is more, he reveals that he has English blood; his grandfather was an Englishman and therefore he feels compelled by his conscience to tell them the truth. The lords believe him and decide to return to John.

Act V, Scene 5

At the battle's end, when Louis believes the French have won, a messenger informs him his supplies have been lost and the English lords have abandoned him.

Act V, Scene 6

In the darkness, after the battle, Hubert bumps into the Bastard. They recognize each other by their voices. Hubert informs the Bastard that a monk has poisoned John and the nobles have returned with Prince Henry, John having pardoned them. Though the English seem to have won the battle, the tide may have turned against them. The Bastard reports half of his army drowned in the Lincoln Washes and that he barely escaped.

Act V, Scene 7

Prince Henry and the nobles discuss John's worsened condition. Servants bring him out to an orchard where he predicts his imminent death. The Bastard enters, and John dies after listing his losses and Louis's looming counterattack. Henry notes he must go on as king, though some day he will die as well. The angry Bastard vows to revenge the king's death. Salisbury informs him that Pandulph is close and has negotiated peace with Louis so that the French are preparing to return home. The lords and the Bastard pledge fealty to Henry, and the Bastard declares that a unified England will never be conquered.

CHARACTER LIST

King John As the king of England and youngest brother of the previous monarch, Richard I (Coeur de Lion/Lionheart), John's position is threatened by his nephew Arthur's claim to be the rightful king. Living in the shadow of his beloved predecessor, John must also contend with shifting political fortunes that have left the empire, which was consolidated by his father, Henry II, and his brother, shrinking rapidly.

Eleanor Eleanor of Aquitaine, once queen of France, divorced King Louis IV and married King Henry II to become the queen of England. She is John's mother. Though in her 70s, Eleanor serves as her son's primary and most vocal adviser.

Philip (the Bastard) Faulconbridge/Sir Richard Plantagenet An unhistorical character, Philip Faulconbridge is the illegitimate son of Richard I. He rejects the wealth of an inheritance to accept the honor of a knighthood and an opportunity to fight for England. His self-assurance contrasts with John's self-doubts.

Arthur John's nephew and Eleanor's grandson, Arthur claims to be the lawful king of England through his father, John's elder brother. Historically a teenager, in the play, he is a child still dominated by his mother.

Constance As Arthur's mother, she is as zealous an advocate for him as Eleanor is for John. Her speeches are passionate and often judgmental of other characters' hypocrisies.

Hubert John's faithful servant and Arthur's sympathetic jailor.

King Philip The king of France is Constance and Arthur's ally but abandons them to sign a treaty with John. Pandulph persuades him to break the treaty and invade England.

Pandulph As the pope's emissary, Cardinal Pandulph represents the Catholic Church's interests and serves as a diplomat between England and France.

Louis The dauphin (crown prince of France), Louis is Philip's eldest son. He marries Blanche to create an alliance between France and England but eagerly prepares to invade England once the alliance is broken.

Blanche John's niece who is married to Louis as a pawn in the treaty between France and England.

Robert Faulconbridge The half brother of Philip Faulconbridge who contests his claim to their father's estate.

Lady Faulconbridge The mother of Robert and Philip, she reveals that Philip's true father is Richard I.

James Gurney Lady Faulconbridge's servant.

Duke of Austria Sometimes known as Limoges, the Duke of Austria claims to have slain Richard I and wears his lion skin as a trophy. The Bastard seeks revenge against him.

Citizen of Angiers The representative of the French city of Angiers who negotiates with John and Philip.

Chatillion Philip's ambassador to England.

Melun A French count, Melun is the messenger between Louis and the traitorous English lords.

Salisbury Early in the play, Salisbury is an English lord sympathetic to Constance. He rebels against John but later returns to the English side.

Pembroke, Essex, and Bigot Along with Salisbury, these seditious English lords betray John to fight for Louis, then return to him.

Peter of Pomfret A prophet arrested by the Bastard who predicts John will surrender his crown.

Prince Henry John's eldest son and the future Henry III.

French and English Heralds Officers who make official public statements for their respective kings.

CHARACTER STUDIES
King John

Rather than dramatize the king John familiar from the Robin Hood tales and the signing of the Magna Carta, Shakespeare tells the story of an uneasy monarch's troubles with his legitimacy as king, his struggles to preserve the empire formed by his father and brother, and his contentions with the pope for power over the English church. At the play's beginning, John behaves as a confident king, though strongly influenced by his mother, Eleanor. But, as the play develops and circumstances conspire against John, he becomes unable to manage his fears about his legitimacy, neglects his duties as king, and leads England into near chaos.

John's legitimacy is the focus of the opening scene, when the French ambassador Chatillion strikes to the heart of John's anxiety, referring to him as "The borrowed majesty, of England" (1.1.4) and demanding that John acknowledge his nephew Arthur as the true king. Initially, John is quiet, while his mother remarks on the insult. He is not spineless, however, and sharply returns Chatillion's threat of war with a pledge to attack France immediately. Eleanor magnifies John's worries when she mentions Arthur's mother, the "ambitious Constance" (1.1.32), and her attempts to undermine John in favor of Arthur. She goes on to scold John, reminding him of his diplomatic failures: "This [threat from France] might have been prevented . . . With very easy arguments of

John sits on his throne after hearing of his mother's death in Act IV, Scene 2 of *King John*. This drawing was designed for the Chiswick edition of Shakespeare, published in 1900. *(Illustration by John Byam Lister Shaw)*

love" (1.1.35–36). John replies with assurance, invoking "Our strong possession and our right for us" (1.1.39). This tension over legitimacy persists when John must adjudicate a quarrel between two brothers over their inheritance. Although Robert Faulconbridge argues he should be heir because his older brother, Philip (the Bastard), is illegitimate, John follows the letter of the law, bluntly declaring, "Sirrah, your brother is legitimate" and tutors the brothers in the relevant legal practices (1.1.119–132).

During the first act, John is a decisive and regal king. He refuses to be baited by Chatillion, speaking calmly in language rich with dramatic imagery: "so depart in peace. / Be thou as lightning in the eyes of France, / For ere thou canst report, I will be there; / The thunder of my cannon shall be heard" (1.1.24–27). He calms his mother's concerns about Constance and Arthur and fairly resolves the dispute between the Faulconbridge brothers. What John does not say or do, however, is also important. He remains silent through most of the debate between the brothers, allowing Eleanor to do most of the talking. John's legalistic judgment on the Faulconbridges' situation is deeply ironic in light of his own claim to the throne and reveals the first instance of his hypocrisy.

This flaw manifests itself again when John, initially committed to defending his crown and the English possessions in France, changes his mind. He agrees to a peace treaty with the French that centers on a marriage between John's niece Blanche and the dauphin, Louis. Following Eleanor's suggestion, John offers as Blanche's dowry virtually all the territories he had been fighting to retain. In addition, he "create[s] young Arthur Duke of Brittany / And Earl of Richmond" and makes him lord of Angiers (2.1.576–578). The decision is sensible. It avoids further bloodshed and the possibility of a French victory and eliminates France as Arthur's ally. It also betrays John's initial commitment to defend England. Even though his hold on the crown is more secure, the losses in territory and wealth are more than might have been lost if John had continued to fight and been defeated.

John's self-serving decision and its cost to England is transparent to the Bastard, who exclaims, "Mad world, mad kings, mad composition / John, to stop Arthur's title in the whole, / Hath willingly departed with a part" (2.1.588–590). Reinforcing his claim as king becomes more important to John than preserving the kingdom. His sacrifice here reveals his inability to manage the duality of the king's two bodies. In the Renaissance, kings were understood to have two parts, a physical, mortal body and a social or political body that embodies

his divine right to rule. In an effective ruler, the two bodies function together without conflict, making decisions that benefit the kingdom as a whole. When the mortal king dies, the next monarch assumes the political body. John is unable keep his two bodies united and recognizes as much as he reflects on the French invasion and Arthur's death:

> My nobles leave me; and my state is braved,
> Even at my gates, with ranks of foreign powers:
> Nay, in the body of this fleshly land,
> This kingdom, this confine of blood and breath,
> Hostility and civil tumult reigns
> Between my conscience and my cousin's death.
>   (4.2.255–260)

John's actions, in particular the attempted murder of Arthur, have disrupted both England and his own body.

Despite having negotiated peace with France and diminished Arthur's threat, John must also negotiate a conflict with the church. Pandulph demands he accede to the pope's candidate for the next archbishop of Canterbury. John is decisive and confident, telling Pandulph "no Italian priest / Shall tithe or toll in our dominions; / But we under God are supreme head" (3.1.159–161). As a result, Pandulph excommunicates John, an act that persuades King Philip of France to withdraw from the treaty. Philip's perfidy leaves England vulnerable. The territory and money are gone; France, allied with Constance and Arthur, has again declared war. John's composure deserts him, and he confesses to "a rage whose heat hath this condition, / That nothing can allay, nothing but blood— / The blood . . . of France" (3.1.356–358).

John's army defeats the French and captures Arthur, but this opportunity leads to John's most dire mistake. With Arthur captive, John summons his servant Hubert and tells him, "Good Hubert . . . [Arthur] is a very serpent in my way / And wheresoe'er this foot of mine doth tread, / He lies before me" (3.3.62–65). Hubert pledges to keep Arthur out of John's way, but he does not fully understand John's point. John reiterates:

KING JOHN. Death.

HUBERT.   My lord?

KING JOHN.   A grave.

HUBERT.   He shall not live.

KING JOHN.   Enough. (3.3.70–74)

Predictably enough, when Hubert reports (falsely) that Arthur is dead, John denies having made such an order. When Hubert produces a warrant for the execution with John's signature and seal, the king prevaricates, insisting that Hubert's "abhorred aspect" (4.2.235) compelled him to sign it. John continues to be decisive, but he acts out of his own self-interest rather than England's. By ordering the death of an innocent child and using his authority as a king to force a servant to carry it out, John has joined the ranks of historical tyrants whose endings are always bloody.

Others are aware of John's potential for treachery. As Louis is preparing to invade England, Pandulph tells him, "If that young Arthur be not gone already, / Even at that news he dies; / and then the hearts / Of all [John's] people shall revolt from him" (3.4.166–169). Pandulph is prescient. Hubert reports to John that "Arthur's death is common in their mouths, / And when they talk of him, they shake their heads" (4.2.198–199). When the English lords, John's "doubtful friends" (5.1.37), discover Arthur's dead body, Salisbury has no doubts: "It is the shameful work of Hubert's hand, / The practice and the purpose of the King, / From whose obedience I forbid my soul" (4.3.63–65). This act compels them to join the invading French to fight against John.

At the play's end, John dies painfully, poisoned by a monk, but not before handing command of the army to the Bastard and forgiving the nobles who have returned to him. At the point of death, John recognizes his mortality and the loss of the divine aspect of kingship. To the Bastard, he says: "all this thou seest is but a clod / And module of confounded royalty" (5.7.61–62). Speaking over his body, Salisbury sees the transformation, "But now a king, now thus" (5.7.70). Prince Henry and the Bastard both echo the sentiment: Henry recognizing his own fate in what "is now clay" (5.7.73) and the Bastard vowing "To do the office for thee of revenge" (5.7.75). But, he is also quick to recall the king's political body lives on in Henry and the nation of England, which if they do not defend, will fall to the French.

Unlike the kings in Shakespeare's other history plays, John is never completely tragic nor completely heroic. At times, he acts resolutely for the good of England, as when he struggles against the French and the influence of the church. At other times, he is consumed by the question of his legitimacy. He relies heavily on the advice of his mother and the Bastard but also is capable of independent thought. His decision to have Arthur murdered, however, makes him irredeemable. He is too willing to forfeit the good of England in exchange for his own security.

The Bastard

A fictional character, probably created from several historical figures, the Bastard gives the play energy and humor. At the same time, he is difficult to categorize, alternating between an idealist and a cynic, a swaggering newcomer and a sober patriot, and a sarcastic outsider and a loyal soldier. Literally a bastard, he is born Philip Faulconbridge and experiences his first alteration, becoming Sir Richard Plantagenet, when his status as the illegitimate son of Richard Lionheart is acknowledged. Though the other characters refer to him as Sir Richard, the speech prefixes and most scholars refer to him simply as the Bastard. The knighthood gives him honor and access to the highest elements of society but also strips him of wealth and property. It is a decision that he willingly makes, telling his brother, "take you my land. I'll take my chance. . . . My father gave me honor, yours gave land" (1.1.155, 169).

The Bastard's boastful attitude appears as he disrupts an argument between King Philip and King John. He singles out the Duke of Austria, who claims to have killed Richard Lionheart and to wear his lion skin, "ass, I'll take that burden from your back / Or lay on that shall make your shoulders crack" (2.1.148–149). He is so persistent that Austria abandons the conversation, exclaiming, "What cracker is this same that deafs our ears / With this abundance of superfluous breath?" (2.1.150–151). When Philip and John are obstructed by the refusal of the citizens of Angiers to recognize John or Arthur as the true king of England, the Bastard inspires them by suggesting that they unite to attack Angiers rather than fight each other. At the same time, he cleverly arranges the assault so that the armies of France and Austria fire into each other's faces.

The Bastard loses his idealism after he watches Philip and John end a "resolved and honorable war" for the sake of "a most base and vile-concluded peace" (2.1.613–614). In a lengthy soliloquy, he castigates the rulers, beginning in disbelief, "Mad world, mad kings, mad composition!" (2.1.588). He blames their self-interest, personifying it as a "sly devil," and "That smooth-faced gentleman, tickling Commodity, . . . the bias of the world" (2.1.594, 601–602). The two kings have shocked the naive Bastard, who expected them to fight for honor and country, as they had promised. But he learns quickly and by the soliloquy's end has joined them: "Since kings break faith upon Commodity / Gain, be my lord, for I will worship thee!" (2.1.625–626). As the Bastard learns more about the world, he becomes less of an outsider.

The Bastard may have declared himself for self-interest, but he never quite demonstrates his own greed. He remains a loyal solider and is heroic, rescuing Eleanor from the French. He is also dutiful, returning to England at John's request to raid the monasteries for money. The Bastard remains capable of being shocked by the depravity of kings, but he has become more measured in his responses. When he and the English lords stumble upon Arthur's corpse, the nobles assume that John has killed the boy, but the Bastard is skeptical, "It is a damned and a bloody work, / The graceless action of a heavy hand, / If that it be the work

of any hand" (4.3.58–60). The Bastard has nothing to gain by defending John at this moment, but he does so regardless and prevents Salisbury from attacking Hubert. He suspects Hubert but withholds judgment. Instead, he instructs Hubert to carry away Arthur's body and reflects on the implications of Arthur's death:

How easy dost thou take all England up!
From forth this morsel of dead royalty,
The life, the right, and the truth of all this
    realm
Is fled to heaven, and England now is left
To tug and scramble. (4.3.150–154)

The Bastard is not concerned with his own advancement or personal honor; he worries about England and the impact of Arthur's death. His earlier cynicism has not entirely disappeared. He recognizes John is a flawed ruler, but he also sees that England is more than a king and needs loyal men to fight for it.

In fact, when he returns to John with the news of Louis's invasion, Arthur's death, and the lords' defection, the Bastard must reassure the discouraged John. He is so convincing that John gives him command of the English army and license to follow his own instincts. The Bastard willingly accepts this challenge and when confronting Pandulph and Louis, claims: "Now hear our English king, / For thus his royalty doth speak in me" (5.2.129–130).

By the play's end, the Bastard has a hero's qualities. In his final speech, he rallies Henry and the assembled English lords:

This England never did nor never shall
Lie at the proud foot of a conqueror
But when it first did help to wound itself.
Now these her princes are come home again,
Come the three corners of the world in arms
And we shall shock them. Naught shall make
    use rue,
If England to itself do rest but true.
    (5.2.118–124)

While delivering this inspirational rhetoric, the Bastard remains realistic about human imperfections. Loyalty is crucial, and he reminds the lords of their betrayal when he notes how England "did help to wound itself" and that success will come only "If England to itself do rest but true."

The Bastard begins the play as a voice of arrogant confidence and idealism. His ideals are challenged by the hypocrisy of kings and their minions. Even though he claims to follow their corrupt example, the Bastard becomes a loyal, courageous, and moral force in the play. If King John lacks an analog in Shakespeare's history plays, critics have seen the Bastard as a prototype Prince Hal, a young man of uncertain promise who nevertheless becomes an honorable English hero.

Constance

Emotional and relentless in support of Arthur's bid for the crown, Constance is one of Shakespeare's most popular female roles, at least in the history plays. Although King Philip of France has pledged to support her and Arthur, few characters like her or speak well of her motives. For Eleanor, Constance only has her own advancement in mind and states "ambitious Constance would not cease / Till she had kindled France and all the world / Upon the right and party of her son" (1.1.32–34). Constance acts out of self-interest, hoping that Arthur "shall be king / That [she] mayest be a queen and check the world" (2.1.123–124). She is an "unadvised scold" (2.1.191) who "utter[s] madness and not sorrow" and is "as fond of grief as of [her] child" (3.4.44; 94).

She never wavers in her quest to put Arthur on the throne and serves as a foil to the hypocritical characters of the play. Like the Bastard, Constance idealistically expects princes to behave consistently and with honor. So, when Philip withdraws his support for Arthur, she questions his identity as a king: "You have beguiled me with a counterfeit / Resembling majesty, which, being touched and tried, / proves valueless" (3.1.102–104). When the dauphin wavers in the face of Pandulph's threat, Constance demands that he follow his oath to the

Constance in Act III, Scene 1 of *King John*. This is a print from Charles Heath's 1848 edition of *The Heroines of Shakspeare: Comprising the Principal Female Characters in the Plays of the Great Poet*. *(Painting by J. W. Wright; engraving by W. H. Egleton)*

church, "O, thine honor, Louis, thine honor!" (3.1.330).

She is also one of the most colorful speakers in the play. Most notably, she is vivid in her grief when she learns of Arthur's capture. She will not be comforted, instead seeking

> Death, death, O amiable, lovely death,
> Thou odoriferous stench, sound rottenness,
> Arise forth from the couch of lasting night,
> Thou hate and terror to prosperity,
> And I will kiss thy detestable bones
> And put my eyeballs in thy vaulty brows,
> And ring these fingers with thy household.
>   worms. (3.4.25–31)

Eleanor

Though she has only about a fifth as many lines as Constance, Eleanor is still a vibrant and polarizing presence. While Constance must care for Arthur and constantly seek support, Eleanor needs only to maintain the power she has through her son. John depends on her counsel and leadership. He does not hesitate to leave her in charge of Angiers when he returns to England, recalling Eleanor's description of herself as "a soldier and now bound to France" (1.1.154). She gives voice to his anxieties about his legitimacy but also recognizes the value of Blanche's marriage to Louis, "by this knot thou shalt so surely tie / They now unsured assurance to the crown / That yon green boy shall have no sun to ripe" (2.1.492–494).

Her influence on John is so strong that Chatillion refers to her as "An Ate stirring him to blood and strife" (2.1.63). Eleanor is Constance's most vicious enemy, a "monstrous injurer of heaven and earth" and "a cankered grandam" (2.1.181, 202). The two women's extended and spiteful clash leaves King John and King Philip, who should be negotiating, nearly speechless. Through their arguments, their willingness to confront the male characters, and their devotion to their sons, Eleanor and Constance dominate the first half of the play to such an extent that their absence from the second half is often given as a reason for its lack of dramatic energy.

Hubert

While editors sometimes conflate him with the Citizen of Angiers, the historical Hubert was one of John's closest advisers, and in the play, John trusts him completely. He is a commoner whose moral consistency magnifies the vacillations of his betters—Philip, John, and the English lords. He refuses to obey John's order to kill Arthur, and though evidence points toward him, Hubert's sincere protests help him escape blame. Near the play's end, he and the Bastard become thematically linked as loyal Englishmen. Wandering in the darkness, the two encounter each other, and when challenged, Hubert offers his national identity rather than his name, "Of the part of England" (5.6.4).

The Bastard recognizes his voice, and the two go together to attend to the dying king John.

DIFFICULTIES OF THE PLAY

As with most of Shakespeare's history plays, the most confusing elements for modern readers and audiences relate to the play's historical and cultural contexts. John's legitimacy, the conflict with the church, and the lords' rebellion are discussed in the "Background" section. Beyond the contexts of the play, the ambiguously motivated characters and inconsistent structures can make *King John* difficult to follow.

Ambiguous Characterization

Shakespeare's histories and tragedies typically have charismatic characters that we are supposed to identify as heroes or villains. Richard III leaves a swath of bodies in his wake as he ascends to power, leaving no question as to his villainy. His corrupt reign ends on a predictably optimistic note, with the providential advent of the Tudor dynasty. As the hero of *Henry V*, Prince Hal must forsake his friends, but his courage and morality mark him as admirable. He occasionally acts ruthlessly but only for England's greater good. *King John*, in contrast, does not give us the drama of a man's rise to the monarchy. John is already king but is never confident of his position. He is an embattled monarch, confronted by threats from his own relatives, the French, and the pope. Rather than rise to the challenge and overcome his enemies, he breaks promises, lies, and sentences a child to death. Because of this, his death, though painful and at the hands of a monk, is neither heroic nor tragic. His replacement, Henry, appears too suddenly and does too little to indicate if he will be any better.

Scholars have argued that the Bastard is the play's hero. He is compared to Prince Hal as a young, ambitious man with a penchant for misbehavior but whose loyalty and patriotism are never in question. Unlike Hal, the Bastard is not directly connected to the action of the play. Most of his time on stage is spent commenting, often cynically, on the action, more like a chorus than an active character (2.1.289–412, 2.1.588–624, 5.1.67–78). Once he is elevated to knighthood, his ambitions taper. He fights loyally and fiercely for England but only in support of the established leadership. He displays no desire for wealth, fame, or power, and no one suggests he might be a potential ruler.

The potential antagonists are similarly ambiguous. King Philip and his son Louis begin the play behaving nobly, but Pandulph easily persuades them to break their promises. He shows Philip how to escape his treaty with John by citing a greater and earlier commitment to the church (3.1). Perhaps most cynically, he explains to Louis the benefits of John's capture of Arthur. Once Arthur is dead, popular opinion will turn against John, and via his marriage to Blanche, Louis can legally claim the English crown (3.4). He is defeated, though, not by a superior English force but by the loss of his reinforcements at sea.

Rather than present a clear hero or villain, Shakespeare has created morally ambiguous characters that require us to decide which qualities in which situations we find admirable. Nearly all of the characters make despicable choices, some more than others. But, in nearly every instance, they have good reasons for their decisions. For some, it is self-preservation. For others, it is a choice of whether to obey an immoral order or disobey and risk punishment. These ambiguities make the characters difficult to categorize, but they make possible a rich discussion and debate of personal and public morality.

Episodic Plot

If the characterization of the play can seem contradictory and inchoate, the structure of the play is no more clear. Unlike most of Shakespeare's other history plays, in which an episode out of England's past is dramatized to demonstrate the hazards of internal conflict and division and the consequent optimistic conclusion, *King John* lacks any strong sense of destiny. Instead, the play seems to present a collection of episodes linked by themes and characters rather than cause and effect. There is little sense of an overall trajectory or a greater meaning.

The Bastard, for example, first appears arguing energetically for his right to inherit his father's property. Yet, when Eleanor offers him the chance to be "reputed" as the son of Richard I and go to war with France, he abandons his argument, letting his brother have everything. In another instance, John is vociferous in his refusal to submit to a "meddling priest" (3.1.169) and goes to war with France. Yet, at the beginning of Act V, he has reconciled with the pope, and Pandulph has promised to prevent Louis from invading England. Louis invades anyway, making both John and Pandulph's actions seem pointless. Adding to the pointlessness, Louis is not defeated by the English but by the drowning of his reinforcements off Goodwin Sands (5.5). After this point, he disappears. Salisbury reports that Louis has agreed to end his invasion and return to France. The play ends without a climactic battle or even a confrontation between sides.

King John, therefore, is best regarded as different sort of play than Shakespeare's other histories. It is an episodic play, with a series of related scenes that each has a logic and a continuity of its own. The play lacks great battles with clear victors or definitive moments that unify it.

Inconsistencies in the Play

Beyond the incoherent structural elements of the play, two particular inconsistencies often confuse readers. The first revolves around John's intentions for Arthur and Hubert's approach to fulfilling them. In his instructions to Hubert, John clearly uses the word *death* (3.3.70), and other characters assume that John will kill Arthur. Further, when Hubert appears in Arthur's cell, characters identified as executioners accompany him (4.1). But the rope and red-hot irons they carry, the warrant, and the conversation between Arthur and Hubert all indicate that Arthur is to be blinded. Some scholars have suggested that the blinding is the prelude to execution, thus death is implied. Others see the blinding as Hubert's attempt to be as merciful as

Prince Arthur pleads with Hubert in Act IV, Scene 1 in *King John*. This is a print from Malcolm C. Salaman's 1916 edition of *Shakespeare in Pictorial Art*. (Painting by William Yeames)

possible without directly disobeying John—a blind Arthur would be alive but ineligible to become king.

John's death is another inconsistency. In Act 5, Scene 3, John tells Hubert "This fever that hath troubled me so long / Lies heavy on me" (3–4). Three scenes later, Hubert tells the Bastard that a monk has poisoned John, which John himself affirms in the final scene. It is certainly possible that John had the fever and was poisoned as well.

Scholars typically mention Shakespeare's sources in trying to explain these events. If we accept that Shakespeare based *King John* on *The Troublesome Raigne of John King of England* (see "Background"),

the inconsistencies could have been carried over from that play, as neither play is clear about either point. Similarly, the historical source, Holinshed's *Chronicles,* is ambiguous, citing several contradictory stories about Arthur's blinding and death and John's death.

KEY PASSAGES
Act I, Scene 1, 1–15

KING JOHN. Now, say, Chatillion, what
  would France with us?

CHATILLION. Thus, after greeting, speaks
  the King of France
In my behavior to the majesty,
The borrowed majesty, of England here.

QUEEN ELEANOR. A strange beginning:
  "borrowed majesty!"

KING JOHN. Silence, good mother. Hear the
  embassy.

CHATILLION. Philip of France, in right and
  true behalf
Of thy deceasèd brother Geoffrey's son,
Arthur Plantagenet, lays most lawful claim
To this fair island and the territories,
To Ireland, Poitiers, Anjou, Touraine, Maine,
Desiring thee to lay aside the sword
Which sways usurpingly these several titles,
And put these same into young Arthur's hand,
Thy nephew and right royal sovereign.

This opening exchange between John, Eleanor, and Chatillion establishes the primary anxiety that drives John's actions. By the rule of primogeniture, the eldest son inherits his father's property. Thus, after the death of Richard I (who had no legitimate heir), the crown of England should have passed to the next-oldest son of Henry II. This son, Richard's brother Geoffrey, had died, but Geoffrey's son Arthur lives, and the king of France advocates his right to the throne. John, also a brother of Richard, but younger than Geoffrey, became king by the virtue of Richard's deathbed will and his age. In the play, Arthur is a boy too young to govern effectively.

Though she claims to have Richard's will, both Eleanor and John recognize that his hold on the throne relies most heavily on "Our strong possession and our right for us" (1.1.39). As long as John is able to control the English territories and people, he will be king. Constance, Arthur's mother, is aware of this too and says as much: "Law cannot give my child his kingdom here / He that holds the kingdom holds the law" (3.1.194–195). Power overcomes ideals and even the law.

This passage also establishes John's character and his mother's influence. King Philip feels comfortable sending an ambassador to insult John and demand that he give up his crown to a boy. To the French, England's insecurity is a situation that could be turned to France's advantage. The insult reinforces John's perceived weakness. He only reacts to quiet his mother once she responds with surprise. We see John as surrounded by people who doubt his authority, and he gives little reason for us to respect him.

Act I, Scene 1, 99–129

ROBERT. And once dispatched him in an
   embassy
To Germany, there with the Emperor
To treat of high affairs touching that time.
Th' advantage of his absence took the King
And in the mean time sojourned at my father's;
Where how he did prevail I shame to speak.
But truth is truth: large lengths of seas and
   shores
Between my father and my mother lay,
As I have heard my father speak himself,
When this same lusty gentleman was got.
Upon his deathbed he by will bequeathed
His lands to me, and took it on his death
That this my mother's son was none of his;
And if he were, he came into the world
Full fourteen weeks before the course of time.
Then, good my liege, let me have what is mine,
My father's land, as was my father's will.

KING JOHN. Sirrah, your brother is
   legitimate.
Your father's wife did after wedlock bear him,
And if she did play false, the fault was hers,
Which fault lies on the hazards of all husbands
That marry wives. Tell me, how if my brother,
Who, as you say, took pains to get this son,
Had of your father claimed this son for his?
In sooth, good friend, your father might have
   kept
This calf bred from his cow from all the world;
In sooth he might; then, if he were my
   brother's,
My brother might not claim him, nor your
   father,
Being none of his, refuse him. This concludes:
My mother's son did get your father's heir;
Your father's heir must have your father's land.

This exchange between Robert Faulconbridge and King John clarifies the laws governing inheritance in the play and provides a counter-example to John's own claim to the English throne. Ordinarily, as the eldest son, Philip Faulconbridge would inherit his father's money and property. But, on his deathbed, the Faulconbridges' father gave his land to Robert, claiming that Philip was another man's son. As evidence, their father recalled that he was in Germany on King Richard's business and that Philip was born too soon after he returned (about five months) for him to have been the father. John explains that these circumstances are not the point in this case. Lady Faulconbridge gave birth to Philip after she was married, and therefore, he is a legitimate son. It may seem unfair that even if a wife deceives her husband, he still has to raise the child, but, as John points out, the system ensures that all children born to married couples will be cared for, reducing the number of orphans.

Ironically, John became king under similar circumstances, but with the opposite result. Richard named John his heir in his will and Arthur, the legal descendant of the eldest son, was prevented from becoming king. John, however, takes no notice of this inconsistency on his part. He is too concerned with his own situation—a characteristic that will come back to haunt him. John appears to have an inclination toward making decisions without regard to their impact on other people.

Although they are not present during the conversation, Richard I and Lady Faulconbridge exert great influence over it. We can see in Richard a destructive self-interest reminiscent of John. He sent Faulconbridge away to Germany so that he could seduce his wife but never had a legitimate son of his own to inherit the crown. Though the stakes are different, Lady Faulconbridge has allowed Robert and Philip to grow up without ever revealing Philip's biological father.

The passage is also an example of the parallel characters that Shakespeare often uses to add depth to his plays. The Bastard and John are in analogous situations, though each behaves differently. Shakespeare never directly acknowledges the similarities, but he gives us enough clues so that we understand that we are to compare and contrast the two characters. Their development through the play further relies on their initial similarities. John's fortunes continue to decline, while the Bastard's continue to rise.

Act I, Scene 1, 182–216

BASTARD. A foot of honor better than I was,
But many a many foot of land the worse.
Well, now can I make any Joan a lady.
"Good den, sir Richard!" "God-a-mercy,
    fellow!"
And if his name be George, I'll call him
    "Peter,"
For new-made honor doth forget men's names;
'Tis too respective and too sociable
For your conversion. Now your traveler,
He and his toothpick at my worship's mess,
And when my knightly stomach is sufficed,
Why then I suck my teeth and catechize
My picked man of countries: "My dear sir,"
Thus, leaning on mine elbow, I begin,
"I shall beseech you"—that is Question now,

And then comes answer like an absey-book:
"O sir," says Answer, "at your best command,
At your employment, at your service, sir."
"No, sir," says Question, "I, sweet sir, at
    yours."
And so, ere Answer knows what Question
    would,
Saving in dialogue of compliment
And talking of the Alps and Apennines,
The Pyrenean and the river Po,
It draws toward supper in conclusion so.
But this is worshipful society
And fits the mounting spirit like myself;
For he is but a bastard to the time
That doth not smack of observation,
And so am I whether I smack or no;
And not alone in habit and device,
Exterior form, outward accoutrement,
But from the inward motion to deliver
Sweet, sweet, sweet poison for the age's tooth,
Which, though I will not practice to deceive,
Yet, to avoid deceit, I mean to learn,
For it shall strew the footsteps of my rising.

In the Bastard's first soliloquy, he ruminates on the advantages his new status will bring him but also worries about the new perils he will face. He observes that he has risen in social status and gained "a foot of honor" but at the same time, has lost all his money and property. Rather than dwell on the disadvantages, the Bastard imagines all the things he will be able to do now that he is a knight. He fantasizes about being able to call people whatever name he chooses and dining at an important man's house, where a boastful traveler defers to the Bastard's superior social status. He even seems to be mocking the artificial language used by the upper classes. This observation leads him to realize that his external appearance will not change his character, whatever his status. He will continue to behave flatteringly as he continues to improve his situation. He does not intend to deceive anyone but knows that in order to avoid others' deceit, he must be able to recognize it.

The Bastard's reflections on status and appearance point to his place outside the social system. As a landless knight, he has nothing to lose and everything to gain; he is a "mounting spirit." He may be part of the nobility, but he does not have to act as they do. Honor is the primary virtue that interests him, and his devotion to it will set him apart from the other characters, members of the nobility, in particular. As an outsider, he can comment and judge the actions of others.

Here, the Bastard introduces themes of ambition and self-knowledge. He is an ambitious character, as his decision to go to war demonstrates. He is also aware that the world of aristocrats is deceptive and that he must be aware that things are not always as they seem. In order to protect himself, he must be skeptical of what he sees but aware of his own strengths and weaknesses.

Act II, Scene 1, 561–598

BASTARD. Mad world! mad kings! mad
  composition!
John, to stop Arthur's title in the whole,
Hath willingly departed with a part;
And France, whose armor conscience
  buckled on,
Whom zeal and charity brought to the field
As God's own soldier, rounded in the ear
With that same purpose-changer, that sly devil,
That broker that still breaks the pate of faith,
That daily break-vow, he that wins of all,
Of kings, of beggars, old men, young men,
  maids—
Who, having no external thing to lose
But the word "maid," cheats the poor maid of
  that—
That smooth-faced gentleman, tickling
  Commodity,
Commodity, the bias of the world—
The world, who of itself is peisèd well,
Made to run even upon even ground,
Till this advantage, this vile-drawing bias,
This sway of motion, this Commodity,
Makes it take head from all indifference,
From all direction, purpose, course, intent.

And this same bias, this Commodity,
This bawd, this broker, this all-changing word,
Clapped on the outward eye of fickle France,
Hath drawn him from his own determined aid,
From a resolved and honorable war
To a most base and vile-concluded peace.
And why rail I on this Commodity?
But for because he hath not wooed me yet.
Not that I have the power to clutch my hand,
When his fair angels would salute my palm,
But for my hand, as unattempted yet,
Like a poor beggar, raileth on the rich.
Well, whiles I am a beggar, I will rail
And say there is no sin but to be rich;
And being rich, my virtue then shall be
To say there is no vice but beggary.
Since kings break faith upon Commodity,
Gain, be my lord, for I will worship thee!

In possibly the play's most famous speech, the Bastard uses a mixture of ordinary language and sophisticated rhetoric to vent his anger at the kings' self-serving decision to make peace instead of ending the conflict in honorable combat. He isolates and personifies the problem as "commodity," or self-interest. Through more than 20 lines, he describes commodity as a "sly devil," a "smooth-faced gentleman," and a "bawd" who lures kings into breaking their promises. It is a "vile-drawing bias" that makes the well-balanced world spin crookedly. He brings himself up short in a moment of self-realization, deciding that he is upset only because he has not had an opportunity to indulge his own self-interest. Embracing his own hypocrisy, he claims that as long as he is poor, he will criticize the rich. Once he is rich, he will claim that wealth is a virtue.

In this and his first soliloquy (1.1), the Bastard serves as a chorus, commenting on the action of the play. He serves as the audience's surrogate and a voice of morality, summarizing the agreement, excoriating both monarchs for changing their minds for their own benefit, and trying to understand what these changes mean for him. Though he may judge others' actions, he is not immune to their effect. If kings may break promises out of self-interest, the Bastard can, too. His comments on the events become fewer and shorter as the play progresses, and though he claims to pursue his own self-interest, he is consistently loyal to John and to England.

Act III, Scene 3

KING JOHN. Come hither, Hubert. O my
   gentle Hubert,
We owe thee much. Within this wall of flesh
There is a soul counts thee her creditor
And with advantage means to pay thy love.
And my good friend, thy voluntary oath
Lives in this bosom, dearly cherishèd.
Give me thy hand. I had a thing to say,
But I will fit it with some better tune.
By heaven, Hubert, I am almost ashamed
To say what good respect I have of thee.

HUBERT. I am much bounden to your
   Majesty.

KING JOHN. Good friend, thou hast no
   cause to say so yet,
But thou shalt have; and creep time ne'er so
   slow,
Yet it shall come from me to do thee good.
I had a thing to say, but let it go:
The sun is in the heaven, and the proud day,
Attended with the pleasures of the world,
Is all too wanton and too full of gauds
To give me audience. If the midnight bell
Did, with his iron tongue and brazen mouth,
Sound on into the drowsy race of night;
If this same were a churchyard where we stand,
And thou possessèd with a thousand wrongs;
Or if that surly spirit, melancholy,
Had baked thy blood and made it heavy, thick,
Which else runs tickling up and down the
   veins,
Making that idiot, laughter, keep men's eyes
And strain their cheeks to idle merriment,
A passion hateful to my purposes;
Or if that thou couldst see me without eyes,

Hear me without thine ears, and make reply
Without a tongue, using conceit alone,
Without eyes, ears and harmful sound of words;
Then, in despite of brooded watchful day,
I would into thy bosom pour my thoughts.
But, ah, I will not. Yet I love thee well,
And, by my troth, I think thou lov'st me well.

HUBERT. So well, that what you bid me
   undertake,
Though that my death were adjunct to my act,
By heaven, I would do it.

KING JOHN. Do not I know thou wouldst?
Good Hubert, Hubert, Hubert, throw thine
   eye
On yon young boy. I'll tell thee what, my
   friend,
He is a very serpent in my way,
And whereso'er this foot of mine doth tread,
He lies before me. Dost thou understand me?
Thou art his keeper.

HUBERT. And I'll keep him so
That he shall not offend your Majesty.

KING JOHN. Death.

HUBERT.   My lord?

KING JOHN.   A grave.

HUBERT.   He shall not live.

KING JOHN.   Enough.
I could be merry now. Hubert, I love thee;
Well, I'll not say what I intend for thee.
   Remember.

In this passage, John reveals himself to be as merciless as Pandulph and Constance have predicted, and his decision marks the beginning of his fall. With Arthur, John faces a problem encountered by other monarchs: a rival lives, but he or she is too young to slay in combat or a duel. To murder the rival outright is beneath the station of a king, so a surrogate must do the dirty work. For John, Hubert is that man. Convincing a servant, no matter how faithful, to kill a child in cold blood is difficult, as Richard discovered in *Richard III*. John's use of sweet talk and suggestion in this passage shows how devious and effective he is when doing dishonorable work. The success of the persuasion reveals John's eloquence but also his depravity. This is John at his most ruthless and the moment, in nearly the center of the play, where he loses his moral authority.

John begins with flattery and employs the royal *we* to describe his feelings. Already using the familiar *thy/thou,* John switches to the even more intimate *I* to demonstrate how much he values Hubert's friendship. He then baits Hubert, by claiming to have something to tell him, then retracting, insisting that the day is too sunny for the dark ideas he has in mind. Hubert says nothing, so John continues suggesting that if Hubert were a melancholy man, then he could reveal what he thinks. Hubert has begun to understand that John wants him to do something and pledges to undertake it, no matter what the cost. This is the reply for which John has been looking, and he tells Hubert how great a danger Arthur is to him. Intentionally misunderstanding John, Hubert says he will keep Arthur clear of John's path. This forces John to abandon his wordy language and speak short lines. Hubert again claims ignorance, and John must reiterate, without explicitly telling Hubert to kill Arthur.

To heighten the tension of the scene, at the end, Shakespeare carefully uses *antilabe* (one line of verse shared by two characters), suggesting that the conversation is quick and that Hubert is following John's lead. This gives the dialogue a feeling of steady acceleration; John's speeches become shorter and shorter until he speaks in single words. This increase in tempo and the presence of Arthur on stage makes the exchange more chilling and prevents John from garnering sympathy later in the play, even at the end as he dies poisoned.

Act IV, Scene 1, 13–70

ARTHUR. Mercy on me!
Methinks no body should be sad but I:
Yet, I remember, when I was in France,
Young gentlemen would be as sad as night,
Only for wantonness. By my christendom,
So I were out of prison and kept sheep,
I should be as merry as the day is long.
And so I would be here, but that I doubt
My uncle practices more harm to me.
He is afraid of me and I of him.
Is it my fault that I was Geoffrey's son?
No, indeed, is't not; and I would to heaven
I were your son, so you would love me, Hubert.

HUBERT. [*Aside*] If I talk to him, with his
  innocent prate
He will awake my mercy which lies dead.
Therefore I will be sudden and dispatch.

ARTHUR. Are you sick, Hubert? You look
  pale today.
In sooth, I would you were a little sick
That I might sit all night and watch with you.
I warrant I love you more than you do me.

HUBERT. [*Aside*] His words do take
  possession of my bosom.
[*He shows Arthur a paper.*]
Read here, young Arthur. [*Aside*] How now,
  foolish rheum!
Turning dispiteous torture out of door?
I must be brief, lest resolution drop
Out at mine eyes in tender womanish tears.—
Can you not read it? Is it not fair writ?

ARTHUR. Too fairly, Hubert, for so foul effect.
Must you with hot irons burn out both mine
  eyes?

HUBERT. Young boy, I must.

ARTHUR.   And will you?

HUBERT.   And I will.

ARTHUR. Have you the heart? When your
  head did but ache,
I knit my handkercher about your brows—
The best I had, a princess wrought it me—
And I did never ask it you again;
And with my hand at midnight held your head,
And like the watchful minutes to the hour
Still and anon cheered up the heavy time,
Saying, "What lack you?" and "Where lies your
  grief?"
Or "What good love may I perform for you?"
Many a poor man's son would have lien still
And ne'er have spoke a loving word to you;
But you at your sick service had a prince.
Nay, you may think my love was crafty love
And call it cunning. Do, an if you will.
If heaven be pleased that you must use me ill,
Why then you must. Will you put out mine
  eyes—
These eyes that never did nor never shall
So much as frown on you?

HUBERT. I have sworn to do it;
And with hot irons must I burn them out.

ARTHUR. Ah, none but in this Iron Age
  would do it.
The iron of itself, though heat red-hot,
Approaching near these eyes, would drink my
  tears
And quench his fiery indignation
Even in the matter of mine innocence;
Nay, after that, consume away in rust
But for containing fire to harm mine eye.
Are you more stubborn-hard than hammered
  iron?
An if an angel should have come to me
And told me Hubert should put out mine eyes,
I would not have believed him. No tongue but
  Hubert's.

This dramatic passage is located at the beginning
of Act IV. Two scenes earlier, in an edgy exchange,
we hear John instruct Hubert to kill Arthur. We

Arthur pleads with Hubert for his life, while an
attendant stands by with a hot iron in Act IV, Scene
I of *King John*. This is a print from the Boydell
Shakespeare Gallery project. *(Painting by James
Northcote; engraving by Robert Thew)*

then witness Constance's fervent grief, and Pandulph and Louis's cold-blooded calculation of how
they would make use of Arthur's inevitable death.
Shakespeare initially rewards this accumulation of
tension by implying that Arthur would be killed
or at least spectacularly blinded with red-hot irons.
Instead, Shakespeare gives us a very personal scene
of Arthur's appealing to Hubert's better nature and
leading him to a morally correct, though politically
disobedient decision. In this passage and through
the rest of the scene, we are shown the power of
personal relationships and how they provide a small
measure of hope in an otherwise bleak play.

Similar to John's persuasion of Hubert in Act III, Scene 3, the beginning of this scene is strongly ironic. Arthur and Hubert both know what is supposed to happen, but they pretend they do not and talk about other things. Arthur attempts to garner sympathy by telling Hubert that he would be happy with a shepherd's life. He did not ask to be born a prince and, in fact, would be happy as Hubert's son. Arthur's tactics are effective, and Hubert cannot even speak his intentions. Shakespeare again manipulates the speeches' lengths to control the pace of the scene. Instead of building a sense of acceleration, he mixes longer speeches, typically from Arthur, with brief statements from Hubert to create an uncomfortable stop-and-start rhythm. Another tension-generating *antilabe* passage brings the pattern to a halt when Arthur asks Hubert to confirm his intentions. Making a point that resonates throughout the play, Arthur claims that "none but in this Iron Age would do" such a thing. Only in a degraded and primitive world could the murder of a boy by his uncle occur.

The conversation is tense and revelatory. Unlike most other negotiations in the play, it takes place between just two characters. Sympathies are established, and Arthur is able to use pity to sway Hubert in a way that his mother never could with Philip. The scene shows that the world is corrupt, but that people are still capable of mercy. In parallel to John's conversation with Hubert, it reestablishes John's callousness and Hubert's compassion. But the world itself is still cruel, and soon after, Arthur falls accidentally to his death.

DIFFICULT PASSAGES
Act V, Scene 7, 110–118
BASTARD. O, let us pay the time but needful
   woe,
Since it hath been beforehand with our griefs.
This England never did, nor never shall
Lie at the proud foot of a conqueror
But when it first did help to wound itself.
Now these her princes are come home again,
Come the three corners of the world in arms
And we shall shock them. Nought shall make
   us rue,
If England to itself do rest but true.

The final speeches of Shakespeare's history plays typically provide the audience with a sense of hope for the immediate future, a rationalization that the terrible things they have just watched were all meaningful because the future will be much better. *King John* is atypical. The Bastard, who will not become king, returns to the role of commentator and judge. He reflects on what he has learned and what he believes about England. Honor makes the nation great. When its subjects are obedient and when all are united, "England . . . never shall / Lie at the proud foot of a conqueror." The speech's optimism and the presence of the newly returned lords and of Prince Henry create the impression that the events of the play mark England's nadir, and now its fortunes will soon improve. The Bastard is no longer an idealist. He is careful to include reservations aimed at the formerly rebellious lords and perhaps King John. The words *but* and *if* establish what went wrong: "But when [England] first did . . . wound itself" and "If England to itself do rest but true." England is a collection of parts—its king, its princes, and its people. When one or more of these is untrue, then "[t]his England" suffers. Rebellion and betrayal are fatal. When loyalty and obedience are present, the nation thrives.

CRITICAL INTRODUCTION TO THE PLAY
Understanding a Shakespeare history play requires not only knowledge of literary devices, characterization, and structure but also a sense of the complex historical events the play depicts. Because it is chronologically separate from Shakespeare's other nine histories, *King John* presents a unique challenge to our expectations. Some of the history has been touched on in the "Background" section, and some of the particular complexities have been described in the section "Difficulties of the Play." This section will expand on that material.

History

England at the beginning of the 13th century was very different from England at the end of the 16th century or the present day. It was a larger, multi-cultural, multilingual empire that extended from the Scottish border across the English Channel and took in a large part of what is now France all the way to Spain: Normandy, Poiters, Anjou, Brittany, Touraine, Aquitaine, and Toulouse. Many of these lands were also claimed by the French king Philip II but were at least nominally under English control. English kings did not always dwell in England or speak English as their first language. In fact, most lived on the Continent and spoke French. The Christian Church had not yet split into Protestant and Catholic factions, and the influence of the pope was quite strong.

The play begins in John's palace in England. The action shifts to Angiers (modern Angers), in the county of Anjou, an area that England and France had fought over for centuries. Acts 4 and 5 take place in various locations across England, though Shakespeare's compression of time gives the impression that the action all occurs in the same area.

Structure and Characters

Many critics of *King John* have pointed to disunity as one of its flaws. The play seems to lack a central character, the action develops unevenly, and what begins as a rhetorically centered play ends with an irregular mixture of speech and action. The first two acts consist of single, lengthy scenes of relatively formal debates and speeches involving kings and national politics. Even what seems to be a private issue, the Faulconbridge family dispute, takes on national relevance when the Bastard's relationship to Richard I is revealed. The patterns of the first two acts are disrupted by the Bastard's formal speeches, which meditate chorus-like on the events of the play. Acts III, IV, and V, however, alter this precedent. The scenes and speeches are shorter. The characters are less reflective, and the play's pace quickens. The action of the play and the characters' loyalties fragment. The French-English divide becomes complicated with the capture of Arthur, the defection of the English lords, and the intrusions of the church. The events of the play do not build a chain of cause and effect, as they do in most of Shakespeare's histories. There seems to be a series of discrete incidents—the battle over Angiers, the conflict with the pope, the death of Arthur, the French invasion, and John's death—that relate to one another through characters and themes more than narrative events.

King John's characters present a similar situation. None fits easily into categories such as protagonist or antagonist. Philip and John switch from enemies to friends in a single act. Louis is willing to marry Blanche to bring peace to France and England, but Pandulph quickly persuades him to invade in the hopes of claiming the crown for himself. The Bastard has heroic moments, but he lacks the ambition to do more than act as a second-in-command. As a mother, Eleanor advises her son, but she also leads the English army to France and remains there to defend Angiers.

Shakespeare gives us parallel characters, as he does in many of his plays, but in *King John,* the parallels are often defective. John and Philip are both kings who, through their self-interest, make promises and break them. Philip has authority over Louis until the marriage, when Philip disappears and Louis replaces him. John is replaced by his son but only at the play's end. The Bastard, not John's son Henry, seems to parallel Louis throughout the play as the heir to the kingdom, but he has no similar desire to be monarch. Adrien Bonjour has argued that, rather than defective parallels, the Bastard and John actually mirror each other. John's fortunes fall as the play develops, while the Bastard's rise. Constance and Eleanor are similar as mothers whose sons have claims to the English crown. Eleanor is active and influential, while Constance, despite having more lines, is ineffective.

Shakespeare also gives us a set of comparatively rare characters, three pairs of mothers and sons. Phyllis Rackin has argued that these mothers, while very different on the surface, each exert a disruptive effect on the play. Lady Faulconbridge reveals the truth to the Bastard about his father, verifying the suspected interruption of patrilineal inheritance. Eleanor, at least twice in the play, advises John on policy, and he acts on her suggestions. Constance, although not as influential as Lady Faulconbridge or Eleanor, tenaciously supports Arthur and becomes one of the play's first victims of self-interest. Despite their early active roles, all three disappear from the play by the end of the third act.

Themes

The structure and characterization of *King John* may be fragmented, but Shakespeare provides a series of related themes that unifies the play. Questions of legitimacy, fitness to rule, and self-interest dominate *King John* and shape nearly every conflict and the play's other themes of fortune and bloodshed. The early discussion between Eleanor and John addresses legitimacy in terms of power. After Chatillion's insulting visit, Eleanor voices her concern that Constance's ambition will eventually put Arthur on the throne in John's place. His reply is both cynical and realistic, "Our strong possession and our right for us," to which Eleanor replies, "Your strong possession much more than your right" (1.1.39–40). John has another advantage: the tacit allegiance of the silent lords Salisbury, Essex, and Pembroke in the opening scene. Arthur may have the law on his side, but lacking allies, his claim is futile. Possession can be lost, however. Later in the play, once circumstances have changed, Salisbury echoes John's language when he rationalizes his defection: "[t]he King hath dispossessed himself of us" (4.3.23). This loss of allies, forces John to turn to Pandulph for aid against the French.

The Faulconbridge brothers experience a similar, though private, situation. Each of their claims to their father's property has a measure of validity, but Philip, the eldest, holds the land, while his possessionless brother can only petition a legal body. By appealing to the king, who has the power, Robert hopes his argument will be recognized. To his dismay, John sides with legal precedent, linking, for one of the only times in the play, possession and legitimate claim. The scene concludes with a brief, private conversation between the Bastard and his mother in which she reveals that "by long and vehement suit I was seduced" by Richard I (1.1.262). The revelation affirms the Bastard's possession of his new name, Sir Richard Plantagenet, but brings no money or property.

The play establishes that John's right derives from his possession of the crown. He also, at least at the beginning, demonstrates he can rule effectively. John can argue that as an adult, he is better able to govern England than the child Arthur. Arthur confirms as much in his reaction to his mother's argument with Eleanor: "I would that I were low laid in my grave. / I am not worth this coil that's made for me" (2.1.169–170), at which point he begins to cry. Shakespeare does not let this theme develop so simply, however. John may be an adult and may have power, but his fitness to rule soon becomes questionable. Deciding to have Arthur murdered is tyrannical. His second coronation, his willingness to give in to Pandulph in Act V, Scene 1, and his body's decay (5.3) all point to a ruler who devotes his energies to reassuring himself rather than maintaining his kingdom. Paradoxically, the one most fit to rule England, the Bastard, cannot actually become king. He has the qualities of a heroic leader and even has the opportunity to speak as the king, "Now hear our English king, / For thus his royalty doth speak in me" (5.2.129–130). At the end of the play, with John dead, the Bastard is in control of the English army and, as the eldest son of Richard I, could claim to be king. He does not, however, instead affirming Prince Henry as John's successor. The question of Henry's ability is left unanswered, however. With Arthur dead, he is the legitimate, legal king of England, but Shakespeare gives us no indication of his fitness to rule.

Closely bound up with the theme of legitimacy and fitness to rule is self-interest, or, in the Bastard's words, "commodity." Nearly every character in the play acts out of self-interest, and this narrowness of purpose contaminates the moral world. John's self-interest is the most fully exposed. Three decisions, in particular, demonstrate John's willingness to forgo the good of England for his own security as king: signing the treaty with Philip and marrying off Blanche (2.1), his second coronation (4.2), and his submission to the pope (5.1). He does not betray any awareness of the consequences of these actions. It is up to the Bastard in his "Commodity" soliloquy (2.1.588–626) and the English lords (4.2) to point out John's self-centeredness. But the moments are pointless, as the Bastard speaks only to the audience and the lords' arguments are ignored.

John is not alone in his self-interest. Philip ends his conflict with John fully aware that he has abandoned Constance and Arthur (2.1). He then gives in to Pandulph's threats and breaks his treaty with John (3.1). Eleanor and Constance both accuse each other of self-interest (1.1, 2.1). In contrast, the Bastard, along with Arthur, Hubert, and Blanche, are all characterized by their lack of self-interest. After witnessing John and Philip break their vows, the Bastard pledges himself to "gain" (2.1.598), but he never does anything that might bring about personal advancement. John sends him to raise money from the monasteries, a perfect opportunity for profiteering, but Shakespeare never provides a scene of his collecting the money. The task is only mentioned once more and in passing. The Bastard is content to serve England and support its king, whoever he may be. Hubert is perhaps even less self-interested, knowingly disobeying John's order to kill Arthur and then conspiring to lie to him (4.1). His actions nearly cost him his life, but they were the right things to do (4.3). Perhaps most surprising, even after John has betrayed him, Hubert remains loyal.

Blanche is so selfless in the play as to be almost tragic. Largely silent until her marriage to Louis is suggested, she easily accedes to John's desire, telling the dauphin, "My uncle's will in this respect is mine, / If he see aught in you that makes him like, . . . I can with ease translate it to my will" (2.1.533–536). If Constance and Eleanor are able to voice their self-interest, Blanche barely has a chance to say anything. When John asks her if she would like to marry Louis, her lines reiterate her loyalty to John, "That [I am] bound in honor still to do / What you in wisdom would vouchsafe to say" (2.1.547–548). Similar to Constance and Hubert, her allegiance is betrayed, and she must join her family's enemies.

The characters themselves articulate another of the play's themes—fortune—to try to explain the play's events. Fortune was typically regarded as chance or luck, a quality that could at any moment favor or abandon a person. The Bastard makes a pun of the term when he says good-bye to his brother, "adieu, good fortune come to thee!" (1.1.186), referring to the family fortune but also to good luck. Later, he uses a familiar construction of fortune, personified as a woman, when he suggests that, after having attacked Angiers, the English and French armies attack each other so that "Fortune shall cull forth / Out of one side her happy minion, / To whom in favor she shall give the day" (2.1.407–409). Victory will go to the side that fortune favors.

Constance uses the figure extensively to describe Arthur:

> [A]t thy birth, dear boy,
> Nature and Fortune joined to make thee great:
> Of Nature's gifts thou mayst with lilies boast,
> And with the half-blown rose. But Fortune, O,
> She is corrupted, changed and won from thee;
> Sh' adulterates hourly with thine uncle John,
> And with her golden hand hath plucked on
>   France
> To tread down fair respect of sovereignty,
> And made his majesty the bawd to theirs.
> France is a bawd to Fortune and King John,
> That strumpet Fortune, that usurping John.
>   (3.1.53–63).

Constance looks for an explanation as to why Philip has abandoned Arthur's cause, and she blames bad luck. Fortune is a woman who once favored Arthur, but like a prostitute, she was "corrupted, changed" by John. In her debased state, she also favored Philip but in the process spoiling his reputation. Constance's bitterness

Constance and Arthur from a 19th-century print of
*King John (Painting by Edward Henry Corbould; engraving
by Henry Wright Smith)*

is powerful here as she implies neither ruler is behaving honorably. Both are seeking fortune's favors but paying for them rather that acquiring them honestly.

A final theme emerges from consideration of Constance, Blanche, and Arthur, one of bloodshed and unnecessary loss. Constance's use of the word *blood* invokes the potential needless cost that Philip was willing to risk in attacking Angiers:

Stay for an answer to your embassy,
Lest unadvised you stain your swords with
   blood.
My Lord Chatillion may from England bring,
That right in peace which here we urge in war,
And then we shall repent each drop of blood

That hot rash haste so indirectly shed.
   (2.1.44–49)

She first uses blood as a symbol, representing the loss of life that war with England would cause. She reiterates this usage three lines later, attacking the idea of waste. To go to war without just cause would not only be immoral; for Constance, it would be a pointless waste of life. Through this notion of blood as not only death, but also wasteful, unnecessary death takes on greater importance as the play develops. The deaths in the second half of the play are personal. Constance and Eleanor die offstage. Arthur's death is profound and tragic because he died accidentally after having been spared earlier. In Act V, the deaths again occur offstage but are impersonal when Philip's reinforcements are drowned and "the best part of [the Bastard's] power . . . were . . . Devourèd by the unexpected flood" (5.7.65–68). These anonymous men were not killed in combat defending their countries but by acts of nature while fighting for the personal interests of their leaders. Bloodshed and death feature in all of Shakespeare's history plays, but the ends nearly always justify the means. England ends up a better place for the loss of English life. Without a reassuring ending, the loss of life in *King John* seems all the more wasteful.

The Language of the Play

King John and *Richard II* are the only two of Shakespeare's plays written entirely in verse. The elevation of tone created by poetry helps portray Richard II as all the more tragic when he falls, but it has a more complicated effect in *King John*. Typically in Shakespeare's plays, characters of high status speaking in verse and using elegant rhetorical devices sound formal, while characters of low status speaking in prose use ordinary and sometimes crude language. When all the characters speak in verse, the social distinctions begin to blur, and it becomes more difficult to place characters into clear-cut social categories. As a result, Shakespeare deploys other linguistic techniques to differentiate characters and prevent them from becoming too similar.

One example of language and status comes late in the play. John has completed his second coronation, and Salisbury, upset at the unnecessary ceremony, tells him:

> Therefore, to be possessed with double pomp,
> To guard a title that was rich before,
> To gild refinèd gold, to paint the lily,
> To throw a perfume on the violet,
> To smooth the ice, or add another hue
> Unto the rainbow, or with taper-light
> To seek the beauteous eye of heaven to garnish,
> Is wasteful and ridiculous excess. (4.2.9–16).

Salisbury must be careful to criticize John's actions but at the same time avoid insulting him or speaking treasonously. He does this by not speaking directly to the king and by using elegant, courtly language. He begins with the rhetorical device anaphora, repeating words at the beginning of a clause. In this way, Salisbury cleverly reiterates his point about the redundancy of the coronation. He softens the tone by decorating his points with natural images of flowers and rainbows. The figures he chooses verge on clichés, and indeed, "to gild the lily" has become one, however misquoted. It might even be argued that these lines are a parody of courtly language and that Salisbury is being sardonic. The final line, however, is forceful and clear, leaving no doubt that Salisbury is unhappy, and this speech foreshadows his defection.

The Bastard's language is also colorful and at times reflects the high style Salisbury and other nobles prefer. Yet, he can also be coarse and common in his choice of words. Criticizing the Citizen of Angiers's use of the language of Petrarchan love poetry that is heavily loaded with rhetorical figures to suggest a marriage between Blanche and Louis (2.1.440–473), the Bastard exclaims, "Zounds! I was never so bethumped with words / Since I first called my brother's father dad" (2.1.487–488). "Zounds," short for *God's wounds,* is a strong curse, and the Bastard follows it with two

more colloquial, and rare in Shakespeare, words, *"bethumped"* and *"dad,"* which remind the audience that his origins are not aristocratic. The Bastard is capable of eloquence, however, especially as he gains experience among the nobility. When challenging Louis, who has invaded England, he claims the English are

> [W]ell prepared
> To whip this dwarfish war, . . .
> To cudgel you and make you take the hatch,
> To dive like buckets in concealèd wells,
> To crouch in litter of your stable planks,
> To lie like pawns locked up in chests and trunks,
> To hug with swine, to seek sweet safety out
> In vaults and prisons. (5.2.135–44)

As did Salisbury, the Bastard uses anaphora to drive his point home, adding some alliteration in line 143 for further eloquence. The imagery is not elevated, however. He describes ordinary, filthy places such as barns, wells, and pigsties to emphasize the humiliation the French will experience. The Bastard's mixture of formal and informal language reveals his origins as a commoner who has risen to a higher status. It enables him to insult Louis, speaking to him with the rhetoric of the aristocracy but the vocabulary of a farmer.

The most pervasive literary device in *King John* is personification. According to Caroline Spurgeon, Shakespeare uses it more often in this play than in any other. It adds liveliness to a play that relies on speeches and dialogue rather than stage action. Characters employ it so frequently that they sometimes build on one another's usage. Confronting the citizens of Angiers, Philip begins by threatening that "Our cannon shall be bent / Against the brows of this resisting town" (2.1.37–38). John echoes this same personification later in the scene when he makes his warning, identifying the "eye and prospect of your town," the "winking gates," "threatened cheeks" and the walls around the city, the "sleeping stones / That as a waist doth girdle you about" (2.1.217–234). The figure of a besieged city personified, often a woman, was commonplace in Shakespeare's time. It implies the threat of cruelty and violence against innocents if the town does not surrender. Philip clarifies the idea when he says that if Angiers recognizes Arthur as king, he will "leave your children, wives, and you in peace" (2.1.266).

Spurgeon also notices how, in the same scene, the Bastard adopts this device but in a grisly fashion. Frustrated by the citizens' delaying tactics, he declares that the two armies will "brawl down / The flinty ribs of this contemptuous city" (2.1.399–400). The image of a crushed skeleton is of a kind with his earlier characterization of the death that will accompany the battle:

> O now doth Death line his dead chaps with
>   steel,
> The swords of soldiers are his teeth, his fangs,
> And now he feasts, mousing the flesh of men
> In undetermined differences of kings.
>   (2.1.367–370)

Death figured as a terrifying skeleton was another Renaissance commonplace, but the Bastard takes it a step further. His personification of a death that devours people, because kings cannot come to an agreement, is chilling. Dying in battle becomes violent and horrific. Soldiers do not simply die; death consumes them. The final line suggests the waste, that the deaths would be pointless. Ordinary soldiers and citizens are being eaten while the self-interested kings remain safe. The Bastard uses the same image later in the same scene when commenting on the treaty that "shakes the rotten carcass of old Death / Out of his rags!" (2.1.475–476). He employs it yet again when confronting Louis at the end of the play, stating that in John's "forehead sits / A bare-ribbed Death, whose office is this day / to feast upon whole thousands of the French" (5.2.179–181).

Constance finds the figure useful as well. As Philip tries to comfort her, she appeals to

> Death, death, O amiable, lovely death,
> Thou odoriferous stench, sound rottenness,

> . . . I will kiss thy detestable bones
> And put my eyeballs in thy vaulty brows
> . . . and be a carrion monster like thyself.
> Come, grin on me, and I will think thou
>   smil'st,
> And buss thee as thy wife. (3.4.25–35)

The rhetorical form of this speech is expressive, beginning with *epanalepsis,* or the use of a word at the beginning and end of a phrase to emphasize its subject. Constance then employs personification to recall the image of death as a devouring skeleton. She develops it to the point where death is her husband, and the repetition and images sound like a horrid parody of romantic language. Her condition has become so miserable that death has become attractive, and her language reflects this change.

Shakespeare's audiences expected lengthy formal speeches in history plays. Sophisticated, repetitive language indicated the importance of the speakers and of the topics. Such passages also slow the action, as typically one character will speak while the others stand and listen. To provide a change of pace, Shakespeare introduces quick one-line exchanges, stichomythia, of insults. In Act II, Eleanor and Constance's contention interrupts what had been a series of speeches and long conversations (2.1.121–124). The most rapid exchange occurs about 10 lines later when the Bastard and the Duke of Austria join the fray. The two alternate words and phrases to create a single metric line. Typically, such exchanges, called *antilabe,* are printed so that the rhythm is clear:

AUSTRIA. Peace!

BASTARD.   Hear the crier.

AUSTRIA.   What the devil art thou?

BASTARD. One that will play the devil, sir, with you. (2.1.135–138)

The Bastard repeats Austria's interjection and uses it as the basis for an extended slur. Such brief and energetic arguments require more movement on stage, creating more action. Shakespeare uses the antagonism between the Bastard and Austria and Constance and Eleanor to insert passages of stichomythia throughout Acts 2 and 3. In later acts, stichomythia and *antilabe* occur less frequently and for more serious matters, such as John's persuading Hubert to kill Arthur (3.3) and Arthur's persuading Hubert not to (4.1).

EXTRACTS OF CLASSIC CRITICISM
William Hazlitt (1778–1830)   [Excerpted from *Characters of Shakespear's Plays* (1817). Hazlitt was a famous romantic-era essayist and critic. His writings on Shakespeare were extremely influential among critics of his time and after.]

King John is the last of the historical plays we shall have to speak of; and we are not sorry that it is. If we are to indulge our imaginations, we had rather do it upon an imaginary theme; if we are to find subjects for the exercise of our pity and terror, we prefer seeking them in fictitious danger and fictitious distress. It gives a *soreness* to our feelings of indignation or sympathy, when we know that in tracing the progress of sufferings and crimes, we are treading upon real ground, and recollect that the poet's "dream" *denoted a foregone conclusion*—irrevocable ills, not conjured up by the fancy, but placed beyond the reach of poetical justice. That the treachery of King John, the death of Arthur, the grief of Constance, had a real truth in history, sharpens the sense of pain, while it hangs a leaden weight on the heart and the imagination. Something whispers to us that we have no right to make a mock of calamities like these, or to turn the truth of things into the puppet and plaything of our fancies. "To consider thus" may be "to consider too curiously;" but still we think that the actual truth of the particular events, in proportion as we are conscious of it, is a drawback on the pleasure as well as the dignity of tragedy.

King John has all the beauties of language and all the richness of the imagination to relieve the painfulness of the subject. The character of King John himself is kept pretty much in the back-ground; it is only marked in by comparatively slight indications. The crimes he is tempted to commit are such as are thrust upon him rather by circumstances and opportunity than of his own seeking: he is here represented as more cowardly than cruel, and as more contemptible than odious. The play embraces only a part of his history. There are, however, a few characters on the stage that excite more disgust and loathing. He has no intellectual grandeur or strength of character to shield him from the indignation which his immediate conduct provokes: he stands naked and defenceless, in that respect, to the worst we can think of him: and besides, we are impelled to put the very worst construction on his meanness and cruelty by the tender picture of the beauty and helplessness of the object of it, as well as by the frantic and heart-rending pleadings of maternal despair. We do not forgive him the death of Arthur because he had too late revoked his doom and tried to prevent it, and perhaps because he has himself repented of his black design, our moral sense gains courage to hate him the more for it. We take him at his word, and think his purposes must be odious indeed, when he himself shrinks back from them. The scene in which King John suggests to Hubert the design of murdering his nephew, is a master-piece of dramatic skill, but it is still inferior, very inferior to the scene between Hubert and Arthur, when the latter learns the orders to put out his eyes. If anything ever was penned, heart-piercing, mixing the extremes of terror and pity, of that which shocks and that which soothes the mind, it is this scene. . . .

Elsie Leslie as Prince Arthur in an early 20th-century production of *King John (Illustration by Bernard Patridge)*

Arthur's death afterwards, when he throws himself from his prison walls, excites the utmost pity for his innocence and friendless situation, and well justifies the exaggerated denunciations of Falconbridge to Hubert whom he suspects wrongfully of the deed. . . .

The excess of maternal tenderness, rendered desperate by the fickleness of friends and the injustice of fortune, and made stronger in will, in proportion to the want of all other power, was never more finely expressed than in Constance. The dignity of her answer to King Philip, when she refuses to accompany his messenger, "To me and to the state

of my great grief, let kings assemble," her indignant reproach to Austria for deserting her cause, her invocation to death, "that love of misery," however fine and spirited, all yield to the beauty of the passage, where, her passion subsiding into tenderness, she addresses the Cardinal in these words:—

> O father Cardinal, I have heard you say
> That we shall see and know our friends
>   in heav'n;
> If that be, I shall see my boy again,
> For since the birth of Cain, the first male
>   child,
> To him that did but yesterday suspire,
> There was not such a gracious creature
>   born.
> But now will canker-sorrow eat my bud,
> And chase the native beauty from his
>   cheek,
> And he will look as hollow as a ghost,
> As dim and meagre as an ague's fit,
> And so he'll die; and rising so again,
> When I shall meet him in the court of
>   heav'n
> I shall not know him; therefore never,
>   never
> Must I behold my pretty Arthur more.

> KING PHILIP. You are as fond of grief
>   as of your child.

> CONSTANCE. Grief fills the room up
>   of my absent child:
> Lies in his bed, walks up and down with
>   me;
> Puts on his pretty looks, repeats his
>   words,
> Remembers me of all his gracious parts;
> Stuffs out his vacant garments with his
>   form.
> Then have I reason to be fond of grief"

The contrast between the mild resignation of Queen Katherine in *Henry VIII* to her own wrongs and the wild, uncontrollable affliction of Constance for the wrongs that she sustains as a mother is no less naturally conceived than it is ably sustained throughout these two wonderful characters.

The accompaniment of the comic character of the Bastard was well chosen to relieve the poignant agony of suffering, and the cold, cowardly policy of behavior in the principal characters of this play. Its spirit, invention, volubility of tongue, and forwardness in action, are unbounded. *Aliquando sufflaminandut erat,* says Ben Jonson of Shakspear. But we should be sorry if Ben Jonson had been his licenser. We prefer the heedless magnanimity of his wit infinitely to all Jonson's laborious caution. The character of the Bastard's comic humour is the same in essence as that of other comic characters in Shakspear; they always run on with good things, and are never exhausted; they are always daring and successful. They have words at will and a flow of wit, like a flow of animal spirits. The difference between Falconbridge and the others is that he is a soldier, and brings his wit to bear upon action, is courageous with his sword as well as tongue, and stimulates his gallantry by his jokes, his enemies feeling the sharpness of his blows and the sting of his sarcasms at the same time. Among his happiest sallies are his descanting on the composition of his own person, his invective against "commodity, tickling commodity," and his expression of contempt for the Archduke of Austria, who had killed his father, which begins in jest but ends in serious earnest. His conduct at the siege of Angiers shows that his resources were not confined to verbal retorts.—The same exposure of the policy of courts and camps, of kings, nobles, priests, and cardinals, takes place here as in the other plays we have gone through, and we shall not go into a disgusting repetition.

This, like the other plays taken from English history, is written in a remarkably smooth and flowing style, very different from some of the tragedies—*Macbeth,* for instance. The passages consist of a series of single lines, not running into one another. This peculiarity in the versification, which is most common in the three parts of *Henry VI.* has been assigned as a reason why those plays were not written by Shakspear. But the same structure of verse occurs in his other undoubted plays, as in *Richard II.* and in *King John.*

Anna Brownell Jameson (1794–1860) [Excerpted from *Characteristics of Women, Moral, Poetical, and Historical* (1832). A critic of literature and art, Jameson wrote particularly for women, though her Shakespearean criticism has had an especially broad appeal. Her works were widely read in the 19th and early 20th centuries but then fell out of favor.]

Whenever we think of Constance, it is in her maternal character. All the interest which she excites in the drama turns upon her situation as the mother of Arthur. Every circumstance in which she is placed, every sentiment she utters, has a reference to him; and she is represented through the whole of the scenes in which she is engaged, as alternately pleading for the rights, and trembling for the existence of her son. . . .

But while we contemplate the character of Constance, she assumes before us an individuality perfectly distinct from the circumstances around her. The action calls forth her maternal feelings, and places them in the most prominent point of view: but with Constance, as with a real human being, the maternal affections are a powerful instinct, modified by other faculties, sentiments, and impulses, making up the individual character. We think of her as a mother, because, as a mother distracted for the loss of her son, she is immediately presented before us, and calls forth our sympathy and our tears; but we infer the rest of her character from what

Constance tears her hair in grief over her son's capture, while King Philip, Pandulph, and Lewis look on in Act III, Scene 4 of *King John*. Print from the Boydell Shakespeare Gallery project *(Painting by Richard Westall; engraving by A. Smith)*

complexion of the character, notwithstanding its amazing grandeur, is so exquisitely feminine. The weakness of the woman, who by the very consciousness of that weakness is worked up to desperation and defiance—the fluctuations of temper, and the bursts of sublime passion, the terrors, the impatience, and the tears, are all most true to feminine nature. The energy of Constance not being based upon strength of character, rises and falls with the tide of passion. Her haughty spirit swells against resistance, and is excited into frenzy by sorrow and disappointment; while neither from her towering pride, nor her strength of intellect, can she borrow patience to submit, or fortitude to endure. It is, therefore, with perfect truth of nature that Constance is first introduced as pleading for peace.

> Stay for an answer to your embassy,
> Lest unadvised you stain your swords
>   with blood:
> My Lord Chatillon may from England
>   bring
> That right in peace, which here we urge
>   in war,
> And then we shall repent each drop of
>   blood,
> That hot, rash haste so indirectly shed.

And that the same woman, when all her passions are roused by the sense of injury, should afterwards exclaim,

> War, war! No peace! peace is to me a
>   war!

That she should be ambitious for her son, proud of his high birth and royal rights, and violent in defending them, is most natural; but I cannot agree with those who think that in the mind of Constance, *ambition*—that is, the love of dominion for its own sake—is either a strong motive or a strong feeling; it

we see, as certainly and as completely as if we had known her whole course of life.

That which strikes us as the principal attribute Constance is power—power of imagination, of will, of passion, of affection, of pride: the moral energy, that faculty which is principally exercised in self-control, and gives consistency to the rest, is deficient—or rather, to speak more correctly, the extraordinary development sensibility and imagination, which lends to the character its rich poetical coloring, leaves the other qualities comparatively subordinate. Hence it is that the whole

could hardly be so where the natural impulses and the ideal power predominate in so high a degree. The vehemence with which she asserts the just and legal rights of her son is that of a fond mother and a proud-spirited woman, stung with the sense of injury, and herself a reigning sovereign,—by birth and right, if not in fact; yet when bereaved of her son, grief not only "fills the room up of her absent child," but seems to absorb every other faculty and feeling—even pride and anger. It is true that she exults over him as one whom nature and fortune had destined to be great, but in her distraction for his loss, she thinks of him only as her "Pretty Arthur."

> O lord! my boy, my Arthur, my fair son!
> My life, my joy, my food, my all the world
> My widow-comfort, and my sorrows' cure!

No other feeling can be traced through the whole of her frantic scene: it is grief only, a mother's heartrending, soul-absorbing grief, and nothing else. Not even indignation, or the desire of revenge, interfere with its soleness and intensity. An ambitious woman would hardly have thus addressed the cold, wily Cardinal:

> And, Father Cardinal, I have heard you
>   say,
> That we shall see and know our friends
>   in heaven:
> If that be true, I shall see my boy again;
> For since the birth of Cain, the first male
>   child,
> To him that did but yesterday suspire,
> There was not such a gracious creature
>   born.
> But now will canker sorrow eat my bud,
> And chase the native beauty from his
>   cheek,
> And he will look as hollow as a ghost;
> As dim and meagre as an ague's fit;
> And so he'll die; and rising so again,

> When I shall meet him in the court of
>   heaven
> I shall not know him: therefore never,
>   never,
> Must I behold my pretty Arthur more!

The bewildered pathos and poetry of this address could be natural in no woman, who did not unite, like Constance, the most passionate sensibility with the most vivid imagination.

It is true that Queen Elinor calls her on one occasion "ambitious Constance;" but the epithet is rather the natural expression of Elinor's own fear and hatred than really applicable. Elinor, in whom age had subdued all passions but ambition, dreaded the mother of Arthur as her rival in power, and for that reason only opposes the claims of the son. But I conceive, that in a woman yet in the prime of life, and endued with the peculiar disposition of Constance, the mere love of power would be too much modified by fancy and feeling to be called a *passion*.

In fact, it is not pride, nor temper, nor ambition nor even maternal affection, which in Constance give the prevailing tone to the whole character; it is the predominance of imagination. I do not mean in the conception of the dramatic portrait, but in the temperament of the woman herself. In the poetical, fanciful, excitable cast of her mind—in the *excess* of the ideal power, tinging all her affections, exalting all her sentiments and thoughts, and animating the expression of both, Constance can only be compared to Juliet. . . .

On the whole, it may be said that pride and maternal affection form the basis of the character of Constance, as it is exhibited to us; but that these passions, in an equal degree common to many human beings, assume their peculiar and individual tinge from an extraordinary development of intellect and fancy. It is the energy of passion which lends the character its concentrated power as it is the prevalence of imagination throughout which dilates it into magnificence.

Some of the most splendid poetry to be met with in Shakspeare, may be found in the parts of Juliet and Constance; the most splendid, perhaps, excepting only the parts of Lear and Othello; and for the same reason,— that Lear and Othello as men, and Juliet and Constance as women, are distinguished by the predominance of the same faculties— passion and imagination. . . .

One more magnificent was never placed before the mind's eye than that of Constance, when, deserted and betrayed, she stands alone in her despair, amid her false friends and her ruthless enemies! [in *King John,* Act III. Scene 1.]—The image of the mother-eagle, wounded and bleeding to death, yet stretched over her young in an attitude of defiance, while all the baser birds of prey are clamoring around her eirie, gives but a faint idea of the moral sublimity of this scene. Considered merely as a poetical or dramatic picture, the grouping is wonderfully fine; on one side, the vulture ambition of that mean-souled tyrant, John: on the other, the selfish, calculating policy of Philip; between them, balancing their passions in his hand, the cold, subtle, heartless Legate: the fiery, reckless Falconbridge; the princely Louis; the still un-conquered spirit of that wrangling queen, old Elinor; the bridal loveliness and modesty of Blanche; the boyish grace and innocence of young Arthur; and Constance in the midst of them, in all the state of her great grief, a grand impersonation of pride and passion, helpless at once and desperate,—form an assemblage of figures, each perfect in its kind, and, taken all together, not surpassed for the variety, force, and splendor of the dramatic and picturesque effect.

Horace Howard Furness, Jr. (1865–1930)
[Excerpted from *A New Variorum Edition of Shake-*

speare: The Life and Death of King John (1919). An editor of several editions of the landmark New Variorum Shakespeare series, Furness was the son of a noted Shakespeare scholar and editor.]

Shakespeare's *King John* . . . among his English Histories . . . has never been one of the favorite or stock-plays, such as *Henry IV.* or *Richard III.* Various are the reasons assigned for this, but chiefly that the titular hero is not the protagonist.

Faulconbridge carries all before him from his first scene, where he at once captivates the King and Queen Elinor, to the final words of the play put in his mouth as the one best typifying the rugged warrior Englishman of the time. Critics have not been slow to note the gradual change in his character. The braggart of the early scenes is drawn on the same plan as that of the Faulconbridge of *The Troublesome Raigne,* and in the older play he maintains practically the same character throughout. It was the intuitive perception of Shakespeare that grasped the dramatic possibilities of such a character and showed how a man of Faulconbridge's temperament attains to full strength and fineness by responsibility placed upon him, and by the confidence of one who trusts him implicitly. "Have thou the ordering of the present time" are almost the last conscious words addressed to Faulconbridge by the King, as he hands over to him the conduct of the campaign against the Dauphin's invasion, and this after Faulconbridge's scathing comment on the King's announcement that Pandulph has offered to make a compromise with the invaders. Once only can we detect a slight wavering in his allegiance. The dead body of Arthur, found under such suspicious circumstances, almost shakes his faith, and wrings from him the admission that he begins to lose his way amid the thorns and dangers of this world; and that Heaven itself frowns upon the land where such deeds can be committed. His righteous indignation is forgotten as he stands beside the dead body of the King; his last words breathed in the dead ears are, that he but stays to avenge the murder, and then his soul shall wait on his benefactor to heaven as it has been but his servant upon earth. In adapting the older play it must have been at once apparent to the Playwright that King John's was not a character which lent itself to dramatic treatment. He was utterly perfidious, a poltroon, and a moral coward without one redeeming feature. Richard, Duke of Gloucester, ruthless and cruel though he was, had at least the saving grace of a grim humor; and his resourcefulness on all occasions excites a dreadful interest in his fate. But John was without even these signs of strength; his defiance of the Pope is mere bluster, he cringes abjectly when he is made actually to realize the power of the Church, and accedes to all the conditions, forcing himself to believe that all this was done not on compulsion, but as a voluntary act on his part.

MODERN CRITICISM AND CRITICAL CONTROVERSIES

Although it is often regarded as one of Shakespeare's least popular plays, *King John* has always attracted a steady stream of critical attention. Interest in the play began to increase in the 1980s with the second wave of feminism and the advent of New Historicism, both of which brought fresh perspectives to old questions about religion, gender, character, and textuality.

Text and Authorship

As discussed in the "Background" section, the modern-day text of *King John* was included in the first collection of Shakespeare's plays, printed in 1623, seven years after his death. Back in 1591, however, an anonymous play entitled *The Troublesome Raigne of John King of England* had been printed. Although there are very few word-for-word similarities between the two plays, *The Trou-*

blesome Raigne events, characters, and structure are so similar to Shakespeare's play that the two cannot be unrelated. Thematically, *The Troublesome Raigne* is more strongly anti-Catholic than *King John,* whose position on Catholicism has been debated by critics. *The Troublesome Raigne* includes a scene with the Bastard visiting a monastery to collect money and finding the monks engaged in lewd and immoral acts. Another scene shows a monk deciding whether it would be better to stab or poison John. *King John* lacks these scenes and tones down the other instances of anti-Catholic language.

The similarities between these texts raise two important questions: Which was written first and by whom? Throughout the 18th, 19th, and early 20th centuries, most scholars agreed that *King John* was Shakespeare's adaptation of *The Troublesome Raigne.* A minority opinion, however, persists. In 1954, E. A. J. Honigmann challenged the orthodoxy in his edition of the play. Honigmann pointed out *King John* contained passages taken from sources such as Holinshed's *Chronicles* and others that were absent from *The Troublesome Raigne.* He went on to argue that as a result of this discovery and other evidence, *King John* must have been written first, in 1590–91 and that *The Troublesome Raigne* had been adapted from it, possibly from memory. Some scholars accepted Honigmann's conclusions, most notably William H. Matchett (1966) and L. A. Beaurline (1990) in their editions of *King John* and Brian Boyd in 1995. Honigmann has continued to defend his conclusions, most recently in an exchange with Sidney Thomas and Paul Werstine and in an article on self-repetition.

The authorship of *The Troublesome Raigne* has also caused disagreement among scholars. Some assume that Shakespeare wrote it and revised it himself into *King John.* The contention is supported by the reprinting in 1611 and 1623 of *The Troublesome Raigne* with Shakespeare identified as the author. This argument is not conclusive, however, because Shakespeare's reputation helped sell books, and therefore, numerous works by other playwrights and poets were printed under his name. The opposing view points out that the publication date of *The Troublesome Raigne* indicates that it would have to have been written very early in Shakespeare's career and that it lacks much of his style and use of language. Using a complex analysis that compares writing styles and word use, Brian Vickers argues that Shakespeare's contemporary George Peele wrote *The Troublesome Raigne*. He goes on to suggest that after Peele died in 1596, Shakespeare revised *The Troublesome Raigne* into *King John*. No one has yet challenged Vickers's conclusions, and they are likely to remain the majority opinion on the relationship between the two plays.

Religion

Its historical context and relationship to *The Troublesome Raigne* means that *King John* has also generated a large body of scholarship regarding Shakespeare's attitudes toward Catholicism and Protestantism. *The Troublesome Raigne* is persistently anti-Catholic, and in the 16th century, the historical King John was regarded as an early Protestant martyr, the victim of a tyrannical Catholic Church. Shakespeare's *King John* is much more reserved in its position on religion and nowhere near as polemic as *The Troublesome Raigne*. Yet, *King John* has several episodes that are easily construed as anti-Catholic. John's death at the hands of a murderous monk is the most egregious. As the pope's representative, Pandulph is an interfering presence, excommunicating John and forcing him to submit to the church's authority. The play's historical context also lends support to its being anti-Catholic. When she became queen, Elizabeth returned England to Protestantism after six years of Catholicism. Her persecution of Catholics suspected of fomenting rebellion, her excommunication by the pope, and the threat of the papally supported Spanish Armada, all contributed to an atmosphere that welcomed anti-Catholic sentiment. Responding to these tensions, much of the scholarly discourse on religion and *King John* has attempted show how the play participates in, or by comparison with *The Troublesome Raigne* does not participate in, anti-Catholic sentiment.

In the late 20th century, however, critics began to write about the play not so much as Catholic or Protestant but as possessing a purposefully ambiguous depiction of Christianity. The play's use of unique characters rather than representative types has given rise to interpretations that have found competing Catholic and Protestant elements in the play. Self-interest replaces religion as a theme for Roy Battenhouse, who claims Shakespeare avoided explicit engagement with religion. Instead, John is a secular figure whose self-interest is his, and the play's, dominant ideology. Arthur and Hubert are the most religious of the characters, and the emphasis on commodity marginalizes them. Other studies, influenced by New Historicism, have moved past the Protestant-Catholic binary to argue that the play does not critique a specific religion, or religion itself, but instead the politicization of religion in Elizabethan England.

The question of religion in Shakespeare's plays inevitably turns to the faith of the playwright. In *Shakespeare: The "Lost Years"* (1985), Honigmann, who contends that Shakespeare grew up in a Catholic household, sees *King John* as presenting a separation between a religious identity, Roman Catholicism, and a national identity (English). *King John* portrays characters who are patriotically English as opposed, not to the Catholic Church, but to the undue influence of the pope in national affairs. Later studies have sought to modify this thesis, pointing out that "in Shakespeare's time, there was a great muddled middle in English Christianity" who were neither rigorously Catholic nor strictly Protestant (Marotti 219). Therefore, in appealing to such a diverse audience, Shakespeare, whatever his own beliefs, sought to create plays that would appeal as widely as possible.

The Bastard

Before the 1950s, most critics, such as E. M. W. Tillyard, regarded the Bastard as the play's hero or at least the most heroic of its characters. Most notable was Adrien Bonjour's consideration that

"John's career represents a falling curve, the Bastard's career a rising curve; and both curves . . . are linked into a single pattern . . . [the] rise of a hero" (270). Some writers are reluctant to grant the Bastard a hero's status. He may be loyal to England, but he is also cynical and not important enough to the narrative to be a hero. Rather than serving as its focus, some suggest, he is a type of chorus who comments on the events of the play. Julia C. Van der Water extends this interpretation to argue that thinking of the Bastard as a single character type is misleading. Not only is the Bastard a chorus, argues Van de Water, he is also a messenger, a patriot, a loyal supporter of the king, as well as a Vice figure.

Some who see the Bastard as a medieval Vice figure, based on the tradition of the morality play, argue that as the play progresses, he changes into a contemporary figure who intentionally becomes a loyal supporter of the monarch. That the Bastard chooses his roles in the play, instead of being shaped by its events, has led some to argue that he is a modern character. He surveys his situation and his options and chooses what he feels is best for himself at the time, an aspect of his character that appeals to modern readers.

Feminism

Feminist literary criticism since the 1960s has expanded on an extensive 19th-century body of work that paid particular attention to Constance. This focus derived in part from the writings and reviews of actors, such as Sarah Siddons, Helen Faucit, Fanny Kemble, and Ellen Kean. Writer Anna B. Jameson is one of the most notable early (19th-century) women critics. Interested in all of Shakespeare's female characters, Jameson devoted special attention to Constance, finding in her a specifically female "power of imagination" that made her such an electrifying presence on stage (*Characteristics of Women*, 220). In 1990, Christy Desmet brought new attention to Jameson's work, which had been largely ignored in the 20th century. Desmet found in Jameson an early feminist, challenging her male contemporaries' narrow

Constance holds Arthur as the English and French forces enter the camp in Act III, Scene 1 of *King John*. Print published by the London Printing and Publishing Company, 19th century *(Painting by Edward Henry Corbould; engraving by Frederick F. Walker)*

understanding of female characters and redefining Shakespeare's characters for a female readership.

Much feminist criticism has focused on female characters' ability to influence the events of Shakespeare's plays. Because they have so little physical power compared to male characters, their words have been closely examined. Constance, for example, is one of the most colorful characters in *King John*, but she is powerless to do anything about her situation. She, like Eleanor, can only try to use words to persuade the male characters to do what she wants. While Eleanor is sometimes successful in guiding John's decisions, Constance, even when she speaks the truth, is continually thwarted.

The understanding of women as powerless in Shakespeare's history plays has been revised in recent decades, most thoroughly by Phyllis Rackin, who notes that women characters can subvert patriarchal structures through their knowledge of true legitimacy; Lady Faulconbridge, for example, through her adultery with Richard I, produced a son but kept that knowledge secret. Another woman, Eleanor, first suspected the truth when she noticed the Bastard's similarity to the dead king Richard I. Lady Faulconbridge finally revealed the truth to the Bastard, confirming Eleanor's suspicion. Another form of female power is described by Juliet Dusinberre using a combination of performance history and feminism. She begins with the fact that boy actors played women's roles in Shakespeare's theater and that in *King John* they may well have overacted. On stage, the boys playing Constance, Eleanor, and Blanche would have been particularly effective at embarrassing the male characters and audiences through their powerful arguments and speeches. In so doing, they helped focus the play on their concerns.

Comparing *King John* to *Richard III*, Jean E. Howard and Rackin write that in *King John*, "the entire action seems designed to foreground every kind of moral and political and historiographic ambiguity. . . . [E]very attempt to resolve the action or make sense of it is immediately frustrated by the moral ambiguities of an episodic plot where success and failure ride on the shifting winds of chance" (119). These sentences neatly sum up the critical difficulties with *King John* and, at the same time, suggest why it has retained scholarly interest over the centuries.

THE PLAY TODAY

In the public eye, *King John*'s fortunes have risen, fallen, and risen again since the 16th century. The historical setting and dramatic speeches made it very popular on stage from the 18th to the late 19th centuries, though it lost popularity at the beginning of the 20th. Criticism of the play, focusing on its relationship to *The Troublesome Raigne of John King of England,* religion, and the female charac-

ters, has followed a similar trajectory. Scholarly and theatrical interest in the play faded through the middle part of the 20th century in part because of the play's apparent lack of focus and the absence of a distinct hero. But in the postmodern culture of the late 20th and early 21st centuries, scholarly and theatrical interest in a play that was once considered uneven and unfocused has returned.

Scholars today continue to be interested in the play's female characters and how they shape the play's actions. Prominent essays have examined how women function as mothers and mourners and how they appear outside of the domestic spaces typically reserved for them. A related stream of criticism has addressed the play's use of masculinity and its representation of children. Other scholars continue to investigate Shakespeare's various sources for the play, looking back at medieval mystery plays as sources of characterization and structure.

As with so many of Shakespeare's plays, we have no record of a performance of *King John* during the playwright's lifetime. The earliest known performance was in London in 1737, and the production ran for four years. *King John* was revived regularly in the 18th century, notably by the great Shakespearean actor David Garrick. In 1745, one of Garrick's competitors, Colley Cibber, staged his own adaptation of *King John,* entitled *Papal Tyranny in the Reign of King John.* Cibber produced the play to take advantage of a wave of anti-Catholic sentiment moving through Britain at the time. He eliminated the first act, and the characters of Eleanor and Austria and sharply reduced the Bastard's part, giving many of his lines to Constance, who was played by Cibber's wife. The play was not very successful but did stimulate interest in Shakespeare's uncut original.

Through the 18th and 19th centuries, *King John* was a regular fixture on British and American stages. Nearly all the great actor-managers of the time produced and starred in the play. Along with Garrick, John Philip Kemble, William Charles Macready, and Charles Kean all used the play to perpetuate their celebrity status. Kemble's younger brother Charles, in collaboration with James

Robinson Planché, directed what is perhaps the best-known 19th-century production. In 1823, the two men staged *King John* with costumes and sets that reflected the play's 13th-century setting, rather than their own time, as was commonly done. Planché had conducted extensive research, and the result was a popular production that influenced the stagings of Shakespeare for the rest of the century.

In the latter half of the 19th century, *King John* again fell out of favor. In 1899, Herbert Beerbohm Tree revived the play in a spectacular production that included a scene showing the signing of Magna Carta. As part of its advertising campaign, Tree made an especially innovative decision. He made a brief film of several scenes from the play and had it shown in London to attract audiences to his stage production. We do not know if Tree's strategy was successful, but it did provide us with the first Shakespeare film ever made, which is now available on DVD.

The 20th century saw *King John* on stage again fade in popularity, but not many years would pass before it returned. With the emergence of director's theater after World War II, an increasing interest in politically inflected productions of Shakespeare's histories, and the proliferation of Shakespeare festivals, the play became more popular. Since the 1950s, the number of productions per decade has increased steadily. To help audiences bridge the historical divide, productions often give the play a modern setting, seeking parallels in modern political conflicts. Shakespeare festivals will sometimes pair *King John* with another play (such as *Henry VIII*) or provide extensive program notes to help illuminate its more difficult aspects.

It is perhaps ironic that after being the subject of the first Shakespeare film ever, *King John* has never been filmed again, though it has been produced for radio and television. David Giles directed it for the last chapter of the complete BBC Shakespeare series in 1984. Critics found the acting strong, particularly Claire Bloom's portrayal of Constance and Mary Morris's of Eleanor, though the poor sets distracted from the production's merits.

While 19th-century audiences were intrigued by the pageant of spectacular productions of *King John* with celebrity actors in leading roles, modern audiences seem to be drawn to the political wrangling over legitimate claims to the throne, the religious conflicts, moral questions involving the use of power, and a general interest in all things Shakespeare. The presence of two strong, vocal female characters, comparatively rare in Shakespeare's plays, also draws the interest of a culture in which female heads of state and commerce are much more common than they were in Shakespeare's day, Queen Elizabeth I notwithstanding.

Several critics have argued that the Bastard is Shakespeare's first modern character. He rises on his own merits from obscurity to attend the king of England and to lead the English army against the French. He addresses the audience, often sarcastically, describing his conflicts over the right thing to do. For most readers and audiences, he consistently makes the right decision. In these ways, the Bastard embodies the modern notion of the self-made man or a rags-to-riches story.

FIVE TOPICS FOR DISCUSSION AND WRITING

1. **Keeping and breaking promises:** Much of the conflict in *King John* begins with promises and oaths that are made and then broken. John and Philip both break promises but do not suffer any consequences. The English lords betray their king but are forgiven. Choose several examples of oaths or promises. Think about the characters' motives for the promises they make and break. How can their decisions be defended? What moral reasons for breaking a promise are there?

2. **Tragedy:** Though it is a history play rather than a tragedy, critics have often sought to find tragedy in *King John*. Which of the characters in the play can we regard as tragic? What definition of tragedy must we use to do so?

3. **Fortune versus Nature:** Constance draws a distinction between Fortune as luck or chance and Nature as the abilities one is born with (3.1.54). What are some examples of them at work in the

play? Which seems to be most influential in the play? In our lives?

4. **Self-interest:** The Bastard claims that self-interest is what is wrong with the world. What are some examples of self-interest in the play? Is it possible to act out of self-interest but also act in the interest of others? Is it unrealistic to expect people not to act out of self-interest?

5. **Personification:** Shakespeare uses the technique of personification more in *King John* than in any other of his plays. Where do we see it in the play? Select several examples, and analyze why the speaker uses this literary device in a particular moment. How does it help him or her make a point?

Bibliography

Anderson, Thomas. "'Legitimation, Name, and All Is Gone': Bastardy and Bureaucracy in Shakespeare's *King John*." *Journal for Early Modern Cultural Studies* 4, no. 2 (Fall–Winter 2004): 35–61.

Banks, Carol. "Warlike Women: 'Reproofe to these degenerate effeminate dayes'?" In *Shakespeare's Histories and Counter-Histories,* edited by Dermot Cavanagh, Stuart Hampton-Rees, and Stephen Longstaffe, 169–181. Manchester, U.K.: Manchester University Press, 2006.

Battenhouse, Roy. "*King John:* Shakespeare's Perspective and Others." *Notre Dame English Journal* 14 (1982): 191–215.

Beaurline, L. A., ed. *King John.* Cambridge: Cambridge University Press, 1990.

Blake, Ann. "Shakespeare and the Medieval Theatre of Cruelty." In *Renaissance Poetry and Drama in Context: Essays for Christopher Wortham,* edited by Andrew Lynch, 7–22. Newcastle, U.K.: Cambridge Scholars, 2008.

Bloom, Gina. "Words Made of Breath: Gender and Vocal Agency in *King John*." *Shakespeare Studies* 33 (2005): 125–155.

Bonjour, Adrien. "The Road to Swinstead Abbey: A Study of the Sense and Structure of *King John*." *English Literary History* 18, no. 4 (December 1951): 253–274.

Boyd, Brian. "*King John* and *The Troublesome Raigne:* Sources, Structure, Sequence." *Philological Quarterly* 74 (1995): 37–56.

Braunmuller, A. R. "*King John* and Historiography." *English Literary History* 55 (1988): 309–322.

Braunmuller, A. R., ed. *The Life and Death of King John.* Oxford: Oxford University Press, 1994.

Bullough, Geoffrey, ed. *Narrative and Dramatic Sources of Shakespeare,* vol. 4. London: Routledge & Kegan Paul, 1962.

Burckhardt, Sigurd. "The Ordering of the Present Time." *English Literary History* 33, no. 2 (June 1966): 133–153.

Calderwood, James L. "Commodity and Honour in *King John*." *University of Toronto Quarterly* 29, no. 3 (April 1960): 341–356.

Campana, Joseph. "Killing Shakespeare's Children: The Cases of *Richard III* and *King John*." *Shakespeare* 3 (2007): 18–39.

Campbell, Lily B. *Shakespeare's "Histories": Mirrors of Elizabethan Policy.* San Marino, Calif.: Huntington Library, 1947.

Candido, Joseph, ed. *King John.* Shakespeare, the Critical Tradition. London: Athlone, 1996.

Clemen, Wolfgang. *The Development of Shakespeare's Imagery.* 2nd ed. London: Methuen, 1977.

Cousin, Geraldine. *Shakespeare in Performance:* King John. Manchester, U.K.: Manchester University Press, 1994.

Curren-Aquino, Deborah T., ed. King John: *New Perspectives.* Newark: University of Delaware Press, 1989.

Curren-Aquino, Deborah T., comp. King John: *An Annotated Bibliography.* New York: Garland Publishing, 1994.

Desmet, Christy. "'Intercepting the dew-drop': Female Readers and Readings in Anna Jameson's Shakespearean Criticism." In *Women's Re-Visions of Shakespeare: On the Responses of Dickinson, Woolf, Rich, H.D., George Eliot, and Others,* edited by Marianne Novy, 41–57. Urbana: University of Illinois Press, 1990.

Dickson, Lisa. "Industrious Scenes and Acts of Death: *King John*'s Visible Economy and the (Dis)Appearing 'I.'" *English Studies in Canada* 24 (1998): 1–23.

Dusinberre, Juliet. "*King John* and Embarrassing Women." *Shakespeare Survey* 42 (1989): 37–52.

Evett, David. "'We Owe Thee Much': Service in *King John*." *Shakespearean International Yearbook* 5 (2005): 44–65.

Gieskes, Edward. "'He is but a bastard to the time': Status and Service in *The Troublesome Raigne of John* and Shakespeare's *King John*." *English Literary History* 65 (1998): 779–798.

Goodland, Katharine. *Female Mourning and Tragedy in Medieval and Renaissance English Drama: From* The Raising of Lazarus *to* King Lear. Aldershot, U.K., and Burlington, Vt.: Ashgate, 2005.

Groves, Beatrice. "Memory, Composition, and the Relationship of *King John* to *The Troublesome Raigne of King John*." *Comparative Drama* 38, nos. 2–3 (Summer–Fall 2004): 277–290.

Honigmann, E. A. J., ed. *King John*. London: Methuen, 1954.

———. "*King John, The Troublesome Reigne,* and 'Documentary Links': A Rejoinder." *Shakespeare Quarterly* 38, no. 1 (Spring 1987): 124–126.

———. *Shakespeare: The "Lost Years."* Manchester, U.K.: Manchester University Press, 1985.

———. "Shakespeare's Self-Repetitions and *King John*." *Shakespeare Survey* 53 (2000): 175–183.

Howard, Jean E., and Phyllis Rackin. *Engendering a Nation: A Feminist Account of Shakespeare's English Histories.* London: Routledge, 1997.

Jones, Emrys. *The Origins of Shakespeare.* Oxford, U.K.: Clarendon Press, 1977.

Lane, Robert. "'The Sequence of Posterity': Shakespeare's *King John* and the Succession Controversy." *Studies in Philology* 92, no. 4 (Autumn 1995): 460–481.

Levin, Richard. "*King John*'s Bastard." *Upstart Crow* 3 (Fall 1980): 29–41.

Marotti, Arthur F. "Shakespeare and Catholicism." In *Theatre and Religion: Lancastrian Shakespeare,* edited by Richard Dutton, Alison Findlay, and Richard Wilson, 218–241. Manchester, U.K.: Manchester University Press, 2003.

Matchett, William H., ed. *The Life and Death of King John.* New York: New American Library, 1966.

McAdam, Ian. "Masculine Agency and Moral Stance in Shakespeare's *King John*." *Philological Quarterly* 86, nos. 1–2 (Winter–Spring 2007): 67–95.

Mowat, Barbara A., and Paul Werstine, eds. *The Life and Death of King John.* New York: Washington Square Press, 2000.

Piesse, A. J. "Character Building: Shakespeare's Children in Context." In *Shakespeare and Childhood,* edited by Kate Chedgzoy, Susanne Greenhalgh, and Robert Shaughnessy, 64–79. Cambridge: Cambridge University Press, 2007.

Rackin, Phyllis. "Patriarchal History and Female Subversion in *King John*." In *King John: New Perspectives,* edited by Deborah T. Curren-Aquino, 76–90. Newark: University of Delaware Press, 1989.

Saccio, Peter. *Shakespeare's English Kings: History, Chronicle, and Drama.* New York: Oxford University Press, 1977.

Schwarz, Kathryn. "A Tragedy of Good Intentions: Maternal Agency in *3 Henry VI* and *King John*." *Renaissance Drama* 32 (2003): 225–254.

Shakespeare, William. *King John.* Folger Shakespeare Library. Edited by Paul Werstine and Barbara A. Mowat. New York: Simon & Schuster, 2005.

Shirley, Frances A., ed. King John *and* Henry VIII: *Critical Essays.* New York: Garland Publications, 1988.

Spurgeon, Caroline F. E. *Shakespeare's Imagery and What It Tells Us.* Cambridge: Cambridge University Press, 1952.

Thomas, Sidney. "'Enter a Sheriffe': Shakespeare's *King John* and *The Troublesome Raigne*." *Shakespeare Quarterly* 37, no. 1 (Spring 1986): 98–100.

Tillyard, E. M. W., *Shakespeare's History Plays.* London: Chatto & Windus, 1948.

Van de Water, Julia C. "The Bastard in *King John*." *Shakespeare Quarterly* 11, no. 2 (Spring 1960): 137–146.

Vanhoutte, Jacqueline. *Strange Communion: Motherland and Masculinity in Tudor Plays, Pamphlets, and Politics.* Newark: University of Delaware Press, 2003.

Vaughan, Virginia Mason. "Between Tetralogies: *King John* as Transition." *Shakespeare Quarterly* 35 (Winter 1984): 407–420.

———. "*King John:* Subversion and Containment." In *King John: New Perspectives,* edited by Deborah T. Curren-Aquino, 62–75. Newark: University of Delaware Press, 1989.

Vickers, Brian. "*The Troublesome Raigne,* George Peele, and the Date of *King John*" In *Words That Count: Essays on Early Modern Authorship in Honor of MacDonald P. Jackson,* edited by Brian Boyd, 78–116. Newark: University of Delaware Press, 2004.

Waith, Eugene, M. "*King John* and the Drama of History." *Shakespeare Quarterly* 29, no. 2 (Spring 1978): 192–211.

Weimann, Robert. "Mingling Vice and 'Worthiness' in *King John.*" *Shakespeare Studies* 27 (1999): 109–133.

Werstine, Paul. "'Enter a Sheriffe' and the Conjuring Up of Ghosts." *Shakespeare Quarterly* 38, no. 1 (Spring 1987): 126–130.

Womersley, David. "The Politics of Shakespeare's *King John.*" *Review of English Studies* 40, no. 160 (1989): 497–515.

Wymer, Rowland. "Shakespeare and the Mystery Cycles." *English Literary Renaissance* 34 (2004): 265–285.

FILM AND VIDEO PRODUCTIONS

Dando, Walter Pfeffer, and William K. L. Dickson, dirs. *King John.* With Sir Herbert Beerbohm Tree and Julia Neilson. British Mutoscope and Biograph Company, 1899.

Giles, David, dir. *The Life and Death of King John.* With Leonard Rossiter and Claire Bloom. BBC, 1984.

—Mark G. Aune

King Lear

INTRODUCTION

Many critics call *King Lear* Shakespeare's masterpiece. Certainly is one of the most moving works of literature even written. Violence, betrayal, and murder stand on one side of the play; on the other, friendship, honor, and redemption. Praised as a perfect description of the human condition, *King Lear* begins with a scene of painful domestic intimacy that turns into a war between two kingdoms.

At the start of the play, King Lear confesses that he is tired and wants to retire. But, in the primeval age in which Shakespeare sets the play, a monarch is a ruler for life, granted power by divine will, not by a society. Unlike the rich and powerful women and men of the contemporary age, monarchs like Lear do not retire; the notion is completely unacceptable. Lear is still a supreme ruler, however, and his choice to hand the kingdom over to his daughters goes unchallenged—though not unpunished.

Treachery and suffering are the fruits of Lear's decision. Deep in the soil of the play, however, Shakespeare plants seeds of rebirth. These elements grow through the course of the play, creeping out from dark corners and amassing strength in unsuspecting characters. A play that, at first, reeks of death and destruction begins to take on a new fragrance. The loyalty, courage, and love shown by characters such as Kent and Edgar begin to dominate.

These positive elements are perhaps expressed most powerfully by Cordelia, Lear's youngest daughter. Unwilling to watch her father destroy himself, Cordelia casts away a massive inheritance by speaking to Lear with brutal honesty. She chooses the thorny path of honor by refusing to flatter her father with empty words and meaningless promises. The depth of her commitment is revealed through the course of the play.

The final and most powerful theme of the play is redemption. In the play's primary plot, that of Lear and his family, and in the secondary plot, that of Gloucester and his two sons, Shakespeare portrays two powerful acts of forgiveness and redemption. When it seems that the world of the play is dominated by evil schemers and dark villains, the audience is overwhelmed by a surpassingly moving turn of events and hearts. One of Shakespeare's great tragedies, *King Lear* is also one of the titanic achievements of the human mind.

BACKGROUND

Shakespeare wrote *King Lear* during the reign of King James I, who ruled England and Scotland from 1603 to 1625. *King Lear* was performed for King James I at his residence, Whitehall Palace, on December 26, 1606. It is interesting to wonder what the king thought of Shakespeare's play and its very political content. Before James I took the English throne, he went by the title of James VI, king of Scotland; his accession to the English throne united all of Great Britain. James I, therefore, ruled over a massive kingdom, and his full title, or "full style," was quite impressive: His Majesty, James VI, by the Grace of God King of England, Scotland, France and Ireland, Defender of the Faith, etc.

With the Fool standing behind him, Lear asks Goneril why she is unhappy in Act I, Scene 4 of *King Lear.* This drawing was designed for the Chiswick edition of Shakespeare, published in 1900. *(Illustration by John Byam Lister Shaw)*

Political censorship was a powerful force in Shakespeare's time. His choice to set *King Lear* in an ancient civilization, 800 B.C., may have been influenced by his desire to avoid angering the authorities. The ancient setting created distance between the reign of King Lear and the reign of King James, making comparisons between the two monarchs more difficult—although the similarities are striking and interesting.

Shakespeare's chief source for the script was probably an earlier play entitled *The Chronicle History of King Leir,* composed around 1593 by an unknown author. This play has a similar plot but the ending is quite different; in *The Chronicle History,* Cordelia and her husband, the king of France, return to England and easily defeat the forces commanded by Goneril, Regan, and Cornwall. The story of King Lear also appears in Raphael Holinshed's *Chronicles of England, Scotland, and Ireland* (1587), which also clearly influenced Shakespeare. Holinshed probably based his account on that of the medieval historian Geoffrey of Monmouth.

The subplot about Gloucester and his sons was based on a story in Philip Sidney's 1590 *Arcadia.* Other parts of the plot are also clearly influenced by other writings of Shakespeare's time, such as Edmund Spenser's *The Faerie Queene* (1589).

Date and Text of the Play

King Lear was probably written around 1605, before Shakespeare wrote *Macbeth* and just after *Othello*—in other words, when Shakespeare was at the height of his powers as a writer. *Lear* has an unusually complicated textual history, making it especially difficult for scholars today to settle on the "best" text. The earliest published text is dated 1608 and is referred to by scholars as the First Quarto (Q1). Twelve copies of the First Quarto survive. A later version also exists, dated 1619. This version includes a number of differences from the first. It is not known if these changes were made by Shakespeare or someone else, an editor or printer. *King Lear* also appears in the 1623 First Folio publication of Shakespeare's plays; the text there has still more differences from both quarto versions. In the First Folio, 285 lines are omitted from the text of the First Quarto, and an additional 115 lines are added. Scholars disagree about which version is the most accurate. Some claim that the First Folio represents changes that Shakespeare made prior to his death in 1616. Others question whether the revisions were truly Shakespeare's.

In 1681, a playwright named Nahum Tate wrote a new version of Shakespeare's *King Lear* that was preferred by critics and producers for more than 150 years. This "improved" version offered what was considered a more satisfying ending. At

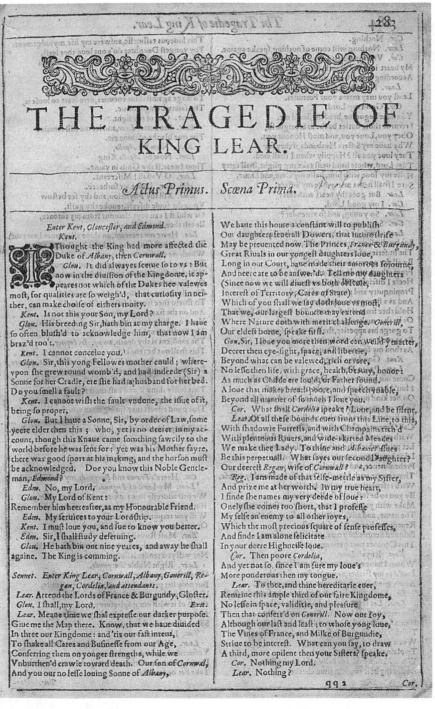

Title page of the First Folio edition of *King Lear*, published in 1623

M. William Shak-speare:

HIS
True Chronicle Historie of the life and
death of King L E A R and his three
Daughters.

With the vnfortunate life of Edgar, *sonne*
and heire to the Earle of Gloster, and his
sullen and assumed humor of
T O M of Bedlam:

As it was played before the Kings Maiestie at Whitehall vpon
S. Stephans night in Christmas Hollidayes.

By his Maiesties seruants playing vsually at the Gloabe
on the Bancke-side.

LONDON,
Printed for *Nathaniel Butter*, and are to be sold at his shop in *Pauls*
Church-yard at the signe of the Pide Bull neere
S^t. *Austins* Gate. 1 6 0 8.

Title page of the First Quarto of *King Lear,* printed in
1608

the close of Tate's play, Edmund, Goneril, and
Regan are dead, but Lear and Cordelia survive,
and Albany turns the kingdom back over to Lear.
Cordelia then marries Edgar, and Lear gives them
the kingdom. Even the great critic Samuel Johnson
preferred Tate's version, claiming that an audience
would "always rise better pleased from the final triumph of persecuted virtue" (190).

SYNOPSIS
Brief Synopsis

King Lear, in his 80s, plans to retire and divide his
kingdom among his three grown daughters. Before
he gives each daughter her portion, each must profess her love of him. The youngest, Cordelia, loves
her father but refuses to play the game. Angered,
Lear disinherits Cordelia, whose honesty nonetheless attracts a suitor, the king of France. Cordelia
and France leave Lear's kingdom. When Lear's
trusted adviser, Kent, warns him against the rash
act, Lear banishes Kent.

Lear quickly learns that his two older daughters, Goneril and Regan, are not as faithful as they
pretended when it came time to dividing the kingdom. Indeed, Lear's plans to live out his retirement
between both daughters' homes are dashed when
each refuses to allow him and his retinue of knights
to share their palaces. Lear flees in the company of
Kent, who has returned in disguise out of his love
for Lear, and his Fool.

The play's double plot involves the Earl of
Gloucester, who has two sons: Edgar and the
younger, Edmund, who was born out of wedlock.
Edmund plots to steal his legitimate brother's
inheritance by tricking Gloucester into believing the
Edgar plans to kill him. As Lear does to Cordelia,
Gloucester disowns his virtuous son, Edgar, who
escapes with his life by disguising himself as a beggar-madman, Tom O'Bedlam. Edgar comes upon
Lear, descending into insanity as he finally understands the folly of trusting his ungrateful daughters and disowning Cordelia. Edmund, meanwhile,
allies himself with Regan's husband, the Duke of
Cornwall. He has also taken both Regan and Goneril as lovers. The daughters plot to assassinate Lear.

Loyal to Lear, Gloucester discovers the plot
and finds Lear. He warns Kent and the Fool, who
arrange to send Lear to Dover, where Cordelia has
set up camp with a French army to fight for her
father's return to the throne. While Gloucester is
helping Lear, Cornwall awards Edmund the title
of the new earl of Gloucester. When Gloucester
returns, Cornwall deems him a traitor and gouges
out his eyes. A servant loyal to Gloucester stabs
Cornwall, who dies (offstage) from the wound.
Blinded, Gloucester wanders the kingdom, where
Edgar, still disguised, finds him and saves him
from committing suicide.

Goneril's husband, the Duke of Albany, runs afoul of his wife, who, like Regan, is in love with Edmund. She plans to kill Albany. She dispatches her steward, Oswald, with a letter for Edmund. Coming upon Gloucester, Oswald prepares to kill the old man; instead, Edgar kills Oswald. He takes the letter, which reveals Goneril's plot against her husband, and delivers it to Albany.

In the war between Cordelia's forces and Edmund, Lear and Cordelia are taken captive. Albany declares that Edmund is not the true earl of Gloucester and calls for witnesses to speak against Edmund's claim. Edgar steps forward and challenges Edmund, killing him in a duel. The bodies of Goneril and Regan are brought in: Goneril has killed her sister and then herself. Lear then enters, carrying the body of Cordelia, whom Edmund had ordered hanged as a traitor. His heart broken, Lear dies embracing Cordelia. Albany declares Edgar the new king of England.

Act I, Scene 1

King Lear describes his plan for retirement, breaking the kingdom into three parts, with each daughter—Goneril, Regan, and Cordelia—receiving a part. But each daughter must first make a public declaration of how much she loves him. Goneril and Regan respond accordingly. Cordelia will not perform such a "test." She tells Lear that she loves him but will not put her affection up for sale. Lear strips her of her dowry and declares her an enemy of the state. The Earl of Kent, Lear's faithful servant and adviser, warns Lear against the impulsive act. Lear declares Kent, too, an enemy of the state.

The volatile scene takes place in front of Cordelia's two suitors, the Duke of Burgundy and the King of France. Burgundy will not take Cordelia as his wife now that she has no dowry. France, however, is attracted to Cordelia's strength and honesty. France and Cordelia marry and leave the kingdom. With Cordelia gone, Goneril and Regan plot to take away all of Lear's authority.

Act I, Scene 2

Edmund, illegitimate son of the Earl of Gloucester, plots to steal his legitimate brother Edgar's inheritance. Edmund writes a letter that incriminates his half brother in a treasonous plot to steal his father's land. When Gloucester comes to greet Edmund, Edmund pretends to try to hide the letter. Gloucester demands to see the letter, and the plan is set into motion. Edmund convinces Gloucester to spy on a meeting that Edmund will set up with Edgar. After Gloucester departs, Edmund finds Edgar and explains that Gloucester is angry with him. Edmund tells Edgar to meet him at his home, armed and ready for a violent conflict with their father.

Act I, Scene 3

At Goneril's home, she expresses her anger at Lear and his battalion of 100 knights, complaining that they are "riotous" (1.3.6). She tells her steward, Oswald, to rebuff Lear's attempts at talking through their differences. She also indicates the she will write a letter to Regan, explaining that she should treat their father in the same cold manner.

Act I, Scene 4

Kent arrives at Goneril's house disguised and offers himself to Lear as a servant. Proving loyal, Kent joins Lear in lashing out at Oswald, Goneril's steward. Lear accepts Kent's service, and the Fool, Lear's man-child and prophetic jester,

Lear accepts Kent, in disguise, as a servant in a 19th-century depiction of Act I, Scene 4 of *King Lear*. *(Illustration by John Ralston; engraving by J. Quartley)*

makes his first appearance. When Goneril finally meets with her father, she complains again of his "insolent retinue" (1.4.221). Her husband, the Duke of Albany, enters and reports to Lear that he does not understand his wife's accusations. When Albany questions his wife, she replies sharply that Albany should not concern himself with the issue and that her father is becoming senile. Furious, Lear departs for Regan's house, hoping for a better reception there. Albany tells Goneril that she may have gone too far in her mistreatment of her father. Goneril sends Oswald to Regan's home with the letter previously written; she also criticizes her husband for being too kind and gentle toward Lear.

Act I, Scene 5

On the way to Regan's home, the Fool tells Lear that he is the true fool for giving up his kingdom. The Fool also declares that Lear has grown old before he has grown wise. Lear sends Kent to Gloucester's house with a letter describing the offensive treatment.

Act II, Scene 1

At Gloucester's castle, Edmund prepares to welcome Regan and her husband, the Duke of Cornwall. Before they arrive, Edmund tells Edgar that he faces Cornwall's wrath because of "intelligence" circulating in the kingdom that Edgar has spoken out against him (2.1.23). Edgar, believing Edmund's lie, flees. Once he is gone, Edmund cuts himself with his own sword; when Gloucester arrives, he claims that Edgar cut him in a duel. He says that when Edgar revealed his plot to kill Gloucester, Edmund drew his sword on him; the two fought, and he chased Edgar away. Gloucester sends his men to arrest Edgar and promises to give Edmund the land that was intended for Edgar.

Regan and Cornwall, having left their homes to avoid Lear, arrive. Gloucester laments Edgar's apparent turn against him. Disturbed at news of such treason, Regan and Cornwall welcome Edmund into their service.

Act II, Scene 2

Oswald and Kent bump into each other at Gloucester's house, both carrying letters for Regan. Kent confronts Oswald for disrespecting Lear at Goneril's house and beats him. Regan, Cornwall, Edmund, and Gloucester hear the scuffle and intervene. Cornwall puts Kent in the stocks as punishment. Gloucester tries to intercede on Kent's behalf, warning Cornwall that Lear will not want to see his valued messenger treated in such a way. Cornwall ignores his protests.

Act II, Scene 3

Edgar disguises himself as a madman-beggar named Tom O'Bedlam to escape the death sentence handed down by his father because of Edmund's deceit.

Act II, Scene 4

Lear arrives at Gloucester's castle and, as Gloucester predicted, is furious to find Kent in the stocks. When Regan and Cornwall refuse to see him, his anger is stoked further. When Regan and Cornwall finally see Lear, Cornwall sets Kent free from the stocks. Lear describes the horrible treatment he received from Goneril, but Regan takes Goneril's

Regan and Cornwall tell a pleading Lear to return to Goneril in Act II, Scene 4 of *King Lear.* This is a plate from *Retzsch's Outlines to Shakespeare: King Lear,* published in 1838. *(Illustration by Moritz Retzsch)*

side and tells Lear that he should return to Goneril, apologize, and stay with her for another month.

Goneril enters, and each daughter now reports that Lear can stay with her only if he dismisses all his knights. Lear leaves the castle into a storm; Cornwall, Regan, and Goneril shut the doors. Gloucester tries to convince them to allow Lear to stay the night, but they refuse.

Act III, Scene 1

Kent, still in disguise, searches for Lear. He meets a Gentleman, who informs him that Lear and the Fool are wandering in the storm. Kent tells the Gentleman that Albany and Cornwall are conspiring against Lear. He asks the Gentleman to take a message to Cordelia at Dover, where French forces have a secret foothold.

Act III, Scene 2

Lear rages against the storm and complains about his mistreatment while the Fool pleads with him to return to his daughters and get out of the elements. Kent finds the two and leads Lear and the Fool to a nearby hovel. Lear admits for the first time that his "wits begin to turn."

Act III, Scene 3

At Gloucester's house, the earl tells Edmund that he has received an incriminating letter about a French invasion, and he knows that there is a power struggle among the dukes. He declares that he will find Lear and help him. After Gloucester leaves, Edmund announces his plan to betray his father to Cornwall.

Act III, Scene 4

Kent sends the Fool into the hovel first, but the Fool returns, frightened by a tramp who turns out to be Edgar disguised as Tom O'Bedlam. Tom confesses that he was a servant who gave himself over to lustful desires. In the grip of madness, Lear ponders the nature of humankind ("Is man no more than this?") and rips at his clothes. The Fool stops him.

Gloucester enters and begs Lear to come with him to a house. To Kent, he confides that he has

uncovered Goneril's and Regan's plot to assassinate Lear.

Act III, Scene 5

Edmund tells Cornwall of his father's plan to help Lear and the incriminating letter from France. Cornwall, in turn, awards Edmund the title of the new earl of Gloucester and tells him to find his father so he can be arrested.

Act III, Scene 6

Lear imagines putting Goneril and Regan on trial, with the Fool, Edgar, and Kent serving as the honored "assembly." Gloucester arrives and advises Kent to take Lear to the safety of Dover, where Cordelia's forces will protect him.

Act III, Scene 7

Cornwall sends men to find Gloucester, branded a traitor. He then dispatches Edmund and Goneril to Goneril's home; they will advise her husband, Albany, to prepare for war against the French. Cornwall's agents bring in Gloucester, who admits to Cornwall and Regan that he has sent Lear to the safety of Dover. Cornwall stabs Gloucester in the eye. One of Gloucester's servants attacks Cornwall, but Regan kills the servant. Cornwall stabs Gloucester in the other eye. Calling out for Edmund, Regan informs the blinded old man that it was Edmund who betrayed him. Gloucester realizes that he has been tricked and that he was unfair to Edgar. Gloucester leaves the castle, attended by a few faithful servants.

Act IV, Scene 1

In the woods, Gloucester meets Edgar in disguise and asks that the beggar lead him to the cliffs of Dover so that he can jump to his death.

Act IV, Scene 2

At the castle of Albany and Goneril, Goneril kisses Edmund before he leaves to return to Cornwall. After he departs, she professes her love for him. Albany enters and lashes out at his wife for her treatment of Lear. The two argue bitterly. A Messenger arrives to report that Cornwall has died of the servant's attack. Goneril expresses her worry that Edmund will turn his affections to Regan, now a widow. Albany vows to avenge Gloucester.

Act IV, Scene 3

In the French camp, Kent meets the Gentleman whom he had earlier sent to deliver the message to Cordelia. Kent learns that the King of France has returned to his country but Cordelia and others remain to fight for Lear. He also learns that Cordelia loves her father but that Lear, in Dover, refuses to see Cordelia because of his shame at how he treated her.

Act IV, Scene 4

Cordelia dispatches a search party to find her father and bring him to the French camp. A messenger informs her that the British forces are advancing. She expresses her love for Lear and her hopes that she will soon "hear and see him" (4.4.29).

Act IV, Scene 5

Regan questions Oswald, Goneril's steward, about Albany's armies and Edmund's location. Oswald reports that Goneril has given him a letter to deliver to Edmund. This worries Regan, who declares that she and Edmund intend to marry now that Cornwall is dead. She tells Oswald to dissuade Goneril from pursuing Edmund.

Act IV, Scene 6

Edgar leads suicidal Gloucester up a hill and convinces him that he is on the edge of a cliff. When Gloucester jumps, he falls on his face. When he rises, Edgar pretends to be a different person who has witnessed Gloucester's great fall. Edgar claims that Gloucester fell from the cliff, but the gods saved him. Gloucester, transformed, vows to bear his affliction through the end of his days.

The two then meet Lear, who rails in his madness about lust, adultery, and abuses of power. Cordelia's men find Lear, but he thinks they are trying to capture him, and he runs off.

Oswald catches up with Gloucester and tries to kill him. Edgar protects his father and kills Oswald, who, before he dies, gives Edgar the letter intended for Edmund. Edgar reads the letter, which describes Goneril's love for Edmund and her plan to kill Albany.

Act IV, Scene 7

Lear has been captured by Cordelia's men and put under her doctor's care. Cordelia thanks Kent for his faithful service. Lear is brought, still sleeping, to Cordelia and Kent. At their reunion, Cordelia forgives her father.

The doctor calls for louder music while he looks after a sleeping Lear in Act IV, Scene 7 of *King Lear*. This drawing was designed for the Chiswick edition of Shakespeare, published in 1900. *(Illustration by John Byam Lister Shaw)*

Act V, Scene 1

Edmund assures Regan that he has not been intimate with Goneril. Albany, Goneril, and soldiers enter; Albany announces that Lear has been reunited with Cordelia and that his forces will fight against the French. Edgar arrives, disguised, and delivers the letter from Oswald to Albany. He advises Albany to read it before he goes to battle.

Edmund reflects on being the lover of both Goneril and Regan and wonders which one he will marry.

Act V, Scene 2

Edgar reports to his father that Cordelia's French forces have been defeated, with Lear and Cordelia taken captive.

Act V, Scene 3

Edmund sends Lear and Cordelia to prison and gives a soldier a note, secretly ordering their execution. Lear accepts the prison sentence with optimism, hoping he and Cordelia can spend their days talking, praying, and singing.

Albany confronts Edmund, arresting him on charges of treason. He calls for witnesses to speak against Edmund's claim of true inheritance. A disguised Edgar steps forward, and the two fight. Edgar delivers the death blow to Edmund and then sheds his disguise. Questioned by Albany, Edgar reveals how he cared for Gloucester, whose "flawed heart" (5.3.196) could not bear the joy when Edgar finally revealed himself to him. As he dies, Edmund confesses to being moved by Edgar's story of their father's death.

A servant arrives with a bloody knife, explaining that it is the knife Goneril used to kill herself after poisoning Regan. Kent enters and tells Edgar that he, too, has been operating under disguise and asks where he can find Lear. Edmund divulges that he ordered Cordelia executed and, trying to do one good thing before he dies, orders servants to intervene with the order. They rush to save her, but Lear walks in with her dead body in his arms. His heart broken, Lear dies as he embraces Cordelia's body. Kent declares that he will soon follow Lear

in death. Albany declares Edgar the new king of Britain.

CHARACTER LIST

King Lear Hoping to retire and to rest in his later years, Lear, king of Britain, plans to divide his country into three parts among his daughters. This plan goes awry when he banishes his daughter Cordelia in anger, unable to bear her honesty when she refuses to compete for his love. Later, he realizes that his other two daughters, Goneril and Regan, do not love him and that they manipulated him by telling him what he wanted to hear. Lear ultimately loses his kingdom and his dignity; his life is threatened by his two eldest daughters; and he curses his fate and the instability of life.

Goneril Married to the Duke of Albany, Lear's eldest daughter, Goneril, and her sister Regan understand that their father is a foolish man, and they manipulate him into giving them his kingdom. She and Regan then plot to kill their father, but they are unable to find him when he escapes into the woods and then to Dover. Goneril falls in love Edmund and plots to kill her husband so that she can be with her lover. Afraid that Regan will try to seduce Edmund, she poisons Regan. Goneril stabs herself when her crimes are uncovered and when she realizes that she will not be able to have Edmund.

Regan Regan, Lear's second daughter, is married to the Duke of Cornwall. In addition to plotting with Goneril against their father, Regan helps her husband blind the Earl of Gloucester. When Gloucester's servant tries to stop Cornwall from stabbing Gloucester, Regan kills the servant. Regan attempts to seduce Edmund, but Goneril kills her with a deadly poison.

Cordelia It is known that Cordelia, Lear's youngest daughter, is also his favorite, but the reason for this preference is not made known in the play. Cordelia's honesty—her refusal to compete for Lear's love—results in her banishment. But the King of France appreciates her honesty and marries her even though she has no inheritance or title. Cordelia knows that her older sisters will plot against her father, and although she is banished, she returns to Britain with an army to defend her father. She finds her father on the run from her sisters and their murderous plot. Cordelia's courage results in her arrest and imprisonment, and ultimately her execution. She makes amends with her father before her death, and he is humbled by her love and loyalty.

Duke of Albany Although Goneril's husband, Albany, agrees to fight France, he does not favor the mistreatment of King Lear or the Earl of Gloucester. When Gloucester is arrested and blinded, Albany vows to avenge his abusers. Albany warns Edmund against harming Lear and Cordelia. When Edmund is made earl by unlawful means, Albany challenges the decision, resulting in the duel between Edmund and Edgar. Albany ends the war and gives the kingdom back to Lear.

Duke of Cornwall Cornwall and his wife, Regan, plot to assassinate Lear. When the Earl of Gloucester runs off into the woods to warn Lear, Cornwall has him arrested. Cornwall stabs Gloucester in the eye, planning to blind him for his treason. Before he can finish the job, Gloucester's servant attacks Cornwall. Regan kills the servant, and Cornwall blinds Gloucester in the other eye, but Cornwall does not survive the wounds inflicted by the servant.

King of France A suitor of Cordelia, the king hears the discussion between Lear and his daughters at the beginning of the play. France interprets Cordelia's honesty with her father as true virtue and agrees to marry her, although she lacks title or inheritance. France helps bring Cordelia and the French forces to Britain, but he does not remain in Britain to fight.

Duke of Burgundy Another suitor of Cordelia, Burgundy is unwilling to take Cordelia as a wife when she is stripped of her title and inheritance.

Earl of Gloucester Gloucester is tricked by Edmund, his illegitimate son, into thinking that Edgar, his legitimate son and the elder of the two, plans to steal Gloucester's land and title. Following Edmund's advice, he tries to have Edgar arrested. When Lear is offended by his daughters Goneril and Regan, Gloucester tries to make room for him at his home. Goneril and Regan do not permit Gloucester to give Lear refuge, and the king wanders off into the woods. Gloucester uncovers a letter that describes the plot to assassinate Lear. He takes the news to Lear in the woods and arranges for the king's safe passage to Dover where he will be given asylum. Gloucester is arrested and blinded for his efforts to save the king. Regan tells Gloucester that Edmund tricked him, and Gloucester realizes that he has unjustly condemned his son Edgar. Gloucester wanders into the woods, where Edgar, in disguise, meets him and leads him through the woods. Gloucester wants Edgar to take him to the cliffs of Dover so that he can jump to his death. Edgar makes him think that he has jumped from the cliff but been saved by the gods. Gloucester's travels lead him to Lear and the invading forces of France. When Edgar reveals his true identity to Gloucester, hoping to receive his blessing, Gloucester dies, his heart too weak to endure the conflicting joy and grief.

Edgar Edgar, the elder and legitimate son of the Earl of Gloucester, is tricked by his younger half brother, Edmund, when Edmund turns their father against him. When Edgar flees the kingdom, he goes into the woods and takes the disguise of the beggar-madman Tom O'Bedlam. When his father is blinded and cast out of the kingdom, Edgar serves as his guide, withholding his true identity. Edgar protects Gloucester when Oswald tries to kill him. Challenging Edmund's right to the title of earl of Gloucester, Edgar defeats his brother. Albany returns the kingdom to Lear, but when Lear dies, the kingdom falls to Edgar.

Edmund Motivated by his desire for power, Edmund, the illegitimate son of the Earl of Gloucester, tricks his father into suspecting his older half brother, Edgar, of treason. Edmund is successful, and he is promised his brother's inheritance. When Edmund turns against his father, he is named the new earl of Gloucester. Edmund attracts the affection of both Goneril and Regan, prompting both to leave their husbands for his hand in marriage. The promises of love are cut short when Albany is notified of the plot to murder him and when Goneril poisons her sister out of jealousy. Edmund's position as earl of Gloucester is challenged by Albany, and Edgar steps in to challenge Edmund to a duel. Edmund is killed in the duel, and he confesses to plotting against Edgar.

Earl of Kent Kent establishes himself as a faithful friend and adviser to King Lear when he steps into the conflict between father and daughter. Kent knows that Cordelia is a faithful daughter, and he tries to warn Lear against banishing her. When Lear threatens to banish and kill Kent for meddling in the king's business, Kent persists, claiming that he is willing to die for the king. After his banishment, Kent returns to serve the king in disguise, knowing that the king's life is in danger. Kent guides the king through the woods and stays with him when he is transported to Dover. Kent is a "plain-dealing" character, and by his own admission, he values King Lear's safety above his own life (2.2.98). Kent presents a picture of the ideal servant through his own actions and also through his criticism of Oswald. Kent criticizes Oswald for merely smiling at his mistress's foolishness, of adding oil to the fire of his mistress's temper or ice to his mistress's frigid depression.

Fool The Fool speaks plainly and honestly with King Lear throughout the play. Lear is unable and, at times, unwilling to listen to the words of the Fool.

Gentleman An attendant of Cordelia.

Oswald Oswald follows Goneril's orders by mistreating the king, Kent, and the king's knights. Oswald receives a beating from Kent when the two meet at Gloucester's house. Oswald is ordered to kill Gloucester, but when he tries, Edgar overpowers him and kills him.

CHARACTER STUDIES
King Lear

King Lear is a transformative figure who, too late, finally understands his faults. Egotistical, vain, lacking self-awareness, Lear in the opening scene wants his daughters to fill his ears with flattery, telling how much they love him. Goneril and Regan respond accordingly, and Lear apportions part of his kingdom to each. Cordelia, however, refuses to feed his ego, declaring that she loves him "According to my bond, no more nor less" (1.1.102). In response, he strips her of her inheritance and dowry. When Kent steps in to warn Lear against this rash act, Lear banishes him. Lear's flaws do not justify his treatment at the hands of ungrateful Goneril and Regan, but, as the critic David Bevington points out, "his failures are, however, tokens of his worldly insolence, for which he must fall. The process is a painful one, but, since it brings self-discovery, it is not without its compensations. Indeed, a central paradox of the play is that by no other way could Lear have learned what human suffering and need are all about" (1,203). The famed Shakespearean actor Derek Jacobi, playing Lear for the first time in 2010, at age 72, stresses that the character is more than simply a "remote power figure who is reduced to little, mad old man. I think it's more interesting than that. The most obvious thing is for big to become small, but his journey is infinitely more complex" (Cavendish n.p.).

Lear's tragedy is rooted in a domestic, not political, calamity; while he seems unlovable in the play's first two acts, Lear loves and, in fact, is loved—by Cordelia, Kent, the Fool, Gloucester, and Edgar. "Of course, whoever you may be, you can be loved and loving and still demand more," the critic Harold Bloom writes. "If you are King Lear, and have ever but slenderly known yourself, then you are almost apocalyptically needy in your demand for love, particularly from the child you truly love, Cordelia" (*Shakespeare* 479). Both Kent and the Fool, in their ways, warn Lear against treading down the path of disaster.

Sight—the ability to see and its loss—is a significant theme linked to Lear as well as to Gloucester.

Lear (E. H. Sothern) and Cordelia (Julia Marlowe) in a late 19th-century production of *King Lear (Photographed by Dana)*

While Gloucester suffers a violent, shocking blinding, Lear simply refuses to see: "Lear, at the beginning of the play, possesses physical eyesight, so far as we know, as perfect as Gloucester's. But morally, he is even blinder. He is a victim, to the point of incipient madness, of his arrogance, his anger, his vanity, and his pride" (Goddard 19). When Lear banishes Kent, the faithful servant implores him to "See better, Lear" (1.1.180). His two murderous daughters recognize and exploit Lear's weakness. When Goneril muses that her father must be mad for casting aside Cordelia, the daughter he loved most, Regan explains that he is acting out of "infirmity" of old age and that "he hath ever but slenderly known himself" (1.1.340–341).

Only through his anguished journey does Lear truly become a king—finally "seeing," finally thinking of others before himself. In his madness, he finds a degree of sanity. Tossed into the storm in Act 3, stripped of his family and the trappings of royalty, Lear endures what Harold Goddard describes as flashes of lightning that illuminate the darkness of his soul (20). Even as he acknowledges that his "wits begin to turn," he speaks his first kind words to the Fool (Bevington 1,204). Later, he contemplates the "poor naked wretches" whom he never concerned himself with while king: "Oh, I have ta'an / Too little care of this! Take physic, pomp; / Expose thyself to feel what wretches feel, / That thou mayst shake the superflux to them / And show the heavens more just" (3.4.28–36). According to Goddard, "More and more from that moment, the tempest in Lear's mind makes him insensible to the tempest without. Increasingly, he sees that madness lies in dwelling on his own wrongs, salvation in thinking of the suffering of others" (20). In Act 4, Scene 7, when Lear is brought, asleep, to the French camp, he first believes he has awakened in hell and that his beloved daughter, with whom he is reunited, is a spirit. Cordelia assures him that she has "no cause" to hate him (4.7.76); Kent assures him that he is not in France but in his own kingdom. Kent means England, "but we know that Shakespeare means that Lear is now in a kingdom not of this earth" (Goddard 29). After his reunion with Cordelia, Lear is never again incoherent, "never utters a word that does not enforce attention either by its truth or its pathos" (Goddard 37). In Act 5, Lear holds Cordelia's dead body, looking for signs of life. For a moment, he believes he sees Cordelia's lips move. "Pray you undo this button. Thank you, sir / Do you see this? Look on her, look, her lips, Look there! Look there!" (5.3.374–375). At that, he dies. Bloom remarks: "Lear, surging on through fury, madness, and clarifying though momentary epiphanies, is the largest figure of love desperately sought and blindly denied ever placed on stage or in print" (*Shakespeare* 507).

Edmund

Ranking among Shakespeare's vilest villains, Edmund has an intriguing complexity, as expressed by his crisis of conscience at the play's end. Scholars describe him as Machiavellian, Epicurean, as even worse than Shakespeare's Iago (in *Othello*); some claim he is a literary representation of Shakespeare's rival playwright, Christopher Marlowe. Bloom argues that Edmund is the most "attractive" of the Jacobean "hero-villains": "As the purest and coolest Machiavel in stage history, at least until he knows he has received his death-wound, Edmund is both a remarkably antic and charming Satan, and a being with real self-knowledge, which makes him particularly dangerous in world presided by Lear" who, as Regan remarks, enjoys no such ability for introspection ("Introduction" 7).

Edmund's status as Gloucester's bastard son defines him and drives him to destroy himself and his family. His only desire is for power. He professes that Nature is his "goddess" (1.2.1), but his notion of nature is a twisted one. He complains that it is unfair that his father's land will go to his legitimate son, Edgar. Edmund's universe is one where the "race goes to the swiftest and in which conscience, morality, and religion are empty myths" (Bevington 1,205). He represents a foil to his father, who believes in the power of gods and the cosmos, and to Lear, who believes that Nature will punish ungrateful daughters and defend fathers (1.4). "He is Machiavellian, an atheist, and Epicurean—everything inimical to traditional Elizabethan ideals of order. To him, 'natural' means precisely what Lear and Gloucester call 'unnatural,'" Bevington observes (1,205). Indeed, when Edmund lies to his father about Edgar's alleged plan to kill him, he shrewdly invokes mythological imagery that Gloucester would appreciate: "But that I told him the revenging gods / 'Gainst parricides did all the thunder bend" (2.1.54–55).

Edmund and Lear never speak to each other in the play, but Edmund, too, undergoes a transformation, albeit belated and smaller in scope than Lear's. After he learns that his lovers, Goneril and Regan, have died terrible deaths—Goneril killing Regan and then herself—Edmund's metamorphosis begins. Delivered a death blow by his brother, Edmund moves toward accepting the wretched life he will leave behind. He confesses to being moved by Edgar's account of their father's death and appears ready to reprieve Cordelia, whom he has ordered executed. But he does not reach that point fully. When the bodies of Goneril and Regan are presented to him, his reaction—"Yet Edmund was beloved" (5.3.238)—could be almost comical, Bloom acknowledges, if taken out of context: "The dying nihilist reminds himself that in spite of all he was and did, he *was* beloved. He does not say that he cared for either, or for anyone else, and yet this evidence of connection moves him. In context, its mimetic force is enormous" (*Shakespeare* 505). Goddard praises the scene for Shakespeare's ability to present a character's change "through the representation of a growing inwardness" (7).

Edgar

Edmund's brother, Gloucester's legitimate heir, and Lear's godson, Edgar parallels the Cordelia character in the play's double plot, albeit with key differences, not the least being that Edgar survives what many describe as the play's nihilistic conclusion. But, while he remains one of the few main characters (along with Kent and Albany) who escapes death, Edmund's psyche has paid a dear price. Sharing neither his half brother's bloodthirsty ambition nor his cruelty, Edgar becomes, according to Bloom, Shakespeare's most "reluctant royal successor" when Albany abdicates the crown to him at the play's end, adding, "For Edgar, it is the final catastrophe; his godfather and his father both are gone" (*Shakespeare* 507).

Edgar's disguise as the madman-beggar Tom O'Bedlam both enriches and complicates his character. The play's subtitle in the 1608 First Quarto suggests the significance of the role: "With the unfortunate life of Edgar, son and heir to the Earle of Gloucester, and his sullen and assumed humor of Tom of Bedlam." Edgar adopts the charade after Edmund convinces Gloucester that Edgar planned to kill him. Gloucester condemns his firstborn to death, launching Edgar's humbling descent from son of an earl to man on the run. Edgar declares that he will take on the "basest and most poorest shape" possible, covering his face with filth, matting his hair, and submitting himself to the "winds and persecutions of the sky" (2.3.7–12). Bloom describes the O'Bedlam masquerade as the central emblem of the play: "philosopher, fool, madman, nihilist, dissembler—at once all of these and none of these" (*Shakespeare* 489). Yet, Bloom also observes, "There is something so profoundly disproportionate in Edgar's self-abnegation throughout the play that we have to presume in him a recalcitrance akin to Cordelia's, but far in excess of hers. Whether as bedlamite or as poor peasant, Edgar refuses his own identity for more than practical purposes" (*Shakespeare* 480). As Tom O'Bedlam, Edgar eventually finds his blinded father, saving the old man from killing himself by convincing him that the gods intervened in his "fall" off the Dover cliffs. Edgar finally reveals himself to his father only before challenging Edmund to combat; so emotionally powerful is the encounter—not staged, but rather described by Edgar in its aftermath—that it breaks Gloucester's heart, and he dies.

At the play's end, Edgar has cast aside his disguise, reconciled with his father, killed his brother, and been crowned king, yet he emerges not so much triumphant as battle scarred and weary. His contrivances as Tom O'Bedlam, concealing his identity from his father for so long, have defeated themselves, Bevington argues (1,202). Susan Snyder wonders if Edgar's journey is more "gratuitous" than redemptive: "Does Gloucester's death in the extremes of joy and grief fittingly conclude [Edgar's] long painful spiritual odyssey, or is it yet another indication that random absurdity governs events, making nonsense of Edgar's redemptive agenda?" (298). While Edgar's slaying of Edmund does represent a turn from gullible, good-hearted son to avenger, he ends his pilgrimage "overwhelmed by the helplessness of his love, a love progressively growing in range and intensity, with the pragmatic effect of yielding him, as the new king, only greater suffering" (Bloom, *Shakespeare* 483). Edgar's lines that end the play—"The oldest hath borne most; we that are young / Shall never see so much nor live so long" (5.3.394–395)—

Lear and the Fool talk to Edgar, disguised as Tom O'Bedlam, in a farmhouse in Act III, Scene 6 of *King Lear*. Drawing designed for the Chiswick edition of Shakespeare. *(Illustration by John Byam Lister Shaw)*

can have a double meaning. While ostensibly the "oldest" refers to Lear and Gloucester, it can also refer to Edgar himself, the elder of two brothers who has, indeed, borne much in the context of the narrative. At the same time, he is young, and youth, in his eyes, seems now not rich with promise but empty.

Cordelia

When Cordelia's gentle kiss awakens Lear at the French camp, he believes for a moment that his beloved daughter is a spirit. In fact, Cordelia has a spiritual quality. She appears infrequently in the play, but she owns a powerful presence that drives the narrative. She is the daughter Lear loves most, and in turn, she loves Lear more than her sisters do. Even her eyes are described as "heavenly" (4.3.32). Lear and Cordelia's all-too-brief reunion reminds us how her spirit, her love, has compelled Lear in his journey. "His sense of guilt with regard to her keeps her perpetually in Lear's memory—and so in ours. And the Fool's love for her, both on its own account and because he is forever insinuating thoughts of her in the King's mind, works the same way" (Goddard 27). When Lear calls Cordelia a spirit, she cries under her breath that he is still in the throes of madness. Yet, Lear, in a sense, sees her perfectly: "Cordelia, *we* know, *is* a spirit,

Cordelia in Act IV, Scene 7 of *King Lear.* This is a print from Charles Heath's 1848 edition of *The Heroines of Shakspeare: Comprising the Principal Female Characters in the Plays of the Great Poet. (Painting by A. Johnston; engraving by B. Eyles)*

and, in that shining line, Shakespeare harvests the promise of the four full acts which have been subtly contrived to convince us of the same truth" (Goddard 28).

Virtuous, certainly, Cordelia is also defined by contradictions. Although she loves her father dearly—" . . . I am sure my love's / More ponderous than my tongue" (1.1.86–87)—she refuses to play sycophant. Her blunt talk enrages Lear at the same time that it attracts France, who expresses the paradoxes of her character when he asks to marry this "dowerless daughter" (1.1.259): "Fairest Cordelia, that art most rich being poor; / Most choice, forsaken; and most loved, despised" (1.1.290–291). And, while Lear warns Cordelia, when she refuses to amplify her profession of love for him, that "Nothing will come of nothing" (1.1.99), in fact everything comes from Cordelia. She is the antithesis of her sisters, and in banishing her, Lear will undergo a painful odyssey. Kent recognizes this. He warns Lear not to take Cordelia's reticence for shallow feelings: "Thy youngest daughter does not love thee least / Nor are those empty-hearted whose low sounds / Reverb no hollowness" (1.1.171–173).

The Fool

"Don't take your eyes off the Fool for a moment," the actor Michael Gambon advised those who would play Lear, as he did in 1982. "It also helps if the Fool isn't too funny," he added (Cavendish, n.p.). Indeed, while clever puns, songs, and riddles characterize the Fool's speech, beneath this, he articulates a calamitous, visionary terror, the significance of which largely escapes Lear. If Cordelia is associated with reticence, the Fool represents the opposite, given license by Shakespeare to express what the audience, and other characters, might be thinking but cannot or will not say. The Fool is merciless, starting from the moment he enters the play, after Lear, at Goneril's home, has welcomed the disguised Kent as a servant. The Fool offers to give Kent a coxcomb, or fool's cap, because, as he explains, anybody who would follow Lear must be a fool himself (1.4.105–107). The battering continues: Lear, the Fool declares, has made his "daughters thy mothers" (1.4.176). He has given away his kingdom, leaving "nothing i' th' middle" (1.4.191). The Fool says he would rather be anything other than a fool—except Lear (1.4.189–190). And when Lear, like a playground bully, blusters, "Dost thou call me 'fool' boy?" the Fool cuts him again: Lear has given away all other titles; this one, he was born with (1.4.152–154). Kent interrupts, and the next exchange between the Fool and Lear has Lear responding to a riddle, Lear's feigned anger at the Fool's insolence gone. "Precisely apocalyptic in his forebodings, the Fool ironically is understood only by the audience (and Kent) but almost never by Lear, who listens yet never hears, and cannot identify himself with the bungler the Fool evokes" (Bloom, *Shakespeare* 497).

The Fool disappears, physically, after Act 3, yet his significance never really disappears. Bloom wonders if the character is "altogether human, or a sprite or changeling? His utterances differ sharply from those of any court fool in Shakespeare; he alone seems to belong to an occult world" (*Shakespeare* 495). Snyder observes that, to some extent, the Fool's role is taken over by Lear himself: "In later scenes the very language of wayward association and non-sequitur that manifests his madness keeps him hovering between tragic grandeur and absurdity" (296). Some scholars point to a six-line reference by Lear as he holds Cordelia's dead body as illustrative of the depth of the Fool's character. "And my poor fool is hanged" Lear cries, moments before he dies (5.3.369). Many scholars believe that *fool* here is a term of endearment for Cordelia, but Goddard and Bloom argue that Lear is referring here to both Cordelia and the Fool, blended as one. "His wandering mind has confused them, if you will. But what a divine confusion! Has *wedded* them would be the better word. Think of how the Fool loved his master! Think how he adored Cordelia and pined away after she went to France! Surely this is the main reason for Shakespeare's banishing the Fool from his play—that he might reappear united to Cordelia on his dear master's lips" (Goddard 34).

DIFFICULTIES OF THE PLAY

Lear's madness, the relationship between the Fool and Lear, and the play's dark ending and brutal action can all present difficulties for modern audiences and readers. Lear's madness often confuses those who wonder why, precisely, he goes mad and what the larger meaning of his madness is. In Act IV, Scene 6, Lear rants about female sexuality and lechery: "But to the girdle to the gods inherit; / Beneath is all the fiend's" (ll. 128–129). The actor Pete Postlethwaite, who played Lear in 2008, insists that the key to portraying Lear is to understand his attitude toward gender: "Lear is fixated. He can't bear the feminine side of himself for some reason" (Cavendish n.p.). Other interpreters suggest different reasons, and of course, his daughters' betrayal is an obvious one. But Lear's own brand of madness is clearly particular to his character in a way that the reader is invited to ponder. In addition, his language during his spells of madness can seem tangled or incoherent. In fact, it is often highly allusive and profound, if bitter, but the reader must take care to puzzle it out.

Each time we see the mad Lear, other characters seem to make progress toward understanding him. On the heath in Act III, Scene 4, Lear is consumed with anger toward his daughters; before ripping off his clothes, he cries out, "Is man no more than this?" (l. 107). He has lost the physical attributes of kingship, such as royal vestments and a palace, not to mention the love of his daughters. He is humbled. In the same scene, when Gloucester arrives and Kent confesses that Lear's "wits begin t'unsettle" (l. 170), Gloucester immediately replies, "Canst thou blame him? His daughters seek his death" (ll. 171–172), an effective act of understanding. In Act III, Scene 7, at perhaps the pinnacle of Lear's insanity, he stages a mock trial of Goneril and Regan. Edgar, Kent, and the Fool play along as the "honorable assembly" (l. 51), with a stool standing in for Goneril (l. 55). Yet, Lear's madness here is expressed not so much in the folly of putting his daughters on trial but by his pitiable quest to understand why they turned against him, a fair, if unanswerable, question: "Is there any cause in nature that make these hard hearts?" (l. 81–82). When Lear and Gloucester meet in Act IV, Scene 6, Gloucester explains that he has been blinded. Lear advises: "A man may see how this world goes with no eyes. Look with thine ears. See how yond justice rails upon yon simple thief. Hark in thine ear" (4.6.166–168). Lear's counsel—do not simply trust your eyes—seems true and clear. Lear's madness, then, can be understood as a paradox: a devastating journey that he must endure before he can, in fact, become sane. The modern reader's charge is to look deeper than the stage action—the bluster and histrionics—to the meaning beneath the language. This is not to say that Lear does not end up broken and humiliated; he does. But, by understanding that Lear becomes a better human being at the play's end, today's audience can perhaps better appreciate the role that his madness plays.

Another challenge to modern readers and viewers is presented by the character of the Fool. First, his language is extremely dense, allusive, and witty, challenging modern readers at all times. Second, he seems also to challenge or even attack Lear directly, but Lear does not always see himself in the Fool's jibes. Finally, the Fool disappears completely from the play after Act 3. Analyzing the play's structure can help readers understand the Fool's character and relationship with Lear. In Acts 1 and 2, the Fool delivers caustic, yet truthful observations about Lear. Speaking in riddles and metaphors, he portends the king's difficult journey: "I would not be thee, nuncle. Thou hast pared thy wit o' both sides and left nothing I' th' middle" (1.4.191–192). At this stage in the play, Lear, of course, is characterized by vanity and lack of self-knowledge. When the Fool follows an enraged Lear into the storm in Act III, the Fool's speech becomes direct. He begs Lear to find shelter: "Ask thy daughters' blessing. Here's a night pities neither wise men nor fools" (3.2.14–15). Here, in the middle of the play, Lear conveys kindness toward the Fool for the first time. Next, the Fool enters the hovel with Lear and Kent. Lear here shows compassion, for the first time, for the "poor naked wretches" of England whose fate he now can appreciate (3.4.28). When

Lear tears at his clothes moments later, the Fool comes to his comfort, no longer tormenting him. After Lear stages the mock trial of his daughters, he lies down to sleep, promising to go to supper in the morning. "And I'll go to bed at noon," the Fool responds (3.6.90), his last line of the play. Structurally, political events are developing against Lear as his madness reaches its peak. The Fool, in effect has prepared the audience for Lear's journey; the rest of it is now up to Lear alone. The Fool's absence after Act III is a significant signal that Lear has accepted this painful road to self-knowledge and cannot turn back. In Act IV, Scene 7, Lear is reunited with Cordelia. Events spin rapidly from there until the tragic ending, with Cordelia executed at Edmund's direction. "And my poor fool is hanged," Lear cries (5.3.369). Some critics argue that this line means that the Fool and Cordelia, in Lear's mind, have become one. The play's structure and narrative work together. The Fool may be gone, but Cordelia has reappeared; both love Lear, and both are loved by Lear.

Ancient versions of the King Lear story ended happily, and Shakespeare's chosen dark conclusion has challenged audiences for years. In the source texts Shakespeare drew on, the youngest daughter triumphed over her evil sisters and married her princely suitor; Lear, temporarily overthrown by sons-in-law, was restored to the throne through help of the French king and ended his reign in comfort, with the love of the virtuous daughter until his natural death (Bevington 1,201). Shakespeare's ending is, of course, quite different. The great critic and editor Samuel Johnson confessed that he was unable to accept Shakespeare's version, with Cordelia's death violating the audience's need for poetic justice (Bevington 1,201). In addition, the brutality of Gloucester's blinding has seemed to some impossible to portray onstage. The editors Barbara A. Mowat and Paul Werstine, in their introduction to the Folger Shakespeare Library edition of *King Lear,* note that other tragedies typically allow characters a degree of triumph before their misery; *King Lear* does not: "In this play, only death seems to provide escape from 'the rack of this tough world.' What, then, keeps bringing us back to *King Lear*?" (xiii). The answer is that by presenting elements such as jealousy, demand for love, and sibling rivalry taken to extremes, Shakespeare is able to amplify his characters' own passions and suffering and our sympathy for them: "We can see ourselves and our small vices magnified to gigantic proportions" (Mowat and Werstine xiv). The critic David Bevington suggests that we can appreciate the story for Shakespeare's "relentless honesty and refusal to accept easy answers" (1,201). For those readers who see no reason for optimism at the play's end, Bevington offers: "we can at least choose whether to be like Cordelia and Edgar . . . or to settle for being our worst selves, like Edmund, Goneril, and Regan. . . . The power of love, though learned too late to avert catastrophe, is at last discovered in its very defeat" (1,206).

Lear sends Cordelia away in Act I, Scene I of *King Lear*. This plate is from *Retzsch's Outlines to Shakespeare:* King Lear, 1838. *(Illustration by Moritz Retzsch)*

KEY PASSAGES
Act I, Scene 1, 156–169

CORDELIA. *[to Lear]* I yet beseech your
  Majesty—
If for I want that glib and oily art
To speak and purpose not, since what I well
  intend
I'll do 't before I speak—that you make known
It is no vicious blot, murder or foulness,
No unchaste action or dishonored step
That hath deprived me of your grace and favor,
But even for want of that for which I am richer:
A still-soliciting eye, and such a tongue
That I am glad I have not, though not to have it
Hath lost me in your liking.

LEAR. Better thou
Hadst not been born than not t' have pleaed me
Better.

The passage reveals the depths to which Lear has hardened his heart against Cordelia. France, a potential suitor for Cordelia, has questioned Lear, wondering how he could withdraw his affection for his "best, dearest" daughter (1.1.219). Before Lear can respond, Cordelia interrupts, addressing her father in one last bid to be understood. She explains that her refusal to participate in "glib and oily art" is not vicious, foul, unchaste, or dishonorable. It is not in her nature to beg or entice ("still-soliciting eye"). And, in fact, she is glad that she does not have these qualities, even though she has lost her father's love in the process. Lear wants his daughters to put their love into words, to make a production of their affection. He has promised the largest inheritance to the daughter who is the best at flattery. Cordelia loves her father, but she respects him too much to play this kind of game with her love. In response, Lear brutally declares that it would have been better if she had never been born. Incapable of obsequiousness, Cordelia's act sets the play in motion.

Act I, Scene 1, 226–237

KENT. My life I never held but as a pawn
To wage against thine enemies, nor fear to lose
  it,
They safety being motive.

LEAR.   Out of my sight!

KENT. See better, Lear, and let me still remain
The true blank of thine eye

LEAR. Now, by Apollo—

KENT.   Now, by Apollo, king,
Thou swear'st thy gods in vain.

LEAR.   Oh vassal! Miscreant!

KENT. Kill thy physician, and thy fee bestow
Upon the foul disease. Revoke thy gift,
Or whilst I can vent clamor from my throat,
I'll tell thee thou dost evil.

Kent steps into the misunderstanding between Lear and Cordelia, trying to help Lear see that Cordelia's response is not one of rebellion but rather one of love and faithfulness. As an adviser to the king, Kent prides himself as one who will sacrifice himself for the king. He has sworn himself for Lear's safety; he is willing to incur Lear's wrath if it means that he will save Lear from disaster. References to eyes and blindness, important imagery throughout the play, appear here with Lear's cry "Out of my sight!" and Kent's plea for his king to "see better" and allow him to remain the "true blank of thine yet," meaning the white bull's-eye in the center of a target. Kent compares himself to a doctor, one whom Lear has appointed to watch over him. Kent portends, correctly, that if Lear will "kill the physician," he runs the risk of falling ill with some "foul disease." As long as Lear remains committed to this course of action, Kent will use every last breath to tell him that he "dost evil."

Act I, Scene 2, 1–22
EDMUND. Thou, Nature, art my goddess. To thy law
My services are bound. Wherefore should I
Stand in the plague of custom, and permit
The curiosity of nations to deprive me
For that I am some twelve or fourteen moooonshines
Lag of a brother? Why 'bastard'? Wherefore 'base',
When my dimensions are as well compact,

My mind as generous and my shape as true
As honest madam's issue? Why brand they us
With 'base,' with 'baseness,' 'bastardy,' 'base,'
  'base,'
Who, in the lusty stealth of nature, take
More composition and fierce quality
Than doth within a dull, stale, tired bed
Go to th' creating a whole tribe of fops
Got tween asleep and wake? Well then,
Legitimate Edgar, I must have your land.
Our father's love is to the bastard Edmund
As to th' legitimate. Fine word, 'legitimate.'
Well, my legitimate, if this letter speed
And my intervention thrive, Edmund the base
Shall top th' legitimate. I grow, I prosper.
Now, gods, stand up for bastards!

This soliloquy is our first look into the evil of Edmund's soul. Here, he reveals his ambition to take his brother's land and the plot that will make it possible—involving a letter, whose contents we discover later. Edmund rationalizes his plan by complaining about the unfairness of being a bastard. Why should legal or social distinctions ("curiosity of nations") deprive him of a healthy inheritance, just because he was born some 12 or 14 months ("moonshines") after his brother and out of wedlock? He is, he argues, just as handsome, or put together ("compact"), and with just as noble or courageous ("generous") mind as a child born in wedlock (an "honest madam's issue").

He declares his devotion to "Nature," but, like most villains, Edmund inverts conventions to meet his own ends: "Edmund is the 'natural' son of Gloucester, meaning literally that he is illegitimate. Figuratively, he therefore represents a violation of traditional moral order. In appearance, he is smooth and plausible, but in reality, he is an arch-deceiver like the Vice in a morality play, a superb actor who boasts to the audience in soliloquy of his protean villainy" (Bevington 1,205). In Edmund's mind, the creation of a bastard is really more special than the creation of a legitimate child. The bastard is created when a man and a woman are driven together out of "natural" passion. In contrast, a legitimate child is born in a bed that is "dull, stale, tired." Unfairly ostracized, Edmund feels he deserves a good inheritance. In the final line of the speech, Edmund invokes "gods," but as a parody of his father's interest in astrology and the cosmos; dedicated to "Nature," Edmund is not invested in religious or spiritual matters.

Act II, Scene 2, 78–86

KENT. That such a slave as this should wear a
  sword,
Who wears no honesty. Such smiling rogues as
  these,
Like rats, oft bite the hold chords a-twain
Which are too intrinse t' unloose; smooth
  every passion
That in the natures of their lords rebel;
Bring oil to the fire, snow to their colder
  moods;
Renege, affirm, and turn their halcyon beaks
With every gale and vary of their masters,
Knowing nought, like dogs, but following.

The responsibility of a faithful friend is one of the play's themes. In this passage, Kent speaks of the duty of any faithful friend and servant. Wearing a sword was an honor given to Kent when he became a servant of the king. He was bound to serve the king and to look out for the king's interests above his own. Kent describes Goneril's servant, Oswald, as a man without honor. Instead of frowning upon the dishonest and evil behavior of his mistress, Oswald simply smiles. Kent believes that Oswald should challenge his mistress's actions and sacrifice himself by speaking out against foolish behavior, bad decisions, and rash action. Kent is willing to die for the king when he opposes the king's decision to banish Cordelia in the first act of the play. In response, Lear threatens Kent, claiming that any interference would result in the servant's death. The king uses the image of a bow and arrow to describe the danger Kent is walking into by interrupting him and his banishment of Cordelia, "The bow is bent and drawn; make from

the shaft" (1.1.139). Kent does not back down; he replies:

> Let it fall rather, though the fork invade
> The region of my heart. Be Kent unmannerly
> When Lear is mad . . .
> Think'st thou that duty shall have dread to
>   speak
> When power to flattery bows? To plainness
>   honour's bound
> When majesty falls to folly (1.1.140–142,
>   146–148).

Kent understands that it is his duty to be unmannerly or to step out of line if the king acts "mad," or unwisely. By bowing to the flattery of Goneril and Regan, Lear rejects Cordelia's honest words. As a faithful friend, Kent values "plainness," or straight-talk, not flattery or mere smiles, as Oswald gives to Goneril. Kent's abuse of Oswald highlights another theme in the play, the commendation of plain dealing. A plain dealer speaks the truth without fear of rejection and does not accept the easy path but is willing to confront a friend or master when he or she is in error. In Kent's view, a plain dealer confronts his master's "colder moods," while an unfaithful or cowardly servant would simply "bring snow," meaning that the servant would seek the simplest path and the way that requires the least sacrifice.

Act II, Scene 4, 261–289

LEAR. *[to Goneril]* I'll go with thee.
Thy fifty yet doth double five-and-twenty,
And thou art twice her love

GONERIL. Hear me, my lord.
What need you five-and-twenty, ten, or five,
To follow in a house where twice so many
Have command to tend you?

LEAR. O, reason not the need! Our basest
  beggars
Are in the poorest thing superflouous.
Allow not nature more than nature needs,

Man's life is cheap as beast's. Thou are a lady;
If only to go warm were gorgeous,
Why, nature needs not what thou gorgeous
    wear'st,
Which scarcely keeps thee warm. But for true
    need—
You heavens, give me that patience, patience I
    need!
You see me here, you gods, a poor man
As full of grief as age, wretched in both.
If it be you that stirs these daughters' hearts
Against their father, fool me not so much
To bear it tamely. Touch me with noble anger,
And let not women's weapons, water drops,
Stain my man's cheeks.—No, you unnatural
    hags,
I will have such revenges on you both
That all the world shall—I will do such
    things—
What they are yet I know not, but they shall be
The terrors of the earth! You think I'll weep.
No, I'll not weep.
I have full cause of weeping but this heart
[Storm and tempest]
Shall break into a hundred thousand flaws
Or ere I'll weep. O Fool, I shall go mad!

This sequence marks Lear's departure out of domestic life and into a literal and figurative storm. At Gloucester's castle, he argues with Goneril and Regan about his attendants; each daughter refuses to allow him to live with her unless he dispatches all of his knights. When Regan asks why he needs even one attendant, Lear launches into this great speech about the nature of "need." Even beggars, he argues, own something more than what they actually need ("are in the poorest thing superfluous"). And, if dressing warmly were the only beauty a lady needed, then she would not need gorgeous clothes, because they "scarcely keeps thee warm."

Lear prays for patience, and Harold Bloom observes that some critics have linked his suffering to that of biblical Job. Bloom, however, disagrees: "Patient Job is actually not very patient, despite his theological reputation, and Lear is the pat-

tern of all impatience, though he vows otherwise" (*Shakespeare* 477). Lear wonders if it was the gods who turned his daughters' hearts against him; he begs the gods not to make him a fool and, instead, "touch [him] with noble anger" so that he can exact his revenge on these "unnatural hags." Full of sound and fury, Lear cannot even articulate how he will exact his revenge. The best he can spew out is that the "things" he will do will be the "terrors of the earth!" And then, vowing not to cry even though he has reason to, he makes his exodus from the castle with Kent and the Fool. Outside, a storm is brewing. The sisters urge Gloucester to shut the castle doors, and it is done.

Act III, Scene 2, 41–72

KENT. Alas, sir, are you here? Things that love
    night
Love not such nights as these. The wrathful
    skies
Gallow the very wanderers of the dark
And make them keep their caves. Since I was
    man,
Such sheets of fire, such bursts of horrid
    thunder,
Such groans of roaring wind and I rain I never
Remember to have heard. Man's nature cannot
    carry
Th' afflication or the fear.

LEAR. Let the great gods
That keep this dreadful pudder o'er our heads
Find out their enemies now. Tremble, thou
    wretch,
That hast within thee undivlged crimes
Unwhipped of justice. Hide thee, thou bloody
    hand,
Thou perjured, and thou similar of virtue
That art incestuous. Caitiff, to pieces shake,
That under covert and convenient seeming
Has practiced on man's life. Close pent-up
    guilts,
Rive your concealing continents and cry
These dreadful summoners grace. I am a man
More sinned against than sinning.

KENT. Alack, bareheaded?
Gracious my lord, hard by here is a hovel.
Some friendship it will lend you 'gainst the
    tempest.
Repose you there while I to his hard house—
Which even but now, demanding after you,
Denied me to come in—return and force
Their scanted courtesy.

LEAR. My wits begin to turn.—
Come on, my boy. How dost, my boy? Art
    cold?
I am cold myself.—Where is this straw, my
    fellow?
The art of our necessities is strange
And can make vile things precious. Come,
    your hovel.—
Poor Fool and knave, I have one part in my
    heart
That's sorry yet for thee.

This passage represents a significant turn in Lear's excrutiating journey. He begins fuming against the gods and, in the next breath, suddenly finds more earthly, humane concerns as his "wits begin to turn."

Kent, in disguise, finds Lear and the Fool wandering in the storm. To ensure that his audience can "see" the horrors of the tempest, Shakespeare has Kent poetically describe it: Such terrible skies, for instance, will execute by hanging anyone so unwise as to venture out in it ("Gallow the very wanderers of the dark"). Lear rails against the gods, using imagery associated with storms ("pudder o'er our heads," "tremble," "shake," "rive"). He is their enemy now; they have hidden his daughters' crimes against their father ("undivulged crimes / Unwhipped of justice"). He calls on the "Caitiff," or villain, to reveal the deception ("seeming") that has been practiced on him. He confesses that he is not a perfect man but beseeches that his hidden "guilts" be closed up and asks for mercy from the elements from "These dreadful summoners" ("summoners" referring to officers of church courts). The final line of the first passage indicates

that Lear sees himself as a victim of his daughters' sin and greed; more "sinned against than sinning."

But, after Kent suggests that Lear and the Fool find shelter in a nearby hovel, Lear expresses for the first time that his sanity is on edge. He also, for the first time, expresses concern for Kent and the Fool. Goddard describes the implications of this moment: "The lightning has struck his soul, and it is at the very moment when he cries 'my wits begin to turn' that he thinks for the first time of someone else's suffering before his own. 'Come on, my boy. How dost, my boy? Art cold?' he cries to Poor Tom" (20). Bevington observes that Lear, in his madness, here begins to understand both the value of this insight—companionship with other human beings who are just as cold and outcast—and the need for suffering to attain it (1,204): "The art of our necessities is strange, / And can make vile things precious."

The lesson becomes increasingly clear to Lear when we next see him, in Act III, Scene 4. The three (Lear, the Fool, and Kent) reach the hovel, where they find Edgar, disguised as poor Tom O'Bedlam. A broken man, Lear learns compassion. It occurs to him here that there are many people in the world who have very little protection from physical storms. Lear reflects:

Poor naked wretches, wheresoe'er you are,
That bide the pelting of this pitiless storm,
How shall your houseless heads and unfed
    sides,
Your looped and windowed raggedness, defend
    you
From seasons such as these? O, I have ta'en
Too little care of this! Take physic, pomp
Expose thyself to feel what wretches feel,
That thou mayst shake the superflux to them
And show the heavens more just. (3.4.28–36)

Act III, Scene 6, 109–116

EDGAR. When we our betters see bearing our
    woes,
We scarcely think our miseries our foes.
Who alone suffers suffers most I' th' mind,

Leaving free things and happy shows behind;
But then the mind much sufferance doth
    o'erskip
When grief hath mates, and bearing fellowship.
How light and portable my pain seems now,
When that which makes me bend makes the
    King bow . . .

Edgar is in the wilderness with Lear, Kent, the Fool, and Gloucester, though they have just exited the scene. In this rhyming speech, Edgar expresses the importance of entering into the suffering of others. He describes the added difficulty of a man who must suffer alone, pointing out that a mental burden is added to this kind of isolation. Much mental suffering can be avoided, or skipped, if one has friends to help bear the suffering. The final two lines of this passage reveal Edgar's wide perspective. The pain of rejection and misunderstanding he has suffered seem much smaller in light of the great pain and anguish that King Lear has suffered.

Act IV, Scene 1, 13–25

OLD MAN. O my good lord, I have been
    your tenant
And your father's tenant these fourscore years.

GLOUCESTER. Away, get thee away. Good
    friend, begone.
Thy comforts can do me no good at all;
Thee they may hurt.

OLD MAN. You cannot see your way.

GLOUCESTER. I have no way and therefore
    want no eyes.
I stumbled when I saw. Full oft 'tis seen
Our means secure us, and our mere defects
Prove our commodities. O dear son Edgar,
The food of thy abused father's wrath,
Might I but live to see thee in my touch,
I'd say I had eyes again.

Deemed a traitor and blinded by Cornwall, Gloucester now realizes that his beloved son Edgar,

whom he had earlier banished, did not deserve his anger. Again, Shakespeare uses the theme of true sight versus moral blindness. Those who can physically see, as Gloucester could before the violence enacted on him, do not always truly see. Gloucester understands the difference now: "I stumbled when I saw." Now, blinded, he sees more clearly. Gloucester speculates that our very resources make us careless: "Our means secure us." At the same time, our "defects" can become our "commodities," or advantages. As Bevington notes, "Gloucester perceives, as does Lear, that adversity is paradoxically of some benefit, since prosperity had previously caused him to be so spiritually blind" (1,204).

Finally, Gloucester reveals his love for Edgar and begs forgiveness. If only he could "see" his son—even by touching him—he would truly once again have vision: "I'd say I had eyes again." Edgar, significantly, hears the entire passage, standing nearby disguised as Tom O'Bedlam. He steps in and agrees to guide his father to Dover.

Act IV, Scene 6, 4–26

EDGAR.   Horrible steep.
Hark, do you hear the sea?

GLOUCESTER.   No, truly.

EDGAR. Why then, your other senses grow
    imperfect
By your eye's anguish.

GLOUCESTER.   So may it be indeed.
Methinks thy voice is altered and thou speak'st
In better phrase and matter than thou didst.

EDGAR. You're much decieved; in nothing
    am I changed
But in my garments.

GLOUCESTER. Methinks you're better spoken.

EDGAR. Come on, sir. Here's the place. Stand
    still. How fearful
And dizzy 'tis to cast one's eyes so low.

The crows and choughs that wing the midway
  air
Show scarce so gross as beetles. Half-way down
Hangs one that gathers samphire, dreadful
  trade;
Methinks he seems no bigger than his head.
The fishermen that walk upon the beach
Appear like mice, and yon tall anchoring
  barque
Diminished to her cock, her cock a buoy
Almost too small for sight. The murmuring
  surge
That on th'unnumbered idle pebble chafes,
Cannot be heard so high. I'll look no more,
Lest my brain turn and the deficient sight
Topple down headlong.

GLOUCESTER. Set me where you stand.

EDGAR. Give me your hand. You are now
  within a foot
Of th' extreme verge. For all beneath the moon
Would I not leap upright.

The exchange illustrates how Shakespeare's use of layered meanings and deception enriches the narrative; according to Goddard, it is a "superb example of Shakespeare's power to do whatever he likes with his auditors or readers" (22). Edgar, disguised as a beggar, leads Gloucester to the edge of an imaginary cliff ostensibly so that Gloucester can commit suicide by jumping off. Gloucester confesses that he does not hear the sea; Edgar reasons that his hearing must be as bad as his eyesight. But, Shakespeare shows us that Gloucester's hearing is perfect: He notices that his guide's speech has curiously changed. "The natural emotion of being with his father, together perhaps with his change of dress, has led [Edgar] to forget to maintain, vocally, the role he is playing, and his father's quick ear has detected the change" (Goddard 23). Edgar denies it, and when Gloucester persists—"Methinks you're better spoken"—Edgar changes the subject, indicating that Gloucester now stands at the edge of the cliff.

Continuing the scam, Edgar pretends to be dizzied by the great height and distance to the beach below. Gloucester's now within a foot of the edge; if it were Edgar, he would not "leap upright," lest he would tumble down. Gloucester does not catch Edgar's slip of the tongue when he says that the "murmuring surge" of the sea cannot be heard so high up on the cliff. "The conclusion of his tale has forgotten the beginning of it—Shakespeare's sly way of proving that the two men are not standing where Edgar says they are" (Goddard 23–24).

Of course, Gloucester does not fall. Edgar puts on yet another mask, this one of a beggar on the beach who convinces Gloucester that the gods rescued the old man. Both Gloucester and Lear make much about their falls from greatness. But, the play mocks the greatness each man once held as well as humanity's assumed security from disaster and humiliation. Just as Gloucester's fall from the Dover cliffs is "pretended," so is the fall Lear and Gloucester experience when they lose their royal titles. Man is a humble creation, as each comes to realize over the course of the play. For Gloucester, this understanding occurs at the end of this scene, when Edgar informs him that the gods "have preserved thee" (4.6.74):

GLOUCESTER. I do remember now.
  Henceforth I'll bear
Affliction till it do cry out itself
'Enough, enough' and die. That thing you
  speak of,
I took it for a man. Often 'twould say
'The fiend, the fiend!' He led me to that place
  (4.6.75–79).

Act IV, Scene 6, 96–136
GLOUCESTER. I know that voice.

LEAR. Ha! Goneril with a white beard? They
  flattered me like a dog and told me I had the
  white hairs in my beard ere the black ones
  were there. To say 'ay' and 'no' to everything
  that I said 'ay' and 'no' to was no good

divinity. When the rain came to wet me once and the wind to make me chatter, when the thunder would not peace at my bidding, there I found 'em, there I smelt 'em out. Go to. There are not men o' their words; they told me I was everything. 'Tis a lie. I am not ague-proof.

GLOUCESTER. The trick of that voice I do well remember. Is't not the King?

LEAR. Ay, every inch a king. When I do stare, see how the subject quakes. I pardon that man's life. What was thy cause? Adultery? Thou shalt not die. Die for adultery? No. The wren goes to 't, and the small gilded fly does lecher in my sight. Let copulation thrive, for Gloucester's bastard son was kinder to his father than my daughters got 'tween the lawful sheets. To 't, luxury, pell-mell, for I lack soldiers. Behold yond simp'ring dame, whose face between her forks presages snow, that minces virtue and does shake the head to hear of pleasure's name. The fitchew nor the soiled horse goes to 't with a more riotous appetite. Down from the waist they are centaurs, though women all above. But to the girdle do the gods inherit; beneath is all the fiend's. There's hell, there's darkness, there is the sulpherous pit; burning, scalding, stench, consumption! Fie, fie, fie, pah, pah! Give me an ounce of civet, good apothecary; sweeten my imagination. There's money for thee.

GLOUCESTER. Oh, let me kiss that hand!

LEAR. Let me wipe it first; it smells of mortality.

Still on the cliffs, Gloucester and Edgar meet the mad Lear, who erupts with two of his major outbursts during the play. Bevington comments: "When at last the two old men come together . . . the sad comfort they derive from sharing the wreckage of their lives calls forth piercing eloquence against the stench of mortality" (1,202).

First, Lear recalls how, as a king, "they flattered me like a dog." They told him he was "everything." He knows now that flattery lies. He is not, after all, immune to chills and fever ("ague-proof"). Here, Lear admits that he believed that he was wise because he allowed himself to be manipulated through flattery. White hairs in one's beard symbolize wisdom, yet Lear was more concerned about words than he was about truth. Goneril and Regan told him he was wise, and he was satisfied. Cordelia told him the truth, but he preferred to be flattered. While he wanted to be flattered early in the play, he now recognizes flattery as something for dogs. The speech signals another transformation in Lear's character. "How fitting that Shakespeare chose the moment when the King discovers the truth which the whole world is bent on hiding from kings to have Gloucester finally identify him: 'Is't not the king?' 'Ay, every inch a king!'" observes Goddard (25–26).

In the second outburst, Lear condemns female sensuality, complaining that Edmund, born illegitimate, was better to his father than Lear's two daughters, conceived between "lawful sheets," were to him. He associates women with "centaurs," mythical beasts that had the torso of a human but the body of a horse. "Hell," in Shakespeare's day, was slang for the vagina (Bloom *Shakespeare* 514). Some critics interpret the speech as antifeminist or even antisex; Goddard argues that Shakespeare is making a link between lust and violence: "The horror of this outpouring, augmented as it is by the age of the man, is a measure not more of the part that sex, expressed or suppressed, has played in his life than of the part that war and power have" (26). Bloom argues that the speech shows how Lear's authority has eroded in the area where he thought it most absolute: his relationship with his daughters: "Goneril and Regan have usurped authority; their nature is akin to Edmund's idea of nature, rather than Lear's, and so the mad king's revulsion is from nature itself, not an idea but the fundamental fact of sexual difference" (*Shakespeare* 514).

Act IV, Scene 7, 30–69

CORDELIA. Had you not been their father,
   these white flakes
Did challenge pity of them. Was this a face
To be opposed against the warring winds?
To stand against the deep dread-bolted
   thunder,
In the most terrible and nimble stroke
Of quick cross-lightening?
To watch, poor *perdu,*
With this thin helm? Mine enemy's dog
Though he had bit me, should have stood that
   night
Against my fire; and wast thou fain, poor
   father,
To hovel thee with swine and rogues forlorn
In short and musty straw? Alack, alack!
'Tis wonder that thy life and wits at once
Had not concluded all.—He wakes. Speak to
   him.

DOCTOR. Madam, do you; 'tis fittest.

CORDELIA. How does my royal lord? How
   fares your Majesty?

LEAR. You do me wrong to take me out o' th'
   grave.
Thou art a soul in bliss, but I am bound
Upon a wheel of fire, that mine own tears
Do scald like molten lead.

CORDELIA. Sir, do you know me?

LEAR. You are a spirit, I know. When did you
   die?

CORDELIA. Still, still far wide.

LEAR. Where have I been? Where am I? Fair
   daylight?
I am mightily abused; I should e'en die with
   pity
To see another thus. I know not what to say.
I will not swear these are my hands. Let's see.

I feel this pinprick. Would I were assured
Of my condition!

CORDELIA. O, look upon me, sir,
And hold your hand in benediction o'er me.
No sir, you must not kneel.

LEAR. Pray do not mock:
I am a very foolish fond old man,
Fourscore and upward, not an hour more nor
   less,
And to deal plainly,
I fear I am not in my perfect mind.
Methinks I should know you and know this
   man,
Yet I am doubtful, for I am mainly ignorant
What place this is, and all the skill I have
Remembers not these garments; nor I know not
Where I did lodge last night. Do not laugh at
   me,
For, as I am a man, I think this lady
To be my child Cordelia.

Lear and Cordelia are reunited at the French camp;
Cordelia reveals the strength of her character, and
blessed by her forgiveness, Lear emerges out of his
mad fog. More than illustrating disapproval of how
her sisters treated their father, this passage reveals
Cordelia's great love for Lear, even after she has
suffered shame and injustice at his hands. Even if
Lear had not been the father of Goneril and Regan,
he deserved to be pitied if only by virtue of his age
(the white hair, or "flakes") and station. He did
not deserve to be cast aside with swine and vaga-
bonds. The passage also illustrates that Cordelia
understands her father's painful odyssey, as when
she observes that it is a "wonder" that he has sur-
vived at all. She further shows her deep respect for
her father when she refuses to allow him to kneel
before her.

When Lear wakes, he first believes that he is in
hell, indicated in his reference to the "wheel of fire,"
a torture device for those condemned to death.
When he calls her a spirit, Cordelia believes that
her father is still "wide," or insane. Paradoxically,

however, Lear's mind is actually sounder than it ever was—certainly sounder than in the play's beginning, when he disinherited Cordelia and exiled Kent. Lear's admission of ignorance (a "foolish fond old man") is evidence of his transformation. From a prideful and arrogant king, Lear now recognizes his frailty; "as his mind begins to break, truth begins to break in on it." (Goddard 37).

DIFFICULT PASSAGES
Act I, Scene 1, 93–95

CORDELIA. Unhappy that I am, I cannot heave
My heart into my mouth. I love your Majesty
According to my bond; no more nor less.

Cordelia speaks these lines when she is asked to participate in the "love test" created by her father. This passage is easy to misunderstand. At first read, one might mistake Cordelia's response for stubbornness, but given the events that follow, it is truly essential to her loving character to withhold empty praise. Furthermore, Cordelia's refusal to flatter Lear initiates a series of events that will save the kingdom and stop the evil pursuits of Goneril and Regan. Cordelia understands that her words have power, and she refuses to engage in the

Lear sends Cordelia away in Act 1, Scene 1 of *King Lear*. This is a print from Malcolm C. Salaman's 1916 edition of *Shakespeare in Pictorial Art*. (*Painting by Ford Madox Brown*)

manipulation her sisters so quickly embrace. Like Kent, Cordelia is willing to say the difficult word, deliver the unpopular message, and put herself in danger to help her father. To heave one's heart into one's mouth describes the process of paying lip service to one's love and one's affection. In Cordelia's view, to simply say she loves her father and to give him praise for material gain is grotesque and crude.

Act I, Scene 4, 130–140

FOOL. Mark it, nuncle:
Have more than thou showest,
Speak less than thou knowest,
Lend less than thou owest,
Ride more than thou goest,
Learn more than thou trowest,
Set less than thou throwest;
Leave thy drink and thy whore,
And keep in-a-door,
And thou shalt have more
Than two tens a score

The Fool has some of the most complicated, brilliant, and perplexing speeches in all of Shakespeare. Here, he addresses King Lear, who has just banished Cordelia and Kent and given his kingdom to Goneril and Regan. Lear has not been willing to listen to Cordelia or Kent, and the Fool recognizes the foolishness at the center of Lear's pride and arrogance. The Fool's speech affirms the wisdom of modesty, humility, and moderation, three characteristics that Lear lacks. To "have more than thou showest" is to refuse the temptation to brag and show off one's riches, pretending and making a large show to impress others. To "speak less than thou knowest" is to control one's tongue, refusing to dominate conversations as a way to impress with one's intelligence. Lending less than one owes requires the humility to admit one's limitations. The Fool gives the audience a picture of Lear that is not presented onstage: a man who loves to show off, loves to impress others, loves to give large loans, and loves to appear larger than life. The Fool knows that Lear's character has earned him the hatred of Goneril and Regan, but Lear does not heed the warning.

Act I, Scene 5, 37–49

FOOL. Thy asses are gone about 'em. The reason why the seven stars are no more than seven is a pretty reason.

LEAR. Because they are not eight.

FOOL. Yes, indeed. Thou wouldst make a good Fool.

LEAR. To take 't again perforce! Monster ingratitude!

FOOL. If thou wert my Fool, nuncle, I'd have thee beaten for being old before thy time.

LEAR. How's that?

FOOL. Thou shouldst not have been old till thou hadst been wise.

This sequence illustrates the Fool's role as the truth teller whose truths Lear does not hear or understand. Enraged that Goneril plans to reduce his retinue of attendants, Lear has left for Regan's home and sent disguised Kent ahead with a letter. Along the way, he and the Fool engage in this almost slapstick routine that, in another context, might foreground vaudeville:

FOOL. Canst tell how an oyster makes his shell?

LEAR. No.

FOOL. Nor I either. But I can tell why a snail has a house. (1.5.26–28)

But, lest the audience get too comfortable with the comedy, Shakespeare always equips the Fool with a sharp tongue that tells the tragic truth of the situation. Here, the Fool starts with an innocuous

reference to the seven stars in the cluster known as the Pleiades. Lear's reward for playing along (Why are there seven stars? Because there aren't eight . . .) is a back-handed compliment: He'd make a good fool. Unfortunately for Lear, the Fool means it literally. Lear is a fool for trusting Goneril and Regan, giving up his kingdom, and banishing Cordelia. He has not, the Fool says, developed the wisdom that should come with old age.

Act II, Scene 4, 79–86

FOOL. *[singing]* That sir which serves and seeks for gain,
And follows but for form,
Will pack when it begins to rain,
And leave thee in the storm.
But I will tarry; the fool will stay
And let the wise man fly.
The knave turns fool that runs away;
The fool no knave, perdy.

The Fool sings this song to Kent, who is bound in the stocks at Gloucester's castle. On close examination, it becomes clear that the song describes the conflict of the play, commenting on the pretended

Lear comes upon Kent in the stocks in Act II, Scene 4 of *King Lear*. Plate from *Retzsch's Outlines to Shakespeare:* King Lear, 1838 *(Illustration by Moritz Retzsch)*

loyalty of those who followed King Lear "for gain." Loyal friends are like fools, putting themselves in harm's way and remaining faithful no matter how dangerous the predicament. The Fool compares the wisdom of self-preservation with the foolishness of faithfulness. It is natural to run away when times are difficult, or when a friend requires more of us than we are willing to give. The Fool's song describes the foolishness that is required of a good friend.

Act IV, Scene 7, 13–16

CORDELIA. O you kind gods,
Cure this great breach in his abused nature!
Th' untun'd and jarring senses, O, wind up
Of this child-changed father!

Cordelia speaks this crucial but somewhat obscure prayer over her sleeping father. While she prays for Lear's health, she also prays that his mind be healed. The last time she saw Lear was on the day that he called her his "sometime daughter" and banished her from the kingdom with insults and curses. Cordelia acknowledges that within Lear's nature is a breach or chasm that inhibits his ability to see clearly and make good decisions. The prayer reveals that Cordelia sees her father clearly, as she points out the abuse he has suffered, jarring his senses and changing his mind. He is a "child-changed father" in two ways. First, he is changed by Goneril and Regan and the abuse they dealt him. This abuse has humbled Lear and changed him. Lear is also changed by his interaction with Cordelia. Cordelia's prayer foreshadows the powerful interaction she has with him in the next few scenes, but it was Cordelia's plain dealing at the beginning of the play that served to change Lear as well.

Act V, Scene 3, 119–128

HERALD. What are you?
Your name, your quality, and why you answer
This present summons?

EDGAR. Know, my name is lost,
By treason's tooth bare-gnawn and canker-bit;

Yet am I noble as the adversary
I come to cope

ALBANY. Which is that adversary?

EDMUND. Himself. What sayest thou to him?

EDGAR. Draw thy sword,
That if my speech offend a noble heart,
Thy arm may do thee justice. Here is mine.
[*He draws his sword.*]

Casting aside his disguise as Tom O'Bedlam and now in full armor, Edgar arrives in the final act to challenge Edmund's claim on Gloucester's title and lands. In the phrase "my name is lost," Edgar means that since his name was destroyed by treason and lies, he has spent much of the play without a name, in disguised self-abasement. Yet, even without a name, he is as noble as his "adversary," Edmund.

CRITICAL INTRODUCTION TO THE PLAY

While *King Lear* follows the story line of the classic tragedy, the play is by no means typical or formulaic. As the Greek philosopher Aristotle wrote, tragic heroes are both admirable and flawed. To an audience member, this dichotomy inspires feelings of understanding and sympathy. But King Lear is not the typical tragic hero, even for Shakespeare. Unlike Hamlet or Othello, whose heroic qualities, both admirable and flawed, are fully realized if not fully understood, King Lear shows himself unsympathetically to us from the very start of the play, when he demands that each of daughters verbally profess her love to him in order to satiate his vanity. From this scene, the tone of the play is set. King Lear's atypical qualities—he is irrational, contentious, and arrogant—inform not only the character of Lear but the play itself. His redemption will come, but it is a long and painful process.

Themes

King Lear touches on a number of themes: the complexities of family relationships and the love between parent and child; rationality and reason versus madness; age versus youth; betrayal and revenge; disguises; nature versus the cosmos; and the yearning for power. Of these, perhaps the family-related themes are the most prominent.

The play depicts various relationships between family members: Lear and his three daughters, Goneril, Regan, and Cordelia; Gloucester and his sons, Edgar and Edmund; Goneril her husband, Albany; Regan and her husband, Cornwall; and the various siblings in the play. Relationships are divided due to misunderstandings and betrayals, creating a microcosmic representation of Lear's initial division of the kingdom, which is based on a kind of "love test" for his three daughters. In Stephen Greenblatt's "The Cultivation of Anxiety: King Lear and His Heirs," the critic explains that Lear "wishes to be the object—the preferred and even the sole recipient—of his child's love," desiring a kind of public deference as well as the inward love of his children (108).

The relationship between King Lear and his daughters Regan and Goneril is sullied by their lack of respect, also evident in this initial scene. Both Regan and Goneril indulge their father's blatant pursual of praise, willingly participating in his love test in order to gain a portion of the kingdom. Their respect is insincere, and they display this as they compete for Lear's favor. Cordelia, the youngest daughter, on the other hand, shows her respect by being honest to her father. Her love does not depend on empty words "since I am sure my love's / More ponderous than my tongue" (1.1.75–76). But Lear takes her refusal to indulge him not as true love but as betrayal and proceeds to disown her completely: "Here I disclaim all my paternal care, / Propinquity and property of blood, / And as a stranger to my heart and me, / Hold thee from this forever" (1.1.111–114). Kent interjects with a rational plea on behalf of Cordelia: "And in thy best consideration check / This hideous rashness. Answer my life, my judgment: / Thy youngest

Julia Margaret Cameron's 1872 photograph of Lear (played by Charles Hay Cameron) and his three daughters (Marina Liddell, Edith Liddell, and Alice Liddell)

daughter does not love thee least" (1.1.144–146). Still, Lear is unable to see through his own vanity and need for public acknowledgment. According to Greenblatt, even at the end of Lear's life, when he has realized Cordelia's true love for him, he is still seeking Cordelia's approval; he "dies still looking on his daughter's lips for the words that she never speaks" (131).

The other important parent-child relationship in the play is between Gloucester and his two sons, Edgar, his eldest, and Edmund, who is illegitimate. Gloucester does not demand a public acknowledgment of love, as Lear does, but he still falls prey to Edmund's lies. Edmund fights for land and power because he knows his status as an illegitimate son will deny him an inheritance. In the very first scene of the play, when speaking with Kent, Gloucester comments on Edmund's illegitimacy: "His breeding, sir, hath been at my charge. I have so often blushed to acknowledge him, that now I am brazed to it" (1.1.8–10). As the story unfolds, Edmund decries the injustice of the situation. ". . . Wherefore should I / Stand in the plague of custom and permit / The curiosity of nations to deprive me? / For that I am some twelve of fourteen moonshines / Lag of a brother? Why 'bastard'? Wherefore 'base'?" (1.2.2–5). Here, Edmund challenges the validity of Edgar's status as Gloucester's heir. He then boldly proclaims his plan to get land and title by convincing Gloucester that Edgar, in fact, has illicit designs. Gloucester is indeed fooled, demonstrating the power of treachery disguised as love.

Structure

King Lear's structure follows the parallel tracks that Lear and Gloucester take throughout the narrative: The story starts in a domestic setting, moves outside (to the heath for Lear and the cliffs for Gloucester) where characters are subjected to the elements, and ends at a prison camp. Domesticity represents safety but also, for both Lear and Gloucester, the locus of their emotional traps. The outdoors, in Acts II and III, is represented by physical and emotional storms, as Lear falls into madness and blinded Gloucester hopes to commit suicide by jumping off a cliff. But the outdoors is also where both characters come to a better understanding of themselves and their lives. Finally, the prison at the end (Act V) represents the final paradox; both Gloucester, who has died, offstage, and Lear, who dies onstage, have completed their devastating odysseys and are, in a sense, more free than they were when the story began.

In an essay titled "An Approach through Dramatic Structure," compiled in *Approaches to Teaching Shakespeare's King Lear,* James E. Hirsh notes that "As soon as possible and as smoothly as possible, a playwright is supposed to give us our bearings, to let us know who's who and what's what and especially whom to root for and whom against" (86). Shakespeare, however, denies us this kind of smooth introduction. *King Lear* opens with

Gloucester and Kent talking, with Gloucester commenting on the illegitimacy of his son, Edmund. In the same room, Edmund listens while his father, in a casual, matter-of-fact tone, demeans his mother and belittles the significance of his birth: "Though this knave came something saucily to the world before he was sent for, yet was his mother fair, there was good sport at his making, and the whoreson must be acknowledged" (1.1.16–19). On the surface, the exposition seems straightforward and reliable. Yet, as the story continues, we see that this is not the case: Gloucester, the man who is presented as an insensitive cad, becomes a "pitiable victim," and Edmund, with whom we sympathize, becomes a "cold-blooded villain" (Hirsh 87).

It is a similar story with Lear himself. In his first scene, in which he divides his kingdom, irrationality, misjudgment, and harshness embody Lear as a character and continue to do so until his insanity peaks in Act III, Scene 2. At that point, we begin to see Lear as not just mad and belligerent but also pitiable and misjudged. And, it is in this scene that the reliability of the dramatic structure is tested most. The rising action of a typical play, in dramatic structure, consists of a conflict the protagonist deals with on his or her way toward some understandable, or at least recognizable, goal. In Lear's case, as we see in his first scene, his goal is to divide his kingdom so that he may retire in luxury. This plan never comes to fruition, and Lear rushes out into the storm for no apparent reason other than to bemoan his fate, a seemingly pointless, causeless act that speaks of neither a goal nor a rising action.

In a typical play, the climax is the central turning point of the action. *King Lear* has several central dramatic moments, but they are not traditional climaxes. One occurs when Lear runs out into the storm, but Lear's fate does not then take a dramatic turn for the worse, as is customary; indeed, things seem to get somewhat better for him. Another takes place in the final act, when Lear manages to come to some version of his senses after losing Cordelia. But if this were the climax, the falling action part of the dramatic structure would be skipped altogether; there is no subsequent denouement, as Lear dies immediately after. The resolution consists only of the sliver of mental clarity Lear experiences, through his love for Cordelia.

Thus, it cannot be said that *King Lear* follows any typical dramatic structure. Nonetheless, in its subversion of our expectations as readers or members of the audience, the play manages to be as moving as any work of literature ever written. Shakespeare's genius here transcends even the typical rules of drama.

Style and Imagery

Recurring images in the play include animals, bestiality, sight, clothing, nature, astrology, and the gods. Even figurative references become associated with literal images. For example, Lear's physical gesture of tearing off his own clothing echoes with the many metaphors related to clothing in the early scenes (Petronella 45).

Especially prominent images throughout *King Lear* are those of sight and blindness. An obvious reference in the play occurs when Gloucester's eyes in Act III are literally removed; examining the text more closely offers greater insight into the use of sight and blindness as symbolic imagery throughout. Lear possesses a kind of spiritual blindness; he chooses not to see the true intentions of Goneril and Regan and turns a blind eye toward the honest affection of Cordelia and the dogged loyalty of Kent. Sight is also physically obstructed by the various disguises characters don throughout the play, hindering their ability recognize one another physically and even morally (Petronella 82–83).

Goneril's ironic profession of love for her father—"Sir, I love you more than word can wield the matter, / Dearer than eyesight, space, and liberty"(1.1.50–51)—invokes her own eyesight as a testament to her love, soon revealed to be false. When Cordelia refuses to indulge Lear's vanity, Lear orders her to "avoid my sight" (1.1.118). Lear cannot bear to look at Cordelia, who has failed his test, but Lear also cannot see that she is his only sincere daughter. Kent attempts to reason with Lear, but it only results in Kent's banishment. "See better, Lear, and let me still remain / The true blank of thine eye," Kent responds (1.1.153–154). Kent sees the truth, that Cordelia is being faithful while her sisters have no loyalty toward their father. Lear's "Out of my sight!" (1.1.157), addressed angrily to Kent, is linked once again to the blindness of the king, unable to see "those who love him most" (Petronella 44). Lear exclaims to the King of France, "Thou hast her, France, let her be thine; for we / Have no such daughter, nor shall ever see / That face of hers again" (1.1.257–259). Finally, Cordelia says that she is unable to possess "A still-soliciting eye, and such a tongue" as her sisters' because of her inability to be anything but genuine and true (1.1.226).

Gloucester begins the play with a figurative blindness much like King Lear's. He is unable to differentiate between Edgar's and Edmund's handwriting, causing him to believe Edmund's lies. Gloucester has been figuratively blinded by Edmund and then becomes literally blinded by Cornwall. While being interrogated about the aid he gave to the supposed traitor King Lear, Gloucester explains himself thus: "Because I would

Lear carries a dead Cordelia in his arms in Act V, Scene 3 of *King Lear,* as depicted in a plate from *Retzsch's Outlines to Shakespeare:* King Lear, published in 1838. *(Illustration by Moritz Retzsch)*

not see thy [Regan's] cruel nails / Pluck out his poor old eyes" (3.7.55–56). Cornwall then removes one of Gloucester's eyes, and by doing so, attempts to remove his dignity and humanity. Regan invites him to "smell / His way to Dover," as if he is nothing more than an animal (3.7.92–93).

One critic points out that "Gloucester's blindness parallels Lear's madness, in that both characters turn away from the external world to find a clearer moral vision within themselves" (Teague 84). By the fourth act, these two men are able to move forward toward a spiritual reawakening. Gloucester is reunited with Edgar; and Lear, with Cordelia, almost offering a happy resolution. By the fifth act, however, Gloucester dies, and Lear reverts back to madness due to Cordelia's death. Edgar ends the play with a final reference to sight, saying, "The oldest hath borne most; we that are young / Shall never see so much, nor live so long" (5.3.299–300). These final lines seem to refer to the clarity that does eventually come to King Lear, even if it is too late. One at least hopes that those reading or watching the play will learn from King Lear.

The Fool's Language

The Fool has some of the funniest and most difficult speeches in the play. From the eloquent verse in his various songs to the knotty riddles of his joking prose to his forthright expressions of concern for Lear, the Fool presents himself as well spoken, witty, and rational. His logic provides a contrast to the maddening, blind irrationality of Lear. The Fool, in fact, both combats and highlights the king's lack of reason, as well as emphasizing the paradox of a logical, rational "fool." As Sheldon P. Zitner observes, "The Fool is sometimes referred to as clinically mad, as having a 'maimed but agile mind,' perhaps because we too easily equate decorum with sanity. But the Fool is a model court Fool: a sage without laurels, obscuring, trivializing, and blunting home truths in order to forestall the blows that are their traditional reward. The logic of his defenseless loyalty is this: the more telling his insight, the more quirky its statement" (Colie 12).

One example of such quirkiness is the Fool's rhyme on the importance of discretion, coming just after Lear's casual division of his kingdom:

Have more than thou showest,
Speak less than thou knowest,
Lend less than thou owest,
Ride more than thou goest,
Learn more than thou trowest,
Set less than thou throwest,
Leave thy drink and thy whore,
And keep in-a-door,
And thou shalt have more,
Than two tens to a score. (1.4.103–112)

Here, the Fool expresses his concern over Lear's irrational behavior, yet he does so in a soft and indirect manner. Later in the scene, the Fool shifts to a different approach. Using prose this time, he expresses his opposition once again to the division, saying, "When thou clovest thy crown i'th'middle and gav'st away both parts, thou bor'st thine ass on thy back o'er the dirt" (1.4.123–125). This back and forth between prose and poetic verse continues in the scene, with the Fool criticizing Lear for giving "thy golden one away" (1.4.126) and then, in a rhymed song, equating Lear to the "wise" man who has "grown foppish" (1.4.129).

As the story progresses and King Lear's madness heightens, the Fool continues to be a rational, positive, honest, logical counterbalance. Lear, a slave to emotion, false premise, misguided love, and rage, depends on the Fool. In the face of Lear's often raucous and distasteful behavior, the Fool seems to try to soften Lear's emotions.

After realizing that both Goneril and Regan intend to strip him of all authority, Lear rushes out into a storm, cursing and melodramatically damning the continued existence of man: "Strike flat the thick rotundity o'th'world, / Crack nature's moulds, all germens spill at once / That makes ungrateful man" (3.2.7–9). The Fool responds with direct prose, urging Lear to "ask thy daughters' blessing" (3.2.11). Although his language does, in fact, soften the apparent severity of his meaning, the statement is explicitly critical, direct, and to the point. This is all to no avail, as King Lear's continuing madness washes away the Fool's insightful, honest, and counterbalanced advice.

EXTRACTS OF CLASSIC CRITICISM

Nahum Tate (1652–1715) [Excerpted from the preface to Tate's infamous 1681 version of the play, in which Tate gave the play a happy ending.]

You have a natural Right to this Piece, since by your Advice I attempted the Revival of it with Alterations. Nothing but the Pow'r of your Persuasions, and my Zeal for all the Remains of Shakespear cou'd have wrought me to so bold an Undertaking. I found that the New-modelling of this Story wou'd force me sometimes on the difficult Task of making the chiefest Persons speak something like their Character, on Matter whereof I had no Ground in my Author. Lear's real and Edgar's pretended Madness have so much of extravagant Nature (I know not how else to express it), as cou'd never have started but from our Shakespear's Creating Fancy. The Images and Language are so odd and surprizing, and yet so agreeable and proper, that whilst we grant that none but Shakespear could have form'd such Conceptions; yet we are satisfied that they were the only Things in the World that ought to be said on those Occasions. I found the whole to answer your account of it, a Heap of Jewels, unstrung, and unpolisht; yet so dazzling in their Disorder, that I soon perceiv'd I had seiz'd a Treasure. 'Twas my good Fortune to light on one Expedient to rectify what was wanting in the Regularity and Probability of the Tale, which was to run through the whole, as Love betwixt Edgar and Cordelia, that never chang'd a Word with each other in the Original. This renders Cordelia's Indifference, and her Father's Passion in the first Scene, probable. It likewise give Countenance to Edgar's Disguise, making that a generous Design that was before a poor Shift to save his Life. The Distress of the Story is evidently heightened by it; and it particularly gave Occasion of a New Scene or Two, of more Success (perhaps) than Merit. This method necessarily threw me on making the Tale conclude in a Success to the innocent distrest Persons: Otherwise I must have incumpred the Stage with dead Bodies, which Conduct makes many Tragedies conclude with unseasonable Jests. Yet was I wract with no small Fears for so bold a Change, till I found it well receiv'd by my Audience; and if this will not satisfy the Reader, I can produce an Authority that questionless will. Neither is it of so Trivial an Undertaking to make a Tragedy and happily, for 'tis more difficult to save than 'tis to Kill: The Dagger and Cup of Poison are always in Readiness; but to bring the Action to the last Extremity, and then by probable means to recover All, will require the Art and Judgment of a Writer, and cost him many a Pang in the Performance.

Samuel Johnson (1709–1784) [Excerpted from Johnson's landmark 1765 edition *The Plays of William Shakespeare*. Johnson was one of the greatest literary critics of all time, and his edition of Shakespeare would inform much of the future critical study of Shakespeare.]

The Tragedy of Lear is deservedly celebrated among the dramas of Shakespeare. There is perhaps no play which keeps the attention so strongly fixed; which so much agitates our passions and interests our curiosity. The artful involutions of distinct interests, the striking opposition of contrary characters, the sudden changes of fortune, and the quick succession of events, fill the mind with a perpetual tumult of indignation, pity, and hope. There is no scene which does not contribute to the aggravation of the distress or conduct of the action, and scarce a line which does not conduce to the progress of the scene. So powerful is the current of the poet's imagination, that the mind, which once ventures within it, is hurried irresistibly along.

On the seeming improbability of Lear's conduct it may be observed, that he is represented according to histories at that time vulgarly received as true. And perhaps if we turn our thoughts upon the barbarity and ignorance of the age to which this story is referred, it will appear not so unlikely as while we estimate Lear's manners by our own. Such preference of one daughter to another, or resignation of dominion on such conditions, would be yet credible, if told of a petty prince of Guinea or Madagascar. Shakespeare, indeed, by the mention of his Earls and Dukes, has given us the idea of times more civilised, and of life regulated by softer manners; and the truth that though he so nicely discriminates, and so minutely describes the characters of men, he commonly neglects and confounds the characters of ages, by mingling customs ancient and modern, English and foreign.

Lear howls over Cordelia's body in Act V, Scene 3 of *King Lear*. This illustration was designed for a 1918 edition of Charles and Mary Lamb's *Tales from Shakespeare. (Illustration by Louis Rhead)*

Charles Lamb (1775–1834) [Excerpted from *On the Tragedies of Shakespeare* (1811). Since their first publication, Lamb's critical works have received great praise. In the 1930s, F. R. Leavis's critique of Lamb's work served to remove Lamb from serious study; however, in the 1960s, Lamb's work was reintroduced and rehabilitated by critics such as Gerald Monsmon and George Barnett. Here, Lamb expresses his famous conviction that *King Lear* is "impossible to be represented on a stage."]

So to see Lear acted,—to see an old man tottering about the stage with a walking-stick, turned out of doors by his daughters in a rainy night, has nothing in it but what is painful and disgusting. We want to take him into shelter and relieve him. That is all the feeling which the acting of Lear ever produced in me. But the Lear of Shakespeare cannot be acted. The contemptible machinery by which they mimic the storm which he goes out in, is not more inadequate to represent the horrors of the real elements, than any actor can be to represent Lear: they might more easily propose to personate the Satan of Milton upon a stage, or one of Michael Angelo's terrible figures. The greatness of Lear is not in corporal dimension, but in intellectual: the explosions of his passion are terrible as a volcano: they are storms turning up and disclosing to the bottom that sea his mind, with all its vast riches. It is his mind which is laid bare. This case of flesh and blood seems too insignificant to be thought on; even as he himself neglects it. On the stage we see nothing but corporal infirmities and weakness, the impotence of rage; while we read it, we see not Lear, but we are Lear,—we are in his mind, we are sustained by a grandeur which baffles the malice of daughters and storms; in the aberrations of his reason, we discover a mighty irregular power of reasoning, immethodised from the ordinary purposes of life, but exerting its powers, as the wind blows where it listeth, at will upon the corruptions and abuses of mankind. What have looks, or tones, to do with that sublime identification of his age with that of the heavens themselves, when in his reproaches to them for conniving at the injustice of his children, he reminds them that "they themselves are old?" What gestures shall we appropriate to this? What has the voice or the eye to do with such things? But the play is beyond all art, as the tamperings with it show: it is too hard and stony; it must have love-scenes, and a happy ending. It is not enough that Cordelia is a daughter, she must shine as a lover too. Tate has put his hook in the nostrils of this Leviathan, for Garrick and his followers, the showmen of scene, to draw the mighty beast about more easily. A happy ending!—as if the living martyrdom that Lear had gone through,—the flaying of his feelings alive, did not make a fair dismissal from the stage of life the only decorous thing for him. If he is to live and be happy after, if he could sustain this world's burden after, why all this pudder and preparation,—why torment us with all this unnecessary sympathy? As if the childish pleasure of getting his gilt-robes and sceptre again could tempt him to act over again his misused station,—as if at his years, and with his experience, anything was left but to die.

Lear is essentially impossible to be represented on a stage.

William Hazlitt (1778–1830) [Excerpted from *Characters of Shakespear's Plays* (1817). Hazlitt, like Coleridge (following), led a revival of Shakespearean critical study, and his erudite analysis of the characters of *King Lear* informed generations of critics.]

We wish that we could pass this play over, and say nothing about it. All that we can say must fall far short of the subject; or even of what we ourselves conceive of it. To attempt to give a description of the play itself or of its effect upon the mind is mere impertinence: yet we must say something.—it is then the best of all Shakespear's plays, for it is the one in which he was the most in earnest. He was here fairly caught in the web of his own imagination. The passion which he has taken as his subject is that which strikes its root deepest into the human heart; of which the bond is the hardest to be unloosed; and the cancelling and tearing to pieces of which gives the greatest revulsion to the frame. This depth of nature, this force of passion, this tug and war of the elements of our being, this firm faith in filial piety, and the giddy anarchy and whirling tumult of the thoughts at finding this prop failing it, the contrast between the fixed, immoveable basis of natural affection, and the rapid, irregular starts of imagination, suddenly wrenched from all its accustomed holds and resting-places in the soul, this is what Shakespear has given, and what nobody else but he could give. So we believe—the mind of Lear, staggering between the weight of attachment and the hurried movements of passion, is like a tall ship-driven about by the winds, buffeted by the furious waves, but that still rides above the storm, having its anchor fixed in the bottom of the sea; or it is like the sharp rock circled by the eddying whirlpool that foams and beats against it, or like the solid promontory pushed from its basis by the force of an earthquake.

The character of Lear itself is very finely conceived for the purpose. It is the only ground on which such a story could be built with the greatest truth and effect. It is his rash haste, his violent impetuosity, his blindness to every thing but the dictates of his passions or affections, that produces all his misfortunes, that aggravates his impatience of them, that enforces our pity for him. The part which Cordelia bears in the scene is extremely beautiful: the story is almost told in the first words she utters. We see at once the precipice on which the poor old king stands from his own extravagant and credulous importunity, the indiscreet simplicity of her love (which, to be sure, has a little of her father's obstinacy in it) and the hollowness of her sisters'pretensions. Almost the first burst of that noble tide of passion, which runs through the play, is in the remonstrance of Kent to his royal master on the injustice of his sentence against his youngest daughter—"Be Kent unmannerly, when Lear is mad!" This manly plainness, which draws down on him the displeasure of the unadvised king, is worthy of the fidelity with which he adheres to his fallen fortunes. The true character of the two eldest daughters, Regan and Goneril (they are so thoroughly hateful that we do not even like to repeat their names) breaks out in their answer to Cordelia who desires them to treat their father well— "Prescribe not us our duties"—their hatred of advice being in proportion to their determination to do wrong, and to their hypocritical pretension to do right. Their deliberate hypocrisy adds the last finishing to the odiousness of their characters. It is the absence of this detestable quality that is the only relief in the character of Edmund the Bastard, and that at times reconciles us to him. We are not tempted to exaggerate the guilt of his conduct, when he himself gives it up as a bad business, and writes himself down "plain villain." Nothing more can be said about it. His religious honesty in this respect is admirable. One speech of his is worth a million. His father, Gloster, whom he has just deluded with a forged story of his brother Edgar's designs against his life, accounts for his unnatural behaviour and the strange depravity of the times from the late eclipses in the sun and moon. Edmund, who is in the secret, says when he is gone—"This is the excellent foppery of the world, that when we are sick in fortune (often the surfeits of our own behaviour) we make guilty of our disasters the sun, the moon, and stars: as if we were villains on necessity; fools by heavenly compulsion; knaves, thieves, and treacherous by spherical predominance; drunkards, liars, and adulterers by an enforced obedience of planetary influence; and all that we are evil in, by a divine thrusting on. An admirable evasion of whore-master man, to lay his goatish disposition on the charge of a star! My father compounded with my mother under the Dragon's tail, and my nativity was under Ursa Major: so that it follows, I am rough and lecherous. Tut! I should have been what I am, had the maidliest star in the firmament twinkled on my bastardising."—The whole character, its careless, light-hearted villainy, contrasted with the sullen, rancorous malignity of Regan and Goneril, its connection with the conduct of the under-plot, in which Gloster's persecution of one of his sons and the ingratitude of another, form a counterpart to the mistakes and misfortunes of Lear,—his double amour with the two sisters, and the share which he has in bringing about the fatal catastrophe, are all managed with an uncommon degree of skill and power.

Samuel Taylor Coleridge (1772–1834) [Excerpted from *Lectures and Notes on Shakespeare and Other English Poets* (1818). The great poet Coleridge was also a perceptive literary critic.]

It may here be worthy of notice, that Lear is the only serious performance of Shakespeare,

With Goneril and Regan behind him, Lear sends Cordelia away in Act 1, Scene 1 of *King Lear*. This print was published in an 1873 edition of *Die Gartenlaube*.

the interest and situations of which are derived from the assumption of a gross improbability; whereas Beaumont and Fletcher's tragedies are, almost all of them, founded on some out of the way accident or exception to the general experience of mankind. But observe the matchless judgment of our Shakespeare. First, improbable as the conduct of Lear is in the first scene, yet it was an old story rooted in the popular faith,—a thing taken for granted already, and consequently without any of the effects of improbability. Secondly, it is merely the canvass for the characters and passions,—a mere occasion for,—and not,

in the manner of Beaumont and Fletcher, perpetually recurring as the cause, and sine qua non of,—the incidents and emotions. Let the first scene of this play have been lost, and let it only be understood that a fond father had been duped by hypocritical professions of love and duty on the part of two daughters to disinherit the third, previously, and deservedly, more dear to him;—and all the rest of the tragedy would retain its interest undiminished, and be perfectly intelligible. The accidental is nowhere the groundwork of the passions, but that which is catholic, which in all ages has been, and ever will be, close and native to the heart of man,—parental anguish from filial ingratitude, the genuineness of worth, though confined in bluntness, and the execrable vileness of a smooth iniquity. Perhaps I ought to have added the Merchant of Venice; but here too the same remarks apply. It was an old tale; and substitute any other danger than that of the pound of flesh (the circumstance in which the improbability lies), yet all the situations and the emotions appertaining to them remain equally excellent and appropriate. Whereas take away from the Mad Lover of Beaumont and Fletcher the fantastic hypothesis of his engagement to cut out his own heart, and have it presented to his mistress, and all the main scenes must go with it.

John Keats (1795–1821) [One of the greatest English poets, Keats died at the age of 25. His famous sonnet on *King Lear* (1818) expresses his admiration for the play.]

> On Sitting Down to Read *King Lear*
>   Once Again
>
> O golden-tongued Romance with serene
>   lute!
>   Fair plumed Syren! Queen of far away!
>   Leave melodizing on this wintry day,
> Shut up thine olden pages, and be mute:
> Adieu! for once again the fierce dispute,
>   Betwixt damnation and impassion'd clay
>   Must I burn through; once more humbly assay
> The bitter-sweet of this Shakespearian
>   fruit.
> Chief Poet! and ye clouds of Albion,
>   Begetters of our deep eternal theme,
> When through the old oak forest I am
>   gone,
>   Let me not wander in a barren dream,
> But when I am consumed in the fire,
>   Give me new Phoenix wings to fly at my
>   desire.

A. C. Bradley (1851–1935) [Excerpted from *Shakespearean Tragedy* (1904), considered one of the best book-length studies of Shakespeare. Bradley has fallen out of fashion in some quarters, but many astute critics deem him an indispensable guide.]

King Lear has again and again been described as Shakespeare's greatest work, the best of his plays, the tragedy in which he exhibits most fully his multitudinous powers; and if we were doomed to lose all his dramas except one, probably the majority of those who know and appreciate him best would pronounce for keeping *King Lear*.

Yet this tragedy is certainly the least popular of the famous four. The "general reader" reads it less often than the others, and, though he acknowledges its greatness, he will sometimes speak of it with a certain distaste. It is also the least often presented on the stage, and the least successful there. And when we look back on its history we find a curious fact. Some twenty years after the Restoration, Nahum Tate altered *King Lear* for the stage, giving it a happy ending, and putting Edgar in the place of the King of France as Cordelia's lover. From that time Shakespeare's tragedy in its original form was never seen on the stage for a century and a half. Betterton acted Tate's version; Garrick acted it and Dr. Johnson approved it. Kemble acted it, Kean acted it. In 1823 Kean, "stimulated by Hazlitt's remonstrances and Charles Lamb's essays," restored the original tragic ending. At last, in 1838, Macready returned to Shakespeare's text throughout.

What is the meaning of these opposite sets of facts? Are the lovers of Shakespeare wholly in the right; and is the general reader and playgoer, were even Tate and Dr. Johnson, altogether in the wrong? I venture to doubt it. When I read *King Lear* two impressions are left on my mind, which seem to answer roughly to the two sets of facts. *King Lear* seems to me Shakespeare's greatest achievement, but it seems to me not his best play. And I find that I tend to consider it from two rather different points of view. When I regard it strictly as a drama, it appears to me, though in certain parts overwhelming, decidedly inferior as a whole to *Hamlet, Othello* and *Macbeth.* When I am feeling that it is greater than any of these, and the fullest revelation of Shakespeare's power, I find I am not regarding it simply as a drama, but am grouping it in my mind with works like the *Prometheus Vinctus* and the *Divine Comedy,* and even with the greatest symphonies of Beethoven and the statues in the Medici Chapel.

This twofold character of the play is to some extent illustrated by the affinities and the probable chronological position of *King Lear.* It is allied with two tragedies, *Othello* and *Timon of Athens;* and these two tragedies are utterly unlike. *Othello* was probably composed about 1604, and *King Lear* about 1605; and though there is a somewhat marked change in style and versification, there are obvious resemblances between the two. The most important have been touched on already: these are the most painful and the most pathetic of the four tragedies, those in which evil appears in its coldest and most inhuman forms, and those which exclude the supernatural from the action. But there is also in *King Lear* a good deal which sounds like an echo of *Othello*—a fact which should not surprise us, since there are other instances where the matter of a play seems to go on working in Shakespeare's mind and reappears, generally in a weaker form, in his next play. So, in *King Lear,* the conception of Edmund is not so fresh as that of Goneril. Goneril has no predecessor; but Edmund, though of course essentially distinguished from Iago, often reminds us of him, and the soliloquy, "This is the excellent foppery of the world," is in the very tone of Iago's discourse on the sov-

ereignty of the will. The gulling of Gloster, again, recalls the gulling of Othello. Even Edmund's idea (not carried out) of making his father witness, without overhearing, his conversation with Edgar, reproduces the idea of the passage where Othello watches Iago and Cassio talking about Bianca; and the conclusion of the temptation, where Gloster says to Edmund:

> and of my land,
> Loyal and natural boy, I'll work the
>   means
> To make thee capable,

reminds us of Othello's last words in the scene of temptation, "Now art thou my lieutenant." This list might be extended; and the appearance of certain unusual words and phrases in both the plays increases the likelihood that the composition of the one followed at no great distance on that of the other.

MODERN CRITICISM AND CRITICAL CONTROVERSIES

Stirring great controversy, *King Lear* has been acclaimed as one of the great works of Western literature and at the same time decried as impossible to act and stage successfully. Harold Bloom said that the play "ultimately baffles commentary," revealing "an apparent infinitude that perhaps transcends the limits of literature" (*Shakespeare* 476).

In the 18th and 19th centuries, *Hamlet* was typically considered Shakespeare's masterpiece, but *King Lear* seems now to carry the highest critical reputation of Shakespeare's plays, although, of course, there is no general agreement. Northrop Frye, Alexander Leggatt, and others credit *Lear's* rise to cultural shifts in the mid-20th century. While previous generations, for instance, found the blinding of Gloucester revolting, Leggatt says that modern generations need only see reports from Amnesty International to find that "Shakespeare is simply telling us what the world is like, in our time as in his" (xi). Frye argues that the focus of some critics turned from *Hamlet* to *King Lear* as feelings of alienation and absurdity rose in the 20th century (119). R. A. Foakes, in *"Hamlet* Versus *Lear,"* goes so far as to list world events from 1954 to 1965, including the war in Vietnam, inauguration of President John F. Kennedy, and global buildup of nuclear arms as reasons for *Lear*'s rise in critical esteem; consciously or unconsciously, he says, critics embraced *King Lear* when fear of a great war dominated the cultural landscape (240). Marjorie Garber suggests that Foakes could have looked beyond 1965 to include the assassinations of Kennedy, his brother Robert F. Kennedy, and civil rights leader Martin Luther King (231). "Against the array of world-disrupting events that took place in the late fifties and sixties, *King Lear* came to look, perhaps, all too familiar," Garber says (241).

Garber also observes that the play continues to be relevant in the 21st century. In one essay, she focuses her analysis on the concept of "nothing," with which the play is preoccupied. When Shakespeare wrote the play, the new computation system of Hindu/Arabic numerals based on the zero was entering the European culture and marketplace. From Act I, when Cordelia says "Nothing, my lord" and Lear rebukes her with "Nothing will come of nothing", the question of what it means to have or be nothing appears central. Scholars, in fact, have long argued that *King Lear* is about nothing: G. Wilson Knight comments that Lear's judgment is "nothing" (36); Frye comments that "nothing" relates to a king being deprived of his kingship and, therefore, his identity (109). For Garber, this theme resonates powerfully for modern readers and audiences who see the play in the context of the threat of nuclear holocaust, global terrorism, poverty, and impending ecological disaster. *King Lear* speaks to us, Garber argues, from a new "ground zero—as, in a sense, it has always done" (269).

Scholars debate whether to read *King Lear* through a Christian lens. Greenblatt, in *The Norton Shakespeare*, acknowledges that the play's structure—in which suffering and humiliation lead to

ultimate spiritual redemption—could have a Christian interpretation ("King Lear" 2,331). Roy Battenhouse argues that "the tragedy as a whole is shaped by a Christian sense of history" (444) and compares Lear's "pagan quest for love" (444) to the fall of Adam and Eve, who chose self-gratification over obedience to God. As Battenhouse notes, "Lear begins to repent his error before the end of Act I, so that the bulk of the drama becomes a purging of his initial mistake" (445). He also affirms other Christian readings, namely by John Danby, who contended that *King Lear* is "our profoundest expression of an essentially Christian comment on life" (446). Battenhouse, in addition, cites Virgil Whitaker, who read *King Lear* as "a profoundly Christian tragedy about a pre-Christian world, undeniable proof that it is possible to write Christian tragedy" (446).

But other modern critics suggest that a religious reading is too narrow to fully understand the play. Leggatt notes that Christian interpretations began falling out of favor in the early 1960s, particularly with a 1960 article by Barbara Everett (xx). For Greenblatt, *Lear* resists the optimism offered by a Christian vision because the moments of moral resolution and spiritual calm are so brief and give way to grief and rage ("King Lear" 2,331). By the time Lear finally sees his beloved Cordelia in Act IV, his world, as Greenblatt observes, has been destroyed. And, while some compare Lear's suffering to that of biblical Job, Bloom argues that Job's afflictions and Lear's are vastly disproportionate, at least until Cordelia's execution. According to Bloom, the Christian God and Christ are "not relevant" in Lear's world; Job is rewarded for his virtue, while Lear suffers his daughter's murder. If Shakespeare did invoke Job, Bloom argues, it is to stress the "absolute negativity" of Lear's ordeal ("Introduction" 3). Rather than Job, Bloom suspects that Shakespeare's biblical model was King Solomon, the "wise yet exacerbated" aged monarch who wrote Ecclesiastes (*Shakespeare* 477). Bloom describes the connection between Lear, a "kind of mortal god" and an "image of male authority," and Solomon, glorious, wise, and wealthy: "Each in their eighties, each needing and wanting love, and each worthy of love" (*Shakespeare* 479). Bloom further observes that the play "announces the beginning and then end of human nature and destiny" as do the Yahwist's text and the Gospel of Mark (*Shakespeare* 476).

Similarly, Frank Kermode observes that the play asks audiences to imagine the last days, when human beings will be reduced to acting like animals, having shed the binds of civility in an age of unimaginable suffering (184). Unlike Bloom, Kermode argues that Shakespeare must have been inspired by the Book of Job, although Kermode, too, notes that Lear does not enjoy the rewards that Job does. For Kermode, the more helpful religious parallel to *King Lear* is not Job but the Last Judgment (198).

If a Christian reading of *King Lear* is debatable, modern critics find other powerful forces that Shakespeare drew upon to enhance the story's power. Frye focuses on three words that repeat so often throughout the text that they seem to guide the play's meaning: *nature, nothing,* and *fool.* For Frye, nature in *King Lear* represents the tension between the "higher" level of nature—the way humanity is intended to live, with the aid of morality, etc.—and the "lower" level—our present environment where humans are essentially like animals, eating or being eaten (106). Nothing represents the answer to the question of what is the cause of love, friendship, good faith, and loyalty: "Love and loyalty don't have motives or expectations or causes, nor can they be quantified" (109). And, the word *fool* is applied to every decent character in the play, Frye notes, but it also means "victim," the kind of person upon whom bad things happen (111).

Other critics examine more wordly themes. Greenblatt, for instance, looks to the political context of the Jacobean era. Just years before Shakespeare penned the play, King James reportedly told his eldest son that God made him a "little God" to rule over men; the sovereign expected unquestioning obedience and love from family and his subjects ("King Lear" 2,325). *King Lear* invokes royal and paternal sovereignty only to chronicle its destruction. When Lear laments how "They told me I

was everything" only to learn that it was all a "lie" (4.5.98–102), Shakespeare expresses the Jacobean respect for power and authority as well as its fragility, Greenblatt argues (2,325). Ritualized spectacles of deference to authority (kneeling, bowing, etc.) are exposed "as if no one quite believed all the grand claims to divine sanction for the rule of Kings and fathers, as if those who ruled both states and families secretly feared that the elaborate hierarchical structure could vanish like a mirage" (2,325). Foakes argues that *King Lear*'s post-1950s popularity was due precisely to political themes that resonated "in a world in which old men have held on to and abused power, often in corrupt or arbitrary ways" (243). Greenblatt acknowledges, as have many others, that retirement for a king would have been shunned in Shakespeare's era. In Shakespeare's hands, Lear's mistake is not the act of parceling out his land but rather in disowning the only child who loves him ("King Lear" 2,327). Ewan Fernie describes *King Lear* as a play that "moves through shame toward relationship" (173). Before Lear can "really see" and know Cordelia, and the injustice he has dealt her, Fernie explains, he must "be stripped and reduced to nothing in a process which is as long as the play itself" (174). Fernie affirms the work of William F. Zak in *Sovereign Shame,* especially Zak's claim that the "old king and father we encounter initially in *King Lear* is a man in hiding" (174). Fernie observes: "through shame Lear is finally released from the illusions of pride into truth" (190), adding "More clearly than in any other Shakespeare play, in *King Lear* it is egoism that obstructs virtue" (194). Janet Adelman argues that the domestic drama pulls us into the play. We are forced, she says, to understand the characters by understanding ourselves ("Introduction" 6). And Knight, who examines the incongruities that provide humor in *King Lear,* notes that Lear's request for expressions of his daughters' love is childish, foolish, and very human: "It is, indeed, curious that so storm-furious a play as *King Lear* should have so trivial a domestic basis" (35).

The ending of the play has also fascinated modern critics. Why does Shakespeare insist on such a bleak ending for *Lear* when various source texts offer a more hopeful story? In 1681, Tate rewrote Shakespeare, restoring and enhancing the old happy ending. Although too moralizing and sentimental for today's audiences, Leggatt argues, Tate's adaptation made sense on its own terms and indeed was the story audiences knew until Shakespeare's version returned in the 19th century (4). Contemporary scholars repeatedly note the hesitation of 19th-century and even 20th-century critics to embrace the tragedy, even to the extent of declaring that it could not be staged. In the 21st century, such pessimistic views have faded. In *The Norton Shakespeare,* Greenblatt points to brilliant modern stage productions and films that show the play's power, particularly in illustrating mental and physical anguish (2,329). Leggatt, too, says that the play has "proved its worth" in the theater for so long that it no longer needs to be defended (9). When Lear asks in Act V why a dog, horse, and rat should have life but not his daughter, Shakespeare refuses to offer conventional answers. By doing so, Greenblatt contends, Shakespeare forces us not to turn away from evil and human pain but to see them face to face, "to strengthen our capacity to speak the truth, to endure, and to love" ("King

Heartbroken, Lear leans over Cordelia and dies in Act V, Scene 3 of *King Lear.* This is a print from Malcolm C. Salaman's 1916 edition of *Shakespeare in Pictorial Art.* (*Painting by James Barry*)

Lear" 2,332). Stephen Booth calls Lear's entrance with Cordelia's body in his arms the "most terrifying five minutes in literature" (101)—agreeing with other scholars that Shakespeare resists easy answers for the audience. For Booth, Cordelia's death reminds us of our own physical and mental vulnerability; *King Lear,* he argues, makes its audience suffer as an audience (102). Adelman would agree, arguing that the play's ending is tolerable because it provides us "proof positive" that we are feeling human beings ("Introduction" 5).

Leggatt points out that Cordelia does die in source texts that Shakespeare would have known: She kills herself in prison in Geoffrey of Monmouth's and Holinshed's texts (6). Further, Leggatt argues that, while Cordelia's death surprises us, as it should for dramatic effect, Shakespeare offers clues to his plan. For instance, in the First Folio version of Act 3, Scene 6, Kent carries off his sleeping master, which anticipates the image of Lear carrying off dead Cordelia (7). "If a surprise is too clearly anticipated, it will not be a surprise at all; but if there is no preparation, it will simply leave the audience feeling cheated. We should feel that we didn't see it coming—but we should have" (8). For Leggatt, Shakespeare stays true to the dramatic, not narrative or moral, needs of the text. For Knight, Cordelia's death is the "last and most horrible" of all the incongruities that drive the narrative and, in some cases—not here, of course—supply its grotesque humor (48). Incongruities throughout *Lear,* Knight argues, illustrate that humor is interwoven with human pain (49).

That women do not fare well in *King Lear* has invited various commentaries. Kathlee McLuskie, in her feminist reading, argues that the play's emotional impact is tied to acceptance of a patriarchal order even as it contains material that a feminist could use to subvert values of that order (Leggatt xxi). Similarly, Marianne Novy observes that the play actually critiques patriarchal society (85). For Novy, Shakespeare tells us that in a patriarchal world, men and women must be mutually forgiving and repentant because the powerful often abuse their power (93). Regarding Lear's rant against sexuality in Act IV, Scene 6, Novy suggests that Lear is actually ranting against pretense and sexuality in general, not just women. When he cries, "Why dost thou lash that whole? Strip thy own back / Thou hotly lusts to use her in that kind / For which though whip'st her" he is complaining that we punish others for our own faults (89). His disgust with women is so strong "because it is really disgust with himself," Novy says (90). In *Suffocating Mothers,* Adelman reflects on the play's lack of a wife for Lear and mother for his daughters. That absence, she argues, gives the reader an "uncanny sense of a world created by fathers alone" (210). For Adelman, "Lear's confrontation with his daughters repeatedly leads him back to the mother ostensibly occluded from the play: in recognizing his daughters as a part of himself, he will be led to recognize not only his terrifying dependence on female forces outside himself but also an equally terrifying femaleness within himself—a femaleness he will come to call 'mother'" in Act II, Scene 4 (210). She believes that the play's power stems from its confrontation with the landscape of maternal deprivation: "from the vulnerability and rage that is a consequence of this confrontation and the intensity and fragility of the hope for a saving maternal presence that can undo pain" (210–211).

Much has been written about Shakespeare's staging of Gloucester's blindness and his imaginary fall from the Dover cliffs. Knight, as others, praise Shakespeare's artfulness of the scene in terms of its physical comedy and thematic value. "The Gloucester-theme throughout reflects and emphasizes and exaggerates all the percurrent qualities of the Lear-theme. Here the incongruous and fantastic element of the Lear-theme is boldly reflected into the tragically-absurd," Knight states (45). Frederick Buechner proposes that Gloucester's physical blindness drives home the point that Lear's tragedy "is no isolated instance of a single life gone wrong" (132). Buechner argues that Gloucester's blinding and subsequent "fall" frame Lear's emotional-spiritual blindness and his ultimate fall. Richard Wilson claims that the "cruel deceit of Gloucester" symbolizes the futility of any "thought of aid or approbation" from a divine hand

(285). Wilson agrees with William Elton's claim that the deception of Gloucester and Lear's suffering represents "the death of an illusion" (286) and of any hope that there is a God who desires to help or guide his creation. Wilson concludes that Gloucester's fall and Lear's suffering are meant to seal the play from any misunderstanding about "the concern of God, working of providence, influence of the planets, power of the Pope, decision of the king of France, or effect of the Armada over the cruelties suffered on stage, and to ram home the helplessness of Lear's cry: 'No rescue? What, a prisoner? I am even / The natural fool of fortune' [4.6.184–185]" (286).

Finally, while readers, critics, scholars, and audiences can enjoy *King Lear* for its rich interpretations, modern editors face a particular quandary: Which version is the best? The play's complicated textual history has elicited more debate than any of Shakespeare's other works (Greenblatt, "King Lear" 2,332). At issue is the authority of multiple early texts and the relationship between them. The first version appeared in 1608 in a pocket-sized book, or "quarto," known as the First Quarto (Q1). An apparent reprint of that version in the quarto format appeared in 1619 and is known as the Second Quarto (Q2). Yet another version appeared in the First Folio (F) of Shakespeare's plays, dated 1623. Overall, Q1 contains about 283 lines not found in F, and F, in turn, has about 115 lines that do not exist in Q1. Scholars believe that Q1 was extensively corrected as it was going to press, resulting in different copies containing different readings, as editors Barbara Mowat and Paul Werstine explain in their preface to the Folger Shakespeare Library edition. Some corrections appear "competent," they state, while others are better called "miscorrections" (lvii). Kermode calls Q1 a "poor text, careless, contaminated, and generally prone to error" (183). And, Greenblatt observes that while scholars and editors agree that Q1 represents a legitimate early version of the text, its authority is "compromised" by often confusing and sometimes "nonsensical" readings ("King Lear" 2,333). What, then, of the First Folio? It, too, is faulty, according to Kermode, although many modern editors use it. Mowat and

Werstine note that editors preferred F for much of the 20th century, believing it to have been written in shorthand or via actors' memories (lx). In the last decade or so, they say, editors leaned more toward Q1 under the theory that it was printed directly from Shakespeare's own manuscript. A third theory is that Q1 and F are independent versions that should never be combined (lx). The editors of the Oxford edition print both versions; the 1992 Cambridge edition uses F (Kermode 183). Greenblatt's Norton edition (based on the Oxford edition) prints Q1 and F on facing pages so readers can compare the two and also prints a conflated text. For Michael Warren, Q1 and F are, indeed, distinct texts and should be printed separately; he calls conflated texts "invalid" (182, 184).

The different versions do suggest different interpretations. In his close examination of both texts, Warren illustrates how the roles of Albany and Edgar change enough to indicate that the author (or authors) substantially recast certain elements of the play (186). Albany, for instance, emerges as a more developed character in Q1 than in F. In Q1, he speaks the play's closing lines, a triumphant duke assuming control of the kingdom. In F, he avoids responsibility. Edgar, meanwhile, has a shorter role in F than in Q1, where he is portrayed as a young man overwhelmed by his painful experience. In F, speaking the play's last lines, Edgar surfaces as the kingdom's new, wizened leader (Warren 186).

The notion of producing an "ideal" version is problematic for two reasons, Warren asserts: First, there is no way to confirm its existence, and second, there is no evidence for the assumption that textual alterations were made by someone other than Shakespeare (183). Warren argues that there may not be one "ideal" *King Lear,* and there may never have been one; that Q1 is the authoritative text; and that F represents a revised version, with corrections possibly done by Shakespeare himself ("we certainly cannot know that they are not") (183). Nonetheless, other scholars have different views, and many still regard F as the superior text. The idea that Shakespeare consciously revised his earlier work to improve it has become more appeal-

Surrounded by Kent, Gloucester, the Fool, and Edgar dressed as Tom O'Bedlam, Lear attempts to tear off his clothes in Act III, Scene 4 of *King Lear.* This is a print from the Boydell Shakespeare Gallery project, which was first conceived in 1786 and lasted until 1805. *(Painting by Benjamin West; engraving by William Sharpe)*

ing to a number of scholars. Despite this, conflated texts of the play, adopting the "best" lines from both sources, continue to be the norm.

In the classroom, *King Lear,* arguably Shakespeare's greatest drama, is not usually the most popular. As far as the great tragedies go, most high school and college students tend to favor *Macbeth* or *Hamlet.* In Garber's *Shakespeare in Modern Culture,* she reports that secondary school teachers describe *King Lear* as a difficult play to teach, while students find it somewhat estranging (232). According to Garber, Hamlet is seen as "a heroic figure, struggling against a corrupt world" (234). Lear, on the other hand, symbolizes "the emptiness, illogic, terror, and absurdity of the modern condition" (234). Simply put, students today often find Lear, especially at the beginning of the play, a difficult character to admire, unlike Othello and Hamlet, and even, at the very beginning of his play, Macbeth. If students dig deeper, however, they can find *King Lear* very relevant to their own lives and preoccupations. The generational conflict, for example, is a very prominent theme in *Lear.* Moreover, the violence and darkness that so shocked and disturbed critics in the past are unlikely to be so offputting to students today. Indeed, present-day students may be now more able than ever before to face the darkness and the terrifying intellectual and emotional storms at the heart of *King Lear.*

Critics today continue to examine the traditional themes and problems presented by *Lear,* but a few issues have become more prominent. Since the late 20th century, there have been various feminist interpretations of *Lear,* some even taking the side of the eternally maligned sisters Goneril and Regan. Jane Smiley's 1991 novel *A Thousand Acres,* made into a film in 1997, is a contemporary reimagining of Lear, presenting the patriarch as a sexually abusive father. However, such radical rethinkings of Lear have become less common in recent years.

THE PLAY TODAY

King Lear continues to be very popular on stage. Actors often regard the character of Lear as the profession's greatest challenge, and the play has often inspired legendary performances. Laurence Olivier's performance for Granada Television came in 1983, while he was dying of cancer. As Bevington reports, "Olivier, weakened but determined, had to be helped through the rigors of the screening, with the result that his Lear is tender, vulnerable, frail, though capable of the outbursts of rage that often come with advanced age" (661). In late 2010, Derek Jacobi's turn at the role caused a "stampede" at the box office of the Donmar Warehouse in London (Cavendish n.p.). In an interview, Jacobi said, "When you're a young classical actor, I think you go through the Hamlet hoop. If your Hamlet is anywhere near all right, then you're admitted to the classical club. And you know that towards the end of your career, you've got to go through the 'Lear hoop' to confirm they were right to let you in" (Cavendish n.p.). Other famous actors who have played Lear include John Gielgud, James Earl Jones, Paul Scofield, Anthony Hopkins, Kevin Kline, and many more.

A recent adaptation for television, shown on the BBC in 2008 and on PBS in 2009, featured much of the cast from the Royal Shakespeare Company, including Sir Ian McKellen as Lear. In 1953, Orson Welles offered his interpretation of Lear for CBS television. And, in 1985, the legendary Japanese director Akira Kurosawa adapted the Lear story in his epic *Ran,* which tells of a Japanese warlord and his three sons, one of them loving and the others treacherous (Bevington 1,206).

Perhaps one of the most unusual modern *Lear* productions was staged by the Muddy Flower Theater Troupe, consisting of inmates from Racine Correctional Institution, a medium-maximum-security prison in Wisconsin. In his essay "When Muddy Flowers Bloom: The Shakespeare Project at Racine Correctional Institution," the director and organizer Jonathan Shailor describes the experience of working with these men, saying that "inmates use performance as the primary means to explore and transform their habitual ways of dealing with conflict" (633). The experience of reading and performing *King Lear* profoundly affected the lives of the inmates, as indicated by Damian, an inmate who played Regan. He wrote: "But twice a week in the prison library they have found / a safe haven to conquer our own defeat . . . a sanctuary . . . a place to rehearse / With a dozen or so in Shakespearean verse . . . / We have been given a chance and a means / to release from confinement our thoughts and our dreams" (Shailor 632). Other actors used their characters as a form of emotional therapy by observing them from various perspectives, especially through their own eyes. Within *King Lear'*s complex Shakespearean verse, the inmates were able to identify with the characters, regardless of the differences in time period, language, and, for some, gender.

FIVE TOPICS FOR DISCUSSION AND WRITING

1. **Sympathetic characters:** What does it mean to be a "sympathetic" character, and is Lear one? What about Gloucester, Edgar, and Edmund? How do our impressions of them change during the course of the play? Do we feel sympathetic toward Edgar when he laments about the

torment of watching his father while in disguise? What about for Edmund, when he tries, too late, to rescind his order to execute Cordelia?

2. **The play's ending:** Samuel Johnson complained that the play's ending, particularly regarding Cordelia's death, violates our sense of poetic justice. Do you agree? What do we make of the play's ending? Can we find any degree of optimism or hope in it?

3. **Fathers and children:** Discuss the relationship between Lear and his daughters, and compare and contrast it to the relationship between Gloucester and his sons. What does it mean for a father to seek and demand love from children? How are children obligated to respond to their parents' desire for love, if at all?

4. **Clothing:** Describe the function of garments and their removal throughout the play. Consider how clothing functions, in particular, in scenes that deal with the outdoors (the heath, the cliffs). What does it mean, in Lear's world, to be clothed, and what does it mean to be naked?

5. **Women in** *Lear:* The two major female characters, Goneril and Regan, are evil. The one "good" female, Cordelia, is so virtuous as to be almost saintly, and, as Bloom points out, she can be seen as a victim of Lear (*Shakespeare* 491). Is *King Lear* misogynistic, as some feminist critics argue? Why or why not? Bloom asks, "Are Shakespeare's perspectives in *Lear* incurably male?" (*Shakespeare* 491). How do you respond?

Bibliography

Adelman, Janet. "Introduction." *Twentieth Century Interpretations of King Lear.* Englewood Cliffs, N.J.: Prentice-Hall, 1978.

———. *Suffocating Mothers: Fantasies of Maternal Origin in Shakespeare's Plays,* Hamlet *to* The Tempest. New York: Routledge, 1992.

Battenhouse, Roy. *Shakespeare's Christian Dimension: An Anthology of Commentary.* Bloomington: Indiana University Press, 1994.

Bevington, David, ed. *The Complete Works of Shakespeare.* 6th ed. New York: Pearson, 2009.

Bloom, Harold. "Introduction." *Modern Critical Interpretations: William Shakespeare's* King Lear. New York: Chelsea House Publishers, 1987.

———. *Shakespeare: The Invention of Human.* New York: Riverside Books, 1998.

Booth, Stephen. "On the Greatness of *King Lear.*" In *Twentieth Century Interpretations of King Lear,* edited by Janet Adelman, 98–111. Englewood Cliffs, N.J.: Prentice-Hall, 1978.

Bradley, A. C. *Shakespearean Tragedy.* New York: Meridian Books, 1955.

Bruce, Susan, ed. *William Shakespeare:* King Lear. New York: Columbia University Press, 1998.

Buechner, Frederick. *Speak What We Feel.* New York: HarperCollins, 2001.

Cantor, Paul A. "Nature and Convention in *King Lear.*" In *Poets, Princes, and Private Citizens,* edited by Joseph M. Knippenberg and Peter Augustine Lawler, 213–233. Lanham, Md.: Rowman & Littlefield, 1996.

Carballo, Robert. "Chaos and Order in *King Lear:* Shakespeare's Organic Conceptions of Man and Nature." In *King Lear,* Ignatius Critical Editions, edited by Joseph Pearce. San Francisco, Calif.: Ignatius Press, 2008.

Cavendish, Dominick. "Sir Derek Jacobi: *King Lear,* the Mountain You Have to Climb," (London) *Telegraph,* 3 December 2010.

Coleridge, Samuel Taylor. *Coleridge on Shakespeare.* Edited by Terence Hawkes. London: Penguin Books, 1959.

———. *Lectures and Notes on Shakespeare and Other English Poets.* London: Bell & Sons, 1883.

Colie, Rosalie, ed. *Some Facets of King Lear.* Toronto: University of Toronto Press, 1974.

Danson, Lawrence, ed. *On* King Lear. Princeton, N.J.: Princeton University Press, 1981.

Doran, Madeleine *The Text of* King Lear. New York: AMS Press, 1967.

Elton, William R. King Lear *and the Gods.* San Marino, Calif.: Huntington Library, 1966.

Everett, Barbara. "The New *King Lear.*" *Critical Quarterly* 2 (1960): 325–339.

Fornie, Eman. *Shame in Shakespeare.* London: Routledge, 2002.

Foakes, R. A. *"Hamlet* versus *Lear."* In *A Norton Critical Edition: William Shakespeare's* King Lear, 240–243. New York: W. W. Norton & Co., 2008.

Frye, Northrop. *"King Lear."* In *Northrop Frye on Shakespeare,* edited by Robert Sandler, 101–121. New Haven, Conn.: Yale University Press, 1986.

Garber, Marjorie. *Shakespeare After All.* New York: Pantheon, 2004.

Goddard, Harold C. *"King Lear."* In *Modern Critical Interpretations: William Shakespeare's* King Lear, edited by Harold Bloom, 9–43. New York: Chelsea House Publishers, 1987.

Greenblatt, Stephen. "The Cultivation of Anxiety: King Lear and His Heirs." In *Learning to Curse: Essays in Early Modern Culture.* London: Routledge, 1990.

———. "King Lear." *The Norton Shakespeare: Based on the Oxford Edition,* 2d ed. New York: W. W. Norton & Co., 2008.

Greg, W. W. *The Variants in the First Quarto of King Lear: A Biographical and Critical Inquiry.* New York: Haskell House, 1966.

Hazlitt, William. *Selected Writings.* Edited by Ronald Blythe. Baltimore, Md.: Penguin Books, 1970.

Johnson, Samuel, ed. *Johnson on Shakespeare: Essays and Notes Selected and Set Forth with an Introduction.* Edited by Walter Raleigh. London: Henry Frowde, 1908.

———. *Preface to Shakespeare:* King Lear. London, 1765.

———. *Selected Writings.* Edited by R. T. Davies. Evanston, Ill.: Northwestern University Press, 1965.

Keats, John. "On Sitting Down to Read *King Lear* Once Again." In *Life, Letters and Literary Remains of John Keats,* edited by Richard Monckton Milnes. New York: Putnam, 1848.

Kermode, Frank. *Shakespeare's Language.* New York: Farrar, Straus & Giroux, 2000.

Kermode, Frank, ed. *Shakespeare:* King Lear, *a Casebook.* London: Macmillan, 1969.

Knapp, Jeffrey. *Shakespeare's Tribe.* Chicago: Chicago University Press, 2002.

Knight, G. Wilson. *"King Lear* and the Comedy of the Grotesque." In *Twentieth Century Interpretations of* King Lear, edited by Janet Adelman, 34–49. Englewood Cliffs, N.J.: Prentice-Hall, 1978.

Lamb, Charles. "On the Tragedies of Shakespeare, Considered with Reference to Their Fitness for Stage Representation." In *English Critical Essays,* edited by Edmund D. Jones, London: Oxford University Press, 1950.

Leggatt, Alexander. *Twayne's New Critical Introductions to Shakespeare:* King Lear. Boston: Twayne Publishers, 1988.

Mowat, Barbara A., and Paul Werstine, eds. *Folger Shakespeare Library:* The Tragedy of King Lear *by William Shakespeare.* New York: Simon & Schuster Paperbacks, 2009.

Muir, Kenneth, ed. King Lear: *Critical Essays.* New York and London: Garland, 1984.

Novy, Marianne. "Patriarchy, Mutuality, and Forgiveness in *King Lear."* In *Modern Critical Interpretations: William Shakespeare's* King Lear, edited by Harold Bloom, 85–95. New York: Chelsea House Publishers, 1987.

Nuttall, A. D. *Shakespeare the Thinker.* New Haven, Conn.: Yale University Press, 2007.

Orwell, George. "Lear, Tolstoy and the Fool." *The Collected Essays, Journalism and Letters of George Orwell.* Edited by Sonia Orwell and Ian Angus. Hammondsworth, U.K.: Penguin Books, 1970.

Peterson, Kaara L. "Historica Passio: Early Modern Medicine, *King Lear,* and Editorial Practice." *Shakespeare Quarterly* 57, no. 1 (Spring 2006): 1–22.

Petronella, Vincent, ed. King Lear: *Evans Shakespeare Edition.* Belmont, Calif.: Wadsworth, 2011.

Ribner, Irving. *Patterns in Shakespearian Tragedy.* London: Methuen, 1960.

Ryan, Kiernan, ed. King Lear: *New Casebooks.* New York: St. Martin's, 1992.

Schlegel, August William. *A course of lectures on dramatic art and literature.* Translated by John Black. London: H. G. Bohn, 1846.

Schneider, Ben Ross, Jr. *"King Lear* in Its Own Time: The Difference That Death Makes." *Early Modern Literary Studies* 1, no. 1 (1995): 1–49.

Shelley, Percy Bysshe. "The Defense of Poetry." *Selections.* Edited by Donald H. Reiman and Neil Fraistat. New York: Norton, 2002.

Snyder, Susan. *"King Lear:* A Modern Perspective." In *Folger Shakespeare Library:* The Tragedy of King

Lear *by William Shakespeare,* edited by Barbara A. Mowat and Paul Werstine, 289–299. New York: Simon & Schuster Paperbacks. 2009.

Stone, P. W. K. *The Textual History of* King Lear. London: Scolar Press, 1980.

Tate, Nahum. *The History of King Lear.* Edited by James Black. Lincoln: University of Nebraska Press, 1975.

Teague, Frances. "Sight and Perception in *King Lear:* An Approach through Imagery and Theme." In *Approaches to Teaching Shakespeare's* King Lear, edited by Robert H. Ray, 80–85. New York: Modern Language Association, 1986.

Tomarken, Edward. *Samuel Johnson on Shakespeare: The Discipline of Criticism.* Athens: University of Georgia Press, 1991.

Tromly, Fred B. "Grief, Authority and the Resistance to Consolation in Shakespeare." In *Speaking Grief in English Literary Culture: Shakespeare to Milton,* edited by Margo Swiss and David A. Kent. Pittsburgh, Pa.: Duquesne University Press, 2002.

Trotter, Jack. "The Tragic Necessity and the Uncertainty of Faith in Shakespeare's *King Lear.*" In *King Lear,* Ignatius Critical Editions, edited by Joseph Pearce, 321ff. San Francisco, Calif.: Ignatius Press, 2008.

Warren, Michael. "Quarto and Folio *King Lear* and the Interpretation of Albany and Edgar." In *A Norton Critical Edition: William Shakespeare's* King Lear, 181–194. New York: W. W. Norton & Co., 2008.

Welsford, Enid. *The Fool: His Social and Literary History.* 1935. Reprint, New York: Farrar & Rinehart, 1965.

Wilson, Richard. *Secret Shakespeare.* Manchester, U.K.: Manchester University Press, 2004.

Young, David, ed. *Shakespeare's Middle Tragedies: A Collection of Critical Essays.* Englewood Cliffs, N.J.: Prentice-Hall, 1993.

Zitner, Sheldon P. "*King Lear* and Its Language." In *Some Facets of* King Lear: *Essays in Prismatic Criticism,* edited by Rosalie L. Colie and F. T. Flahiff, 3–22. London: Heineman, 1974.

FILM AND VIDEO PRODUCTIONS

Blessed, Brian, dir. *King Lear.* With Brian Blessed and Phillipa Peak. Cromwell Productions, Ltd., 1999.

Brook, Peter, dir. *King Lear.* With Paul Scofield and Anne-Lise Gabold. Athena Films, 1971.

Elliot, Michael, dir. *King Lear.* With Laurence Olivier and Anna Calder-Marshall. Granada Television, 1983.

McCullough, Andrew, dir. *King Lear.* With Orson Welles and Natasha Parry. CBS, 1953.

Nunn, Taylor, dir. *King Lear.* With Ian McKellen and William Gaunt. The Performance Company, 2008.

Sherin, Edwin, dir. *King Lear.* With James Earl Jones and Douglass Watson. New York Shakespeare Festival, 1974.

—John J. Norton and Melissa Birks

Love's Labour's Lost

INTRODUCTION

Love's Labour's Lost is one of Shakespeare's earliest comedies, written in either 1595 or 1596. The play contains entertaining characters, witty dialogue, rich symbolism, and universal themes. It differs from Shakespeare's other comedies in that it has fewer characters, the structure is more simplistic, and the ending is less formulaic. Nonetheless, the play's romantic plot contains several recognizable Shakespearean elements: numerous couplings, comedic "base" characters, and pastoral interludes.

Many similarities to the works Shakespeare wrote around this time, most notably *A Midsummer Night's Dream,* can be seen in this play. *Love's Labour's Lost* continues in the pastoral tradition of *Midsummer,* with the action of the play taking place in the fields surrounding Navarre Castle. Furthermore, both of these works contain a play within the play, a staging device used by Shakespeare several times, most notably in *Hamlet.* However, *Love's Labour's Lost* does not result in the traditional marital endings found in *A Midsummer Night's Dream.* Instead, the play ends with the women returning to France for a year. The audience is left wondering what will happen to the three sets of lovers: Will they reunite in one year's time, or is love's labor truly lost?

More than any other Shakespearean comedy, this play explores the power of language; the written word is used as a symbol for love in its varied forms. Ferdinand, the King of Navarre, and his friends profess their love for the Princess of France and her attendants through poems and letters of

varying quality. *Love's Labour's Lost* has been called Shakespeare's most intellectual play, due mainly to the text's emphasis on wordplay, including a wide variety of puns, allegories, and more. Moreover, the study of language is explored and revered. The play opens with the King of Navarre and his companions dedicating themselves to study for one year. It ends with the King returning to his initial intention: The men will forgo the luxuries of their material world, and possibly even love, to immerse themselves in the pursuit of knowledge.

Love's Labour's Lost is a joy to read, and it provides insights into Shakespeare's mind as a wordsmith more than his other plays do. It is a tightly crafted celebration of knowledge and words. Nearly every scene and romantic interaction reinforce this important theme. The play is clearly flawed in some ways, with its minimal plot and characters that do

The Princess of France and her ladies meet the King and his men at the court of Navarre in Act II, Scene I of *Love's Labour's Lost.*

not develop significantly, but the overall magic is always apparent.

BACKGROUND

There is no specific source material that Shakespeare used to write *Love's Labour's Lost,* but there are several real-life characters that may have provided inspiration for the colorful courtiers of Navarre. Much of the play seems inspired by the French court, with the real-life Navarre who became Henry IV at its center. Shakespeare's play takes place in Navarre, and the king (Ferdinand) is referred to only by his country's name. A historical Biron was a French general, and a Longaville was the governor of Normandy. Shakespeare's audience, particularly those at court, would have recognized these names and who they represented. The unexpected arrival of the Princess of France and her ladies mirrors a trip Marguerite (Margaret) of Valois made to see her estranged husband, Henry of Navarre, which fits with the play's French characters well. Many scholars have argued that Rosaline in the play was inspired by the Dark Lady of Shakespeare's sonnets, as her dark hair and eyes are, somewhat artlessly, described by Berowne in his letters and poems. What is most plausible is that Shakespeare combined several events in his recent history to create this play about courtly interactions between men and women. Without a singular source, Shakespeare was left to create the world of Navarre and its residents in the manner that best suited the message he wished to convey.

Even if contemporary audiences did not immediately recognize the leading men and women as embodiments of these real individuals, the rituals of court life and courtship would have been apparent. Duty, decorum, and the intricacies of male-female relationships are all explored within the play. Also at issue is the use of language to woo. The men write love letters and sonnets to the Princess and her ladies. The ladies, however, raise an interesting question about courtly love: Is it necessarily part of the ritual of court life, or can it also be sincere? This question is posed to the men at the end of the play, and they, as well as the audience, are left to ponder why their language was not interpreted as sincere.

Beyond courtly ritual, a deeper issue related to learning is raised in the play. In the opening, the King and his men vow to sequester themselves for three years in order to study. The "little academe" is possibly a reference to the *Académie française,* by P. de La Primaudaye, which had recently been translated into English. A more intriguing interpretation has Berowne, the King's attendant, who is ardently against the endeavor, speaking out against the School of Night, a supposedly atheist group led by Sir Walter Raleigh and dedicated to the study of science. The title of the alleged group was coined in *Love's Labour's Lost,* with Berowne describing "the hue of dungeons, and the school of night" (4.3.251). The scholar Holofernes and his curate, Nathaniel, also present problematic views of education, as both men consistently misuse Latin and are generally seen as comedic characters. If these two men represent learning, what conclusions can the audience draw about formalized study? When combined with the King's halfhearted attempt at study, the audience is left to wonder what value formal education plays in real learning.

Date and Text of the Play

The original performance date for *Love's Labour's Lost* is unclear, but records indicate that it was performed in either 1597 or 1598 for Queen Elizabeth during the Christmas celebrations. The play was printed in a quarto edition in 1598, "newly corrected and augmented by W. Shakespere," although what corrections or additions were made remain unknown. The quarto text is somewhat problematic. As Charles Boyce points out, it apparently

> reflects two renderings of the play. Most prominently, there are several passages that are printed in two versions. Also, there is variation in the names provided for several characters in stage directions and dialogue headings, and there is an evident change in the casting of the pageant of the Nine Worthies between its planning in 5.1 and its presentation in 5.2.

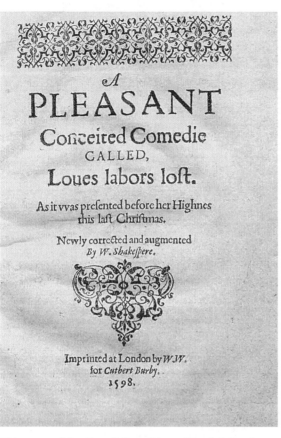

A
PLEASANT
Conceited Comedie
CALLED,
Loues labors loft.

As it vvas prefented before her Highnes
this laft Chriftmas.

Newly corrected and augmented
By W. Shakeſpere.

Imprinted at London by W.W.
for *Cutbert Burby*.
1598.

Title page of the First Folio edition of *Love's Labour's Lost,* published in 1623

Further, it has been speculated that the play may originally have ended at 5.2.870, before the anticlimactic songs of Winter and Spring, and that a scene involving Armado and Moth was cut, leaving Costard's puzzling lines at 4.1.145–150 (342).

The quarto publication states that the text is "As it was presented before her Highnes this last Christmas." We also know that the play was performed again in 1604, to celebrate the release of the earl of Southampton (Shakespeare's friend and patron) from prison. The text of the play in the 1623 First Folio edition of Shakespeare's plays appears to be based on the 1598 quarto.

SYNOPSIS
Brief Synopsis

Love's Labour's Lost begins when the King of Navarre and his men declare that they will spend the next three years cloistered to study. They will abstain from frivolity, drinking, and most important, the company of women. This plan is immediately challenged as the Princess of France arrives with her retinue of women, on official state business. The King compromises his oath by having the women camp outside the castle walls. The Princess is not pleased with her arrangements. Nevertheless, the king's men—Berowne, Longaville, and Dumaine—fall in love with the Princess's ladies, Rosaline, Maria, and Katherine, whom they have met before. The King and the Princess also fall for each other.

Prior to the women's arrival, the King receives a letter from Don Armado, a Spanish visitor, accusing the fool Costard of inappropriate relations with Jaquenetta, a peasant. Costard is sentenced to a week's fasting, which he feels is too harsh. Don Armado confesses to his page, Moth, that is in love with Jaquenetta, but she does not reciprocate his feelings.

The men hide their feelings for the women from one another, but each is caught declaring his love. First the King is discovered by Berowne, then Longaville is discovered reciting a poem, as is Dumaine. Finally, Berowne's love for Rosaline is revealed. The men decide to "study" love, essentially breaking their vows made so recently.

The women, out in the forest, discuss the love letters and gifts the men have given them. They decide to mask themselves and swap the gifts, in order to confuse the King and his courtiers. The men arrive dressed as Muscovites, and each immediately begins wooing the woman wearing his specific gift. Of course, the men are courting the wrong women. The men leave, and the women return the gifts to the correct recipient. The men return, and the Princess begins insulting the Muscovites. Unable to take any more ridicule, the King reveals that he and his men were the Muscovites, which the women knew.

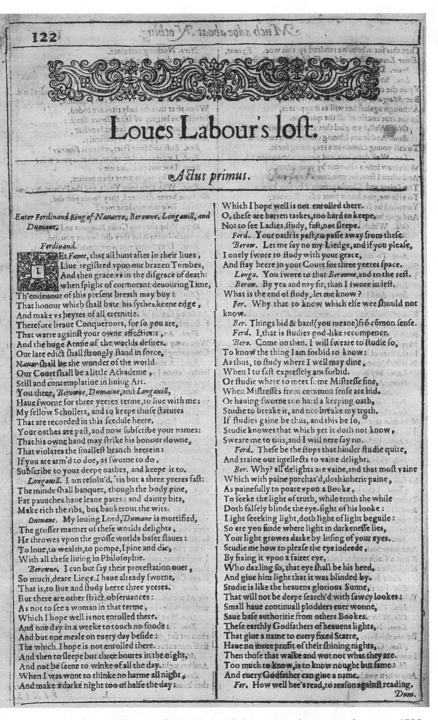

Loues Labour's lost.

Actus primus.

Enter Ferdinand King of Nauarre, Berowne, Longauill, and Dumaine.

Ferdinand.

Et *Fame*, that all hunt after in their liues,
Liue regiſtred vpon our brazen Tombes,
And then grace vs in the diſgrace of death:
when ſpight of cormorant deuouring Time,
Th'endeuour of this preſent breath may buy:
That honour which ſhall bate his ſythes keene edge,
And make vs heyres of all eternitie.
Therefore braue Conquerours, for ſo you are,
That warre againſt your owne affections,
And the huge Armie of the worlds deſires.
Our late edict ſhall ſtrongly ſtand in force,
Nauar ſhall be the wonder of the world.
Our Court ſhall be a little Achademe,
Still and contemplatiue in liuing Art.
You three, *Berowne, Dumaine,* and *Longauill,*
Haue ſworne for three yeeres terme, to liue with me:
My fellow Schollers, and to keepe thoſe ſtatutes
That are recorded in this ſeedule heere:
Your oathes are paſt, and now ſubſcribe your names:
That his owne hand may ſtrike his honour downe,
That violates the ſmalleſt branch heerein:
If you are arm'd to doe, as ſworne to do,
Subſcribe to your deepe oathes, and keepe it to.
Longauill. I am reſolu'd, 'tis but a three yeeres faſt:
The minde ſhall banquet, though the body pine,
Fat paunches haue leane pates: and dainty bits,
Make rich the ribs, but bankerout the wits.
Dumane. My louing Lord, *Dumane* is mortified,
The groſſer manner of theſe worlds delights,
He throwes vpon the groſſe worlds baſer ſlaues:
To loue, to wealth, to pompe, I pine and die,
With all theſe liuing in Philoſophie.
Berowne. I can but ſay their proteſtation ouer,
So much, deare Liege, I haue already ſworne,
That is, to liue and ſtudy heere three yeeres.
But there are other ſtrict obſeruances:
As not to ſee a woman in that terme,
Which I hope well is not enrolled there.
And one day in a weeke to touch no foode:
And but one meale on euery day beſide:
The which, I hope is not enrolled there.
And then to ſleepe but three houres in the night,
And not be ſeene to winke of all the day,
When I was wont to thinke no harme all night,
And make a darke night too of halfe the day:

Which I hope well is not enrolled there.
O, theſe are barren taskes, too hard to keepe,
Not to ſee Ladies, ſtudy, faſt, not ſleepe.
Ferd. Your oath is paſt, to paſſe away from theſe.
Berow. Let me ſay no my Liedge, and if you pleaſe,
I onely ſwore to ſtudy with your grace,
And ſtay heere in your Court for three yeeres ſpace.
Longa. You ſwore to that *Berowne,* and to the reſt.
Berow. By yea and nay ſir, than I ſwore in ieſt.
What is the end of ſtudy, let me know?
Fer. Why that to know which elſe wee ſhould not know.
Ber. Things hid & bard (you meane) frō cōmon ſenſe.
Ferd. I, that is ſtudies god-like recompence.
Bero. Come on then, I will ſweare to ſtudie ſo,
To know the thing I am forbid to know:
As thus, to ſtudy where I well may dine,
When I to faſt expreſſely am forbid.
Or ſtudie where to meet ſome Miſtreſſe fine,
When Miſtreſſes from common ſenſe are hid.
Or hauing ſworne too hard a keeping oath,
Studie to breake it, and not brcake my troth.
If ſtudies gaine be thus, and this be ſo,
Studie knowes that which yet it doth not know,
Sweare me to this, and I will nere ſay no.
Ferd. Theſe be the ſtops that hinder ſtudie quite,
And traine our intellects to vaine delight.
Ber. Why? all delights are vaine, and that moſt vaine
Which with paine purchas'd, doth inherit paine,
As painefully to poare vpon a Booke,
To ſeeke the light of truth, while truth the while
Doth falſely blinde the eye-ſight of his looke:
Light ſeeeking light, doth light of light beguile:
So ere you finde where light in darkeneſſe lies,
Your light growes darke by loſing of your eyes.
Studie me how to pleaſe the eye indeede,
By fixing it vpon a fairer eye,
Who dazling ſo, that eye ſhall be his heed,
And giue him light that it was blinded by.
Studie is like the heauens glorious Sunne,
That will not be deepe ſearch'd with ſawcy lookes:
Small haue continuall plodders euer wonne,
Saue baſe authoritie from others Bookes.
Theſe earthly Godfathers of heauens lights,
That giue a name to euery fixed Starre,
Haue no more profit of their ſhining nights,
Then thoſe that walke and wot not what they are.
Too much to know, is to know nought but fame:
And euery Godfather can giue a name.
Fer. How well hee's read, to reaſon againſt reading.
                                                    Dum.

Title page of the first publication of *Love's Labour's Lost*, printed in quarto format in 1598

Once true identities and intentions are re-established, the group watches a play, performed in their honor by Nathaniel, Holofernes, and Don Armado. The fun is interrupted with news that the King of France has died. The Princess leaves immediately but vows to return in one year, when her mourning period is over. She and her ladies convince the men to return to their sequestered studies for the year, in demonstration of their love for the women.

The play ends with songs of winter and spring that Don Armado had prepared for the pageant.

Act I, Scene 1

Love's Labour's Lost opens with the King of Navarre and his lords Berowne, Longaville, and Dumaine discussing the oath they have made to dedicate themselves to study for three years. The audience learns that during the three-year term, the men are to live monastic lives, abstaining from food one day a week, limiting sleep, and, most important, avoiding all contact with women. Longaville and Dumaine enthusiastically agree to the plan, but Berowne is less amenable, arguing that he learns much about the world through observations of women, fine food, and courtly life. Reluctantly, however, Berowne agrees to participate in the King's plan.

The King and his men next draft a public proclamation, which will be sent to the people of Navarre. The most significant statute of the public document declares that no woman shall be allowed within one mile of court. Berowne informs the King that he will have to break this very rule as the Princess of France is on her way to Navarre, conducting royal business for her ill father.

A messenger arrives with a letter to the King from Don Adriano de Armado, a Spaniard visiting the court. The letter accuses the fool Costard of inappropriate behavior with Jaquenetta, a wench. The fool has violated the King's order that all men stay away from women, and such a crime carries a one-year prison term. After some debate, the King sentences Costard to a week's fasting, with Don Armado serving as his jailor.

Act I, Scene 2

Don Armado speaks to his page, Moth, and confesses that he is in love with Jaquenetta. The constable Anthony Dull returns with Costard and Jaquenetta, and he explains to Armado the King's sentence. Don Armado declares his love for Jaquenetta, and she replies with a vague acknowledgment but does not seem to reciprocate the feelings. All other characters leave, and Don Armado decides to write a love letter to Jaquenetta, declaring that the best way to woo her is through the written word.

Act II, Scene 1

The Princess and her ladies, Rosaline, Maria, and Katherine, arrive at the court of Navarre. Boyet, a lord who is traveling with the Princess, is sent to announce their arrival. The ladies confess to the Princess that they have met the King's men previously. The Princess suspects that her ladies have romantic inclinations toward the men. Boyet returns and announces that the King will not receive the women at court due to his new oath. Instead, the women must camp in the field. Not surprisingly, the King receives a cold welcome from the Princess when he greets his guest. Berowne and Rosaline recognize each other, and flirting via a quick, witty exchange of words ensues. Dumaine and Longaville also notice the attending ladies. When the men leave, Boyet tells the Princess that the King appears to be in love with her. The Princess laughs at the statement, but she neither denies nor protests the assertion about the King.

Act III, Scene 1

Don Armado and Moth discuss the Spaniard's love for Jaquenetta. An exchange of witty, carefully crafted wordplay occurs. Don Armado calls forth his prisoner, Costard. The two men, along with Moth, have a witty discussion about the word *l'envoi,* as Costard is ordered to deliver a message. Armado releases Costard from custody so that the clown may deliver the letter Armado penned to Jaquenetta. Costard is paid and sent on his way. On his way to deliver the letter, Costard meets

Berowne, who also pays him to deliver a letter. Berowne's letter is written to Rosaline.

Act IV, Scene 1

The Princess, her ladies, and Boyet are in the woods hunting. The Princess chides a Forester for complimenting her hunting skills unnecessarily. Costard mistakenly delivers the letter meant for Jaquenetta, rather than the letter from Berowne to Rosaline. Boyet reads the letter aloud to the ladies. The party then continues the hunt. Rosaline, Boyet, and Maria enter into a conversation in which the hunt becomes an allusion to courtship and sex.

Act IV, Scene 2

Nathaniel, Holofernes, and Dull discuss the Princess's hunt. They debate whether the deer just killed was a "Pricket," a young deer, or an older animal. Holofernes delivers an "extemporal epitaph on the death of the deer" (4.2.49–50). Jaquenetta appears and asks Holofernes to read the letter she has just received from Don Armado, as she is illiterate. The letter, of course, is the one Berowne wrote to Rosaline.

Act IV, Scene 3

Berowne enters alone carrying a sheet of paper. Talking to himself, he reveals that he has written a poem to Rosaline. The King enters, and Berowne hides. The King begins reading the poem he has crafted for the Princess. Next, Longaville enters, and the King hides. The former reads his sonnet to Maria. Finally, Dumaine enters and recites his poem to Katherine. Longaville confronts Dumaine about his love, and the King comes forth to chide Longaville. He then asks what Berowne would think of the men violating their oaths. Berowne hears this and reveals the King's love for the Princess. Jaquenetta enters with the letter Berowne wrote to Rosaline, which was accidentally delivered to her, and Berowne is exposed. Costard and Jaquenetta accuse Berowne of treason, since he has violated the King's public oath to avoid all contact with women.

The King turns to Berowne, asking how they can reconcile their loves with the vow to education they have made. Berowne gives a speech whereby he declares that the best education on beauty is found in looking at women; therefore, the men have broken no laws by falling for the Princess and her ladies. Moreover, in their studies, the men will be reading texts about the beauty of women. They would be better served to observe specimens of female beauty firsthand. All four agree that the best course of action is to immediately court the women, officially abandoning their studies.

Act V, Scene 1

Holofernes and Nathaniel discuss Don Armado, whom they view in a negative light. Nathaniel reveals that he has just spoken with Armado. Both men criticize Armado for being vain yet lacking in intellect. They mock his pronunciation and word choice, although Holofernes makes several pronunciation errors in his condemnation of the Spanish visitor. Don Armado enters with Costard, and then Holofernes and Nathaniel taunt Armado, although the Spaniard does not realize this. Armado tells the men that the King has ordered them to put on a play for the ladies. The men decide to put on a play about the Nine Worthies and then divide the parts among themselves.

Act V, Scene 2

The ladies share the items that the men sent along with their love letters: The Princess received a jewel from the King; Rosaline received a poem from Berowne; Maria received pearls from Longaville; and Katherine received a glove from Dumaine. Katherine reveals to the ladies that her sister died from love, casting a temporary darkness on the otherwise festive scene. Boyet enters and tells the ladies that the King and his men are coming to their camp in disguise, dressed as Russians. The Princess decides that they should mask themselves and exchange the aforementioned gifts in order to outwit the men.

The men arrive, and Moth attempts to make a speech about the women's beauty. Berowne inter-

Boyet greets Katherine, Rosaline, Maria, and the Princess of France in Act V, Scene 2 of *Love's Labour's Lost,* in this engraving from the 1744 Hanmer edition of Shakespeare's works. *(Illustration by Francis Hayman; engraving by Hubert Gravelot)*

recites the words that the King had spoken to her earlier, believing her to be the Princess. The ladies reveal that they had exchanged favors, so the men, in fact, were not wooing their intended loves.

Costard enters and asks the King if they should begin the pageant of the Nine Worthies. The play begins with Nathaniel playing Alexander. Boyet begins mocking the characters from the audience. Berowne is impressed with Boyet's wit. Holofernes and Moth come onto the stage, as Judas Maccabeus and Hercules. Don Armado next enters as Hector. Costard announces in the middle of the play that Jaquenetta is two months' pregnant, which incenses Don Armado. The two men begin fighting, although they stay in character, which leads to humorous commentary from Berowne and Dumaine.

At this moment, a messenger arrives with news that the king of France is dead. The Princess decides that she must leave at once. The King of Navarre pleads with her to stay, but she is unmoved, saying that she and her ladies are not convinced that the men were sincere in their advances. Their letters and declarations were too outrageous to be believed. Instead, she asks the King to go to a hermitage for one year. At the end of that year, they will meet again and renew their courtship. Rosaline, Maria, and Katherine make the same promise to Berowne, Longaville, and Dumaine.

Don Armado asks the King if the remaining party can perform the songs they rehearsed for the pageant. The King agrees, and the play ends with the songs of spring and winter.

rupts him several times. The King begins wooing Rosaline, whom he believes is the Princess. The other mismatched couples flirt and converse in separate areas. The men leave, and the women return one another's gifts. They agree to speak poorly of the Muscovites when the men return as themselves. When the King and his men return, the ladies begin insulting the Russians. The King then proclaims that they were wearing the Russian disguises in order to save himself and his men from further embarrassment. The Princess asks the King what he said to her while in disguise and then asks the same question to Rosaline. Rosaline

CHARACTER LIST

Ferdinand, King of Navarre The King decides to dedicate himself to study for three years and his lords decide to join him. He then falls in love with the Princess of France while she is visiting his kingdom.

Berowne A lord attending the King of Navarre. Of the three supporting lords, he is the most vocal in his opposition to the plan of seclusion. He falls in love with the Princess of France's lady Rosaline.

Longaville   Another lord attending the King of Navarre. He falls in love with Maria.

Dumaine   A third lord attending the King of Navarre. He falls in love with Katherine.

Don Adriano de Armado   A Spanish braggart visiting the court of Navarre. He is not well liked and often ridiculed. He falls in love with Jaquenetta, a dairy maid.

Moth   Don Armado's page.

Princess of France   The Princess travels to Navarre with her ladies on behalf of her bedridden father. Although she appears to fall for the King of Navarre, she is critical of his romantic games and tokens.

Rosaline   A lady attending the Princess of France. She is pursued by Berowne.

Katherine   Another lady attending the Princess of France. She falls in love with Dumaine.

Maria   A third lady attending the Princess of France. She falls in love with Longaville.

Boyet   An attendant to the Princess of France. He is often critical of the King of Navarre and his men, and he reveals the men's plans to the Princess.

Costard   A clown, or fool. He switches the love letters of Berowne and Don Armado. Earlier, he was discovered with Jaquenetta.

Jaquenetta   An illiterate dairy maid. Both Don Armado and Costard are vying for her.

Sir Nathaniel   A curate. Along with Holofernes, he offers criticism of the love letters circulating around the court. He participates in the play of the Nine Worthies.

Holofernes   A schoolteacher. With Sir Nathaniel, he participates in the literary commentary and mocks Don Armado.

Anthony Dull   A constable who appears with Nathaniel and Holofernes. As his name implies, he is dull and often cannot understand the witty remarks of the characters around him.

CHARACTER STUDIES
Ferdinand, King of Navarre

The King sets the conflicts of the play into action. His decision to sequester himself in study sets an example that his men have little choice but to follow. Only Berowne voices an opposition, though one wonders whether Dumaine and Longaville would have so readily agreed if Navarre were not a king. Moreover, the King's decision to issue a public proclamation with dire consequences for women breaking the new law creates an even larger conflict, as the female proxy for the king of France is on her way. Although Navarre enthusiastically begins his years of study, he quickly breaks his oath, leaving the audience to wonder if he ever did want to study in the first place. The King is never seen studying in the play; instead, he is portrayed as writing love poetry, joking with his men, and putting on costumes to trick the women. The audience is never convinced of his dedication to his education.

As a king, Navarre seems to lack some of the mature traits necessary in a good ruler. He is willing to leave his kingdom without a leader while he retreats into his books. Readers and viewers learns at the beginning of the play that there is a diplomatic issue involving the region of Aquitaine that needs to be resolved urgently, hence the Princess's trip. Surely this would not be an ideal time to leave his kingdom without a consistent, active monarch. He insults the Princess of France by forcing her to camp in a field, instead of residing within the castle. Although he is upholding his vow, such action could prove detrimental to his diplomatic efforts. A better ruler would have not made such a stringent declaration or would have made exceptions for foreign dignitaries.

Of course, the King exists in the play as a lover, not as a scholar or ruler. For dramatic purposes, he is a monarch only to match the societal level of the Princess. Navarre's actions are dominated by thoughts of the Princess, and he composes love poetry to her and sends her gifts. Even in courtship, however, the King demonstrates a lack of maturity. He participates in the Cossack episode and appears incapable of recognizing the way the men trivialize love or idealize the women, never seeing them as the real individuals they are. Only when the Princess points out the problems with their games does the King seem to understand his errors.

The King, Berowne, Longaville, and Dumaine appear as Russians in Act V, Scene 2 of *Love's Labour's Lost*. Print published by Lemerre in the 19th century (*Illustration by Henri Pille; engraving by Louis Monziès*)

At the end of the play, the King reluctantly agrees to spend one year in study while the Princess mourns her father's death. The audience is left wondering just how different the King will be in 12 months' time. He desperately needs to mature, as both a lover and a ruler. The play's ambiguous ending leaves the audience speculating as to whether he will grow into the man he is not in the play. In order for his relationship with the Princess to flourish, he will need to mature. Surely, he will also need to grow into his role as king in order to be an effective ruler for his people.

The Princess of France

The Princess is by far the most insightful character in the play, male or female. Upon arriving at Navarre, she is immediately aware of the undiplomatic reception she has received and does not accept the King of Navarre's proclamation as reason enough to be housed in the field. She respects the law, nevertheless, and agrees to stay outside of court.

The Princess's strongest and most consistently displayed attribute is truthfulness. When she arrives in Navarre, she laments her accommodations directly to the King. While hunting with Boyet, she chides a Forester for complimenting her unnecessarily. She demands honesty from others and speaks truthfully to those she encounters, even if her statements may not seem diplomatic. Even though she is the mastermind of the masking at the end of the play, her aim is truthfulness. By switching favors with her ladies, she is able to show the King that he is treating their courtship as a childish game, when, in fact, love, and with it courtly marriage, is a very serious matter. Since she does not believe the King's words, she persuades him to demonstrate his love by action: retreating into his studies.

The Princess demonstrates the keenest intellect and wit of all other characters in the play. She is perceptive, honest, and consistent. There is little doubt that she is the stronger, more effective monarch, demonstrating the traits Navarre should possess. She understands her duty to rule, as is demonstrated both upon her arrival in Navarre and her immediate decision to leave when she learns of her father's death. Unlike the King, she will not shirk her responsibilities in order to participate in the romantic games occurring in Navarre. She is unwilling to see the King for one full year, the customary mourning period. It is her duty to honor her father fully, and leaving her romance with Navarre aside for 12 months is her only option, as forgoing the mourning period is not in her nature.

Berowne

Berowne is the King of Navarre's most outspoken attendant. As such, he reveals what the others are

The Princess and her ladies during the hunt in Act IV, Scene 1 of *Love's Labour's Lost*

possibly thinking but may be afraid to say. As the play opens, he expresses his objection to the King's monastic enterprise, although Longaville and Dumaine enthusiastically support the plan. The audience is left wondering if the two other attendants feel as Berowne does but are afraid to voice opposition to the King. As the play progresses, Berowne is the first of the men to openly admit love for one of the ladies: He gives Costard a letter meant for Rosaline. Soon, the other men will write their own love letters and sonnets to the women. When Longaville and Dumaine are discovered by the King, Berowne reveals Navarre's own writings

to the Princess of France. The King condemns his attendant for revealing the secret, but then Berowne boldly chides all the men for lying about their passions: "I that am honest, I hold it sin / To break the vow I am engaged in, / I am betrayed by keeping company / With men like you, men of inconstancy." (4.3.172–175) He persuades the men to give up their scholarly pursuits and to woo the women openly.

Berowne is one of the wittiest characters in the play, mainly because of his honesty. Unlike the other men, he openly admits to having an aversion to traditional education and declares his intention to court Rosaline openly. In these instances in the play, his long monologues reveal both his wit and his adventurous nature. When the men's masked encounter is revealed, it is Berowne, not the King, who apologizes to the women for neglecting their duties and toying with the ladies. As the play ends, Berowne once again shares the thoughts that all are probably thinking. As the women prepare to leave for one year, Berowne says to the King, "Our wooing does not end like an old play: / Jack hath not Jill" (5.2.858–859). When the King offers hope of reuniting with the women in one year, Berowne declares, "That's too long for a play" (5.2.863). Although all characters seem optimistic about these lovers' fates, Berowne states what all others are afraid to utter, that their loves may fade after so long a separation. Indeed, Berowne is the only one to declare that love's labors may indeed be lost. Many scholars believe that Shakespeare's voice can be found in many of Berowne's lines, as he offers endorsement for humanistic education that focuses on observing the human condition rather than studying traditional texts.

Readers and audience members enjoy Berowne because of his combination of wit and honesty. Without the latter, his humorous lines would seem callous or lacking depth. For the most part, he refuses to be dishonest, and when he is, he feels deeply sorry. He speaks truths that reinforce the significant themes of the text, such as the importance of using language effectively and the problematic role of games in courtship.

Rosaline

Rosaline is the most developed of the Princess of France's attending ladies. As she is matched with Berowne, the King of Navarre's most vocal attendant, she consequently receives more attention in the play than Katherine and Maria do. What is most intriguing about Rosaline in *Love's Labour's Lost* is not necessarily what she does within this play but how she marks a development in Shakespeare's heroines. Rosaline's physical traits are described in detail by Berowne. Her dark eyes and hair have led many to believe that she is the Dark Lady, for whom many of Shakespeare's sonnets were written. Furthermore, many scholars believe that *Romeo and Juliet* was written around the time he produced *Love's Labour's Lost*. The similarities between Rosalind and Romeo's first love are most likely not coincidental.

When Rosaline and Berowne first meet in Navarre, the tension between the two characters is palpable:

BEROWNE. Did not I dance with you in
  Brabant once?

ROSALINE. Did not I dance with you in
  Brabant once?

BEROWNE. I know you did.

ROSALINE. How needless was it then to ask
  the question!

BEROWNE. You must not be so quick.

ROSALINE. 'Tis long of you that spur me
  with such questions.

BEROWNE. Your wit's too hot, it speeds too
  fast, 'twill tire.

ROSALINE. Not till it leave the rider in the
  mire.

BEROWNE. What time o'day?

ROSALINE. The hour that fools should ask.

BEROWNE. Now fair befall your mask!

ROSALINE. Fair fall the face it covers!

BEROWNE. And send you many lovers!

ROSALINE. Amen, so you be none.

BEROWNE. Nay, then will I be gone.
  (2.1.114–128)

Berowne is seen largely as the wittiest character in the play, and Rosaline is quite comfortable keeping up with his quick remarks. Even though she has just revealed to the Princess that she in fond of Berowne, the language here indicates an air of antagonism between the two. Berowne raises a question that he knows the answer to already. Instead of playing along with the casual flirtation, Rosaline retorts with the same question to him. The quick back and forth between the two reveals an equality of wit, which will only help their love to develop, if it does not get in the way. Shakespeare perfects this dueling couple motif with Beatrice and Benedick in *Much Ado About Nothing*, and their opening lines together are remarkably similar to the ones above.

Rosaline will demonstrate this same acumen in several scenes throughout the play, with Berowne and with other characters, including Boyet and the King (when she is pretending to be the Princess). She has a mastery of witty language that many of the men are trying desperately to achieve. Although Rosaline is a minor character, her finely crafted language and sharp intellect make her an important part of the play's theme on language.

Don Armado

Don Armado is a Spaniard visiting the court of Navarre. Even though he is supposed to be a courtier of higher rank, he plays the fool throughout the play. He is introduced to the stage by a description from the King of Navarre: "But I protest, I love to hear him lie, / And I will use him for my minstrelsy" (1.1.172–173). The audience is immediately made aware of Armado's reception in Navarre: Everyone from the King to the court fool, Costard, view Armado as someone to ridicule. His actual language usage is first presented to the audience via a letter delivered to the King. The letter reveals his love for Jaquenetta, a lowly milkmaid. As a "refined traveler," Armado should have no interaction with Jaquenetta, and he certainly should not allow his feelings for a woman far below his social class to become known. Adding to his insult, Jaquenetta is not interested in Armado; instead, she is in love with Costard.

Throughout the play, Armado is mocked primarily for his poor usage of English. *Love's Labour's Lost* is a play about language, and Armado's inability to communicate effectively is mocked by everyone, from the King to Holofernes. In the end, he challenges Costard to a duel over Jaquenetta, but the fight is interrupted by news of the King of France's death.

Many critics believe that Armado represents the fallen Spanish Empire. His name is surely meant to invoke Spain's great navy, the Armada. He is a braggart with very little to brag about. Armado is ineffective in wooing Jaquenetta, and he seems out of place with the King, Princess, and their attendants, characters who are of similar social rank to him. Instead, he bickers with Costard and spends his time with Moth. Like the fallen Spanish Armada (1588), Don Armado can brag about his past accomplishments but is ineffective in his current life. He is mocked because he embodies so many stereotypical traits of England's enemy: He is boastful, unsuccessful, and decidedly not English.

Many modern critics, however, view Don Armado as a sympathetic character, as so many are cruel to him. He may be foolish and struggle with language, but he is not insulting or unfair to anyone. Like Malvolio in *Twelfth Night,* he does not fit in with any group in society. However, he still deserves decency. Malvolio will reclaim his self-respect by publicly condemning Olivia's advances. Don Armado insists that the play be finished, and he leads the characters in singing the closing songs of the play.

DIFFICULTIES OF THE PLAY

Love's Labour's Lost differs from Shakespeare's other comedies in that plot is all but absent. Very little happens over the course of five acts. Many of the scenes involve characters discussing the intricacies of language or concepts related to language, such as oaths and promises. In Shakespeare's other comedies, plot is central to character development, thematic exposition, and, of course, creating the romantic couplings in the final act. There is no switching of lovers, as in *Midsummer Night's Dream,* no complex mistaken identities such as those found in *Twelfth Night,* no evil plots by villains like the one formed by Don John the Bastard in *Much Ado About Nothing.* In *Love's Labour's Lost,* what little plot there is serves only to prompt the characters' discussions of study, love, and duty.

In addition, the language of the play is extremely complicated and allusive, even more so than in most of Shakespeare's plays. The plot structure may be simple, but conversations had by the various characters are often very complex. On the surface, discussions about courtly romance or keeping oaths seem quite straightforward; however, a closer examination of the language reveals Shakespeare's strong criticism of language usage. If a reader is not looking for these deeper meanings, many passages will seem incomprehensible or absurd. From the poor poetry the King and his men write (Berowne describes Rosaline's eyes as "two pitch balls stuck in her face" (4.1.194)) to the wordplay between Holofernes and Nathaniel, the play is filled with scenes that focus on amateurish or improper language construction.

Another difficulty that the play presents is in understanding references that signal a time long after the play has ended. Much of the play builds toward the pact that the King and the Princess make to rekindle their courtship after one year. In earlier scenes, references are made to cuckolding, which seems to make little sense as none of the courtships end in marriage. Don Armado, for example, refers to himself as a cuckold after learning that Jaquenetta and Costard have been intimate, but of course, Jaquenetta is married to neither man. These various references to spousal cheating are placed within the play to further erode the audience's confidence in a positive resolution in a year's time. The men may already be worried about cheating wives, but it is uncertain that they will gain wives when the 12-month period of mourning and study is complete. Certainly Don Armado, who learns that Jaquenetta is pregnant, presumably with Costard's child, has virtually no chance of marrying the woman he loves.

The King and his men dress as Russians to meet the Princess and her ladies in Act V, Scene 2 of *Love's Labour's Lost,* in this print published by Jacob Tonson in 1709.

The cuckold references may be present within the text to reinforce the sexually charged situation of courtship. Throughout the play, the Princess, her ladies, and their attendant, Boyet, make references to the hunt as an allusion for wooing. These passages are often sexual in nature, and explicitly so. Boyet says to Maria while hunting, "Let the mark have a prick in't to mete at if it may be" (4.1.133), referring to the bull's-eye she has just shot. Of course, the sexual allusion is not difficult to discern, and this discussion travels into even more taboo innuendo within a few lines. The purpose of the sexual language is to remind the characters, and the audience, that courtship is closely connected to passion and that it is not necessarily pure, as so many stories have depicted courtly love to be. The lovers in the play are walking a fine line between igniting the passions necessary for romance and losing their virtue.

With little action and many difficult passages, readers are often unprepared for the final scene in Act V, the longest continually running scene in any Shakespearean play. The scene begins with the ladies switching favors and masking themselves for the Muscovites, followed by the mismatched lovers' courtships. The truth is revealed to the men, just as the play of the Nine Worthies begins. Don Armado and Costard, as Hector and Pompey, begin arguing about Jaquenetta in the middle of the play, breaking character. Finally, the messenger arrives with news of the king of France's death, and all resolve to meet again in one year. The scene is packed with brief moments of disguise, both in masks (the ladies) and playacting (the Muscovites and the Worthies). The play-within-the-play structure can lead to confusion, for it is not always immediately clear if the characters are speaking as themselves or in their prescribed roles. A staged version of the play will undoubtedly clarify the characters' intentions, but a reading of the text can be quite confusing. The lighthearted mood turns somber when news of the king of France's death reaches Navarre; however, the play ends on a seemingly light note with the songs of spring and winter. Readers must look closely at the language of these two songs in order to see their connection to the larger play, which is not immediately evident.

KEY PASSAGES
Act I, Scene 1, 1–23

FERDINAND. Let fame, that all hunt after in
  their lives,
Live register'd upon our brazen tombs
And then grace us in the disgrace of death;
When, spite of cormorant devouring Time,
The endeavor of this present breath may buy
That honour which shall bate his scythe's keen
  edge
And make us heirs of all eternity.
Therefore, brave conquerors,—for so you are,
That war against your own affections
And the huge army of the world's desires,—
Our late edict shall strongly stand in force:
Navarre shall be the wonder of the world;
Our court shall be a little Academe,
Still and contemplative in living art.
You three, Berowne, Dumain, and Longaville,
Have sworn for three years' term to live
  with me
My fellow-scholars, and to keep those statutes
That are recorded in this schedule here:
Your oaths are pass'd; and now subscribe your
  names,
That his own hand may strike his honour
  down
That violates the smallest branch herein:
If you are arm'd to do as sworn to do,
Subscribe to your deep oaths, and keep it too.

The opening lines are crucial to the play, as they reveal both the major conflict in the play and key components of the King of Navarre's character. The brief speech reveals the King's intention to leave public life for three years and embark on an academic retreat. Of course, such solitude will immediately have consequences, as a king can hardly leave his duties without producing negative effects. The audience will soon learn that the particular statutes "recorded in this schedule here" include having no interaction with women. Since *Love's Labour's Lost* is a comedy, the audience can immediately conjecture as to what effect this oath will have on romance within the play, since the rule and romance stand in direction opposition to each other.

More poignant, however, the passage reveals several significant character flaws found in Ferdinand. He is king, but he is willing to give up his public duty in order to study. Moreover, the language used by the King reveals an ulterior motive to his plan. He does not seem to desire knowledge for its own sake but rather for the glory that it will bring to himself and his kingdom. The King tells his men that they are warriors in pursuit of education and that they will achieve glory like soldiers on the battlefield. He wishes to embark on this project so that "Our court shall be a little Academe." He is interested in study for the public praise they will receive, not the actual knowledge they will gain. Throughout the play, the King and his men will shy away from the oaths they have taken to learn in solitude. Knowing that the King may not truly wish to expand his studies for the sake of knowledge allows the audience to understand why he is so willing to break his vow. If his motive is to gain prestige for his land, several other ways of achieving this may be more amenable to the King. These opening lines reveal to the audience the King's flawed motivation in making his plan, which, in turn, allows the audience to accept his decision to break the oath with little difficulty. The audience is neither surprised nor disappointed when the King breaks his vow, and this speech portrays his lack of enthusiasm for the endeavor, making his later decisions appropriate for his character.

Act I, Scene 2, 1–31

ARMADO. Boy, what sign is it when a man of
  great spirit grows melancholy?

MOTH. A great sign, sir, that he will look sad.

ARMADO. Why, sadness is one and the selfsame thing, dear imp.

MOTH. No, no; O Lord, sir, no.

ARMADO. How canst thou part sadness and melancholy, my tender juvenal?

MOTH. By a familiar demonstration of the working, my tough senior.

ARMADO. Why tough senior? why tough senior?

MOTH. Why tender juvenal? why tender juvenal?

ARMADO. I spoke it, tender juvenal, as a congruent epithet on appertaining to thy young days, which we may nominate tender.

MOTH. And I, tough senior, as an appertinent title to your old time, which we may name tough.

ARMADO. Pretty and apt.

MOTH. How mean you, sir? I pretty, and my saying apt? or I apt, and my saying pretty?

ARMADO. Thou pretty, because little.

MOTH. Little pretty, because little. Wherefore apt?

ARMADO. And therefore apt, because quick.

MOTH. Speak you this in my praise, master?

ARMADO. In thy condign praise.

MOTH. I will praise an eel with the same praise.

ARMADO. What, that an eel is ingenious?

MOTH. That an eel is quick.

ARMADO. I do say thou art quick in answers: thou heatest my blood.

This scene between Don Armado and his page is but one demonstration of the intricate wordplay that is so apparent throughout the play. Although these passages can be difficult to discern, they contain a good deal of humor and intellect. Here, we also see Shakespeare playing with word definitions and homonyms, offering multilayered passages whose meanings often change with close analysis.

Don Armado tells his page that he is melancholy because he has agreed to study with the King for three years. As the conversation ensues, Armado calls Moth "juvenal," meaning juvenile but, in fact, referencing the Roman satirist. Of course, the Spanish Empire is being satirized through Armado's character. Moth retorts by calling Armado "senior," simultaneously reinforcing the play on words *(señor)* and Armado's nationality. Since Moth was mislabeled, he will in essence mislabel his employer as well. Commonly used words such as *pretty, apt,* and *little* are examined to determine what exactly they mean. Armado uses these words to describe Moth, and, with each word, Moth asks for clarification. Other words such as *tough* and *tender* are used with multiple interpretations within the passage, revealing a multilayered analysis of discourse. The word analysis adds humor to the scene but also brings attention to the power of language, when it is used effectively or, more important, when it is misinterpreted or abused.

Several similar scenes are found within the play, usually with Armado or Holofernes at the center of the wordplay. Each scene reinforces the dynamic nature of language, demonstrating how word meanings can change with context and motive. These scenes are enjoyable to read or see performed as they offer a glimpse of Shakespeare having fun with language and playing with his specific medium in a way that only he can.

Act IV, Scene 3, 289–365

BEROWNE. 'Tis more than need.
Have at you, then, affection's men at arms.
Consider what you first did swear unto,
To fast, to study, and to see no woman;
Flat treason 'gainst the kingly state of youth.
Say, can you fast? your stomachs are too young;

And abstinence engenders maladies.
And where that you have vow'd to study, lords,
In that each of you have forsworn his book,
Can you still dream and pore and thereon look?
For when would you, my lord, or you, or you,
Have found the ground of study's excellence
Without the beauty of a woman's face?
From women's eyes this doctrine I derive;
They are the ground, the books, the academes
From whence doth spring the true Promethean
 fire
Why, universal plodding poisons up
The nimble spirits in the arteries,
As motion and long-during action tires
The sinewy vigour of the traveller.
Now, for not looking on a woman's face,
You have in that forsworn the use of eyes
And study too, the causer of your vow;
For where is any author in the world
Teaches such beauty as a woman's eye?
Learning is but an adjunct to ourself
And where we are our learning likewise is:
Then when ourselves we see in ladies'eyes,
Do we not likewise see our learning there?
O, we have made a vow to study, lords,
And in that vow we have forsworn our books.
For when would you, my liege, or you, or you,
In leaden contemplation have found out
Such fiery numbers as the prompting eyes
Of beauty's tutors have enrich'd you with?
Other slow arts entirely keep the brain;
And therefore, finding barren practisers,
Scarce show a harvest of their heavy toil:
But love, first learned in a lady's eyes,
Lives not alone immured in the brain;
But, with the motion of all elements,
Courses as swift as thought in every power,
And gives to every power a double power,
Above their functions and their offices.
It adds a precious seeing to the eye;
A lover's eyes will gaze an eagle blind;
A lover's ear will hear the lowest sound,
When the suspicious head of theft is stopp'd:
Love's feeling is more soft and sensible
Than are the tender horns of cockl'd snails;

Love's tongue proves dainty Bacchus gross in
 taste:
For valour, is not Love a Hercules,
Still climbing trees in the Hesperides?
Subtle as Sphinx; as sweet and musical
As bright Apollo's lute, strung with his hair:
And when Love speaks, the voice of all the gods
Makes heaven drowsy with the harmony.
Never durst poet touch a pen to write
Until his ink were temper'd with Love's sighs;
O, then his lines would ravish savage ears
And plant in tyrants mild humility.
From women's eyes this doctrine I derive:
They sparkle still the right Promethean fire;
They are the books, the arts, the academes,
That show, contain and nourish all the world:
Else none at all in ought proves excellent.
Then fools you were these women to forswear,
Or keeping what is sworn, you will prove fools.
For wisdom's sake, a word that all men love,
Or for love's sake, a word that loves all men,
Or for men's sake, the authors of these women,
Or women's sake, by whom we men are men,
Let us once lose our oaths to find ourselves,
Or else we lose ourselves to keep our oaths.
It is religion to be thus forsworn,
For charity itself fulfills the law,
And who can sever love from charity?

In this passage, Berowne convinces the men to give up their studies in order to woo the women. The audience has earlier learned that Berowne is most resistant among the lords to the King's educational plan, but his reasoning here for abandoning their vows actually reinforces the importance of education. Berowne is arguing for a natural education, in which the men study the inspiration for the many tomes they will encounter in seclusion: woman's beauty. Instead of reading the numerous texts about love, Berowne argues, the men should experience it firsthand. *Love's Labour's Lost* is a play primarily about language and learning; therefore, Berowne insists that the men not give up their search for knowledge. They will merely change the way in which they learn.

Berowne's speech separates knowledge into two categories: traditional learning and the study of human nature. As the wooing ensues, it becomes evident that the men are in need of the latter, as they toy with the women and do not seem to take courtship seriously. The king and his attendants need to learn about love, women, and their own wants and desires. These are concepts that will not be found on a library shelf. Berowne's monologue puts knowledge of the world on the same level as academic knowledge, reinforcing a theme found in many of Shakespeare's plays: humanistic study. Textual study is important, but forgoing the lessons found outside the classroom or library leaves the individual lacking knowledge.

Just as human nature is elevated in Berowne's speech, so is the importance of beauty and love. The women are beautiful, but their external appearances provide more than mere enjoyment for the men. It is through their beauty that the King and his attendants, and all men, are able to truly understand the great works of drama, poetry, and philosophy. In order to fully comprehend these essential texts, the men must understand the transformative effect of beauty. According to Berowne, love is the primary theme of the works they would be studying, love obviously inspired by beauty. By fully giving themselves over to courtship, the men will become fully engaged in the study of beauty and love. Without gazing upon beautiful faces or falling in love, the men will never truly grasp the pieces they were to study. Since they are studying living examples of beauty and love, the foursome will receive a more complete education than they would have with only books to study.

Berowne's words certainly fit his desire to woo Rosaline, but they also portray what many believe to be Shakespeare's own opinion on formal education and the importance of humanism found within Renaissance society. The numerous neoclassical references found in the love letters to the women, combined with Berowne's treatise on studying beauty, demonstrate the cultural acceptance of individualism while still upholding the need to understand the classics.

Act V, Scene 2, 798–822

PRINCESS. A time, methinks, too short
To make a world-without-end bargain in.
No, no, my lord, your grace is perjured much,
Full of dear guiltiness; and therefore this:
If for my love, as there is no such cause,
You will do aught, this shall you do for me:
Your oath I will not trust; but go with speed
To some forlorn and naked hermitage,
Remote from all the pleasures of the world;
There stay until the twelve celestial signs
Have brought about the annual reckoning.
If this austere insociable life
Change not your offer made in heat of blood;
If frosts and fasts, hard lodging and thin weeds
Nip not the gaudy blossoms of your love,
But that it bear this trial and last love;
Then, at the expiration of the year,
Come challenge me, challenge me by these
  deserts,
And, by this virgin palm now kissing thine
I will be thine; and till that instant shut
My woeful self up in a mourning house,
Raining the tears of lamentation
For the remembrance of my father's death.
If this thou do deny, let our hands part,
Neither entitled in the other's heart.

As the Princess prepares to depart from Navarre, she leaves the King with these words. The monologue not only marks the end of the comedy but also ends the focus on language. So much of the play has focused on words: men professing their love, writing letters, speaking lines as other characters (the Muscovites). Here, the Princess urges the men to turn away from words and toward action. She tells the King that she does not trust his oath to remain faithful to her while in mourning. Indeed, his public speech has held little value throughout the play. He broke his vow to study in solitude, he has lied to his men about his intentions toward the Princess, and he tried to deceive her with the Muscovite interlude. Now, the Princess calls on the King, as well as his men, to focus on action. The only way she will believe

initial moments of courtship, but will a lack of passion ultimately destroy their love? The audience is also left wondering whether the King, or any of his attendants, is truly in love or merely moved by the excitement of new romance.

The Princess's words are central to understanding the ambiguous ending of the play and its relation to the title. The three sets of lovers all vow to reunite in one year's time. All seem satisfied with this arrangement, except for Berowne, who declares, "That's too long for a play" (5.2.862). The Princess's long speech and Berowne's short line leave the audience wondering if their labors of love are truly lost. We are hopeful but ultimately doubtful that the lovers will reconnect after 12 months have passed. Both the Princess and Berowne express reluctance about this outcome. Berowne's use of the word *play* indicates that the one year is far too long for the plot of a play, a direct reference to Aristotle's unities of time, place, and action, which Shakespeare rarely followed. However, the word can also be seen as a reflection of the Princess's speech. It is possible that the men were performing a play of love and may not be real-world lovers. The Princess demands action from the King, since his words, like those of an actor on the stage, are lacking truth. His promises of love are only truthful if he can live the promises he has made.

The Princess of France in Act V, Scene 2 of *Love's Labour's Lost.* This is a print from Charles Heath's 1848 edition of *The Heroines of Shakspeare: Comprising the Principal Female Characters in the Plays of the Great Poet.* (Painting by J. W. Wright; engraving by W. H. Mote)

DIFFICULT PASSAGES
Act V, Scene 1, 1–39
HOLOFERNES. Satis quod sufficit.

SIR NATHANIEL. I praise God for you,
  sir: your reasons at dinner have been sharp
  and sententious; pleasant without scurrility,
  witty without affection, audacious without
  impudency, learned without opinion, and
  strange without heresy. I did converse this
  quondam day with a companion of the king's,
  who is intituled, nominated, or called, Don
  Adriano de Armado.

HOLOFERNES. Novi hominem tanquam te:
  his humour is lofty, his discourse peremptory,

his oath is if he follows through on the broken promise to study.

The passage also speaks to the difficulties of passion. The Princess is not convinced that, after a year of solitude and reflection, the King will still want her. Her language, however, indicates that her feelings will not change. She refers to his feelings as "gaudy blossoms of your love," a description that does not evoke strength or longevity. Since the King has acted rashly from the beginning of the play to the end, the Princess is correct is doubting whether the King will still want to court her after one long year apart. Moreover, the passage calls into question the relationship between passion and true love. Passion has aided love in the

his tongue filed, his eye ambitious, his gait majestical, and his general behavior vain, ridiculous, and thrasonical. He is too picked, too spruce, too affected, too odd, as it were, too peregrinate, as I may call it.

SIR NATHANIEL. A most singular and choice epithet.
[*Draws out his table-book.*]

HOLOFERNES. He draweth out the thread of his verbosity finer than the staple of his argument. I abhor such fanatical phantasimes, such insociable and point-devise companions; such rackers of orthography, as to speak dout, fine, when he should say doubt; det, when he should pronounce debt,—d, e, b, t, not d, e, t: he clepeth a calf, cauf; half, hauf; neighbour vocatur nebor; neigh abbreviated ne. This is abhominable,—which he would call abbominable: it insinuateth me of insanie: anne intelligis, domine? to make frantic, lunatic.

SIR NATHANIEL. Laus Deo, bene intelligo.

HOLOFERNES. Bon, bon, fort bon, Priscian! a little scratch'd, 'twill serve.

SIR NATHANIEL. Videsne quis venit?

HOLOFERNES. Video, et gaudeo.
[*Enter DON ADRIANO DE ARMADO, MOTH, and COSTARD.*]

DON ADRIANO DE ARMADO. Chirrah!
[*To MOTH*]

HOLOFERNES. Quare chirrah, not sirrah?

DON ADRIANO DE ARMADO. Men of peace, well encountered.

HOLOFERNES. Most military sir, salutation.

MOTH [*Aside to COSTARD*] They have been at a great feast of languages, and stolen the scraps.

The dialogue between Holofernes and Nathaniel portrays two concepts that run throughout *Love's Labour's Lost,* although neither is readily apparent in the lines above. First, the criticism of the Spanish Empire is revealed in the negative discussion about Don Armado. Second, the entire play is filled with examples of problematic language usage. The passage above and especially Moth's telling words criticize the poor use of language, particularly language used by those who are supposed to be masters of it.

The conversation between Holofernes and Nathaniel is primarily a critique of Don Armado. The two men are criticizing the Spaniard for his general demeanor, but the bulk of their commentary focuses on Armado's use of language. Holofernes mocks Armado's pronunciation of English, never giving the foreigner credit for speaking a second language. Within the description of his oral shortcomings, however, Holofernes and Nathaniel provide a symbolic criticism of the Spanish Empire, since Armado is the personification of that nation. He is "vain, ridiculous, and thrasonical." Members of Shakespeare's audience would recognize the description as that of a stereotypical Spaniard: boastful to the point of comical. The critique continues with the mockery of Armado's pronunciation of English words. When Armado enters the scene, he, of course, mispronounces the common salutation as "chirrah," for which Holofernes and Nathaniel mock him openly. When the Spaniard addresses the men as "men of peace," Holofernes responds with "most military," a reminder to the audience that Armado represents the Spanish Armada and a reversal of Armado's polite address.

Within their discussion, however, Holofernes and Nathaniel grossly misuse language, as well. The scene opens with Holofernes declaring "Satis quid sufficit." The actual Latin phrase is *"Satis est quod sufficit,"* which means "Enough is as good as a feast." Moth will close the feast motif with his comments at the end of the scene. Holofernes and Nathaniel are criticizing Armado's use of language, while they misuse it themselves. As the scene progresses, Holofernes gives examples of the words that the Spaniard has mispronounced in his presence. However, it is the English schoolteacher and not the Spanish visitor who is mispronouncing the words. He declares that the silent *b* in both *debt* and *doubt* should be pronounced. A few moments later, he tells Nathaniel that *abominable* is pronounced "abhominable."

As the scene progresses, Nathaniel and Holofernes continue speaking to each other in both English and Latin, referencing the grammarian Priscian. However, their lack of knowledge in grammar is most apparent through their misquoting of Latin and wrong pronunciations. Moth tells Costard that the men "have been at a great feast of languages and stolen the scraps." Shakespeare, via Moth, criticizes those who have little understanding of language and rhetoric. Holofernes and Nathaniel are guilty of the same crime they accuse Armado of: not using language properly. The two men are not able to see their own limitations and look just as foolish as the Spaniard does when he mispronounces words and jumbles phrases in the rest of the play. Moth, Armado's page, is able to see just how poorly the two educators use language.

This scene is difficult for modern readers because of the Latin, which many may not understand. In a staging of this scene, the actors will accentuate the mispronunciations, which are decidedly comical, but a reader may miss some of the subtle pronunciations as written in the text. This scene demonstrates the motif of problematic discourse that is present throughout the play. The texts of the love letters the King and his men write to the French ladies, for example, are fraught with bad poetry. Dumaine writes to his intended in couplets:

> On a day—alack the day!—
> Love, whose month is ever May,
> Spied a blossom passing fair
> Playing in the wanton air:
> Through the velvet leaves the wind,

> All unseen, can passage find;
> That the lover, sick to death,
> Wish himself the heaven's breath.
> Air, quoth he, thy cheeks may blow;
> Air, would I might triumph so!
> But, alack, my hand is sworn
> Ne'er to pluck thee from thy thorn;
> Vow, alack, for youth unmeet,
> Youth so apt to pluck a sweet!
> Do not call it sin in me,
> That I am forsworn for thee;
> Thou for whom Jove would swear
> Juno but an Ethiope were;
> And deny himself for Jove,
> Turning mortal for thy love.
> This will I send, and something else more plain,
> That shall express my true love's fasting pain.
> O, would the king, Biron, and Longaville,
> Were lovers too! Ill, to example ill,
> Would from my forehead wipe a perjured note;
> For none offend where all alike do dote.
>   (4.3.97–122)

The reader must remember that these poems, along with the misused language by Armado, Holofernes, and Nathaniel, demonstrate lesser forms of writing. Shakespeare is intentionally creating flawed language, drawing particular attention to the romantic poems so prevalent at the Elizabethan court. The play draws attention to these amateurish writings as direct contrasts to the elevated, masterly writing professional writers such as Shakespeare were producing. It is important that the reader or audience recognize the difference and not interpret these passages as poor writing by Shakespeare. He is intentionally using flawed passages to make his point.

CRITICAL INTRODUCTION TO THE PLAY

Love's Labour's Lost is a play that seems far more simple than it actually is. Beneath the romantic story lie deep cultural criticism and several important themes, which are revealed through analysis of the symbols, songs, setting, and plot devices, such as the play within the play. Particularly important to the play is the question of how social enterprises intersect with the needs of the individual.

Symbols

There are numerous symbols and allegorical motifs within the text. Many ordinary objects take on added significance, including the letters and poems written by the various suitors to their intendeds, the gifts the men give to the ladies, the hunt, and masks. Also notable is the absence of heroes from the text.

The numerous love letters and poems read aloud throughout are written by the King, his men, and Don Armado. The letters represent two primary concepts: the futility of language and the problems of ineffective word craft. The first letter the audience hears is the one written to the King by Don Armado about catching Jaquenetta and Costard together. The letter has the opposite effect of its writer's intention. The law, written by the King, proclaims that any man found with a woman will be subject to a year's imprisonment. The King sentences Costard to a week's fasting, with Armado serving as jailor. In this first encounter with a letter, the audience sees that the written word holds no power. The King dismisses his own written law by sentencing Costard to a term 51 weeks short of the official proclamation. Armado's letter proved to be futile, if we assume his goal was to rid himself of Costard, who now is the Spaniard's ward. The King continually breaks his written oaths via oral analysis and decrees. The same will happen when he chooses first to interact with the Princess and then to pursue her openly, repeatedly violating the law he has created.

The love letters written by the men demonstrate the limitations of writing that many amateur authors face. When the King and his attendants each fall in love, they all are moved to write love letters and sonnets. Berowne declares: "By heaven, I do love, and it hath taught me to rhyme, and to be melancholy" (4.3.11–12). He is usually quite in control of his language, giving eloquent speeches and rousing the King to various actions. With

Longaville enters reading his sonnet, while the King and Berowne watch from their hiding places in Act IV, Scene 3 of *Love's Labour's Lost*. Print published by F. & C. Rivington in 1803 *(Painting by Henry Fuseli; engraving by J. Dadley)*

poetry, however, he is a failure. Longaville finds that he, too, struggles to write eloquent verse: "I fear these stubborn lines lack power to move" (4.3.51). Even though the men are aware of the shortcomings in their writings, they send their lines to the women. Here, Shakespeare is mocking the trend of writing poetry as part of the courting process. The women are not convinced of the men's affections because the poems are so poorly written.

Katherine calls Dumaine's writing "A huge translation of hypocrisy, / Vilely compiled, profound simplicity" (5.2.51–52). The women doubt the men's sentiments because they were delivered in poorly crafted, hyperbolic language. The reader senses that the men would have been taken more seriously if their feelings had been delivered in clear, unadorned prose.

Along with the poorly crafted verses, the men give their intendeds gifts that are symbolic of the men's difficulties in wooing the ladies. The Princess and her attendants mock the gifts, as they do not view them as tokens of true love. When Maria displays the necklace Longaville has sent her, the Princess replies, "Dost thou not wish in heart / The chain were longer and the letter short?" (5.2.56). Since the gifts are delivered with the love letters that the ladies deem insincere, the tokens are received with slight contempt. A major conflict within the play is, indeed, the interpretation of feelings, as the men believe they are courting for love, while the women think the men are only being flirtatious. The gifts then become a part of the courtship game, as the women switch favors and mask themselves in Act V. The King and his attendants, of course, woo the wrong lovers. The switched favors shows that the men do not know their ladies well at all. Just as they cannot tell one from another when masked, the four men do not know the true feelings of the ladies.

While camping outside Navarre Castle, the Princess and her ladies, along with Boyet, embark on a hunt. The hunt becomes an allegory for courtship, with the commonly assumed roles of men and women reversed: When courtship is usually described as a hunt, it is the woman who becomes the hunted animal; in *Love's Labour's Lost,* however, the women are the hunters.

> BOYET. My lady goes to kill horns, but, if thou marry,
> Hang me by the neck if horns that year miscarry.
> Finely put on!
>
> ROSALINE. Well then, I am the shooter.

> BOYET. And who is your deer?
>
> ROSALINE. If we choose by the horns, yourself. Come not near.
> Finely put on, indeed! (4.1.112–118)

In both the literal and figurative sense here, the ladies are the ones on the hunt, and the implied meaning of the passage is decidedly sexual. Boyet makes the pun about cuckolding her husband with the mention of horns. Since Rosaline is not married, the reference is meant as a sexual allusion, which is carried throughout the hunting scene. Rosaline declares that she is the shooter; therefore, she is the one who is hunting for either a husband or a lover. Boyet's response offers a play on words: *deer* in the literal hunt and *dear* in the allegorical. Rosaline is hunting for her mate. The scene continues with Maria joining the conversation, and the language develops along this sexual trajectory. Although the cuckold pun does not exactly fit since the ladies are not married, the intent of the hunt motif is clear: The women, not the men, are in control of the courtship. The women are making decisions and allowing the men to court them, which in essence places them in positions of power. The bawdy language implies that the women are more comfortable with the sexual aspect of courting than the men are, which, of course, is a reversal of the commonly accepted traits of men and women.

Masks are a prominent symbol found in the last scene of Act V. The women decide to don masks and switch favors in order to the trick the men. The men arrive dressed as Cossacks in order to fool the ladies. Of course, they do not recognize their lovers, since the ladies' faces are covered. Masks symbolize the theme of appearance versus reality in nearly every work of literature where masks are found, and *Love's Labour's Lost* is no different. However, the masks serve as a way for the characters to be honest finally with one another. When the King and his attendants return dressed as themselves, the ladies insult the Muscovites who have just left. Embarrassed, the men reveal that they were the Russians. The women reveal their own masked game, telling the men that they were not speaking to their intendeds. In turn, the Princess informs the men that their wooing has not been taken seriously by the ladies. The men of Navarre seem to only be playing games of courtship, rather than trying to win the women's hearts. By masking and then de-masking, the truth about all the character's intentions becomes evident.

Another symbolic motif throughout the play revolves around heroes, or the lack of them. All the men in the play try to act heroically but fail to do so. The men, and Don Armado specifically, invoke the names of heroic men throughout the play. The references culminate in the play of the Nine Worthies, which includes great men from history. The constant references to these fabled heroes bring attention to the fact that none of the men in Navarre are heroic. The King and his attendants are childlike and easy to persuade. Armado and Costard bicker but never actually fight for Jaquenetta as romantic heroes should. Holofernes and Nathaniel are ridiculous and overly verbose. Shakespeare's references to great heroes in fiction and history reveal that Navarre is lacking such men. Moreover, the mention of so many heroes shows that these men are desperately in need of real heroic men to emulate. The fictional heroes, and their stories, mentioned throughout the play have not taught the men how to act in matters of bravery or love. Real-life mentors are in short supply and are needed to instruct the King and the others in the very real matters they are involved in.

Character names are symbolic of the characters they represent. While some are obvious, like the King and Princess, others would be recognizable only to Shakespeare's contemporary audience. The two royal lovers are known by their country names, as neither are given formal names within the text. The King is listed as Ferdinand in the dramatis personae, but he is never called this name in the play. The reader is constantly reminded that this is a French play, as the King and the Princess are referenced by their countries. What is also reinforced by their names is the serious issue of courtly alliances that hides behind their romance. Theirs is not just a romance. If the two decide to marry, a strong alliance between the two countries would be made. Along with France and Navarre, the kingdom of Spain is of course represented in Don Armado, whose name is the key to understanding the symbolic reference. Without his obviously Spanish name, the insults about Spain, through his mangled language and haughty mannerisms, might not be as apparent.

Other minor characters have symbolic names, as well. Armado's page is Moth, which would have been pronounced *mote* in Shakespeare's day. *Mote* means "small" or "diminutive," which is how Moth is described by Armado throughout the play. As a page, Moth is assumed to be a young man or boy. Anthony Dull is the constable consistently seen with Holofernes and Nathaniel. As the name suggests, he is dull, both in personality and intellect. When rehearsing for the play of the Worthies, Armado says to Dull, "Thou hast spoken no word all this while," to which Dull replies, "Nor understood none neither, Sir" (5.1.140–141). Dull is present in the play to act as a foil to the "intellectuals" Holofernes and Nathaniel. The latter characters, of course, believe they know far more than they do and often offer entertainment through their intellectual pursuits. Dull, on the other hand, has no interest in participating in the academic exercises or trying to learn more. Since he does not enter into the primary activity of the subplot, he is, indeed, dull. The messenger who arrives at the end of Act 5 also has a name filled with symbolism. *Marcade* is an alternative pronunciation of *macabre,* and his news of the French king's death changes the tone of the scene from one of celebration to one of mourning. The death of the king brings another type of death to the stage: the end of the romance. The games and exchanging of gifts must come to an end as the Princess and her ladies immediately depart for France. Marcade's name, like so many others in the play, symbolizes the role he plays and the information he brings to the other characters.

Songs

The play ends with two songs, which are performed by the actors of the Nine Worthies play, led by Don Armado. Although the Princess and her ladies have left and the play within the play is over, Armado asks the King if his company may still perform the finale, bringing down the curtain on both the Nine Worthies performance and the larger play. The cast sings first the song of spring and then the song of winter:

SPRING. When daisies pied and violets blue
And lady-smocks all silver-white
And cuckoo-buds of yellow hue
Do paint the meadows with delight,
The cuckoo then, on every tree,
Mocks married men; for thus sings he,
  Cuckoo;
Cuckoo, cuckoo: O word of fear,
Unpleasing to a married ear!

When shepherds pipe on oaten straws
And merry larks are ploughmen's clocks,
When turtles tread, and rooks, and daws,
And maidens bleach their summer smocks
The cuckoo then, on every tree,
Mocks married men; for thus sings he,
  Cuckoo;
Cuckoo, cuckoo: O word of fear,
Unpleasing to a married ear!

WINTER. When icicles hang by the wall
And Dick the shepherd blows his nail
And Tom bears logs into the hall
And milk comes frozen home in pail,
When blood is nipp'd and ways be foul,
Then nightly sings the staring owl, Tu-whit;
Tu-who, a merry note,
While greasy Joan doth keel the pot.

When all aloud the wind doth blow
And coughing drowns the parson's saw
And birds sit brooding in the snow
And Marian's nose looks red and raw,
When roasted crabs hiss in the bowl,

Then nightly sings the staring owl, Tu-whit;
Tu-who, a merry note,
While greasy Joan doth keel the pot.

The songs symbolize the passing of time in the year of mourning that will separate the ladies and the men. A full year passes with the songs, as spring gives way directly to winter. The poems are nearly identical in structure, both consisting of two eight-line stanzas with the same A-B-A-B structure repeated in the first four lines of each stanza. Similar sounds are made by the birds in each poem, with spring's "cuckoo" mirrored by the winter owl's "tu-who."

There is, however, a significant difference in the tones of the two poems, which will present an ironic ending to the play. The song of spring, the season usually associated with renewal and courtship, is filled with images of the cuckoo. The singing of the bird acts as a warning to men of their wives' possible infidelity. The warning stands in direct contrast to the soft, pastoral images of "daisies pied" and "violets blue." The song of winter describes the cold, harsh conditions of the season, particularly for those of the working class. The names *Dick, Tom,* and *Joan* would have been immediately recognized

The King and his men perform the Nine Worthies for the Princess and her ladies in Act V, Scene 2 of *Love's Labour's Lost,* as depicted in this print published by Virtue & Company in the 19th century. *(Painting by Robert Alexander Hillingford; engraving by Peter Lightfoot)*

by Shakespeare's audience as names belonging to commoners. Although the poem contains images of frozen milk and chafed skin, the overall tone of the song is uplifting. The owl sings in "a merry note," providing entertainment or respite to those working hard in the winter air.

In these two songs, the symbolic interpretations of the seasons are reversed so that spring is a time of worry and confusion while winter is a time for lighthearted celebration. They feel disjointed from the rest of the play and, initially, appear to be included only to provide the play with a musical ending, common to nearly all comedies. However, the songs are closely related to the subtext of sex found through the play. The audience has seen references to cuckolding earlier in the play, with allusions made in the scenes involving the hunt. In this song, the reference to the cuckoo is meant to remind the audience once again of the sexual nature of courtship, hearkening the explicit language spoken by Boyet, Rosaline, and Maria in previous scenes. The winter song, by contrast, shows the difficulty of married life, particularly for those of the working class. The song contains four characters: two men and two women. They could very well be couples attending to their daily household obligations, which do not end although the weather has turned harsh. The characters in the song, although seemingly content, are not engaged in romance or courtship. Instead, each is attending to his or her own responsibilities in a solitary manner.

The songs of winter and spring end the play on a light, positive note while also reinforcing the complex message about courtship and marriage that Shakespeare has made throughout the play. They serve as symbolic representations of what may be ahead for the lovers in *Love's Labour's Lost* after their year of separation has ended. If the couples do marry, the men may have to worry about their wives' fidelity, especially since the play has shown the women to be more comfortable with their sexuality than the men are, or the relationships may fall into the comfortable but hard work of marriage.

Setting

The pastoral setting of the play reinforces the theme that the laws of human nature do not always coexist with the laws of society. Shakespeare often moves his comedies to the forests, in order to show young men and women acting according to their hearts, not the rules of their lands. The kingdom of Navarre is cursed with numerous unnecessary laws, all of which were enacted by the King. When the Princess arrives and is forced to camp outside the palace, the constructs of courtly society are removed. The standard devices of courtly love, letters, and gifts prove to be ineffective in the woodland setting. Scholars are mocked by servants. Women become the strong hunters. The most powerful men in society are ineffective at communication. In many ways, the pastoral setting allows for an inverted society to emerge, akin to the medieval carnival. Other carnival motifs are present in the play, such as masking and playacting. Like Shakespeare's other comedies that take to the woods, the carnival is concluded with a reordering of societal norms. In the end, the Princess and her ladies return to France, and the men go back to their original plan to study in seclusion. Once the characters are removed from the pastoral setting, the rules of society again influence the actions of all. While in the forest, however, the characters can act on their emotions and desires, many of which are suppressed in society.

Plot Devices

The play contains several key plot devices that are used to develop the individual characters and themes. The most important plot device is the play within the play found in Act V. Students of Shakespeare will recognize this device from *Hamlet* and *A Midsummer Night's Dream.* In *Love's Labour's Lost,* the dramatic device is used to blur the lines between the actors in the staged play and characters in the larger play, reminding the audience that what they are seeing is illusory. The play of the Nine Worthies also demonstrates the theme of appearance versus reality by showing how obvious the truth really is. When the play of the Nine Worthies begins, Costard declares that the audience will be seeing a production of the "Three Worthies," since there are only three actors: Armado, Costard, and Holofernes. Armado and Costard begin arguing about Jaquenetta while playing the characters of Pompey and Hector. In the middle of the scene, Costard announces that Jaquenetta is two months' pregnant, presumably with his child. Don Armado then challenges Costard to a fight. This very personal argument takes place on the stage, and the men continue to act out their scene, discussing the Jaquenetta situation using the language of their characters. Costard declares, "Then shall Hector be whipped for Jaquenetta that is quick by him, and hanged for Pompey that is dead by him" (5.2.671–673). The characters move between their stage personas and their true selves, but the audience is aware of where their play ends and reality begins. This is also true of the audience watching *Love's Labour's Lost.* As the play draws to an end, the play within the play reminds the audience that characters on the stage are actors, not really young men and women engaged in romantic conflict. Don Armado asks the King if he may finish the play, even though the Princess and her attendants have departed for France. The Nine Worthies play is used to end the larger play in song, an ending associated with comedies but one that does not fit well with the somber tone and separation of lovers that occurs in the final moments of the play. The audience is reminded that what they have just seen is indeed acting, not the real conflicts of young lovers.

Themes

The most significant themes in the play are appearance versus reality, human nature versus society, the need to test true love, and the value of education. Appearance versus reality is most clearly demonstrated in Act 5, when both the men and women don masks. Throughout the play, though, there is a significant discrepancy between the way the men view the women and who the ladies actually are. The men invoke images of goddesses, madonnas, and other perfect embodiments to describe the ladies. The women, however, understand that they are no such creatures and are not flattered by such

comparisons. Indeed, the Princess and her attendants wish to be seen as they are, not how the men choose to view them. Along with this, they wish for honesty and simple courtship, not the exaggerated language each man has penned for his love. As the play draws to a close, the Princess tells the King that the women do not believe that the men have been serious in their pursuits. They appeared to be courting for sport, not for love. By focusing on the appearance of the ladies and not their inner selves, the men have failed to connect to their loves as they would have liked. The women viewed the men's courting efforts as just courtly fun because their actions gave the appearance of frivolity, hiding their real feelings of love.

The pastoral setting and constant violation of oaths reveal a theme of nature versus society. The King and his men have difficulty upholding the laws of Navarre, most of which they have created. When the play moves to the forest, all oaths are broken, with little consequence. By refusing to follow the arbitrary rules of society, the men become aware of their own wants and desires. While courting the women, the men try to follow courtly rules of romance, which end in disaster. The women rebuke the men and doubt their intentions. When they shed the constraints of courtly norms, the men confess their feelings clearly, and the women seem optimistic that in time, the three sets of couples will be reunited. There is little doubt that the relationships would not have included such honesty if the men had followed the rules of their world. The audience is hopeful that the couples will reunite in the future because all are revealing their true selves, which were explored in the woods. It is through the natural setting and by forgoing the rules of society that the men are able to explore and express their natural feelings of love.

As the play ends in an ambiguous, unresolved way, the reader is left to question what message about love Shakespeare is conveying. If we believe that the lovers will continue their relationships after the year of separation, the theme of testing love becomes apparent. In the last scene of the play, the Princess challenges the King to a test of his love: He must complete one year of solitary study as proof of his love for her. Words have proven to be so ineffective in the play, so the characters must now turn to actions to prove their love. Even Don Armado promises to wait three years for Jaquenetta, although the audience is quite certain that his labor of love will not prove fruitful. Great love must be able to withstand trials and difficult times. The Princess believes that the only way for the King to prove his love is to pass her test. Once he has completed his year of study, she will know that his love is true. As the King's true intentions toward the Princess have been revealed, the audience is optimistic that he will be successful in passing her test and completing his year of study.

The most important theme found in *Love's Labour's Lost* is that of the importance of education, both scholarly and of the world. The play begins and ends with the men preparing to seclude themselves in study. They have neglected their academic pursuits and must return to them. The rest of the play, however, focuses on the education that can only be gained outside the classroom or library. Berowne immediately bristles at the thought at having to leave society in order to study. When the Princess and her ladies arrive, he convinces the others that studying the women and pursuing love are educational pursuits. The natural world offers valuable lessons that cannot be found within a book, and the play celebrates the notion that self-taught education is just as important as traditional education. By watching the men of Navarre grow from immature rule breakers to determined men in love, the audience sees that learning about themselves and their world is paramount to their development.

EXTRACTS OF CLASSIC CRITICISM
Samuel Johnson (1709–1784) [Excerpted from *The Plays of William Shakespeare* (1765). In his landmark edition of Shakespeare's plays, Johnson comments on specific lines from *Love's Labour's Lost*, a few of which are below. His main complaint with most of the text in the play is that the language

is too vague and easily misinterpreted. Although Johnson takes issue with the many obscure phrases and overly wordy passages, overall, he views the play as an enjoyable comedy, containing many brilliant passages.]

> 1.1.31
> To love, to wealth, to pomp, I pine and
>   die;
> With all these, living in philosophy . . .

The stile of the rhyming scenes in this play is often entangled and obscure. I know not certainly to what *all these* is to be referred; I suppose he means, that he finds *love, pomp,* and *wealth* in *philosophy*.

> 1.1.75
> . . . while truth the while Doth falsly
>   blind . . .

Falsly is here, and in many other places, the same as *dishonestly* or *treacherously*. The whole sense of this gingling declamation is only this, that *a man by too close study may read himself blind,* which might have been told with less obscurity in fewer words.

> 1.1.82
> Who dazzling so, that eye shall be his
>   heed,
> And give him light, that it was blinded
>   by . . .

This is another passage unnecessarily obscure: the meaning is, that when he *dazzles,* that is, has his eye made weak, *by fixing his eye upon a fairer eye, that* fairer *eye shall be his heed,* his *direction* or *lode-star,* (see Midsummer-Night's Dream) *and give him light that was blinded by it.*

   . . . In this play, which all the editors have concurred to censure, and some have rejected as unworthy of our poet, it must be confessed that there are many passages mean, childish, and vulgar; and some which ought not to have been exhibited, as we are told they were, to a maiden queen. But there are scattered, through the whole, many sparks of genius; nor is there any play that has more evident marks of the hand of Shakespeare.

William Hazlitt (1778–1830)   [Excerpted from *Characters of Shakespear's Plays* (1817). Hazlitt is arguably one of the most important Shakespearean critics of the 19th century, particularly in regard to both his interest in character and his attempts to politicize the interpretations of Shakespeare's plays. Here, he offers some scathing criticism of *Love's Labour's Lost,* arguing that we could actually do without it in Shakespeare's canon. He dismisses excuses made for it by other critics and insists that it is an inferior play, although it does contain a few successful moments.]

If we were to part with any of the author's comedies, it should be this. Yet we should be loth to part with Don Adriano de Armado, that mighty potentate of nonsense, or his page, that handful of wit; with Nathaniel the curate, or Holofernes the schoolmaster, and their dispute after dinner on "the golden cadences of poesy"; with Costard the clown, or Dull the constable. Biron is too accomplished a character to be lost to the world, and yet he could not appear without his fellow courtiers and the king: and if we were to leave out the ladies, the gentlemen would have no mistresses. So that we believe we may let the whole play stand as it is, and we shall hardly venture to 'set a mark of reprobation on it'. Still we have some objections to the style, which we think savours more of the pedantic spirit of Shakespear's time than of his own genius; more of controversial divinity, and the logic of Peter Lombard, than of the inspiration of the Muse. It transports us quite as much to the manners of the court, and the quirks of courts of law, as to the scenes of nature or the fairyland of his own imagination. Shakespear has set himself to imitate the tone of polite conversation then prevailing among the fair, the witty, and the learned, and he has imitated it but too faithfully. It is as if the hand of Titian had been employed to give grace to the curls of a full-bottomed periwig, or Raphael had attempted to give expression to the tapestry figures in the House of Lords. Shakespear has put an excellent description of this fashionable jargon into the mouth of the critical Holofernes "as too picked, too spruce, too affected, too odd, as it were, too peregrinate, as I may call it"; and nothing can be more marked than the difference when he breaks loose from the trammels he had imposed on himself, "as light as bird from brake," and speaks in his own person. We think, for instance, that in the following soliloquy [3.1.170–202] the poet has fairly got the start of Queen Elizabeth and her maids of honour . . .

The character of Biron [Berowne] drawn by Rosaline and that which Biron gives of Boyet are equally happy. The observations on the use and abuse of study, and on the power of beauty to quicken the understanding as well as the senses, are excellent. The scene which has the greatest dramatic effect is that in which Biron, the king, Longaville, and Dumain, successively detect each other and are detected in their breach of their vow and in their profession of attachment to their several mistresses, in which they suppose themselves to be overheard by no one. The reconciliation between these lovers and their sweethearts is also very good, and the penance which Rosaline imposes on Biron, before he can expect to gain her consent to marry him, full of propriety and beauty.

. . . The famous cuckoo-song closes the play; but we shall add no more criticisms: "the words of Mercury are harsh after the songs of Apollo."

Samuel Taylor Coleridge (1772–1834)
[Excerpted from *Shakspeare, with Introductory Remarks on Poetry, the Drama, and the Stage* (1818). Coleridge, best known for poems such as *The Rime of the Ancient Mariner,* was also an inventive critic. Here he offers an analysis of *Love's Labour's Lost* that closely resembles much modern criticism. He contends that this play, though flawed, has many elements of genius and in general shows Shakespeare honing his craft. Moreover, it contains material that would have been much more accessible to Shakespeare's contemporary audience than it is to Coleridge's. Many flaws in the play may be attributable to changing times and ideas. Within the text, Coleridge sees the development of Shakespeare's use of characterization and logic.]

The characters in this play are either impersonated out of Shakspeare's own multiformity by imaginative self-position, or out of such a country town and a schoolboy's observation might supply,—the curate, the schoolmaster, the Armado (when even in my time was not extinct in the cheaper ins of North Wales), and so on. The satire is chiefly on follies of words. Biron [Berowne] and Rosaline are evidently the pre-existent state of Benedick and Beatrice, and so, perhaps, is Boyet of Lafeu, and Costard of the Tapster in *Measure for Measure;* and the frequency of the rhymes, the sweetness as well as the smoothness of the metre, and the number of acute and fancifully illustrated aphorisms, are all as they ought to be in a poet's youth. True genius begins by generalizing and condensing; it ends in realizing and expanding. It first collects the seeds.

Yet if this juvenile drama had been the only one extant of our Shakspeare, and we possessed the tradition only of his riper works, or accounts of them in writers who had not even mentioned this play,—how many of Shakspeare's characteristic features might we not still have discovered in *Love's Labour's Lost,* though as in a portrait of him taken in boyhood.

I can never sufficiently admire the wonderful activity of thought throughout the whole of the first scene of the play, rendered natural, as it is, by the choice of the characters, and the whimsical determination on which the drama is founded. . . . This sort of story, too, was admirably suited to Shakspeare's times, when the English court was still the foster-mother of the state and the muses; and when, in consequence, the courtiers, and men of rank and fashion, affected a display of wit, point, and sententious observation, what would be deemed

Armado releases Costard from custody so that he may deliver a letter to Jaquenetta in this 19th-century depiction of Act III, Scene 1 of *Love's Labour's Lost.* *(Illustration by John Ralston; engraving by J. Quartley)*

intolerable at present,—but which a hundred years of controversy, involving every great political, and every dear domestic, interest, had trained all but the lower classes to participate. . . .

Hence the comic matter chosen in the first instance is a ridiculous imitation or apery of this constant striving after logical precision, and subtle opposition of thoughts, together, with a making the most of every conception or image, by expressing it under the least expected property belonging to it, and this, again, rendered specially absurd by being applied to the most current subjects and occurrences. The phrases and modes of combination in argument were caught by the most ignorant from the custom of the age, and their ridiculous application of them is most amusingly exhibited in Costard; whilst examples suited only to the gravest propositions and impersonations, or apostrophes to abstract thoughts impersonated, which are in fact the natural language only of the most vehement agitations of the mind, are adopted by the coxcombry of Armado as mere artifices of ornament.

The same kind of intellectual action is exhibited in a more serious and elevated strain in many parts of the play. Biron's speech at the end of the fourth act is an excellent specimen of it. It is logic clothed in rhetoric;—but observe how Shakspeare, in his two-fold being of poet and philosopher, avails himself of it to convey profound truths in the most lively images,—the whole remaining faithful to the character supposed to utter the lines, and the expressions themselves constituting a further development of that character.

George Bernard Shaw (1856–1950) [Excerpted from a review in the journal *Our Corner* (1886). Here, the great playwright Shaw reviews a staged version of *Love's Labour's Lost* performed at the St James's Theatre. Although he cared little for the acting in the play, Shaw did have some positive comments about the play itself, though he also says that the play is outdated and that the characters and their mannerisms can be difficult for a modern audience to relate to. Still, he sees the play as enjoyable and entertaining if performed well. His review is important in that it focuses on the work as a play to be seen, not just a text to be read. Shaw seems to be surprised that the play was successful, presumably because he was aware of the problems found within the written text.]

The play itself showed more vitality than might have been expected. Three hundred years ago, its would-be wits, with their forced smartness, their indecent waggeries, their snobbish sneers at poverty, and their ill-bred and ill-natured mockery of age and natural infirmity, passed more easily as ideal compounds of soldier, court, and scholar than they can nowadays. . . .

The construction of the play is simple and effective. The only absolutely impossible situation was that of Biron [Berowne] hiding in the tree to overlook the king, who presently hides to watch Longaville, who in turn spies on Dumain; as the result of which we had three out of four gentlemen shouting "asides" through the sylvan stillness, No. 1 being inaudible to 2, 3, and 4; no.2 audible to No. 1 but not 3 and 4; No.3 audible to 1 and 2, but not to No. 4; and No. 4 audible to all the rest, but he himself temporarily stone deaf. Shakespear has certainly succeeded in making this arrangement intelligible; but the Dramatic Students' stage manager did not succeed in making it credible. For Shakespear's sake one can make-believe a good deal; but here the illusion was too thin. . . . On the whole, I am not sure that *Love's Labour's Lost* in worth reviving at this time of day; but I am bound to add that if it were announced to-morrow with an adequate cast, I should make a point of seeing it.

The King, Berowne, and Longaville hide as Dumaine enters reciting his poem to Katherine in Act IV, Scene 3 of *Love's Labour's Lost*. This is a print from Malcolm C. Salaman's 1916 edition of *Shakespeare in Pictorial Art*. *(Painting by Thomas Stothard)*

Walter Pater (1839–1894) [Excerpted from *Appreciations: With an Essay on Style* (1889). Pater was one of the great Victorian critics of literature and art and a master prose stylist. Here, he notes the many examples of courtly language in *Love's Labour's Lost*. He claims that this demonstration of the "foppery of delicate language" makes the play a success. While other critics condemn the text for its language, Pater asserts that what they contend are inferior passages are in fact intentionally so; he gives Shakespeare credit for consciously drafting flawed poems and speeches. Moreover, Pater believes that the audience can hear the voice of Shakespeare coming through the characters, specifically Ber-owne, analyzing his own early writing and making profound statements about the human condition.]

Love's Labours Lost is one of the earliest of Shakspere's dramas, and has many of the peculiarities of his poems, which are also the work of his earlier life. The opening speech of the king on the immortality of fame—on the triumph of fame over death—and the nobler parts of Biron [Berowne], display something of the monumental style of Shakspere's Sonnets, and are not without their concerts of thought and expression. This connection of *Love's Labours Lost* with Shakspere's poems is further enforced by the actual insertion in it of three sonnets and a faultless song; which, in accordance with his practice in other plays, are inwoven into the argument of the piece and, like the golden ornaments of a fair woman, give it a peculiar air of distinction. There is merriment in it also, with choice illustrations of both wit and humour; a laughter, often exquisite, ringing, if faintly, yet as genuine laughter still, though sometimes sinking into mere burlesque, which has not lasted quite so well. And Shakespere brings a serious effect out of the trifling of his characters. A dainty love-making is interchanged with the more cumbrous play: below the many artifices of Biron's amorous speeches we may trace sometimes the "unutterable longing"; and the lines in which Katherine describes the blighting through love of her younger sister are one of the most touching things in older literature. Again, how many echoes seem awakened by those strange words, actually said in jest! "The sweet war-man (Hector of Troy) is dead and rotten; sweet chucks, beat not the bones of the buried: when he breathed, he was a man!"—words which may remind us of Shakspere's own epitaph. In the last scene, an ingenious turn is given to the action, so that the piece does not conclude after the manner of other comedies.—

> Our wooing doth not end like an old
>   play;
> Jack hath not Jill:

and Shakspere strikes a passionate note across it at last, in the entrance of the messenger, who announces to the princess that the king her father is suddenly dead.

The merely dramatic interest of the piece is slight enough; only just sufficient, indeed, to form the vehicle of its wit and poetry. The scene—a park of the King of Navarre—is unaltered throughout; and the unity of the play is not so much the unity of a drama as that of a series of pictorial groups, in which the same figures reappear, in different combinations but on the same background. It is as if Shakspere had intended to bind together, by some inventive conceit, the devices of an ancient tapestry, and give voices to its figures. On one side, a fair palace; on the other, the tents of the Princess of France, who has come on an embassy from her father to the King of Navarre; in the midst, a wide space of smooth grass.

The same personages are combined over and over again into a series of gallant scenes—the princess, the three masked ladies, the quaint, pedantic king; one of those amiable kings men have never loved enough, whose serious occupation with the things of the mind seems, by contrast with the more usual forms of kingship, like frivolity or play. Some of the figures are grotesque merely, and all the male ones at least, a little fantastic. Certain objects reappearing from scene to scene—love-letters crammed with verses to the margin, and lovers' toys—hint obscurely at some story of intrigue. Between these groups, on a smaller scale, come the slighter and more homely episodes, with Sir Nathaniel the curate, the country-maid Jaquenetta, Moth or Mote the elfin-page, with Hiems and Ver, who recite "the dialogue that the two learned men have compiled in praise of the owl and the cuckoo." The ladies are lodged in tents, because the king, like the princess of the modern poet's fancy, has taken a vow "to make his court a little Academe" and for three years' space no woman may come within a mile of it; and the play shows how this artificial attempt was broken through. For the king and his three fellow-scholars are of course soon forsworn, and turn to writing sonnets, each to his chosen lady. These fellow-scholars of the king—"quaint votaries of science" at first, afterwards "affection's men-at-arms"—three youthful knights, gallant, amorous, chivalrous, but also a little affected, sporting always a curious foppery of language, are, throughout, the leading figures in the foreground; one of them, in particular, being more carefully depicted than the others, and in himself very noticeable—a portrait with somewhat puzzling manner and expression, which at once catches the eye irresistibly and keeps it fixed.

Play is often that about which people are most serious; and the humourist may observe how, under all love of playthings, there is almost always hidden an appreciation of something really engaging and delightful. This is true always of the toys of children: it is often true of the playthings of grown-up people, their vanities, their fopperies even, their lighter loves; the cynic would add their pursuit of fame. Certainly, this is true without exception of the playthings of a past age, which to those who succeed it are always full of a pensive interest—old manners, old dresses, old houses. For what is called fashion in these matters occupies, in each age, much of the care of many of the most discerning people, furnishing them with a kind of mirror of their real inward refinements, and their capacity for selection. Such modes or fashions are, at their best, an example of the artistic predominance of form over matter; of the manner of the doing of it over the thing done; and have a beauty of their own. It is so with that old euphuism of the Elizabethan age—that pride of dainty language and curious expression, which it is very easy to ridicule, which often made itself ridiculous, but which had below it a real sense of fitness and nicety; and which, as we see in this very play, and still more clearly in the Sonnets, had some fascination for the young Shakspere himself. It is this foppery of delicate language, this fashionable plaything of his time, with which Shakspere is occupied in *Love's Labours Lost*. He shows us the manner in all its stages; passing from the grotesque and vulgar pedantry of Holofernes, through the extravagant but polished caricature of Armado, to become the peculiar characteristic of a real though still quaint poetry in Biron himself, who is still chargeable even at his best with just a little affectation. As Shakespere laughs broadly at it in Holofernes or Armado, so he is the analyst of its curious charm in Biron; and this analysis involves a delicate raillery by Shakspere.

As happens with every true dramatist, Shakspere is for the most part hidden behind the persons of his creation. Yet there are certain of his characters in which we feel that there is something of self-portraiture. And it is not so much in his grander, more subtle and ingenious creations that we feel this—in Hamlet and King Lear—as in those slighter and more spontaneously developed figures, who, while far from playing principal parts, are yet distinguished by a peculiar happiness and delicate ease in the drawing of them; figures which possess, above all, that winning attractiveness which there is no man but would willingly exercise, and which resemble those works of art which, though not meant to be very great or imposing, are yet wrought of the choicest material. Mercutio, in Romeo and Juliet, belongs to this group of Shakspere's characters—versatile, mercurial people, such as make good actors, and in whom

the "nimble spirits of the arteries," the finer but still merely animal elements of great wit, predominate. A careful delineation of minor, yet expressive traits seems to mark them out as the characters of his predilection; and it is hard not to identify him with these more than with others. Biron, in *Love's Labours Lost*, is perhaps the most striking member of this group. In this character, which is never quite in touch, never quite on a perfect level of understanding, with the other persons of the play, we see, perhaps, a reflex of Shakspere himself, when he has just become able to stand aside from and estimate the first period of his poetry.

MODERN CRITICISM AND CRITICAL CONTROVERSIES

Most modern critics are generally in agreement that the play, although flawed, is enjoyable and entertaining. Many point out that it was undoubtedly more successful when originally performed than it can be now simply because the play contains so many references to the politics, events, and characters of Shakespeare's day.

Dating the play to early in Shakespeare's career allows for many of its flaws to be seen as experimentation or lack of practice. The critic Marjorie Garber argues that great moments from future plays, such as the interaction between Beatrice and Benedick in *Much Ado About Nothing* and the wise fool found in *A Midsummer Night's Dream* were anticipated in *Love's Labour's Lost*. Without Berowne and Rosaline's witty discussions or Costard's wisdom dressed in foolish language, these other characters would not exist. Alfred Harbage refutes the notion that this play could have been written toward the middle of Shakespeare's career, an argument that he feels is made in an attempt to elevate the play by moving it away from the Bard's early days. Instead, Harbage contends that the play can only fit into the beginning of Shakespeare's career, since it stylistically matches things written in the 1590s far better than those plays written in the following decade. Harbage points to the

"French" aspects of the play, specifically the names of the King's men, and the juvenile aspects of the play. He goes so far as to label *Love's Labour's Lost* a children's play, although most other critics would likely disagree with this assertion.

Many modern critics believe that the success of the play is due mainly to the playful use of language found within. John Dover Wilson calls the play a "feast of languages," echoing the text itself. Frank Kermode describes Shakespeare's Navarre as a "world of delightful artifice" (82). Wilson identifies a complex pattern of language, with groupings of poems and songs created to deliberately celebrate poetry. Kermode praises the different dialects that Shakespeare has created, ranging from the courtly men to the boastful Don Armado and the overly wordy Holofernes. Harold Bloom describes *Love's Labour's Lost* as "an exuberant fireworks display in which Shakespeare seems to seek the limits of his verbal resources, and discovers that there are none" (121). According to Bloom, the interaction between Berowne and Rosaline more than any of the other characters demonstrates Shakespeare's mastery with language.

W. H. Auden believes the play is successful because of its combination of satire and ties to the neoclassical movement prevalent in Shakespeare's time. The critic sees the text as a satire of humanist education, courtly love, and art. Many of the flaws that others have found in the play Auden attributes to satire, which explains many of the shortcomings in language or character development. Moreover, the play demonstrates many of the ideas it is satirizing, and these are important concepts in Renaissance society. According to Auden, Shakespeare's audience would recognize the importance of cultural norms of courtly society that are simultaneously dramatized and mocked.

Like George Bernard Shaw, several modern critics have noted the dramatically different effects of reading and viewing *Love's Labour's Lost*. Garber states that the play "reads 'hard' and plays 'easy'" (186). Other critics agree that the witty use of language is also improved by live performance. Moreover, the lack of detailed plot and the less developed characters seem less problematic when the play is staged.

Nonetheless, there are still quite a few critics who cannot see past the obvious shortcomings of the play. Koshi Nakanori believes that the lack of plot is the central problem. As characterization is closely linked to plot, the characters see virtually no development. Harbage contends that the characters are "barbarous." He even argues that the most moral character in the play is Don Armado, who, although ridiculous because of his language, treats others with kindness and appropriate decorum, most notably the Princess. The other characters, Harbage surmises, talk ill of one another and vilify one another's intended mates in language that borders on cruelty. A. D. Nuttall describes a panicked energy that exists throughout the entire play, which, like the cruel language, compromises the lightness that a play about love and language should contain.

Love's Labour's Lost contains an unusual amount of topical references to events and people of Shakespeare's day, as many critics have noted. For example, critics such as Harold Goddard see Berowne's refusal to study as a criticism of the School of Night, a group that included Raleigh, Christopher Marlowe, and Thomas Harriot and was supposedly dedicated to studying the sciences. Although the group's existence was never confirmed, it was talked about in court circles, and its members were rumored to be atheists. Such allusions are often lost on modern audiences, making the play at times seem tedious. Stephen Greenblatt believes that Holofernes is a parody of the English schoolmaster, verbose and haughty, that existed in so many schools at the time. Greenblatt even ties Holofernes's lengthy analyses to the popular educational technique of Shakespeare's time, which included translating Erasmus's *On Copiousness*, "a book that taught students 150 different ways of saying (in Latin, of course) 'Thank you for your letter'" (124). Shakespeare's audience would have recognized the parodies of both the archetypal schoolmaster and the day's most popular, if painful, mode of study.

THE PLAY TODAY

Recent critics have tended to focus on the intricate language of the play as well as on more contemporary themes, such as masculinity in the play. Some have also commented on the problems in the original text, in which some passages appear to have been printed twice and other obvious mistakes are made.

Love's Labour's Lost is a difficult play for modern audiences to understand, but its witty language and romantic encounters can still be successful on stage and screen. Modern performances often focus on the jovial friendships between the King and his men and the silliness of men in love.

The BBC produced a televised version of the play in 1985. This adaptation focused on the intricate wordplay and various comic interludes provided by the characters in Shakespeare's text. The cast consisted mainly of Royal Shakespeare Company actors, such as Jonathan Kent as the King, Maureen Lipman as the Princess, and David Warner as Don Armado. This version follows the original text closely and is performed in Elizabethan costumes and sets. It stays true to the tradition of Shakespeare onstage and is a particularly appropriate adaptation to watch while studying Shakespeare's text.

The Royal Shakespeare Company staged the play in England in 2008 and at various U.S. locations in 2009. The play received positive reviews from the *Daily Telegraph, Daily Mail,* and *Guardian.* Most reviewers agreed that the production captured the witty tone and fun nature of Shakespeare's original text.

The most notable film version of the play is the 2000 adaptation, directed by Kenneth Branagh, who also starred as Berowne. The film also features Alicia Silverstone as the Princess and Nathan Lane as Costard. It is set in a 1930s version of Navarre, and the characters sing and dance to easily recognizable songs by Irving Berlin, George and Ira Gershwin, and Cole Porter. The mixtures of Shakespeare's language and the more modern components do not work entirely well together, with the language of the play often pushed aside by musical numbers or plot synopsis done through faux newsreels. Nonetheless, the film does capture the playful essence of Shakespeare's original, particularly with regard to the romances. The archetypal characters, Armado, Holofernes, and Dull, are updated with a traditional comedic approach that classic films generally give to minor characters.

FIVE TOPICS FOR DISCUSSION AND WRITING

1. **Human nature versus society:** What stance does the text take on human nature as it intersects with society? Does the play favor one over the other? Do any characters represent solely either human nature or society?

2. **Traditional education versus worldly education:** What difference does the play make between education found in a traditional setting, such as a classroom, and learning that can only occur in the real world? Is one valued over the over? If so, which characters demonstrate the superiority of one over the other?

3. **Love at first sight versus tested love:** Most characters in Shakespeare's comedies fall in love at first sight. Does this also occur in this play? How does the ending uphold or contradict the notion of love at first sight? Does the text support one notion of love over the other?

4. **Importance of language:** *Love's Labour's Lost* is a play above all else about language. What specifically does the text reveal about language? How is language related to education, interpersonal relations, and status in society?

5. **Appearance versus reality:** The play includes several instances of false appearance—something appears to be so but is not. What can the reader learn about appearance and reality from the play? Does the play make a statement about false impressions or deceptions? How do these relate specifically to courtship?

Bibliography

Auden, W. H. *Lectures on Shakespeare.* Princeton, N.J.: Princeton University Press, 2000.

Bloom, Harold. *Shakespeare: The Invention of the Human.* New York: Riverhead Books, 1998.

Boyce, Charles. *Critical Companion to William Shakespeare*. New York: Facts On File, 2005.

Carroll, William. *The Great Feast of Languages in Love's Labour's Lost*. Princeton, N.J.: Princeton University Press, 1976.

Garber, Marjorie. *Shakespeare After All*. New York: Anchor Books, 2005.

Goddard, Harold. *The Meaning of Shakespeare,* Vol. 1. Chicago: University of Chicago Press, 1951.

Greenblatt, Stephen. *Will in the World*. New York: W. W. Norton, 2004.

Harbage, Alfred. *Shakespeare and the Rival Traditions*. New York: MacMillan, 1952.

Hardison Londres, Felicia, ed. Love's Labour's Lost: *Critical Essays*. New York: Garland Publishing, 1997.

Kermode, Frank. *Shakespeare's Language*. New York: Farrar, Straus & Giroux, 2000.

Nuttall, A. D. *Shakespeare the Thinker*. New Haven, Conn.: Yale University Press, 2007.

Scott, Charlotte. *Shakespeare and the Idea of the Book*. Oxford: Oxford University Press, 2007.

Traversi, Derek. *William Shakespeare: The Early Comedies*. London: Longmans Green, 1964.

Wells, Stanley. *Shakespeare: A Life in Drama*. New York: Norton, 1997.

Wilson, John Dover. *The Essential Shakespeare*. Cambridge: Cambridge University Press, 1962.

Yates, Frances. *A Study of* Love's Labour's Lost. Folcroft, Pa.: Folcroft Press, 1969.

FILM AND VIDEO PRODUCTIONS

Branagh, Kenneth, dir. *Love's Labour's Lost*. With Alicia Silverstone and Nathan Lane. Miramax, 2000.

Illif, Noel, dir. *Love's Labour's Lost*. BBC Radio, 1946.

Jenkins, Roger, dir. *Love's Labour's Lost*. BBC, 1965.

Moshinsky, Elijah, dir. *Love's Labour's Lost*. BBC, 1985.

Spenser, David, dir. *Love's Labour's Lost*. BBC Radio, 1979.

—Jolene C. Mendel

Macbeth

INTRODUCTION

Macbeth is the last of Shakespeare's four great tragedies *(Hamlet, Othello,* and *King Lear),* and many readers find it the most powerful. In *Life of Mrs. Siddons* (1834), the poet Thomas Campbell called *Macbeth* "the greatest treasure of our dramatic literature" (volume II, 6), comparing it to the works of Aeschylus. The contemporary critic Harold Bloom has said that *Macbeth* "surpasses" the other three great Shakespearean tragedies "in maintaining a continuous pitch of tragic intensity, in making everything overwhelmingly dark with meaning" *(Modern Critical* 2).

As in all great tragedies, the struggle in *Macbeth* is played out within the mind of the protagonist. This conflict begins in Act I, Scene 3, when Macbeth first appears, and persists until his death. Even more than *Hamlet, Macbeth* is a play about the struggle between conscience and desire. Like Raskolnikov in Fyodor Dostoyevsky's *Crime and Punishment* (1865), Macbeth gains sympathy through the author's revelation of the tormented mind that rebels against the horrible actions the character commits. Malcolm dismisses Macbeth as a "butcher" (5.9.35) because the young king sees only the cruelty the tyrant has perpetrated against others. The audience, however, sees a complex, suffering human being who "on the torture of the mind [lies] / In restless ecstasy" (3.2.21–22). When Raskolnikov, in *Crime and Punishment,* confesses his killings to Sonya, she exclaims, "What have you done to yourself?" The same could be asked of Macbeth. Perhaps his worst crime is the violation of his own nature. *Macbeth* might take as its epigraph Ophelia's lament for the seemingly mad prince of Denmark: "O, what a noble mind is here o'erthrown!" *(Hamlet,* 3.1.150). Too late, Macbeth discovers that he has gained a small portion of the world in exchange for his soul, that for "a barren scepter" he has given his "eternal jewel / . . . to the common enemy of man" (3.1.61, 67–68). That common enemy turns out to be himself. Banquo asks the witches to "look into the seeds of time, / And say which grain will grow" (1.3.58–59). For Macbeth, these prove to be the seeds of his own

Macbeth and Banquo encounter the witches in Act I, Scene 3 of *Macbeth.* This print was published by Gebbie & Husson Company in 1888. *(Painting by George Romne)*

destruction. As Albert Camus observed in *The Rebel,* "Rebellion, when it gets out of hand, swings from the annihilation of others to the destruction of the self."

BACKGROUND

Although *Macbeth* appears among the tragedies in the First Folio (1623), it could also be considered a kind of history play. Shakespeare's chief source for *Macbeth* was Raphael Holinshed's *Chronicles of England, Scotland, and Ireland* (1577; second edition, 1587), which also supplied material for his historical plays. In *Macbeth,* however, Shakespeare played even faster and looser with Holinshed than he customarily did in his other plays. *Macbeth* fuses many incidents from Holinshed. Perhaps the most obvious is Holinshed's story of Natholocus (242–280), who sends a follower to consult a witch about the outcome of a revolt. The witch

tells this man he will kill the king. The man scoffs at the idea, but then he fears that if he reports this prophecy, Natholocus will execute him, so he fulfills the witch's prediction by stabbing the king with a dagger (the same weapon Macbeth uses to assassinate Duncan).

Shakespeare also drew on Holinshed's account of the reign of King Duff (952–967). Duff kills rebels related to Donwald despite Donwald's plea to spare their lives. Goaded by his desire for revenge and by his wife, Donwald kills Duff when the king is visiting Donwald's castle at Forres, much as Macbeth kills the visiting king, Duncan. But Donwald does not commit the murder himself; he engages four servants to undertake the crime. When the king is found dead the next morning, Donwald feigns ignorance and later kills the chamberlains who were supposed to be guarding Duff and who are suspected of being the murderers,

This 19th-century painting erroneously depicts Shakespeare reciting *Macbeth* before the court of Elizabeth. *(Painting by Eduard Ender; engraving by George Edward and J. L. Giles)*

just as Macbeth executes the chamberlains who are blamed for Duncan's death. Though some suspect Donwald, he is too powerful to be accused. Holinshed records that "for the space of six moneths together, after this heinous murther thus committed, there appeared no sunne by day, nor moone by night in anie part of the realme, . . . and sometimes such outrageous windes arose, with lightenings and tempests, that people were in great feare of present destruction". The *Chronicles* add that the horses in Lothian become cannibalistic and an owl kills a hawk; similar events are recounted in *Macbeth* in Act II, Scene 4, after Duncan's death. Donwald, his wife, and the four murderers are captured and executed. The sun then shines, and flowers bloom "clear contrarie to the time and season of the yeere". This reference may have influenced Shakespeare's linking images of fertility to Duncan and Malcolm.

Yet another episode from Holinshed that Shakespeare uses derives from the reign of Kenneth III, who kills his nephew, Duff's son, so that Kenneth's own offspring will rule. Afterward, Holinshed relates, "a voice was heard as he [Kenneth] was in bed in the night time to take his rest, uttering unto him these or the like woords in effect, 'Thinke not Kenneth that the wicked slaughter of Malcolm Duffe by thee contrived, is kept secret from the knowledge of the eternall God.'" Macbeth tries to kill Banquo and Banquo's son to prevent their line from ruling Scotland, and after killing Duncan, Macbeth hears a voice condemning his deed. The voice Kenneth hears foretells his death and that of his children. Kenneth is killed by Fenella, whose son he had ordered executed, just as Macbeth is killed by Macduff, whose children he murdered. When Kenneth fails to emerge from his chamber, according to Holinshed, his servants "knocked at the doore softlie, then they rapped hard therat." Perhaps this sound suggested to Shakespeare the knocking at the south gate of Macbeth's castle at Inverness after Duncan is murdered.

The historical Duncan became king in 1034. Though Shakespeare makes Duncan an ideal monarch, Holinshed describes him as "soft and gentle," whereas his cousin Macbeth is "somewhat cruel of nature"; his excessive leniency leads to a rebellion by Macdonwald, who is joined by Irish kerns, light foot soldiers. (Interestingly, *Skene's Scots Acts* [1597] describes Duncan as "a good and modest Prince," thus contradicting Holinshed and perhaps explaining Shakespeare's favorable view of the slain monarch.) This is the revolt described in Act I, Scene 2. Macbeth defeats the king's enemies, and Macdonwald kills himself. To add luster to Macbeth's military success, Shakespeare has his hero kill the rebel in hand-to-hand combat. Shakespeare fuses a separate Norwegian invasion with the rebellion; the payment for burial that Norway's king Sweno offers in the play (1.2.60–62) was, in Holinshed, paid by King Canute of England after his unsuccessful attack on Scotland.

After these wars, Holinshed recounts, "It fortuned as Makbeth and Banquho journied towards Fores, where the king then laie, . . . suddenlie in the middest of a laund, there met them three women in strange and wild apparel, resembling creatures of elder world." Shakespeare describes the famous meeting between the women, Macbeth, and Banquo in Act I, Scene 3. Banquo asks about his future and is told, as in the play, that "thou in deed shalt not reigne at all, but of thee those shall be borne which shall govern the Scottish kingdome by long order of continuall descent." Banquo was first described in print by Hector Boece, whose 1527 *Scotorum Historiae* is the source for Holinshed's Scottish history. At the time, the Stuarts who were then reigning in Scotland, and who ruled England from 1603 to 1714, traced their lineage to Banquo. According to Boece, the women are "weird sisters or wiches," making them perhaps instruments of fate. In the First Folio they are called "weyward" or "weyard"; modern editions tend to follow Lewis Theobald's 1733 alteration to "weird," but Shakespeare may not have intended them to be as powerful as Boece imagined.

For Holinshed, the women's prophecy first plants the idea of monarchy in Macbeth's mind. But, Shakespeare indicates, through Macbeth's reaction to their words and by Lady Macbeth's comment (1.7.47–52), that he had been thinking about seizing the throne and had spoken to his wife on this topic before he first heard the prediction. According to Holinshed, despite the prophecy of his kingship, Macbeth "thought with himselfe that he must tarie a time, which should advance him thereto (by the divine providence) as it had come to passe in his former preferment" to Thane of Cawdor, which the women had predicted. So, in the play, he meditates, "If chance will have me king, why, chance may crowne me / Without my stir" (1.3.143–144). Then Duncan names his own son Malcolm as his successor. In Holinshed's account, Macbeth has a better claim to the throne, and since Scotland had an elected monarchy at the time, Duncan had no right to name the next king. Shakespeare denies Macbeth any legitimate claim to rule Scotland.

Macbeth now plots to seize the crown. Holinshed writes that the women's prediction encourages him, "but speciallie his wife lay sore upon him to attempt the thing, as she that was verie ambitious, burning in unquenchable desire to beare the name of a queene." According to Boece, she "calland him oft tymes febill cowart and nocht desirous of honouris, sen he durst nocht assailye the thing with manhood and corage quhilk is offert to him be [by] benevolence of fortoun." Shakespeare obscures Lady Macbeth's motivation, but in Act I, Scene 5 and 7 she gives him "gret artacioun [prompting] to persew" Duncan's murder, as Boece writes, and assails his manhood. In 1046, the historical Macbeth, together with other nobles, including Banquo, killed Duncan, and Macbeth became king. Shakespeare exonerates Banquo; it is obviously significant that in Shakespeare's time, Banquo's descendant James was reigning in Scotland and England and was the patron of Shakespeare's acting company.

The sources give Macbeth 10 years of good rule before he becomes a tyrant and 17 years overall. Shakespeare's chronology is unclear, but the play's brevity and fast pace suggest that his reign was brief, and Macbeth moves from crime to crime without interruption. Fearing Banquo, Macbeth invites him to dinner and has him killed outside the palace. Banquo's son, Fleance, whom Macbeth also wanted dead, flees (3.1, 3.3). These details appear in Holinshed. Macbeth is warned against Macduff. In Boece, the warning comes from witches; in Holinshed, from wizards. Shakespeare simplifies his casting by using the same women who predicted his kingship.

Learning of Macduff's flight to England, Macbeth, in Holinshed, besieges Macduff's castle and is admitted by the unsuspecting inhabitants, all of whom he kills. In Shakespeare's play, however, Macbeth employs others to commit this greatest of his atrocities. Macduff has left his family to persuade Malcolm to claim the Scottish throne. To test Macduff's sincerity, Malcolm feigns unworthiness, calling himself lustful, greedy, and deceitful. As this scene plays out, Malcolm's third self-accusation is more serious: "had I pow'r, I should / Pour the sweet milk of concord into hell, / Uproar the universal peace, confound / All unity on earth" (4.3.97–100). These lines would sound especially offensive in 1606 during the reign of James I, who prided himself as a peacemaker and the unifier of England and Scotland. On July 31, 1606, when James and his brother-in-law passed through London, a pageant reflecting this self-image was staged for them. In it, "Divine *Concord* as sent from Heaven, descended in a cloud from the toppe unto the middle stage, and with a loud voice, spake an excellent speech in Latine, purporting their heartie welcome, with heavenly happiness of *peace* and *unitie* among Christian Princes," according to Edmond Howes, in *Continuation of Stowe's Chronicle* (1615). Yet, when assured of Macduff's integrity, Malcolm retracts his self-accusations, he says he is "unknown to woman, never was forsworn" (4.3.126), as though he were rejecting the third charge he had leveled against himself in Holinshed. Did Shakespeare initially copy his source and then change his text, perhaps after viewing the pageant?

Malcolm invades Scotland with 10,000 men led by his uncle Old Siward. Both Holinshed and Boece call Siward Malcolm's grandfather, but

Shakespeare actually got the genealogy correct. In *The Royal Play of* Macbeth (1950), Henry N. Paul notes that Lawrence Fletcher, an English actor who had gone to Scotland to serve James and had returned south when James assumed the English throne, was a member of Shakespeare's company when the playwright was composing *Macbeth*. Fletcher may have explained the Siward-Malcolm relationship and that the Seytons were traditional armor-bearers to the Scottish kings (5.3, 5.5); he may even have told Shakespeare that Lady Macbeth had been previously married and had had a child by her first husband, which is cryptically alluded to in the play (1.7.54–58). According to Holinshed, when Macbeth sees Birnam Wood coming to Dunsinane (5.4, 5.5), he flees. Shakespeare gives him more resolution. In both play and Holinshed, Macduff confronts Macbeth. In the play, Macbeth initially refuses to fight because "my soul is too much charg'd / With blood of thine already" (5.8.5–6). He retains a sense of guilt as well as bravery to the end. Macduff insists on battle and declares he was not born of woman. Macbeth has no words in Holinshed; Macduff decapitates him forthwith. In the play, Macbeth refuses to yield and dies fighting. In both play and history, Malcolm succeeds to the throne and for the first time in Scottish history creates earls (5.9).

Holinshed, unlike Shakespeare, does not concentrate on Macbeth's mental state. He does observe, however, "[T]he prick of conscience (as it chanceth euer in tyrants, and such as atteine to anie estate by vnrighteous means) caused him euer to feare, least [lest] he should be serued of the same cup, as he had ministred to his predecessor." This image of the cup and the fear of retribution may underlie Macbeth's lines "This even-handed justice / Commends th' ingredience of our poison'd chalice / To our own lips" (1.7.10–12).

Shakespeare may have supplemented Holinshed with other histories. George Buchanan's *Rerum Scoticarum Historia* (1582) records that Donaldus (Donwald in Holinshed) is goaded by his wife's "bitter words" to kill Duff. Buchanan tells of Donaldus's making the king's attendants drunk before

killing the ruler. These incidents appear in the play. Buchanan rejected the supernatural elements in Holinshed, claiming that Macbeth dreams of three beautiful women who promise him the kingship. Andrew of Wyntoun's *Orygynale Cronykill of Scotland* (ca. 1420) treats the three weird sisters as a fantasy of Macbeth's imagination, too. Shakespeare almost certainly did not see Andrew's account, since it was still in manuscript during Shakespeare's life, but Buchanan might have read it. Shakespeare leaves ambiguous the question of the witches' reality. Buchanan, unlike Holinshed, claims Macbeth was thinking of kingship even before his dream of the prophecy. For Buchanan, guilt rather than fear turns Macbeth into a tyrant. Shakespeare's Macbeth suffers from both.

Shakespeare turned to Scottish history for a play because in 1603 James VI of Scotland assumed the English throne, as well, becoming King James I. The story of Macbeth seemed especially likely to please James for a variety of reasons. James traced his lineage to Banquo. James had, like Duncan, been the subject of assassination plots: In 1600, John Ruthven, earl of Gowrie, invited James to his castle and tried to kill him there. In 1604, the King's Men, Shakespeare's company, twice performed a play based on this event (*The Tragedy of Gowrie,* now lost), but the Privy Council forbid further productions because it dealt with a living monarch and addressed contemporary political issues too overtly. Another, even more recent attempt on James's life was the Gunpowder Plot, in which a group of disaffected Catholics sought to blow up the houses of Parliament and the king when he addressed the opening session on November 5, 1605. In July 1606, a plot by Captain William Neuce to kill James was uncovered.

James also had a deep interest in witches. In 1597, he published *Daemonologie* on this subject. He credited them with the ability to predict the future and warned that the devil can make himself "so to be trusted in these little thinges, that he may haue the better commoditie therafter to deceiue them in the end with a tricke once for all." Banquo echoes this sentiment: "And oftentimes, to win us to our harm, / The instruments of darkness tell us truths, / Win us with honest trifles, to betray's / In deepest consequence" (1.3.123–126). James also wrote that witches can raise storms, which they do in Act I, Scene 1 and threaten to do in Act I, Scene 3. He claimed that witches prefer solitary places; in the play, all four of their scenes are set in such terrain. He also asserted that the devil can "thicken and obscure the air . . . that the beams of any other man's eye cannot pierce through the same to see them." The word *thicken* appears repeatedly in the play, and in Act I, Scene 5, Lady Macbeth calls upon night to hide the murder of Duncan. For all his concern with the power of evil, James wrote that the devil can deceive "only such, as first willfully deceive themselves, by running unto him." The witches in the play predict but do not compel.

The idea for *Macbeth* may have come from a visit James paid to St. John's College, Oxford, on August 27, 1605. To welcome him, Matthew Gwinn, a fellow of St. John's, wrote *Tres Sibyllae,* in which three students dressed as sibyls greeted the king. The first student referred to the prophecy that Banquo's descendants would rule forever, a message repeated in the procession of kings in Act IV, Scene 1 of *Macbeth,* and then greeted James as king of Scotland. The second welcomed him as king of England; and the third, as ruler of Ireland. Macbeth, too, receives a three-fold greeting from the witches as Thane of Glamis, Thane of Cawdor, "King hereafter" (1.3.48–50). James's entertainment at Oxford included 10 disputations. One of the debates dealt with the question of whether the imagination can produce real effects. In *Macbeth,* the answer is yes. Another session considered whether a child took in manners with its mother's milk. Perhaps Lady Macbeth's reference to breast-feeding (1.7.54–55) owes something to this discussion.

As he always did, Shakespeare drew on classical authors in composing this play. Thomas Newton had translated Seneca's tragedies in 1581, and Shakespeare might have read them in Latin as well. Banquo's avenging ghost derives from a stock feature in Senecan drama. Seneca's Medea prepares a brew resembling the witches' concoction in Act IV, Scene 1, and in book 7 of Ovid's *Metamorphoses,* she does so as well. Shakespeare knew this Ovidian passage; he adapts part of it in *The Tempest* (5.1.33–57). In Seneca's *Agamemnon,* Cassandra sees "The gobs of bloode downe dropping on the wynde," just as Macbeth sees "gouts of blood" on the mind-drawn dagger (2.1.46). In John Studley's 1566 translation of *Agamemnon,* the Chorus in Act 1 observes that rulers are never secure enough to say "To morrow shall we rule, as we have don to daye. / One clod of croked [crooked] care another bryngeth in, / One hurlye burlye done, another doth begin." These lines may have inspired Macbeth's famous soliloquy in Act V, Scene 5 as well as the second witch's statement that they will meet again "When the hurly-burly's done" (1.1.3). Seneca, in that speech, refers to "Slepe that doth overcome and breake the bondes of greefe (2.1.38–41). In *Hercules Furens,* the title character kills his wife and children. Afterward, he laments that rivers and the North Sea cannot "my right hande now wash from gylt." A similar passage appears in Seneca's *Phaedra.* Macbeth (2.2.57–60) and Lady Macbeth (5.1.50–51) both express a similar sentiment.

Shakespeare used Plutarch as a source for *Julius Caesar,* written just before *Macbeth,* and he would turn to that historian again for *Antony and Cleopatra,* the tragedy he wrote after *Macbeth.* Macbeth's refusal to "play the Roman fool and die / On mine own sword" (5.8.1–2) refers to either Brutus or Antony, both of whom killed themselves this way. Like Cleopatra, Macbeth refuses to yield to become a spectacle for his conquerors. Macbeth observes that his "Genius is rebuk'd" by Banquo's, just as Mark Antony's was by Octavius (3.1.55–56)—another allusion to Plutarch's *Lives.*

Macbeth also draws on the Bible. According to the Geneva Bible's gloss of Genesis 3:6, by Adam's eating the fruit of the Tree of Knowledge, he sinned, "not so muche to please his wife, as moued by ambition at her persuasion." Macbeth may kill Duncan for the same reason. Both Macbeth and his wife invoke darkness: "Come, thick night" (1.5.50); "Stars, hide your fires" (1.4.50).

They thus reverse God's "Let there be light." They choose uncreation, as when Macbeth tells the witches he will be answered "though the treasure / Of nature's germains [seeds] tumble all together, / Even till destruction sicken" (4.1.58–60). Later, he declares, "I gin to be a-weary of the sun, / And wish th' estate o' th' world were now undone" (5.5.48–49). Such inverted echoes of the story of creation link them with the demonic. In his soliloquy in Act 1, Scene 7, Macbeth speaks of "heaven's cherubin, hors'd / Upon the sightless couriers of the air" (1.7.22–23). This image derives from Psalm 18:10: "And he rode upon Cherub and did flie, and he came flying upon the wings of the wind."

Thinking of killing Duncan, Macbeth says in as aside, "The eye wink at the hand; yet let that be / Which the eye fears, when it is done, to see" (1.4.52–53). This line recalls Matthew 13:15: "With their eyes they have winked, lest they should see with their eyes." The famous "To-morrow, and to-morrow, and to-morrow" speech in Act V, Scene 5, about the brevity and vanity of life and the judgment that "Life's but a walking shadow" (5.5.24), repeats sentiments from the Bible. Psalm 144:4 in the Geneva Bible translation declares, "Man is like to vanitie: his daies are like a shadowe, that vanisheth." Job 8:9 similarly states, "For our days upon earth are but shadow." The Wisdom of Solomon, 2:5, reads, "For our time is as a shadowe that passeth away, and after our end there is no returning." The darkness after Duncan's death derives from Holinshed's account of the murder of King Duff but also from the biblical story of the Crucifixion, thereby linking Duncan with Christ. So, too, the witches' greeting of Macbeth in Act I, Scene 3 with their "All hail," while again coming from Holinshed, repeats Judas's greeting of Jesus. Macbeth's visit to the witches in Act IV, Scene 1 to learn the future recalls Saul's going to the Witch of Endor in 1 Samuel 28. Isaac Disraeli in his *Amenities of Literature* (1841), in fact, calls Saul "the Israelite Macbeth."

The play also draws on topical references. In Act II, Scene 3, the Porter welcomes an equivocator to hell. On March 28, 1606, Father Henry Gar-net, superior of the Jesuits in England, was tried for his role in the Gunpowder Plot. He had learned through the confessional of the plan to blow up the king and Parliament but had kept silent and denied knowledge of it. He defended his behavior by invoking the doctrine of equivocation, which allows for telling "lies like truth" (5.5.43) through mental reservation. The published account of the trial explains this procedure, "wherein under the pretext of the lawfulnesse of a mixt proposition to express one part of a mans mind, and retaine another." This principle was so odious to Parliament that its 1606 Oath of Allegiance barred "any equivocation or mental evasion or secret reservation whatsoever." The witches in Act IV, Scene 1 equivocate, seeming to promise Macbeth security but in fact, pronouncing his doom.

The First Witch in Act I, Scene 3 refers to the wife of the master of the ship *Tiger,* which has sailed to Aleppo. A ship of this name traveled to the East on December 5, 1604, and returned to the Welsh port at Milford Haven, after an unsuccessful voyage, on June 27, 1606, reaching Portsmouth on July 9. The storm mentioned in Act II, Scene 4 and the winds Macbeth would unleash against the churches (4.1.52–53) may reflect the hurricane that struck England and the Continent on March 29–30, 1606.

Malcolm's account in Act I, Scene 4 of the noble death of the thane of Cawdor was a Shakespearean invention. Shakespeare may have been thinking of the execution of Robert Devereux, earl of Essex in 1601. He might also have had in mind a more recent death, that of Everard Digby, whom James I had knighted in 1603. James had trusted Digby, just as Duncan had Cawdor. Digby joined the Gunpowder Plot and was executed on January 30, 1606, after apologizing for his actions. Like Cawdor, he "very frankly . . . confess'd his treasons, / Implor'd . . . pardon, and set forth / A deep repentance" (1.4.5–7).

Shakespeare had no historical source for the confrontation between Macbeth and Banquo's ghost in Act III, Scene 4. The idea for this scene may have derived from *A Treatsie of Spectres* (1605) by

Pierre de Loyer and translated into English by Z. Jones. Here, Shakespeare could have read: "How often have they [tyrants] supposed and imagined, that they have seene sundry visions and apparitions of those whom they have murdered, or of some others whome they have feared?" The book refers to Theodoric the Great (455–526), who had Simmachus killed. Afterward, "on an evening as he sat at supper [Theodoric saw] the face of Simmachus in a most horrible shape and fashion, with great mustachioes, knitting his browes, frowning with his eyes, biting his lippes for very anger, and looking awry upon him," as Banquo's ghost glowers at Macbeth.

Macbeth's overactive imagination, one of Shakespeare's own additions, perhaps results from his melancholy disposition. Samuel Harsnett writes in his *Declaration of Egregious Popish Impositions* (1603): "Why men of a melancholie constitution be more subject to fears, fancies and imaginations of devils, and witches, than others tempers be? . . . because from their black & sooty blood, gloomie fuliginous spirits do fume into their brains which bring black, gloomy, and frightful images, representations, and similitudes in them." Shakespeare had drawn on Harsnett's book for *King Lear,* (written circa 1605).

Robert Burton's *Anatomy of Melancholy* (1621) observes that melancholy is called "the Devil's Bath" because "melancholy persons are most subject to diabolical temptations and illusions, and most apt to entertain them, and the Devil best able to work upon them." Reginald Scot's *The Discoverie of Witchcraft* (1584) notes, "Many thorough [through] melancholie do imagine that they see or heare visions, spirits, ghosts, strange noises, &c," a perfect description of Macbeth. Lady Macbeth's sleepwalking was another of Shakespeare's inventions. Burton's *Anatomy of Melancholy* sets forth the popular view that this behavior results from fantasy overcoming reason.

Date and Text of the Play

The contemporary allusions noted above suggest that *Macbeth* was written in 1606. William War-

ner's *A Continuation of Albion's England* (1606) and William Camden's *Britannia* (1607 edition) refer to *Macbeth* in ways that suggest the authors had seen Shakespeare's play. *The Puritan* (1607) and Francis Beaumont and John Fletcher's *Knight of the Burning Pestle,* produced in 1607, also allude to *Macbeth*. Paul, in *The Royal Play of* Macbeth, argues that the play was first performed at Hampton Court on August 7, 1606, before James and his brother-in-law, King Christian IV of Denmark, who visited England between July 17 and August 10 of that year. The King's Men performed three plays for the monarchs, two at Greenwich, one at Hampton Court; the titles of these works are not recorded. James disliked long plays. During his 1605 visit to Oxford, he was "entertained" with three lengthy productions. He tried to leave in the middle of one, fell asleep during another, and "spoke many words of dislike" against the third. *Macbeth* is Shakespeare's fifth shortest play; it may well have been intended for a royal spectator with a short attention span.

The play was first printed in the First Folio (1623). No earlier quarto publications have been discovered. The First Folio text was probably based on a promptbook or transcript thereof. Its stage directions and speaker designations are detailed, and the play is divided into acts and scenes. Modern editions further separate the First Folio's Act V, Scene 7 into two or three scenes. The portions of the play involving Hecate (3.5 and 4.1.39–43, 125–132) are usually attributed to another writer, Thomas Middleton. The songs called for in stage directions (3.5.33 and 4.1.43) certainly are Middleton's.

The First Folio text contains some contradictions. While these may result from hasty composition to meet a deadline, more likely the typesetters could not decipher changes in the manuscript. For example, Ross says that Macbeth fought against the thane of Cawdor "rebellious arm 'gainst arm" (1.2.56), yet in Act I, Scene 3, Macbeth is unaware that Cawdor joined Sweno's invasion. The bleeding sergeant in Act I, Scene 2 was initially a captain. Shakespeare demoted him in the text but not in the

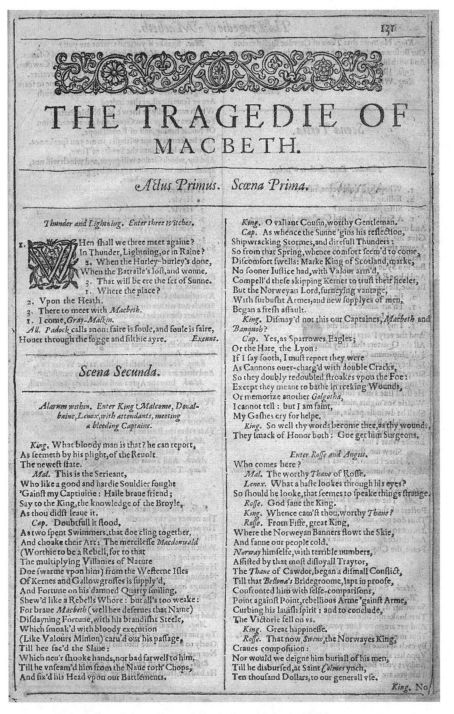

THE TRAGEDIE OF
MACBETH.

Actus Primus. Scœna Prima.

Thunder and Lightning. Enter three Witches.

1. Hen shall we three meet againe?
In Thunder, Lightning, or in Raine?
    2. When the Hurley-burley's done,
When the Battaile's lost, and wonne.
    3. That will be ere the set of Sunne.
    1. Where the place?
2. Vpon the Heath.
3. There to meet with *Macbeth.*
1. I come, *Gray-Malkin.*
All. Padock calls anon: faire is foule, and foule is faire,
Houer through the fogge and filthie ayre. *Exeunt.*

Scena Secunda.

Alarum within. Enter King Malcome, Donalbaine, Lenox, with attendants, meeting a bleeding Captaine.

King. What bloody man is that? he can report,
As seemeth by his plight, of the Reuolt
The newest state.
Mal. This is the Serieant,
Who like a good and hardie Souldier fought
'Gainst my Captiuitie: Haile braue friend;
Say to the King, the knowledge of the Broyle,
As thou didst leaue it.
Cap. Doubtfull it stood,
As two spent Swimmers, that doe cling together,
And choake their Art: The mercilesse *Macdonwald*
(Worthie to be a Rebell, for to that
The multiplying Villanies of Nature
Doe swarme vpon him) from the Westerne Isles
Of Kernes and Gallowgrosses is supply'd,
And Fortune on his damned Quarry smiling,
Shew'd like a Rebells Whore: but all's too weake:
For braue *Macbeth* (well hee deserues that Name)
Disdayning Fortune, with his brandisht Steele,
Which smoak'd with bloody execution
(Like Valours Minion) caru'd out his passage,
Till hee fac'd the Slaue:
Which neu'r shooke hands, nor bad farwell to him,
Till he vnseam'd him from the Naue toth' Chops,
And fix'd his Head vpon our Battlements.

King. O valiant Cousin, worthy Gentleman.
Cap. As whence the Sunne 'gins his reflection,
Shipwracking Stormes, and direfull Thunders:
So from that Spring, whence comfort seem'd to come,
Discomfort swells: Marke King of Scotland, marke,
No sooner Iustice had, with Valour arm'd,
Compell'd these skipping Kernes to trust their heeles,
But the Norweyan Lord, surueying vantage,
With furbusht Armes, and new supplyes of men,
Began a fresh assault.
King. Dismay'd not this our Captaines, *Macbeth* and *Banquoh*?
Cap. Yes, as Sparrowes, Eagles;
Or the Hare, the Lyon:
If I say sooth, I must report they were
As Cannons ouer-charg'd with double Cracks,
So they doubly redoubled stroakes vpon the Foe:
Except they meane to bathe in reeking Wounds,
Or memorize another *Golgotha*,
I cannot tell: but I am faint,
My Gashes cry for helpe.
King. So well thy words become thee, as thy wounds,
They smack of Honor both: Goe get him Surgeons.

Enter Rosse and Angus.

Who comes here?
Mal. The worthy *Thane* of Rosse.
Lenox. What a haste lookes through his eyes?
So should he looke, that seemes to speake things strange.
Rosse. God saue the King.
King. Whence cam'st thou, worthy *Thane*?
Rosse. From Fiffe, great King,
Where the Norweyan Banners flowt the Skie,
And fanne our people cold.
Norway himselfe, with terrible numbers,
Assisted by that most disloyall Traytor,
The *Thane* of Cawdor, began a dismall Conflict,
Till that *Bellona's* Bridegroome, lapt in proofe,
Confronted him with selfe-comparisons,
Point against Point, rebellious Arme 'gainst Arme,
Curbing his lauish spirit: and to conclude,
The Victorie fell on vs.
King. Great happinesse.
Rosse. That now, *Sweno*, the Norwayes King,
Craues composition:
Nor would we deigne him buriall of his men,
Till he disbursed, at Saint *Colmes* ynch,
Ten thousand Dollars, to our generall vse.
King. No

Title page of the First Folio edition of *Macbeth*, published in 1623

speech headings and stage directions. In Act III, Scene 6, a lord reports that Macbeth is exasperated by Macduff's flight to England, but in Act IV, Scene 1 Macbeth is shocked to learn of this development.

SYNOPSIS

Brief Synopsis

The play opens with a thunderstorm. Three witches resolve to meet again that evening to speak with Macbeth, a leader of the Scottish forces confronting the rebellious Macdonwald and the invading Norwegians, led by Sweno. The scene then shifts to the camp of King Duncan, who learns of Macbeth's success and of the treachery of the thane (lord) of Cawdor. Duncan orders Cawdor's execution; that thane's title will be given to Macbeth.

On a heath, Macbeth and his fellow military leader, Banquo, meet the witches, who proclaim Macbeth Thane of Glamis, his present title; Thane of Cawdor, an honor he does not yet know is his; and Scotland's future king. To Banquo. they promise that his descendants will rule the country. As soon as they leave, Ross arrives to tell Macbeth he is now thane of Cawdor.

When Macbeth and Banquo rejoin Duncan, the king names his son Malcolm as his successor, thus raising an obstacle to Macbeth's royal aspirations. The king says he will spend the night at Macbeth's castle at Inverness. When Lady Macbeth learns from her husband's letter of the witches' prophecies and the imminent arrival of Duncan, she plots the king's murder. Macbeth initially refuses to kill Duncan, but Lady Macbeth persuades him to do so. The two make the crime appear to be the work of Duncan's chamberlains, whom Macbeth also kills. When Duncan's two sons flee, fearing for their lives, suspicion falls on them. Macbeth becomes king.

Fearing Banquo and hoping to thwart the witches' prediction that Banquo's heirs will reign, Macbeth hires men to kill Banquo and Banquo's son, Fleance. Banquo is murdered, but Fleance escapes. That night, Macbeth gives a feast at the palace. When he says he misses Banquo, Banquo's bloody ghost appears and disrupts the festivities.

Macbeth resolves to revisit the witches to learn his fate.

The witches tell him to fear Macduff, but no one born of woman will harm Macbeth, whose reign is secure until Birnam Wood comes to Dunsinane. Discovering that Macduff has fled to England, Macbeth orders the execution of Macduff's family. In England, Macduff tries to persuade Malcolm to return and topple Macbeth. Malcolm at first demurs but then announces that he is preparing to invade Scotland with 10,000 English soldiers.

To disguise their numbers, the English cut boughs from Birnam Wood as they advance on Macbeth's castle at Dunsinane. Macbeth, preparing for a siege, learns that his wife has died, probably by her own hand. Hearing that Birnam Wood is coming to Dunsinane, Macbeth resolves to confront his enemies. In the battle, he encounters Macduff. Macbeth does not want to fight him, having spilled so much of Macduff's family's blood already. Macbeth warns Macduff that no man born of woman can harm him. Macduff responds that he was born by cesarean section. Again, Macbeth wants to avoid combat, but Macduff offers the choice of surrender or battle. Macbeth chooses the latter. Offstage, Macduff kills Macbeth and cuts off his head. Malcolm is declared king of Scotland.

Act I, Scene 1

Amid thunder and lightning, Three Witches meet on a plain in Scotland. They have just concluded a witches' sabbath and discuss when they will gather again. The Second Witch says they will assemble at the conclusion of the battle, which will soon be over. They plan to reconvene that evening on the heath to meet with Macbeth. Hearing the call of their familiars (spirits who serve them), they depart.

Act I, Scene 2

A wounded Sergeant enters the camp of Duncan, the Scottish king. Duncan's older son, Malcolm, asks the soldier how the battle is proceeding. The Sergeant replies that Macbeth has killed the rebel Macdonwald and, together with Banquo, is valiantly fighting the Norwegian invaders led by

Sweno. Ross arrives to report Sweno's defeat; the Norwegians are suing for peace. Duncan orders the execution of the traitorous thane of Cawdor, whose title and lands he will give to Macbeth.

Act I, Scene 3

The Three Witches unite on the heath. The First Witch declares her anger against a sailor's wife who refused to share chestnuts with her. All three agree to raise a storm to torment that woman's husband. Macbeth and Banquo enter. The First Witch greets Macbeth with his present title, thane of Glamis. The second hails him as thane of Cawdor, an honor he does not yet know he has. The last of the witches hails him as Scotland's future king.

Banquo asks about his future and is told that although he will not be a king, his descendants will rule the country. Macbeth wants to speak further with the witches, but they vanish. Ross and Angus appear to tell Macbeth that he is now thane of Cawdor. He asks Banquo whether this fulfillment of the witches' prophecy gives him hope his children will be kings. Banquo replies with the warning that the forces of evil sometimes reveal small truths to betray their victims with great lies. As

Macbeth and Banquo encounter the witches in this 19th-century depiction of Act 1, Scene 3 of *Macbeth*. *(Illustration by T. H. Nicholson; engraving by Charles William Sheeres)*

Banquo speaks with Ross and Angus, Macbeth, in a soliloquy, ponders the witches' words. Eventually, Banquo recalls Macbeth from his reverie. The men set off to join Duncan; as the scene ends, Macbeth tells Banquo he wants to talk more about the prophecies.

Act I, Scene 4

At the king's palace at Forres, Malcolm and Duncan discuss Cawdor's execution. Macbeth, Banquo, Ross, and Angus join them. Duncan praises Macbeth, who replies that he has done only his duty. Duncan then declares Malcolm as successor to the throne. In a brief soliloquy, Macbeth ponders this impediment to the fulfillment of the witches' words. The king and his entourage set off to spend the night as Macbeth's guest.

Act I, Scene 5

At Macbeth's castle, Inverness, Lady Macbeth reads a letter from her husband informing her of his encounter with the witches. Lady Macbeth recognizes her spouse's ambition but fears he lacks the ruthlessness necessary to achieve his desires. When he arrives, she will goad him to gain the crown he wants. A messenger announces the imminent arrival of the king. When the man leaves, Lady Macbeth plots Duncan's death. She is joined by her husband. She tells him to give a hearty welcome to Duncan, who never will leave the castle alive.

Act I, Scene 6

Duncan, with his sons and attendants, reaches Inverness. Lady Macbeth receives him warmly.

Act I, Scene 7

That evening as everyone is feasting, Macbeth, alone, expresses reservations about killing Duncan. When Lady Macbeth joins him, he tells her to abandon their plot, but she rebukes him for his cowardice. After a brief argument, she prevails.

Act II, Scene 1

As Banquo and his son, Fleance, are preparing for bed, Macbeth enters. Banquo hands him a diamond

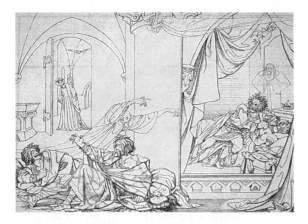

Voices haunt Macbeth as he kills Duncan in Act II, Scene 1 of *Macbeth*. This is a plate from *Retzsch's Outlines to Shakespeare:* Macbeth, published in 1833. *(Illustration by Moritz Retzsch)*

from Duncan for Lady Macbeth, a token of the king's appreciation for her hospitality. Banquo and Macbeth talk about the witches; then Banquo and Fleance exit. Alone, Macbeth sees a dagger like the one he will soon use to murder Duncan. Even as he stares at this mind-forged weapon, it becomes covered with blood before it disappears. A bell rings, and Macbeth goes to kill the king.

Act II, Scene 2

Lady Macbeth awaits her husband in the inner court of the castle. He soon enters to report that he has done the deed. He adds that when the king's chamberlains awoke, frightened, and prayed, he could not say amen. He also has heard a voice saying he will never sleep again. She tells him to stop worrying and wash his bloodstained hands. Seeing that he is carrying the murder weapons, she instructs him to return the daggers to the chamberlains' room, since it must appear that these attendants committed the crime. Macbeth refuses to revisit to the scene of the murder. Dismissing his weakness, Lady Macbeth takes the daggers back. In her absence, Macduff and Lennox begin knocking on the castle gate. Lady Macbeth returns to urge her husband to pretend to go to bed so no

one will suspect they are awake. They exit to the sound of more knocking.

Act II, Scene 3

In the play's only comic scene, the drunken Porter imagines himself the keeper of the gate of hell. He responds to the sounds of knocking by welcoming an imaginary suicide, a liar, and a thief. At length, he recovers his senses enough to feel too cold to be in hell and admits Macduff and Lennox. Macbeth joins them. While Macduff goes off to wake Duncan, Lennox and Macbeth discuss the stormy night just past. Macduff reenters, horrified, to announce the king's murder. Macbeth and Lennox rush away to look, as Macduff orders the ringing of the castle's bell to rouse everyone. Lady Macbeth and Banquo are the first to appear. Soon, Macbeth, Lennox, Ross, and the king's two sons, Malcolm and Donalbain, all are standing in the inner court.

Told of their father's death, the young men ask who committed the murder. Lennox replies that the chamberlains appear to be guilty. Macbeth says he has killed these attendants, thus arousing Macduff's suspicion. Macbeth tries to justify his action, but Lady Macbeth cuts short the discussion by fainting. The men agree to meet shortly in the hall to discuss what to do. Malcolm and Donalbain, fearing for their lives, decide to flee, Donalbain to Ireland, Malcolm to England.

Act II, Scene 4

Ross and an Old Man discuss recent bad weather and unnatural occurrences. When Macduff joins them, they speak of Duncan's recent murder, which appears to be the work of Malcolm and Donalbain, since they have so guiltily fled. Macduff says he will not attend Macbeth's coronation at Scone and worries about the new king's reign.

Act III, Scene 1

In the royal palace at Forres, Banquo, alone, reveals his suspicion that Macbeth killed Duncan to get the throne the witches promised. His musings are interrupted by the arrival of the new king and queen, who invite him to a feast that evening. Macbeth tries to learn where Banquo will be until then and whether Banquo's son, Fleance, will accompany him. Once everyone else leaves, Macbeth, in a soliloquy, expresses his fear of Banquo and declares his intention of thwarting the witches' prophecy that Banquo's heirs will reign in Scotland. To achieve his goal, Macbeth speaks with two poor men, whom he has convinced that Banquo is the cause of their misery. They agree to kill Banquo and Fleance.

Act III, Scene 2

Lady Macbeth summons her husband and asks him why he remains solitary and worried. He replies that danger lurks. She tells him that he should appear cheerful among his guests that night. He promises to do so and urges her to pay particular attention to Banquo, though Macbeth says he fears the man. To Lady Macbeth's observation that Banquo and Fleance are not immortal, he responds that they may soon die but offers no details.

Act III, Scene 3

In a grove near the palace, the two men engaged to kill Banquo and Fleance are surprised to be joined by an unidentified third person. As the Three

Fleance escapes from the murderers in Act III, Scene 3 of *Macbeth*. Plate from *Retzsch's Outlines to Shakespeare: Macbeth*, 1833. *(Illustration by Moritz Retzsch)*

Murderers talk, Banquo and Fleance approach. The men attack and kill Banquo, but Fleance escapes.

Act III, Scene 4

Back in the hall of the palace, Macbeth, Lady Macbeth, and their guests are about to enjoy a feast. Macbeth glimpses one of Banquo's murderers at the door and speaks to him. The murderer reports the death of Banquo and the flight of Fleance. Once the killer leaves, Lady Macbeth reminds her husband to give a welcoming toast, which he does. He adds that he misses Banquo. Ross invites Macbeth to sit, but the king finds no empty chair. When Lennox points to one, Macbeth starts back in horror because in it, he sees the bloody specter of Banquo.

Addressing this ghost, which is visible to Macbeth alone, the king denies responsibility for his murder. Lady Macbeth tries to explain her husband's reaction, which is as puzzling to her as to everyone else, telling the company to ignore him. In an aside to Macbeth, she urges him to regain his composure. He responds that he is acting bravely under the circumstances; she retorts that whatever appalls him is a figment of his imagination. While he tries to make her see the ghost, she attempts to convince him there is nothing to see.

The ghost departs. Macbeth glosses over his odd behavior and gives another toast to his guests and to Banquo, whose absence he regrets. His words once more conjure up the specter, which Macbeth again addresses. Lady Macbeth tries to cover for him. After the ghost leaves, Macbeth urges everyone to sit and eat, but he also expresses amazement that others can look calmly on such horror. Ross, who has witnessed no bloody vision, asks Macbeth to explain. To avoid any further disclosure, Lady Macbeth dismisses the guests. After the company departs, Macbeth tells his wife he intends to consult the witches. She replies that he needs sleep, and the two go off to bed.

Act III, Scene 5

On the heath, Hecate rebukes the Three Witches for trafficking with Macbeth. She instructs them to meet her the next morning at the pit of Acheron, where Macbeth will come to learn his fate. She will go to the Moon to secure a drop that will produce visions that will lead Macbeth to his doom.

Act III, Scene 6

Somewhere in Scotland, Lennox and an unnamed Lord meet. Lennox comments on the deaths of Duncan and Banquo and on Macduff's fall from Macbeth's favor. The Lord replies that Macduff is going to England to urge Malcolm to invade his homeland and topple Macbeth. The Lord adds that Macbeth, aware of Macduff's intentions, is preparing for war. Both men wish Macduff success.

Act IV, Scene 1

In a cave, the Three Witches prepare a brew. Hecate and three other witches join them; Hecate commends the witches' efforts. After a song and dance, Hecate leaves, and Macbeth enters. He orders the witches to answer his questions, but before he can speak, an armed head appears to warn him against Macduff. When this vision vanishes, a bloody child rises and declares that no one born of woman can

The witches answer Macbeth's questions with visions in Act IV, Scene 1 of *Macbeth*, as depicted in this plate from *Retzsch's Outlines to Shakespeare: Macbeth*, (1833). *(Illustration by Moritz Retzsch)*

harm Macbeth. This apparition is succeeded by a third, a crowned child holding a tree, who says that Macbeth will be safe until Birnam Wood moves to his castle at Dunsinane.

Reassured, Macbeth asks whether Banquo's children will rule Scotland. The witches try to dissuade him from learning the truth, but he insists. His answer comes in a vision of a procession of eight kings, the last of whom holds a mirror showing an unending parade of monarchs; Banquo appears and points at them as his descendants. To cheer Macbeth, the witches conjure up music and perform a dance before they vanish.

Lennox enters. Macbeth asks whether he saw the witches; Lennox has not. Lennox informs Macbeth of Macduff's flight to England. Macbeth is surprised, although the Lord in Act 3, Scene 6 claimed that Macbeth knew of this event. Macbeth resolves to attack Macduff's castle and kill all the thane's relatives.

Act IV, Scene 2

At Macduff's castle in Fife, Lady Macduff asks Ross why her husband has abandoned his family. Ross urges patience and maintains that Macduff has acted wisely. Lady Macduff retorts that even a wren will remain in the nest to defend its young against predators. She attributes her husband's flight to fear. Ross again tries to pacify her.

After he leaves, Lady Macduff tells her son that his father is dead. The Boy refuses to believe her. As they talk, a messenger arrives to warn Lady Macduff to flee with her family. Before she can do so, murderers enter. Now, she says, she is glad her husband has escaped. Her son is killed, and she flees, pursued by the villains and is killed.

Act IV, Scene 3

In London, Macduff urges Malcolm to return to Scotland to depose Macbeth. Malcolm, suspecting Macduff to be in league with the tyrant, tests his visitor by claiming he would prove a ruler even worse than the present king. Despairing, Macduff prepares to leave; Malcolm now reassures Macduff of his fitness to rule. Malcolm intends to lead an invasion, and Old Siward has already assembled an army of 10,000 to assist.

As Malcolm and Macduff discuss the English king (Edward the Confessor), Ross joins them. Macduff asks about his family. Ross tries to avoid the subject and notes that rebellion is brewing in Scotland. He adds that Malcolm's presence would encourage Macbeth's opponents. Malcolm replies that he is coming with an English army. Ross then reveals the murder of Macduff's family. As Macduff grieves, Malcolm tells him that these deaths should strengthen his resolve to topple Macbeth, and Macduff vows to confront the tyrant.

Act V, Scene 1

At Macbeth's castle in Dunsinane, one of Lady Macbeth's ladies-in-waiting tells a doctor that her mistress has been sleepwalking. He is skeptical, but as they talk, Lady Macbeth appears with a candle. They watch her rub her hands as if washing them and overhear her speak about the deaths of Duncan, Lady Macduff, and Banquo. After Lady Macbeth departs, the Scots Doctor instructs the Gentlewoman to watch the queen carefully.

Act V, Scene 2

Near Dunsinane, Scottish forces opposing Macbeth await the arrival of the English army led by Malcolm, Old Siward, and Macduff. Caithness reports that Macbeth has fortified his castle to withstand a siege. The men march off to meet the English near Birnam Wood.

Act V, Scene 3

In his castle, Macbeth receives reports of desertions among his troops. Macbeth does not fear, however, because he recalls the witches' prophecies. When a servant announces the arrival of the English army, Macbeth calls for his armor. He asks the doctor about Lady Macbeth; the physician replies that her imagination troubles her. Cure her, the king instructs him, and then asks whether the doctor knows of any remedy for an afflicted mind. The doctor says that in such cases,

the patient must cure himself. Macbeth now wonders whether the doctor can purge the English from Scotland. After Macbeth and his attendants leave, the doctor wishes he were far away from Dunsinane.

Act V, Scene 4

Near Birnam Wood, Malcolm orders the Scottish and English forces to camouflage their ranks by cutting down branches and carrying these in front of them.

Act V, Scene 5

As Macbeth prepares for a siege, he hears a scream. Seyton, Macbeth's armor-bearer, goes off to learn what has happened; he returns with the news that Lady Macbeth is dead. Macbeth delivers a soliloquy on life's meaninglessness.

A Messenger reports that as he looked toward Birnam Wood, he thought the grove was coming to Dunsinane. Macbeth begins to recognize that the witches gave him a false sense of security. He decides to confront the invaders rather than remain within the safety of his castle.

Act V, Scene 6

In front of Macbeth's castle, Malcolm sets forth the order of battle. The invaders discard their leafy camouflage and prepare to attack.

Act V, Scene 7

Amid the fighting, Macbeth encounters Young Siward and kills him in hand-to-hand combat. Macduff enters seeking Macbeth. After he leaves to continue his pursuit, Malcolm and Old Siward appear to report that Macbeth's forces have defected and surrendered the castle.

Act V, Scene 8

Macduff and Macbeth meet. Macbeth refuses to fight Macduff, having already shed so much of Macduff's family's blood. Macduff assails the king, who declares he cannot be harmed by anyone born of woman. Macduff informs Macbeth of his birth by cesarean section. Again, Macbeth refuses to fight; Macduff says the king must then surrender. Rather than yield, Macbeth resumes the battle, and they exit fighting.

Act V, Scene 9

The victorious English enter. Malcolm reports that Young Siward and Macduff are missing. Ross announces the death of the former. Macduff arrives, carrying Macbeth's severed head. All hail Malcolm as Scotland's king. Malcolm declares that Scotland's thanes will now be earls, and he promises to restore peace to the kingdom. The play ends with Malcolm inviting all to witness his coronation at Scone.

CHARACTER LIST

Macbeth Military leader under King Duncan, whom he kills. Macbeth then becomes a tyrannical ruler.

Lady Macbeth Macbeth's intelligent, ruthless, scheming wife.

Duncan King of Scotland.

Malcolm Duncan's older son, whom the king names as his successor. He eventually assumes the Scottish throne.

Donalbain Duncan's younger son.

Banquo Macbeth's fellow leader of the Scottish forces.

Fleance Banquo's son.

Macduff A powerful Scottish lord opposed to Macbeth. He allies himself with Malcolm.

Lady Macduff Devoted wife to Macduff, killed by Macbeth's henchmen.

Boy Clever, charming son of Macduff, killed by Macbeth's hired assassins.

Lennox A Scottish aristocrat.

Ross A Scottish aristocrat.

Angus A Scottish nobleman.

Menteith A Scottish nobleman.

Caithness A Scottish aristocrat.

Old Siward Earl of Northumberland, leader of the English forces that invade Scotland to depose Macbeth.

Young Siward Old Siward's son, killed by Macbeth in the battle to depose the tyrant.

English Doctor He serves in the court of Edward the Confessor.

Scots Doctor He attends on Lady Macbeth.

Sergeant Wounded in the battle against the rebels fighting Duncan's forces, he fought successfully to save Malcolm from being captured. He brings news of the fighting to the king.

Porter A hard-drinking, witty servant of Macbeth.

Old Man He converses with Ross in Act 2, Scene 4 and serves as a commentator on developments to that point in the play.

Three Murderers Hired by Macbeth to kill Banquo and Fleance.

Three Witches Ambiguous figures who foretell Macbeth's kingship and later enigmatically warn him of his doom. They also predict that Banquo's descendants will rule Scotland.

Hecate Queen of the witches.

CHARACTER STUDIES
Macbeth

Macbeth dominates his play. He speaks some 700 lines, more than 30 percent of the total, and is on stage for more than half the dialogue despite his vanishing from the end of Act IV, Scene 1 to the beginning of Act V, Scene 3. As noted in the "Background" section, Shakespeare took the skeleton of his plot from historical sources. Our interest in his character lies, however, not in what he does to others but rather in why and how his actions affect himself. Just as Shakespeare did with his other great tragic characters such as Hamlet and Iago, here he obscures motivation and complicates his originals. The actor Richard Burbage was the first to play the role of Macbeth, but it is impossible to know how he understood the character. In the late 17th and early 18th centuries, Shakespeare's play yielded the stage to William Davenant's adaptation. Only with David Garrick's 1744 restoration of a modified version of Shakespeare's original do actors' and critics' interpretations become a matter of record.

For Garrick, Macbeth was a sensitive and reluctant murderer, driven to crime by the promptings of his wife and the witches. In *Lettres sur la Danse et sur les Ballets* (1783), Jean Georges Noverre wrote of Garrick's performance: "I have seen him, I say, playing a tyrant, who, frightened by the enormity of his crimes, dies shattered with remorse. The final act was given over to regrets and sadness; humanity triumphed over killings and barbarism; the tyrant, sensible to the voice of conscience, detested his crimes, which became his judges and his executioners." In *An Essay on Acting* (1744), Garrick described the character as "an experienced general crown'd with Conquest, innately ambitious and religiously Humane, spurr'd on by metaphysical prophecies and the unconquerable pride of his Wife, to a deed horrid in itself and repugnant to his nature". As Noverre indicates, Garrick highlighted Macbeth's humanity and his suffering.

To emphasize these traits, Garrick's production omitted Act IV, Scene 2, the murder of Macduff's family, and Macbeth's killing of Young Siward in Act V, Scene 7. Garrick also gave Macbeth a penitent dying speech in which he acknowledges his crimes and stoically accepts his punishment:

'Tis done. The scene of life will quickly close.
Ambition's vain, delusive dreams are fled, and
now I wake to darkness, guilt and horror. I
cannot bear it. Let me shake it off—'Two' [it
will] not be; my soul is clogg'd with blood—
and cannot rise. I dare not ask for mercy. It is
too late, hell drags me down. I sink, I sink—
Oh!—my soul is lost forever. Oh!

In the early 19th century, John Philip Kemble followed Garrick's lead in presenting a noble Macbeth. Both he and William Macready portrayed him as a noble savage. Kemble emphasized the nobility; Macready, the savage who is trapped by fate. George Vandenhoff wrote, in *Leaves from an Actor's Notebook* (1860), that Macbeth is "a very courteous person, a man of poetic mind, and considerable culture." In 1934, Tyrone Guthrie directed the play at the Old Vic, London. In his program notes, he wrote Macbeth is destroyed "by the imagination and intellectual honesty

which enable him to perceive his own loss of integrity and to realize the fullest implication of the loss."

Ruth Ellis regarded Robert Harris's Macbeth (Stratford-upon-Avon, 1946) as "human-hearted, never reconciled to the murky hell of his own deed." Yet another of the noble Macbeths was Paul Scofield's at Stratford-upon-Avon in 1967 under the direction of Peter Hall. According to Gareth Lloyd Evans in "*Macbeth:* 1946–1980 at Stratford-upon-Avon," Scofield's character "was a Sir Thomas More with a conscience and martial instincts" (104), always trying to recapture a goodness that keeps eluding him. This interpretation coincides with Hall's, who argued that Macbeth's moral sense would not have allowed him to kill Duncan without his wife's urging him on. The scholar Cleanth Brooks shared this positive view of Shakespeare's creation in *The Well Wrought Urn* (1947):

For it is not merely his great imagination and
his warrior courage in defeat which redeem
him for tragedy and place him beside the
other great tragic protagonists: rather, it is
his attempt to conquer the future, an attempt
involving him, like Oedipus, in a desperate
struggle with fate itself. It is this which holds
our imaginative sympathy, even after he has
degenerated into a bloody tyrant and has
become the slayer of Macduff's wife and
children. (40)

Other critics and actors regard Macbeth differently. Marvin Rosenberg quotes an anonymous letter to Garrick objecting to his sympathetic interpretation: "you almost everywhere discover dejectedness of mind . . . more grief than horror . . . heart heavings, melancholy countenance and slack carriage of body. . . . The sorrowful face and lowly gestures of a penitent, which have ever a wan and pitiful look . . . are quite incompatible with the character" (65–66). Charles Macklin, who began playing the role at Covent Garden in the later 18th century, abandoned Garrick's noble

Publicity photo from 1948 Republic Pictures film adaptation of *Macbeth*, starring Orson Welles as Macbeth

figure for a sinister Macbeth. Edmund Kean in the early 19th century similarly rejected Garrick's vision. Kean also took the lead in *Richard III*, and he portrayed both characters alike. His Macbeth was planning to kill Duncan before the witches' and his wife's promptings, and after the murder, he feels no remorse. He does, however, become a moral coward. When confronted with Banquo's ghost, Kemble showed courage, whereas Kean retreated, and he even recoiled at his wife's touch. The 19th-century critic George Fletcher called Macbeth a "heartless slave." Ralph Richardson's 1952 Machiavellian Macbeth (Stratford-upon-Avon) again resembled Richard III.

Michael Redgrave summarized well this negative vision. Redgrave played Macbeth in London and New York in the immediate postwar period (1947–48) and may have been influenced by the recent rise and fall of Adolf Hitler and Benito Mussolini. Writing in *The Actor's Ways and Means* (1953), he declared: "Macbeth is described as noble and valiant and during the whole play we see him do nothing that is either noble or valiant. . . . I could find none of the noble resignation, the philosophy, I expected to find in the part. . . . You will find yourself appalled at how little the text says in Macbeth's own part that will enable you to build up this great, terrifying figure" (Rosenberg 76–77).

Some have sought to steer a middle course between these two extremes; their understanding of the character has produced the most fascinating versions of this complex creation. John Upton in *Critical Observations on Shakespeare* (1746) described Macbeth as "a man, not a monster, a man of virtue, till he hearkened to the lures of ambition . . . his mind agitated and convulsed, now virtue, now vice prevailing, how beautifully from such a wavering character." Caroline Spurgeon summarizes this viewpoint of the dual-natured Macbeth:

> Undoubtedly Macbeth is built on great
> lines and in heroic proportions, with great
> possibilities—there could be no tragedy else.
> He is great, magnificently great, in courage,
> in passionate, indomitable ambition, in
> imagination and capacity to feel. But he could
> never be put beside, say Hamlet or Othello,
> in nobility of nature; and there *is* an aspect in
> which he is but a poor, vain, cruel, treacherous
> creature, snatching ruthlessly over the dead
> bodies of kinsman and friend at place and
> power he is utterly unfitted to possess. (327)

R. S. Crane, too, regards Macbeth as a good man "who has fallen under the compulsive power of an imagined better state for himself which he can attain only by acting contrary to his normal habits and feelings" (172). Once he achieves his initial goal of kingship, he discovers that he must continue to kill to keep what he has gained. As a result, he "becomes progressively hardened morally" (Crane 172). At the end of the play, Crane argues, Macbeth recaptures some of his original nobility.

In the 19th century, Henry Irving offered onstage someone who is "a poet with his brain and a villain with his heart" (Furness 470). He is a cold-blooded killer who was plotting the murder of Duncan before he encountered the witches. He is "self-torturing, self-examining, playing with conscience so that action and reaction of poetic thought might send emotional waves through the brain while the resolution was as firmly fixed as steel and the heart as cold as ice" (Furness 470–471).

Under Glen Byam Shaw's direction, Laurence Olivier, in 1955, presented Macbeth as both noble and flawed. Byam Shaw described Macbeth as "a superb leader with the courage of a lion and the imagination of a poet. . . . He has greatness of soul even though he is damned" and conceded that once Macbeth kills Duncan, "all that is bad in his character bursts out" (Rosenberg 105–106). Still, he never becomes a coward or a villain in the same category as Iago in *Othello* or Aaron in *Titus Andronicus*. As Olivier played him, he is torn between evil and sensitivity. A 1974 English production of the play used three actors for Macbeth to represent, respectively, the wife-dominated figure, the murderer of Duncan, and the lost soul after the ghost of Banquo appears.

However one views Macbeth, certain traits remain indisputable. The physical world does not frighten him. In battle in Act I, Scene 2 and in Act 5, he is dauntless. When Banquo's ghost haunts him in Act III, Scene 4, he exclaims: "Approach thou like the rugged Russian bear, / The arm'd rhinocerous, or th' Hyrcan tiger, / Take any shape

Lady Macbeth attempts to calm Macbeth, who reacts strongly to the sight of Banquo's ghost in this 19th-century depiction of Act III, Scene 4 of *Macbeth*. (*Painting by Max Adamo; engraving by Tobias Bauer*)

but that, and my firm nerves / Shall never tremble" (99–102). It is the metaphysical world that torments him. As he observes, "Present fears / Are less than horrible imaginings" (1.3.137–138). When the witches hail him as king, he imagines, perhaps not for the first time, the killing of Duncan. The Norwegian assault had troubled him "As sparrows eagles, or the hare the lion" (1.2.35). The vision of the slain Duncan, however, "doth unfix my hair / And make my seated heart knock at my ribs" (1.3.135–136). As Lady Macbeth says, "th' attempt, and not the deed, / Confounds [him]" (2.2.10–11).

His conscience conjures up the imaginary dagger in Act II, Scene 1 and covers it with blood. It converts the hooting of an owl and the chirping of crickets into a disembodied voice condemning him to "Sleep no more!" (2.2.32, 38, 40). It summons the ghost of the slain Banquo into the banquet hall (3.4) and paints that vision with "gory locks" and "twenty mortal murthers on [its] crown" (3.4.50, 80). He tells Lady Macbeth that he is shaken nightly with "terrible dreams" (3.2.18) and lives in constant fear of retribution. He spends the duration of his brief play lying "on the torture of the mind . . . / In restless ecstasy" (3.2.21–22). Late in the play, he asks the doctor tending his wife

> Canst thou not minister to a mind diseas'd,
> Pluck from the memory a rooted sorrow,
> Raze out the written troubles of the brain,
> And with some sweet oblivious antidote
> Cleanse the stuff'd bosom of that perilous
>   stuff
> Which weighs upon the heart? (5.3.40–45)

He is asking not for his wife—or not only for her. His success has not brought surcease from worry. He knew, even before he killed Duncan, "We still have judgment here" (1.7.8). For Macbeth, self-judgment is the most damning form. He can murder Duncan, Banquo, Macduff's wife and children, and Young Siward, but he cannot kill his conscience. Consequently, he is more tormented than Richard III and Iago and also greater.

Shakespeare gives Macbeth a conscience like Hamlet's, but unlike Hamlet, Macbeth is a man of action. The first speeches about him recount his heroic deeds in battle, and he dies, as he has lived, a soldier in armor. Whereas Hamlet declares, "That would be scann'd" (3.3.75), Macbeth says, "Strange things I have in head, that will to hand, / Which must be acted ere they may be scann'd" (3.4.138–139). Hamlet spends half his play determining whether the ghost is honest; Macbeth never questions the witches' prognostications. Forms of the verb *to do* are associated with Macbeth. Early in the play, he reflects, "If chance will have me king, why, chance may crown me / Without my stir" (1.3.143–144). He cannot, however, refrain from acting even though he knows that what he is doing is wrong. His poetic soul cannot restrain his soldier's heart, though the battle between these two natures "Shakes so [his] single state of man" (1.3.140) that he is destroyed by this internal conflict. The civil wars that open and close the play are objective correlatives for the mental condition of the work's title character.

This struggle that divides him from himself isolates him from others. Before he rebels against himself, he is not alone. Duncan joins Macbeth's name with Banquo's (1.2.34), the Sergeant's report fuses them, and together they encounter the witches. After hearing the prediction of kingship, Macbeth instantly writes to his wife, whom he calls "my dearest partner of greatness" (1.5.11). Already in Act I, Scene 3, he speaks to himself, but his first soliloquy appears in Act 1, Scene 7 as he wrestles with his conscience. Thereafter, these speeches mark him as solitary. As he says in Act III, Scene 1, "To make society / The sweeter welcome, we will keep ourself / Till suppertime alone" (41–43). Lady Macbeth asks him "Why do you keep alone, / Of sorriest fancies your companions making?" (3.2.8–9).

He conceals from his wife his plan to kill Banquo and Fleance; she has quickly ceased to be his partner even in crime. At the feast in Act III, Scene 4 he can find no seat among his guests. As that scene ends—the last in which he and his wife appear together—he asks her opinion of Macduff's avoiding him. She replies, "Did you send to him, sir?" (3.4.128). This question reveals her ignorance of his activities, and that "sir" exposes the distance between them. She will speak only one more line to him in that scene and in the play.

By the fifth act, his supporters have deserted him. To the doctor, he acknowledges his loneliness: "that which should accompany old age, / As honor, love, obedience, troops of friends, / I must not look to have" (5.3.34–36). In Act V, Scene 6 he observes that if "those that should be ours" (5) had not joined Malcolm's army, he would not be compelled to endure a siege; he could have confronted his enemies in the field. It is fitting that in the only fighting the audience sees, Macbeth stands alone. He thus dies as he has lived.

The Sergeant describes Macbeth as "Disdaining fortune" (1.2.17). He casts aside human limitations in daring to be more than his lot would decree. He aspires to kingship and attains that goal. He strives to keep the monarchy from Banquo's heirs despite the witches' prediction, and to retain his throne even when Birnam Wood comes to Dunsinane and he is confronted by a man not born of woman. These efforts to transcend the restrictions that govern mortals make him heroic, even as transgressing those boundaries makes him tragic.

Lady Macbeth in Act II, Scene 2 of *Macbeth*. This print is from Charles Heath's 1848 edition of *The Heroines of Shakspeare: Comprising the Principal Female Characters in the Plays of the Great Poet*. *(Painting by K. Meadows; engraving by W. H. Mote)*

Lady Macbeth

According to the contemporary critic Garber, "Lady Macbeth is the strongest character in the play" (712). She so dominates the scenes in which she appears that her role at times seems equal to, perhaps even larger than, Macbeth's. She is on stage for more than a quarter of the dialogue though she speaks about a third of the number of lines as her husband (254) and vanishes between the end of Act III, Scene 4 and Act 5, Scene 1, her final scene.

Interpretations of Lady Macbeth have proved as diverse as those of her husband. In productions, noble Macbeths have generally been paired with fiendlike wives; and more villainous Macbeths,

with gentler wives. Thus, Hannah Pritchard's Lady Macbeth dominated Garrick; she instigated the murder of Duncan and overwhelmed her husband's scruples. In so acting, she was conforming to the 18th-century view of the character. Samuel Johnson, in the end note to his 1765 edition of the play, wrote: "Lady Macbeth is merely detested." Earlier, in 1730, Charles Gildon commented that both Macbeth and his wife were "too monstrous for the stage."

In a later production, the actress Sarah Siddons controlled her brother John Philip Kemble in their portray of the Macbeths. The actress Ellen Terry described Siddons in the role as "a remorseless, terrible woman, who knew no tenderness, and who was already 'unsex'd' [1.5.41] by the enormity of her desires." Siddons herself described Lady Macbeth as her husband's "evil genius" who overcomes all his "loyalty, and pity, and gratitude." Siddons maintained:

> In this astonishing creature one sees a woman in whose bosom the passion of ambition has almost obliterated all the characteristics of human nature; in whose composition are associated all the subjugating powers of intellect and all the charms and graces of personal beauty. . . . Such a combination only, respectable in energy and strength of mind, and captivating in feminine loveliness, could have composed a charm of such potency as to fascinate the mind of a hero as dauntless, a character so honourable, as *Macbeth*. (Furness 472)

The early 19th-century critic William Hazlitt wrote of Siddons's "unrelieved fierceness," saying that she displays "no intercourse with human sensation or human weakness." He continued, "Vice was never so solitary and so grand. The step, look, voice of the Royal Murderess so forces our eye after them as if of a being from a darker world, full of evil, but full of power—unconnected with life, but come to do its deed of darkness, and then pass away." Hazlitt's contemporary Leigh Hunt compared her to Aeschylus's Clytemnestra. Thomas Campbell wrote of her "superb depravity." Lady Macbeth's fainting in Act II, Scene 3 was cut, in fact, when Siddons played the part because audiences would not believe that so strong a character would lose consciousness.

Siddons did not agree fully with her stage portrayal. She called Lady Macbeth "fair, feminine, nay, perhaps even fragile. . . . Her feminine nature, her delicate structure, it is too evident, are soon overwhelmed by the enormous pressure of her crimes" (Furness 472–476). In George Henry Harlow's portrait of her in the role she appears gentle. Siddons recognized that Malcolm's dismissal of the character as "fiendlike" (5.9.35) is overly facile. Siddons's domineering physical presence and her

brother's understanding of his character, however, required her to adopt Pritchard's approach. Audiences, too, expected an evil, forceful woman who drives her husband to murder.

Fanny Kemble, Siddons's niece, described her own Lady Macbeth as possessing "energy, decision, daring, unscrupulousness; a deficiency of imagination, a great preponderance of the positive and practical mental elements; a powerful and rapid appreciation of what each exigency of circumstance demanded, and the coolness and resolution necessary for its immediate execution" (242). Kemble followed her aunt's interpretation of a Lady Macbeth, in Kemble's words, "incapable of any salutary spasm of moral anguish, or hopeful paroxysm of mental horror . . . never, even in dreams, does any gracious sorrow smite from her stony heart the blessed brine of tears that wash away sin" (Rosenberg 167). She will commit without compunction any crime she thinks necessary. Kemble's Lady Macbeth dies of guilt, but she never recognizes this fact. The (London) *Times* commented on Kemble's portrait of "that bad, bold woman, the slave of evil passions" (Rosenberg 168).

The American Charlotte Cushman, a large woman, adopted the Pritchard-Siddons-Kemble model. The late 19th-century theater critic John Coleman described her as "a domineering, murderous harridan [who] browbeats everyone," especially her husband. At the end of Act 2, Scene 2, Cushman even dragged him off the stage. Other reviewers wrote of her "full-fledged ferocity of a truculent nature in sight of prey" and her "appalling impartment of predestinate evil and sinister force"; yet another claimed, "Not only was she fully capable of killing her own infant at sight, but if occasion offered she could perpetrate by her own unaided efforts another 'Slaughter of the innocents' merely for the gratification of an insatiable thirst for blood" (Rosenberg 168–169).

Adelaide Ristori, a mid-19th-century Italian actress, called Lady Macbeth a "monster in human shape": She wants to be queen and uses her husband to achieve that end. A New York reviewer described Ristori's Lady Macbeth as "a bloody minded virago, without heart, without sensibility . . . in the form of a Lucretia Borgia, an adept at crime" (Rosenberg 170). At the end of the 19th century, the French actress Eugénie Marie Caroline Segond-Weber wrote of her agreement with Ristori. As Segond-Weber understood the character, "She does not love her husband . . . because he is her creature; she wants him to be king because she will be queen. . . . [S]he is a kind of fourth witch, a daughter of witches." When Judith Anderson played the role opposite Olivier at the Old Vic in 1937, she, too, displayed this lack of tenderness and an ambition of self-advancement.

Occasionally, on the early 19th-century stage, an actress ventured to oppose the then-accepted vision of the monstrous queen. Some critics did not take well to this view. Rosenberg cites a review of Campbell's 1817 Lady Macbeth as tender wife that faulted her for having "none of the dignity, none of the masculine energy, none of the unrelenting cruelty, none of the devouring ambition which belongs to the cool murderess" (178). Yet, as the decades passed, this milder interpretation of the role gained advocates. As early as 1823, Franz Horn wrote in *Shakespeare's Schauspiele Erläutert* that Lady Macbeth seeks the throne for her husband, not herself. Ludwig Tieck echoed this interpretation (*Dramaturgische Blätter,* 1826). Tieck maintained that she has to invoke the forces of darkness because of her innate sensitivity. Tieck's Lady Macbeth is noble and loves her husband. Anna Brownell Jameson, in *Shakespeare's Heroines* (1833), challenged the conventional view of the character as "cruel, treacherous, and daring" (371). Jameson noted that Macbeth, not his wife, first conceives of killing Duncan. Lady Macbeth then assumes the lead in this enterprise, not because she is more wicked than her husband, but because she is more intelligent than he. Her ambition is less for herself than for her husband: "The strength of her affections adds strength to her ambition" (377). In the end, she is consumed by her conscience. In Jameson's vein, George Fletcher wrote in "*Macbeth:* Shakesperian Criticism and Acting" (1844) that Lady Macbeth is a loving wife who seeks the crown for her husband. She goes mad when she discovers that he cannot love anyone, not even her.

In *Studies in Shakespeare* (1847), Fletcher commended the acting of Helen Faucit because she presented an "essentially feminine person." He noted that in rejecting Siddons's model, Faucit offered "the far more interesting picture of a naturally generous woman, depraved by her very self-devotion to the ambitious purpose of a merely selfish man" (228). A review of Faucit in the *Morning Post* of August 5, 1851, praised her rendition in which "the ambition of the heroine o'erswayed but did not extinguish the sentiments of the woman." Dennis Bartholomeusz quotes from a letter written by a person who had seen Faucit on stage: "This woman, it seems to me, is simply urging her husband forward through her love of him, which prompts her to wish for the gratification of his ambition, to commit a murder" (174). Faucit played opposite William Macready, a forceful Macbeth whom Fletcher called a "heartless slave." The two actors, thus, complemented each other's interpretation of their roles.

In *Shakespeare Papers* (1860), Walter Maginn endorsed what was becoming the new orthodoxy. He writes of Lady Macbeth,

> She sees that [her husband] covets the throne, that his happiness is wrapped up in the hope of becoming a king; and her part is accordingly taken without hesitation. With the blindness of affection she persuades herself that he is full of the milk of human kindness, and that he would reject false and unholy ways of attaining the object of his desires [1.5.17–22]. She deems it, therefore, her duty to spirit him to the task. (194)

In the late 19th century, Ellen Terry presented a loving Lady Macbeth opposite Henry Irving's cowardly villain in the play's title role. In a letter to William Winter, Terry declared that Lady Macbeth was above all else a devoted wife. To her daughter, she wrote, "I by no means make her a gently lovable woman, as some of them say. That's

Lady Macbeth greets the King and his party in Act I, Scene 6 of *Macbeth*. This is a plate from *Retzsch's Outlines to Shakespeare: Macbeth,* published in 1833. *(Illustration by Moritz Retzsch)*

all pickles; she was nothing of the sort, although she was not a fiend and did love her husband" (Rosenberg 185). Lady Macbeth invokes the spirits to unsex her because she is too weak to act without their aid. She urges her husband to kill Duncan because she knows he craves the throne. A review in the *World* for January 2, 1889, shows that Lady Macbeth as loving wife was now the prevailing view, perhaps reflecting the late Victorian vision of women generally. The *World* praised Terry as "the Lady Macbeth Shakespeare would have drawn had he had Ellen Terry in his company. . . . We can readily accept this clinging and cajoling enchantress, whose enkindled ambition affects her with a temporary paralysis of conscience." According to Terry, Lady Macbeth retains "the nervous force of a woman, the devotion of a woman, and above all the conscience of a woman," and this conscience destroys her (Rosenberg 186).

In the 20th century, Vivien Leigh, who played opposite her husband, Laurence Olivier, in the Glen Byam Shaw 1955 Stratford production, followed Terry's loving approach. Byam Shaw declared that Lady Macbeth's "loyalty to her husband is magnificent. The way she behaves in the banquet scene is beyond praise. In spite of her complete lack of

compassion and goodness of heart one cannot but have the greatest admiration for her courage and loyalty" (Mullin 152–153). Supporting the view of Lady Macbeth as affectionate, Robin Grove argues, in "Multiplying Villainies of Nature," "what binds these two together is not ambition or bloodlust or fear alone, it is love" (133).

Despite Lady Macbeth's prayer in Act I, Scene 5 to be unsexed and the role's having been created to be played by a boy, some interpreters have emphasized her sexual nature. Under Trevor Nunn's direction in 1976, Judi Dench in the role exerted "a powerful sexual sway over her husband," according to Jack Tinker's review of the play in the *Daily Mail* for September 16, 1976. Two years earlier, Helen Mirren had also emphasized the character's sexual nature, but Mirren attributed Lady Macbeth's disintegration to sexual deprivation as Macbeth increasingly distances himself from her. This portrayal dates from Sarah Bernhardt's late 19th-century approach. Her Lady Macbeth resembled Delilah and Cleopatra in her seductive power. Bernhardt's Polish contemporary Helena Modjeska also stressed Lady Macbeth's femininity, humanity, and tenderness.

Whether she is seeking to promote her own desires or her husband's, Lady Macbeth displays resolution. She seizes the opportunity that Duncan's visit presents, plans his murder, which Macbeth might not have executed without her goading, and covers up the killing afterward. Her fainting in Act II, Scene 3 as Macduff sharply questions Macbeth is often taken as a clever ruse to prevent her husband from exposing himself, as he seems to falter under interrogation. She recognizes the price of success and is willing to pay it, for she also understands its rewards. Even if the Macbeths are suspected of regicide, she knows that they will be too powerful to be accused (1.7.78–80, 5.1.37–39). She is a rationalist and a literalist, perhaps by nature, perhaps by suppressing her imagination. She sees no mind-forged dagger, no ghost. The owl and cricket speak no words to her ear. She does not fear returning the daggers to the death chamber: "The sleeping and the dead / Are but as pictures"

(2.2.50–51). Her bloody hands do not appall her: "A little water clears us of this deed" (2.2.64).

Through Act III, Scene 4 she is so strong that her disintegration in Act V, Scene 1 may seem out of character. Yet, the text offers clues to the sensitivity and remorse that destroy her. She does not kill Duncan herself because he looks like her father. Though the sounds she hears after the king's murder are not words, she says, "I heard the owl scream and the crickets cry" (2.2.15). Earlier, she notes, "It was the owl that shriek'd" (2.2.3). Her verbs convey a sense of horror. Her fainting in Act II, Scene 3 may not, in fact, be a ruse but the delayed reaction to the enormity of the murder. By Act III, Scene 1, she has discovered that monarchy has not brought happiness: "Nought's had, all's spent, / Where our desire is got without content" (4–5).

Her husband, whom she sought to advance or control, grows distant. He no longer needs her. He kills Banquo and attacks Macduff's castle without telling her of his plans. The witches have become his sole advisers. In her sleepwalking, she still shows resolution as she relives Duncan's murder: "Fie, my lord, fie, a soldier and afeard?" (5.1.36–37); "No more o' that, my lord, no more o' that; you mar all with this starting" (5.1.43–45). In her reverie, she also chides her husband for fearing Banquo's ghost (5.1.62–64). Yet, the memory of Duncan's blood haunts her. She sees it. She smells it. What is that letter that she writes in her sleep? Is she belatedly warning Lady Macduff of danger? Or, is she writing to her husband, who, a gentleman reports, has left Dunsinane to suppress rebellion? Perhaps guilt overwhelms her; perhaps she finds that she has paid too high a price for her dream. Hers is the tragedy of getting what she wants; her success kills her.

The Witches

These equivocators have received varying treatment over the centuries. In William Davenant's adaptation, they are comic rather than threatening, and this tradition persisted through the 18th and into the 19th century. Thomas Davies, David Garrick's biographer, remarked in his *Dramatic Miscellanies* at the end of the 18th century, "Since all the tragic actors of a company were needed elsewhere in the play, none but the comic actors are left" for the witches' parts (119). Davies defended this humorous interpretation. In a journal entry for February 18, 1833, Fanny Kemble observed: "It has always been customary—heaven only knows why,—to make low comedians act the witches, and to dress them like old fishwomen." According to Kemble, they were outfitted with peaked hats and broomsticks. Hazlitt complained that in the early 19th-century production he saw, the witches were "ridiculous."

An armed head, conjured by the witches, tells Macbeth to beware of Macduff in Act IV, Scene 1 of *Macbeth*. This illustration was designed for a 1918 edition of Charles and Mary Lamb's *Tales from Shakespeare*. (Illustration by Louis Rhead)

Holinshed called the witches "eyther the weird sisters, that is (as ye would say) ye Goddesses of destinie, or else some Nimphes, or Feiries." Tyrone Guthrie in his 1934 Old Vic production cut the opening scene because, he maintained, to have the witches open the play implied that they controlled the action. In his 1939 edition of the work, George Lyman Kittredge claimed they did just that. For him, they are like the Scandinavian Norns, or fates.

Kittredge inconsistently insisted that Macbeth, nonetheless, has free will. Most critics share this view. Hence, they deny the witches the power to determine behavior. In *Shakespearean Tragedy* (1904), A. C. Bradley proleptically rejected Kittredge's position. Bradley wrote: "The Witches . . . are not goddesses or fates, or, in any way whatever, supernatural beings" (341). He regards them as old women with supernatural powers. Their words prove fatal to Macbeth "because there is in him something which leaps into light at the sound of them; but they are at the same time witness of forces which never cease to work in the world around him, and, on the instant of his surrender to them entangle him inextricably in the web of Fate" (349). As noted in the "Background" section, in *Daemonlogie,* King James maintained that Satan can deceive only those who "first willfully deceive themselves by running unto him, whom God then suffers to fall in their owne snares, and justly permits them to be illuded with great efficacie of deceit." Garber likens the witches to Iago; they "allow [Macbeth] to interpret things as he wants to see them" (698).

Upon first seeing the witches, Banquo declares, "You should be women," (1.3.45), and that is how some directors and critics see them, as merely human. Theodore Komisarjevsky's 1933 *Macbeth* at Stratford-upon-Avon banished the supernatural. Banquo's ghost is Macbeth's shadow, and the witches are only old women. Joan Littlewood (1957) and Peter Hall (1967) treated them this way as well. Hall said he wanted them to resemble old women one might find along the Thames Embankment or the New York Bowery (before these were gentrified). Harbage calls the witches "musty crones of popular superstition, not ministers of fate" (373).

Though Banquo speaks of their hairy chins, "choppy finger[s]," and thin lips (1.3.44–46), not all directors have made the witches old and ugly. In the 1577 edition of Holinshed, they appear young and attractive in the woodcut showing their first meeting with Macbeth. Thomas Heywood retold the Macbeth story in his *Hierarchie of the Blessed Angels* (1635); he describes the witches as "Virgins wondrous faire." A 1965 Edinburgh production cast three beautiful young blonds in these roles. Trevor Nunn, prompted by their line, "Fair is foul, and foul is fair" (1.1.11), used one beautiful and two ugly witches.

Shakespeare may have read George Buchanan's version of the Macbeth story, in which the witches are figments of Macbeth's mind. By the 1580s, writers such as Buchanan and Reginald Scot (*The Discoverie of Witchcraft,* 1584) were challenging the idea of witches, and by 1606, even King James was having doubts. Samuel Taylor Coleridge in the early 19th century regarded them as symbolizing "the shadowy obscure and fearfully anomalous of physical nature, the lawless of human nature." Garber rejects this purely metaphoric interpretation, but it appeals to modern sensibility and heightens the psychological aspects of the play.

Duncan

Duncan's main function in the play is to be killed. He speaks 69 lines, or about half those given to Ross (134 lines) and just five more than Lennox. He is present in only three scenes (1.2, 1.4, 1.6). Symbolically, he represents the good king. Macbeth praises him even while contemplating regicide (1.7.16–20), and Duncan's excellences almost persuade Macbeth not to commit murder. Shakespeare improved on the weak figure of the play's sources; in the play, Duncan does not fight the rebels himself because he is old, not because he is weak. He shows concern for the wounded Sergeant, sending him off with attendants to secure medical help. He generously rewards Macbeth for valor and Lady

Macbeth for hospitality, and he acknowledges the burden a royal visit places on his entertainers (1.6.11–12). He dispenses justice, condemning the traitorous thane of Cawdor while rewarding loyal supporters.

Duncan's language of fertility contrasts with Macbeth's images of barrenness, just as Duncan's just reign highlights Macbeth's tyranny. In making his son his heir, Duncan was violating the 11th-century Scottish practice of tanistry, or elective monarchy, yet, even if English audiences in 1606 were aware of this ancient practice, they would have regarded hereditary monarchy as the norm and would have approved of Duncan's effort to preclude a succession crisis such as England had experienced in 1553 and again in 1603.

Duncan is, however, innocent and naive. He trusted the first thane of Cawdor and does not suspect the second of harboring treacherous thoughts. Arriving at Inverness, Duncan observes: "This castle hath a pleasant seat, the air / Nimbly and sweetly recommends itself / Unto our gentle senses" (1.6.1–3). The dramatic irony of this speech is palpable. He also commends the love the Macbeths show him. In his final speech, he asks Lady Macbeth for her hand, which shortly will be coated with his blood.

Banquo

Shakespeare improved Banquo's character from the co-conspirator he found in Holinshed to Macbeth's foil. He warns Macbeth not to trust the witches' prophecies, even after the first of these comes true when Macbeth is named thane of Cawdor. To Macbeth's suggestion that Banquo will gain honor by siding with him, Banquo replies: "So I lose none / In seeking to augment it, but still keep / My bosom franchis'd and allegiance clear" (2.1.26–28). Whereas Macbeth will sacrifice conscience and loyalty to make the witches' words come true, Banquo refuses to do so.

Not that he is ignorant of temptation. Unable to sleep, perhaps because the witches' prediction troubles him, he prays: "Merciful powers, / Restrain in me the cursed thoughts that nature /

Gives way to in repose" (2.1.7–9). Just before these lines, he gives his dagger to his son. Soon afterward, Macbeth sees his mind-drawn dagger that presages his regicide and draws his real weapon. Shakespeare thus creates a visual contrast between these two men.

Like so much else in this play, Banquo nonetheless remains equivocal. Although he suspects Macbeth of killing Duncan, he says nothing. Nor does he shun the new king. For him, the death of Duncan is made less a heinous crime in that it relates to an opportunity for his descendants to gain the throne (3.1.1–10). His final act is nonetheless noble: As he battles his assassins, he urges his son to fly.

Macduff

This character, too, contrasts with Macbeth. Horrified by Duncan's murder, he quickly suspects Macbeth and, unlike Banquo, distances himself from the usurper. For the good of his country, he leaves his home, unguarded, to go to England to urge Malcolm to supplant the tyrant. His wife initially condemns this action but before her death recognizes that he acted properly. She is glad that he has not remained in Scotland to be killed with the rest of his family. He successfully persuades

Macduff kills Macbeth in Act V, Scene 8, as depicted in a plate from *Retzsch's Outlines to Shakespeare: Macbeth*, published in 1833. *(Illustration by Moritz Retzsch)*

Malcolm to return to Scotland with an army and kills Macbeth, thereby freeing Scotland from bad rule and also avenging his personal losses. He proves a loyal follower of Malcolm, whereas Macbeth was a faithless subject of Malcolm's father.

Macduff also offers a vision of manhood that contrasts with Macbeth's. In Act I, Scene 7, Macbeth and his wife discuss this concept. Initially, he refuses to kill Duncan because Macbeth recognizes the limits that manhood imposes: "I dare do all that may become a man; / Who dares do more is none" (46–47). Lady Macbeth disagrees: "When thou durst do it, then you were a man; / And to be more than what you were, you would / Be so much more the man" (49–51). Her definition of manhood endorses violence and excludes feelings for others. Macbeth accepts her interpretation, agreeing to kill Duncan and declaring, "Bring forth men-children only! / For thy undaunted mettle should compose / Nothing but males" (72–74).

When Macduff learns of the death of his family, he presents a more humane face of manhood as he openly displays his grief. Malcolm urges him to "Dispute it like a man" (4.3.220). Macduff's weeping and pulling his hat upon his brows (4.3.207) strike the king's son as unmanly. Macduff's line "He has no children" (4.3.216) may refer to Macbeth, but it might as well mean that childless Malcolm cannot recognize the emotions of a bereft father. Macduff retorts: "I shall do so [dispute it like a man]; / But I must also feel it like a man" (4.3.220–221). Manliness is not only fighting, killing, pursuing ambition, and revenge. To be a man, Macduff maintains, to be fully human, is also to grieve.

Macbeth loses this ability. Hearing a shriek provoked by his wife's death, he observes: "I have almost forgot the taste of fears. / . . . I have supp'd full with horrors; / Direness, familiar to my slaughterous thoughts, / Cannot once start me" (5.5.9–15). Learning that Lady Macbeth is dead, he can say only, "She should have died hereafter" (5.5.17). His (and his wife's) vision of manliness leads to isolation and death.

DIFFICULTIES OF THE PLAY

The poet and dramatist John Dryden already found Shakespeare's language challenging in the late 17th century. Dryden in "The Grounds of Criticism in Tragedy" observed that Shakespeare "often obscures his meanings by his words, and sometimes makes it unintelligible. . . . The fury of his fancy often transported him beyond the bounds of judgment, either in coining of new words and phrases, or racking words which were in use into the violence of a catachresis." *Catachresis* is the application of a word to a thing it does not properly denote, as when Macbeth speaks of "daggers . . . breech'd with gore" (2.3.115–116), suggesting by *breech'd* that the blood on them served as pants covering their nakedness.

Macbeth presents speeches of unusual obscurity and complexity, even for Shakespeare. Macbeth's soliloquy in Act I, Scene 7 (discussed in "Key Passages") provoked Samuel Johnson, who produced an edition of Shakespeare in 1765, to comment, "The meaning is not very clear: I have never found the readers of Shakespeare agreeing about it." Of a later speech (2.1.33–64), Johnson remarks, "I believe every one that has attentively read this dreadful soliloquy is disappointed at the conclusion, which, if not wholly unintelligible, is, at least, obscure, nor can be explained into any sense worthy of the author." Like many others, Johnson cannot explain what Macbeth means by "the perfect spy o' th' time" (3.1.130). Malcolm's lines, "That which you are, my thoughts cannot transpose: / Angels are bright still, though the brightest fell. / Though all things foul would wear the brows of grace, / Yet grace must still look so" (4.3.21–24), elicit Johnson's direct remark, "This is not very clear."

Other characters give similarly puzzling speeches. Lady Macbeth seems to mix her metaphors when she asks, "Was the hope drunk / Wherein you dressed yourself? Hath it slept since?" (1.7.35–36). How does one dress in drunken hope? Macbeth tells his wife, "ere to black Hecat's summons / The shard-borne beetle with his drowsy hums / Hath rung night's yawning peal, there shall be done / A deed of dreadful note" (3.2.41–44).

How does a drowsy hum become the pealing of a bell? Later, Ross describes the time as one in which "we hold rumor / From what we fear, / But float upon a wild and violent sea / Each way and move" (4.2.19–22). These lines are cut in a promptbook dating from about 1630, perhaps indicating that an early director found them hard to comprehend. The witches' equivocal lines also puzzle.

One question that has always puzzled readers is that of Lady Macbeth's children. Lady Macbeth clearly says she has suckled an infant, but no son or daughter of the Macbeths appears in the play. Historically, Macbeth was her second husband, so Lady Macbeth may have had one or more children from her first marriage. The play, however, leaves the matter unclear. (Some critics have declared the question pointless; in a famous essay "How Many Children Had Lady Macbeth?" (1932), L. C. Knights mocked treatments of Shakespeare's characters as real people.) Similarly, the play seems to leave open the Third Murderer involved in killing Duncan. Only two murderers seem to be needed. The First Murderer expresses the feelings of many a reader and viewer upon seeing this mysterious figure: "But who did bid thee join with us?" (3.3.1).

Finally, *Macbeth*'s connection to contemporary politics often poses a problem for students. Although the play is set in 11th-century Scotland, it draws on such English events of the early 17th century as the Gunpowder Plot and King James's fascination with witches. For example, the Porter scene (2.3; discussed in Difficult Passages below) makes much more sense if one understands the then burning concern with Jesuitical equivocation. Knowledge of historical context can be useful in appreciating the play.

KEY PASSAGES
Act I, Scene 7, 1–27

MACBETH. If it were done, when 'tis done, then 'twere well
It were done quickly. If th' assassination
Could trammel up the consequence, and catch
With his surcease, success; that but this blow
Might be the be-all and the end-all—here,
But here, upon this bank and shoal of time,
We'ld jump the life to come. But in these cases
We still have judgment here, that we but teach
Bloody instructions, which, being taught,
    return
To plague th' inventor. This even-handed
    justice
Commends th' ingredience of our poison'd
    chalice
To our own lips. He's here in double trust:
First, as I am his kinsman and his subject,
Strong both against the deed; then, as his host,
Who should against his murtherer shut the
    door,
Not bear the knife myself. Besides, this
    Duncan
Hath borne his faculties so meek, hath been
So clear in his great office, that his virtues
Will plead like angels, trumpet-tongu'd,
    against
The deep damnation of his taking-off;
And pity, like a naked new born babe,
Striding the blast, or heaven's cherubin, hors'd
Upon the sightless couriers of the air,
Shall blow the horrid deed in every eye,
That tears shall drown the wind. I have no
    spur
To prick the sides of my intent, but only
Vaulting ambition, which o'erleaps itself,
And falls on th' other—

Macbeth has stolen away from the feast with Duncan, just as in Act I, Scene 3, he had withdrawn from his comrades to contemplate the killing of the king. This scene opens with music and with servants crossing the stage bearing platters of food, symbols of revelry and companionship. A feast represents communion, both sacred and profane. Here, and again in Act III, Scene 4, Macbeth's imaginings do not allow him to partake of that unity with others. Already isolated, he will grow only more so as the play progresses.

In *Othello*, Desdemona declares: "I cannot say, 'whore.' / It does abhor me now I speak the word. / To do the act that might the addition earn, /

Not the world's mass of vanity could make me" (4.2.161–164). Macbeth similarly cannot say the word *murder;* he can call his contemplated regicide only "it." He says "the assassination," not "my assassination"; "his murtherer," not "me." He uses "we" in "We'ld jump the life to come. But in these cases / We still have judgment here." Perhaps he already thinks himself king and is using the royal plural personal pronoun. Perhaps he is including his wife. He may also be stating a general proposition that again removes him from the immediate situation. When he shifts to "I" later in this soliloquy, he abandons his plan to kill Duncan. The hypermetric lines of 11 and even 12 syllables (for example, lines 2, 7, 10, and 11) and deranged syntax reflect his agitation.

In this soliloquy's opening lines, Macbeth seeks to reduce the future to the instant, to deny actions any consequence beyond the moment. Lady Macbeth shares this view: "This night's great business . . . / shall to all our nights and days to come / Give solely sovereign sway and masterdom" (1.5.68–70). Later, she declares: "what's done, is done" (3.2.12). Even before he commits his first murder, Macbeth recognizes the fallacy of this position. Even if he could avoid damnation for his crime—and his use of the subjunctive "we'ld" *(we would)* shows he understands he cannot—he will face condemnation in this world. His regicide will sanction his own deposition.

As he continues to think aloud, he discovers other reasons that dissuade him from killing the king. Typical of this play, he finds three arguments: hospitality, kinship, and Duncan's excellences as a ruler. Social, familial, and political concerns argue against Macbeth's bloody thoughts. Most important among reasons, as the imagery of the end of the speech indicates, is the biblical injunction against murder. Macbeth speaks of trumpet-tongued angels, damnation, and cherubim. In "Education and the University," F. R. Leavis commented: "What we have in this passage is a conscience-tormented imagination, vivid with terror of the supernatural, proclaiming a certitude that 'murder will out,' a certitude appalling to Mac-

beth not because of the consequences on 'this bank and shoal of time' (1.7.6) but by reason of a sense of sin—the radical hold on him of religious sanctions" (318).

By the end of this passage, Macbeth has argued himself into rejecting the plan to kill Duncan. Rosenberg observes of this speech,

> What Macbeth is envisioning, in his wild poetry, is in fact a projection of the struggle being fought out in his interior battleground— his impulses of innocence and humankindness striving to manage and tame the Dionysian storm. The progression of the soliloquy parallels what happens within Macbeth himself; violent impulses are eventually subdued by the more powerful force of a rising tenderness (261).

Macbeth acknowledges that he has "no spur / to prick the sides of my intent," a trope suggested by the earlier reference to the horsed cherubim. But, before he can complete his final sentence, Lady Macbeth enters. She will provide the spur that will goad him to do what he knows is wrong and will lead to his downfall.

Act II, Scene 1, 33–64
MACBETH. Is this a dagger which I see
 before me,
The handle toward my hand? Come, let me
 clutch thee:
I have thee not, and yet I see thee still.
Art thou not, fatal vision, sensible
To feeling as to sight? Or art thou but
A dagger of the mind, a false creation,
Proceeding from the heat-oppressed brain?
I see thee yet, in form as palpable
As this which now I draw.
Thou marshal'st me the way that I was going,
And such an instrument I was to use.
Mine eyes are made the fools o' th' other
 senses,
Or else worth all the rest. I see thee still;
And on thy blade and dudgeon gouts of blood,

Which was not so before. There's no such
thing:
It is the bloody business which informs
Thus to mine eyes. Now o'er the one half
world
Nature seems dead, and wicked dreams abuse
The curtain'd sleep; witchcraft celebrates
Pale Hecat's off'rings; and wither'd Murther,
Alarum'd by his sentinel, the wolf,
Whose howl's his watch, thus with his stealthy
pace,
With Tarquin's ravishing strides, towards his
design
Moves like a ghost. Thou sure and firm-set
earth,
Hear not my steps, which way they walk, for
fear
The very stones prate of my whereabout,
And take the present horror from the time,
Which now suits with it. Whiles I threat, he
lives:
Words to the heat of deeds too cold breath
gives.
[A bell rings.]
I go, and it is done; the bell invites me.
Hear it not, Duncan, for it is a knell,
That summons thee to heaven or to hell.

Macbeth's vivid imagination has been evident from his first appearance, when the thought of killing Duncan entranced him so because he could picture the deed in his mind's eye. Now that same thought of murder conjures up a mind-forged dagger, such as he is about to use, and then coats it with Duncan's soon-to-be-spilled blood. He has resolved to commit the murder, but his subconscious that raised the vision remains as horrified by the deed as it was in Act I, Scene 3.

He dismisses the dagger as unreal, but his description of night again reveals how vexed his thoughts remain. He speaks of bad dreams troubling sleep, a foreshadowing of his own inability to sleep once he kills Duncan. His mind reverts to the witches, whom he links to murder. These references to witches and Hecate join him to the forces of darkness and evil, marking him as damned as they are. Then, his mind shifts to Tarquin, ravisher of Lucrece. For a momentary pleasure, this king of ancient Rome was deposed. Macbeth's allusion indicates that his action will not produce lasting happiness; rather it will bring about his downfall. Still, he imagines that the bell he hears summons him to kill Duncan, even though the last words of the speech raise once more the prospect of divine judgment, not just for Duncan, but for Macbeth.

Act V, Scene 5, 17–28

MACBETH. She should have died hereafter;
There would have been a time for such a word.
To-morrow, and to-morrow, and to-morrow,
Creeps in this petty pace from day to day,
To the last syllable of recorded time;
And all our yesterdays have lighted fools
The way to dusty death. Out, out, brief candle!
Life's but a walking shadow, a poor player,
That struts and frets his hour upon the stage,
And then is heard no more. It is a tale
Told by an idiot, full of sound and fury,
Signifying nothing.

These, among the best known of Shakespeare's lines, serve as Macbeth's elegy to his dead wife and to his squandered life. A comparison between Macduff's heartfelt response to the news of his spouse's murder and Macbeth's unfeeling reflection reveals how far the latter has isolated himself from humanity. He recognizes his transformation earlier in this scene when, hearing a cry of women prompted by the discovery of the queen's body, he reflects:

The time has been, my senses would have
cool'd
To hear a night-shriek, and my fell of hair
Would at a dismal treatise rouse and stir
As life were in't. I have supp'd full with
horrors;
Direness, familiar to my slaughterous
thoughts,
Cannot once start me. (5.5.9–15)

The opening lines of this monologue are ambiguous. Perhaps Macbeth wishes his wife had died at another time when he would not be distracted by imminent battle. Then he would have been able to mourn properly. Perhaps he wishes she had lived longer. Alternatively, he might mean that Lady Macbeth was going to die sometime anyway. In this last interpretation, he expresses the same fatalism as Hamlet: "If it be now, 'tis not to come; if it be not to come, it will be now; if it be not now, yet it will come—the readiness is all" (*Hamlet* 5.2.220–222). The rest of the speech reflects at least as much on his condition as it does on his wife's, again indicating how far removed Macbeth has grown from the woman he once called "my dearest partner of greatness" (1.5.11). Indicating this division, the two never appear onstage together after Act III, Scene 4.

Macbeth and his wife had thought to arrest time, to reduce the future to the instant (1.5.58), to make the killing of Duncan "the be-all and the end-all" (1.7.5). Now, Macbeth acknowledges that time—the play contains 44 mentions of this word—moves inexorably onward. Macbeth's speeches follow a stream-of-consciousness pattern. In his soliloquy opening Act I, Scene 7, the image of trumpet-tongued angels leads to horsed cherubim and the reference of horses conjures up the reference to a spur. Here, "yesterdays" lighting the way suggests a candle, which reminds the audience of the one Lady Macbeth carries in her sleepwalking scene. That earlier candle now emerges as a beacon that possibly guided her to suicide. The candle calls to mind a shadow, one meaning of which is an actor (see *A Midsummer Night's Dream*, 5.1.423), hence the reference to the poor player. The Globe Theatre's Latin motto, *"Totus Mundus Agit Historionum,"* means, "All the world plays the player." Or, as Jacques's loose translation states, "All the world's a stage" (*As You Like It*, 2.7.139). Rosenberg regards this imagistic linking as "reflecting the agonized, roaming mind" (613).

Macbeth nihilistically reduces life to a meaningless script created by an idiot and acted by fools. Macbeth here reaches the nadir of despair, deny-ing himself, as well as everyone else, volition and free will, rejecting any meaning in life. Rosenberg writes: "Macbeth puts into words the mortal frustration with a world that seems to lie in wait to baffle and enervate the trusting" (613). Immediately after Macbeth delivers these lines, a messenger arrives to announce that Birnam Wood is coming to Dunsinane. The witches had assured Macbeth that he would not be defeated until "Great Birnam wood to high Dunsinane hill / Shall come against him" (4.1.93–94). Yet, the moving grove presaging his overthrow instills in him new determination. Resolving to confront the enemy despite the witches' warning, he disdains fortune as he had in fighting Macdonwald and Norway (1.2.17). The heroic soldier resurfaces for one final battle. The candle blazes up one last time before it is extinguished. For Macbeth, like the previous thane of Cawdor, "Nothing in his life / [Becomes] him like the leaving it" (1.4.7–8).

DIFFICULT PASSAGES
Act I, Scene 5, 39–55

LADY MACBETH. The raven himself is
  hoarse
That croaks the fatal entrance of Duncan
Under my battlements. Come, you spirits
That tend on mortal thoughts, unsex me here,
And fill me from the crown to the toe topful
Of direst cruelty! Make thick my blood,
Stop up th' access and passage to remorse,
That no compunctious visitings of nature
Shake my fell purpose, nor keep peace between
Th' effect and it! Come to my woman's breasts,
And take my milk for gall, you murth'ring
  ministers,
Wherever in your sightless substances
You wait on nature's mischief! Come, thick
  night,
And pall thee in the dunnest smoke of hell,
That my keen knife see not the wound it
  makes,
Nor heaven peep through the blanket of the
  dark
To cry, "Hold, hold!"

Viola Allen as Lady Macbeth *(Photographed by White Studio)*

This scene begins with Lady Macbeth entering with the letter her husband has sent her to report his meeting with the witches and their predictions. Having read this account, she declares: "Glamis thou art, and Cawdor, and shalt be / What thou art promised" (1.5.15–16). This threefold naming of Macbeth echoes the witches' greeting to him in Act I, Scene 3, thus linking Lady Macbeth with those forces of darkness. She then declares she will spur Macbeth to regicide. A messenger interrupts her reflections to announce that Duncan will spend that very night in her castle.

As soon as she is alone again, she states her intention to seize this opportunity to kill the king. In this complicated speech, she imagines that the raven, a harbinger of death, has crowed itself hoarse predicting Duncan's demise. To achieve

her goal, she calls upon evil spirits (perhaps the witches?) to remove any feminine pity she may possess. Her invocation rejects fertility and nurture ("Make thick my blood"; "take my milk for gall"), foreshadowing the "barren scepter" (3.1.61) that Macbeth will gain. This speech's imagery of hell and night again unite her with the forces of evil and destruction that she summons, turning Lady Macbeth into a witch herself. She even knows how she will commit the crime ("my keen knife").

At the end of this speech, Macbeth enters, and her greeting once more repeats that of the witches, joining her with them: "Great Glamis! worthy Cawdor! / Greater than both, by the all-hail hereafter!" (1.5.54–55). Yet, her attempts to demonize herself fail. She can goad Macbeth into killing Duncan, but she cannot commit the crime herself because, she says, the king resembles her father (2.2.12–13). This excuse may be rationalization. Even if true, her inability to kill shows that she retains a measure of compunction. This feeling will overwhelm her in Act 5, Scene 1 and cause her death, perhaps by her own hand. The last lines of her soliloquy anticipate her failure to abandon her humanity, as she summons darkness to prevent God from seeing what she does and stopping her. Like Macbeth, she knows that she is violating divine as well as human law. Neither of them can permanently suppress that knowledge, and it is this inner struggle that will destroy them both.

Act II, Scene 3, 1–25

PORTER. Here's a knocking indeed! If a man
were porter of Hell Gate, he should have
old turning the key. *[Knock]* Knock, knock,
knock! Who's there, i' th' name of Belzebub?
Here's a farmer, that hang'd himself on th'
expectation of plenty. Come in time! Have
napkins enow about you, here you'll sweat
for't. *[Knock]* Knock, knock! Who's there,
in th' other devil's name? Faith, here's an
equivocator, that could swear in both the
scales against either scale, who committed
treason enough for God's sake, yet could
not equivocate to heaven. O, come in,

equivocator. *[Knock]* Knock, knock, knock!
Who's there? Faith, here's an English tailor
come hither for stealing out of a French
hose. Come in, tailor, here you may roast
your goose. *[Knock]* Knock, knock! Never at
quiet! What are you? But this place is too cold
for hell. I'll devil-porter it no further. I had
thought to have let in some of all professions
that go the primrose way to th' everlasting
bonfire. *[Knock]* Anon, anon! *[Opens the
gate.]* I pray you remember the porter.

The only comic episode in the play (unless one
regards the witches as humorous), this speech
comes between the high tension of Duncan's murder (2.1–2.2) and the discovery of his death later in
Act II, Scene 3. (Thomas de Quincey wrote a well-
known exegesis of this opening of Act II, Scene 3;
see "Extracts of Classic Criticism" below.) It thus
provides a needed emotional oasis for the audience.
It also provides time for Macbeth and his wife to
wash their hands and put on their night clothes.
(When productions cut this part of the scene,
which retards rather than advances the plot, actors
are hard-pressed to switch outfits.) But the dense,
allusive nature of the speech makes it quite difficult
for audiences to grasp.

The Porter, who has drunk not wisely but too
well during the revelry celebrating Duncan's visit,
hears the knocking that began at the end of the
previous scene and that alerted Macbeth and his
wife to retire. As he rises from bed, still half asleep
and perhaps half dressed, he imagines he is opening not the south entry of the castle at Inverness
but the gates of hell. The first person he imagines
admitting is a farmer who hoarded grain, expecting food prices to rise because of a poor harvest.
When crops were plentiful, his investment declined
in value, so he killed himself. In Ben Jonson's *Every
Man out of His Humour* (1599), Sordido, a speculator in crops, enters in Act III, Scene 2 with a
halter around his neck because he expected storms,
but the weather was fair, leading to a bountiful
harvest and low food prices. *Macbeth* premiered at
the Globe, and Shakespeare's company performed

it for King James on January 8, 1605. Shakespeare
was himself a grain speculator and so knew the
emotions of such a person. Harvests in the period
surrounding the play had been good, and food,
cheap. The farmer may have hanged himself with
a large napkin, which he still wears as he comes to
hell's gate.

This farmer who hangs himself "on th' expectation of plenty" draws on another contemporary reference as well: Father Henry Garnet (mentioned in
the "Background" section) used the name *Farmer*
as one of his aliases. He is probably the equivocator who enters hell after the farmer. Equivocation was linked to treason. The third entrant, the
thieving tailor, stole fabric given to him to make
French hose. This fashionable article was either so
tight that any stealing would be obvious or so loose
that it would not be. Another possible meaning of
"stealing out of a French hose" is sexual.

All three men resemble Macbeth. Like the
farmer, Macbeth's expectations will go unmet.
As Lady Macbeth reflects in Act III, Scene 2,
"Nought's had, all's spent, / Where our desire is
got without content" (4–5). Like the equivocator,
Macbeth commits treason, and he steals, not fabric,
but the crown. The cavalcade of the damned, like
a Dance of Death, could go on, but the Porter has
been sufficiently awakened by the cold to recognize
where he is. He admits Macduff and Lennox and
asks them for a tip for his service.

The changes the Porter rings on the knock-
knock joke provide more than laughter and time
for the principals to change costumes, however
important these functions are. In "Hell-Castle
and Its Door-Keeper," Glynn Wickham compares
this episode to "The Harrowing of Hell" in medieval mystery cycles. These plays were still being
performed during Shakespeare's youth, though
they were subsequently banned in Protestant England as Catholic vestiges. In this mystery play (so
called because the plays were staged by craft guilds,
known as "mysteries" for their trade secrets), Christ
knocks at hell's gate, and a comic janitor under the
command of Beelzebub opens it ("Who's there, i'
th' name of Belzebub?"). Jesus then enters, look-

ing for Satan, as Macduff, who will save Scotland by killing the tyrant, comes seeking Macbeth, who, like Lucifer, aspired to a throne not his, committed crimes to obtain it, and was finally defeated "in his own castle by a savior-avenger" (Wickham 74). This episode also recalls Revelation 3:20: "One like the Son of Man [Jesus] says, 'Behold, I stand at the door, and knock.'" Audiences familiar with the mystery play would recognize that by killing Duncan, Macbeth has turned his castle into hell and has damned himself. As he acknowledges later, "For Banquo's issue have I fil'd my mind, / . . . and mine eternal jewel / Given to the common enemy of man" (3.1.64–68). Stylistically, this scene maintains the triadic mode of so much else in the play. The Porter imagines admitting three damned souls and twice says, "Knock, knock, knock!"

CRITICAL INTRODUCTION TO THE PLAY
Themes

A recurring theme in literature is the disparity between appearance and reality. Theater particularly invites an examination of this issue, since it presents illusion in the guise of reality but also reality (in the sense of truth) in the guise of illusion. As noted in the "Background" section, one of the matters debated during King James's 1605 visit to Oxford was whether the imagination could produce real effects. This question remains vital today; consider the placebo effect of sugar pills given as medicine. In the Renaissance, the matter carried particular weight as empiricism was displacing authority as the chief way of knowing. *Macbeth* challenges the validity of the senses. After the witches vanish from Act I, Scene 3, Banquo wonders: "Were such things here as we do speak about? / Or have we eaten on the insane root / That takes the reason prisoner?" (83–85).

In the next scene, Duncan remarks of the traitorous thane of Cawdor, "There's no art / To find the mind's construction in the face: / He was a gentleman on whom I built / An absolute trust" (11–14). Duncan then places his faith in the new thane of Cawdor, who proves equally treacherous.

The witches answer Macbeth's questions with visions in this 19th-century depiction of Act IV, Scene I of *Macbeth. (Illustration by Joshua Reynolds; engraving by Samuel Reynolds)*

He also praises Lady Macbeth's hospitality even as she contrives his murder. He cannot see the serpent hiding beneath "th' innocent flower" (1.5.65).

Macbeth sees a dagger of the mind and the ghost of Banquo. He hears a voice proclaiming he will sleep no more. Banquo shares the first vision of the witches, but only Macbeth encounters them a second time. In both instances (1.3 and 4.1), they tell him what he is already thinking—that he will be king and that Macduff is dangerous. Do his thoughts conjure up the witches, or do the witches fortify his ideas? Lady Macbeth, asleep, sees and smells the blood of Duncan on her hands; awake, she had imagined Duncan resembled her father. An invading army looks like a moving grove. The queen's death is ambiguous, perhaps suicide. Malcolm, echoing his father, acknowledges the limits of empirical evidence as he tries to assess Macduff's loyalty: "Angels are bright still, though the brightest fell. / Though all things foul would wear the brows of grace, / Yet grace must still look so" (4.3.22–24).

The theme of myth versus reality runs throughout Shakespeare's work. In *A Midsummer Night's Dream,* Theseus rejects the story the lovers tell of their time in the woods: "I never may believe

/ These antic fables, nor these fairy toys" (5.1.2–3). Ironically, he is himself a mythical figure. The audience, having seen events unfold, dismisses his skepticism. At the end of the play, though, Puck suggests that the entire play may have been a dream. In Shakespeare's other fairy play, *The Tempest,* Prospero, often viewed as the playwright's surrogate, says that existence itself is a dream. *Macbeth* questions reality in much the same way. Banquo's wondering whether the witches are real is just one obvious example.

The play similarly examines the reliability of language. The witches equivocate (that is, speak what is literally true but in a manner intended to deceive) with Macbeth, but even among themselves they speak ambiguously: "When the battle's lost and won" (1.1.4), "Fair is foul, and foul is fair" (1.1.11), "Double, double, toil and trouble" (4.1.10, 20, 35). Lady Macbeth speaks of her devotion to Duncan as she plots his death. Macbeth tells Banquo he looks forward to the latter's company at an evening's feast while expecting his former friend to be dead by then. Macbeth suborns Banquo's killers by deceiving them into believing Banquo is responsible for their miseries. Lady Macbeth persuades her husband to kill Duncan by telling him he will be more the man if he commits the murder, that no one will suspect them, and kingship will provide "sovereign sway and masterdom" (1.5.70). These arguments are false. Macbeth knows that his supporters offer him only "mouth-honor, breath, / Which the poor heart would fain deny, and dare not" (5.3.27–28). Their words cannot be trusted any more than his own or, as he learns too late, the witches' promises.

Communication fails in this play. Characters do not speak to one another so much as they speak past or ignore. Communication is love, and in this play, communication is tainted. Speech is ironic or riddling, with the meaning sometimes unknown even to the speaker, as when Macbeth, in Act III, Scene 4, wishes for Banquo's presence, only to be appalled when his ghost appears. As Lawrence Dawson notes in *Tragic Alphabet,* "Macbeth's deed is an overturning of normal values and relationships,

and the language of the play (the Weird Sister's speeches being only the most obvious example) follows the action into the chaotic world he establishes, into the realm of impossibility, beyond the powers of ordinary conception, beyond the proper sphere of words" (126).

Like Shakespeare's history plays, which *Macbeth* in many ways resembles, this play examines the nature of kingship. Duncan and Malcolm exemplify good rule, whereas Macbeth illustrates tyranny and its consequences. Nature itself alters when kingship is corrupted, as the conversation between Ross and the Old Man illustrates in Act II, Scene 4. Ross again comments on the inversions resulting from bad rule when he notes, "good men's lives / Expire before the flowers in their caps, / Dying or ere they sicken" (4.3.171–173). Trees move; a man not born of woman kills Macbeth. In a 1621 sermon, Robert Bolton stated:

> Take sovereignty from the face of the earth, and you turn it into a Cockpit. Men would become cut-throats and cannibals one unto another. Murder, adulteries, incests, rapes, robberies, perjuries, witchcrafts, blasphemies, all kinds of villainies, outrages, and savage cruelty, would overflow all Countries. We should have a very hell upon earth, and the face of it covered with blood, as it was once with water.

These words sound like a gloss upon the fruits of Macbeth's regicide.

More frightening than the consequences to Scotland of Duncan's death is its cost to Macbeth and his wife. The depictions of the murder of Banquo and the attack on Macduff's castle are moving, but these events occupy only two scenes; Duncan's killing occurs offstage. The focus of the play is less on external events than on the disintegration of characters who destroy themselves through their effort to transcend moral boundaries. This theme, which pervades tragedy from fifth-century B.C. Athens onward, receives one of its most potent expressions in *Macbeth.*

Structure

Macbeth unfolds rapidly, without a subplot. Though historically, Macbeth ruled 17 years, the play makes his reign seem to last only a few months. (Shakespeare employed this kind of compression in his other historical dramas as well.) The arc of the action traces Macbeth's rise and fall. The opening scene sets the tone of the entire work, with thunder and lightning indicating the political and psychological tempests to come. The witches introduce the note of evil that pervades the play, and their equivocation will echo repeatedly in characters' speeches.

The second scene moves to Duncan's camp and news of battle. Descriptions of the fighting and the sight of the bloody Sergeant enhance the feeling of discord created in the previous scene. Yet, the reports from the field describe the defeat of rebellion and the return of order. As Shakespeare often does, he here allows others to speak of the protagonist before the audience meets him. The third scene introduces Macbeth, whom the Sergeant and Ross have portrayed as a heroic warrior. His first appearance highlights not his deeds but his thoughts, and he will not show his physical heroism again until the end of the play. The witches reappear to dominate this scene. Their presence and words reveal that the order established by the defeat of Duncan's foes will be short-lived.

In Act I, Scene 4, the focus returns to Duncan and order, as the king rewards loyalty and establishes succession. Evil returns in Act 1, Scene 5, with Lady Macbeth's invocation of "murth'ring ministers" (1.5.48). Although the witches are absent, Lady Macbeth serves as a suitable surrogate. Duncan makes his final appearance in Act I, Scene 6, where his courteous speech and optimistic outlook and Banquo's references to fertility contrast with Act I, Scene 5 and 7, in which Macbeth and his wife resolve on regicide.

The second act begins in the darkness that Macbeth and Lady Macbeth have invoked. Night dominates the first two scenes, in which Duncan is murdered. Although morning comes in Scene 3, Ross notes in the following scene that "dark night strangles the traveling lamp," that is, the Sun (2.4.7). Macbeth's murder has blotted out the light.

The third act opens in daylight but moves to darkness again with Banquo's death (3.3) and the feast in which his ghost frightens Macbeth (3.4). That central scene—Act III, Scene 4—epitomizes the play. It begins in order, as Macbeth tells his guests, "You know your own degrees, sit down. At first / And last, the hearty welcome" (1–2). He sounds like Duncan here. The mood quickly changes, though, and by the end of the scene, Lady Macbeth must assume control, this in itself a breach of hierarchy, and orders the guests, "Stand not upon the order of your going, / But go at once" (118–119). The scene also marks the turning point of the action. It is the last time Macbeth and Lady Macbeth appear together, and Macduff is mentioned here as Macbeth's antagonist. After a possibly interpolated scene with the witches (3.5), Lennox and a Lord again speak of Macduff and his journey to England to promote Scotland's liberation. Hope dawns.

With Macbeth's visit to the witches (4.1) and massacre of Macduff's family (4.2), evil remains dominant, but Act IV, Scene 3 heralds its defeat as Malcolm and Macduff in England prepare to invade Scotland. A brief discussion of Edward the Confessor's healing scrofula (known as the "king's evil") foreshadows Scotland's return to political health. This curing is effected in Act V, in which scenes alternate, as they had in Act I, between the forces of darkness and death (5.1, 5.3, 5.5) and those of redemption and renewal (5.2, 5.4, 5.6). Macbeth dominates the former and Malcolm and his allies dominate the latter, just as in Act I the odd scenes belong to the witches and plots of murder and the even scenes to Duncan, order, and justice. In Act V, Scenes 7–9, Macbeth confronts his opponents and is defeated. The play ends with Malcolm's establishing a new order from the old chaos.

Shakespeare's two tetralogies of English history similarly moved from strife to peace but, when combined chronologically, told a rather

Macbeth instructs the murderers in Act III, Scene 1 of *Macbeth*. Print from Malcolm C. Salaman's 1916 edition of *Shakespeare in Pictorial Art (Illustration by George Cattermole)*

different story. Henry V's glorious reign, which caps the second tetralogy, would prove short-lived and yield to the Wars of the Roses of the first set of histories. Shakespeare's epilogue to *Henry V* highlights this circular sense of history. *Macbeth*, in which ambiguity predominates, ends equivocally as well. The play begins with the defeat and decapitation of a traitor, Macdonwald, by Duncan's chief warrior, Macbeth. The work ends with the defeat and decapitation of another traitor, Macbeth, by Duncan's son's chief warrior, Macduff. This circularity suggests that the whole process may repeat itself. Roman Polanski's 1971 film version emphasized this aspect of the play: It concludes with Donalbain's going to consult the witches. Another regicide looms.

The play's structure may be anatomized in diverse ways. The first three acts, which include the killing of Duncan and Banquo, work out the consequences of the witches' prophecy in Act I, Scene 3. The final two acts bring to fruition the predictions of the witches in Act IV, Scene 1. Alternatively, Act 1 may be seen as prologue to the imperial theme. Shakespeare here introduces most of the major characters and the initial con-

flict from which the play's actions will flow. In Act II, Macbeth kills Duncan to gain the throne. Feeling insecure in his new position because of Banquo's knowledge of the witches' prophecy and their promise that Banquo's line, rather than Macbeth's, will rule in the future, Macbeth, in Act III, commits his next crime, the killing of his former friend. Macbeth still feels threatened, now by Macduff, whose family he destroys in Act IV. This series of butcheries redounds upon him in Act V, as Malcolm, the son of his first victim, and Macduff, his last, join to topple the tyrant and restore the kingship to the man Duncan named his heir in the first act.

The play is built around three locations: Inverness in Acts I and II; Forres, where the Macbeths as monarchs reside in Act III; and Dunsinane, where they seek refuge against the growing revolts in Acts IV and V. Three figures also dominate the action. In the first two acts, the action revolves around Duncan. In Act III, Banquo (and his ghost) takes center stage. The final two acts belong to Macduff, first as victim, then as conqueror.

Language and imagery also link scenes. In Act I, Scene 1, the witches declare: "Fair is foul and foul is fair" (11). Macbeth's first words are "So foul and fair a day I have not seen" (1.3.38). Lady Macbeth, in Act I, Scene 5, echoes the witches' threefold greeting to Macbeth in Act I, Scene 3. Macbeth's statement in Act II, Scene 2 that all the oceans cannot wash Duncan's blood from his hands anticipates Lady Macbeth's inability in Act V, Scene 1 to remove its traces and smell from hers. Act II, Scene 4; Act III, Scene 6; and Act IV, Scene 3 rehearse Scotland's plight under Macbeth. The play's second scene introduces a bloody Sergeant. The witches in Act IV, Scene 1 conjure up a bloody baby, and in Act IV, Scene 2 Macduff's child is stabbed. Young Siward is killed onstage in Act V, Scene 7. As noted above, Act I, Scene 2 reports the decapitation of Macdonwald; Macduff enters in Act V, Scene 9 with Macbeth's severed head. In Act I, Scene 4 Duncan holds court to reward those who defeated his enemies; in Act V, Scene 9 Malcolm does the same.

Style and Imagery

In *Shakespeare's Imagery and What It Tells Us,* Spurgeon writes:

> The imagery in *Macbeth* appears to me to be more rich and varied, more highly imaginative, more unapproachable by any other writer, than that of any other single play. . . . The ideas in the imagery are in themselves more imaginative, more subtle and complex than in other plays, and there are a greater number of them, interwoven the one with the other, recurring and repeating. (324)

As always in Shakespeare, the figures of speech in *Macbeth* serve as more than verbal ornament: They carry the burden of the play's meaning.

One important set of images relates to clothing. Hailed by Ross as thane of Cawdor, an incredulous Macbeth replies: "Why do you dress me / In borrow'd robes? (1.3.108–109). Here and elsewhere in the play, clothes serve as a metonym for honors and titles that may be donned and doffed and stolen. They mask the individual and are external to, rather than an integral part of, a person. Banquo picks up on Macbeth's language to explain Macbeth's musings upon learning of his new dignity: "New honors come upon him, / Like our strange garments, cleave not to their mould / But with the aid of use" (1.3.144–146).

Macbeth again links honors and clothes when he tells his wife, "He [Duncan] hath honored me of late, and I have bought / Golden opinions from all sorts of people, / Which would be worn now in their newest gloss, / Not cast aside so soon." Lady Macbeth immediately seizes upon this metaphor, exclaiming, "Was the hope drunk / Wherein you dress'd yourself?" (1.7.32–36). Should Macbeth content himself with the recognition he has received or try to gain the garb of kingship? After he chooses the latter, Macduff tells Ross, who is going to see Macbeth's coronation, "Well, may you see things well done there: adieu! / Lest our old robes sit easier than our new!" (2.4.37–38).

Usurping kingship, Macbeth has indeed dressed himself in borrowed robes, and these fit him poorly. He has brought chaos to Scotland. Caithness reflects on this situation when he observes that Macbeth "cannot buckle his distemper'd cause / Within the belt of rule" (5.2.15–16). Angus concurs: "Now does he feel his title / Hang loose upon him, like a giant's robe / Upon a dwarfish thief" (5.2.20–22). Like a poor player (the Greek word for which is *hypocrite*), Macbeth has disguised himself as a king by dressing as one, but he is not truly royal. His true clothing is soldierly. Ross describes him as "lapp'd in proof," that is, armor (1.2.54). In his final moments, Macbeth becomes a warrior again. He dons his armor and declares to Macduff, "Before my body / I throw my warlike shield" (5.8.32–33). By choosing his proper attire here, he recovers the nobility he lost when he covered himself with what rightly belonged to others.

Various images reveal the corruption of the natural world that results from Macbeth's usurpation and murders. In *Troilus and Cressida,* Ulysses reflects on the results of violating order and degree, as when a subject disobeys his king: "Take but degree away, untune that string, / And hark what discord follows" (1.3.109–110). *Macbeth* shows that discord. Macbeth says that Duncan's wounds "look'd like a breach in nature / For ruin's wasteful entrance" (2.3.113–114). The choric Act II, Scene 4 comments on dissonances in nature after Duncan's death: An owl kills a falcon, horses eat each other, earthquakes shake the land, and days are dark. The Scots Doctor describes Lady Macbeth's illness as "A great perturbation in nature" (5.1.9) and reflects, "Unnatural deeds / Do breed unnatural troubles" (5.1.71–72). Birnam Wood seems to uproot itself to come to Dunsinane.

The witches introduce this theme of distortion of the natural order: They meet in the midst of tempest and proclaim that "Fair is foul, and foul is fair (1.1.11). Their trochaic meter marks a deviation from the orderly iambic pentameter of most of the play. Maurice Morgann, in *An Essay on the Dramatic Character of Sir John Falstaff,* observed in 1777: "The weird sisters rise, and order is extinguished. The laws of nature give way, and leave nothing in our minds but wildness and horror." The very thought of violating the political order causes Macbeth's heart to pound against his ribs "Against the use of nature" (1.3.137). Lady Macbeth prays to become unnatural, with gall for milk and thickened blood. She inverts nature in assuming the masculine role when she plans to "chastise" her husband "with the valor of [her] tongue" (1.5.27) and rid herself of all "compunctious visitings of nature" (1.5.45). Macbeth makes a looking-glass world of Scotland, where men die "or ere they sicken" (4.3.137), where "nothing is / But what is not" (1.3.141–142). His royal feast in Act III, Scene 4 ends in chaos, with order and degree ignored. Nor does he care what befalls the natural order so long as he has his will. He commands the witches:

> Though you untie the winds, and let them
>   fight
> Against the churches; though the yeasty waves
> Confound and swallow navigation up;
> Though bladed corn be lodg'd [destroyed],
>   and trees blown down,
> Though castles topple on their warders' heads;
> Though palaces and pyramids do slope
> Their heads to their foundations; though the
>   treasure
> Of nature's germains [seeds] tumble all
>   together,
> Even till destruction sicken, answer me
> To what I ask you. (4.1.52–61)

As the invading army approaches, he wishes "th' estate o' th' world were now undone" (5.5.49).

Food and sleep fail to nourish in this distorted world of the play. Macbeth's nights are troubled by "terrible dreams" (3.2.18), and he eats his meals "in fear" (3.2.17). His absence from Duncan's banquet in Act I, Scene 7 upsets the festivities. The meal in Act III, Scene 4 ends before it begins, and the witches' stew reveals the depth to which feasting has descended. Lady Macbeth's tormented slumbers culminate in her sleepwalking

Lady Macbeth attempts to calm Macbeth, who reacts strongly to the sight of Banquo's ghost, in this 19th-century depiction of Act III, Scene 4 of *Macbeth*. *(Illustration by Georg Emanuel Opitz; engraving by Auguste Delvaux)*

scene (5.1). A Lord expresses to Ross his hope that when Malcolm dethrones Macbeth, "we may again / Give to our tables meat, sleep to our nights; / Free from our feasts and banquets bloody knives" (3.6.33–35).

In his speech on order, Ulysses declares: "O, when degree is shak'd, / Which is the ladder of all high designs, / The enterprise is sick" (*Troilus and Cressida*, 1.3.101–103). The language of *Macbeth* develops this idea of disease. Learning that Fleance has escaped the plot to murder him, Macbeth declares: "Then comes my fit again" (3.4.20). Having witnessed Lady Macbeth's sleepwalking, the doctor observes, "infected minds / To their deaf pillows will discharge their secrets" (5.1.72–73). Macbeth asks whether this physician can "minister to a mind diseas'd" (5.3.40), referring to both himself and his wife.

His infection has spread to the entire country. He asks the doctor, "What rhubarb, cyme, or what purgative drug / Would scour these English hence?" (5.3.55–56). He wishes the doctor could "cast / The water of my land, find her disease, / And purge it to a sound and pristine health" (5.3.50–52). He does not recognize that he is the sickness he would remove. Macduff wonders when Scotland will "see thy wholesome days again" (4.3.105). Caithness calls Malcolm as "the medicine of the sickly weal" and urges his companions, "And with him pour we, in our country's purge, / Each drop of us" (5.2.26–28). When Macduff learns of his family's murders, Malcolm tells him, "Let's make us med'cines of our great revenge / To cure this deadly grief" (4.3.214–215). The reference to Edward the Confessor's scrofula, which is being cured, serves to contrast the health-giving English court and its legitimate king with the disease-causing usurper to the north. In *A Counterblast to Tobacco,* James I calls himself "The proper Phisician of his Politicke-bodie," whose duty is "to purge it of all those diseases, by Medicines meet for the same." The good ruler brings health, whereas the tyrant undermines it.

Blood pervades the play as another indication of the horrors Macbeth causes. The word itself appears 23 times in the play, which contains another 25 related terms, such as *bloody, bleed,* and *gory.* A bloody Sergeant reports the progress of battle (1.2). Macbeth's dagger of the mind becomes coated with imagined blood, presaging "the bloody business" he is about to undertake (2.1.48). His hands and his wife's are coated with blood after Duncan's murder; Lady Macbeth will see and smell this blood even in her sleep (5.1). Lennox finds the king's grooms, "their hands and faces . . . all badg'd with blood" (2.3.102). Banquo's murderer appears with blood on his face (3.4.13); Banquo's ghost appears with "gory locks" (3.4.50).

Later, Macbeth refers to "blood-bolter'd Banquo" (4.1.123). Macbeth says of himself, "I am in blood / Stepp'd in so far that, should I wade no more, / Returning were as tedious as go o'er" (3.4.135–137). He knows, "It will have blood, they say; blood will have blood" and "The secret'st man of blood" will be exposed (3.4.121, 125). The apparition of a bloody child tells Macbeth, "Be bloody, bold, and resolute" (4.1.79). Malcolm calls Macbeth "bloody" (4.3.57) and laments that Scotland "bleeds" (4.3.39). Macduff, too, grieves, "Bleed, bleed, poor country!" (4.3.31) and calls Macbeth "bloody-sceptred" (4.3.104). Ross describes Scotland after Duncan's murder as a "bloody stage" (2.4.6) and calls Duncan's death "this more than bloody deed" (2.4.22).

Macbeth and his wife war against fertility itself. In Act I, Scene 3, Banquo asks the witches, "If you can look into the seeds of time, / And say which grain will grow, and which will not, / Speak then to me" (58–60). When Duncan says to him, "let me infold thee / And hold thee to my heart," he replies with another image of increase: "There if I grow, / The harvest is your own" (1.4.31–33). Arriving at Dunsinane, he speaks of the martin building "his pendant and procreant cradle" and breeding (1.6.8–9). Duncan tells Macbeth, "I have begun to plant thee, and will labor / To make thee full of growing" (1.4.28–29). Both Duncan and Banquo have children whom they foster and protect.

Macbeth has no children (4.3.216). Lady Macbeth says she has nursed a child but would dash out its brains (1.7.58). Both war against legitimate succession, and Macbeth repeatedly kills or tries to kill not just parents but also children. Lennox remarks that if Macbeth had Malcolm, Donalbain, and Fleance in his power, he would destroy them (3.6.18–20). He hires murderers to kill Banquo and Fleance, he murders Malcolm's family, and Young Siward falls as his final victim. Whereas the good king Duncan speaks of planting, Macbeth acknowledges that his is a "fruitless crown, / . . . a barren scepter" (3.1.60–61). Macduff calls Scotland under Macbeth "our downfallen birthdom" (4.3.4); Ross says that Scotland "cannot / Be call'd our mother, but our grave" (4.3.165–166). Macbeth would tumble "nature's germains . . . all together" (4.1.59). This rejection of growth and renewal consumes him, as he recognizes when he says, "my way of life / Is fall'n into the sear, the yellow leaf" (5.3.22–23).

The forces that gather against him and triumph mark the return of fruitfulness. In Act 4, Scene 1, he sees children representing Macduff and the English army, who will defeat him, as well as Banquo's descendants who will succeed him. He had spoken of "pity, like a new-born babe" denouncing his murder (1.7.21), and this image resurfaces against him. Ross tells Malcolm his presence in Scotland "Would create soldiers" (4.3.186). Caithness and Lennox say that Macbeth's foes will pour as much of themselves as necessary "To dew the sovereign flower and drown the weeds" (5.2.28–30). Disguising themselves with branches, the English forces bring greenery to oppose Macbeth's autumnal foliage. In his final speech, Malcolm adopts his father's language of fertility: "What's more to do, / Which would be planted newly with the time, . . . / We will perform in measure, time, and place" (5.9.30–39).

The connection between goodness and light, evil and gloom has a long history. *Macbeth* draws on this imagery. Duncan, as a good king, associates himself with light when he says, "But signs of nobleness, like stars, shall shine / On all deservers" (1.4.41–42). The witches, Macbeth, and his wife link themselves to darkness. Macbeth calls the witches "secret, black and midnight hags" (4.1.48). They "Hover through the fog and filthy air" (1.1.12). Into their magic potion, they put "Root of hemlock digg'd in the dark" and "slips of yew / Sliver'd in the moon's eclipse" (4.1.25, 27–28).

Lady Macbeth calls upon "thick night / [to] pall thee in the dunnest smoke of hell" (1.5.50–51). Later, Macbeth invokes "seeling night" (3.2.46). Whereas Duncan speaks of stars' shining, Macbeth would extinguish them: "Stars, hide your fires, / Let not light see my black and deep desires" (1.4.50–51). Malcolm refers to "black Macbeth" (4.3.52). Macbeth kills Duncan at night and has Banquo murdered "Whiles night's black agents

to their preys do rouse" (3.2.53). After Macbeth's murder of Duncan, "darkness does the face of earth entomb, / When living light should kiss it" (2.4.9–10). Reflecting on his wife's death, Macbeth again summons darkness: "Out, out, brief candle! / Life's but a walking shadow" (5.5.23–24). Learning of the approach of Birnam Wood, he declares, "I gin to be a-weary of the sun" (5.5.48).

Initially refusing to kill Duncan, Macbeth asserts: "I dare do all that may become a man; / Who dares do more is none" (1.7.46–47). Lady Macbeth retorts: "When you durst do it, then you were a man; / And to be more than what you were, you would / Be so much more the man" (1.7.49–51). He is right. Yielding to her, he becomes less

Viola Allen as Lady Macbeth in the sleepwalking scene *(Photographed by White Studio)*

than a man rather than more, as the animal imagery associated with him attests. Even before his first crime, Lady Macbeth instructs her husband to "look like th' innocent flower, / But be the serpent under it" (1.5.65–66). Later, he tells her, "O, full of scorpions is my mind, dear wife!" (3.2.36). Besieged by his enemies, Macbeth exclaims: "They have tied me to the stake; I cannot fly, / But bear-like I must fight the course" (5.7.1–2). He resolves to "die with harness on our back" (5.5.51), thus likening himself to an animal. A few lines earlier, hearing a cry of women, he remarks that once his "fell of hair / Would at a dismal treatise rouse and stir / As life were in't" (5.5.11–13). The word *fell* refers to the pelt of mammals. Coming upon Macbeth, Macduff challenges him, "Turn, hell-hound, turn!" (5.8.3). When Macbeth refuses to fight him, Macduff says: "Then yield thee, coward, / . . . We'll have thee, as our rarer monsters are, / Painted upon a pole" (5.8.23–26).

Macbeth's speeches use animal imagery as well. He tells the ghost of Banquo, "Approach thou like the rugged Russian bear, / The arm'd rhinoceros, or th' Hyrcan tiger" (3.4.99–100), and he will not be afraid. When the men he has hired to kill Banquo and Fleance assert, "We are men, my liege" (3.1.90), Macbeth replies:

> Ay, in the catalogue ye go for men,
> As hounds and greyhounds, mungrels,
>   spaniels, curs,
> Shoughs, water-rugs, and demi-wolves are clipt
> All by the name of dogs. (3.1.91–94)

As long as Banquo and Fleance live, Macbeth maintains, "We have scorch'd the snake, not kill'd it" (3.2.13). Learning that Banquo lies dead in a ditch but that Fleance has escaped, he tells the murderers, "There the grown serpent lies; the worm that's fled / Hath nature that in time will venom breed, / No teeth for th' present" (3.4.28–30). He assails the messenger who brings news of the approach of the English army, "The devil damn thee black, thou cream-fac'd loon! / Where got'st thou that goose-look?" When the man replies, "There is ten

thousand—" Macbeth interrupts with, "Geese, villain?" (5.3.11–13).

Highlighting the play's concern with appearance versus reality are the many references to images, acting, deception, and concealment. Ross speaks of Macbeth's creating "strange images of death" (1.3.97). Macbeth calls his mental picture of Duncan's murder a "horrid image" and continues, "Present fears / Are less than horrible imaginings" (1.3.135, 137–138). He calls Banquo's ghost "horrible shadow! / Unreal mock'ry" (3.4.105–106). Lady Macbeth dismisses it as "the very painting of your fear" (3.4.60). He calls the imaginary weapon a "fatal vision" (2.1.36). His wife's term is "air-drawn dagger" (3.4.61). He tells his wife he suffers from "terrible dreams" (3.2.18); earlier he speaks of "wicked dreams [that] abuse / The curtain'd sleep" (2.1.50–51). Conjuring Banquo and his descendants, the witches declare: "Come like shadows, so depart" (4.1.111). Macbeth finally dismisses existence as "a walking shadow" (5.5.24).

Macbeth calls the confirmation of the witches' prophecy that he will become thane of Cawdor as well as thane of Glamis "happy prologues to the swelling act / Of the imperial theme" (1.3.128–129). His soliloquy on the meaninglessness of life (5.5) is filled with references to acting. His wife tells him to disguise his intention to kill Duncan (1.5.61–66), and he resolves to "mock the time with fairest show: / False face must hide what the false heart doth know" (1.7.81–82). He instructs his wife to welcome Banquo to the feast. Though they fear him, they will "make our faces vizards to our hearts, / Disguising what they are" (3.2.34–35). The previous and present thanes of Cawdor conceal their traitorous intentions. Malcolm instructs his soldiers to camouflage themselves with boughs: "thereby shall we shadow / The numbers of our host, and make discovery / Err in report of us" (5.4.5–7). Lady Macbeth had smeared the grooms' faces with blood to make them appear guilty of Duncan's murder, and she instructs her husband to put on a nightgown to conceal the fact that they have not gone to bed (2.2.52–54, 67–68).

This theme of ambiguity also emerges from the play's many questions, equivocations, and use of dramatic irony, in which characters do not grasp the import of their words. The play's first four scenes begin with questions: "When shall we three meet again? / In thunder, lightning, or in rain?" (1.1.1–2); "What bloody man is that?" (1.2.1); "Where hast thou been, sister?" (1.3.1); "Is execution done on Cawdor? Are not / Those in commission yet return'd?" (1.4.1–2). This pattern persists: "How goes the night, boy?" (2.1.1); "Is Banquo gone from court?" (3.2.1); "But who did bid thee join with us?" (3.3.1); "What had he done, to make him fly the land?" (4.2.1); "Why should I play the Roman fool, and die / On mine own sword?" (5.8.1–2). Altogether, nine of the play's 28 scenes open in the interrogatory mode, or 10 of 29 if one counts Act 3, Scene 5, which may not be by Shakespeare. In *Hamlet,* only four of 20 scenes commence thus.

Speeches are unclear. The witches seem to promise Macbeth success and invincibility; he learns too late that "these juggling fiends . . . / palter with us in a double sense, / . . . keep the word of promise to our ear, / And break it to our hope" (5.8.19–22). The witches' speeches exemplify ambiguity: "When the battle's lost and won" (1.1.4); "Lesser than Macbeth, and greater. / Not so happy, yet much happier" (1.3.65–66). Malcolm denounces himself as unworthy of kingship, but he does so only to test Macduff's loyalty. Macbeth knows that his followers give him only "mouth-honor" (5.3.27). His doctor feigns loyalty to him but, alone, declares, "Were I from Dunsinane away and clear, / Profit again should hardly draw me here" (5.3.61–62). The Porter offers a comic version of indeterminacy when he remarks, "much drink may be said to be an equivocator with lechery: it makes him, and it mars him; it sets him on, and it takes him off; it persuades him, and disheartens him; makes him stand to, and not stand to; in conclusion, equivocates him in a sleep, and giving him the lie, leaves him" (2.3.31–36).

Uncertainty extends to characters' ignorance of the import of their own words. Speaking of the first thane of Cawdor, Duncan acknowledges, "There's no art / To find the mind's construction in the face: / He was a gentleman on whom I built / An absolute trust" (1.4.11–14). These words apply equally well to the new thane of Cawdor, Macbeth. Feigning grief over Duncan's death, Macbeth says: "Had I but died an hour before this chance, / I had liv'd a blessed time" (2.3.91–92). He is speaking truth without knowing it. Having had Banquo killed, Macbeth now misses him at the feast in Act III, Scene 4, thereby conjuring up Banquo's ghost. At the end of that scene, he says he will consult the witches to learn "By the worst means, the worst" (3.4.134). The witches tell him the worst, that when Birnam Wood comes to Dunsinane he will be killed by a man not born of woman. He mistakes their portents for reassurance.

Though the witches' words bode ill for Macbeth, they anticipate Scotland's redemption. The unnatural events they predict lead, ironically, to the restoration of the natural order. A seeming monster, a man not born of woman (Macduff), kills the real monster, Macbeth. Malcolm then succeeds to the throne, as is proper, and ends the destruction and sterility of Macbeth's reign.

Indicative of the duplicity of the play's language is the frequent doubling of words and phrases. Hearing Macbeth's approach, the Third Witch announces, "A drum, a drum! / Macbeth doth come" (1.3.30–31). All three then say, "Thus do go, about, about" (1.3.34). As they prepare their brew, the Third Witch says, "Harpier cries, ''tis time, 'tis time'" (4.1.3), and they repeat, "Double, double, toil and trouble" (4.1.10, 20, 35). Lady Macbeth prays for darkness to prevent heaven from crying, "Hold, hold!" (1.5.54). Seeing Banquo and Fleance approach, the Second Murderer calls out, "A light, a light!" (3.3.14). Listening to Lady Macbeth's sleepwalking speeches, the Scots Doctor remarks, "Go to, go to; you have known what you should not" (5.1.46–47). In her last lines, she urges her husband, "To bed, to bed" (5.1.66).

Another stylistic device involves the use of triplets. The number three has been associated with the supernatural well before the advent of Chris-

The three witches discuss a recent battle in Act I, Scene I of *Macbeth*. This is a plate from *Retzsch's Outlines to Shakespeare: Macbeth,* published in 1833. *(Illustration by Moritz Retzsch)*

tianity, and the many triplings here contribute to the play's mystical mood. There are Three Witches, Three Murderers. The Porter imagines three souls entering hell. Macbeth lives in three castles (Inverness, Forres, Dunsinane). The witches show Macbeth three apparitions (4.1). Macbeth is promised three titles. Both the witches and Lady Macbeth give him a three-fold greeting (1.3.48–50; 1.5.54–55). The witches also hail Banquo three times (1.3.62–64). Before meeting Macbeth the witches perform a dance: "Thrice to thine, and thrice to mine,/ And thrice again, to make up nine" (1.3.35–36). They know the time has come to prepare their brew because "Thrice the brindled cat hath mew'd. / Thrice, and once the hedge-pig whin'd" (4.1.1–2). They repeat their "Double, double" refrain three times. Banquo's last words to Fleance are, "fly, fly, fly" (3.3.17). Three times in her soliloquy in 1.5.38–54 Lady Macbeth invokes spirits and night with the word "Come" (lines 40, 47, 50). In his soliloquy that opens Act I, Scene 7, Macbeth offers three reasons for not killing Duncan. In the first two lines of that speech, he repeats the word *done* three times. After Duncan's murder, Macbeth and his wife exclaim *Hark!* three times (2.2.2, 11, 18). Macbeth relates hearing

a voice that repeats "sleep no more" three times (2.2.38–40). Finding Duncan dead, Macduff cries, "O horror, horror, horror!" (2.3.64). Addressing Banquo's ghost, Macbeth names three animals he would willingly confront rather than the apparition before him (bear, rhinoceros, tiger). After the ghost vanishes, Macbeth muses, "It will have blood, they say; blood will have blood" (3.4.121–122), another threefold repetition. He reflects, "Augures and understood relations have / By maggot-pies and choughs and rooks brought forth / The secret'st man of blood" (3.4.123–125), noting three avian means of exposure.

EXTRACTS OF CLASSIC CRITICISM

Samuel Johnson (1709–1784) [Excerpted from *Miscellaneous Observations on* The Tragedy of Macbeth (1745). Anticipating the present-day critical movement New Historicism, the great critic Johnson here places *Macbeth* within its historical context to justify the role of the witches.]

In order to make a true estimate of the abilities and merit of a writer, it is always necessary to examine the genius of his age, and the opinions of his contemporaries. A poet who should now make the whole action of his tragedy depend upon enchantment, and produce the chief events by the assistance of supernatural agents, would be censured as transgressing the bounds of probability, he would be banished from the theatre to the nursery, and condemned to write fairy tales instead of tragedies; but a survey of the notions that prevailed at the time when this play was written, will prove that Shakespeare was in no danger of such censures, since he only turned the system that was then universally admitted to his advantage, and was far from overburthening the credulity of his audience.

The reality of witchcraft or enchantment, which though not strictly the same, are confounded in this play, has in all ages and countries been credited by the common people, and in most by the learned themselves.

These phantoms have indeed appeared more frequently, in proportion as the darkness of ignorance has been more gross; but it cannot be shown, that the brightest gleams of knowledge have at any time been sufficient to drive them out of the world. . . .

The Reformation did not immediately arrive at its meridian, and tho' day was gradually encreasing upon us, the goblins of witchcraft still continued to hover in the twilight. In the time of Queen Elizabeth was the remarkable Trial of the Witches of Warbois, whose conviction is still commemorated in an annual sermon at Huntingdon. But in the reign of King James, in which this tragedy was written, many circumstances concurred to propagate and confirm this opinion. The King, who was much celebrated for his knowledge, had, before his arrival in England, not only examined in person a woman accused of witchcraft, but had given a very formal account of the practices and illusions of evil spirits, the compacts of witches, the ceremonies used by them, the manner of detecting them, and the justice of punishing them, in his dialogues of *Daemonologie,* written in the Scottish dialect, and published at Edinburgh. This book was, soon after his accession, reprinted at London, and as the ready way to gain K. James's favour was to flatter his speculations, the system of *Daemonologie* was immediately adopted by all who desired either to gain preferment or not to lose it. Thus the doctrine of witchcraft was very powerfully inculcated, and as the greatest part of mankind have no other reason for their opinions than that they are in fashion, it cannot be doubted but this persuasion made a rapid progress, since vanity and credulity co-operated in its favour, and it had a tendency to free cowardice from reproach. . . .

Thus in the time of Shakespeare, was the doctrine of witchcraft at once established by law and by fashion, and it became not only unpolite, but criminal, to doubt it, and as

prodigies are always seen in proportion as they are expected, witches were every day discovered, and multiplied so fast in some places, that Bishop [Joseph] Hall mentions a village in Lancashire, where their number was greater than that of the houses. . . .

Upon this general infatuation Shakespeare might be easily allowed to found a play, especially since he has followed with great exactness such histories as were then thought true; nor can it be doubted that the scenes of enchantment, however they may now be ridiculed, were both by himself and his audience thought awful and affecting.

William Hazlitt (1778–1830) [Excerpted from *Characters of Shakespear's Plays* (1817). Hazlitt's observations about *Macbeth*'s principals, imagery, mood, and structure retain their power to provoke thought and underlie much subsequent commentary about the work. His focus on character in analyzing Shakespeare's plays persisted throughout the 19th century.]

Macbeth and *Lear, Othello* and *Hamlet,* are usually reckoned Shakespear's four principal tragedies. *Lear* stands first for the profound intensity of the passion; *Macbeth* for the wildness of the imagination and the rapidity of the action; *Othello* for the progressive interest and powerful alterations of feeling; *Hamlet* for the refined development of thought and sentiment. . . . His plays have the force of things upon the mind. What he represents is brought home to the bosom as part of our experience, implanted in the memory as if we had known the places, persons, and things of which he treats. *Macbeth* is like a record of a preternatural and tragical event. It has the rugged severity of an old chronicle with all that the imagination of the poet can engraft upon traditional belief . . . All that could actually take place, and all that is only possible to be conceived, what was said and what was done, the workings of passion, the spells of magic, are brought before us with the same absolute truth and vividness.— Shakespear excelled in the openings of his plays: that of *Macbeth* is the most striking of any. The wildness of the scenery, the sudden shifting of the situations and characters, the bustle and expectations excited, are equally extraordinary. From the first entrance of the Witches and the description of them when they meet Macbeth:

> —What are these
> So wither'd and so wild in their attire,
> That look not like the inhabitants of th'
>   earth
> And yet are on't?

the mind is prepared for all that follows.

This tragedy is alike distinguished for the lofty imagination it displays, and for the tumultuous vehemence of the action; and the one is made the moving principle of the other. The overwhelming pressure of preternatural agency urges on the tide of human passion with redoubled force. Macbeth himself appears driven along by the violence of his fate like a vessel drifting before a storm: he reels to and fro like a drunken man; he staggers under the weight of his own purposes and the suggestions of others; he stands at bay with his situation; and from the superstitious awe and breathless suspense into which the communications of the Weird Sisters throw him, is hurried on with daring impatience to verify their predictions, and with impious and bloody hand to tear aside the veil that hides the uncertainty of the future. He is not equal to the struggle with fate and conscience. He now "bends up each corporal instrument to the terrible feat"; at other times his heart misgives him, and he is cowed and abashed by his success. "The deed, no less than the attempt, confounds him." His mind is assailed by the stings of remorse, and full of "preternatural solicitings." His speeches and soliloquies are dark riddles on human life, baffling solution, and entangling him in their labyrinths. In thought he is absent and perplexed, sudden and desperate in act, from a distrust of his own resolution. His energy springs from the anxiety and agitation of his mind. His blindly rushing forward on the objects of his ambition and revenge, or his recoiling from them, equally betrays the harassed state of his feelings.—This part of his character is admirably set off by being brought in connexion with that of Lady Macbeth, whose obdurate strength of will and masculine firmness give her the ascendancy over her husband's faltering virtue. She at once seizes on the opportunity that offers for the accomplishment of all their wished-for greatness, and never flinches from her object till all is over. The magnitude of her resolution almost covers the magnitude of her guilt. She is a great bad woman, whom we hate, but whom we fear more than we hate. She does not excite our loathing and abhorrence like Regan and Goneril [the villainous daughters in *King Lear*]. She is only wicked to gain a great end; and is perhaps more distinguished by her commanding presence of mind and inexorable self-will, which do not suffer her to be diverted from a bad purpose, when once formed, by weak and womanly regrets, than by the hardness of her heart or want of natural affections. . . .

Macbeth (generally speaking) is done upon a stronger and more systematic principle of contrast than any other of Shakespear's plays. It moves upon the verge of an abyss, and is a constant struggle between life and death. The action is desperate and the reaction is dreadful. It is a huddling together of fierce extremes, a war of opposite natures which of them shall destroy the other. There is nothing but what has a violent end or violent beginnings. The lights and shades are laid on with a determined hand; the transitions from

Lady Macbeth tries to wash her hands while she sleepwalks in Act V, Scene I of *Macbeth*. Plate from *Retzsch's Outlines to Shakespeare:* Macbeth, published in 1833 *(Illustration by Moritz Retzsch)*

triumph to despair, from the height of terror to the repose of death, are sudden and startling; every passion brings in its fellow-contrary, and the thoughts pitch and jostle each other as in the dark. The whole play is an unruly chaos of strange and forbidden things, where the ground rocks under our feet. Shakespear's genius here took its full swing, and trod upon the furthest bounds of nature and passion. This circumstance will account for the abruptness and violent antitheses of the style, the throes and labour which run through the expression, and from defects will turn them into beauties.

Thomas de Quincey (1785–1859) [Excerpted from "On the Knocking on the Gate in *Macbeth*" (1823). In this famous essay, de Quincey anticipates reader-response theory by analyzing the effect of the Porter scene (2.3) on audiences.]

In *Macbeth,* for the sake of gratifying his own enormous and teeming faculty of creation, Shakespeare has introduced two murderers; and, as usual in his hands, they are

remarkably discriminated: but,—though in Macbeth the strife of mind is greater than in his wife, the tiger spirit is not so awake, and his feelings caught chiefly by contagion from her,—yet, as both were finally involved in the guilt of murder, the murderous mind of necessity is finally presumed in both. This was to be expressed; and, on its own account, as well as to make it a more proportionable antagonist to the unoffending nature of their victim, "the gracious Duncan," and adequately to expound "the deep damnation of his taking off," this was to be expressed with peculiar energy. We were to be made to feel that the human nature,—*i.e.* the divine nature of love and mercy, spread through the hearts of all creatures, and seldom utterly withdrawn from man,—was gone, vanished, extinct, and that the fiendish nature had taken its place. And, as this effect is marvelously accomplished in the *dialogues* and *soliloquies* themselves, so it is finally consummated by the expedient under consideration; and it is to this that I now solicit the reader's attention. . . . All action in any direction is best expounded, measured, and made apprehensible, by reaction. Now, apply this to the case of *Macbeth.* Here, as I have said, the retiring of the human heart and the entrance of the fiendish heart was to be expressed and made sensible. Another world has stept in; and the murderers are taken out of the region of human things, human purposes, human desires. They are transfigured: Lady Macbeth is "unsexed"; Macbeth has forgot that he was born of woman; both are conformed to the image of devils; and the world of devils is suddenly revealed. But how shall this be conveyed and made palpable? In order that a new world may step in, this world must for a time disappear. The murderers and the murder must be insulated—cut off by an immeasurable gulf from the ordinary tide and succession of human affairs—locked up and sequestered in some deep recess; we must be made sensible that the world of ordinary life is suddenly arrested, laid asleep, tranced, racked into a dread armistice; time must be annihilated, relation to things without abolished; and all must pass self-withdrawn into a deep syncope and suspension of earthly passion. Hence it is that, when the deed is done, when the work of darkness is perfect, then the world of darkness passes away like a pageantry in the clouds: the knocking at the gate is heard, and it makes known audibly that the reaction has commenced; the human has made its reflux upon the fiendish; the pulses of life are beginning to beat again; and the re-establishment of the goings-on of the world in which we live first makes us profoundly sensible of the awful parenthesis that had suspended them.

A. C. Bradley (1851–1935) [Excerpted from *Shakespearean Tragedy: Lectures on* Hamlet, Othello, King Lear *and* Macbeth (1904). Bradley's focus on characters as real people marked the culmination of the romantic approach to Shakespeare and prompted strong reaction, as in L. C. Knights's mocking essay "How Many Children Had Lady Macbeth?" (1933). Yet, Bradley's emphasis on characters' minds was further developed by psychological criticism, and his close textual reading anticipates the New Critics.]

Macbeth, the cousin of a King mild, just, and beloved, but now too old to lead his army, is introduced to us as a general of extraordinary prowess, who has covered himself with glory in putting down a rebellion and repelling the invasion of a foreign army. In these conflicts he showed great personal courage, a quality which he continues to display throughout the drama in regard to all plain dangers. It is difficult to be sure of his customary demeanour, for in the play we see him either in what appears to be an exceptional relation to his wife, or else in the throes of remorse and desperation; but from his behaviour

during his journey home after the war, from his *later* conversations with Lady Macbeth, and from his language to the murderers of Banquo and to others, we imagine him as a great warrior, somewhat masterful, rough, and abrupt, a man to inspire some fear and much admiration. He was thought "honest," or honourable; he was trusted, apparently, by everyone; Macduff, a man of the highest integrity, "loved him well." And there was, in fact, much good in him. We have no warrant, I think, for describing him, with many writers, as of a "noble" nature, like Hamlet or Othello; but he had a keen sense of both honour and of the worth of a good name. The phrase, again, "too full of the milk of human kindness," is applied to him in impatience by his wife, who did not fully understand him; but certainly he was far from devoid of humanity and pity.

At the same time he was exceedingly ambitious. He must have been so by temper. The tendency must have been greatly strengthened by his marriage. When we see him, it has been further stimulated by his remarkable success and by the consciousness of exceptional powers and merit. It becomes a passion. The course of action suggested by it is extremely perilous: it sets his good name, his position, and even his life on the hazard. It is also abhorrent to his better feelings. Their defeat in the struggle with ambition leaves him utterly wretched, and would have kept him so, however complete had been his outward success and security. On the other hand, his passion for power and his instinct of self-assertion are so vehement that no inward misery could persuade him to relinquish the fruits of crime, or to advance from remorse to repentance.

In the character as so far sketched there is nothing very peculiar, though the strength of the forces contending in it is unusual. But there is in Macbeth one marked peculiarity, the true apprehension of which is the

Macbeth, with his daggers, and Lady Macbeth just after the murder of Duncan, in Act II, Scene 2 of *Macbeth* (Painting by Samuel John Stump)

stands it, and he himself understands it only in part. The terrifying images which deter him from crime and follow its commission, and which are really the protest of his deepest self, seem to his wife the creations of mere nervous fear, and are sometimes referred by himself to the dread of vengeance or the restlessness of insecurity. His conscious or reflective mind, that is, moves chiefly among considerations of outward success and failure, while his inner being is convulsed by conscience. And his inability to understand himself is repeated and exaggerated in the interpretations of actors and critics, who represent him as a coward, cold-blooded, calculating, and pitiless, who shrinks from crime simply because it is dangerous, and suffers afterwards simply because he is not safe. In reality his courage is frightful. He strides from crime to crime, though his soul never ceases to bar his advance with shapes of terror, or to clamour in his ears that he is murdering his peace and casting away his "eternal jewel."

MODERN CRITICISM AND CRITICAL CONTROVERSIES
New Criticism

Criticism of Shakespeare in the 19th century focused on his characters, who were treated as real people with lives outside the confines of the text. In "How Many Children Had Lady Macbeth?" (1932), L. C. Knights objected to this approach and singled out A. C. Bradley's *Shakespearean Criticism* (1904) as an exemplar of what he disliked. For Knights and his fellow New Critics, "The only profitable approach to Shakespeare is a consideration of his plays as dramatic poems, of his use of language to obtain a total complex emotional response" (20). In *Some Shakespearean Themes,* he applies his analysis to *Macbeth.* He notes, for example, that when Lady Macbeth speaks of dashing out her infant's brains (1.7.54–59), her violent imagery connects with the many violent occurrences throughout the work. Also, her willingness to kill

key to Shakespeare's conception. This bold ambitious man of action, has, within certain limits, the imagination of a poet,—an imagination on the one hand extremely sensitive to impressions of a certain kind, and on the other, productive of violent disturbance both of mind and body. Through it he is kept in contact with supernatural impressions and is liable to supernatural fears. And through it, especially, come to him the intimations of conscience and honour. Macbeth's better nature—to put the matter for clearness' sake too broadly—instead of speaking to him in the overt language of moral ideas, commands, and prohibitions, incorporates itself in images which alarm and horrify. His imagination is thus the best of him, something usually deeper and higher than his conscious thoughts; and if he had obeyed it he would have been safe. But his wife quite misunder-

her own child is unnatural in a play that abounds in unnatural actions. According to Knights, noting these connections is more important than figuring out whether Lady Macbeth really had a child, when she might have had it, why it never appears in the play, and so on.

Knights also observes that the witches' "Fair is foul, and foul is fair" (1.1.11) expresses the play's "reversal of values" and carries "premonitions of the conflict, disorder and moral darkness into which Macbeth will plunge himself" (*Some Shakespeare Themes* 122). The play's references to nature reveal that Macbeth's actions are unnatural and also define the values against which those actions are to be judged. He contrasts Lady Macbeth's "The raven himself is hoarse / That croaks the fatal entrance of Duncan / Under my battlements" (1.5.38–40) with Banquo's description of the castle (1.6.3–10). Banquo speaks of the breeding martin, of life rather than death. These two speeches epitomize a central conflict in the play between the Macbeths' destructive impulses and "a natural and wholesome *order,* of which the equivalent in the human sphere is to be found in those mutualities of loyalty, trust and liking that Macbeth proposes to violate" (136). Malcolm's final speech marks the return of those positive values.

Cleanth Brooks's "The Naked Babe and the Cloak of Manliness," in *The Well Wrought Urn: Studies in the Structure of Poetry,* considers the play's use of clothes imagery. Macbeth initially rejects titles and honors not his. Greeted by Ross as thane of Cawdor, Macbeth asks, "why do you dress me / In borrowed robes?" (1.3.108–109). He wants to wear the good reputation he has won, that belongs to him. He tells his wife, "I have bought / Golden opinions from all sorts of people, / Which would be worn now in their newest gloss, / Not cast aside so soon" (1.7.32–35). As the play progresses, he steals the royal crown. As his reign is about to end, he finds, in Angus's words, "his title / Hang[s] loose about him, like a giant's robe / Upon a dwarfish thief" (5.20–22). Brooks links the play's clothing imagery to other forms of concealment, as when Macbeth and Lady

Macbeth both invoke darkness to hide their killing of Duncan.

Brooks also examines the play's references to babies, which he calls "the most powerful symbol in the tragedy" (39). These images are significant because what drives Macbeth to tyranny, according to Brooks, is his attempt to keep the throne in his family rather than let it pass to Banquo's. When Fleance escapes, Macbeth returns to the witches, who show him babies bloody and crowned. Since babies represent the future Macbeth cannot control, he wars against them, killing Macduff's family. Babies also symbolize pity: "And pity, like a naked new-born babe" (1.7.21). Macbeth and his wife reject this emotion that defines humanity. Brooks concludes:

> [B]etween them—the naked babe, essential humanity, humanity striped down to the naked thing itself, and yet as various as the future—and the various garbs which humanity assumes, the robes of honor, the hypocrite's disguise, the inhuman "manliness" with which Macbeth endeavors to cover up his essential humanity—between them, they furnish Shakespeare with his most subtle and ironically telling instruments. (49)

Psychological Criticism

Sigmund Freud applied his own theories to Shakespeare's plays. His "Some Character Types Met With in Psychoanalytic Work" (1915–16) attributes Lady Macbeth's decline to her childlessness. If Shakespeare had followed his source and allowed Macbeth a number of years of good rule before he became a tyrant, the significance of their barrenness would be more evident. Freud in "Some Character Types Met With in Psychoanalytic Work" also argues that Macbeth and his wife may be viewed as one person. He hallucinates; she succumbs to mental disorder. He hears a voice that cries, "Sleep no more!" (2.2.32), and she walks in her sleep. He says, in Act II, Scene 2, that no amount of water can cleanse Duncan's blood from his hands. In Act V, Scene 1, Lady Macbeth imagines attempting

Another depiction of the Macbeths just after the murder of Duncan, in Act II, Scene 2 of *Macbeth* (*Painting by Joshua Cristall*)

unsuccessfully to wash away that stain. She suffers the pangs of conscience he feared. She feels remorse while he is defiant. They thereby display the two possible reactions to crime, "like two disunited parts of the mind of a single individuality, and perhaps they are divided images of a single prototype."

Robert J. Lordi, in "Macbeth and His 'dearest partner of greatness,' Lady Macbeth," (*Upstart Crow* 4 [Fall 1982]: 94–106) develops this idea, describing Lady Macbeth as her husband's alter ego. Early in the play, she is "the pragmatic, unscrupulous side of Macbeth's nature that compels him to perform his tragic deed" (94). Lordi approvingly references James Kirgh's observation, in *Shakespeare's Royal Self,* "[In] the characterization of Lady Macbeth we do not have a separate individual,

a living woman, but the personification of Macbeth's ambition and darkest possibilities" (347).

Derek Russell Davis picks up on Freud's discussion of childlessness; his essay "Hurt Minds" argues that Macbeth's barrenness causes him to question his manliness. He is therefore susceptible to his wife's taunts. One reason he kills Duncan is "to remove, however ineptly, a threat to his conception of himself as a man of valour and to reinstate himself in his own esteem and in the esteem of Lady Macbeth" (216).

Macbeth's sensitivity to sounds after Duncan's murder and his insomnia indicate a mental breakdown. Lady Macbeth protects her sanity for a time by denying the enormity of her crime. Yet, she understands the lurking danger: "These deeds must not be thought / After these ways; so, it will drive us mad" (2.2.30–31). Davis believes that Lady Macbeth's fainting in Act II, Scene 3 is real; unconsciousness offers her a temporary relief from remorse. Unable to confide in her husband, Lady Macbeth's denial of criminality continues until she descends into psychosis. Macbeth is equally isolated. Consequently, his sense of guilt turns to paranoia. Davis writes: "His unquestioning belief in his invulnerability has something of the quality of the delusions of grandeur and omnipotence which are typical of paranoid illnesses" (222).

Crane, in *The Languages of Criticism and the Structure of Poetry,* regards Macbeth as a good person who imagines he can improve his condition by acting against his natural impulses. Having gained the kingship, he discovers that he must continue in that manner, becoming "progressively hardened morally" as a result (173). Bertrand Evans, in *The College Shakespeare,* disagrees: "Macbeth is not basically a good man at all, but a man of criminal mentality, either already corrupted or in any event corruptible, because he possesses a severely defective moral mechanism, or no moral sense at all" (600).

Harvey Birenbaum, in "Consciousness and Responsibility in *Macbeth,*" agrees with both Crane and Evans. Lady Macbeth asks, "Art thou afeard / To be the same in thine own act and valor

/ As thou art in desire?" (1.7.39–41). She thus "focuses him on the very basic relation between act and desire, behavior and experience, the inner subjective reality by which we directly know ourselves and the deeds that issue from us and earn our images in others' eyes" (19). Is the real Macbeth what he feels within or what he shows without? In killing Duncan, Macbeth accepts his inner horror. Birenbaum quotes Jan Kott's claim that Macbeth kills Duncan because he cannot accept his fear of doing so. Having committed the crime, he cannot accept himself as a murderer. Birenbaum concludes that Claudius *(Hamlet),* Angelo *(Measure for Measure),* and Macbeth "remain with a consciousness that consciousness itself is impotent, even though it is the ultimate and the fundamental level of experience" (29).

Feminist Criticism

Many modern critics examine the presentation of gender roles in literature. Caroline Asp exemplifies this approach in "'Be bloody, bold, and resolute': Tragic Action and Sexual Stereotyping in *Macbeth*." Asp maintains that Lady Macbeth rejects her feminine qualities because she recognizes that in her society, these are equated with weakness. Macduff does not want to tell Lady Macbeth about Duncan's murder because "The repetition in a woman's ear / Would murther as it fell" (2.3.85–86). Macduff does not tell his wife why he is going to England, again to protect someone he perceives as weak.

Masculinity in the world of *Macbeth* is defined through violence. Macbeth initially rejects this vision. He is "too full o' th' milk of human kindness" (1.5.17). He treats his wife as an equal, calling her "my dearest partner of greatness" (1.5.11). Lady Macbeth convinces him to adopt his culture's vision of manhood and kill Duncan. His new understanding of masculinity surfaces in his discussion with those he has hired to murder Banquo and Fleance. He asks them what kind of men they are. If they "have a station in the file, / Not i' th' worst rank of manhood" (3.1.101–102), they will be willing to kill. Once Macbeth equates manhood with violence,

he subordinates his wife. He does not tell her about his plan to kill Banquo and Fleance, and after Act 3, Scene 4, Macbeth and his wife do not appear on stage together. Asp concludes, "The tension which raises them [the Macbeths] to the level of tragedy in the eyes of the audience is created by the conflict between the roles they think they must play to actualize the self and achieve their destiny and the limits imposed by both nature and society" (393).

Peter Stallybrass's "Macbeth and Witchcraft" also argues that the world of *Macbeth* marginalizes women. Ideal families in the play are all male: Duncan, Malcolm, and Donalbain; Banquo and Fleance. Women are associated with destruction of the family. Lady Macbeth would kill her infant. The witches' brew includes "Finger of birth-strangled babe" (4.1.30) and the blood of a sow that "hath eaten / Her nine farrow" (4.1.64–65). "Witchcraft," Stallybrass writes, "is associated with female rule and the overthrowing of patriarchal authority which in turn leads to the 'womanish' (both cowardly and instigated by women) killing of Duncan, the 'holy' father who establishes both family and state" (201). Heinrich Institoris and Jacob Sprenger's *Malleus Maleficarum* (1486), a treatise on witchcraft, claimed that women were responsible for the downfall of most kingdoms and described women as deceitful. Macduff, not born of woman, restores order at the end of the play.

Janet Adelman's "'Born of Woman': Fantasies of Maternal Power in *Macbeth*" maintains, contrary to Asp, that at the beginning of *Macbeth,* women are powerful. The witches and Lady Macbeth dominate the central male figure. The play reasserts masculine domination by eliminating women. Macbeth imagines his wife as masculine: "Bring forth men-children only! / For thy undaunted mettle should compose / Nothing but males" (1.7. 73–75). Like Stallybrass, Adelman sees in Macduff further rejection of the female. To be born of woman is to be vulnerable; Macduff lacks this weakness.

Marilyn French, in *Shakespeare's Division of Experience,* offers a different perspective of the play, which she regards as a warning against rejecting the feminine. Duncan is an ideal king because

Mrs. David P. Bowers as Lady Macbeth in an 1887 production of *Macbeth*. This photogravure was published by Gebbie & Company.

he unites both male and female traits: he exercises authority but also nourishes his kingdom. (Adelman also views Duncan as androgynous.) Duncan dies in part because Lady Macbeth "fails to uphold the feminine principle" and aligns herself with the masculine (244–245). With Duncan's death, chaos ensues, as described in Act II, Scene 4. For French, this loss of androgyny leads directly to the massacre of Macduff's family. French concludes that *Macbeth* demonstrates "We may not repudiate the qualities associated with pleasure and procreation, with nature and giving up control, without injuring ourselves, perhaps even destroying ourselves" (251).

New Historicism

Combining social science and literary theory, New Historicism seeks to place a work in its larger historical context. It rejects New Criticism's treatment of a text as a self-contained artifact. In *Renaissance Self-Fashioning: From More to Shakespeare,* Stephen Greenblatt, one of the founders of this critical school, warns against "permanently sealing off one type of discourse from another or decisively separating works of art from the minds of their creators and their audiences" (5). Specifically, Greenblatt's "Shakespeare Bewitched" disagrees with Stallybrass that *Macbeth* endorses the patriarchal fear of the feminine. He also rejects Adelman's claim that the play eliminates the female principle and consolidates masculine authority. For Greenblatt, the play is more ambiguous, and this ambiguity is embodied in the witches. He cites Reginald Scot's 1584 *The Discoverie of Witchcraft,* which challenges the belief in witches. (King James ordered this work burned.) Also, George Gifford's 1593 *A Dialogue Concerning Witches and Witchcraftes* denied that witches have supernatural powers, though they receive knowledge from the devil and so should be destroyed. Greenblatt notes that in *The Comedy of Errors,* Shakespeare mocks Antipholus of Syracuse's fear of witches, although in *Henry VI, Part 1,* Joan of Arc is regarded as a real witch, and in *Henry VI, Part 2,* so is Margery Jordan.

Elizabethan society and Shakespeare's own writing thus offer diverse views of witches. The three in *Macbeth* exhibit many traits associated with witches: They raise storms, call upon familiars, sail in a sieve, and foretell the future. Yet, their role in the play remains uncertain. They may influence events, or they may not. They serve as a useful theatrical device, but Shakespeare takes no position on them. Like theater itself, the witches exist, according to Greenblatt, "on the boundary between fantasy and reality, the border or membrane where the imagination and the corporeal world . . . meet" ("Shakespeare Bewitched" 123).

Steven Mullaney's *The Place of the Stage: License, Play and Power in Renaissance England* also takes a New Historical approach to reveal *Macbeth's* ambiguities. In typical New Historicist fashion, Mullaney starts with an obscure event, in this case Robert Kette's 1549 rebellion against Edward VI. Contemporary accounts claimed that Kette relied on prophecies that the rebels would fill the vale of Dussindale with dead bodies. Kette and his followers assumed the bodies would be those of their opponents, but the rebels were defeated, and their own corpses packed the valley. Macbeth, like Kette, understands the witches' words as favoring him, but at the end of the play, he recognizes the ambiguity of their pronouncements. For Mullaney, *Macbeth* illustrates the uncertainty of all language and therefore challenges any monolithic source of authority.

THE PLAY TODAY

Macbeth is perennially popular on the stage; its relative brevity and its straightforward, highly dramatic nature make it among the most appealing of Shakespeare's plays. In addition, it presents headline roles for both a male and a female actor. Famous actors who have played Macbeth on stage include Orson Welles, Laurence Olivier, and Ian McKellen. Famous Lady Macbeths include Vivien Leigh, Helen Mirren, and Judi Dench. Trevor Nunn's 1976 production, with McKellen and Dench as the Macbeths, has become legendary and is available on DVD.

In production, *Macbeth* is widely associated with regicide and tyranny, betrayal and war. Although Welles set his 1936 stage production of the play in the West Indies, critics assumed he was alluding to the long-standing unrest in Haiti. An article in the *New York Times* for April 5, 1936, noted, "the stormy history of Haiti during and subsequent to the French colonization in Napoleon's day—and the career of Henri Christophe, who became 'the Negro King of Haiti' as a result of civil war, and ended by killing himself when his cruelty led to a revolt—form a striking parallel to the bloody story of 'Macbeth.'" A loose adaptation called *MacBird*

(1967) portrayed an evil Lyndon Johnson as a Macbeth figure who was responsible for the assassination of the good president John F. Kennedy. In a *Washington Post* article on August 9, 1974 ("High Drama and Flawed Character in a Theater Too Accustomed to Tragedy"), William Greider offered an extensive analogy between Macbeth and the discredited Richard Nixon. Such trends have continued in recent productions. The well-known Shakespearean actor and film and television star Patrick Stewart played Macbeth in the West End in London and later in New York on Broadway in a production that seemed to compare Macbeth's regime in Scotland to Joseph Stalin's in the Soviet Union; that production was filmed for television by PBS in 2010.

Lady Macbeth tries to wash her hands while she sleepwalks in Act V, Scene 1 of *Macbeth,* in this print published in 1797. *(Illustration by Richard Westall)*

Other notable film versions emphasized different aspects of the play. Welles's low-budget 1948 version emphasized the play's moral concerns. Roman Polanski's 1971 version seemed typically (for Polanski) preoccupied with blood and sex. The movies *Joe Macbeth* (1955) and *Men of Respect* (1990) set Shakespeare's play in the criminal underworld. The famous Japanese director Akira Kurosawa adapted the story loosely but powerfully in his *Throne of Blood* (1957). Literary critic Bloom called Kurosawa "uncannily the most successful film version of *Macbeth,* though it departs very far from the specifics of Shakespeare's play."

In recent years, scholars analyzing the play have focused on political themes as well as feminist themes inspired by the play's depiction of Lady Macbeth and the Weird Sisters. One relatively recent trend is to explore the play's effect on its audience, both in Shakespeare's time and subsequently. Still other critics continue to explore more traditional concerns, such as the ethics and theology in the play, and offer new analyses of the play's characters, particularly Macbeth and Lady Macbeth.

FIVE TOPICS FOR DISCUSSION AND WRITING

1. **Nature of the tragedy:** Is *Macbeth* the tragedy of a man caught up in forces beyond his control? Is Macbeth a hero with a single flaw that causes his downfall? If so, what is that flaw? Ambition? Credulity?
2. **Appearance vs. reality:** According to G. Wilson Knight in *The Wheel of Fire* (1930), "Reality and unreality change places" in the play (153). Is Knight correct? Are characters deluded into mistaking reality for unreality? Do they attempt to confuse others without being mystified themselves?
3. **Theme of evil:** What is the source of evil in the play? Is it an external force ushered into the world of the play by demonic forces? Is it inherent in the violent society that praises Macbeth for brutally killing Macdonwald? Does it lie within the individual psyche?
4. **Role of women:** The section on "Modern Criticism" discusses some feminist writers who interpret the play as rejecting female values, but Stephen Greenblatt, a New Historicist, disagrees. Is androgyny the play's ideal, as exemplified by Duncan and by Macduff's emotional response to the loss of his family? Does the play regard women as weak? As destructive? As essential for society to function as it should?
5. **The role of the supernatural:** Do the play's supernatural elements detract from an appreciation of the play in a secular age that does not believe in witches and ghosts? Would removing these features eviscerate the play or strengthen its psychological dimension?

Bibliography

Adelman, Janet, "'Born of Woman': Fantasies of Maternal Power in *Macbeth*." In *Cannibals, Witches, and Divorce: Estranging the Renaissance,* edited by Marjorie Garber, 90–121. Baltimore, Md.: Johns Hopkins University Press, 1987.

Aitchinson, Nick. *Macbeth, Man and Myth* Stroud, U.K.: Sutton, 1999.

Batholomeusz, Dennis. Macbeth *and the Players.* Cambridge: Cambridge University Press, 1969.

Blissett, William. "'The Secret'st Man of Blood': A Study of Dramatic Irony in *Macbeth*." *Shakespeare Quarterly* 10 (1959): 397–408.

Bloom, Harold. *Shakespeare: The Invention of the Human.* New York: Riverhead, 1999.

Bloom, Harold. ed. *Modern Critical Interpretations:* Macbeth. New York: Chelsea House, 2006.

Booth, Stephen. King Lear, Macbeth, *Indefinition and Tragedy.* New Haven, Conn.: Yale University Press, 1983.

Bradley, A. C. *Shakespearean Tragedy.* London: Macmillan, 1904.

Braunmuller, A. R., ed. *Macbeth.* Cambridge: Cambridge University Press, 2008.

Brooks, Cleanth. "'The Naked Babe' and the Cloak of Manliness." In *The Well Wrought Urn.* New York: Harcourt, Brace & World, 1947.

Brown, John Russell, ed. *Focus on* Macbeth. London: Routledge & Kegan Paul, 1982.

Bullough, Geoffrey, ed. *Narrative and Dramatic Sources of Shakespeare,* Vol. 7: *Major Tragedies.* London: Routledge & Kegan Paul, 1973.

Calderwood, James L. *If It Were Done:* Macbeth *and Tragic Action.* Amherst: University of Massachusetts Press, 1986.

Coursen, H. R. Macbeth: *A Guide to the Play.* Westport, Conn.: Greenwood Press, 1997.

Crane, R. S. *The Languages of Criticism and the Structure of Poetry.* Toronto, Canada: University of Toronto Press, 1953.

Dawson, Lawrence. *Tragic Alphabet.* New Haven, Conn.: Yale University Press, 1974.

Elliott, G. R. *Dramatic Providence in* Macbeth. Princeton, N.J.: Princeton University Press, 1958.

Evans, Gareth Lloyd. *"Macbeth:* 1946–1980 at Stratford-upon-Avon. In *Focus on* Macbeth, edited by John Russell Brown, 87–110. London: Routledge & Kegan Paul, 1982.

Fawkner, H. W. *Deconstructing* Macbeth: *The Hyperontological Voice.* London: Associated University Presses, 1990.

Furness, Horace Howard, ed. *Macbeth.* Philadelphia: J. B. Lippincott, 1901.

Garber, Marjorie. *Shakespeare after All.* New York: Pantheon Books, 2004.

Grove, Robin. "Multiplying Villainies of Nature." In *Focus on* Macbeth, edited by John Russell Brown, 113–130. London: Routledge & Kegan Paul, 1982.

Harbage, Alfred. *William Shakespeare: A Reader's Guide.* New York: Noonday, 1963.

Hawkes, Terence, ed. *Twentieth Century Interpretations of* Macbeth. Englewood Cliffs, N.J.: Prentice-Hall, 1977.

Jorgensen, Paul. *Our Naked Frailties: Sensational Art and Meaning in* Macbeth. Berkeley: University of California Press, 1971.

Kemble, Fanny. "Lady Macbeth." In *Every Saturday.* Boston: Ticknor and Fields, 1868.

Kinney, Arthur. *Lies Like Truth: Shakespeare's* Macbeth *and the Cultural Moment.* Detroit, Mich.: Wayne State University Press, 2001.

Kliman, Bernice W. *Shakespeare in Performance:* Macbeth. Manchester, U.K.: Manchester University Press, 1992.

Knights, L. C. "How Many Children Had Lady Macbeth." In *Explorations.* New York: New York University Press, 1964.

———. Some *Shakesperean Themes.* Stanford, Calif.: Stanford University Press, 1959.

Leavis, F. R. "Education and the University." *Scrutiny* 9 (March 1941): 306–322.

Leggatt, Alexander, ed. *William Shakespeare's* Macbeth: *A Sourcebook.* London: Routledge, 2006.

Long, Michael. *Macbeth.* Boston: Twayne, 1989.

McElroy, Bernard. *Shakespeare's Mature Tragedies.* Princeton, N.J.: Princeton University Press, 1973.

Muir, Kenneth. "Image and Symbol in *Macbeth.*" *Shakespeare Survey* 19 (1966): 45–54.

Muir, Kenneth, and Philip Edwards. *Aspects of* Macbeth. Cambridge: Cambridge University Press, 1977.

Mullin, Michael, ed. Macbeth *Onstage: An Annotated Facsimiles of Glen Byam Shaw's 1955 Promptbook.* Columbia: University of Missouri Press, 1976.

Norbrook, David. "*Macbeth* and the Politics of Historiography." In *Politics of Discourse: The Literature and History of Seventeenth-Century England,* edited by Kevin Sharpe and Steven Zwicker, 78–116. Berkeley: University of California Press, 1987.

Nostbakken, Faith. *Understanding* Macbeth: *A Student Casebook to Issues, Sources, and Historical Documents.* Westport, Conn.: Greenwood Press, 1997.

Paul, Henry N. *The Royal Play of* Macbeth. New York: Macmillan, 1950.

Rosenberg, Marvin. *The Masks of* Macbeth. Berkeley: University of California Press, 1978.

Schoenbaum, Samuel, ed. Macbeth: *Critical Essays.* New York: Garland, 1991.

Sinfield, Alan, ed. *Macbeth.* London: Macmillan, 1992.

Spurgeon, Caroline. *Shakespeare's Imagery and What It Tells Us.* Cambridge: Cambridge University Press, 1935.

Tanner, Tony. *Prefaces to Shakespeare.* Cambridge, Mass.: Belknap Press of Harvard University Press, 2010.

Wain, John, ed. Macbeth: *A Casebook.* London: Macmillan, 1968.

Walker, Roy. *The Time Is Free: A Study of* Macbeth. London: Andrew Dakers, 1949.

Wickham, Glynn. "Hell-Castle and Its Door-Keeper." *Shakespeare Survey* 19 (1966): 68–74.

FILM AND VIDEO PRODUCTIONS

Casson, Philip, dir. *A Performance of* Macbeth. With Ian McKellen, Judi Dench, and John Brown. Thames Television, 1979.

Doran, Gregory, dir. *Macbeth.* With Richard Armitage, Diane Beck, and Ken Bones. Illuminations and Royal Shakespeare Company, 2001.

Gold, Jack, dir. *Macbeth.* With Brenda Bruce, Eileen Way, and Anne Dyson. BBC, 1983.

Goold, Rupert, dir. *Macbeth.* With Oliver Burch, Suzanne Burden, and Ben Carpenter. BBC and PBS, 2010.

Polanski, Roman, dir. *Macbeth.* With Jon Finch, Francesca Annis, and Martin Shaw. Playboy Productions and Caliban Films, 1971.

Warren, Charles, dir. *Macbeth.* With Brian Badcoe, Brian Godfrey, and Tim Hardy. Thames Television, 1988.

Welles, Orson, dir. *Macbeth.* With Orson Welles, Jeanette Nolan, and Dan O'Herlihy. Mercury Productions, 1948.

Winarski, Paul, dir. *Macbeth.* With Stephen J. Lewis, Dawn Winarski, and John Schugard. Showcase Films, 1998.

—Joseph Rosenblum